Ever
Closer
Union

FOURTH EDITION

Ever Closer Union

An Introduction to European Integration

Desmond Dinan

LYNNE
RIENNER
PUBLISHERS

BOULDER
LONDON

Published in the United States of America in 2010 by
Lynne Rienner Publishers, Inc.
1800 30th Street, Boulder, Colorado 80301
www.rienner.com

Library of Congress Cataloging-in-Publication Data
Dinan, Desmond, 1957–
 ˙Ever closer union : an introduction to European integration / Desmond
Dinan. —4th ed.
    p. cm.
  Includes bibliographical references and index.
  ISBN 978-1-58826-607-1 (pbk. : alk. paper)
  1. European Economic Community. 2. European federation. I. Title.
  HC241.2.D476 2010
  337.1'42—dc22

                                           2010018929

Printed and bound in the United States of America

The paper used in this publication meets the requirements
of the American National Standard for Permanence of
Paper for Printed Library Materials Z39.48-1992.

5 4 3 2 1

To WM,
Conor, Cian, and Clio

Contents

Illustrations

Preface

Will the European Union forever be in flux? I asked this question in the preface to the third edition of *Ever Closer Union,* published in 2005. That edition went to press a couple of weeks after French and Dutch voters rejected the Constitutional Treaty, setting off a further period of flux that lasted until implementation of the Lisbon Treaty in December 2009. Additional uncertainty beset the EU as I worked on this new edition, this time in the form of a global financial crisis, recession, and the Greek debt crisis.

Nevertheless, the notion of flux or uncertainty needs some perspective. Undoubtedly the fate of the Constitutional Treaty and the delay in implementing the Lisbon Treaty preoccupied politicians and officials in the EU, and the impact of the financial crisis has raised concerns about the rise of economic nationalism, the solidity of the single market, and the future of the euro. Yet, the EU is remarkably resilient. Beneath the surface, under the churning waves of political drama and economic anxiety, European integration trundles along. Despite appearances to the contrary, the EU is stronger than ever in a range of policy areas and continues, through the process of enlargement and close cooperation with neighboring countries, to promote stability and security in Eastern Europe and the Western Balkans. The past five years have shown that the EU is as important and vibrant as ever before.

I was struck as I wrote this edition not only by the resilience and pervasiveness of the EU, but also by the plethora of information available on it. When I wrote the first edition, the Web was in its infancy. It is difficult nearly two decades later to imagine how I survived without it. Nevertheless, I remain a firm believer in the utility of books. Indeed, the new and the old complement each other. For instance, readers of the fourth edition may use the Web to keep abreast of current institutional, policy, and political developments in the EU, through an almost infinite variety of sources, while relying on *Ever Closer Union* to provide a solid foundation of information and analysis about the EU—its history, institutions, and policies.

—*Desmond Dinan*

The European Union, 2010

Introduction

The Lisbon Treaty, the latest and probably the last major revision of the foundational treaties of the European Union, came into effect in December 2009. The treaty took eight years to complete. Officials and politicians held an unprecedented Constitutional Convention; national governments conducted two negotiations on new treaty provisions; Dutch and French voters rejected the first proposed treaty; Irish voters rejected the follow-on Lisbon Treaty, then accepted it; and the president of the Czech Republic, a notorious Euroskeptic, refused to sign the treaty into law until the last possible moment. The entire episode showed how fraught the process of treaty reform had become and the touchiness of European integration for politicians and the public alike.

Before considering the implications of the treaty's lengthy gestation and difficult birth, it is worth asking why reform was necessary in the first place. The answer lies in the nature of the EU, a multifaceted, ever changing entity. The most significant changes affect its size and scope, which have expanded greatly following the end of the Cold War and the acceleration of globalization. Treaty reform helps the EU adapt to daunting internal and external challenges, not least the challenge of enlargement (see Box 0.1). The Lisbon Treaty is the fourth major treaty reform since 1992.

The background to this particular reform was the determination of EU leaders—in national governments and EU institutions alike—to streamline the EU; revise its institutional arrangements; strengthen its decisionmaking capacity; make it a credible international actor; clarify and in some cases extend its scope; and make the EU more accountable, appealing, and comprehensible to its citizens. EU leaders were reacting to the organization's manifest inadequacies in the face of growing public disillusionment with European integration, a membership that had more than doubled in less than fifteen years, rapid socioeconomic change, and a radically altered international environment.

Although a tall order, the rationale for a new round of reform therefore seems reasonable, even sensible. If so, why was the process so prolonged and painful? Why does the outcome—the treaty itself—look like a caricature of

1

Box 0.1   The Ever Larger Union

Original Member States (1958)	First Enlargement (1973)	Second Enlargement (1981)	Third Enlargement (1986)	Fourth Enlargement (1995)	Fifth Enlargement (2004–2007)[a]
Belgium	Britain	Greece	Portugal	Austria	Bulgaria (2007)
France	Denmark		Spain	Finland	Czech Republic
Germany	Ireland			Sweden	Cyprus
Italy					Estonia
Luxembourg					Hungary
Netherlands					Latvia
					Lithuania
					Malta
					Poland
					Romania (2007)
					Slovakia
					Slovenia

Note: a. Ten countries joined the EU in 2004; Bulgaria and Romania joined in 2007.

the EU: unappetizing and impenetrable? Far from having produced a text that is simple, short, and inspiring, the treaty's authors drafted a document that is long, complicated, and difficult for experts, let alone intrepid lay readers, to understand.

The answer lies in the EU's complexity. The Lisbon Treaty is the latest layer to rest upon previous layers of treaty change, going back to the founding charters of the three European communities—the Coal and Steel Community, the Atomic Energy Community, and the European Economic Community—in the 1950s. Each layer has emerged from intensive negotiations among national governments over the realization of European integration in concrete institutional and policy terms. New treaty changes are path-dependent; they follow the course of preceding ones. Unable to start from scratch and possibly produce a short, simple, readable, and enduring document, national governments have found themselves revising previously revised treaties, adding declarations and protocols at each stage in order to gain a slight advantage and allay domestic concerns (see Box 0.2).

The saga and substance of the Lisbon Treaty and the Constitutional Treaty before it reveal much about the state of the EU more than sixty years after the first, tentative steps toward "ever closer union." Clearly, treaty reform—changing the rules of what the EU does and how the EU does it—is extremely difficult. Governments care about the form and scope of European integration because potential losses and gains, and the domestic political stakes, are high. As European integration has intensified, the EU's impact on policy and politics has become far more conspicuous and important.

The EU is pervasive in people's lives. Residents of the euro area—the countries in which the common currency is used—are reminded of the EU's exis-

---

Box 0.2   The Founding Treaties and Major Treaty Reforms

The Lisbon Treaty (2007) is the latest in a long series of reforms of the original treaties on which the EU is built: the Treaty Establishing the *European Coal and Steel Community* (Paris Treaty, 1951), and the Treaties Establishing the *European Economic Community* and the *European Atomic Energy Community* (Rome Treaties, 1957).

The Merger Treaty (formally the Brussels Treaty, 1965) reformed the three founding treaties.

The budget treaties include the Treaty Amending Certain Budgetary Provisions, signed in Luxembourg in 1970, and the Treaty Amending Certain Financial Provisions, signed in Brussels in 1975.

The Single European Act (1986) reformed the Treaty Establishing the European Economic Community.

The Maastricht Treaty (1992), formally the Treaty on *European Union,* established the EU and included a major reform of the Treaty Establishing the European Economic Community—renaming it the Treaty Establishing the *European Community.*

The Amsterdam Treaty (1997) reformed the Treaty Establishing the European Community and the Treaty on European Union.

The Nice Treaty (2001) reformed the Treaty Establishing the European Community and the Treaty on European Union.

The Lisbon Treaty reformed the Treaty on European Union and the Treaty Establishing the European Community, renaming it the Treaty on the *Functioning of the European Union.*

Note: The years in parentheses indicate when the treaties were signed.

---

tence whenever they reach into their pockets and pull out notes and coins. The EU is also omnipresent in less obvious ways. Most regulation affecting everyday life, such as rules about product safety, food labeling, and environmental standards, is produced not in national capitals but by government officials and ministers, Commission officials, and members of the European Parliament working together in Brussels and Strasbourg. The rulings of the European Court of Justice in Luxembourg are shaping the legal landscape throughout Europe.

People tend to take for granted the benefits of European integration, such as unfettered cross-border travel, low roaming charges for cell phone use, and cheap air travel. Often oblivious to the economic growth generated by the existence of a large, EU-wide market, people fret about the fallout from globalization: they worry about job losses, downward pressure on wages and social services, and the rise of transnational crime, often seeing the EU as part of the problem rather than the solution. While wanting the EU to help strengthen internal and external security, many Europeans are either unaware or dismissive of the strides that governments have taken together regarding asylum and immigration, external border control, police and judicial cooperation, foreign policy, and international peace operations.

Referendums on treaty change give people an opportunity to express dissatisfaction with the EU by either voting against the proposed reform or not voting at all. Not that referendums on treaty change always end in defeat (voters in Luxembourg and Spain approved the Constitutional Treaty). Nevertheless, fear of defeat has made governments wary of putting painstakingly negotiated treaty reform before the electorate. Ireland was the only country to hold a referendum on the Lisbon Treaty because it was the only country whose own constitution obliged it to do so.

Many Europeans are mistrustful of the EU for other reasons. Its sheer size—comprising nearly thirty countries and 500 million people—is intimidating and offputting. The idea of a federal Europe, no matter how decentralized, is uncongenial to most Europeans. All politics are local, which in the context of European integration means national. People may not understand how national legislative procedures work, but generally accept the legitimacy of those procedures without question. People may not like national politicians, but tolerate them nonetheless, taking solace in the knowledge that if necessary they can throw the rascals out. Ordinary Europeans relate differently to the EU, considering it remote, technocratic, and unaccountable.

There are few proponents today of a United States of Europe, a possibility that exists only in the paranoid dreams of ardent Euroskeptics. Arguably the EU has reached equilibrium. It is best understood as an association of states that have pooled a great degree of national sovereignty in supranational institutions, thereby forming an entity with federal characteristics that is nonetheless well short of a full-fledged state. European integration is not static; it ebbs and flows according to national preferences and initiatives, institutional leadership and entrepreneurship, and prevailing regional and global circumstances. The balance established in the Lisbon Treaty between and among national governments and supranational actors (the Commission, the Parliament, and the Court) is unlikely to change fundamentally.

Such an elaborate organization exists for the simple reason that national governments believe that it is in their interest for it to exist. Although European countries differ greatly, they have enough in common, in terms of geography, history, and political culture, to agree that an entity such as the EU serves them well, or at least better than the alternative of either a looser regional organization or going it alone in an increasingly interdependent and turbulent world. Despite the frequent irritations and inconveniences of European integration, countries would not have formed or joined the EU unless they had calculated that belonging to a supranational entity would greatly increase national security and economic well-being.

For some people, the EU is anathema precisely because it involves the sharing of sovereignty, no matter how limited or circumscribed and no matter how pressing the reasons for it. In their view, sovereignty is sacrosanct and indivisible. Believers in the inviolability of sovereignty are found mostly in great powers such as China, India, and the United States, countries whose size generally insulates them from having to cede power to others. Within the EU, proponents of that viewpoint are found mostly in Britain, a country with a markedly different historical experience and political culture from most other member states and one that continues to struggle with the philosophical and practical implications of European integration.

Opponents of European integration naturally exaggerate the threat that they think the EU poses to national identity, independence, and interests. In their mind, ever closer union is dangerous and undesirable, paving the way for a federal Europe. In reality, "ever closer union"—first used in the Rome Treaty of 1957—is a catchphrase for institutionalized European integration, a means of overcoming historical animosities, addressing common problems on a small and crowded continent, and strengthening regional stability. Ever closer union plays out in the daily grind of intensive transnationalism, involving endless, countless meetings among a host of public and private actors in the multilevel dance of EU governance. It is a far cry from incipient federalism or empire building.

To say that a federal United States of Europe is a chimera is not to deny the existence of an ideology of European integration, a belief that the sharing of sovereignty among European countries is inherently good and beneficial for the countries concerned and for the world as a whole. Proponents of this viewpoint believe passionately in what they call the European project and tend to conflate "Europe" with "European Union." Just as national sovereignty is sacrosanct for many Euroskeptics, it is an abomination for many advocates of ever closer union.

The premise of this book is that European integration is a good thing, for practical, not ideological, reasons. On balance, European integration has benefited the countries concerned in ways that go well beyond narrow calculations of economic self-interest. The EU should be judged not by what it is and certainly not by what it says, but by what it does or what it fails to do. All politicians are prone to rhetorical flights of fancy. The atmosphere at summit meetings seems to lend itself to extravagant statements and impressive communiqués, in the G20 as much as in the European Council. What matters is the follow-through, whether a summit can generate sufficient political momentum to achieve concrete results. More broadly in the case of European integration, what matters is whether the EU's elaborate policymaking procedures generate outcomes that improve the lives of Europeans and others.

It is impossible to know what Europe would look like without the EU. With the EU, the culmination of more than fifty years of European integration, Europe is more prosperous and secure than it has ever been. Yet coincidence is not causation. Just because the EU exists does not mean that Europe is better off because of it. Other developments and organizations, such as the movement for social justice or the North Atlantic Treaty Organization, have been influential in shaping Europe today. Nevertheless, the EU is so deeply woven into the cultural, economic, political, and social fabric of contemporary Europe that it is impossible to deny the impact of European integration.

Critics would claim that such an impact has not necessarily been beneficial, that Europe would be better off without the EU or with a different kind of EU. Undoubtedly the EU as we know it has its faults and failings. Yet it is difficult to refute the benefits of the single market program or monetary union, let alone the achievement—little short of miraculous—of bringing the poor, unstable postcommunist countries of Central and Eastern Europe into the EU, and thus securely into a stable Western political and economic order. The institutions of the EU are by no means perfect, and the behavior of EU officials and politicians—like officials and politicians everywhere—is not beyond reproach, but the achievements of European integration are invaluable.

The purpose of this book is not to convince readers of the EU's virtues but to elucidate in a lively and comprehensive way what the EU is, how it came about, how it works, and what it does. The distinction among the European Economic Community, European Community, and European Union can be confusing (see Box 0.3). This book aims to clarify and explain the origins and development of the European communities and the conduct of the contemporary EU. The book is organized logically into three parts—history, institutions, and policies—but inevitably there is overlap among these somewhat artificial categories. For instance, the history part recounts institutional and policy developments; the institutions part explores policymaking processes; and the policies part mentions the roles of institutional actors. Nor is it possible to include every significant historical development, institutional feature, or policy issue in a book of this size. Nevertheless *Ever Closer Union* seeks to satisfy those who want a solid understanding of the EU while whetting their appetite for further inquiry.

Box 0.3   EEC, EC, or EU?

The European Union (EU) came into existence in May 1993, following implementation of the Treaty on European Union, better known as the Maastricht Treaty. Among other things, the Maastricht Treaty changed the name of the European Economic Community (EEC) to the European Community (EC), although the acronym "EC" was already widely used to describe not only the EEC but also, collectively, the three original communities. After Maastricht, the EC became an integral part of the EU. Most policy areas—ranging from agriculture to monetary union—were conducted under the auspices of the EC, until implementation of the Lisbon Treaty in December 2009 did away with the EC and brought every policy area under the auspices solely of the EU. In this book, "EEC" is used when referring specifically to activities relating to the original treaty that established the EEC, and "EC" is used when referring generally to developments before 1993. "EU" is used when referring to developments after implementation of the Maastricht Treaty, although "EU history" refers to the history of European integration since the launch of the original communities. At the risk of sacrificing accuracy for narrative flow, policies and decisions are attributed to the EU even when undertaken, strictly speaking, by the EC.

PART 1

History

1 Reconstruction, Reconciliation, and Integration, 1945–1957

Schuman Plan ($ECSC$ + Germany)

On May 9, 1950, French foreign minister Robert Schuman announced an extraordinary idea to place "the whole of Franco-German coal and steel production under a common High Authority, within the framework of an organization open to the participation of the other countries of Europe."[1] It is difficult to appreciate today the boldness of Schuman's proposal. The intervening years have obliterated our awareness not only of the depth of distrust toward Germany in the immediate aftermath of World War II, but also of the importance of coal and steel for postwar reconstruction. Schuman's dramatic announcement contained a strategy intended to reconcile German economic recovery and French national security. By accepting the recently established Federal Republic of Germany as an equal and suggesting that responsibility for regulating both countries' coal and steel industries be transferred to a supranational authority, the Schuman Plan gave substance to the vague notion of European integration. Fleshing out the Schuman Declaration resulted first in the European Coal and Steel Community (ECSC) and later in the European Atomic Energy Community (Euratom) and the European Economic Community (EEC). Schuman Day is celebrated annually as the birthday of what is now the European Union (see Box 1.1).

■ What Future for Europe?

General Charles de Gaulle, leader of the provisional French government formed at the end of the war, realized that his country could never become great again without radical economic restructuring. Keenly aware of the need to increase national production, boost foreign trade, maximize employment, and raise living standards, de Gaulle put Jean Monnet at the head of the newly established economic planning office. Monnet was an ideal choice, having spent years working in the private and public sectors in France and abroad. Monnet's experience as a senior Allied administrator during both world wars

Box 1.1   Chronology, 1945–1957

1945	May	End of World War II in Europe
1946	September	Churchill's "United States of Europe" speech
1947	June	Marshall Plan announced
	July	Committee for European Economic Cooperation established in Paris
	October	General Agreement on Tariffs and Trade (GATT) launched
	December	International Committee of the Movements for European Unity established in Paris
1948	January	Benelux customs union launched
	March	Brussels Treaty (defensive alliance of France, Britain, and Benelux) signed
	April	Organization for European Economic Cooperation (OEEC) established in Paris
	May	Congress of Europe held in The Hague
	June	Berlin blockade begins
1949	April	North Atlantic Treaty signed in Washington, D.C.; International Ruhr Authority established; Federal Republic of Germany (West Germany) established
	May	Council of Europe launched; end of Berlin blockade
1950	May	Schuman Declaration
	June	Negotiations begin to establish the European Coal and Steel Community (ECSC)
	October	Pleven Plan for a European Defense Community (EDC)
	November	European Convention for the Protection of Human Rights and Fundamental Freedoms signed in Rome
1951	April	Treaty establishing the ECSC signed in Paris
1952	May	Treaty establishing the EDC signed in Paris
	August	ECSC launched in Luxembourg
	September	ECSC assembly holds first session in Strasbourg
1954	August	French national assembly rejects EDC treaty
	October	Brussels Treaty amended to establish the Western European Union
1955	May	Germany joins the North Atlantic Treaty Organization (NATO)
	June	Messina Conference to relaunch European integration; Spaak Committee meets for first time
1956	May	Venice Conference: Spaak Committee recommends a European Economic Community (EEC) and a European Atomic Energy Community (Euratom)
	June	Intergovernmental conference to negotiate EEC and Euratom treaties opens in Brussels
	October–November	Suez crisis
1957	January	The Saar rejoins Germany
	March	Treaties of Rome (establishing the EEC and Euratom) signed

convinced him of the potential of peacetime economic planning. Nor was he encumbered by political baggage; inasmuch as he was politically motivated, it was by the remorseless ideology of efficiency.[2]

Monnet concluded during World War II that economic integration was the only means to avoid future conflict between France and Germany. There

econ → geopolitical goals

would be no peace in Europe, Monnet wrote in August 1943, if countries "reestablished themselves on the basis of national sovereignty with all that this implies by way of prestige politics and economic protectionism." Instead, he argued, European countries "must form a federation . . . which will make them a single economic entity."[3]

The idea of European integration gained considerable currency after the war. Repugnance at the slaughter of two European civil wars in as many generations and the economic depression and political extremism of the intervening years fueled political rhetoric in favor of new patterns of international relations. Words such as "integration," "union," and even "supranationalism" were bandied about as panaceas for Europe's ills. This gave rise to the European movement, a loose collection of individuals and interest groups ranging across the political spectrum.[4]

The intellectual ancestry of the European movement may have stretched into antiquity, but its immediate roots lay in the prewar years and during the war itself. The wartime resistance, a loose collection of individuals and groups opposed to Axis occupation, took up the cause of European unity as one plank of a proposed radical reorganization of postwar politics, economics, and society. Resistance literature espoused the goal of European integration as a basis for future peace and prosperity. Altiero Spinelli, a fervent anti-fascist and European federalist, helped draft a manifesto in 1941 for a "free and united Europe," while imprisoned on the island of Ventotene. After his release, Spinelli traveled secretly to Switzerland for a meeting of resistance leaders, out of which came the "Draft Declaration of the European Resistance," calling for a "Federal Union among the European peoples."[5]

The legacy of the resistance contributed to growing support for European unity in the early postwar years. Winston Churchill, then Europe's best-known and most respected statesman, came to personify the European movement. Renowned for his inspiring leadership of Britain during the war, Churchill called explicitly for a "United States of Europe" in a famous speech in Zurich in September 1946.[6]

Yet Churchill advocated a far more limited form of integration than did many of his continental colleagues. Differences between Churchill and like-minded intergovernmentalists (defenders of national sovereignty), on the one hand, and supranationalists (European federalists), on the other, came to the fore at the Congress of Europe, a glittering gathering of over 600 influential Europeans held in The Hague in May 1948. There was general agreement among participants on the desirability of European unity, however vaguely understood, and on the need to form a new European organization with a parliamentary body. Churchill and other anti-federalists envisioned nothing more than a consultative assembly subordinate to a committee of government ministers. The federalists, by contrast, called for a constituent assembly charged with drafting a charter for the United States of Europe.

What emerged from the Hague congress and from follow-up negotiations had the appearance of a compromise but was in fact a capitulation to Churchill's position. The ensuing Council of Europe was far from a supranational entity. While pledged "to achieve a closer union between its members in order to protect and promote the ideals and principles which constitute their common heritage and to further their economic and social progress," the Council of Europe did little more than exchange ideas and information on social, legal, and cultural matters.[7] Only in one important area, that of human rights, did the new organization stand out. Its Court of Human Rights soon became a bulwark for the protection of civil liberties throughout Europe.

The founding members wanted to locate the Council of Europe away from national capitals. To symbolize European reconciliation, they settled on Strasbourg, a frequently fought-over city on the border between France and Germany. Later, the European Community's founders decided to place the European Parliament there also.

Almost alone among influential Europeans at the time, Monnet did not participate in the Congress of Europe. Monnet was an elitist and a pragmatist. His road to European unity would follow the unglamorous but more effective path of functional economic integration. Close cooperation between countries in specific sectors, Monnet believed, held the key to overcoming national differences and ultimately achieving European federation. Decisions to share national sovereignty should be taken not by hundreds of delegates at the Congress of Europe but by powerful politicians in the privacy of their government ministries.

Uninvolved in the broader European movement, Monnet worked instead on the French modernization plan. Given his conviction that Europe could not be united unless France was resurgent, the plan was an indispensable component of Monnet's strategy for European integration. Based on lengthy consultations with employers, workers, and consumers, Monnet's team set production targets, foreign trade goals, and employment objectives. Few were ever met, but the plan indirectly helped France achieve an enviable economic recovery (although not by later German standards).[8]

Monnet loved aphorisms. One of his favorites—"People only accept change when they are faced with necessity, and only recognize necessity when a crisis is upon them"—offers a clue to how he operated.[9] Monnet was convinced that it would take a crisis for politicians to act against their cautious instincts and embrace European integration. No crisis had occurred so far to give Monnet the chance to push politicians in his preferred direction, although two formidable challenges confronted European governments. The first was the state of the European economy after six years of the most destructive war in modern history. The second was the onset of the Cold War. Neither, by itself, was sufficient to trigger the kind of political reaction that would convince European governments to share sovereignty in a novel supranational entity. But the combined impact of the economic and strategic situation in postwar Europe provided exactly the kind of political catalyst—if not crisis—that Monnet hoped to exploit.

▓ The Cold War, the Marshall Plan, and European Integration

As enmity between the Western Allies and the Soviet Union intensified after the war, Western European governments grew increasingly alarmed about internal Communist subversion and possibly even direct Soviet attack. Thanks to their prominent participation in the wartime resistance movements, communist parties were popular in Western Europe immediately after the war. They fared well in early postwar elections, especially in Italy and France. Indeed, in 1946 and 1947 the French Communist Party shared power with the Christian Democrats and the Socialists, and the Italian Communist Party seemed on the verge of an outright election victory. With relations between the Soviet Union and the Western powers rapidly deteriorating, relations between communist and noncommunist parties in Europe deteriorated as well. Electoral support in Western Europe for communist parties gradually waned as the Cold War intensified, notably after the Berlin blockade of 1948–1949. However, the economic consequences of the war offered ideal conditions for communist parties to exploit.

The emergence of the Cold War and its domestic political repercussions aided the European movement, which called for European countries, once at the center of the international system, to join together in an increasingly rigid bipolar world. As the Cold War intensified and the Iron Curtain descended, integration came to be seen as a means by which Western Europe could strengthen its security, in close collaboration with the United States, against external Soviet aggression and internal Communist subversion. Western Europe's vulnerability drew the United States deeper into the continent's affairs and turned Washington into a zealous champion of European integration.

The Marshall Plan was the main US instrument to encourage that goal.[10] But the Marshall Plan had many origins and objectives, all of them connected. One was humanitarian. Indeed, reports of privation in occupied Germany contributed directly to the famous speech of June 1947, in which US secretary of state George C. Marshall pledged wholehearted US support for European postwar reconstruction. Healthy economic and political self-interest also guided the US undertaking. Without economic growth in Europe, US exports would stagnate and decline. Nevertheless, the US economy depended much less on exports in the late 1940s than it does today, so the export argument alone would not have sufficed to convince a skeptical Congress to flesh out the Marshall Plan in the form of massive financial assistance.

Compelling political and strategic arguments ultimately made the difference. Twice in the previous thirty years the United States had become directly involved in Europe's wars, at a cost of hundreds of thousands of American lives. Despite its strong emotional appeal, isolationism had patently failed. Apart from an emerging consensus that postwar US security depended on increasing international involvement, the onset of the Cold War provided a powerful incentive for the United States to play a leading part in postwar European affairs.

Americans and Europeans agreed about the problem and the prescription. The direct Soviet threat could best be countered by immediate US intervention (as in Greece in 1947) and military alliance building and leadership (as in the case of the North Atlantic Treaty Organization [NATO] two years later). The indirect communist danger, by contrast, could best be defused by restoring Western Europe to sound economic health. The United States would play the role of pharmacist, dispensing drugs in the form of badly needed dollars. On both sides of the Atlantic, the prescription emphasized the importance of integration for future peace and prosperity in Europe.

Monnet had befriended a number of influential Americans when he worked in Washington, D.C., in the early 1940s, most of whom were in key policymaking positions in the postwar period. They agreed with Monnet on the limits of national sovereignty and advantages of supranationality in Western Europe. They also wanted to apply the lessons of modern US history to war-torn Europe. Just as the United States had grown strong and prosperous by promoting interstate commerce and establishing a single market, so too could Europe. In that simple, straightforward way, European integration became an essential part "of a grand design for remaking the Old World in the likeness of the New."[11]

The Marshall Plan occupies a special place in the historiography of the Cold War. Some revisionist historians see in it an effort by the United States to acquire an empire in Europe by design; others argue that Europe's economic weakness allowed the United States to acquire an empire by default.[12] Some Europeans at the time were reluctant to rely too much on US economic largesse and military protection and saw European integration as a means of asserting the continent's independence. Similarly, perhaps paradoxically, many contemporary Americans looked to European integration, which the Marshall Plan aimed to promote, as a way of obviating future US intervention in the Old World.

In the event, the Marshall Plan aided European recovery but failed to break down national barriers to regional integration.[13] For all their platitudes about integration, governments were unwilling to move beyond rhetorical support for supranationalism. Neither Marshall's insistence that aid recipients had to act together and present a common recovery program nor the enormous influence of the United States could overcome the reluctance of European governments formally to share sovereignty. In order to meet the prerequisite for US assistance, recipient governments established the Organization for European Economic Cooperation (OEEC), which was entirely intergovernmental in ethos and operation and failed to live up to its foster parents' expectations. (Shortly after the EEC was established in 1958, the OEEC became the Organization for Economic Cooperation and Development [OECD], the Paris-based body for international economic research and analysis.)[14]

Despite the disappointing impact of the OEEC, the Marshall Plan contributed to the crisis that Monnet knew was necessary to prompt his own government to act. Because it involved the reconstruction of West Germany as part of the reconstruction of Western Europe, the Marshall Plan set the stage for a series of diplomatic decisions that would rehabilitate the former enemy, much to the consternation of Germany's neighbor to the west. The threat to France's own economic recovery and security was immense. Here was a situation that Monnet could exploit to the full.

Even as the United States and Britain revised their harsh policies toward Germany, France stuck stubbornly to a number of severe strictures. France had suffered grievously from German militarism, far more than either Britain or the United States. The humiliation and horror of World War II would not quickly be forgotten. Denied a place at the negotiating table where the "Big Three" (Britain, the Soviet Union, and the United States) decided the fate of the world, France at least won the right to occupy a small part of defeated Germany. The gradual softening of British and US policy toward Germany served only to strengthen French determination to stick to a rigid course. Not surprisingly, France refused to merge its occupation zone into the newly established Anglo-American zone in May 1947.[15]

Even Monnet was not unaffected by the rampant Germanophobia that swept France immediately after the war. Indeed, Monnet had predicated his plan for economic modernization upon a punitive policy toward Germany. Coal and steel, the two key industrial sectors in mid-twentieth-century Europe, lay at the heart of the plan. Postwar French policy toward Germany sought to win control over the coal-rich Saar, which France then occupied, and to prevent the recovery of the Ruhr, which had become a synonym for the German military-industrial complex and whose resuscitation would threaten France's own economic revival. Monnet based his economic planning squarely on the assumption that Ruhr coal would be available to fuel French steel mills, whose increased output would find buyers in displaced German markets. German economic rehabilitation, if it came before full implementation of the Monnet Plan, would greatly imperil France's economic fortunes and, by extension, France's international stature.

As long as the Soviet Union was involved in formulating Allied policy toward Germany, France had some chance of thwarting the increasingly benign approach of Britain and the United States. Although there had never truly been four-power cooperation on Germany, the Western Allies were reluctant to break openly with the Soviet Union. As the Cold War escalated, however, the Anglo-Americans felt increasingly free to act unilaterally in the West while the Soviet Union pursued its own policy in the East.

French difficulty in sticking to a repressive policy toward Germany came to a head in early 1948. As long as France refused to join the combined British and US occupation zone, officials in Paris could only watch angrily as their counterparts in London and Washington gradually loosened the Ruhr's economic shackles. Pragmatism seemed to triumph when France, in an effort to influence Anglo-American policy from within, agreed to merge the Western zones of occupation into the new Federal Republic of Germany.

Born in September 1949, the Federal Republic of Germany lacked many attributes of sovereignty. Apart from accepting limits on foreign policy and a complete absence of defense policy, the new German state had to accept the International Ruhr Authority. French hopes that the authority would maintain strict controls on Ruhr production proved unrealistic. Realizing that the Ruhr was the industrial heartland of Europe, the United States pushed hard for German industrial recovery as a prerequisite for European economic recovery. The United States appreciated the implications of this for France. Accordingly, officials in Washington pressed their counterparts in Paris to devise a mutually acceptable solution to the Ruhr problem and to take the initiative in proposing a new Allied policy toward the new Federal Republic.

By the end of 1949, therefore, France faced the failure of its postwar strategy. The International Ruhr Authority, a body intended to perpetuate control over the area under the guise of Allied cooperation with the Federal Republic, made little headway. French officials realized that policy toward Germany would have to be revised. In the following months they searched for a strategy that would satisfy their country's overriding concern with security, meet its industrial demands for adequate supplies of coal and markets for steel, and relieve US pressure for an approach that would accommodate Germany's rapid economic recovery.[16]

Monnet himself had the most to gain—and the most to lose—from the predicament that France faced. After all, the French modernization plan, now at risk, was his. Apart from a keen personal interest in the plan's success, Monnet bore primary responsibility in the French civil service for overcoming obstacles to economic recovery. The particular obstacle facing France in 1949 and 1950—Anglo-American support for rapid German economic revival—gave Monnet the chance to push his cherished project of European integration. Capitalizing on the growing sentiment in official French circles that policy toward Germany should in future be based on economic association rather than antagonism, Monnet approached Schuman with the idea of a supranational coal and steel community. Thus, the relaxation of Allied restrictions on German steel production and the ensuing pressure on France precipitated the political crisis that, Monnet hoped, would convince his government to take a dramatic step on the road to Franco-German rapprochement and European integration. That step was the Schuman Declaration.[17]

▪ The Coal and Steel Community and European Defense

Robert Schuman's background lent poignancy to the coal and steel proposal that bore his name. Coming from the disputed province of Lorraine, where he experienced firsthand the incessant conflict between France and Germany, Schuman sought above all else to promote reconciliation between the two countries.[18] As a Christian Democrat, Schuman held political principles that reinforced his personal convictions. Constrained by the climate of retribution toward Germany that pervaded postwar France, Schuman had refrained from taking any conciliatory steps in the direction of the erstwhile enemy. Now, emboldened by Monnet's suggestion and by the swing in official French opinion toward economic accord with Germany, Schuman floated the fateful proposal with secrecy and speed.

Before it could be made public, Monnet and Schuman needed the approval of three key parties: the French, German, and US governments. On May 9, 1950, Schuman simultaneously placed the proposal before his own cabinet in Paris and brought it to Chancellor Konrad Adenauer's attention in Bonn. Adenauer responded enthusiastically. Like Schuman, he had a strong personal yearning for Franco-German reconciliation. Keenly aware of the depth of French distrust toward the Federal Republic, Adenauer knew that shared sovereignty held the key to Germany's international rehabilitation. Only by integrating closely with neighboring countries could Germany hope to remove the remaining controls on its domestic and foreign policies.[19]

Monnet had alerted US secretary of state Dean Acheson to the proposed French initiative. Acheson, they knew, strongly supported not only European integration but also the necessity of French efforts to bring it about. The previous October, Acheson had shared with Schuman his belief that "our policy in Germany, and the development of a German Government which can take its place in Western Europe, depends on the assumption by your country of leadership in Europe on these problems."[20]

As expected, Acheson endorsed the political thrust of the Schuman Plan, though he feared that the plan was a clever cover for "a gigantic European cartel." Accordingly, Acheson drafted a statement of support for President Harry Truman to release once the plan became public, partly to allay the secretary of state's "apprehension that upon receiving partial information, the Antitrust Division in the Department of Justice might stimulate some critical comments, which would have been damaging at that stage."[21] Monnet's assiduous cultivation of the US establishment had borne fruit in their enthusiasm for the French initiative.

Buoyed by Acheson's endorsement and Adenauer's approval, Schuman convinced his cabinet colleagues to support the scheme. A public announcement immediately followed at a hastily convened press conference in Paris. The result was "a public relations coup of heroic proportions."[22] Although French officials had been moving in the direction of Franco-German economic association for some time, the Schuman Declaration had all the appearances of a dramatic reversal of policy. Instead of trying to keep the traditional enemy down, France would build a new Europe on the basis of equality with Germany. Coal and steel, the two key sectors of industrial production and warmaking potential, would be removed from national management and placed under the regulatory control of a single, supranational authority. As Monnet put it, "If . . . the victors and the vanquished agreed to exercise joint sovereignty over part of their joint resources . . . then a solid link would be forged between them, the way would be wide open for further collective action, and a great example would be given to the other nations of Europe."[23]

Schuman's offer to open the proposed organization "to the participation of the other countries of Europe" was not as far-reaching as it seemed. The countries of Eastern Europe were excluded by the onset of the Cold War; Portugal and Spain were international pariahs because of their fascistic regimes; and the Scandinavian countries had so far shown little interest in supranationalism. For Schuman and Monnet, European integration meant, in essence, Franco-German integration. Germany was the traditional enemy, the economic powerhouse of Europe, and the country that posed the greatest threat to France. European integration aimed first and foremost at resolving the German question. Beyond Germany, it was limited in practice to the neighboring countries of Belgium, the Netherlands, and Luxembourg (known as the Benelux), and Italy. The founding members of the European Communities became known as the Six.

Yet Monnet and Schuman were eager to include Britain as well. The Americans felt the same way. As late as 1948, "Western European integration without Britain was unacceptable in Washington," where the ultimate decision about Western Europe's future would be made.[24] By 1950, however, both France and the United States had dropped Britain from their plans for European integration. Britain's obvious reluctance to become involved, despite Churchill's memorable endorsement of a United States of Europe, convinced officials in Washington and Paris that progress would have to be made without British participation.

Britain preferred to remain aloof because of a political culture that emphasized national sovereignty, a long history of detachment from continental European affairs, and the special wartime experience of having escaped invasion. In addition, Britain saw itself as an intermediary between the United States and continental Europe, an aspect of the Anglo-American "special relationship" that officials in London feared would be endangered by participation in European integration despite their US counterparts' assertions to the contrary. British officials also thought that too close an involvement in European integration would jeopardize Britain's strong attachment to the dwindling empire and growing Commonwealth.[25]

Schuman's decision to give the British government no more than a few hours' notice of his groundbreaking declaration vividly illustrates French indifference to British involvement in the future coal and steel community. British foreign minister Ernest Bevin was furious, doubly so when he discovered that Acheson had known about the impending declaration when he had arrived in London the day before Schuman's press conference.[26] Any French embarrassment at slighting Bevin rapidly dissipated when the British government belittled the plan.

Yet the French held open the door to British participation in the negotiations for the coal and steel community. Other prospective member states, especially the Benelux countries, hoped that Britain would take the decisive step. But in order to cross the threshold, all participants had to accept the principle of shared sovereignty, whatever that would mean in practice. Monnet stuck to the position that if the principle of supranationality was debatable, the proposed organization would go the way of the ineffectual OEEC. Following a series of cabinet meetings and diplomatic exchanges with France, the British government reached a predictable but discouraging conclusion. At the definitive cabinet meeting, "there seems to have been a general, resentful agreement to give a negative answer [to France]."[27] The French had little choice but to proceed without Britain.

John Gillingham, author of an authoritative history of the Schuman Plan, titled his chapter on the coal and steel negotiations "From Summit to Swamp."[28] The summit was the high point of the declaration itself, made in the glare of publicity and self-congratulation; the swamp was the low point of intergovernmental squabbling as each country jockeyed for advantage in pursuit of its own interests. Monnet negotiated for France and prevailed upon Adenauer to appoint Walter Hallstein, state secretary in the foreign office and later the Commission's first president, as Germany's representative. The main issues were the proposed community's competence, institutions, and decision-making procedures. Based on a French document, the negotiators gradually gave substance and shape to the new organization. What emerged was a supranational High Authority, the institutional embodiment of shared sovereignty in the coal and steel sectors. The High Authority would be responsible for establishing a common market in coal and steel and for regulating prices, wages, investment, and competition. As Monnet saw it, the purpose of the community was not "to substitute the High Authority for private enterprise, but . . . to make possible real competition throughout a vast market, from which producers, workers and consumers would all gain."[29]

Because of the High Authority's small size, national bureaucracies would have to cooperate closely with it to implement community regulations. A separate institution, the Court of Justice, would adjudicate disputes and ensure member states' compliance with the terms of the treaty. The other negotiators forced Monnet to accept the Council of Ministers, representing national governments, in the institutional framework. Initially intended to be advisory, the Council would increasingly act as a brake on supranationalism within the community. Finally, a Common Assembly consisting of delegates of the national parliaments would give the ECSC the appearance of democratic accountability.

A contemporaneous controversy over whether to allow the Federal Republic to have an army imperiled the coal and steel negotiations. At first France fiercely resisted US demands that Germany rearm itself following the outbreak of the Korean War. That caused Adenauer to doubt France's commitment to Franco-German rapprochement and European integration. If shared sovereignty was good enough for German industry, Adenauer asked, why was it not also acceptable for German rearmament, especially as Cold War tensions escalated? Faced with possible German recalcitrance in the coal and steel talks, Monnet pressed French prime minister René Pleven to propose a supranational organization for European defense. In October 1950, France announced the Pleven Plan for a European defense community, analogous to the proposed coal and steel community.[30]

Negotiations to form the European Defense Community (EDC), in which German units would be integrated into a European army, began in February 1951. Although Monnet was not directly involved in the talks, he again used his influence behind the scenes to win essential US support for the plan. Based on a deep distrust of supranationalism, Britain resisted US entreaties to enter the EDC negotiations. After hard bargaining, the Six signed the EDC treaty in May 1952.

The EDC negotiations spawned another initiative that raised federalists' hopes for the future of European integration. Article 38 of the EDC treaty called for the establishment of a supranational political authority to direct the new community. In September 1952 the foreign ministers of the Six asked a special committee of the newly established Common Assembly of the Coal and Steel Community to draft a treaty for an overarching political community. The so-called constitutional committee soon drew up plans for a political community that would not only encompass the EDC and ECSC but also embrace foreign, economic, and monetary policy coordination. Even in the heated climate of the early 1950s, however, with the Korean War and the attendant acceptance of German rearmament acting as a spur to European integration, the Six balked at the constitutional committee's extravagant recommendations. At a series of meetings in 1953 and early in 1954, the Six successfully diluted the more far-reaching clauses of the draft treaty establishing the political community. The proposed community soon withered away, a casualty of its stillborn sibling, the EDC.[31]

Having survived the penultimate negotiating stage, the EDC foundered on the rock of ratification. Gaullist hostility toward sharing sovereignty over sacrosanct national defense policy, coupled with implacable communist opposition to German rearmament, resulted in defeat of the EDC treaty in the French parliament in August 1954. It was paradoxical that the EDC failed in France, where the initiative had originated. In the interim, Stalin's death and the end of hostilities in Korea had lessened Cold War tensions and made the issue of German remilitarization less urgent. Moreover, in the early 1950s, France had become increasingly preoccupied with its war in Indochina (later Vietnam).

But the genie of German rearmament could not be stuffed back in the bottle. With the collapse of the EDC, Britain proposed instead that Germany join with Britain, France, Italy, and the Benelux countries in the Western European Union (WEU), a new defense organization intended to facilitate German entry into the North Atlantic Treaty Organization. Mollified by Britain's membership in the intergovernmental WEU, France reluctantly endorsed the initiative. In a fitting finale to the EDC debacle, France thereby acquiesced in Germany's entry into NATO in May 1955, a prospect that five years previously had filled it with fright.

The EDC left an interesting legacy. Having marked the high point of European federalist aspirations, it quickly acquired the aura of a great opportunity lost. As the European Community struggled through setbacks in the 1960s and 1970s, and a belated revival in the 1980s, supporters of supranationalism harked back to the early 1950s as the European movement's golden age. If only the EDC and related political community had been ratified, the argument went, European integration would have reached a level considered unattainable in later years. Yet the collapse of both proposals and the failure of subsequent initiatives along similar lines clearly indicated the limits of European integration in the 1950s and beyond. It was no accident that the EDC fell at the final hurdle of French ratification or that the political community languished in the wings. Only with great reluctance had the Six confronted the question of a defense community and the equally daunting challenge of a supranational political community. The outcome allowed them to concentrate instead on the kind of initiative politically possible in the 1950s and for many years thereafter: functional economic integration.

Concerned about the possible consequences of the EDC controversy for the Schuman Plan, Monnet pushed for early ratification of the ECSC treaty. In each prospective member state, the ratification debate was lively: producer associations complained about the High Authority's ability to interfere in their affairs, labor groups fretted about the impact of keener competition, and nationalist politicians railed against the supposed onslaught of supranationalism. While the EDC debate raged, the ECSC treaty was nonetheless ratified in national parliaments with relatively little fanfare.

One of the issues still to be worked out was the site of the institutions themselves. Despite Monnet's hope that a special area analogous to the District of Columbia would be set aside for the ECSC, national governments eventually settled on Luxembourg as the site of the High Authority, with Monnet as its first president. It was there, in the capital of the small, sleepy Grand Duchy, that the ECSC began to function in August 1952.

The ECSC disappointed European federalists both in its conceptual framework and in its actual operation. It was an unglamorous organization that inadequately symbolized the high hopes of supranationality in Europe. Yet the ECSC served a vital purpose in the postwar world in terms of Franco-German reconciliation and the related goal of European integration. To quote John Gillingham: "A supranational authority had been created, a potential nucleus for a European federal system. It would serve in lieu of a peace treaty concluding hostilities between Germany and Western Europe. This was no grand settlement in the manner of Westphalia or Versailles. The agreement to create a heavy industry pool changed no borders, created no new alliances, and reduced only a few commercial and financial barriers. It did not even end the occupation of the Federal Republic. . . . By resolving the coal and steel conflicts that had stood between France and Germany since the Second World War, it did, however, remove the main obstacle to an economic partnership between the two nations."[32] These were by no means inconsiderable achievements.

■ The Economic and Atomic Energy Communities

A favorite metaphor of European federalists depicts the EU as a fragile craft constantly running aground on the treacherous shoals of national sovereignty and self-interest. With each repair and relaunch the ship gets stronger, while navigational hazards are charted and exposed. Eventually, one supposes, the United States of Europe will resemble a supranational supertanker plying stormy economic, political, and security seas, invulnerable to the perils lurking beneath the surface.

The first relaunch of the community concept took place immediately after the EDC foundered in 1954, but there was nothing inevitable about the revival of European integration at that time. Certainly the ECSC continued to operate unabated, but it was not a striking success. The High Authority struggled in vain to formulate and implement effective pricing and competition policies and managed only with difficulty to regulate other aspects of the coal and steel sectors. Yet the political lessons of functional integration were not lost on national governments. Despite the bitterness engendered by the EDC debate, governments were willing to maintain, or even extend, functional economic cooperation, not least for the sake of Franco-German rapprochement.

A specific idea for economic integration, floated earlier by the Dutch, survived the defeat of the EDC. It called for the Six to establish a customs union, unify trade policy toward the rest of the world, devise common policies for a range of socioeconomic sectors, and organize a single market. Monnet thought this idea too ambitious; enamored as always of more precise proposals, he continued to advocate sectoral integration. Even while the ECSC treaty was being negotiated, Monnet knew that coal was rapidly losing its position as the basis of industrial power and, by extension, military might. Atomic energy had already revolutionized strategic doctrine and seemed poised to replace coal and oil as the elixir of the future. Accordingly, Monnet proposed an atomic energy community, to be structured along the lines of the ECSC, in order to achieve immediate economic objectives and promote the distant goal of European federation.

Impatient to play a more active political role in advocating European unity, in November 1954 Monnet announced his intention to resign from the High Authority. As he explained at the time, "It is for Parliaments and Governments to decide on the transfer of new powers to the European institutions. The impulse must therefore come from without. [By resigning from the High Authority,] I shall be able to join in the efforts of all those who are working to continue and enlarge what has been begun."[33] Monnet's vehicle for influencing parliaments and governments would be the Action Committee for a United States of Europe, a small, "private supranational organization" of political party and trade union leaders.[34] Monnet envisioned the committee as a powerful pressure group lobbying for implementation of his new initiative.

At a meeting in Messina, Sicily, in June 1955, foreign ministers of the Six discussed Monnet's replacement and, more broadly, the future of European integration. Paul-Henri Spaak, Belgium's foreign minister, had prepared a memorandum on behalf of the Benelux countries suggesting further integration along the lines of the proposed atomic energy community and common market. The foreign ministers asked Spaak to form a committee and write a report on possible options. Given the impact of the Spaak report, in later years the Messina meeting came to be seen as a turning point in the history of European integration.

Spaak's enthusiasm for integration had already won him the nickname "Mr. Europe." As chairman of the conference that opened in Brussels later in 1955 to draft the report that subsequently bore his name, Spaak steered the work of the various committees and subcommittees. The Spaak report, submitted in May 1956, proposed that the objectives of atomic energy and wider economic integration be realized in separate organizations with separate treaties. Spaak and the other foreign ministers agreed that governments should begin negotiations on what eventually became the European Atomic Energy Community and the European Economic Community.[35]

Despite the bitter EDC bequest, French politicians generally favored Euratom, which offered an opportunity to share the exorbitant costs of atomic energy research and development while enjoying all the benefits. Not only was the United States willing to share nuclear technology for peaceful purposes, but also the State Department recognized that "the most hopeful avenue for relaunching the movement toward European integration now appears to be the creation of a European common authority, along the lines of the Schuman Plan, to be responsible for the development of atomic energy for peaceful purposes."[36] By contrast, reaction in France to the possible establishment of a common market was almost uniformly negative. Robert Marjolin, who advised the French government on European affairs and subsequently participated in the Euratom and EEC negotiations, emphasized in his memoirs "the hostility of almost the whole of French opinion to the removal, even gradual, of the protection which French industry enjoyed." That hostility led to intense confrontations between the negotiators in Brussels on the one hand and recalcitrant ministers and bureaucrats in Paris on the other. In addition to fighting for France in the intergovernmental conference, Marjolin found himself waging a rearguard action that he called the "Battle of Paris."[37]

Marjolin and others argued the case for a customs union and common market on its own merits, while pointing out that France could not have the desirable atomic energy community without the undesirable economic community. With the exception of Britain, which participated in the EEC negotiations until November 1955, France's partners in the intergovernmental conference were keen to have a common market in Europe. The advantage of such an outcome was obvious to Germany, although Ludwig Erhard, the economics minister, objected to the EEC on the grounds that it would be protectionist and retard global trade liberalization under the auspices of the General Agreement on Tariffs and Trade (GATT). As for Euratom, the other countries in the negotiations did not share France's enthusiasm and doubted that the French government would exploit atomic energy only for civil projects.

Guy Mollet, the French prime minister, who strongly supported both Euratom and the EEC, became preoccupied late in 1956 with the Suez crisis, the result of an ill-fated Anglo-French military intervention in Egypt. Only when the crisis was resolved did Mollet focus his attention fully on the EEC negotiations. A vote in the French parliament on the negotiations, in January 1957, demonstrated the divisiveness of the issue. In the end, a vague desire to improve the country's image after the EDC debacle, the legacy of the Suez crisis, and a concern that France might be left permanently behind its more economically advanced neighbors contributed to the government's success. Yet the outcome was close. Only by guaranteeing clauses in the EEC treaty that favored France's overseas possessions and promising to include agriculture in the proposed EEC did the government carry the day.

Having accepted these conditions during the parliamentary debate, the French government had to convince its partners to incorporate them into the draft treaty. The other countries agreed to do so in part because of the benefits that would accrue to all from a common agricultural policy and in part because Belgium and the Netherlands would benefit as well from extending EEC privileges to member states' overseas possessions. But the main reason for the other countries' acquiescence was the importance of including France in the community. An EEC without Britain was possible; an EEC without France was not. As Franco-German rapprochement lay at the core of the EEC, and as the EEC was the key to Germany's postwar rehabilitation, Adenauer would pay almost any price to placate the government in Paris.

The intergovernmental conference came to an end in a series of high-level meetings in February 1957. The result was two treaties, one for Euratom and the other for the EEC. Both were signed at an elaborate ceremony in Rome in March. Monnet's Action Committee was instrumental, if not decisive, in ensuring swift and successful ratification of the two treaties. First the committee's influence helped win the support in Germany of the Social Democratic Party, which had previously opposed both the ECSC and the EDC. With German ratification secure, the Action Committee turned its attention to France, where the fall of Mollet's government during the early summer threw the treaties' prospects in doubt. Thanks in part to lobbying by the committee, a comfortable majority of French parliamentarians endorsed the treaties in July 1957.[38] By the end of the year, each of the prospective member states had ratified the treaties, allowing the two new communities to begin operating in January 1958.

As he had done in the early 1950s during the negotiations that led to the ECSC, Monnet championed the cause of a special "European District" to house the new community institutions. Government representatives could not agree on an appropriate location. Still dealing with an influx of ECSC officials and associated personnel into the Grand Duchy, the Luxembourg government declined to accept any more. Almost by default, Brussels, site of the conference that gave birth to the new communities, became their home.

By the time of the Brussels negotiations, held in the aftermath of the EDC debacle, "supranationality" was a term from which even the most ardent federalists recoiled. As Marjolin noted, "Nowhere did it appear in the documents drafted during the negotiations; no one so much as mentioned the word."[39] The preamble of the EEC treaty was far less fanciful than its ECSC counterpart, referring only to the signatories' determination "to lay the foundations of an ever closer union among the peoples of Europe." The treaty itself outlined the essential principles of the common market: the free movement of goods, persons, services, and capital; a customs union and common external tariff; and various community policies. The institutional architecture of Euratom and the

EEC emulated that of the ECSC but included a stronger Council and a weaker Commission, the latter a more acceptable name than "High Authority" for the new communities' executive body. In effect, "an institutional system was set up [in the communities] with the aim of doing justice to both the intergovernmental and supranational concepts."[40]

In his monumental history of postwar Europe, Tony Judt warns readers not to "overestimate the importance of the Rome Treaty [in establishing the EEC]."[41] Indeed, the significance of the Rome Treaty was not fully apparent at the time. Most Europeans in 1958 were unlikely to have heard of it; those who did would most likely have thought of it as a technical agreement among Western European countries intended to facilitate investment and trade. The EEC's importance was nonetheless profound. In his memoirs, Marjolin, whose feet were firmly planted on the ground and who had fought so hard to make the EEC possible, described March 25, 1957, the day that the treaties were signed, as representing "one of the greatest moments of Europe's history. Who would have thought during the 1930s, and even during the ten years that followed the war, that European states which had been tearing one another apart for so many centuries and some of which, like France and Italy, still had very closed economies, would form a common market intended eventually to become an economic area that could be linked to one great dynamic market?"[42] Politically as well as economically, the launch of the EEC was a major historical event.

■ Notes

1. The definitive and draft versions of the Schuman Declaration are available in *European NAvigator: The Authoritative Multimedia Reference on the History of Europe,* http://www.ena.lu/.

2. On Monnet's life, career, and contribution to European integration see François Duchêne, *Jean Monnet: The First Statesman of Interdependence* (New York: Norton, 1994); Frederic J. Fransen, *The Supranational Politics of Jean Monnet: Ideas and Origins of the European Community* (Westport: Greenwood, 2001); and Jean Monnet, *Memoirs* (Garden City: Doubleday, 1978).

3. Monnet, *Memoirs,* p. 222.

4. For a comprehensive history of the European movement, see Walter Lipgens, *History of European Integration,* 2 vols. (London: Oxford University Press, 1981 and 1986).

5. See Michel Dumoulin, ed., *Plans des temps de guerre pour l'Europe d'après guerre, 1940–1947* (Brussels: Bruylant, 1995).

6. The speech is available in *European NAvigator,* http://www.ena.lu/.

7. See Council of Europe, *Congress of Europe, The Hague, 7–11 May 1948* (Council of Europe Publishing, 1999).

8. On the Monnet Plan and postwar French economic recovery, see Frances Lynch, *France and the International Economy: From Vichy to the Treaty of Rome* (London: Routledge, 1997), pp. 16–109.

9. Monnet, *Memoirs,* pp. 286, 304–305.

10. For an account of the Marshall Plan and its relationship to European integration, see Greg Behrman, *The Most Noble Adventure: The Marshall Plan and the Reconstruction of Postwar Europe* (New York: Free Press, 2007); and Michael Hogan, *The Marshall Plan: America, Britain, and the Reconstruction of Western Europe, 1947–1952* (Cambridge: Cambridge University Press, 1987).

11. Hogan, *Marshall Plan,* p. 52.

12. See John Killick, *The United States and European Reconstruction, 1945–1960* (Chicago: Routledge, 2000); and Geir Lundestad, *"Empire" by Integration: The United States and European Integration, 1945–1997* (Oxford: Oxford University Press, 1998).

13. This is a major thesis of Alan S. Milward, *The European Rescue of the Nation State* (London: Routledge, 2000).

14. See Richard T. Griffiths, ed., *Explorations in OEEC History* (Paris: OECD Publishing, 1997).

15. See John W. Young, *France, the Cold War, and the Western Alliance, 1944–49: French Foreign Policy and Post-War Europe* (New York: St. Martin's, 1990).

16. On the circumstances that led to the Schuman Plan, see Pierre Gerbet, *La genèse du plan Schuman: Des origines à la déclaration du 9 mai 1950* (Lausanne: Centre des Recherches Européens, École des H.E.C., University of Lausanne, 1962).

17. For an account of the historic declaration, see John Gillingham, *Coal, Steel, and the Rebirth of Europe, 1945–1955: The Germans and French from Ruhr Conflict to Economic Community* (Cambridge: Cambridge University Press, 1991).

18. On Schuman's life and career, see Raymond Poidevin, *Robert Schuman: Homme d'état, 1866–1963* (Paris: Imprimerie Nationale, 1986).

19. On Adenauer's commitment to European integration, see Dennis Bark and David Gress, *A History of West Germany,* vol. 1, *1945–1963* (Oxford: Blackwell, 1989).

20. Office of the Historian, *Foreign Relations of the United States* (hereafter cited as *FRUS*), *1949,* vol. 3, p. 625.

21. Dean Acheson, *Present at the Creation: My Years in the State Department* (New York: Norton, 1969), pp. 383–384.

22. Gillingham, *Coal, Steel, and the Rebirth of Europe,* p. 231.

23. Monnet, *Memoirs,* p. 293.

24. Alan S. Milward, *The Reconstruction of Western Europe, 1945–51* (London: Methuen, 1984), p. 255.

25. For a discussion of British policy toward postwar Europe, see Alan Milward, *The United Kingdom and the European Community,* vol. 1, *The Rise and Fall of a National Strategy, 1945–1963* (London: Cass, 2002).

26. See Alan Bullock, *The Life and Times of Ernest Bevin,* vol. 3, *Ernest Bevin: Foreign Secretary, 1948–1951* (London: Heinemann, 1983), pp. 731–733.

27. Milward, *Reconstruction,* p. 404.

28. Gillingham, *Coal, Steel, and the Rebirth of Europe,* p. 229.

29. Monnet, *Memoirs,* p. 329.

30. See Edward Fursdon, *The European Defense Community: A History* (New York: St. Martin's, 1980).

31. See Richard Griffiths, *Europe's First Constitution* (London: Federal Trust, 2001).

32. Gillingham, *Coal, Steel, and the Rebirth of Europe,* pp. 297–298.

33. Monnet, *Memoirs,* p. 400.

34. Walter Yondorf, "Monnet and the Action Committee: The Formative Years of the European Communities," *International Organization* 19 (1965): 909.

35. See Enrico Serra, ed., *The Relaunching of Europe and the Treaties of Rome* (Baden-Baden: Nomos, 1989); and Thomas Horber, *The Foundations of Europe: European Integration Ideas in France, Germany and Britain in the 1950s* (Wiesbaden: Vs Verlag, 2006).

36. *FRUS, 1955–1957*, vol. 4, p. 323.

37. Robert Marjolin, *Architect of European Unity: Memoirs, 1911–1986* (London: Weidenfeld and Nicolson, 1989), p. 284.

38. See Yondorf, "Monnet and the Action Committee," pp. 896–901.

39. Marjolin, *Architect of European Unity,* p. 296.

40. Hanns-Jurgen Küsters, "The Treaties of Rome (1955–57)," in Roy Pryce, ed., *The Dynamics of European Union* (London: Croom Helm, 1987), p. 94.

41. Tony Judt, *Postwar: A History of Europe Since 1945* (London: Penguin, 2005), p. 303.

42. Marjolin, *Architect of European Unity,* p. 306.

2

Uncertain Terrain, 1958–1972

Three individuals, all French, have contributed most to shaping the European Union. Yet if the EU ever built a pantheon for its heroes, only two of them would be buried there. The first, Jean Monnet, would have pride of place. The second, Jacques Delors, Commission president from 1985 to 1995, would repose beside Monnet in almost equal esteem. But the third, Charles de Gaulle, president of France from 1958 until 1969, would be relegated to the rogues' gallery of EU villains. For in the opinion of EU enthusiasts, de Gaulle's anachronistic championing of the nation-state thwarted ever closer union until the revival of European integration in the 1980s.

In fact, de Gaulle's contribution to European integration was far from negative. Though subsequently a drain on EU resources and an impediment to international trade accord, the Common Agricultural Policy (CAP) owes its existence to de Gaulle. In the 1960s, the CAP was a cherished symbol of Community solidarity and helped restructure declining Western European agriculture. More important, without the CAP there would not have been a European Community (EC). Just as France had successfully insisted on agricultural provisions in the Rome Treaty, so too de Gaulle demanded implementation of those provisions as a precondition for completing the customs union, the core of the new community.

De Gaulle is best known in EU history for keeping Britain out of the Community and for curbing the role of the Commission. Both seem negative achievements. But allowing Britain to join in the early 1960s would in all likelihood have thwarted the CAP, undermined the Community, and turned the customs union into a broad free trade area. De Gaulle's stand against the Commission epitomized his hostility to supranationalism, yet intergovernmentalism, which he so bluntly asserted, helped the EC survive in the 1970s and thrive in the 1980s. Ironically, as Stanley Hoffmann observed, the EU that emerged in the 1990s was "an improbable, yet not ineffectual, blend of de Gaulle and Monnet."[1]

both french

29

After the political frustrations of the 1960s, the EC seemed set to shake off the shackles of Gaullism and begin an invigorating new phase of its development. "Completion, deepening, enlargement," a slogan endorsed by national leaders at the Hague summit of 1969, summed up the optimism of the post–de Gaulle era. Imbued with the so-called spirit of The Hague, the EC completed unfinished business, launched new initiatives, and finally concluded accession agreements with Britain, Denmark, and Ireland, which joined the EC in January 1973. Nevertheless, solidarity was sorely tested on the eve of enlargement by Franco-German differences over monetary policy, a harbinger of difficulties in the decade ahead as the EC endured the impact of British accession and severe economic recession (see Box 2.1).

■ France, Germany, and European Integration

De Gaulle's first contribution to the EC was to bring France, the politically and economically most important member state at the time, back from the brink of catastrophe. Since the end of World War II a series of costly colonial conflicts had progressively undermined the already precarious Fourth Republic. In May 1958 a revolt by French army officers opposed to possible Algerian independence proved the last straw. Threatened by a right-wing coup d'état, the government collapsed.

Twice before at times of national crisis de Gaulle had come to the rescue: first when he rejected the Franco-German armistice of June 1940 and set up the Free French Movement, second when he bridged deep political divisions and established a provisional government in newly liberated France in August 1944. Fourteen years later, only de Gaulle wielded the authority necessary once again to save the nation. Drawing on the legend of 1940 and the lessons of 1944, de Gaulle formed a new government and drafted a new constitution, characterized by a strong presidency having almost exclusive responsibility for foreign policy and defense. French voters ushered in the Fifth Republic by overwhelmingly endorsing de Gaulle's constitution in a referendum in September 1958.[2]

Monnet understood the importance for the EC of a politically stable France. He saw de Gaulle's constitution as being essential in order to "give the executive greater legitimacy and also facilitate the decisions required for the unification of Europe. For sovereignty to be relegated, authority must be well-established."[3] Of course de Gaulle was averse to surrendering any sovereignty whatsoever. But Monnet's point about a strong executive forming the necessary basis for the sharing of sovereignty was prescient, for it was precisely from such a position that President François Mitterrand advanced European integration so effectively in the 1980s.

Box 2.1 Chronology, 1958–1972

1958	January	Launch of the European Economic Community (EEC) and the European Atomic Energy Community (Euratom)
	May	Collapse of the French Fourth Republic
	June	Charles de Gaulle forms a provisional government in France
	July	A conference in Stresa, Italy, lays the foundations for the Common Agricultural Policy (CAP)
	September	Referendum endorses the establishment of the French Fifth Republic
	December	De Gaulle is elected president of France
1959	January	First stage of transition to a common market begins
1961	August	Britain applies to join the EEC (followed by Denmark, Ireland, and Norway)
	November	France drafts a treaty for a political community (Fouchet Plan)
1962	January	Second stage of transition to a common market begins
	April	Fouchet Plan collapses
	July	US president John F. Kennedy outlines "Grand Design" for US-European relations
1963	January	De Gaulle vetoes Britain's EEC membership application; de Gaulle and Konrad Adenauer sign the Elysée Treaty; accession negotiations with Britain (and Denmark, Ireland, and Norway) end
	July	Yaoundé Convention signed between the European Community (EC) and seventeen African states and Madagascar
1965	April	Merger Treaty signed, fusing the executives of the EEC, ECSC, and Euratom
	July	"Empty chair" crisis begins
1966	January	EC enters the third and final stage of transition to a common market; agreement is reached on the Luxembourg Compromise, ending the empty chair crisis
1967	May	Britain applies a second time for EEC membership (followed by Denmark, Ireland, and Norway)
	July	Merger Treaty enters into force
	November	De Gaulle vetoes Britain's application a second time
	December	Accession negotiations with Britain (plus Denmark, Ireland, and Norway) suspended
1968	May	Student and worker riots in Paris
	July	Customs union completed, eighteen months ahead of schedule
1969	April	De Gaulle resigns
	July	Britain, Denmark, Ireland, and Norway reactivate membership applications
	December	At a summit in The Hague, EU leaders decide to reinvigorate European integration
1970	April	Agreement reached to finance the EEC through "own resources"
	June	Accession negotiations with Britain, Denmark, Ireland, and Norway resume
	October	Pierre Werner presents plan for Economic and Monetary Union (EMU)
	November	Foreign ministers launch European Political Cooperation (EPC)
1971	January	Second Yaoundé Convention and Arusha Agreement enter into force
	August	United States announces suspension of dollar convertibility, formally ending the Bretton Woods system
1972	January	Accession treaties with Britain, Denmark, Ireland, and Norway signed in Brussels
	March	Launch of the monetary "snake"
	September	Norwegians reject EEC membership in referendum
	October	At Paris summit, EEC leaders agree "to transform [by the end of the decade] the whole complex of . . . relations [among member states] into a European Union"

De Gaulle's concomitant financial and monetary reforms proved equally important for the success of the EC. Without de Gaulle's drastic devaluation of the franc in 1958 and related government spending cuts and taxation hikes, the fragile French economy could not have survived the transition to a customs union. There is some truth to de Gaulle's later claim that when the EC came into being, "it was necessary—in order to achieve something—that we French put in order our economic, financial and monetary affairs. . . . From that moment the Community was in principle viable."[4]

Adherence to the terms of the Rome Treaty may have provided a pretext for financial and monetary measures that would otherwise have been difficult to take, but the EC meant much more than that to de Gaulle. Despite its implications for national sovereignty, French membership in the EC offered the prospect of economic modernization, something that de Gaulle desperately wanted. Thus the EC flourished in its early years not because de Gaulle grudgingly went along with it but because he strongly supported a certain amount of economic integration.

Apart from seeking industrial renewal, de Gaulle saw in the EC an invaluable opportunity to modernize the antiquated French agricultural sector. "How could we maintain on our territory more than two million farms," de Gaulle wondered, "three-quarters of which were too small and too poor to be profitable, but on which, nonetheless, nearly one-fifth of the French population live? How . . . could we [provide] . . . technical training, organized markets, and the support of a rational credit system required for it to be competitive?"[5] The solution lay in the proposed Common Agricultural Policy, which would provide a Community-wide outlet for French produce at guaranteed high prices and subsidize exports outside the EC. The negotiations ahead would be arduous, but the advantage for France was clear. Hence de Gaulle's admission that "if, on resuming control of our affairs, I indeed embraced the Common Market, it was as much because of our position as an agricultural country as for the progress it would impose on our industry. . . . The CAP was a sine qua non of [our] participation."[6]

Britain's proposal in the late 1950s to establish a European free trade area to incorporate and possibly supplant the nascent EC threatened de Gaulle's economic objectives. Robert Marjolin, a vice president of the new Commission, saw the proposal as "a great danger, that of being more or less sucked into a vast European free trade area in which [the Community] would have lost its individuality, and which might have prevented it from fully establishing itself according to the terms of the Treaty of Rome."[7] De Gaulle especially feared the proposal's implications for agriculture, a sector specifically excluded from the free trade area. Accordingly, soon after coming to power de Gaulle brought the talks about a free trade area to an abrupt end. Britain pressed ahead and in November 1959 formed the European Free Trade Association (EFTA) with Austria, Denmark, Norway, Portugal, Sweden, and

Switzerland. EC member states rejected an early EFTA overture for some kind of economic association, resolving instead to continue with closer integration. This proved so successful that Britain soon applied for EC membership, leaving EFTA in the lurch.

De Gaulle's policy toward the EC complemented his policy toward Germany. Whereas de Gaulle had advocated a punitive policy toward a weak, divided Germany when he left office in 1946, he returned in 1958 to a radically different European scene. With Germany reindustrialized and rearmed, de Gaulle abandoned his earlier position and espoused instead the then-orthodox policy of Franco-German rapprochement. In September 1958, German chancellor Konrad Adenauer visited de Gaulle for the first time. The remarkably warm relationship that blossomed between the octogenarian chancellor and septuagenarian president confirmed both in the belief that their countries' future, and the future of Europe, depended above all on close Franco-German accord. At their second meeting, in November 1958, de Gaulle assured Adenauer of France's commitment to the Rome Treaty and won German support for the CAP.[8]   *both economically-based*

In de Gaulle's view, economic integration could succeed only in a broader framework of intergovernmental cooperation on political and security affairs. Such cooperation was essential for the emergence of an economically strong, politically assertive, and militarily independent Europe. Accordingly, de Gaulle sought to establish a "Union of States" as a central plank of his European policy and as a means of challenging the United States and breaking down global bipolarity.   *ultimate goal = econ. int.*

De Gaulle launched his initiative for an overarching European security community in September 1960. A committee under the chairmanship of Christian Fouchet, a senior French official, eventually drafted a plan for foreign and defense policy cooperation, as well as cooperation on cultural, educational, and scientific matters. The Fouchet Plan included an institutional framework with a supreme ministerial council, a subordinate commission of senior foreign ministry officials, and a consultative assembly of delegated national parliamentarians. This was clearly incompatible with supranational integration as envisioned by the EC's founders. Fearing either French or Franco-German hegemony, the other member states followed the Netherlands' lead and fiercely resisted the idea. As a result, the Fouchet Plan collapsed.[9]   *security failed*

De Gaulle resolved to press ahead with an exclusive Franco-German arrangement. He proposed to Adenauer that the two countries hold regular meetings at the highest political level to discuss international issues, and at the level of senior officials to discuss a wide range of policies. In the ensuing Franco-German Treaty of Friendship and Reconciliation, signed at the Elysée Palace in January 1963, both sides pledged "to consult each other, prior to any decision, on all questions of foreign policy . . . with a view to reaching an analogous position."[10]

The Elysée Treaty cemented the Franco-German rapprochement. But concern in Germany about the treaty came to a head during the ratification debate in May 1963, robbing the treaty of much of its value for de Gaulle. Alarmed by Adenauer's apparent willingness to go along uncritically with de Gaulle's European initiatives, a majority in parliament insisted on attaching a codicil to the treaty asserting Germany's overriding commitment to existing North Atlantic Treaty obligations. To make matters worse for de Gaulle, Adenauer resigned in April 1963. His successor, Ludwig Erhard, was a steadfast Atlanticist whose tenure as chancellor, from 1963 to 1966, saw a steady deterioration in Franco-German relations. "There is no point deceiving ourselves," de Gaulle remarked after a meeting with Erhard in July 1964, "the [Elysée] Treaty has not yet developed as we had hoped. . . . Europe will only be a reality when France and Germany are truly united."[11]

The Elysée Treaty would prove its worth as a building block of European integration. Despite his dislike of Erhard, de Gaulle attended regular bilateral meetings under the terms of the treaty. Subsequent French presidents and German chancellors, as well as a host of government ministers and officials, similarly stuck to a fixed schedule of bilateral meetings. With the rapid improvement of Franco-German relations in the 1970s and a growing consensus in both countries about the utility of deeper integration, these frequent, institutionalized contacts became a major factor in strengthening the EC.

■ Constructing the European Community

Franco-German rapprochement in the late 1950s, de Gaulle's acceptance of the Rome Treaty, and a buoyant European economy helped get the EC off the ground. Robert Marjolin recalled the EC's first four years as "a honeymoon . . . a time of harmony between the governments of the member countries and between [EC] institutions."[12] Walter Hallstein, a former German state secretary for foreign affairs, presided over the first Commission. With nine members (two each from Germany, France, and Italy, and one each from the other member states), the Commission spent the first few months of its existence settling into temporary quarters in Brussels, allocating portfolios among its members, and organizing the necessary staff and services.

The Council of Ministers, the EC's legislative body, began regular meetings in Brussels and formed a small secretariat there. The Council also organized the Committee of Permanent Representatives (Coreper), consisting of ambassadors resident in Brussels charged with promoting their countries' EC interests on a day-to-day basis. In Luxembourg the Court of Justice slowly began to produce an impressive body of EC case law that would later shape the course of European integration. The EC Assembly, later called the European Parliament (EP), met for the first time in Strasbourg in January 1958.

customs union

In some policy areas the Rome Treaty dictated a specific timetable for implementing certain measures; in others, it provided no more than general guidelines and statements of principle. The most immediate task was to establish the customs union, which was due to be phased in over a twelve-year period. Thanks to French financial and economic reforms, the first intra-EC tariff reductions took place, on schedule, in January 1959. As other rounds of tariff cuts and quota increases followed, the EC put a common external tariff in place. The customs union came into being in July 1968, eighteen months ahead of schedule.

The late 1950s and the early 1960s were years of extraordinarily high and sustained economic growth in Western Europe, not least because of the boom in international trade. From 1958 to 1960 alone, trade among the Six grew by 50 percent, a dramatic rise that was as much a result of "the increased activity of businessmen as [of] the actual reduction of tariffs. As soon as managers were convinced that the common market was going to be established, they started to behave in many ways as if it was already in existence."[13] Externally, the EC's early initiatives pointed in two directions: multilateral trade negotiations and global development. Under the former, the Commission assumed responsibility for member state participation in the General Agreement on Tariffs and Trade. Under the latter, in 1964 the EC concluded the Yaoundé Convention with seventeen African states and Madagascar, all former European colonies. With the exception of the Soviet Union and its satellites, other countries quickly acknowledged the Commission's responsibility for commercial policy and opened diplomatic missions in Brussels.

Successful first steps in commercial policy and external relations contrasted with the difficulty of achieving other treaty objectives. Whereas tariff barriers between countries could easily be identified and tackled, policies in areas such as competition, social affairs, transport, and energy were harder to formulate. A combination of sometimes vague treaty provisions, national apathy or outright opposition, and differences between and within the Commission and the Council inevitably impeded progress.

Given the sensitivity of agricultural policy, it is hardly surprising that, according to a key participant, "during the [Community's] first five years the question that dominated all others, by far, was the progressive construction of the CAP."[14] Agriculture was a touchy issue for most European governments. Near-famine conditions in much of postwar Europe had made food security a national priority. The centrality of peasant proprietorship in European political culture, the romantic allure of the land, and the emergence of a highly influential farmers' lobby gave agriculture added political salience. A decline in the relative economic weight of the agricultural sector and a corresponding drop in farmers' incomes raised the political stakes. Not surprisingly, by the mid-1950s agriculture had become a heavily protected and subsidized sector in most Western European countries.

Notwithstanding their general support for market integration, governments had no intention of giving up the traditional interventionist measures widely used to protect agricultural price levels and buttress farmers' earnings. Some governments, such as the German and the Dutch, would have been happy to exclude agriculture from the EC, continuing instead to subsidize it at the national level. The French government, by contrast, wanted to include agriculture in the EC in order to shift the cost of subsidizing France's large and unproductive agricultural sector from the national to the European level. As France made this a condition of accepting a common market in manufactured goods, which it wanted to have in any case, France's partners had little choice but to commit themselves in the treaty to establishing the CAP.

Bringing the CAP into being, however, proved extremely difficult. The first big battle took place over the modalities of price supports, import levies, and export subsidies. Detailed negotiations among national governments culminated in a series of legendary marathon meetings of the Council in December 1961 and January 1962. By the simple stratagem of "stopping the clock" at midnight on December 31, the ministers ostensibly reached agreement by the statutory deadline, although talks continued until mid-January. The result was a package deal that included a common system of price supports covering 85 percent of total EC agricultural production. The second, decisive battle of the CAP campaign took place in December 1964, resulting in an agreement on prices for cereals, the most important agricultural commodity.

The political importance of the CAP cannot be underestimated. In his own words, de Gaulle had come to power resolved to "put up a . . . desperate fight" in order to implement the agricultural policy provisions of the Rome Treaty, "sometimes going so far as to threaten to withdraw our membership [in the EC]" until ultimately "France and common sense prevailed."[15] The successful outcome of the marathon CAP negotiations locked France, the most important member state at the time, and the most temperamental, into the Community system. Notwithstanding its unintended consequences, without the CAP there would not have been a customs union; without a customs union there would not have been an internal market; without an internal market there would not have been a monetary union. Quite simply, the EU as we know it today would not have come into existence.[16]

The "Empty Chair" Crisis and the Luxembourg Compromise

De Gaulle's refusal to acknowledge the Commission's contribution to implementing the CAP demonstrated his well-known hatred of the Brussels bureaucracy. De Gaulle dismissed Commission officials as stateless and denationalized; he especially detested Hallstein, who seized every opportunity to enhance the Commission's power and push European integration along federal lines. The extent to which each side used the other during the CAP negotiations led to a miscalculation by the Commission, which sought to link a further sharing of national sovereignty with an ambitious proposal for the EC budget. The dispute over the Commission's proposal was the proximate cause of what became known as the "empty chair" crisis, the most serious constitutional conflict in the EU's history.[17]

Under the terms of the Rome Treaty, duties on agricultural and industrial imports would belong to the Community rather than to national governments, following completion of the EC's transitional phase, initially planned for 1970. Therefore, such revenue constituted the Community's "own resources." Pending completion of the transitional phase, the EC would be funded by temporary agreements among the member states, the first of which was due to expire at the end of June 1965.

The Commission saw the need for a new agreement as an opportunity to bring forward the advent of the own resources system to July 1968, when the customs union was due to be completed ahead of schedule. In the meantime, governments would conclude a temporary funding arrangement, covering the period from July 1965 until July 1968. Suggesting that governments give up their import duties early and switch to the system of own resources was inherently controversial. Emboldened by the successful implementation to date of the treaty's commercial and agricultural provisions and by de Gaulle's obvious interest in securing Community funding for the CAP, the Commission rashly went too far in the spring of 1965 when it proposed a new budgetary arrangement whereby the Commission itself and the EP would greatly enhance their powers.

De Gaulle's reaction was hardly unexpected. Marjolin had already warned his colleagues that to persist with the funding proposal would antagonize de Gaulle and violate the Commission's "golden rule" of not taking any action "likely to encounter an outright veto [by a national government]."[18] Undeterred, Hallstein pressed ahead and took the additional inflammatory step of announcing the proposals first to the EP in Strasbourg. Storm clouds immediately gathered, with the French foreign minister warning that the Commission was "indulging in wishful thinking by putting forward proposals which they know France will not accept."[19]

The crucial Council meeting opened on June 28 with the French minister in the chair. Substantive discussions had not even begun by midnight on June 30. The other ministers were not particularly concerned. After all, negotiations concerning the CAP had a habit of running over the stipulated deadline. To the dismay of the other governments, the French government promptly recalled its minister and permanent representative from Brussels and announced that French officials would no longer participate in the Council or its numerous subcommittees.

Faced with French abstention, the Council could do little more than conduct routine business. De Gaulle raised the stakes by linking an additional, hitherto unrelated point to the original cause of the conflict. In a press conference in September 1965, full of invective against the Commission and the EP, de Gaulle announced that France would not accept a provision of the treaty, due to be implemented in January 1966, allowing voting in the Council on a limited range of issues. It quickly became apparent that the method of Council decisionmaking, as much as or even more than the Community budget, was the root cause of the empty chair crisis.

Even though the voting system in question called for a qualified majority in order to reach a decision, thereby making it possible for countries opposed to a proposal to form a blocking minority, de Gaulle rejected voting in principle as an unacceptable abnegation of national sovereignty. He insisted instead on unanimity in Council decisionmaking, which would allow any government to veto a proposal. This greatly exacerbated the crisis, which now went to the core of the Community system.

Other governments shared the French concern about being outvoted in the Council but argued that the principle of Council voting was sacrosanct in the Community and that, in practice, deep-seated national concerns were unlikely ever to be ignored. At a Council meeting held without France in late October, ministers reaffirmed their commitment to the treaty and refusal to abandon one of its key supranational instruments. At the same time, they seemed willing to compromise on the Commission's earlier proposals and offered France every opportunity to return to the negotiating table.

The other countries' solidarity may have been a factor in de Gaulle's decision to resume talks. French public opinion was arguably a more important consideration. Farmers' organizations and business interests feared the consequences of a protracted crisis, and the presidential election of December 1965 gave them an opportunity to express their concern. Much to his surprise, de Gaulle did not win over 50 percent of the vote in the first round and had to participate in a second round, which he won, but not by a huge margin.

The election result demonstrated the domestic limits of de Gaulle's European policy. Although supposedly indifferent to public opinion, de Gaulle undoubtedly got the message. A week after the election, France announced its willingness to negotiate an end to the crisis, which the foreign ministers finally resolved at a meeting in Luxembourg in January 1966. There, the Six agreed to adopt an interim financial regulation for the CAP, deferring the question of the EC's own resources and, by extension, the Brussels institutions' budgetary powers. Majority voting in the Council remained the outstanding issue. After restating their positions, both sides approved a short declaration, the Luxembourg Compromise, which amounted to an agreement to disagree:

1. When issues very important to one or more member countries are at stake, the members of the Council will try, within a reasonable time, to reach

solutions which can be adopted by all members of the Council, while respecting their mutual interests, and those of the Community.

2. The French delegation considers that, when very important issues are at stake, discussions must be continued until unanimous agreement is reached.

3. The six delegations note that there is a divergence of views on what should be done in the event of a failure to reach complete agreement.

4. However, they consider that this divergence does not prevent the Community's work being resumed in accordance with the normal procedure.[20]

The outcome of the crisis was apparently a draw, perhaps even a victory for the Community as a whole. The other governments had not reneged on the principle of voting, and the Council soon resumed full operation. In reality, the crisis ended in victory for de Gaulle. The Council approved temporary funding for the CAP in May 1966, and the Commission's ambitious proposals to revise budgetary procedures sank out of sight. Moreover, the crisis profoundly undermined both Hallstein's credibility and the Commission's confidence. Thereafter, the Commission was politically unassertive for over a decade.

Crucially, the Luxembourg Compromise impeded effective decisionmaking in the Council for a long time to come. De Gaulle's insistence on unanimity heightened governments' awareness of each other's special interests and increased their reluctance to call a vote even when no vital interest was at stake—whatever a "vital interest" was understood to mean. As Joseph Weiler observed, the crisis and its outcome "symbolized a transformation from a 'Community' spirit to a more selfish and pragmatic 'cost-benefit' attitude of the member states. It was a change of ethos, at first rejected by the Five [the member states minus France] but later, especially after the first enlargement, eagerly seized upon by all. In this sense the danger to the Community, even if not always tangible, was significant."[21] Six months of near-paralysis in Brussels, a heavy blow to the Commission's morale, and a substantial setback to Council voting had an invidious long-term effect.

▪ Keeping Britain Out

The question of EC enlargement arose for the first time in 1961, when Britain applied to join.[22] By the end of the 1950s it was apparent that the Commonwealth and the EFTA were inadequate to fulfill Britain's commercial potential. By contrast, the EC exerted a powerful pull. But British politicians were generally unenthusiastic about the EC, with the opposition Labour Party deeply divided on the issue. The Conservatives generally favored joining, although the government of Prime Minister Harold Macmillan included more than a few "anti-marketeers," forerunners of today's Euroskeptics.

Macmillan accepted that EC membership was in Britain's economic interest and that it would advance his main foreign policy objective: nurturing the

Anglo-American "special relationship." US president John F. Kennedy's unequivocal endorsement of British membership in the EC strengthened Macmillan's determination to join but aroused de Gaulle's antipathy. Kennedy's "Grand Design" for closer US-European relations and a stronger Atlantic Alliance, outlined in a famous Independence Day speech in 1962, was at odds with de Gaulle's vision of Europe.[23]

Macmillan tried to overcome his differences with de Gaulle by appealing to past friendship. De Gaulle had been in North Africa during the war, fighting for his political life as leader of the Free French Movement. Macmillan had been there as well, as a high-level British representative. As Macmillan's biographer noted, "But for Macmillan's support for de Gaulle against Roosevelt and Churchill [in 1943], almost certainly de Gaulle would not have been in Paris, at the helm, in 1958."[24] De Gaulle may have owed Macmillan a huge political debt, but he was not about to pay it off by easing Britain's path to EC membership.

As it was, the accession negotiations in Brussels quickly became mired in a mass of technical detail, mostly over agriculture, the Commonwealth, and the EFTA. A British government paper outlined the problems in all three areas. In agriculture, Britain's twin policies of buying low-priced food on the world market and paying farmers direct price support were incompatible with the principles of the CAP. As for the Commonwealth, Britain feared the impact on its former possessions of a sudden disruption of traditional trade patterns. Finally, as a British white paper (official government document) noted, "given [Britain's] obligations to our EFTA partners, we should not be able to join the Community until [we agree upon] . . . ways and means of meeting their legitimate interests."[25]

Developments in Anglo-American relations overshadowed the accession negotiations. Matters came to a head in December 1962 at a meeting in Nassau between Macmillan and Kennedy to negotiate a new Anglo-American missile accord. Under the terms of the agreement, Britain would use US missiles as the delivery system for British nuclear warheads. Moreover, Britain's nuclear force would be integrated into NATO, except when the government "may decide that supreme national interests are at stake."[26]

For de Gaulle, who at the time was struggling to develop the French nuclear force, the Nassau agreement represented a damning surrender of sovereignty. Britain had relinquished to the United States technological and strategic responsibility for a supposedly independent nuclear deterrent. There could have been no more graphic demonstration of Britain's irreconcilability with de Gaulle's vision of an independent Europe. De Gaulle now had an ideal excuse to break off the enlargement negotiations.

He did so dramatically in a press conference in January 1963. Having been asked if he could "define explicitly France's position towards Britain's entry into the Common Market," de Gaulle said that he would "endeavor to reply clearly." He then launched into an answer that was almost 2,000 words long. The gist of it was that if Britain joined at this stage, the EC "would not endure for long [but] instead would become a colossal Atlantic community under American domination and direction."[27] This amounted to a veto of Britain's application.

Paul-Henri Spaak, one of the authors of the Rome Treaty, wrote that the date of de Gaulle's press conference would "go down in history as the 'black Monday' of both European policy and Atlantic policy."[28] But as another observer remarked, the "crisis atmosphere" provoked by de Gaulle's statement "was not of long duration . . . because the concern of France's partners to push the Community forward was stronger than their irritation with French high-mindedness."[29] Though they regretted how the negotiations had come to an end, many national and EC officials agreed that Britain was not yet ready for membership. As Marjolin noted, de Gaulle's decision to close the door on Britain "offended France's continental partners possibly more through its form than through its content."[30]

The suspension of Britain's application was a political disaster for Macmillan, who could not have failed to notice that de Gaulle was far from isolated in his rejection of Britain's candidacy. There was nothing to do but await a favorable time for Britain to reapply for membership. Dejected, Macmillan resigned in October 1963, reportedly because of bad health—but he went on to enjoy twenty-three years of robust retirement.

When Britain applied again, in May 1967, the Labour Party was in power. Harold Wilson was still equivocal about the EC but saw little economic alternative to joining. If anything, Britain's growing commercial contacts with the continent increased the urgency of accession. Like Macmillan before him, Wilson hoped to overcome French opposition to British entry by cultivating de Gaulle, based on Wilson's own ambivalence about the Anglo-American special relationship.

The Commission issued a favorable opinion of Britain's application, and preparations went ahead to resume accession negotiations. Then, in another of his famous stage-managed press conferences, in December 1967, de Gaulle announced that Britain's entry "would obviously mean the breaking up of a Community that has been built and that functions according to rules which would not bear such a monumental exception."[31] There was no longer any doubt about the issue. A week later Britain again shelved its application. De Gaulle blocked Britain's second attempt to join the EC for essentially the same reasons as before. Despite Wilson's personal ambivalence about the United States, Anglo-American relations remained fundamentally sound and, in de Gaulle's view, constituted an insuperable barrier to British membership.[32]

■ De Gaulle's Departure and the Spirit of The Hague

Domestic and international developments in 1968 abruptly ended the Gaullist illusion of French grandeur. De Gaulle's focus on foreign policy had blinded him to the extent of growing domestic dissatisfaction. Protesting a rigid educational system and stagnant living standards, in May 1968 millions of students and workers poured onto French city streets. After a month of unrest, the Fifth Republic seemed on the brink of collapse. What saved it, perhaps, was the unwillingness or inability of the Communist Party to exploit the situation fully. The government also survived, but not because of de Gaulle, who fled Paris at the height of the crisis, leaving his prime minister, Georges Pompidou, to find a solution. Pompidou did so by gambling on time and capitalizing on the inevitable public reaction against incessant instability. Having dissolved the parliament and called new elections in June 1968, the Gaullists and their allies won an overall majority.

It proved a Pyrrhic victory. The events of May 1968 irrevocably weakened de Gaulle's standing. Although his term of office was not due to expire for another four years, after the events of May 1968 de Gaulle increasingly looked like a lame-duck president. In the EC, other governments awaited de Gaulle's departure before taking any new initiatives. That came sooner than expected when, in April 1969, de Gaulle resigned, having staked his presidency on the outcome of two referendums on relatively minor matters. US and Western European leaders watched de Gaulle go with a mixture of relief and regret—relief because progress within the EC and harmony within the Atlantic Alliance finally seemed assured; regret because for all his foibles and illusions, few could doubt de Gaulle's eminence or achievements.

Pompidou, de Gaulle's successor as president of France, held the key to the EC's progress in the immediate aftermath of the general's resignation. Pompidou was steeped in Gaullism but was not a slave to de Gaulle's EC policies. He sought to balance Gaullist hostility toward political integration on the one hand, with growing resentment throughout the EC against French obduracy on the other. Enlargement posed an obvious dilemma. For Gaullist diehards, the veto of Britain's application had become sacrosanct. Yet for a growing portion of the French public and for France's EC partners, revoking the veto was the only means by which France could possibly retain influence in the EC.

Regardless of his personal preferences, there was an objective difference in France's circumstances in the late 1960s that impelled Pompidou to accept enlargement. The events of May 1968 had enfeebled France economically and lowered the country's international standing, making a positive French contribution to the EC more important than ever before. Consequently, Pompidou was in a much weaker position than de Gaulle to veto British membership.

At the same time, Germany surged ahead economically. Under a new chancellor, Social Democrat Willy Brandt, Germany was also politically assertive. Gone were the days of Adenauer's subservience to de Gaulle. Germany's refusal to arrest the declining value of the franc by revaluing the mark and its decision to launch an ambitious foreign policy initiative toward Eastern Europe and the Soviet Union emphasized the point. Germany's growing economic power and rising political confidence made British accession a more appealing prospect for Pompidou. Together, Britain and France might counterbalance Germany's weight within the EC.

Brandt's major foreign policy initiative was known as Ostpolitik. However unfairly, Ostpolitik raised the specter for Germany's allies of a neutral Federal Republic loosening its moorings in the EC and NATO. That led Brandt to emphasize the importance of European integration, which in any case he genuinely supported. Moreover, Brandt saw British accession into the EC as a form of reassurance for those countries fearful of Germany's resurgence. Similarly, Wilson argued that, in view of Ostpolitik, British accession would restrain German's foreign policy ambition.[33]

Apprehensive about the possible impact of Ostpolitik and under pressure to assert French leadership in the EC, Pompidou called for a special summit of the EC's leaders. The meeting took place in The Hague (the Netherlands held the rotating EC presidency at the time), in December 1969. In contrast to the ubiquity of summits today, the December 1969 summit was the first meeting of EC leaders since the tenth-anniversary celebration of the Rome Treaty in 1967.

With de Gaulle gone, most leaders looked forward to a decisive breakthrough on a range of issues. Indeed, the summit spawned the "spirit of The Hague," a belief that the EC was once again on the ascendant. Especially in view of the Community's difficulties in the mid-1960s and later in the mid-1970s, the summit assumed a retrospective aura of harmony and rapid progress. Yet this belies the reality of a tense encounter between Pompidou, trying to square the Gaullist circle, and the others, led by Brandt. The EC leaders' endorsement of Pompidou's catchphrase "completion, deepening, enlargement" disguised the continuing tension between France and the others but met the disparate demands of the main protagonists—including Britain, hovering in the wings.[34]

It was no accident that "enlargement" came after "completion" and "deepening." At the summit, Pompidou endorsed enlargement in principle but called first for a strengthening of existing Community competences. "Completion" meant reaching an agreement to fund the EC through its own resources. "Deepening" meant extending EC competences beyond existing policies and activities. Accordingly, Pompidou advocated a system of foreign policy cooperation through regular meetings of foreign ministers and, possibly, the establishment of a secretariat in Paris. This smacked to the others of a revival of de Gaulle's political plans. In the absence of de Gaulle and the onset of Ostpolitik, however, governments were willing to explore the idea of keeping each other informed of significant foreign policy initiatives.

Monetary policy was another area in which countries could deepen European integration. Pompidou proposed coordinating member states' monetary policies in part because international financial instability could have endangered the CAP by exposing farm prices to parity fluctuations. Brandt had little sympathy for the CAP; during the Hague summit he repeatedly attacked the rapid accumulation of agricultural surpluses. Nevertheless, he supported the idea of closer monetary policy coordination if only to demonstrate Germany's commitment to the EC in the face of concerns about Ostpolitik. But Brandt would not consider monetary cooperation in isolation. An ingrained fear of inflation led him also to urge greater economic convergence in the EC.

As for enlargement, Pompidou insisted that a budget agreement—essential for financing the CAP—would have to be reached before talks with the candidate countries (Denmark, Ireland, Norway, and Britain) could begin. The Dutch countered with the opposite argument—that a budget agreement should be concluded only when the EC agreed upon a timetable for enlargement. The outcome was a classic EC compromise: in return for a commitment from the others to sort out the budget by the end of the year, France promised that enlargement negotiations would begin by June 1970.

The spirit of The Hague soon bore fruit in an agreement to fund the CAP by granting the EC its own resources, consisting of all levies on agricultural products and duties on industrial goods imported into the EC, plus a small portion (not to exceed 1 percent) of national receipts of value-added tax. The agreement granted the EP modest budgetary powers. Foreign ministers approved the new arrangement in an amendment to the Rome Treaty in April 1970, subject to ratification by the member states. Even in France, ratification proceeded smoothly.

The budget agreement marked an important stage of the EC's development. Yet progress in other areas proved difficult. Efforts to coordinate foreign, economic, and monetary policies encountered differences of interpretation and enthusiasm among national governments as well as an increasingly hostile international environment. The attempt to coordinate foreign policy fared best, with governments agreeing in October 1970 to launch European Political Cooperation (EPC), consisting of biannual meetings of foreign ministers and more frequent meetings of their officials, with the Council presidency managing the procedure and providing the necessary support.[35]

Despite the launch of EPC, France remained highly skeptical of Germany's new foreign policy orientation. A desire to reassure France, and thereby indirectly appease the domestic opposition, motivated Brandt's approach to monetary policy coordination as well as to foreign policy cooperation. At the summit in The Hague, EC leaders had asked Pierre Werner, prime minister of Luxembourg, to draft a report on Economic and Monetary Union (EMU). In October 1970, Werner presented an ambitious plan to achieve EMU within ten years by means of institutional reform and closer political integration.[36] The Werner Plan glossed over the contending French and German emphases on monetary measures and economic policy coordination by proposing parallel progress in both spheres. A related difference between the governments in Paris and Bonn soon emerged over the scope and possible implementation of the plan. Although a firm supporter of monetary policy coordination, Pompidou was loath to share sovereignty in a new policy area. Brandt and other national leaders, by contrast, had no qualms about strengthening supranationalism.[37]

■ The First Enlargement

The accession negotiations began in June 1970 in Luxembourg and ended almost a year later in Brussels.[38] Familiar issues from Britain's previous applications soon resurfaced. However, the talks were far less contentious than in the early 1960s. For one thing, Edward Heath, who became prime minister in 1970, was the most Euroenthusiastic of British politicians. Heath championed his country's application and deeply regretted the lost opportunity of the early 1960s, when he had negotiated Britain's first entry effort. For another thing, Commonwealth and EFTA concerns about British membership in the EC had abated in the intervening decade. The impact on the Commonwealth of Britain's accession now focused on specific problems, such as imports of Caribbean sugar and New Zealand dairy products. Nevertheless, the negotiations occasionally stalled, particularly on the controversial questions of Britain's budgetary contribution and the related issue of the dubious benefit to Britain of the CAP.

A meeting between Heath and Pompidou in Paris in May 1971 helped resolve these issues. According to the usually understated *Times* of London, relations between the two leaders reached a "dizzy pinnacle of mutual admiration" at the Paris tête-à-tête.[39] The surprising rapport between Pompidou and Heath led some observers to speculate that France had finally jettisoned its lingering opposition to enlargement. Together with a deterioration in relations between Pompidou and Brandt, it also sparked speculation that the Paris-London axis would replace the Paris-Bonn axis as the main bilateral motor of Community development, or at least that the Paris-Bonn axis might broaden into a trilateral axis that included Britain. Nothing of the sort happened.[40]

The negotiations in Brussels rekindled the highly flammable domestic debate on EC membership. The opposition Labour Party suffered most in the ensuing conflagration. Whether motivated by conviction or opportunism, Harold Wilson denounced Heath's entry terms and declared that a Labour government would renegotiate Britain's membership. On the other side of the parliamentary aisle, few of Heath's fellow Conservatives shared the prime minister's ardor for European integration; they saw EC membership largely in negative terms—as Britain's least bad option.

Pompidou surprised everyone by announcing in March 1972 that he would hold a referendum on enlargement. Domestic rather than international factors inspired the French president's decision. A snap referendum provided a clever means of splitting the opposition by driving a wedge between the Communists, who opposed the mere existence of the EC, and the Socialists, who favored British entry. Referendums were a hallmark of Gaullist government; it seemed especially appropriate for Pompidou to use a widely recognized Gaullist instrument to undermine an equally identifiable Gaullist position on the EC (keeping Britain out).

The great danger, as de Gaulle's last referendum clearly demonstrated and as future referendums would also show, was that the government could lose. In the event, Pompidou won the April 1972 referendum, but not as convincingly as expected. Only 60 percent of the French electorate turned out, and 32 percent voted against. The result, like the reason for the referendum, should be seen in domestic political terms. The relatively small number of French voters who endorsed enlargement reflected Pompidou's unpopularity more than the merits of Britain's case.[41]

British opponents of accession pressed Heath's government to hold a referendum in Britain on EC membership. With the three other applicant countries—Denmark, Ireland, and Norway—all holding referendums, British Euroskeptics cited the French case as an additional reason to adopt such a procedure. Heath refused to budge, arguing that parliament had the sovereign right to decide such questions on behalf of the electorate. Yet Pompidou's decision to consult the electorate helped push Wilson into the pro-referendum camp, which paved the way for the referendum on Britain's EC membership once the Labour Party came back to power.

The question of EC membership was even more contentious in Norway, where the government sought to reassure the electorate about the consequences of membership, especially for fishing and agriculture—even more protected in Norway than in the EC—and the fledgling oil industry. After a campaign that polarized Norwegian opinion, 54 percent voted against accession in the September 1972 referendum.

Passions also ran high in Denmark, but the referendum there—held only one week after the Norwegian vote—resulted in an impressive endorsement of membership. Like the British, the Danes were, and remain, skeptical about European integration. Once Britain applied for membership, however, Denmark had little choice but to follow suit. With the bulk of the country's exports going to Britain and Germany, it would have been economic suicide for Denmark to stay out of the enlarged EC. Despite familiar fears about the erosion of national sovereignty and the possible severance of traditional ties with the Nordic countries, 63 percent voted in favor of accession.

The Irish referendum, held in May 1972, registered strong support for EC membership. Far more than Denmark's, Ireland's economic fortunes were tied to those of Britain. It would have been absurd economically for Ireland to stay outside the EC once Britain went in. Added to this were elements of opportunism and political calculation. The former had to do with the expected wind-fall for Irish farmers of participation in the CAP. The latter consisted of the anticipated impact of EC membership on Anglo-Irish relations. Despite becoming independent in 1922, Ireland remained relatively isolated from Europe, bound up instead in a suffocatingly close relationship with Britain. EC membership gave Ireland the chance to place its relations with Britain in a broader, multilateral context. It was little wonder that a resounding 83 percent of those voting endorsed accession.[42]

The ratification drama continued in Britain until almost the last minute. Having survived a series of procedural hurdles, the act of accession finally won parliamentary approval in October 1972. But that was not the end of either Labour Party posturing or British misgivings about the EC. On the contrary, British—and Danish—aversion to deeper integration, the inevitable strains of absorbing three new member states, and a difficult international economic environment combined in the mid-1970s to put the newly enlarged EC sorely to the test.

Rhetoric vs. Reality

The Paris summit of October 1972, which Pompidou convened in anticipation of enlargement, marks the high point of Euro-optimism in the post–de Gaulle period. The summit is famous—or infamous—for the last sentence of a "solemn declaration" attached to the concluding communiqué: "The member states of the Community, the driving force of European construction, affirm their intention before the end of the present decade to transform the whole complex of their relations into a European Union."[43] Although nobody knew quite what "European Union" meant, the commitment to achieve it within eight years put an unnecessary and ultimately embarrassing onus on the member states. As the 1970s passed and nothing remotely resembling European union appeared on the horizon, the Paris Declaration served only to highlight the extent of the EC's disarray.

Yet at the time, the Paris Declaration played well in national capitals. The text was sufficiently warm and woolly to escape excessive criticism even in London and Copenhagen. The communiqué also struck a positive chord by expressing the EC's readiness to launch an impressive array of new initiatives. Apart from referring to monetary union and foreign policy cooperation, the communiqué mentioned regional policy, industrial policy, energy, and the environment. These were striking examples of Community "deepening."

Pompidou's apparent retreat from Gaullism should not be exaggerated, however. A close reading of the communiqué, supplemented by reports of the two-day meeting, suggests that the summit did not represent a radical departure from previous French policy. Pompidou supported establishing a fund for regional economic development within the EC, mostly in deference to Heath, who badly needed to achieve something at the summit from which Britain might profit directly. In the wake of the bitter accession debate, Heath saw the Paris summit largely in domestic political terms. A promise of financial assistance for depressed industrial and agricultural regions would offset criticism in Britain of the high cost of the CAP.

Pompidou's willingness to help Heath emphasized the rapport between the two leaders and fueled further speculation about a new Anglo-French axis. By contrast, the vaunted Franco-German axis seemed moribund. Personally, Pompidou had little time for Brandt; politically, Brandt's repeated criticism of the CAP angered the French president. In keeping with his complaints about unwarranted EC expenditure, voiced all the more loudly in the prelude to the approaching German elections, Brandt distrusted the proposed regional fund, which looked too much like "an exercise in old-fashioned, pork-barrel politics rather than a political instrument for the unification of Europe."[44]

The vexing question of economic and monetary policy remained the greatest cause of friction between Germany and France. In the eighteen months before the summit, monetary matters had dominated European and wider international affairs. The collapse of the postwar Bretton Woods system of fixed exchange rates triggered markedly divergent reactions in Bonn and Paris. Whereas Brandt proposed that EC members together float their currencies, Pompidou opposed the idea because of its likely impact on the competitiveness of French products and because of lack of sympathy with the economic plight of the United States, which Pompidou blamed for the international financial unrest. The currency crises of 1971, culminating in President Richard Nixon's announcement in August that year of the suspension of dollar convertibility and the imposition of restrictive trade measures, had long-lasting effects and helped send European economies slipping into recession.

Circumstances were hardly propitious for the fledgling EMU, although the collapse of the international monetary system inevitably increased calls among the Six for closer coordination of economic and monetary policy. In April 1972 the Six hatched the "snake," a regimen to keep EC currency movements within a 2.5 percent margin inside the "tunnel" established during the Smithsonian talks of December 1971 that sought to repair the international system. Worried about the consequences of currency fluctuations for the CAP, Pompidou put monetary policy cooperation high on the agenda of the Paris summit. In response to Pompidou's call for exchange rate stability, Brandt stressed the importance of anti-inflationary measures. The result was a reaffirmation at the summit of the need for parallel progress on economic and monetary measures. Echoing the member states' call for European Union by the end of the decade, the summit communiqué reiterated the commitment to EMU "with a view to its completion not later than December 31, 1980."[45]

The rhetoric of European integration was increasingly at odds with reality. The EC was weakened at the top by a politically unassertive Commission and by deep differences between the leaders of France and Germany, the two countries on which the EC depended for direction. At the same time, the EC was about to digest two new members—Denmark and Britain—noted for their skepticism toward the political objectives of European integration.

Under the circumstances, it would be easy to underestimate the achievements of European integration in the fifteen years since the founding of the EC. By the early 1970s the customs union, the CAP, and a common trade policy were firmly in place. The EC had survived the empty chair crisis and was about to undertake an ambitious enlargement. Since its inception in 1958, the EC had become a major political and economic factor for the member states, in dealings among them, and in broader international relations. By any measure, the EC was a striking success.

■ Notes

1. Stanley Hoffmann, review of *De Gaulle: The Rebel, 1890–1944,* by Jean Lacouture, *New Republic,* December 17, 1990, p. 34.

2. See Nicholas Atkin, *The Fifth French Republic* (Basingstoke: Palgrave Macmillan, 2005), pp. 38–59.

3. Jean Monnet, *Memoirs* (Garden City: Doubleday, 1978), p. 430.

4. Quoted in *Le Monde,* January 15, 1963.

5. Charles de Gaulle, *Mémoires d'espoir* (Paris: Edition Omnibus, 1999), pp. 165–166.

6. De Gaulle, *Mémoires,* p. 167.

7. Robert Marjolin, *Architect of European Unity: Memoirs, 1911–1986* (London: Weidenfeld and Nicolson, 1989), p. 318.

8. On the Adenauer–de Gaulle relationship, see Hermann Kusterer, *Der Kanzler und der General* (Baden-Baden: Klett-Cotta, 1995); and Paul Legoll, *Charles de Gaulle et Konrad Adenauer: La Cordiale entente* (Paris: Editions L'Harmattan, 2004).

9. Jeffrey Vanke, "An Impossible Union: Dutch Objections to the Fouchet Plan, 1959–62," *Cold War History* 2, no. 1 (2001): 95.

10. Edward Kolodziej, *French International Policy Under de Gaulle and Pompidou: The Politics of Grandeur* (Ithaca: Cornell University Press, 1974), p. 316.

11. Quoted in *Le Monde,* July 7, 1964, p. 1.

12. Marjolin, *Architect of European Unity,* p. 310.

13. John Pinder, "Implications for the Operation of the Firm," *Journal of Common Market Studies* 1, no. 1 (1962): 41.

14. Marjolin, *Architect of European Unity,* p. 312.

15. De Gaulle, *Mémoires,* pp. 159, 186–187.

16. On the origins and development of the CAP, see Kiran Patel, ed., *Fertile Ground for Europe? The History of European Integration and the Common Agricultural Policy Since 1945* (Baden-Baden: Nomos, 2009).

17. On the empty chair crisis and Luxembourg Compromise, see W. Loth, ed., *Crises and Compromises: The European Project, 1963–1969* (Baden Baden: Nomos, 2001); N. Piers Ludlow, *The European Community and the Crises of the 1960s: The*

Gaullist Challenge (London: Routledge, 2006), pp. 40–124; and Jean-Marie Playret, Helen Wallace, and Pascaline Winand, eds., *Visions, Votes, and Vetoes: The Empty Chair Crisis and the Luxembourg Compromise Forty Years On* (Brussels: Peter Lang, 2006).

18. Marjolin, *Architect of European Unity,* p. 314.

19. Quoted in Françoise de la Serre, "The EEC and the 1965 Crisis," in F. Roy Willis, ed., *European Integration* (New York: New Viewpoints, 1975), p. 134.

20. The text of the agreement is reproduced in Playret, Wallace, and Winand, *Visions, Votes, and Vetoes,* app. 2, pp. 325–326.

21. Joseph Weiler, "The Genscher-Colombo Draft European Act: The Politics of Indecision," *Journal of European Integration* 4, nos. 2–3 (1989): 134.

22. See N. Piers Ludlow, *Dealing with Britain: The Six and the First UK Application to the EEC* (Cambridge: Cambridge University Press, 1997).

23. On competing US and French designs for Europe, see E. Mehan, *Kennedy, de Gaulle, and Western Europe* (Basingstoke: Palgrave, 2002).

24. Alastair Horne, *Harold Macmillan,* vol. 2 (New York: Viking, 1989), p. 312.

25. The white paper is reproduced in Frances Nicholson and Roger East, *From the Six to the Twelve: The Enlargement of the European Communities* (Chicago: St. James, 1987), pp. 14–21.

26. See Richard Neustadt, *Alliance Politics* (New York: Columbia University Press, 1970), pp. 52–55.

27. The text of the press conference is available in *European Navigator: The Authoritative Multimedia Reference on the History of Europe,* http://www.ena.lu/.

28. Paul-Henri Spaak, "Hold Fast," *Foreign Affairs* 41, no. 4 (1963): 611.

29. Lois Pattison de Menil, *Who Speaks for Europe? The Vision of Charles de Gaulle* (London: Macmillan, 1978), p. 136.

30. Marjolin, *Architect of European Unity,* p. 338.

31. The text of the press conference is available in *European NAvigator,* http://www.ena.lu/.

32. See Oliver Daddow, *Harold Wilson and European Integration: Britain's Second Application to Join the EEC* (London: Routledge, 2002); Helen Parr, *British Policy Towards the European Community: Harold Wilson and Britain's World Role, 1964–1967* (London: Routledge, 2005); and Melissa Pine, *Harold Wilson and Europe: Pursuing Britain's Membership of the European Community* (London: Taurus Academic, 2008).

33. On the relationship between Ostpolitik and European integration, see N. Piers Ludlow, ed., *European Integration and the Cold War: Ostpolitik-Westpolitik, 1965–1973* (London: Routledge, 2007).

34. See J. Van Der Harst, *Beyond the Customs Union: The European Community's Quest for Deepening, Widening, and Completion, 1969–1975* (Brussels: Bruylant, 2007).

35. See Daniel Mockli, *European Foreign Policy During the Cold War: Heath, Brandt, Pompidou, and the Dream of Political Unity* (London: Tauris, 2008).

36. Council of Ministers, "The Werner Report on Economic and Monetary Union," Bulletin EC S/11-1970.

37. See Loukas Tsoukalis, *The Politics and Economics of European Monetary Integration* (London: Allen and Unwin, 1977).

38. See David Hannay, ed., *Britain's Entry into the European Community: Report on the Negotiations of 1970–1972 by Sir Con O'Neill* (London: Routledge, 2000).

39. *The Times* (London), October 21, 1972, p. 6.

40. Haig Simonian, *The Privileged Partnership: Franco-German Relations in the European Community, 1969–1984* (Oxford: Clarendon, 1985), p. 114.

41. Kolodziej, *French International Policy,* pp. 432–438.

42. For an account of the 1972 referenda issues and results in Norway, Denmark, and Ireland, see Nicholson and East, *From the Six to the Twelve,* pp. 97–100, 113–115, 117–133.

43. European Commission, *1972 General Report* (Luxembourg: Office for Official Publications of the European Communities, 1973), point 5.16.

44. Werner Feld, *West Germany and the European Community: Changing Interests and Competing Policy Objectives* (New York: Praeger, 1981), p. 67.

45. European Commission, *1972 General Report,* point 5.1.

3 A Community in Flux, 1973–1984

The terms "Eurosclerosis" and "Europessimism" were widely used to describe the state of European integration in the late1970s. Following global financial upheaval early in the decade and the first oil crisis in 1974, the European Community struggled to cope with oscillating exchange rates and widely uneven economic performance among member states plagued by low growth, high unemployment, and rampant inflation—collectively called stagflation. The history of the EC in the 1970s and early 1980s is that of a Community in flux, lacking internal coherence and buffeted by international economic headwinds.

The EC weathered the storm in part because of the emergence of the European Council, involving regular summit meetings of the heads of state or government, as a forum for solving problems and providing direction at the highest political level. Equally important, the trials and tribulations of the 1970s convinced leaders in national governments, the Commission, and the European Parliament of the urgent need for institutional reform and policy innovation. As a result, the late 1970s and early 1980s formed a critical bridge between the Community's early attainments and later triumphs.

The impending improvement in the EC's fortunes was by no means apparent at the time. The twenty-fifth anniversary of the Rome Treaty, observed in March 1982, was a dismal affair. Remarking on a report that the Council had canceled the official celebration, the president of the EP compared the Community to "a feeble cardiac patient whose condition is so poor that he cannot even be disturbed by a birthday party."[1] Under the circumstances, Greenland's decision in February 1982 to become the first (and so far only) territory to leave the EC seemed entirely appropriate.

The EC's problems were legion: a dysfunctional decisionmaking process; a weak Commission; an agricultural policy apparently out of control; a new French president (François Mitterrand) pursuing a "dash for growth" that further strained Community solidarity; and a new British prime minister (Margaret Thatcher) insisting on a budget rebate, an issue that preoccupied the EC for the next five years and fifteen summits. Only when the European Council resolved the British budgetary question in June 1984 did the EC suddenly revel in the impact of other, less perceptible, but no less important developments that, over the previous four years, had generated momentum for greater integration. As a result, as Commissioner Christopher Tugendhat observed at the time, "One has the feeling of ice breaking up and spring approaching"[2] (see Box 3.1).

Box 3.1   Chronology, 1973–1984

1973	January	Britain, Denmark, and Ireland join the European Community (EC)
	October	Arab oil producers quadruple the price of oil and embargo port of Rotterdam
	December	EC leaders discuss oil crisis at Copenhagen summit
1974	April	New British government opens renegotiation of EC membership terms
	September	EC leaders decide to form European Council
	December	EC leaders hold last informal summit in Paris
1975	February	Lomé Convention between the EC and forty-six developing countries signed
	March	Inaugural meeting of European Council in Dublin concludes renegotiation of Britain's membership terms; European Regional Development Fund established
	June	Britons decide in referendum to accept new EC membership terms
		Greece applies to join the EC
	July	Agreement to establish Court of Auditors and strengthen budgetary powers of the European Parliament (EP)
	December	Tindemans Report on European Union
1976	July	Accession negotiations with Greece begin
1977	January	Jenkins Commission takes office
	March	Portugal applies to join the EC
	July	Spain applies to join the EC
1978	July	European Council agrees to establish European Monetary System (EMS)
	October	Accession negotiations with Portugal begin
1979	February	Accession negotiations with Spain begin
	March	Eight member states launch the exchange rate mechanism of the EMS
	May	Accession treaty with Greece signed in Athens
	June	First direct elections to the EP
	September	Spierenburg Report on Commission reform
	October	Second Lomé Convention signed
	November	"Three Wise Men" report on EC reform
		Beginning of British budgetary question
1981	January	Greece joins the EC
	November	Genscher-Colombo proposals
1982	February	Greenlanders decide in referendum to leave the EC
1983	June	Stuttgart Declaration
1984	February	EP adopts Draft Treaty Establishing the European Union
	June	Second direct elections to the EP
		At Fontainebleau summit, EC leaders resolve British budgetary question
	December	Third Lomé Convention signed

▓ Britain's Renegotiation and Referendum

Far from celebrating its first enlargement in 1973, the EC found itself grappling with a serious economic downturn. Soaring inflation, rising unemployment, yawning trade deficits, and a worsening oil crisis shook the Community to the core. Continuing exchange rate fluctuations and divergences of member states' monetary and economic policies made nonsense of the 1980 target date for economic and monetary union. A massive hike in oil prices and the imposition of an oil embargo, in the aftermath of the October 1973 Arab-Israeli war, made matters even worse (oil from the Middle East supplied over 60 percent of the EC's energy needs). Eager to protect their close relationships with the Arab oil-producing countries, Britain and France stifled discussion of a common energy policy. Meeting in December 1973, EC leaders failed to restore solidarity or agree on joint action.

It was under these circumstances that the new British government, once again led by Harold Wilson, sought a renegotiation of the country's accession agreement. Apart from a recalculation of Britain's budgetary contribution, Wilson's demands included reform of the Common Agricultural Policy, concessions to Commonwealth commercial interests, and less concretely, the protection of British sovereignty.

What followed epitomized the EC's languor in the mid-1970s. The renegotiations lasted eleven months, dominated two summits, and drove Britain's partners to distraction. Roy Jenkins, who became Commission president later in the 1970s, observed that the entire episode "produced the minimum results with the maximum ill-will."[3] At the expense of Britain's standing in Europe, Wilson seemed to be engaged in a frantic effort to hold his fractious Labour Party together. In the run-up to the October 1974 general election, the second in less than a year, Wilson pledged either another general election or a referendum to validate the result of Britain's renegotiation of EC membership terms. Wilson's election victory kept the question of continued EC membership at the top of the political agenda.

Jenkins credits German chancellor Helmut Schmidt not only with ensuring a successful outcome of the renegotiation but also with convincing a majority of Labour Party members that Britain should stay in the EC. Schmidt, a Social Democrat, visited Britain in November 1974 and made an impassioned speech at the Labour Party conference. At the same time, he coached Wilson privately on the approach to take with French president Valéry Giscard d'Estaing, who strongly opposed Britain's renegotiation. Although conceding the validity of Britain's claim that it was contributing too much to the EC budget, Giscard was unconvinced that a successful renegotiation would end British dissatisfaction with the EC. Agreement on the Regional Development Fund, reached at a summit in December 1974, undoubtedly helped Wilson politically—nearly 30 percent of the fund would go to Britain.

Also at the December 1974 summit, EC leaders charged the Commission with designing a formula to prevent Britain, or any other member state, from paying too much into the EC. The Commission published its report, quaintly titled "The Unacceptable Situation and the Correcting Mechanism," in January 1975.[4] This provided the basis for the negotiations among EC leaders, at the crucial summit in March 1975, to try to reach agreement on an acceptable British rebate. Success hinged on satisfying Wilson's demand for access into the EC market of New Zealand dairy products, which both amused and infuriated Giscard. Finally, out of tedium or despair, the other eight leaders agreed to make the concession and Wilson agreed that the proposed rebate yielded a reasonable figure on which to base a referendum campaign for Britain to stay in the EC.

Regardless of its impact on British public opinion, the result of the renegotiation had failed to unite the Labour Party on the question of continued Community membership. The opposition Conservative Party had more than its fair share of Euroskeptics, yet the vast majority of its members favored staying in the EC. Margaret Thatcher's first major speech as the newly elected Conservative Party leader was on the referendum issue. Though deploring the constitutional precedent of holding a referendum, which she considered a violation of parliamentary sovereignty, Thatcher strongly advocated a "yes" vote. With the leadership of the two main parties and the small Liberal Party urging a positive result, the outcome of the June 1975 referendum was hardly in doubt: 67 percent voted for and 33 percent against staying "in Europe" (the turnout was 64 percent).[5]

Four days after the referendum, Wilson told the House of Commons that "the debate is now over . . . the historic decision has been made. . . . We look forward to continuing to work with [our partners] in promoting the Community's wider interests and in fostering a greater sense of purpose among the member states."[6] By then it was difficult to repair the damage that the renegotiation and referendum had done. At home, according to Jenkins, "the handling of the European question by the leadership throughout the 1970s did more to cause the [Labour] Party's disasters of the 1980s than did any other issue."[7] Abroad, the renegotiation "added to the spirit of irritation and impatience with Britain that had been growing within the Community" since enlargement.[8] Even before Thatcher came to office in 1979 and promptly reopened the budgetary question, nothing about Britain's behavior after the referendum suggested a willingness to play a positive role in the Community.

■ A General Malaise

Although relieved to have put Britain's troubles to rest, the EC found itself in a rut in the mid-1970s because of the governments' inability or unwillingness to tackle economic and political problems on a Community-wide basis. Still suffering from the effects of the Gaullist challenge, the Commission was politically frail. France and Germany, either separately or together, failed to provide decisive leadership. A growing divergence among the member states undermined political solidarity and risked jeopardizing current levels of economic integration. Faced with high inflation and unemployment, governments applied an array of nontariff barriers and other protectionist measures that impeded the emergence of a single market. Disputes over budget contributions and compensation to farmers for the impact of fluctuating exchange rates on the CAP illustrated the extent of the malaise.

Plans for Economic and Monetary Union were an early victim of this situation. The Werner Plan, launched in 1972 with a target date for full implementation in 1980, hardly got off the ground. National currencies wiggled in and out of the "snake." The mark, buoyed by Germany's low inflation and large trade surplus, pushed through the top; the pound, franc, and lira, weakened by their countries' high inflation and large trade deficits, fell through the bottom. No wonder that EMU was quietly put to bed.[9]

The launch of the European Council in 1975 helped hold the EC together. The move from ad hoc to institutionalized summitry—regular meetings of national leaders (prime ministers and the president of France)—reflected the need for top-level direction in order to maintain the EC's integrity at a time of increasing economic complexity and bureaucratic lethargy. Originally Giscard's idea, regular summits appealed also to Schmidt. With their unrivaled grasp of economic and monetary issues, Giscard and Schmidt saw the European Council as an ideal forum in which to dominate the EC.

As expected, meetings of the European Council provided a stage for dazzling Schmidt-Giscard performances that helped maintain a semblance of unity during an acutely inauspicious time. The affinity between the two leaders was not immediate. They had strikingly different characters and personalities—Giscard haughty, Olympian, condescending; Schmidt pretentiously unpretentious, moody, and temperamental, "a figure out of Wilhelm Busch, Elbe bargeman's cap and pipe."[10] But both were shrewd, incisive, and highly intelligent. Before reaching the highest office in their respective countries, they had been unusually effective finance ministers. Giscard and Schmidt spoke two common languages: economics and English.

The Privileged Partnership, the title of Haig Simonian's book on Franco-German relations in the 1970s, sums up the exclusive relationship between them. Going well beyond the framework of the 1963 Elysée Treaty, Giscard and Schmidt got together often for dinner, spoke frequently on the phone, and caucused regularly on the fringes of multilateral meetings. Despite the appearance of an easy Franco-German relationship based on a genuine friendship between the president and the chancellor, both sides worked hard to resolve occasional disputes and ease inevitable friction. As William Wallace observed,

"The success of the Franco-German relationship [in the 1970s and 1980s] is a record of determination to accommodate divergent interests through positive political action, to explain and to tolerate differences and to minimize their impact; not a simple record of convergence in economic, industrial, political or security interests and outlooks."[11] It was an approach conspicuously absent from Britain's dealings with other member states.

With the economic recession continuing unabated, in the mid-1970s Giscard and Schmidt were engaged in little more than damage control. Even in the best of times, Giscard and Schmidt's approach to EC affairs would not have facilitated the kind of renaissance that the Community enjoyed a decade later. Schmidt's reported statement that "Europe can only be brought forward by the will of a few statesmen, and not by thousands of regulations and hundreds of ministerial councils,"[12] was only half right. Schmidt's and Giscard's impatience with the Commission and preference to avoid Brussels in favor of Paris and Bonn contributed to the EC's dysfunctionalism. The two leaders' infatuation with each other also irritated other leaders.

Regardless of the rise of the European Council and the state of relations among national leaders, the inefficiency of the Brussels bureaucracy in the 1970s became a metaphor for the EC's malaise. The Commission was dispirited and demoralized. As if to underscore its seeming unimportance, in 1972 the outgoing president, Franco Malfatti, left office early in order to stand for election to the Italian parliament. Not for the last time, widely publicized complaints about a commissioner's extravagant expenses reinforced the public image of the Commission as wasteful and mismanaged. Schmidt's intense dislike of the Commission reinforced Germany's reluctance to send top-rate people to Brussels as either commissioners or permanent representatives. For his part, Giscard inherited de Gaulle's antipathy toward the Commission and used every opportunity to put its president in his place.

More than the Commission's ineffectualness, however, the Council's indecisiveness lay at the root of the Community's institutional immobility. By the early 1970s nearly a thousand Commission proposals were said to be stuck in the Council's decisionmaking pipeline because, under the terms of the Luxembourg Compromise, a government could easily prevent a vote from being taken. For all their supposed commitment to the Community, Giscard and Schmidt tinkered with various possible solutions but never injected into the process the political will so desperately lacking.

The fate of the Tindemans Report was typical. Having been charged by other national leaders with recommending ways to advance European integration, Belgian prime minister Leo Tindemans focused less on the lofty goal of a federal Europe than on the need for institutional reform and a modest extension of Community competence.[13] Few national leaders were open to his ideas. Giscard took the lead and stifled the report with the kind of bureaucratic asphyxiation that Tindemans had so bitterly complained about. National leaders asked their foreign ministers to consider the report; the foreign ministers asked their senior officials to do so. The senior officials reported on the report to the foreign ministers; the foreign ministers reported on the report's report to the national leaders, who thanked Tindemans for his efforts and let the matter drop.

Another high-level report, that of the "Three Wise Men," suffered a similar fate.[14] The report had originated in a suggestion by Giscard that a small group of eminent Europeans recommend procedural changes that would not require treaty reform. The wise men set about the task with enthusiasm, presenting their report on time. At the next meeting of the European Council, Giscard noted with pleasure the report's criticism of the Commission and endorsement of the European Council. Beyond that, he did not delve too deep. After all, the report also criticized successive Council presidencies for lack of direction (the French presidency, in the first half of 1979, had been particularly poor). Nor did Giscard like the report's pointed observation that poor leadership was the main obstacle to the EC's revival. Thus, after a perfunctory discussion at the Dublin summit, the report of the Three Wise Men joined the Tindemans Report in the EC's archive.

Requesting high-level reports and then failing to act on them was a fitting comment on the European Council's performance in the late 1970s. As the decade drew to a close, the EC's fortunes looked unpropitious. Economic integration had stalled, as national governments struggled separately to combat stagflation. The political will to take a common approach and revive European integration was missing in national capitals. There were few economic, political, or institutional signs that the EC would soon turn the corner and transform itself dramatically within the next few years.

◾ The European Monetary System

The launch in 1979 of the European Monetary System (EMS), an initiative to establish a zone of relative monetary stability in a world of wildly fluctuating exchange rates, stood out at an otherwise unremarkable time. After a shaky start, the EMS helped participating countries to fight inflation and recover economic growth. The EMS would also provide a vital underpinning for the single market program and lay a basis for the eventual achievement of EMU.

Peter Ludlow chronicled the origins of the EMS in a masterly monograph that reads like a novel.[15] The story of the EMS has the ingredients of a political thriller: Jenkins's courage and prescience in proposing a monetary initiative after the failure of the Werner Plan and the currency "snake"; Schmidt's sudden espousal of a scheme for exchange rate stability and determination to see it through, despite domestic opposition; Giscard's strong support but apparent U-turn at the last moment; the efficacy of the Franco-German alliance; Britain's refusal yet again to take the plunge; and the value of the European Council for rapid decisionmaking at the highest level.

Much of the credit for the EMS belongs to Jenkins, Commission president from 1977 to 1981. Having spent his entire career in British politics, Jenkins was a Brussels outsider. Especially because Jenkins succeeded the uninspiring François-Xavier Ortoli, however, his arrival in Brussels aroused inflated expectations. In fact, Jenkins got off to a slow start, making it look by mid-1977 as if his presidency would be as forgettable as any in the years since Walter Hallstein's resignation. Yet Jenkins yearned for an initiative that would boost the Commission's morale and reinvigorate the EC. Jenkins's knowledge of economics, experience as chancellor of the exchequer (finance minister) in Britain, and concern about the impact on the EC of global financial turbulence made him want to act in the monetary field.

Jenkins sent up a trial balloon at a public lecture in October 1977. Apart from making predictable points about advancing European integration and helping to realize the common market's full potential, Jenkins argued that monetary union would help to lower inflation, increase investment, and reduce unemployment throughout the EC. Nor, if properly implemented, would monetary union exacerbate regional economic disparities.[16]

Jenkins's advocacy of what he called a bold "leap forward" initially elicited only a lukewarm response from most national leaders. There was little discussion of it at the December 1977 European Council, where Jenkins noted Schmidt's "benevolent skepticism" and detected only "a fair if not tremendously enthusiastic wind behind our monetary union proposals."[17] The initiative would have withered entirely but for Schmidt's sudden conversion to it, or at least to a modified version of what Jenkins wanted.

Jenkins was at a loss to explain the reason for Schmidt's sudden change of heart in early 1978. Was it a function of the chancellor's mercurial personality? Was it an antidote to his domestic security problems? Was it anger with the United States over yet another drop in the dollar's value?[18] One or more of those reasons may explain the timing of Schmidt's espousal of a quasi-fixed exchange rate regime. The fundamental cause of his "conversion," however, went much deeper. Persistent depreciation of the dollar and a corresponding appreciation of the mark cut German industrial competitiveness and fed speculation that a US economic recovery was happening at Germany's expense.

Overnight, Schmidt replaced Jenkins as the principal proponent of what became the EMS. Yet Schmidt's crucial collaborator was not the president of the Commission but the president of France. Alone or with Jenkins's sole support, Schmidt might not have been able to bring the monetary initiative rapidly to fruition. But with Giscard's backing, the proposal quickly gathered speed. The birth of the EMS one year later "came from a clear convergence of French and German interests, confirming the two countries' leading roles in the Community."[19]

The European Council gave Schmidt and Giscard the ideal forum in which to push the idea of the EMS at the highest possible level. The two leaders possessed vast powers of political persuasion. When they unveiled their exchange rate idea at a summit in April 1978, only British prime minister James Callaghan expressed serious misgivings. Resentment of close Franco-German collaboration and doubts about the scheme's validity led Callaghan to end British participation with France and Germany in planning the EMS. Thus, the blueprint for the EMS bore an exclusive Franco-German imprint.

Schmidt's forceful chairmanship of the decisive summit, in Bremen in July 1978, contributed to general acceptance of the Franco-German proposal for an exchange rate mechanism as the centerpiece of the EMS, using a parity grid and a divergence indicator based on the European currency unit.[20] By contrast, Callaghan's sullenness presaged Britain's self-exclusion from the system. Britain's decision not to take part was of more than symbolic importance. As Helen Wallace pointed out, "for many of those involved the EMS was viewed, rightly or wrongly, as a critical stage in the development of the EC as a whole."[21]

While Commission and national officials worked in a number of specialized committees to thrash out details of the scheme, a last-minute political row erupted over compensation for poorer participating countries, with Ireland and Italy demanding an increase in regional development funding. The problem of redistribution came to a boil when France and Britain insisted on getting additional funding as well and Germany balked at paying the bill. This did not augur well for the final European Council before the EMS was to have been implemented in January 1979. A last-minute compromise by Schmidt broke the deadlock, although the EMS came into operation slightly later than planned, in March 1979.

The EMS was substantially different from what Jenkins had originally envisioned. What emerged was "a hybrid—not entirely Community, nor entirely outside it."[22] Only EC member states could participate in the EMS, but none was obliged to do so. The EMS was not based on the Rome Treaty, although closer monetary coordination, leading eventually to EMU, was a cherished EC objective. Nor did it emerge from a formal Commission proposal. Nevertheless, EC institutions, notably the Council of Economic and Finance Ministers, were central to its successful operation. Despite its peculiarities, the EMS represented an important breakthrough for the Community. Regardless of its subsequent development, the fact of its existence and the relative speed with which it came into being marked an important milestone in the EC's history.

■ The British Budgetary Question

The launch of the EMS ended an otherwise disappointing decade on a high note. Nevertheless, the long-term impact of the EMS could not have been predicted in 1979. On the contrary, the emergence that year of the British budgetary question, following Margaret Thatcher's election victory, suggested that the EC was in for a rough time. Thatcher never liked the EC, seeing the Commission as an agent of supranationalism and enemy of the nation-state. But she grasped the potential for British business of continued EC membership and later became one of the foremost proponents of the single market program. In Thatcher's view, the EC should confine itself to the removal of barriers to trade and investment and leave governments to coordinate economic and foreign policies on an intergovernmental basis.

Thatcher grasped another thing about the EC even before she became prime minister: the obvious unfairness of Britain's budgetary contribution. Simply put, Britain paid too much into the Community budget and received too little in return. That imbalance should have been rectified in the mid-1970s, but Harold Wilson's renegotiation of Britain's membership terms had been largely a cosmetic exercise to appease British public opinion and to try to keep the Labour Party together. Thereafter, special transitional arrangements for Britain cushioned the financial burden of membership. Only at the end of the 1970s did the extent of Britain's overpayment become fully apparent.

Here was a cause dear to Thatcher's heart. Britain's demand for reform was clear-cut, easily comprehensible, and sure of widespread domestic support. How could her EC colleagues not concede the point? Even the Commission's own figures bolstered Britain's case. Thatcher surely had a natural ally in Helmut Schmidt, whose country also paid a great deal into the EC (although Germany could afford to do so and was unlikely to complain in any event because of lingering war guilt). Righting Britain's wrong would strengthen, not weaken, the EC. Thatcher correctly argued that without budgetary reform the British public, already equivocal about European integration, would turn solidly against the EC. For Thatcher, this was a question of fairness and of saving the EC from itself.[23]

Under the circumstances it seems surprising that the British budgetary question—what Jenkins called the "Bloody British Question," or BBQ[24]—nearly wrecked the EC and filled a reservoir of ill feeling toward Britain in Brussels. Admittedly, Britain's partners were predisposed not to reopen the issue. Wilson's handling of the renegotiation had left a bitter aftertaste. Yet such was the justice of Britain's case that even the most resentful of Commission and national officials conceded the need for further reform.

What turned a relatively straightforward case into one of the most complex and divisive issues in the EC's history was Thatcher's abrasive personality and truculent approach to the negotiations. Being a new participant in European Council meetings, and a woman in a hitherto exclusively male world, may have fired Thatcher's innate belligerence. She also suspected the Commission and the other governments of uniformly opposing Britain's position. Thatcher was fully aware that an aggressive approach enhanced her reputation at home as a dogged defender of British interests and helped her political standing at a time of sagging ratings.

At a succession of European summits in the coming years, Thatcher's tactics were to repeat endlessly her main arguments and keep everyone up late after dinner. Thatcher drove her fellow EC leaders to distraction, shrilly demanding Britain's money back. She quickly alienated Helmut Schmidt, whose support was crucial to her getting the outcome that she wanted. It is difficult to avoid the conclusion that Thatcher's fierce determination to settle only on her own terms was part of her political pathology.

Thatcher accepted a truce in 1980, in the form of an interim agreement on Britain's contribution. As expected, she returned to the charge when the agreement expired in 1983, the tenth anniversary of Britain's unhappy EC membership. This time Thatcher sought a permanent solution, not merely a series of annual remedies. Two factors, one domestic and one European, strengthened Thatcher's position. First, her popularity at home had soared in the aftermath of the 1982 Falklands/Malvinas War. Having taken on the Argentineans, Thatcher was set to take on the Europeans. The British public now stood squarely behind her. Even the opposition Labour Party, committed at that time to pulling out of the EC if it ever got back into government, could hardly criticize her efforts to get a better budget deal for Britain. Second, the EC was financially strapped. By the early 1980s the CAP was out of control with an obscene accumulation of surplus production for which farmers received guaranteed high prices. The EC would have to rein in the CAP or increase its overall budget. Thatcher favored CAP reform, a politically unpalatable option for most other leaders.

Yet there was little progress on the budgetary dispute throughout 1983. The situation changed dramatically for the better when France, now led by François Mitterrand instead of the haughty Giscard d'Estaing, took over the Council presidency in January 1984. Having jettisoned an initial effort to boost employment and economic growth through government intervention and high public spending, Mitterrand was in the process of switching to limited deregulation and market integration. He was eager to end the budgetary impasse and focus attention instead on the need to complete the single market.

The French presidency was due to end in June with a summit just outside Paris in the spectacular setting of the palace at Fontainebleau, in June 1984. Mitterrand launched a concerted diplomatic offensive in the run-up to the meeting. Despite his efforts, there was nothing to suggest that a breakthrough on the budget was imminent as the EC leaders began the summit, surrounded by a swarm of journalists. Talk in previous weeks of a possible "two-speed" Europe, with Britain in the slow lane, had not helped matters, nor had Thatcher's clever definition of what a two-speed Europe meant: "Those who pay most are in the top group and those who pay less are not."[25]

As the Fontainebleau summit progressed, a surprising willingness to compromise gradually became apparent. Thatcher seemed eager to settle the long-standing dispute and move the EC in new directions; the others were equally weary and wanted to reach a comprehensive agreement. A possible solution emerged based on a rebate in the form of a yearly fixed percentage of Britain's net contribution. Thatcher held out for 66 percent; German chancellor Helmut Kohl demurred. Finally, after some concessions to Germany on agricultural spending, the chancellor lifted his objections. The British budgetary dispute was over.

Had anything good come of the protracted and painful negotiations? Undoubtedly Thatcher's conduct antagonized other national leaders. Yet without her aggressive approach Britain might not have secured such a favorable result (the agreement saved Britain over £10 billion in the remainder of the 1980s). For all the aggravation and frustration of the previous five years, arguably Thatcher had needed time to build her case, exhaust the opposition, and secure a satisfactory solution.

It could be argued as well that resolution of the dispute helped the Community's long-term development, not only in the obvious sense of removing a persistent irritant in relations among member states but also because it emphasized the need to overhaul the EC's finances. Indeed, the European Council resolved the British problem in the context of a broader budget reform, involving a decision to control agricultural spending while slightly increasing the Community's budget.[26]

In a postsummit press conference Thatcher said she now looked forward to "pressing ahead with the development of the Community."[27] The other leaders could not have agreed more. Mitterrand reveled in the success of "his" European Council not only in ending five years of friction over the budget but also in clearing the way for new initiatives. At Fontainebleau, Mitterrand had spoken eloquently about the need to revive the EC and reinvigorate European integration. Although France would no longer be in the Council presidency, the Fontainebleau summit created a favorable climate in which to advance Mitterrand's agenda.

■ Reviving European Integration

A number of factors in the early 1980s fueled renewed interest in deeper economic integration, particularly in the long-standing goal of a single market. One was the ideological shift then sweeping Western Europe. Its most obvious manifestation was Thatcher's election victory in 1979. After five years of Labour Party rule, a powerful popular reaction against excessive government intervention in economic and social affairs swept Thatcher to power. The new government immediately launched a program of privatization and deregulation to unleash pent-up market forces and stimulate individual enterprise.

Across the Channel, by contrast, Mitterrand pushed a socialist agenda of state intervention and regulation after his election victory in 1981. The consequences were catastrophic: inflation soared, investment slumped, and the value of the franc plummeted, forcing devaluation within the EMS and prompting a tough domestic austerity program. In 1983, pragmatism overcame principle when Mitterrand abandoned a doctrinaire approach to economic recovery and began to bend with the prevailing economic wind. Mitterrand's U-turn influenced other socialist leaders, notably Felipe González in Spain and Mário Soares in Portugal, two countries then on their way to joining the EC.

The success of Etienne Davignon, the commissioner responsible for industrial affairs from 1981 to 1985, in rallying European industry to the cause of cross-border collaboration also contributed to the momentum developing for a single, EC-wide market. Davignon cultivated the chief executive officers of major European manufacturers in the high-technology sector, advocating the advantages of European integration, something the persistent economic recession in any case predisposed them toward. Commission officials kept discreetly in the background; the last thing Davignon wanted was to scare off big business with a display of bureaucratic heavy-handedness.

Davignon's efforts bore fruit in the European Strategic Program for Research and Development in Information Technology (ESPRIT), a basic research program involving major manufacturers, smaller firms, and universities throughout the Community. Technological collaboration, in turn, "created an important and vocal constituency . . . impatient for an end to such things as customs delays at borders, conflicting national standards in data processing or arcane rules on property ownership . . . and pressing for the completion of the internal market, for once these firms had lost their national champions status, it was imperative that they maximized the advantages to be gained from the single market."[28] Guy Gyllenhammer, the head of Volvo, catalyzed such thinking by organizing the European Round Table, a high-level interest group for deeper economic integration, although his own firm was located in Sweden, a nonmember state.

As well as encouraging technological collaboration in the EC, the Commission championed completion of the single market. Moreover, the Commission followed up on a landmark decision of the Court of Justice, in the *Cassis de Dijon* case, that was to have a profound effect on economic integration. Based on the Court's rejection of a German prohibition on imports from other member states of alcoholic beverages that did not meet minimum alcohol-content requirements, the Commission declared that "any product imported from another member state must in principle be admitted . . . if it has been lawfully produced, that is, conforms to rules and processes of manufacture that are customarily and traditionally accepted in the exporting country, and is marketed in the territory of the latter."[29] Thus the Commission developed the principle of mutual recognition, which would avoid the otherwise impossible process of harmonizing the member states' diverse legal norms.

Moving from oratory to action, the Commission urged the Council in 1980 both to pass a number of proposals to strengthen the internal market and to simplify intra-EC frontier formalities involving customs, taxation, and statistics. Thereafter the Commission sharpened its strategy of putting forward concrete proposals, prodding the European Council to act. The Commission's approach bore fruit in 1983 when the Council defined a standardization policy for European industry. The next year the Commission prepared a detailed paper for the Fontainebleau summit on a number of internal market issues, ranging from the abolition of customs barriers to the free movement of people, capital, and services.[30]

Thatcher, a leading proponent of market integration, came to the Fontainebleau summit armed with a paper of her own. It contained the classic assertion that "if the problems of growth, outdated industrial structures and unemployment which affect us all are to be tackled effectively, we must create the genuine common market in goods and services which is envisaged in the Treaty of Rome and will be crucial to our ability to meet the US and Japanese technological challenge."[31] By advocating completion of the single market, Thatcher sought to advance deeply held convictions and establish beyond question her pro-EC credentials.

Resolution of the British budgetary question removed a major barrier to EC action on a wide range of issues and opened the door to achieving a genuinely single market. During the preceding few years a consensus had emerged in Brussels and among national governments on the need for as much deregulation as possible at the national level, coupled with as little reregulation as necessary at the Community level. Ideological, political, and economic changes had brought about a reemphasis on market integration and paved the way for an imminent breakthrough. Other developments, notably tension in the transatlantic relationship, the assertiveness of the first directly elected EP, and Mediterranean enlargement, focused attention on the desirability of institutional reform in the EC. Completing the single market and revising the Rome Treaty were not unconnected. Each gave added impetus to the other, and both were to combine in the Single European Act of 1986.

■ The External Environment

The Community's external relations were every bit as rocky as its internal development in the early 1980s. The sudden heightening of Cold War tension in the late 1970s after a decade of relative calm tested the EC's ability to act internationally. European Political Cooperation was an inadequate instrument for foreign policy coordination, especially in response to crises such as the Soviet invasion of Afghanistan in December 1979 and the imposition of martial law in Poland two years later. At the same time, the unremitting hostility of the United States toward the Soviet Union severely tested EC solidarity and combined with other developments in EC-US relations to put transatlantic ties under great strain. Under Ronald Reagan, the new US administration saw the Soviet Union as the root of all evil and pressured European allies of the United States to cease most economic activities with the Soviet bloc. US officials cited Western Europe's less confrontational approach to the Soviet Union as evidence of weakness and cowardice.

Matters came to a head in June 1982, when the United States announced sanctions against US subsidiaries and license holders in Western Europe involved in a massive infrastructural project to facilitate the export of gas from the Soviet Union to Western Europe through a pipeline thousands of miles long. Such unilateral action galvanized latent anti-Americanism and provided a powerful impetus for high-technology industries to accelerate collaboration in the EC, thereby lessening their dependence on the United States. ESPRIT and other EC-sponsored high-technology research and development programs emerged in a climate of strained US-EC relations, exacerbated by bitter transatlantic disputes over subsidized steel and agricultural exports from the EC.

At the same time, the United States and its European allies were mired in a political dispute over NATO's deployment in Western Europe of medium-range nuclear missiles in response to a similar Soviet deployment in Eastern Europe. The "Euromissile" crisis, played out publicly on the streets of many Western European cities as well as privately in the chancelleries of the Atlantic Alliance, cast a pall over Euro-American relations. So did a dispute between the United States and its allies in the EC over policy toward the Middle East, an especially sensitive issue for Washington. The United States viewed the member states' declarations on the Arab-Israeli conflict, which tended to criticize Israel and support the Palestinians, as examples of the perniciousness of EPC. The Venice Declaration of June 1980, in which the Nine recognized the special position of Palestine in the Arab-Israeli conflict, greatly irritated the United States, as did the resumption of the "Euro-Arab dialogue" shortly afterward. The United States disliked its European allies' taking an independent and relatively radical position on an issue that was both inherently explosive and part of the wider, all-encompassing Cold War conflict.

Irritation with the United States emboldened some member states to try to strengthen EPC. In 1981, Hans-Dietrich Genscher, Germany's foreign minister, and Emilio Colombo, his Italian counterpart, launched an initiative to assert the EC's international identity while reassuring the United States about their intentions. The "Draft European Act," popularly known as the Genscher-Colombo proposals, advocated more effective decisionmaking and greater Community competence in external relations. The Genscher-Colombo initiative culminated in the Solemn Declaration on European Union, proclaimed by national leaders at the Stuttgart summit in June 1983.[32] While seemingly innocuous and yet another example of extravagant EC rhetoric, the Stuttgart

Declaration contributed to the incremental deepening of European integration in the early 1980s. In particular, it prefigured the section on EPC in the 1986 Single European Act.

Drawing on the Stuttgart Declaration, Mitterrand made a famous speech to the EP in May 1984, during his country's Council presidency, calling for institutional reform in the EC and deeper economic and political integration.[33] On external relations, Mitterrand advocated a permanent secretariat for the conduct of foreign policy cooperation and urged member states to make a common defense effort. Mitterrand's proposals, together with the earlier Genscher-Colombo proposals, stoked concern in Washington about the implications of closer foreign and security cooperation among EC member states.

Although she had signed the Stuttgart Declaration, believing it to be meaningless, Thatcher was uncomfortable with the EC's interest in security policy. For varying reasons a number of the smaller member states also disliked the emphasis on closer security cooperation. Despite being a NATO member, Denmark did not want to give the EC competence in the security domain. Under Andreas Papandreou's leadership, Greece (also a NATO member) opposed deeper European integration in general and closer security cooperation in particular. Sensitive to public support for nonmembership in NATO, the Irish government objected to any EC initiative on security and defense.

As a result, the EC did not move beyond a rhetorical commitment to closer foreign and security policy cooperation. Nevertheless, the member states' willingness to consider a possible security and defense dimension for the EC created a climate conducive to change. Together with the growing consensus on the need to deepen economic integration in response to Western Europe's declining competitiveness, the discussions about closer foreign policy cooperation added to the momentum in the early 1980s for an intensification of European integration.

■ An Assertive European Parliament

The activism of the first directly elected EP was another factor that paved the way for deeper European integration later in the decade. The Rome Treaty provided for an elected assembly, but governments had dragged their feet on switching from an appointed to an elected EP. As a gesture to counterbalance the creation of the European Council, national leaders decided in December 1974 to hold elections in the near future. They eventually agreed on the size of the elected EP, which was to comprise 410 seats, over twice the number in the existing assembly, distributed among member states approximately according to their populations. The first direct elections eventually took place in June 1979.[34]

Britain and France disliked the idea of elections, fearing that a stronger EP would challenge national supremacy in the EC system. By contrast, Germany, the Netherlands, and Italy, more sympathetic toward supranationalism, favored a stronger EP. Similarly, the Commission saw a stronger EP as a natural institutional ally.

In the event, the elections of June 1979 did not cause a radical redistribution of power in the EC. Yet direct elections brought a new breed of parliamentarian to Brussels and Strasbourg and noticeably improved the institution's morale. Many of the first directly elected members of the European Parliament (MEPs) appreciated the extent of the EC's difficulties and hoped to revive the process of European integration. Between April 1980 and February 1982, the EP passed no fewer than eight resolutions advocating institutional and policy reform in the EC.

Altiero Spinelli, the veteran Eurofederalist, was one of the best-known and most influential members of the newly elected Parliament. Spinelli interpreted the results of the elections as nothing less than a mandate to overhaul the Rome Treaty. Accordingly, in July 1980 Spinelli gathered together a number of like-minded MEPs, representing a wide spectrum of political opinion. By the end of the year this heterogeneous group, dedicated to reforming and reviving the EC, had grown to seventy members. Their ideas ranged from a return to the EC's first principles—the need to complete the single market— to drafting a constitution for Europe. Gradually a consensus emerged on the urgency of a new treaty to replace the original treaties and for a new European Union to replace the existing communities.

The Spinelli group formed the nucleus of the Institutional Affairs Committee, which met for the first time in January 1983, halfway through the EP's five-year mandate. Members of the committee, under Spinelli's chairmanship, appreciated the pitfalls surrounding their work. Because the EP remained relatively powerless, there was a predisposition in Brussels and in national capitals to dismiss MEPs' agitation for reform as the bleating of overindulged and underemployed politicians. Spinelli himself had a reputation for being idealistic and excitable. National governments expected MEPs to demand a larger say for their institution in EC decisionmaking. Accordingly, the Institutional Affairs Committee risked not being taken seriously.

Yet the malaise in the Community—prolonged economic recession, declining international competitiveness, and institutional inertia—lent credibility to the MEPs' efforts to revive European integration, as did the member states' own initiatives along the same lines. For instance, Belgium, in the Council presidency, set an important precedent in May 1982 by rejecting the practice of unanimity and calling for a vote in the Council on that year's farm prices.[35] The symbolism of Belgium's action was not lost on the Commission and the member states, and certainly not on the EP.

By the middle of 1982, the Institutional Affairs Committee had identified the main lines of a reform program and established subgroups to work on them. Issues included the legal personality of a possible European Union, and its institutional structure, competence, and relationship with the member states. The proposed reforms wound their way through the committee and the Parliament in 1983, emerging at the end of the year as the "Draft Treaty Establishing the European Union."[36]

This bold initiative sought to substitute a single treaty establishing the European Union for the existing treaties establishing the European communities. The EU would maintain the basic institutional structure and legal competence of the three communities but strengthen their decisionmaking procedures and add to them new or expanded authority over certain aspects of economic, social, and political affairs. The purpose of decisionmaking reform was to improve efficiency and to close what politicians perceived as an emerging "democratic deficit" in the EC. Sensitive to national concerns about the centralization of power in Brussels, the draft treaty provided for something that received little attention at the time but became prominent a decade later: the principle of subsidiarity, whereby the EU would be responsible only for tasks that could be undertaken more effectively in common than by governments acting alone. In one of the most famous votes ever taken in the Parliament, the draft treaty passed by a resounding majority, in February 1984.[37]

MEPs sent the draft treaty to national parliaments and governments in an effort to increase the momentum for reform then gathering in the EC. The draft treaty demonstrated the EP's seriousness and commitment to European integration, but had no discernible impact on the second direct elections, held in June 1984 (the turnout was lower than five years before). The draft treaty nevertheless constituted a concrete legacy from the first elected EP to its successors. The vote on the draft treaty also gave Mitterrand, then in the Council presidency and boldly championing deeper integration, additional political ammunition.

EP activism both symbolized and stimulated the movement toward deeper integration that gathered momentum in the early 1980s. The launch of the European Monetary System, collaborative ventures in high technology, renewed interest in the single market, and eagerness to overcome decisionmaking inertia helped pave the way for the revival of European integration that followed resolution of the British budgetary question. Initiatives such as the Genscher-Colombo proposals, the Stuttgart Declaration, and the EP's draft treaty were important precursors of imminent change. They provided a climate and a context in which governments could get back to basics: deeper economic integration as originally envisioned in the Rome Treaty. The scene was set for the Single European Act and the single market program, which facilitated the EC's resurgence in the late 1980s.

▓ Notes

1. Quoted in Steven Lagerfeld, "Europhoria," *Wilson Quarterly* 14 (Winter 1990): 66.
2. Christopher Tugendhat, "How to Get Europe Moving Again," *International Affairs* 61 (Winter 1990): 421.
3. Roy Jenkins, *Life at the Centre* (London: Macmillan, 1991), p. 375.
4. European Commission, "The Unacceptable Situation and the Correcting Mechanism," COM(75)40 final, January 30, 1975.
5. See Mark Baimbridge, ed., *The 1975 Referendum on Europe*, vol. 1, *Reflections of the Participants* (Exeter: Imprint Academic, 2006).
6. Quoted in Frances Nicholson and Roger East, *From the Six to the Twelve: The Enlargement of the European Communities* (Chicago: St. James, 1987), p. 180.
7. Jenkins, *Life at the Centre*, p. 342.
8. Stephen George, *An Awkward Partner: Britain in the European Community* (Oxford: Oxford University Press, 1990), p. 87.
9. See Loukas Tsoukalis, *The Politics and Economics of European Monetary Integration* (London: Allen and Unwin, 1977).
10. James Goldsborough, "The Franco-German Entente," *Foreign Affairs* 54, no. 3 (April 1976): 499.
11. William Wallace, introduction to Roger Morgan and Caroline Bray, *Partners and Rivals in Western Europe: Britain, France, and Germany* (Brookfield, VT: Gower, 1986), p. 4.
12. Quoted in Jonathan Storey, "The Franco-German Alliance Within the European Community," *World Today*, June 1980, p. 209.
13. The text of the report is available in *European NAvigator*, http://www.ena.lu/.
14. See Andrew Duff, "The Report of the Three Wise Men," *Journal of Common Market Studies* 19, no. 3 (1981): 237–254.
15. Peter Ludlow, *The Making of the European Monetary System: A Case Study in the Politics of the European Community* (London: Butterworths Scientific, 1982).
16. Roy Jenkins, "Europe's Present Challenge and Future Opportunity," speech at the European University Institute, Florence, October 27, 1977.
17. Roy Jenkins, *European Diary, 1977–1981* (London: Collins, 1989), p. 183.
18. Jenkins, *Life at the Centre*, pp. 470–471.
19. Haig Simonian, *The Privileged Partnership: Franco-German Relations in the European Community, 1969–1984* (Oxford: Clarendon, 1985), p. 277.
20. On the mechanics of the EMS, see Jacques Van Ypersele, *The European Monetary System: Origins, Operation, and Outlook* (Chicago: St. James, 1985).
21. Helen Wallace, "The Conduct of Bilateral Relations by Governments," in Morgan and Bray, *Partners and Rivals*, p. 154.
22. William Nicoll and Trevor Salmon, *Understanding the European Communities* (Savage, MD: Barnes and Noble, 1990), p. 197.
23. See Margaret Thatcher, *The Downing Street Years* (New York: HarperCollins, 1993), pp. 34–35, 60–64, 78–88, 537–545.
24. Jenkins, *European Diary*, p. 545.
25. Quoted in *Daily Express* (London), June 4, 1984, p. 4.
26. See Geoffrey Denton, "Restructuring the EEC Budget: Implications of the Fontainebleau Summit," *Journal of Common Market Studies* 23, no. 2 (December 1984): 117–140.
27. Quoted in *Financial Times*, June 28, 1984, p. 14.

28. Margaret Sharp, Christopher Freeman, and William Walker, *Technology and the Future of Europe: Global Competition and the Environment in the 1990s* (New York: Pinter, 1991), p. 73.

29. European Commission, *1980 General Report* (Luxembourg: Office for Official Publications of the European Communities, 1981), point 120.

30. European Commission, *1984 General Report* (Luxembourg: Office for Official Publications of the European Communities, 1985), point 133.

31. "Europe: The Future," reproduced in *Journal of Common Market Studies* 23, no. 1 (September 1984): 76.

32. See Ulrich Rosengarten, *Die Genscher-Colombo-Initiative: Baustein für die Europäische Union* (Baden-Baden: Nomos, 2008).

33. François Mitterrand, speech to the European Parliament, May 24, 1984, reprinted in *Vital Speeches of the Day,* August 1, 1984, p. 613.

34. Karlheinz Reif, ed., *Ten European Elections: Campaigns and Results of the 1979/81 First Direct Elections to the European Parliament* (London: Gower, 1985).

35. Bulletin EC 5-1982, points 2.1.73–2.1.97.

36. See Roland Bieber, Jean-Paul Jacqué, and Joseph Weiler, eds., *An Ever Closer Union: A Critical Analysis of the Draft Treaty Establishing European Union,* European Perspectives Series (Luxembourg: Office for Official Publications of the European Community, 1985).

37. Bulletin EC 2-1984, point 1.1.1.

4 From European Community to European Union, 1985–1992

In the late 1980s the European Community underwent an extraordinary transformation. After years of sluggish growth and institutional immobility, governments negotiated the Single European Act (SEA), a major revision of the Rome Treaty that underpinned the single market program. Jacques Delors, who became Commission president in January 1985, is often credited with the EC's metamorphosis. As Stanley Hoffmann wrote in 1989, "Delors is as important to the enterprise today as Jean Monnet was in the 1950s."[1]

Yet Delors's role should not be exaggerated. Undoubtedly he was ambitious, competent, and resourceful. But Delors could not possibly have succeeded had the economic, political, and international circumstances been unfavorable. It was his good fortune to have become Commission president at precisely the time when internal developments (resolution of the British budgetary question, agitation for institutional reform, and pressure to complete the internal market) and external factors (the acceleration of globalization) made a dramatic improvement in the EC's fortunes almost inevitable. Without Delors, the single market program and the acceleration of European integration might not have happened exactly as they did, but this is not to say that they would not have happened at all.

The EC's transformation coincided with the potentially disruptive Mediterranean enlargement (Greece had joined the EC in 1981, Portugal and Spain in 1986). Without compensating mechanisms, completion of the internal market could have aggravated the economic divide between the EC's rich and poor member countries, especially the new entrants. Thus the SEA was more than a device to launch the single market program. It was a complex bargain to improve decisionmaking, strengthen democracy, achieve market liberalization, and at the same time promote economic and social cohesion.

The SEA and the single market program sparked a renewed interest in Economic and Monetary Union. At the same time, in response to different kinds of political and economic pressures, the reform movement in Central

73

and Eastern Europe hastened the collapse of communism. More than any other event, the sudden breach of the Berlin Wall in November 1989 symbolized the end of the Cold War and led to the unification of Germany in 1990. Governments responded to these and other developments by negotiating the Maastricht Treaty—the second major treaty reform in only six years—and establishing the European Union.

The Maastricht Treaty triggered widespread public concern and almost foundered in June 1992 when Danish voters narrowly rejected it in a referendum. The ensuing ratification crisis was an inauspicious beginning for the EU. At issue were public alienation from an increasingly complex and intrusive policymaking process, poor democratic accountability in Brussels, and doubts about the EU's ability to cope with sudden changes in the wider world. Worries about the long-term impact of German unification and eventual EU enlargement to the east contributed to the climate of uncertainty in which the ratification drama unfolded. Implementation of the treaty in November 1993, following a second, successful Danish referendum, allowed European integration to progress beyond the single market program toward monetary union, closer cooperation on foreign and security policy, and cooperation on justice and home affairs. Nevertheless, the treaty ratification crisis was a symptom of public unease with the rapidity, direction, and management of deeper integration, and foreshadowed the EU's difficulties in the years ahead (see Box 4.1).

■ Mediterranean Enlargement

Having shaken off right-wing dictatorships in the mid-1970s, Greece, Portugal, and Spain sought to join the EC in order to end their relative international isolation, stabilize their newly established democracies, and help develop their backward economies.[2] Greece succeeded in differentiating itself from the two Iberian candidates, which posed greater economic problems for the Community. Nevertheless, the Commission advised against early Greek accession. The Council disregarded the Commission's advice. As Germany's foreign minister put it, "Greece, only recently returned to the democratic fold, would march in future with the Community of European nations."[3] Exploiting such sentiments to the full, Greece began accession negotiations in July 1976.

If the Community could have foreseen the problems that Greek membership would pose, the negotiations might not have concluded so swiftly, if at all. In the event, Greece skillfully distanced itself from the contemporaneous Iberian negotiations, did not raise any contentious issues, and managed to conclude an accession agreement in April 1979. Following ratification of the accession treaty in Athens and the Community capitals, Greece became the tenth member of the EC in January 1981.

Box 4.1 Chronology, 1985–1992

1985	January	Delors Commission takes office
	February	Agreement on Integrated Mediterranean Programs
	March	Dooge Committee recommends intergovernmental conference (IGC) on treaty reform
	June	Commission publishes white paper on single market; at Milan summit, EC leaders decide to hold IGC
	September	IGC begins
	December	IGC ends
1986	January	Portugal and Spain join the EC
	February	Foreign ministers sign Single European Act (SEA)
1987	April	Turkey applies to join the EC
	July	SEA comes into effect
1988	February	At Brussels summit, EC leaders agree on Delors I budget package
	June	At Hanover summit, EC leaders decide to establish Delors Committee on Economic and Monetary Union (EMU)
1989	June	Delors Report on EMU; third direct elections to the European Parliament (EP)
	July	Austria applies to join the EC
	November	Fall of Berlin Wall
	December	At Strasbourg summit, EC leaders decide to hold IGC on EMU and adopt Charter of Fundamental Social Rights for Workers
1990	May	Charter for European Bank for Reconstruction and Development signed
	June	France, Germany, and Benelux countries sign Schengen Agreement; at Dublin summit, EC leaders decide to hold IGC on political union concurrently with IGC on EMU, beginning in December 1990
	July	Stage I of EMU begins; Cyprus and Malta apply to join the EC
	October	German unification
		Britain joins exchange rate mechanism of European Monetary System (EMS)
	November	US-EC Transatlantic Declaration signed
	December	IGCs begin in Rome
1991	June	Outbreak of war in Yugoslavia
	July	Sweden applies to join the EC
	December	IGCs end at Maastricht summit; Soviet Union collapses
1992	January	EC recognizes independence of Croatia and Slovenia
	February	Foreign ministers sign Treaty on European Union in Maastricht
	March	Finland applies to join the EU
	May	EC and EFTA countries agree on European Economic Area (EEA); agreement on Common Agricultural Policy (CAP) reform; Switzerland applies to join the EU
	June	Danes reject Maastricht Treaty in referendum
	September	Britain suspends participation in exchange rate mechanism of EMS as currency crisis deepens; French narrowly approve Maastricht Treaty in referendum
	November	Norway again applies to join the EU
	December	Swiss reject EEA membership in referendum, implicitly rejecting EU membership; at Edinburgh summit, national leaders agree on Danish opt-outs from Maastricht Treaty and on Delors II budget package; completion of single market program

Realizing that the EC feared the economic consequences primarily of Spanish membership, Portugal also tried to have its application considered separately and concluded swiftly. Portugal applied to join in March 1977, more than a year before Spain applied. Portugal's accession negotiations also began sooner than Spain's, but the EC considered the two sets of talks closely related. Apart from the Spanish situation and the EC's preoccupation with internal budgetary and institutional problems, a number of factors peculiar to Portugal—notably textiles, migrant workers, fisheries, and agriculture—accounted for the talks' slow progress. This irritated British prime minister Margaret Thatcher, who strongly supported Portuguese accession for traditional British foreign policy reasons: a history of alliance and friendship with Portugal and the desire for a wider and weaker Community.

The Commission identified a host of economic, structural, and administrative issues that would have to be tackled before Portugal joined the Community, and refused to recommend a detailed timetable for accession. The formation of a relatively stable administration in Lisbon by the able and energetic Mário Soares in June 1983 increased EC goodwill toward Portugal, not least because the new government soon reached an agreement with the International Monetary Fund (IMF) that included measures to restructure the economy. In the following months, Soares embarked on a frantic round of visits to Community capitals and cultivated a close relationship with French president François Mitterrand, a fellow Socialist. Soares impressed his interlocutors with Portugal's determination to become a model member state. Rapid agreement on a number of outstanding issues followed, although (much to Soares's annoyance) the fate of the Spanish and Portuguese negotiations became increasingly linked. Without a breakthrough in the talks with Spain, especially concerning agriculture and fisheries, Portugal's prospects for immediate accession looked poor.

French misgivings about enlargement focused primarily on Spain, whose accession would increase the EC's agricultural area by 30 percent and its farm workforce by 25 percent, thereby further straining the Common Agricultural Policy. Yet France recognized the political imperative of Spanish membership, especially after an attempted coup d'état in Madrid in February 1981. For its part, Spain seemed unwilling to accept all of the obligations of membership, especially the need to introduce a value-added tax, curtail subsidies, and curb protectionism. Spain's reluctance prompted the European Council in November 1981 to urge the Spanish government to "make good use of the period until accession for careful preparations for . . . enlargement by introducing the necessary reforms so that the potential benefits for both sides can be realized."[4]

The situation improved when Felipe González formed a new government in Madrid. Young, personable, and capable, González was passionate about bringing Spain into the EC. González emulated Soares by embarking on a series of visits to national capitals, using personal charm, political savvy, and, where appropriate, ideological affinity to promote Spanish accession. An informal summit of the prime ministers—all Socialists—of the EC's Mediterranean members and the applicant countries in October 1983 paved the way for a deal on agriculture.

By contrast, fisheries became increasingly a subject of dispute between the EC on one side and Spain and Portugal on the other. At issue was the EC's effort under the Common Fisheries Policy to limit the post-enlargement access of Spain's fishing fleet, which was larger than the entire EC fleet. Spanish fishermen attacked foreign trucks in protest; French truckers, in turn, blockaded the Spanish border. Such incidents continued throughout 1984.

The decisive breakthrough on enlargement came not in the talks themselves but in the EC's internal affairs, notably through resolution of the British budgetary question. As if to signal a new stage in the EC's development, national leaders announced at the Fontainebleau summit in June 1984 that enlargement would take place by January 1986.[5] As Spain had always suspected France of blocking enlargement, Mitterrand's pivotal role in securing the Fontainebleau settlement greatly improved relations between the two countries. In a move calculated to reassure González of French goodwill, Mitterrand flew to Madrid immediately after the summit to report personally on its outcome.[6]

Negotiations between the EC and the applicant countries accelerated thereafter. Yet it was not until March 1985 that foreign ministers resolved the remaining problems—fisheries, free movement of Spanish and Portuguese workers in the EC, and the applicant countries' budgetary contributions. At that point enlargement became bound up with Greek demands for an accord among member states on the so-called Integrated Mediterranean Programs. Originating in a request in 1982 by the new Greek government of Andreas Papandreou for better membership terms, the Integrated Mediterranean Programs called for financial assistance primarily to Greece but also to Italy and southern France to help develop agriculture, tourism, and small business.[7] As the negotiations with Spain and Portugal reached a conclusion, Papandreou linked an agreement on financial transfers to Greece with an agreement on enlargement.

Delors, who became Commission president in January 1985, had to satisfy the Greek demands before the EC could advance on other fronts. He threw himself enthusiastically into the fray, setting the tone for his leadership of the Commission in the years ahead. Following intensive negotiations, the European Council agreed in March 1985 to a seven-year program of grants and loans to assist existing Mediterranean regions in the EC "to adjust under the best conditions possible to the new situation created by enlargement."[8] The issue showed how a tough-minded member state could leverage accession negotiations for its own advantage.

The outcome was a triumph for Delors. Because he had taken responsibility for resolving the dispute, failure would have seriously undermined his credibility. After the March 1985 summit, a relieved Delors declared that "all the family quarrels have been sorted out. The family is now going to grow and we can think of the future."[9] Indeed, for the first time in nearly twenty years the EC's future looked bright. Imminent enlargement provided a psychological boost and an additional rationale for institutional reform. Following the protracted accession negotiations and short but sharp dispute over the Integrated Mediterranean Programs, the decks were cleared for the European Council to consider, as Mitterrand put it, "what Europe will become."[10]

■ Accelerating European Integration

Coinciding with the breakthrough on enlargement, political pressure intensified to complete the single market. Delors wanted to revitalize the EC in other ways as well, notably by overhauling decisionmaking procedures, launching a new monetary policy initiative, and extending Community competence in the field of foreign and defense policy. As a former finance minister and a committed Eurofederalist, Delors preferred to concentrate primarily on monetary union. Yet Delors knew that monetary policy was too sensitive politically for such a bold initiative to succeed at this stage.

By contrast, the advantages of choosing the internal market option were obvious. By going back to basics and emphasizing one of the original objectives of the Rome Treaty, Delors could hardly be accused of overweening ambition. Regardless of their political preferences and personal opinions of each other, national leaders uniformly sang the praises of the single market. Thatcher was especially eloquent on the subject. By championing a cause dear to her heart, Delors hoped to tie Thatcher closer to the Community and heal the wounds caused by the British budgetary question.

In addition, Delors believed, completion of the single market necessitated greater use in the Council of qualified majority voting (QMV). Otherwise, single market proposals would get bogged down forever in disputes among national governments. Moreover, interest in the single market would most likely fuel interest in monetary union. How could the market be fully integrated without common economic and monetary policies? In Delors's view, the logic of a large, vibrant internal market pointed inexorably toward EMU.[11]

The link between market integration, decisionmaking reform, and a further monetary initiative intrigued Delors and underlay the entire single market strategy. At the same time, Delors understood the importance of maintaining private-sector support. To a great extent the Commission's subsequent proposals for collaborative research and development projects sought to strengthen the Commission-industry alliance in anticipation of the single market program. Of course, industrial leaders were already eager to complete the single market, and had formed a high-level interest group, the European Round Table, to help achieve that objective.

Building on widespread support in political and business circles, Delors submitted to the European Council in June 1985 a set of detailed proposals to complete the single market. This famous white paper was one of the most important policy documents ever prepared by the Commission.[12] Often caricatured as a typical Commission product—unintelligible, obtuse, and tedious— in fact the white paper was a surprisingly lucid piece, containing a ringing defense of market liberalization and a clear exposition of how and why the EC should achieve a single market.

The white paper is best known for its appendix listing approximately 300 legislative proposals that the EC needed to enact before the internal market could be implemented. The Commission was able to compile this list in record time because most of the proposals already existed in draft form, a legacy of the Commission's earlier internal market efforts. The indispensable novelty of the white paper's appendix was not the items listed in it but the way that Delors organized them according to a timetable ending on December 31, 1992, at the end of the next Commission's term in office. Accordingly, the appendix constituted a detailed action plan against which Commission officials, politicians, and businesspeople could measure progress toward achieving the single market (implementation of the single market program is examined in detail in Chapter 13).

The white paper's appendix represented only part of the legislative agenda likely to be unleashed by the single market program, which could touch on a wide range of policies and activities, notably in the fields of competition, research and development, the environment, consumer protection, and social affairs. Despite the simplicity of the "single market" slogan and the brevity of the Commission's action plan, the white paper heralded a major revival of European integration.

As Delors pointed out, the European Council's acceptance of the white paper alone would not suffice to ensure the success of the single market program or of a broader legislative agenda. As long as decisionmaking procedures remained unreformed, the single market might never come to fruition. The main challenge for the European Council, therefore, was to tackle the politically charged question of treaty change, a question already on the European Council's agenda thanks to a report by a high-level committee on institutional reform, set up after the Fontainebleau summit under the chairmanship of James Dooge, a former Irish foreign minister.

The Dooge Committee's report identified a number of "priority objectives" deemed necessary to revive European integration.[13] Apart from completing the single market, these included more use of QMV in the Council, a greater legislative role for the EP, and new initiatives in selected policy areas.

Given the wide differences among committee members, the report was replete with reservations and minority opinions. In particular, three committee members—the representatives of Britain, Denmark, and Greece—disagreed with the report's central suggestion that national leaders convene an intergovernmental conference (IGC) to negotiate a new treaty.

The European Council took up the 1985 white paper and the Dooge Report in June 1985. Quick endorsement of the white paper apparently presaged a smooth summit, but the meeting soon became mired in a major procedural dispute. Arguing against a treaty revision, Thatcher advocated informal arrangements to quicken decisionmaking in the Council. Taking a coordinated position, Mitterrand and German chancellor Helmut Kohl urged major institutional reform. The Italian presidency of the European Council finally forced the issue by proposing an IGC to negotiate a treaty on foreign and security policy cooperation as well as a revision of the Rome Treaty to improve decisionmaking procedures and extend Community competences. Italy called for a vote—an unprecedented step in the European Council. Seven national leaders voted in favor of a conference; three—the British, Danish, and Greek prime ministers—voted against.

It was nothing new for Thatcher, the lone crusader for reform of the EC budget, to be isolated in the European Council, but she was in a novel situation in 1985. In the past, Thatcher's intransigence had thwarted the EC's development. Now she was powerless to prevent an IGC that could change the Community's character completely. Thatcher felt especially aggrieved because the single market program, at the root of the Community's metamorphosis, owed much to her initiative. She also supported closer foreign policy cooperation and appreciated that excessive use of the veto impeded efficient decisionmaking. Nevertheless, she felt that the existing treaties were more than adequate.[14]

The more integration-minded governments fretted that Britain, Denmark, and Greece, smarting from their isolation at the recent summit and renowned for their minimalist positions on European integration, might attempt to sabotage an IGC from within. Ultimately, the three countries in question had too much to lose by pursuing blatantly negative tactics. They defended their interests tenaciously in the conference, in a creditable and constructive manner.

▪ The Single European Act

The IGC began in September 1985 and ended in January 1986. Foreign ministers conducted the negotiations, assisted by two sets of high-ranking officials, one dealing with treaty reform, the other with reorganizing European Political Cooperation, which would remain largely intergovernmental. Commissioners and their officials participated at each level of the conference. One of the Com-

qualified majority voting

mission's earliest contributions to the conference recommended a single concluding document rather than a treaty on foreign and security cooperation and a separate set of Rome Treaty revisions. Most governments saw the advantage of having one document emerge from the conference. Yet it was only at a late stage of the negotiations that foreign ministers endorsed the idea and named the eventual outcome of their deliberations the *Single* European Act.[15]

At a time when Cold War rivalry was gradually giving way to direct US-Soviet bargaining without European involvement, governments generally agreed on the advisability of asserting the EC's international identity by shoring up EPC. Accordingly, the conference concluded that member states would "coordinate their positions more closely on the political and economic aspects of security" and "endeavor jointly to formulate and implement a European foreign policy." In deference to the United States and to those member states—notably Britain and the Netherlands—most sensitive about US opinion, the conference declared that greater foreign policy coordination would not "impede closer cooperation in the field of security" among relevant member states "in the framework of the Western European Union or the Atlantic Alliance."

As for EC policies and procedures, the conference had little difficulty endorsing the goal of an internal market, defined as "an area without internal frontiers in which the free movement of goods, persons, services and capital is ensured." But negotiations on the steps necessary to bring it about were difficult. In the end, the conference revised the treaty to allow the use of QMV for most single market measures, leaving others—the least tractable ones—still subject to unanimity. The conference also approved a number of national derogations for parts of the single market program.

The IGC did not directly confront the Luxembourg Compromise, the informal arrangement whereby a government could prevent a vote from being taken in the Council. Some governments saw in the agreement to use QMV for most of the single market program the beginning of the end of the national veto. Others reached the opposite conclusion, citing the continued applicability of unanimity for the 1985 white paper's most controversial proposals. In any event, governments would remain sensitive to each other's special concerns, thus perpetuating "the very strong inclination of the Council to seek consensus irrespective of the voting rules."[16]

To push the Community more in a federal direction and to increase its democratic legitimacy, Germany and Italy urged greater power for the Parliament. For a combination of political and practical reasons, Britain and France opposed strengthening the EP's legislative role. The issue dominated a number of negotiating sessions, until governments agreed to extend the requirement for consultation between the Council and the EP to new policy areas and, more important, to establish a cooperation procedure to involve the EP more fully in the legislative process, notably for most single market measures.

During the IGC, Delors returned repeatedly to his pet project of including "a certain monetary capacity" in the SEA. Britain strongly opposed any move toward EMU, France was broadly in favor, and Germany was equivocal. Without strong support from a large member state, Delors succeeded only in having a new chapter included in the treaty that recognized the need to converge economic and monetary policies "for the further development of the Community." The SEA also included significant changes with regard to environmental policy, research and development, and efforts to promote cohesion between rich and poor member states.

National leaders failed to resolve a number of outstanding issues and conclude the IGC at a summit in Luxembourg in December 1985. A subsequent foreign ministers' session brought agreement closer, but lingering Danish and Italian reservations (the Danes complained that the SEA's institutional provisions went too far, and the Italians complained that they did not go far enough) carried over into the new year. The wording of an article on working conditions, buried in a subsection on social policy, caused last-minute delays. The final ministerial session of the conference, in January 1986, approved compromises reached in the relevant working party.

Ratification of the SEA, which the foreign ministers signed in Luxembourg in February 1986, proceeded relatively smoothly. There was little public concern throughout the Community about an excessive loss of national sovereignty or a further concentration of power in Brussels. Most national parliaments held lively debates on the SEA, and almost all voted in favor of ratification. Denmark's parliament was the exception, but the positive outcome of the subsequent referendum ensured Danish ratification. (The reverse happened in 1992, when a majority of Danes rejected the Maastricht Treaty following the Danish parliament's acceptance of it.)

Few predicted the far-reaching impact that the SEA could have on the course of European integration. Delors was downcast, believing that national governments had been too timid in the IGC, thus reducing progress to the level of the lowest common denominator. Franco-German leadership had not been decisive; far from pushing a radical reform agenda, Mitterrand and Kohl had seemingly succumbed to Thatcher's minimalist position. Delors even wondered whether the SEA would suffice to bring about completion of the single market by the end of 1992.[17]

Thatcher's delight and Delors's disappointment reflected the importance attached to the SEA at the time of its negotiation. As the *Common Market Law Review* editorialized in 1986, "Measured against Parliament's Draft Treaty, the results [of the conference] are disappointingly meager. They also fall short of the expectations . . . of the Commission and some of the member states. . . . But they reflect the limits of what was possible at the turn of the year [1985–1986]."[18] Yet the SEA had tremendous potential for the EC. First, provision for QMV might not only expedite the internal market but also encourage the Council to be more flexible in areas where unanimity remained the norm. Second, a successful single market program could advance European integration in related economic and social sectors. Third, the SEA's institutional and policy provisions might strengthen the role of the Commission and the EP in the EU system. Finally, the SEA's provisions for closer foreign policy cooperation procedures could enhance the EC's international standing. Within a short time, proponents and opponents of ever closer union would know whether and how the SEA's potential would be realized.

◼ The Single Market Program and Cohesion

It is easy to underestimate the ambition of the 1992 program. Integrating separate national markets into a single market is a Herculean task, even with a customs union and an institutional structure already in place. Completing the single market would involve intensive interaction between the Commission (which submitted the legislative proposals) and the Council (which enacted them). The European Parliament would also play a key part through the new cooperation procedure for legislative decisionmaking.[19]

The 1992 program enjoyed considerable popular and political support and got off to a flying start in the real world of business and commerce. "Italian businessmen talk about it, the French have visionary dreams about it, the West Germans plan quietly for it." "It," *The Economist* informed the unenlightened in February 1988, "is December 31, 1992, the date by which the European Community is supposed to become a true common market."[20] Entrepreneurs and businesspeople were bombarded by conferences, newsletters, and advertisements organized and disseminated by the Commission, national governments, and the private sector on how to exploit a frontier-free Community.

A Commission-sponsored research project on the "costs of non-Europe" fueled business interest in the single market. The purpose of the project, led by Paolo Cecchini, a former Commission official, was to quantify the cost to the Community of maintaining a fragmented market. Based on data from the four biggest member states, Cecchini's team assessed the costs and benefits of maintaining the status quo by analyzing the impact of market barriers and comparing the EC with the United States. Cecchini looked at the financial costs to firms of the administrative procedures and delays associated with customs formalities, the opportunity costs of lost trade, and the costs to national governments of customs controls. In early 1988 Cecchini produced the project's optimistic findings in a massive, sixteen-volume publication.[21]

The private sector's love affair with 1992 disguised the program's slow legislative progress. The problem lay not only with the complexity and sensitivity of many of the 1985 white paper's proposals—the Council dealt swiftly and easily with the least controversial measures—but also with a looming dispute over a Commission proposal for the EC's finances over the next five years. The purpose of the proposal, known as the Delors package, was to put the annual budget into a new, multiannual framework and to ensure sufficient funding to achieve the objectives of the SEA. Implementing the single market would not cost much, but efforts to close the economic gap between the EC's rich and poor countries would be expensive.

Disagreement over the Delors package became the largest obstacle blocking implementation of the single market program, as the poorer member states (Ireland, Greece, Portugal, and Spain) demanded greater spending on regional development policy in return for further liberalization. Delors, a strong supporter of cohesion policy, characterized the budgetary package as a "marriage contract between the Twelve" and struggled throughout 1987 to bring Thatcher to the altar.[22] The British prime minister had an instinctive aversion to increasing the size of the EC's budget and let it be known that regardless of any change, Britain would keep its current rebate, for which she had fought so hard in the early 1980s.

Matters came to a head at a summit in June 1987 where Thatcher complained that the other EC leaders were not sufficiently serious about budgetary discipline and CAP reform. For old-timers at the European Council, this was vintage Thatcher; for newcomers, it was an eye-opener. Leaders of the poorer countries, apparently quiescent at the summit, grew more assertive thereafter in demanding a greater distribution of EC resources and pressing for acceptance of the Delors package. A showdown followed at the next summit, with Thatcher reverting to her early 1980s negativism, Kohl and Mitterrand reluctant for domestic political reasons to cut the CAP, and Spanish prime minister González demanding additional funding. The meeting ended in disarray.[23]

Delors was despondent about the budget negotiations. Governments had debated his proposals for nearly a year without reaching agreement. Hoping to turn Germany's Council presidency in early 1988 to domestic political advantage, Kohl decided to resolve the impasse. He was more willing than he might otherwise have been to pay the bill for cohesion. Even more than Kohl's largesse, Thatcher's surprising tractability helped settle the issue. At a special meeting of the European Council in February 1988, national leaders eventually got down to the kind of detailed negotiations that should properly have been left to subordinates. After intense bargaining, they agreed to double the structural funds—the instruments of cohesion policy—by 1992, to introduce a new source of revenue for the budget, and to reform the CAP.

Thatcher's willingness to increase the EC's budget seemed a remarkable climb down, especially in light of previous such battles. The prime minister may have been grateful for her colleagues' continuing acceptance of Britain's rebate, but most likely a desire to end the dissipating dispute and proceed with the single market program—of particular interest to Britain—convinced her to compromise. Whatever the reason, her decision removed a large obstacle on the road to 1992.

Economic and Monetary Union

Capitalizing on the budget agreement and on enthusiasm for the single market program, Delors focused attention on his primary goal of EMU, the Holy Grail of European integration. Delors argued that exchange rate fluctuations were inconsistent with and contradictory to the objectives of the single market. With the 1992 program off to a strong start, the close relationship between it and EMU became a new orthodoxy. The Commission developed the link: "A single currency is the natural complement of a single market. The full potential of the latter will not be achieved without the former. Going further, there is a need for economic and monetary union in part to consolidate the potential gains from completing the internal market, without which there would be risks of weakening the present momentum of the 1992 process."[24] The Commission's much-quoted cost-benefit analysis of EMU appeared two months later. Its title, *One Market, One Money,* reinforced the 1992-EMU connection and became a mantra for advocates of a single currency.[25]

The European Monetary System, which had helped to make the single market possible, provided another impetus toward EMU. Italian economist Tomaso Padoa-Schioppa pointed out that with complete capital mobility (a feature of the single market), the exchange rate mechanism and the existing degree of monetary policy coordination would be insufficient to promote price stability and ensure orderly trade relations among member states. "In a quite fundamental way," Padoa-Schioppa concluded, "capital mobility and exchange rate fixity together leave no room for independent monetary policies."[26] In other words, a unified market with free flows of capital could put the EMS under unbearable pressure. National governments would discover the extent of that pressure during the currency crisis of 1992.

Businesspeople warmed to the idea of monetary union thanks to the success of the EMS and the single market program. In 1990, management consultants Ernst and Young conducted a survey for the Commission that showed widespread optimism in business circles about the economic impact of monetary union combined with completion of the single market.[27] Moreover, the experience of working together in the exchange rate mechanism had built trust among national officials and reconciled many of them to the prospect of EMU.

Nevertheless, the drive for EMU needed powerful political impetus, which could come only from the European Council. Within that body, Mitterrand was the most influential proponent of monetary union, but not necessarily because of the success of the 1992 program. Only if monetary policy decisions were taken on an EC-wide basis, Mitterrand reasoned, could France hope to regain some of the influence it had lost to Germany in the EMS because of the mark's predominance in the exchange rate mechanism. For precisely that reason, initially Kohl was equivocal about EMU. The German central bank, he knew, would want to keep de facto predominance in European monetary policymaking.

Alone among national leaders, Thatcher wholeheartedly opposed EMU, seeing it as an unacceptable abrogation of national sovereignty and an effort to aggregate power in Brussels. Opposition to EMU had led in part to Thatcher's infamous speech at the College of Europe in Bruges, a citadel of Eurofederalism, in September 1988. The speech was peppered with barbed attacks against Delors, the Commission, and incipient Eurofederalism as Thatcher presented her view of the EC and of Britain's role in it. "We have not successfully rolled back the frontiers of the state in Britain," she declared, "only to see them reimposed at a European level with a European superstate exercising a new dominance from Brussels."[28] Primed by Delors, pressed by Mitterrand, and with Kohl's lukewarm support, the European Council decided in June 1988 to instruct a committee, chaired by Delors and made up primarily of national central banker presidents, to "study and propose concrete changes" that could result in EMU. Believing that the committee would never produce a roadmap for EMU, Thatcher grudgingly acquiesced in its establishment. As she later admitted, this was a fateful miscalculation.[29]

Whatever their institutional positions on EMU, the central bank presidents could not resist the intellectual challenge of devising steps that could result in its achievement. Accordingly, the Delors Report did not take an explicit stand on whether monetary union was necessary to ensure the success of the single market, nor did it develop a cost-benefit analysis of EMU. Instead, it provided a roadmap for reaching EMU. Although the committee did not explicitly endorse a single currency, its definition of monetary union—"the assurance of total and irreversible convertibility of currencies; the complete liberalization of capital transactions and full integration of banking and other financial markets; and the elimination of margins of fluctuation and the irrevocable locking of exchange rate parities"—necessarily involved a centralized monetary policy in the EC.[30]

The report identified four basic elements of economic union: a single market; competition policy; common policies aimed at structural change and regional development; and macroeconomic policy coordination, including binding limits on national deficits and debts. Three of these were already in place or being put in place: the single market program was in full swing; competition policy was being strengthened; and governments had agreed to a big increase in the structural funds to promote regional development. Only macroeconomic policy coordination would represent a significant new departure. Although economic union would not necessitate a common economic policy, the Delors Report stressed the need for close coordination of national fiscal policies in order to operate EMU successfully.

Responsibility for monetary policy would rest squarely with a new EC institution, the European Central Bank (ECB). Reflecting the influence on the committee of Karl-Otto Pöhl, president of the Bundesbank (German central bank), and a high degree of satisfaction with the existing EMS, the report emphatically identified price stability as the ECB's primary objective.

The Delors Report is best known for proposing a three-stage approach to EMU:

- *Stage I:* Free capital movement in the EC and closer monetary and macroeconomic cooperation among member states and their central banks.
- *Stage II:* Close coordination of national monetary policies and a progressive narrowing of margins of fluctuation within the exchange rate mechanism.
- *Stage III:* Establishment of "irrevocably fixed" exchange rate parities and granting of full authority for monetary policy to the ECB.

Mindful of the embarrassment caused by the EC's commitment in 1972 to achieve EMU by the end of the decade, the Delors Report did not adopt a timetable for reaching Stage III. Instead, the report merely recommended that Stage I start no later than July 1990, when capital movements were due to be liberalized anyway as part of the single market program.

Publication of the report sparked a lively debate. The most explosive political issue, inherent in any discussion of EMU, was that of national sovereignty. Most participants in the exchange rate mechanism had already lost control over national monetary policy; in practice, their currencies were pegged to the German mark, the system's unofficial anchor. Participating countries reaped the political and economic rewards of low inflation and stable exchange rates. To a great extent, Germany's partners in the EMS had given up using interest rates and exchange rates as instruments of economic policy.

Most participants in EMU therefore stood to regain a degree of sovereignty rather than lose more of it. By joining a federal monetary system, they would wrest some power back from the Bundesbank. For that reason, Germany should have been the least happy about monetary union. Indeed, the Bundesbank had serious concerns about the venture, at least until it could be sure that an alternative arrangement offered as good a prospect of price stability as did the existing mechanism.[31] But the German government, which supported monetary union for political reasons, could hardly argue in favor of maintaining the status quo, in which Germany had de facto control over monetary policy in the EC.

The debate over national sovereignty was loudest in Britain, where the economic benefits of EMU were also least apparent. Speaking in July 1991, Thatcher complained that the exchange rate mechanism, into which she had reluctantly brought Britain the previous October, was "tearing the heart out of parliamentary sovereignty." As for EMU, handing over responsibility for monetary policy to the putative ECB would reduce "national finance ministers to the status of innocent bystanders at the scene of an accident."[32]

The question of sovereignty also hinged on powerful political symbols. Money was both a means of transacting business and a badge of national identity or, in the event of a single currency, a symbol of European unity. As the Maastricht ratification crisis would show, attachment to the national symbolism of money ran deep throughout the EC, especially in Germany, where the mark epitomized postwar prosperity and stability.

The Commission did not try to calculate the political costs or benefits of EMU apart from an oblique reference to possible "psychological" problems.[33] National governments would have to reach their own conclusions, but for most it was clear that the anticipated benefits of EMU outweighed the intangible political costs. Not only had most countries already sacrificed national sovereignty by participating in the exchange rate mechanism, but some—notably Italy—saw future EC curbs on national fiscal policy as the only way to tackle their exorbitant budget deficits.

Instead, the Commission focused on economic losses and gains, identifying the elimination of transaction costs and exchange rate vulnerability, resulting in greater trade and investment, as a major advantage. Yet the Commission conceded that the EC was not an "optimum currency area" in which labor would move freely in order to offset country-specific shocks, nor would Brussels have a fiscal system capable of making income-stabilizing transfers. Given that economic shocks would continue to affect each country differently, that labor would remain relatively immobile because of cultural and linguistic barriers, and that the EC would not acquire competence for fiscal policy, the advantages of EMU seemed far from obvious. Nevertheless, the Commission concluded that "the case [for EMU] can stand powerfully on economic criteria alone."[34]

The Commission's arguments failed to impress some influential economists on both sides of the EMU debate. Peter Kenen, a supporter of monetary integration, regretted that the Commission publication *One Market, One Money* did not prove conclusively "that the benefits would exceed the costs," its title being "as close as the study came to making a case for EMU."[35] Martin Feldstein, an opponent of EMU, refuted the assertion that a single market needed a single currency, let alone monetary union. Feldstein argued that monetary union would not necessarily increase trade and that the success of the EMS weakened the anti-inflationary argument for EMU.[36] Perhaps the Commission should have produced an aggregate estimate of the impact of EMU, along the lines of the Cecchini Report on the single market. The Commission explained in August 1990, however, that the nature of EMU, conditional as it was on "the responses of governments as well as private economic agents," made such an approach infeasible.[37]

As Feldstein noted disapprovingly, the main push for EMU was political, not economic. It emanated mainly from Paris, Brussels, and Bonn (then Germany's capital), with Thatcher being almost completely marginalized. The conclusions of successive European summits in the late 1980s chronicled the seemingly unstoppable political pressure that had developed for EMU.

German Unification

Reaction to events in Central and Eastern Europe in the late 1980s also set Thatcher apart from other EC leaders. The most immediate issue was the sudden prospect of German unification following the fall of the Berlin Wall. The challenge for Britain, France, and other countries was to overcome latent fear of a strong, united Germany. The challenge for the EC was both procedural (how to absorb the relatively underdeveloped East Germany) and political (how to retain Germany's commitment to the EC and prevent a united Germany from predominating). The challenge for Germany was to reassure other countries of its abiding attachment to European integration.

Delors took the initiative in October 1989, a month before the wall came down, in a speech at the College of Europe in Bruges, where Thatcher had issued her infamous anti-federalist manifesto the previous year. Citing the rapidly changing situation in Central and Eastern Europe, Delors called for a huge "leap forward" in European integration to meet the challenges ahead.[38] In a key address to the German parliament in November 1989, Kohl sought to assuage restive neighboring states when he proclaimed that "the future architecture of Germany must be fitted into the future architecture of Europe as a whole."[39] Kohl failed to reassure all of his EC colleagues: Thatcher was the most troubled, but Mitterrand was anxious as well.

EC leaders had their first opportunity to thrash things out at the December 1989 European Council. Torn between an aversion toward German unification and an affinity for European integration, Mitterrand forged a link between the two. Obstructing German unification at the summit, the highlight of France's Council presidency, would have tarnished Mitterrand's carefully cultivated image as a European statesman, impaired deeper integration, and possibly undermined the drive for EMU. A key passage in the summit's conclusions outlined Mitterrand's position, to which even Thatcher subscribed: German unity through free self-determination "should take place peacefully and democratically, in full respect of the relevant agreements and treaties . . . in a context of dialogue and East-West cooperation [and] in the perspective of European integration."[40]

It was also at the December 1989 summit that Community leaders agreed to hold an intergovernmental conference to negotiate the treaty changes necessary to achieve monetary union. As Mitterrand announced after the summit, the agreement represented "the sole objective link" in the European Council's deliberations between German and European integration.[41] Thatcher did not disguise her opposition but saw no point in being formally outvoted.

A resounding victory for Kohl's Christian Democratic Party in the first free elections in East Germany, in March 1990, signaled the prospect of imminent unification and quickened the momentum for deeper European integration. The time seemed ripe for a major Franco-German initiative. It came in April 1990 when Kohl and Mitterrand publicly linked the need "to accelerate the political construction" of the EC to recent developments in Central and Eastern Europe as well as to moves already under way to achieve EMU.[42] This was striking evidence of the importance of Franco-German leadership at a critical stage in EU history.

Meeting in April 1990, EC leaders discussed preparations for the intergovernmental conference on EMU, which was due to open before the end of the year, and the possibility of a parallel conference on a range of other issues. Kohl and Mitterrand identified four essential objectives: stronger democratic legitimacy; more efficient institutions; unity and coherence of economic, monetary, and political action; and a common foreign and security policy. Only Thatcher adamantly opposed holding yet another IGC. In deference to her, the European Council postponed until June 1990 the formal decision to hold the conference on what they misguidedly called political union, in parallel with the conference on economic and monetary union.[43]

The run-up to the launch of the two IGCs in December 1990 saw the governments' understanding of EMU come into sharper focus and their understanding of political union become more blurred. This situation reflected the concrete nature of EMU, especially after publication of the Delors Report, and the imprecise nature of political union. The ultimate goals of EMU—a single monetary policy and a single currency—were obvious, whereas the endpoint of political union was not. Most governments agreed on what political union could or should include—closing the democratic deficit, strengthening subsidiarity, improving decisionmaking, extending Community competence, and devising a common foreign and security policy—but disagreed on the extent of those changes and how to bring them about.

Moves toward EMU received a further boost at a special meeting of the European Council in October 1990, when eleven of the twelve national leaders agreed to launch Stage II in January 1994. The summit's conclusions identified Britain as the odd one out.[44] Thatcher's resistance had an unexpected side effect: it precipitated her ouster as prime minister. With its popularity plunging, the ruling British Conservative Party saw Thatcher's implacable opposition to deeper European integration as a serious liability. By itself, Thatcher's negativism in European affairs would not have caused the Conservatives to lose a general election, but combined with a hugely unpopular tax reform, it threatened to tip the scales in favor of the opposition Labour Party. Thatcher's strident remarks on her return from the European summit sparked a leadership struggle, which John Major, her finance minister, surprisingly won. Rarely in EU history had "Community affairs" impinged so dramatically and so directly on domestic politics.

Other national leaders welcomed the arrival of a new British prime minister. Although, as *The Economist* facetiously remarked, Thatcher's departure robbed the Community of "the grit around which the other eleven formed their Euro-pearl,"[45] her Community counterparts were glad to see her go. It was impossible at that stage to judge whether Major's ascendancy represented more than a welcome stylistic change in Britain's dealings with Brussels. As it turned out, Major was every bit as obdurate as Thatcher, but was nicer about it.

The launch of two new IGCs did not resonate much with the public. If anything, Europeans generally seemed more guarded about the prospect of deeper integration. The Gulf War, triggered by Iraq's invasion of Kuwait in August 1990, cast a pall over the IGCs, which opened ceremonially in Rome at the end of the year. Exhilaration over the revolution in Central and Eastern Europe and its possible spread to the Soviet Union gradually gave way to concern about the possibility of economic, political, and military instability in the East. Celebration of German unification, which took place in October 1990, rested uneasily with latent fear of the country's resurgence and more realistic anxiety about the high cost of assimilating East Germany into the Federal Republic. It soon became clear that enthusiasm for deeper European integration had been fleeting: it peaked with the launch of the single market program in the late 1980s and was relatively short-lived.

■ The Maastricht Treaty

The Maastricht summit of December 1991 brought the two IGCs—one on EMU, the other on broader institutional and policy issues—to a successful conclusion. The summit crowned a year of intensive negotiations among national governments, with the Commission as a formal participant, the Council secretariat playing a crucial behind-the-scenes role, and the EP looking on from the margins. Although the lowest common denominator often prevailed, the conferences and the ensuing Maastricht Treaty—formally the Treaty on European Union—nonetheless marked a watershed in the history of European integration, notably by paving the way for monetary union and the launch of the euro.

Negotiation

Each national delegation brought to the table a particular set of expectations and objectives.[46] Germany, having the most to lose from EMU and the most to gain from political union, advocated a close connection between the two sets of negotiations. By agreeing to a single currency, Germany would be giving up the mark and surrendering de facto control over European monetary policy. In return, Germany wanted an EU with a familiar federal system of government in which controversial domestic issues (such as asylum policy) might be resolved and in which a more powerful EP (with a large German contingent) would play a greater role.

The Bundesbank rather than the government seemed to determine Germany's position on EMU. Even before the negotiations began, the president of the Bundesbank outlined Germany's objectives in a number of forceful speeches. His main point was the indivisibility of monetary policy, responsibility for which at the European level would have to reside in a single, independent institution with the unambiguous mandate of maintaining price stability. In other words, the proposed European Central Bank should replicate the Bundesbank. He also urged a gradual approach to EMU, stressing the need for economic convergence between potential participants. The Bundesbank's stridency caused a rift in the government, with the finance minister echoing the bank's position and Kohl and the foreign minister taking a more flexible line.

France wanted EMU at almost any cost and did not have an independent central bank counseling caution. Mitterrand was not keen on having an independent ECB but conceded the point early in the negotiations. However, France strongly urged the launch of the ECB at the beginning of Stage II (January 1994), believing that a functioning ECB and a strict timetable for a single currency would spur governments to bring about economic convergence. In the parallel conference on political union, France opposed giving the EP additional power and sought a stronger European Council at the expense of both the Commission and the EP.

In a series of speeches in early 1991, Major had promised to put Britain "at the very heart of the Community." Yet Britain's new prime minister, like Thatcher before him, adamantly opposed a single currency and an EU organized on federal lines. Britain's performance in both IGCs demonstrated the philosophical and ideological distance between it and other member states. On a range of issues—from EMU to legislative reform to foreign and security policy—Britain took a minimalist position. It was obvious in the run-up to the Maastricht summit that Major was as unyielding in his defense of British interests as Thatcher had ever been.

A prolonged controversy over the use of the word "federal" demonstrated the difference between Britain and its Community partners. A draft treaty presented by the Luxembourg presidency in June 1991 described European integration as "a process leading to a Union with a federal goal." The British foreign secretary immediately announced that his country did "not intend to be committed to the implications which, in the English language, the phrase 'federal goal' carries."[47] The issue was not simply linguistic; after all, Americans understood "federalism" to mean something positive and worthwhile. A British member of the EP explained the problem differently: "On the Continent, [federalism] is a harmless label, neither exciting nor controversial. In Britain, it carries connotations of unspeakable disloyalty and unmentionable perversity."[48]

With Thatcher hovering in the wings and a general election looming, it was not surprising that the British government protested so vehemently about the F-word. It was an easy battle to fight because there was nothing of substance at stake. When Major denounced the draft treaty's reference to a "federal goal," the new Dutch presidency merely changed this phrase to "federal vocation." As the conferences gathered speed, Major escalated his campaign to excise the F-word entirely. Eventually his colleagues gave in. "What does the word matter, as long as we have the actual thing?" asked Delors.[49] The word mattered, of course, because Major needed to claim a political victory at home.

No two countries had identical positions on EMU and political union, and no single country—not even Britain—was completely isolated. Regardless of the reason for a country's position—whether principle, pragmatism, tradition, or size—there was considerable scope for ad hoc coalition building, which took place at a series of official and unofficial meetings. Franco-German initiatives were common, although the Community's two leading countries disagreed sharply on many institutional and policy proposals.

Not surprisingly, Delors took a particularly keen interest in EMU. By contrast, Delors was far less involved in the conference on political union. Early in the negotiations the Commission suggested several treaty reforms with which a majority of countries strongly disagreed. These included a radical increase in the Commission's responsibility for international trade relations and greater powers of policy implementation for Brussels. In addition, Delors made a famous speech in London in March 1991 on security and defense, in which he called for the new EU to subsume the Western European Union and advocated greater independence from the United States.[50] Delors's speech and some of the Commission's proposals caused a backlash in certain national capitals. Thereafter, the Commission was on the defensive, fighting a rearguard action to protect its existing prerogatives.

Unlike the Commission, the EP did not participate directly in the conferences. Nevertheless, the EP has a set of objectives for the negotiations, including a radical extension of Community competence, more supranational decisionmaking, and not surprisingly, greater power for the Parliament itself through legislative codecision with the Council. Although the EP was in a relatively weak position and could not veto the outcome of the negotiations, two countries—Belgium and Italy—threatened not to ratify the final treaty unless the EP approved it.[51]

Based largely on contributions from national governments and the Commission, the new treaty began to take shape in mid-1991. With regard to EMU, the length and purpose of Stage II were especially controversial. Whereas France and the Commission wanted to establish the ECB at the beginning of Stage II, Germany insisted that the ECB not come into existence until just before Stage III—the formal launch of monetary union. Otherwise, Germany feared, the ECB would lack credibility and lose sight of its primary objective: price stability. The Luxembourg presidency followed Germany's lead and proposed that during Stage II the European Monetary Institute (EMI), a precursor of the ECB, would merely try to coordinate national monetary positions. The Luxembourg proposals sparked the first serious discussion of convergence criteria for countries hoping to participate in Stage III and of possible opt-outs for the others. A consensus gradually emerged that no country would be allowed to prevent others from moving to Stage III. Nor would any country, notably Britain, be forced to adopt a single currency. That formula ensured the success of the IGC.

The Luxembourg presidency circulated a draft treaty, including the provisions for EMU, in the run-up to the June 1991 summit. Its most striking feature was architectural: the putative EU would consist of three pillars. The first, subject to supranational decisionmaking, would envelop the EC, including EMU and additional competence in a number of areas, notably education, training, cohesion, research and development, environment, infrastructure, industry, health, culture, consumer protection, and development cooperation. The other two, subject to intergovernmental arrangements, would cover the Common Foreign and Security Policy (CFSP) and cooperation on justice and home affairs (JHA). The reason for this design was the unwillingness of many governments—not only the British—to bring politically sensitive internal and external security issues into a decisionmaking regime in which the Commission had the exclusive right of legislative initiative, the EP had considerable power, and the Court of Justice had the right of judicial review.

The European Council was not ready to conclude the conferences in June 1991, although the agreement eventually reached in Maastricht bore a striking resemblance to the Luxembourg presidency's draft. The June meeting was overshadowed in any case by the outbreak of war in Yugoslavia. Like the Gulf War six months earlier, the war in Yugoslavia emphasized the importance of developing an effective CFSP for the EU. Yet also like the Gulf War, the protracted and—for the EC—much more consequential Yugoslav war would make an effective CFSP far harder to achieve.

The Netherlands' presidency of the Council and chairmanship of the IGCs in the second half of 1991 were controversial and, at the outset, ineffectual. In a serious political miscalculation, the Dutch government sought to replace

Luxembourg's draft treaty with a new draft that included a unitary structure. Predictably, the Dutch draft triggered an angry reaction when presented at a foreign ministers' meeting in September 1991. Only Belgium supported the text, which the Dutch prime minister had earlier proclaimed "acceptable to all our partners."[52] The near-unanimous rejection of the Dutch draft inadvertently put the Luxembourg draft on a pedestal, thereby ensuring that the EU would have a three-pillar structure.

Earlier in September, the Dutch finance minister suffered a similar rebuke in the negotiations on EMU when he proposed that any six countries meeting specific economic criteria by 1996 could establish their own central bank and single currency. Most countries, regardless of economic performance, resented a proposal that could have created a permanent underclass of EU member states. A consensus emerged instead calling for EU members to decide collectively when the EU should move to Stage III and establish a single currency, although not all of them would be economically able or politically willing to participate in the currency union at the outset.[53] Governments finally agreed that the third stage of EMU, involving the introduction of a common currency, would take place by 1999 at the latest.

The Maastricht summit of December 1991 almost foundered not because of EMU but because of a proposal to strengthen Community competence in the area of social policy. Reflecting the British Conservative Party's stance on the issue, Major adamantly opposed the treaty's draft social policy provisions. As the summit wore on and Major showed no sign of changing his mind, the Dutch presidency suggested removing the new social policy provisions entirely from the treaty and including them in a separate protocol to which the other countries would subscribe, thereby reinforcing the emergence of differentiated integration, already inherent in the provisions for EMU. Such a development may not have been in the EU's interest, but creating the social protocol prevented a British walkout and saved the Maastricht Treaty.

Some governments had scored more negotiating points than others during the yearlong conferences, but none was an absolute winner or loser. The outcome was more clear-cut for the EU's institutions: the Council and Parliament gained most; the Commission gained least. As well as being an intensive bargaining session, the Maastricht summit was an opportunity to permit each participant, including the Commission, to claim victory on a variety of issues. Clearly there was something in the final agreement for everyone. Even Major's press officer was able to claim "game, set, and match" for Britain.[54]

Ratification

Despite their importance, the IGCs had not attracted much public or parliamentary attention in most countries. Britain was the obvious exception. There, pervasive Euroskepticism and a general election due to take place by mid-1992 at the latest ensured that the conferences were newsworthy. In particular, the British government's insistence on the right to opt out of monetary union attracted widespread notice and support. Given Major's supposed triumph in Maastricht and his victory in the April 1992 election, Britain seemed likely to ratify the treaty, through a vote in parliament, without much difficulty or delay. However, the situation changed dramatically following rejection of the Maastricht Treaty in the fateful Danish referendum of June 1992, which shook the Community to its core and galvanized British Euroskeptics.

There had been little discussion of the IGCs in Denmark until the run-up to the referendum, when opinion seemed evenly divided on the issue. Denmark was known for its ambivalence toward European integration, but the positive results of the 1972 referendum on EC membership and the 1986 referendum on the SEA suggested that a majority would support the Maastricht Treaty. Accordingly, the result—50.7 percent against to 49.3 percent in favor, with a record turnout of 83 percent—came as a shock to the Danish government and the EC establishment. Having spent a year negotiating the treaty, national governments never thought that a majority of Danes, or of any other nationality, would vote against it.

EC leaders immediately grasped the seriousness of the situation. Unless ratified in each member state, the treaty could not come into effect. Abandoning the institutional and policy innovations so painstakingly negotiated in the IGCs was out of the question. Instead, EC leaders announced soon after the referendum that they would search for a solution to what had become the Danish problem while continuing with ratification in the other countries.[55]

Fewer than 30,000 votes had determined the outcome of the referendum. Exhaustive analyses indicated a host of reasons for the result. Some were peculiarly Danish, others common to the EC; some were reasonable, others fanciful; some were consistent, others contradictory. Whatever the explanation, the result showed that national governments were unaware of growing public concern, in Denmark and elsewhere, about the direction and pace of European integration. Hitherto, most Europeans knew little about the EC. Suddenly, with the prominence of the single market program, passage of the SEA, and media coverage of the Maastricht summit, the EC loomed large. Now, the *Community* was about to be subsumed by a more far-reaching and portentous *Union*. Without even having read the treaty, many Europeans fretted about its contents. On EMU, worries ranged from the loss of national currencies to the rigors of the economic convergence criteria. More broadly, people seemed unhappy about the implications of deeper integration for national identity and control of sensitive policy areas, and resented the possibility of bureaucratic intrusion from Brussels. In most cases a perusal of the treaty's unintelligible text merely reinforced popular antipathy toward it.

Ireland was the only country constitutionally obliged to ratify the treaty by referendum. Coming two weeks after the Danish vote, the Irish referendum assumed special significance. Given Ireland's traditional support for European integration, and benefit from the single market program and the structural funds, a positive result seemed inevitable. Indeed, the government's referendum campaign concentrated on crude calculations of economic self-interest. The result was a strong endorsement of the Maastricht Treaty: of 57 percent who voted, 69 percent were in favor and 31 percent against.

A much more important test for the treaty came in September 1992, when French voters went to the polls. Although France could have ratified the treaty by an easily obtainable supermajority vote in parliament, Mitterrand announced immediately after the Danish result that France would also ratify by referendum. Since the mid-1980s, Mitterrand had cast himself as a staunch proponent of European integration. By winning a resounding referendum victory, he hoped both to breathe new life into the treaty and to give his presidency of France an indelible "European" imprint. Clearly Mitterrand believed that the country's historical contribution to the EC and the people's commitment to European integration would produce a comfortable majority and dispel the gloom caused by the Danish result.

Yet developments in France and elsewhere favored the treaty's opponents. The government's popularity slumped as the economy worsened and unemployment rose. The deteriorating situation in Bosnia reflected poorly on the EC, whose peace efforts did nothing to stop the fighting. Opinion polls in summer 1992 showed that the treaty's opponents were inching ahead and that frustration over the EC's inability to broker a Bosnian cease-fire was a powerful impetus to vote against. The concurrent crisis in the EMS—Britain and Italy dropped out of its exchange rate mechanism in September 1992, and the franc came under heavy pressure—further eroded public confidence. It also fueled a reaction against what looked like a German-designed monetary union, although EMU arguably offered the best chance to end currency instability.

The French government and other supporters of the treaty went on the offensive late in the campaign, cajoling the electorate to vote in favor of ratification. The normally staid *Le Monde* editorialized on the eve of the referendum that "a 'no' vote would be for France and for Europe the greatest catastrophe since Hitler's coming to power."[56] Such histrionics may have alienated more people than they assuaged. In the event, Mitterrand's gamble narrowly paid off. In a 70 percent turnout, 51.05 percent voted in favor and 48.95 percent voted against. The result was too close to justify the political and emotional effort invested. Far from boosting Mitterrand or Maastricht, it accelerated the president's political decline—his Socialist government lost heavily in the March 1993 parliamentary election—and further shook the EC establishment.

Delors was quick to respond to Denmark's rejection and France's narrow endorsement of the Maastricht Treaty. Alert to the extent of popular alienation from European policies and institutions, he strove to break the bureaucratic barrier surrounding Brussels, make the legislative process more transparent, and promote subsidiarity, a feature of the new treaty, as the best way to reassure public opinion. In particular, subsidiarity would provide guidelines as to where the EU could or could not act, just as similar constitutional provisions determine the proper functioning of US or German federalism.

At the June 1992 European Council, held immediately after the Danish referendum, national leaders "stressed the need for [subsidiarity] to be strictly applied, both in existing and in future legislation, and called on the Commission and the Council to look at the procedural and practical steps needed to implement it."[57] The Commission duly submitted to the Council and Parliament a lengthy analysis of subsidiarity, asserting that the burden of proof as to the need for action and the intensity (proportionally) of action lay with the EU's institutions. Because of its exclusive right of initiative, the Commission accepted special responsibility in that regard. But the Commission also argued that subsidiarity could not become an excuse for national governments either to blame Brussels for unpopular actions or to curb the Commission's legitimate legislative and executive authority.[58]

The Commission's report and other contributions set the stage for the December 1992 European Council, where national leaders approved a declaration outlining the basic principles of subsidiarity and guidelines for its application. The report included concrete examples of pending proposals and existing legislation in light of subsidiarity's "need for action" and "proportionality" criteria. The European Council also called for the EC's institutions to negotiate an agreement on the effective application of subsidiarity.[59]

The elaboration of subsidiarity went hand in hand with efforts to make the EC's legislative process more transparent, with EC leaders adopting specific measures in December 1992. Foremost among them was a decision to televise the opening sessions of some Council meetings and to publish the record of formal votes taken in the Council. Given the Council's history of secretiveness, these seemed remarkable measures. Even more than the debate about subsidiarity, the European Council's efforts to make the Brussels decision-making machinery more open and comprehensible demonstrated the profound impact on national governments of the Maastricht ratification crisis.

In the short term, however, the European Council's response sought to make the treaty more palatable to Danish voters. Regardless of promoting subsidiarity and transparency, EC leaders would have to address specific Danish concerns in order to enable the government to hold—and win—a second referendum. The only feasible approach was to offer Denmark the right to opt out of treaty provisions in areas of particular concern to voters, notably EMU, the CFSP, and cooperation on justice and home affairs. Based on behind-the-scenes negotiations involving the Danish government, the Council presidency, and the Council secretariat, national leaders reached an agreement in December 1992 on Danish opt-outs from the Maastricht Treaty. The agreement, in turn, allowed the Danish government to hold a referendum in May 1993, in which 56.7 percent voted in favor of ratification.

Britain, in the Council presidency during the second half of 1992, helped negotiate Denmark's opt-outs and thereby resolve the ratification crisis. But Britain itself had still not ratified the treaty. The delay was due to a combination of weak political leadership, unfortunate timing, and arcane parliamentary procedures. John Major wanted Britain to ratify the treaty during the country's presidency, but his plans were blown off course by the crisis in the EMS. It was difficult for Major to push the Maastricht Treaty through parliament, let alone put Britain "at the heart of Europe," after the pound sterling left the exchange rate mechanism so suddenly and disastrously in September 1992 (see Chapter 5).

The prime minister soon became a hostage of the Euroskeptics in his own party, who capitalized on the currency crisis and on the Maastricht Treaty's growing unpopularity. When the treaty barely survived a House of Commons vote in November 1992, Major announced that Britain would delay ratification until after the second Danish referendum. In the meantime, the opposition Labour Party tried to link ratification with a decision to scrap the deal on the social protocol negotiated by Major at the Maastricht summit (as a center-left party, Labour wanted the treaty to include strong social policy provisions). This seemed to galvanize the prime minister. Having fought in Maastricht to exclude Britain from the treaty's proposed social chapter, Major was not about to reverse course because of domestic political difficulties. Although peculiar parliamentary procedures gave steadfast opponents of the treaty great scope to filibuster, even the staunchest Euroskeptics admitted the unlikelihood of ultimately being able to prevent ratification. Yet only after narrowly surviving a vote of confidence did the government cross the final hurdle, in August 1993, and get the necessary number of votes in parliament for ratification.

That left Germany as the sole member state still to ratify the treaty. Only on the eve of the Maastricht summit had the issues under discussion—specifically EMU—attracted much attention in Germany. Before and during the treaty negotiations themselves, the Bundesbank tried to alert public opinion to the dangers, as it saw them, of EMU: Germany would lose the mark; its central bank would no longer formulate monetary policy but would become a regional member of a federal central banking system; the rest of Europe lacked Germany's historical fear of inflation; and the ECB might not be rigorously independent of political control. These harangues stiffened the government's position on EMU but otherwise fell on deaf ears until, in early December, a series of articles in the mass-circulation *Bild* newspaper struck a popular chord. On the second day of the Maastricht summit, a banner headline proclaimed "The End of the D-Mark." Widespread concern in Germany about the implications of EMU, fueled by the rising costs of unification, came too late to affect the Maastricht negotiations but became an element in the ratification debate.

Nevertheless, support for European integration was so deeply ingrained in Germany that the government was never at risk of losing a parliamentary vote on the Maastricht Treaty. Despite grumbling in Germany about the undesirability of EMU and other aspects of the treaty, in December 1992, large majorities voted in favor of ratification in both houses of parliament. The matter did not end there, however. Unable to block the treaty politically, opponents challenged its constitutionality on a variety of grounds. The federal constitutional court took almost a year to deliberate. In a landmark ruling in October 1993, it upheld the treaty's constitutionality but not without criticizing the putative EU's democratic credentials.[60] The court's ruling removed the last obstacle to ratification of the Maastricht Treaty, allowing it finally to come into effect in November 1993.

■ Notes

1. Stanley Hoffmann, "The European Community and 1992," *Foreign Affairs* 68, no. 4 (Fall 1989): 32.
2. On the 1981 and 1986 enlargement, see J. Sampedro, *The Enlargement of the European Community: Case Studies of Greece, Portugal and Spain* (Atlantic Highlands, NJ: Humanities Press International, 1984).
3. Quoted in Werner Feld, *West Germany and the European Community: Changing Interests and Competing Policy Objectives* (New York: Praeger, 1981), p. 55.
4. London European Council, "Presidency Conclusions," Bulletin EC 11-1981, point 1.1.5.
5. Fontainebleau European Council, "Presidency Conclusions," Bulletin EC 6-1984, point 1.1.5.
6. *Le Monde,* June 30, 1984, p. 2.
7. See Bulletin EC 2-1982, point 1.2.4.
8. Brussels European Council, "Presidency Conclusions," Bulletin EC 3-1985, point 1.2.1.
9. *Le Monde,* April 2, 1986.
10. Quoted in Frances Nicholson and Roger East, *From the Six to the Twelve: The Enlargement of the European Community* (Chicago: St. James, 1987), p. 229.
11. On Delors's strategy and impact on European integration, see Helen Drake, *Jacques Delors: Perspectives on a European Leader* (London: Routledge, 2000); Ken Endo, *The Presidency of the European Commission Under Jacques Delors: The Politics of Shared Leadership* (New York: St. Martin's, 1999); George Ross, *Jacques Delors and European Integration* (Oxford: Oxford University Press, 1995); Jacques Delors, *Mémoires* (Paris: Plon, 2004), pp. 171–430.
12. European Commission, "Completing the Internal Market: White Paper from the Commission to the European Council," COM(85)210 final, June 14, 1985.
13. "Ad Hoc Committee for Institutional Affairs Report to the European Council," Bulletin EC 3-1985, point 3.5.1.
14. For Thatcher's perspective on the single market and the SEA, see Margaret Thatcher, *The Downing Street Years* (New York: HarperCollins, 1993), pp. 551–554, and Stephen Wall, *A Stranger in Europe* (Oxford: Oxford University Press, 2008), pp. 41–86.
15. For a description and analysis of the IGC and the SEA, see Jean de Ruyt, *L'Acte Unique Européen: Commentaire,* 2nd ed. (Brussels: Editions de l'Université de Bruxelles, 1996). For the SEA itself, see European Council, Bulletin EC S/2-1986.

16. Roland Bieber, Jean-Paul Jacqué, and Joseph Weiler, eds., *An Ever Closer Union: A Critical Analysis of the Draft Treaty Establishing the European Union* (Luxembourg: Office for the Official Publications of the European Communities, 1985), pp. 372–373.

17. Delors, *Mémoires,* pp. 202–228.

18. *Common Market Law Review* 23 (1986): 251.

19. On the development of the single market, see Arthur Cockfield, *The European Union: Creating the Single Market* (Chichester: John Wiley, 1994), pp. 37–60; and Michelle Egan, *Constructing a European Market: Standards, Regulation, and Governance* (Oxford: Oxford University Press, 2001).

20. *The Economist,* February 13, 1988, p. 11.

21. For a condensed version of the Cecchini Report, see Paolo Cecchini, *The European Challenge, 1992* (Aldershot: Wildwood, 1988).

22. Bulletin EC S/1-1988, p. 14.

23. Wall, *Stranger in Europe,* pp. 74–75.

24. European Commission, *Economic and Monetary Union* (Luxembourg: Office for Official Publications of the European Communities, 1990), p. 11.

25. European Commission, *One Market, One Money: An Evaluation of the Potential Benefits and Costs of Forming an Economic and Monetary Union* (Luxembourg: Office for Official Publications of the European Communities, 1990), p. 9.

26. Tomaso Padoa-Schioppa, ed., *Efficiency, Stability, and Equity: A Strategy for the Evolution of the Economic System of the EC* (Luxembourg: Office for Official Publications of the European Communities, 1987), pp. 3, 13.

27. See European Commission, *One Market,* p. 10.

28. Margaret Thatcher, Speech to the College of Europe, September 20, 1988, http://www.margaretthatcher.org/speeches/displaydocument.asp?docid=107332. For her own account of events in the late 1980s, see Thatcher, *Downing Street Years,* pp. 742–746.

29. Thatcher, *Downing Street Years,* p. 708.

30. Committee for the Study of Economic and Monetary Union, *Report on Economic and Monetary Union in the European Community* (Delors Report) (Luxembourg: Office for Official Publications of the European Communities, 1989), pp. 18–19.

31. See Dorothee Heisenberg, *The Mark of the Bundesbank: Germany's Role in European Monetary Cooperation* (Boulder: Lynne Rienner, 1999).

32. Quoted in *The Guardian,* July 7, 1991, p. 6.

33. European Commission, *Economic and Monetary Union,* p. 17.

34. European Commission, *One Market,* pp. 28–29.

35. Peter Kenen, "Speaking Up for EMU," *Financial Times,* July 28, 1992, p. 15.

36. Martin Feldstein, "Europe's Monetary Union: The Case Against EMU," *The Economist,* June 13, 1992, pp. 19–22.

37. European Commission, *Economic and Monetary Union,* p. 11.

38. Delors, *Mémoires,* pp. 240–245.

39. Chancellor's press release, 134/1989, pp. 1141ff.

40. Strasbourg European Council, "Presidency Conclusions," Bulletin EC 12-1989, point 1.1.20.

41. Quoted in *Le Monde,* December 9, 1989, p. 1.

42. Reproduced in Finn Laursen and Sophie Vanhoonacker, eds., *The Intergovernmental Conference on Political Union* (Maastricht: European Institute of Public Administration, 1992), p. 276.

43. Dublin European Council, "Presidency Conclusions," Bulletin EC 4-1990, points 1.1–1.12; and Dublin European Council, "Presidency Conclusions," Bulletin EC 6-1990, points 1.1–1.8.

44. Rome European Council, "Presidency Conclusions," Bulletin EC 10-1990, points 1.2–1.6.

45. *The Economist,* March 23, 1991, p. 15.

46. On the negotiations and their outcome, see Michael Baun, *An Imperfect Union: The Maastricht Treaty and the New Politics of European Integration* (Boulder: Westview, 1996); Kenneth Dyson and Kevin Featherstone, *The Road to Maastricht: Negotiating Economic and Monetary Union* (Oxford: Oxford University Press, 1998); Laursen and Vanhoonacker, *Intergovernmental Conference on Political Union;* and Colette Mazzucelli, *France and Germany at Maastricht: Politics and Negotiations to Create the European Union* (New York: Garland, 1997).

47. Quoted in *Financial Times,* June 18, 1991, p. 1.

48. Lord O'Hagan, "Federalism," *Manchester Guardian Weekly,* July 7, 1991, p. 12.

49. Quoted in *Agence Europe,* December 6, 1991, p. 4.

50. Jacques Delors, speech at the Royal Institute for International Affairs, London, March 20, 1991.

51. See Sophie Vanhoonacker, "The Role of Parliament," in Laursen and Vanhoonacker, *Intergovernmental Conference on Political Union,* pp. 209–229.

52. Quoted in *Financial Times,* September 21–22, 1991, p. 3.

53. *Agence Europe,* September 15, 1991.

54. See Wall, *Stranger in Europe,* p. 135.

55. Lisbon European Council, "Presidency Conclusions," Bulletin EC 6-1992, point 1.1.3. On the ratification crisis, see Finn Laursen, ed., *The Ratification of the Maastricht Treaty: Issues, Debates, and Future Implications* (New York: Springer, 1994).

56. *Le Monde,* September 20–21, 1992, p. 1.

57. Lisbon European Council, "Presidency Conclusions," Bulletin EC 6-1992, point 1.1.

58. European Commission, "The Principle of Subsidiarity," SEC(92)1990 final, October 27, 1992.

59. Edinburgh European Council, "Presidency Conclusions," Bulletin EC 12-1992, point 1.4.

60. See Karl M. Meessen, "Hedging European Integration: The Maastricht Judgment of the Federal Constitutional Court of Germany," *Fordham International Law Journal* 17 (1993–1994): 511–530.

5 The Emergent European Union, 1993–1999

Implementation of the Maastricht Treaty seems an obvious turning point in the history of European integration. It occurred at a time of profound international change. The 1990s was the first decade of the post–Cold War era, a unipolar moment of unrivaled US supremacy. The end of the Cold War, China's economic ascent, and recent reform in India unleashed the forces of globalization, which would buffet Europe in the years ahead.

The post–Cold War period was unsettling in a number of other respects as well. Close to home, Yugoslavia disintegrated in a series of secessionist wars that cost tens of thousands of lives and cast a pall over the emergent European Union. The Common Foreign and Security Policy, launched with great fanfare in 1993, was utterly inadequate to deal with the Yugoslav imbroglio. Only at the end of the decade, after yet another outbreak of war in the Western Balkans, did the EU seriously address the need for a military capacity and begin the long process of developing an effective defense policy.

The collapse of communism opened up a hitherto unimaginable enlargement scenario. First the European neutrals, no longer constrained by the Cold War, applied for EU membership. Three of them—Austria, Finland, and Sweden—joined in January 1995. At the same time, the newly independent countries of Central and Eastern Europe made clear their desire to join the EU. The prospect of acquiring so many new member states was daunting for the EU. Although Central and Eastern European enlargement did not happen for another decade, its likely impact was palpable by the late 1990s. The Amsterdam Treaty of 1997 provided an opportunity to reform the EU's founding treaties in anticipation of enlargement, but governments ducked the most difficult institutional issues.

Getting to Stage III of Economic and Monetary Union—launch of the common monetary policy and the single currency—was the most significant internal development in the post-Maastricht period. Meeting the criteria and timetable for participation in Stage III preoccupied most national governments throughout the decade. The domestic impact of EMU demonstrated the inextricable link between EU and national politics, as governments strove to meet the convergence criteria for participation in Stage III in the face of growing public dissatisfaction. The anticipated benefits of launching the final stage of EMU, both positive (improving the EU's global competitiveness) and negative (averting a major political crisis if the venture failed), focused governments' attention and convinced them to stay the course. The successful launch of the euro first as a virtual currency in 1999 (notes and coins were introduced only in 2002) was an impressive achievement.

Much of the credit belongs to Chancellor Helmut Kohl, who doggedly advocated EMU despite major misgivings in Germany and weak political leadership elsewhere in the EU. Kohl did not preside over completion of his cherished goal of monetary union, having been voted out of office in September 1998 because of widespread dissatisfaction with Germany's economic performance. Kohl's defeat after sixteen years as chancellor was the most dramatic change in leadership at the end of a decade that saw the departure of nearly every key player in the EU.

Jacques Delors stepped down as Commission president in January 1995 after ten years in office. His departure signaled a move away from policy entrepreneurship. Delors's successor, the unremarkable Jacques Santer, turned his attention to the unglamorous but necessary task of internal Commission reform. It is ironic under the circumstances that Santer will forever be remembered for having been president of the only Commission (so far) ever forced to resign, in 1999, over allegations of corruption and mismanagement. The Commission's ouster by the European Parliament had far-reaching institutional implications. Thereafter the Commission lost its political prominence, whereas the Parliament grew increasingly assertive (see Box 5.1).

■ The 1995 Enlargement

Compared to enlargements past and still to come, the enlargement of January 1995, when Austria, Finland, and Sweden joined the EU, seemed simple and straightforward. The three countries were economically better off than many existing member states; had administrative structures capable of interpreting and implementing EU laws; and, despite varying degrees of public opposition, had governments eager to bring them into the EU. The accession negotiations took a relatively short time (about fifteen months) because, as members of the European Free Trade Association, the candidate countries (including Norway) had already adopted much of the EU's voluminous *acquis communautaire*.

The candidates had begun to adopt the *acquis* in the mid-1980s in an effort to minimize the possible negative consequences for outsiders of the soon-to-be-completed single market program. Dissatisfied with having to react to developments in the European Community, the EFTA countries had

---

Box 5.1 Chronology, 1993–1999

1993	June	At Copenhagen summit, European Council agrees on EU accession criteria; Danes approve Maastricht Treaty in second referendum
	November	Maastricht Treaty comes into effect
1994	January	Launch of Stage II of Economic and Monetary Union (EMU)
	June	Accession treaties with Austria, Finland, Sweden, and Norway signed; elections to the European Parliament (EP)
	July	European Monetary Institute (EMI) established
	November	Norwegians reject membership in referendum
1995	January	Austria, Finland, and Sweden join the EU; Jacques Santer becomes Commission president
1996	March	Beginning of intergovernmental conference (IGC)
1997	June	IGC ends at Amsterdam summit; Stability and Growth Pact adopted
	July	Commission issues favorable opinions on EU membership applications of Central and Eastern European countries
	December	European Council endorses Commission's opinions on enlargement; European Council agrees to Eurogroup, consisting of finance ministers of countries participating in Stage III of EMU
1998	February	Governments release data showing high degree of nominal convergence
	July	European Central Bank established
	March	Accession negotiations with the Czech Republic, Estonia, Hungary, Poland, Slovenia, and Cyprus begin
1999	January	Stage III of EMU begins; eleven EU member states adopt the euro
	March	At Berlin summit, EU leaders agree on Agenda 2000 budget package; resignation of Santer Commission
	May	Amsterdam Treaty comes into effect
	June	Elections to the EP
	December	European Council agrees to recognize Turkey as candidate for EU membership

---

called for a role in formulating single market and related policies that directly affected them. When the Commission refused, a number of EFTA countries reached the obvious conclusion and considered joining the EC. Until it had digested the recent Iberian enlargement and fully implemented the single market program, however, the EC was uninterested in acquiring new members.

Instead, the Commission proposed the European Economic Area (EEA), a huge integrated market intended to encompass the then twelve EC and seven EFTA members (Austria, Finland, Iceland, Liechtenstein, Norway, Sweden, and Switzerland).[1] With 380 million people accounting for 40 percent of global trade, the EEA would be the world's largest and most lucrative commercial bloc. Although meant mainly to forestall EU enlargement, the EEA instead became, for most EFTA members, a waiting room for EU accession. Thus the EEA negotiations constituted a first, unofficial step in the EU's next enlargement. By that reckoning, the 1995 enlargement took almost five years to complete.

Fishing rights, alpine trucking, and financial support for the EC's poorer member states nevertheless posed major obstacles to reaching an agreement. Spain and Portugal demanded generous access to Norwegian and Icelandic fishing grounds; Switzerland and Austria wanted to limit heavy-truck transit from EC member states; and Spain wanted a substantial increase in EFTA's initial offer to the EC's cohesion coffers. Clearly the EFTA countries had more to lose from a breakdown of negotiations. Yet Switzerland and Iceland held out until the last moment before accepting final offers on trucking and fishing. Both sides eventually signed the agreement in May 1992, after a last-minute compromise over the legal mechanism to resolve EEA disputes.[2]

Much to the Commission's dismay, the EEA initiative did not deter Austria, Finland, Norway, Switzerland, and Sweden from applying to join the EC. Why were these countries not satisfied with EEA membership? First, although they had generally outperformed their EC counterparts in the past, most of them stagnated economically in the early 1990s and saw better prospects for improvement inside the EC. Second, they were unhappy with the limited decision shaping offered by Brussels and decided that full EC membership was the only way to acquire decisionmaking power. Third, many EFTA countries feared exclusion from EMU, the next big project, and accordingly from EMU-related economic growth (were there to be any).

With the end of the Cold War, neutrality virtually disappeared as an obstacle to EC membership for Austria, Finland, Switzerland, and Sweden (Norway was a NATO member). Nevertheless, with the newly negotiated CFSP very much in mind, the Commission stressed in a report on possible enlargement that "widening must not be at the expense of deepening."[3] Eager to finish current business before beginning another round of enlargement, the European Council decided in June 1992 not to begin accession negotiations until the member states had ratified the Maastricht Treaty and reached agreement on a new budgetary package.[4] Following rejection of the EEA in a referendum in December 1992, Switzerland chose not to pursue EU membership.

Completion of the EEA agreement gave the EU accession negotiations, which began in early 1993 with Austria, Finland, Norway, and Sweden, a huge head start. Of the twenty-nine "chapters" or issues that made up the negotiations, sixteen had already been covered in whole or in part by the EEA. Of the rest, the most contentious issues were not the EU's intergovernmental policies—the neutral applicants were willing to square their neutrality with the CFSP and had few problems with the area of justice and home affairs—but rather the chapters only partly covered by the EEA. Some of the fiercest battles involved environmental policy (standards were generally higher in the applicant states), agricultural policy (price supports and subsidies were higher in three of the applicant states), energy policy (Norway was unwilling to relinquish control over its vast oil and natural gas reserves), and fisheries policy (again, Norway was unwilling to relinquish control over its lucrative territorial waters).[5]

National governments and the Commission adamantly opposed granting the applicants long-term exceptions from the *acquis communautaire,* let alone permanent opt-outs. Under the circumstances, it is ironic that Denmark, which had won opt-outs from the Maastricht Treaty, presided over the opening round of the enlargement negotiations. It is also ironic that the Nordic applicants seemed more enthusiastic than Denmark about European integration, given Denmark's tendency to object to controversial aspects of the Maastricht Treaty on the dubious grounds of "Nordic solidarity."

One of the bitterest disputes at the end of the negotiations erupted not between the EU and the candidate countries but among the member states themselves over the threshold for a blocking minority in the reweighted system of qualified majority voting. As with previous enlargements, the acceding countries received a number of Council votes roughly proportionate to their populations, and the member states recalculated the number of votes needed for a qualified majority. This time, however, for reasons of principle and policy, Britain and Spain insisted on keeping the number of votes needed for a blocking minority at the pre-enlargement level, thereby making it possible for a relatively smaller number of countries to block decisions in the Council. The dispute ended in the Ioannina Compromise, whereby the new threshold would remain, proportionately, at its pre-enlargement level, although the Council would "do all within its power to reach, within a reasonable time . . . a satisfactory solution that [could] be adopted by at least 65 votes" (Britain's and Spain's preferred qualified majority).[6]

This seemingly arcane issue showed how institutional disputes could overshadow and possibly derail future enlargement negotiations. Apart from the weighting of Council votes, increasingly troublesome institutional questions included the number of commissioners per country and the size of national delegations in the EP. The EP had already urged national governments to undertake major institutional reforms before proceeding with enlargement. The dispute over voting rights strengthened the conviction of members of the European Parliament that large-scale institutional reform was pressing. Although the EP delivered a resounding endorsement of the accession treaties in May 1994, MEPs made clear their dissatisfaction with the Ioannina Compromise and with the institutional situation in general.[7]

The next step was to ratify the accession treaties. In addition to general concerns about loss of sovereignty and neutrality (except in the case of Norway), each of the applicants had various reasons to be wary of joining the EU. All complained that the Common Agricultural Policy would hurt their heavily subsidized agricultural sectors; Austrians feared an additional influx of foreigners and worried about the anonymity of their bank accounts; the Nordics fretted about the integrity of their environmental laws; Swedish snuff-takers abhorred the EU's efforts to put a stop to their bad habit.

Hoping to generate momentum for victory in all four countries, the applicants tacitly agreed to schedule their accession referendums in the summer and fall of 1994 so that the more Euroenthusiastic of them would go to the polls first. By the end of 1994, Austria, Finland, and Sweden had voted to join the EU; Norway, where the fault lines of the bitter 1972 membership campaign had eerily reopened, voted against.

The 1995 enlargement changed the EU in a variety of ways. Most obvious, it extended the EU into the far north of Europe and increased its size by 33 percent, although its population by only 6.2 percent. Economically, enlargement brought into the EU three affluent countries, all net contributors to the budget. Politically, the accession of Finland and Sweden, two countries with strong attachments to accountability and openness, was a welcome development at a time of widespread public concern about democracy and legitimacy in the EU. In terms of public policy, the new members had greater concern for environmental issues; a strong commitment to free trade and global development; progressive social policies; and a fresh perspective on relations with Russia (Finland's immediate neighbor to the east), the Baltic states (across the sea from Finland and Sweden), and Slovenia (across the mountains from Austria).

Enlargement also brought with it another strong streak of Euroskepticism. Swedes were halfhearted about joining the EU (the results of the country's first direct elections to the EP in September 1995 revealed widespread dissatisfaction). Swedish civil servants, used to transparent policymaking in Stockholm, were shocked by the cumbersome and opaque procedures that awaited them in Brussels. In deference to public opinion, the Swedish government decided in 1998 not to participate in the final stage of EMU. Deep economic recession and few tangible benefits of membership exacerbated Swedish Euroskepticism. Although it became commonplace by the end of the 1990s to say that a majority of Swedes would vote to leave the EU, such an outcome was by no means certain.

The experience of negotiating the 1995 enlargement dampened enthusiasm in the EU (if there had been any to begin with) for Central and Eastern European enlargement. For one thing, the negotiations in 1993 and 1994 showed how difficult the next round of accession was likely to be. For another, a last-minute dispute reverberated loudly for the negotiations with the Central and Eastern European countries. In December 1994, the Spanish government threatened not to ratify the accession treaties unless the EU agreed to give Spain a fishing deal similar to Norway's. Foreign ministers resolved the crisis at the end of the month when they agreed to integrate Spain into the Common Fisheries Policy by January 1996, six years earlier than the date stipulated in Spain's own accession agreement. Spain's tactics were an obvious cause of foreboding: during the next round of enlargement, some member states would surely claim a threat to their national interests. Would they provoke a dramatic confrontation to win concessions? If so, would the EU be able or willing to buy them off?

The Road to Monetary Union

The post-Maastricht path to EMU got off to the worst possible start. Not only did the Danish referendum result of June 1992 put the future of the Maastricht Treaty in doubt, but a related crisis in the exchange rate mechanism of the European Monetary System stoked public doubt about the feasibility of EMU.[8] Throughout 1992 the German mark rose steadily and weaker currencies, notably the Italian lira and the British pound, fell to the floor of their exchange rate bands. Dealers sensed that a realignment of the exchange rate mechanism was imminent. The Maastricht Treaty had itself encouraged speculation about a realignment or series of realignments before the advent of fixed exchange rates. Such speculation, in turn, tended further to strengthen strong currencies and weaken weak ones.

Realizing that the Bundesbank (German central bank) was not inclined to prop up weak currencies, dealers moved large amounts of money out of the Italian lira and into the mark. Similar concerns about sterling led to massive sales of the pound. Ironically, the removal of exchange controls as part of the single market program contributed to the volatility in currency markets by making it possible to move money freely among member states.

The evolution of the EMS into what looked like a fixed-rate regime exacerbated tension. The frequency of realignments before 1987 (thirteen altogether) and absence of them afterward gave the impression that the EMS had turned into a quasi–currency union. Except in Germany and some other "core" currency countries, "realignment" became a dirty word, synonymous with political indecision and economic frailty. The pound had joined the exchange rate mechanism in October 1990 at a high central rate against the mark, but it was politically impossible for the British government to contemplate realignment, especially with a general election in the offing.

Most governments feared that a parity change would affect their credibility, undermine confidence in the convergence criteria, fuel inflation, and make Stage III of EMU harder to reach. Realignments appeared to be incompatible with the treaty's convergence strategy and with the goal of EMU; as a tool of macroeconomic management, they seemed anachronistic at a time when the EU was moving toward a single monetary policy. For all of those reasons, governments unwisely but understandably endured mounting pressure in the exchange rate mechanism, often at a cost of high interest rates and declining competitiveness.

Matters came to a head in September 1992, partly because of the negative result of the Danish referendum and the unpredictability of the upcoming French referendum on the Maastricht Treaty. In the EMS, the Italian and British governments desperately shored up their ailing currencies with noticeably unenthusiastic German support. Having spent billions trying to prop up the pound, the British government pulled sterling out of the exchange rate mechanism on "Black Wednesday," September 16. Italy soon followed suit. In a preemptive move, Spain devalued the peseta by 5 percent against the remaining currencies in the exchange rate mechanism.

The narrow French "yes" to Maastricht failed to stem attacks against the franc. Only concerted efforts by the French and German governments and central banks averted a disaster in late September and prevented a French devaluation. Currency turbulence continued in late 1992 and early 1993, with the franc again under pressure, Spain and Portugal devaluing by 6 percent on November 23, and Ireland devaluing by 10 percent two months later.

The currency crisis contributed to the Maastricht ratification crisis by undermining public confidence in the EMS and, by extension, in European integration. With the pound outside the exchange rate mechanism and the Danish krone still inside but under growing pressure, public opinion in Britain and Denmark—already bitterly divided over Maastricht—hardened against ratification. Although the treaty survived, the EMS crisis had other consequences for EMU. Britain's and Italy's abrupt departure from the exchange rate mechanism made it seem highly unlikely that either country would rejoin in time to participate in Stage III of EMU. Of course, Britain's participation was already doubtful for political reasons, Italy's for economic reasons. Yet the embarrassing events of September 1992 had diametrically opposite consequences for each country. Whereas the crisis strengthened British antipathy to EMU, it convinced many Italians that the solution ultimately lay in EMU itself. As a result, Italy's humiliating exit from the exchange rate mechanism strengthened the country's resolve to meet the convergence criteria and join the single currency.

Currency turmoil peaked in summer 1993 when a decision by the Bundesbank not to make an eagerly awaited cut in interest rates put other currencies under additional pressure. Following an emergency meeting in August 1993, finance ministers announced that apart from the Dutch guilder, which would stick to its original 2.5 percent band, EMS currencies would float within a 15 percent band around their parity with the mark. By widening the band for most currencies in the exchange rate mechanism, finance ministers had provided sufficient room for maneuver to reduce speculative attacks.

Staying the Course

Overall, the crisis shook confidence in the EMS but did not undermine the foundations of the system or seriously weaken intellectual and political support for EMU.[9] Government officials pointed out that the crisis merely restored the EMS to its original state: a system of fixed but adjustable exchange rates. Most officials and politicians defended the EMS tenaciously.

Currency turmoil may have strengthened the rationale for EMU, but it widened the already growing gap between political and public opinion in most member states. Ordinary mortals could comprehend neither the complexities of the exchange rate mechanism nor the reasons for its existence. To most people, the crisis had shown the impracticability, if not the impossibility, of currency union. At the same time, deep recession and growing economic divergence made it unlikely that many countries would satisfy the prerequisites for EMU within the stipulated period.

Most striking, Germany's high interest rates forced other participants in the exchange rate mechanism to pursue equally tight monetary policies, which exacerbated the EU's economic downturn and made the convergence criteria harder to meet. The Bundesbank's decision less than a week after the Maastricht summit to raise interest rates was widely denounced as an affront to the spirit of EMU and an egregious example of the bank's blatant "Germany first" approach. Of course, the Bundesbank's duty was solely to Germany and not at all to the wider EU. Nevertheless, the persistence of high German interest rates in the mid-1990s suggested that the Bundesbank would continue to subordinate European interests to German interests, possibly to the detriment of convergence among member states. Inasmuch as the Bundesbank wanted to warn the EU, the message was that high inflation would not be tolerated and that a form of monetary Darwinism would weed out the noncharter members of EMU.

Germans like to point out that their experience of hyperinflation in the early 1920s forged an anti-inflationary consensus that accounted for the Bundesbank's preoccupation with price stability and determination to make it the primary objective of the European Central Bank. The Bundesbank always argued that there was no trade-off between inflation and employment. Economic theory and empirical evidence bear out the Bundesbank's point, except in the short term. And in the short term of the mid-1990s, as the Bundesbank pursued a tight monetary policy at a time of deep economic recession, unemployment rose alarmingly in most member states. This outcome further eroded support for EMU by creating the impression that a future ECB, like the present Bundesbank, would pursue price stability regardless of the EU's unemployment level.

High interest rates made the economic situation worse by increasing the cost of borrowing money, thereby reducing investment. With unemployment rising and consumer spending declining, governments took in less revenue through direct and indirect taxation and paid out more money in unemployment and other benefits. This situation made it impossible for most governments to bring down deficit and debt levels toward the Maastricht-stipulated reference points. In many cases, not least in postunification Germany, public-sector borrowing rose at a time when, according to the EMU timetable, governments should have been exercising strict budget discipline.

Thus, in the mid-1990s, EMU seemed an unlikely prospect. Few governments could satisfy the public finance criterion; most countries' inflation rates ranged outside the targeted band; and although interest rates had converged, they had done so at an unacceptably high level. Ironically, only the currency stability criterion was unproblematic, but that was because finance ministers had widened the band for "normal" fluctuation margins in the exchange rate mechanism to 15 percent, thereby effectively removing exchange rates as a factor in the EMU equation.

The first edition of this book, published in 1994, concluded that "with Europe in the grip of recession and the exchange rate mechanism in disarray, it is difficult to see EMU coming into being within the Maastricht Treaty time frame."[10] Meeting in Madrid in December 1995, the European Council abandoned the goal of launching Stage III in 1997. In their reports on progress toward convergence, the European Monetary Institute, forerunner of the European Central Bank, and the Commission stressed the positive progress that had been made toward meeting the criteria, but emphasized as well the distance that countries still had to travel.[11] Together with the European Council's decision to postpone the launch of Stage III, the reports fed prevailing skepticism about the feasibility of EMU in the foreseeable future.

Political Will and Technical Work

Although the European Council abandoned 1997 as a starting date for Stage III, it nevertheless affirmed its commitment to the 1999 deadline. At the time, the European Council's steadfastness seemed unrealistic. Yet in retrospect, the Madrid summit of December 1995 was a turning point in the fortunes of EMU. The summit's significance lies not in the affirmation of the 1999 deadline— after all, the European Council is notorious for its optimistic announcements— but in the adoption of a technically detailed post-1999 scenario for switching to the single currency. EMU could come about only by political will and intensive planning. The Madrid summit showed that despite popular indifference or even opposition to EMU, political will existed in abundance. Moreover, deep administrative foundations were being laid regardless of rising Europessimism.

The abundance of political will was all the more surprising in view of otherwise weak leadership. Jacques Santer, Delors's successor as Commission president, was unassuming, which is largely why national leaders chose him for the job. Few governments enjoyed large parliamentary majorities. This was especially true of Germany, where Kohl had narrowly won the October 1994 election. Yet Kohl pursued EMU with a passion, staking his political future and his place in history on its achievement. His obsession with EMU was partly emotional and partly rational—emotional in that despite his equivocation in the late 1980s, he had advocated EMU unhesitatingly since the fall of the Berlin Wall; rational in that he strongly believed EMU was essential for Germany's and Europe's political and economic welfare.

French president François Mitterrand shared Kohl's conviction, but he left office in May 1995. Jacques Chirac, Mitterrand's successor, seemed ambivalent about EMU. Once in office, however, Chirac realized that France had no choice but to press ahead with it. Chirac's relationship with Kohl would never be close, but on EMU—an issue of vital importance for Franco-German relations—Chirac was resolute.

Administrative work proceeded apace in national central banks, the Commission, and the new EMI. Although EMU threatened to turn them into branch offices of the European System of Central Banks (the umbrella body for eurozone central banks), national central banks relished the intellectual and analytical challenges of preparing for Stage III. The Commission had a more obvious bureaucratic incentive to lay the groundwork for EMU. Indeed, at the height of EMU skepticism in 1995, the Commission issued a detailed discussion document on technical aspects of launching the single currency.[12]

As stipulated in the treaty, the European Monetary Union (EMI) bore the brunt of the administrative work necessary to ensure EMU's success. The institute had been set up at the beginning of Stage II, in July 1994. Its location, a highly political decision, provoked a row between France and Germany. At Kohl's insistence, the European Council decided to locate the institute in Frankfurt, seat of the Bundesbank and a symbol for Germans of sound monetary policy.

The foremost technical task of the EMI was to specify, by the end of 1996, the regulatory, organizational, and logistical framework for the European System of Central Banks (including the ECB), which would come into existence on the eve of Stage III. Thus the institute drafted the "changeover scenario," which the European Council adopted in December 1995; developed monetary policy instruments and procedures; prepared the TARGET cross-border payment system; and compiled EU-wide statistics (see Box 5.2). In addition, the institute had to encourage closer cooperation among national central banks in an effort to coordinate national monetary policies. Here it was powerless to make decisions, as member states remained responsible for their monetary policies until the beginning of Stage III. Nevertheless, the institute's regular reports on monetary policy and economic performance in the EU helped nudge countries toward compliance with the convergence criteria.

The European Council asked the Economic and Financial Affairs Council (Ecofin) in December 1995 to study two issues central to EMU's success. One was the problem posed by the fact that some member states would not participate initially (if ever) in Stage III. The other, at Germany's insistence, was to ensure the sustainability of EMU through the continuation of budgetary discipline after the launch of Stage III. In due course, Ecofin proposed a revised exchange rate mechanism (dubbed ERM II) to regulate relations between the euro and nonparticipating member state currencies and a stability pact to

---

Box 5.2　Key EMU Decisions and the Changeover to the Euro, 1994–2002

January 1994	Stage II of EMU begins; European Monetary Institute (EMI) established in Frankfurt
December 1995	European Council decides on changeover timetable and the name "euro"
June 1997	European Council agrees on the Stability and Growth Pact and on revised EMU exchange rate mechanism (ERM II)
May 1998	European Council selects participating member states for Stage III of EMU, fixes bilateral conversion rates, and selects president and executive board of European Central Bank (ECB)
June 1, 1998	ECB takes over from EMI; European System of Central Banks established
January 1, 1999	Stage III of EMU begins, irrevocable fixing of exchange rates and entry into force of relevant legislation; launch of single monetary policy; beginning of foreign exchange operations in euros; inauguration of TARGET payment system; new public debt issued in euros
January 1, 2002	Euro notes and coins replace national currencies in the eurozone

---

ensure budgetary discipline after the launch of the euro. The European Council adopted the relatively straightforward proposal for ERM II, which allowed generous fluctuation margins (15 percent) for noneuro currencies in relation to the euro. The European System of Central Banks and the central banks of noneuro member states would intervene if necessary to maintain currency parities within the fluctuation limits.

Sustainability, Employment, and Oversight

By contrast with ERM II, the proposed stability pact caused a political storm. Bearing an obvious German imprint, the draft agreement threatened automatic penalties for eurozone countries running excessive budget deficits. Like the budget deficit criterion in the Maastricht Treaty, the proposed stability pact defined "excessive" as above 3 percent of gross domestic product (GDP). By 1996, when the proposal was being debated, governments were cutting budgets in order to bring deficits below the 3 percent ceiling. As the effects of budget cuts rippled through the economy, unemployment inevitably increased and generous social welfare programs came under financial pressure. These developments reinforced a popular perception that EMU itself exacerbated unemployment and worsened the plight of the unemployed.

Nowhere was this perception stronger, and nowhere was a government more sensitive to its political repercussions, than in France. Already French workers had rioted in December 1995, protesting proposed changes in the social security system. In deference to French sensitivity, Germany watered down the terms of the proposed stability pact, making fines not automatic but subject to approval by governments. Also in deference to the perception that EMU was imposing a fiscal straitjacket that destroyed jobs, Ecofin renamed the proposed agreement, which the European Council adopted in Amsterdam in June 1997, as the Stability and *Growth* Pact.

Eager to have a government whose term would coincide with the remainder of his seven-year presidency, Chirac brought forward the date of parliamentary elections to March 1997. He miscalculated badly: Lionel Jospin, leader of the Socialist Party, won the election and formed a new government. France now entered a period of cohabitation (the presidency and government were held by opposing political parties), and Jospin, the new prime minister, was outspoken in his criticism of EMU.

One of Jospin's first steps as prime minister, at the Amsterdam summit in June 1997, was to demand a renegotiation of the Stability and Growth Pact. This irked the Germans and delayed discussion of the summit's most pressing business: the Amsterdam Treaty. Jospin succeeded only in having the European Council adopt a separate resolution on growth and employment that stressed governments' determination to keep employment firmly at the top of the political agenda. The European Council also decided to hold an extraordinary summit in Luxembourg in November 1997 to discuss job creation.[13]

A call by Jospin for an "economic government" to watch over the supposedly independent ECB caused even greater alarm in Frankfurt and Berlin. Germany and like-minded member states had no intention of undermining the ECB's independence or commitment to price stability, but were willing to establish a forum for discussions among governments in the eurozone about such key issues as maintaining fiscal discipline, coordinating taxation policy, and setting the euro's exchange rate. Accordingly, the European Council decided in December 1997 to establish the Eurogroup, consisting of finance ministers of countries participating in Stage III of EMU.

The EMU Juggernaut

The controversy surrounding the Stability and Growth Pact and the Eurogroup demonstrated both the increasing politicization of EMU and the likelihood that it would be launched on time. By late 1997, pessimism about the prospects for EMU had given way to the conviction that Stage III would begin in January 1999 with eleven countries, that is, with all the member states that wished to participate minus Greece (Britain, Denmark, and Sweden having opted out for political reasons).

French and German efforts to meet the convergence criteria by engaging in what some critics derided as "creative accounting" reinforced the impression that Stage III would be launched in 1999 at all costs. France's creative accounting was successful, Germany's was a failure. The Commission allowed France to apply a huge onetime payment from France Telecom in 1997 against the country's deficit. However, the Bundesbank rejected the German finance minister's effort to revalue Germany's gold reserves in May 1997 and apply the proceeds against the country's deficit.

Even with recourse to such measures as privatization and gold-reserves revaluation, neither France nor Germany looked likely in early 1997 to come under the 3 percent ceiling. If one or both of them proved unable to participate in EMU, the entire project would collapse. By mid-1997, however, Europe's economic recovery began to have an impact on the member states' budget deficits. It seemed that France, Germany, and most other countries would confound the skeptics and meet the 3 percent standard. The Commission's fall 1997 economic forecast bore out this rosy scenario and strengthened the growing conviction that EMU would start in 1999 with a large majority of member states.[14]

Most surprising of all was the likelihood that Portugal, Spain, and Italy, countries notorious for their lack of fiscal discipline, would make the first cut. Even strong supporters of EMU derided the possibility of the Mediterranean countries' participation in it. Snide comments by German officials about Italy's ineligibility for EMU strained relations between the two countries. Yet whereas the German government had tried to revalue the Bundesbank's gold reserves in order to meet the convergence criteria, Italy's center-left coalition government had taken such politically courageous steps as introducing tough austerity measures and levying a special tax to help cut the budget deficit. For Italy, then in the throes of post–Cold War political upheaval, failure to make the EMU grade came to be seen as a potential national disaster.

Germany's concerns about Italy, shared by most northern countries, pertained especially to sustainability. Even if Italy met the convergence criteria, would it sustain the 3 percent budget deficit ceiling after 1999? Opponents of Italy's participation may have had legitimate concerns, but attempting to keep Italy out of Stage III on grounds of nonsustainability would have implicitly acknowledged the worthlessness of the Stability and Growth Pact, which the European Council had already adopted to deal with this issue.

One of the most striking aspects of the EMU juggernaut was the extent to which the public went along with it. The Maastricht ratification crisis had exposed a high degree of public concern about deeper integration, which many observers expected to crystallize around EMU. Moreover, the popular equation of EMU with austerity and unemployment seemed destined to spark protests at the polling booth and in the streets.

In the event, the pain of EMU was unevenly spread, and reaction to it differed widely among aspiring participants. Luxembourg was already a model of fiscal rectitude. Belgium considered that EMU membership was its birthright and so did not bother to tackle seriously its bloated public debt. Alone among the Nordic member states, Finland was highly motivated to participate in EMU. The convergence criteria caused little pain in Ireland and the

Netherlands, which had already embarked on structural reform and were enjoying strong economic growth, but caused considerable pain in Italy, Portugal, Spain, and Greece, countries that badly needed a pretext to put their public finances in order and at the same time feared the humiliation of not coming up to the EMU standard.

Only in France and Germany, the EU's core countries, might hostile public opinion have jeopardized EMU. France seemed especially vulnerable because of its tradition of government surrender in the face of violent political protest. Nor did the appointment of Lionel Jospin as prime minister seem auspicious. In the event, economic recovery made it possible for Jospin to square the circle of EMU-inspired austerity and traditional Socialist extravagance. Anti-EMU protests never materialized, and the government did not have to put its EMU commitment to the ultimate political test of facing down demonstrators.

In contrast to France, Germany's political tradition is one of public obedience to authority. That helps to explain why, despite numerous polls showing how unhappy the majority of Germans were to give up the mark, a powerful anti-EMU movement failed to materialize. Germans confined their protests to writing letters to the editor and bringing a case before the constitutional court. Most Germans reckoned that the political consequences of abandoning EMU were potentially more destabilizing than the economic consequences of staying the course. Gerhard Schröder, the Social Democratic challenger who beat Kohl in the September 1998 election, knew which way the wind was blowing and abandoned his earlier equivocation about EMU.

With the realization by late 1997 that opposition to EMU was muted and that most countries would meet the convergence criteria, the procedure for selecting participants in Stage III lost its political edge. In February 1998, governments released data showing a high degree of nominal convergence. Based on these figures, only Greece failed to qualify, because its budget deficit was a full percentage point above the reference point. Britain, Denmark, and Sweden, which had decided not to adopt the single currency, came in well under the 3 percent ceiling. By contrast, France reported a deficit of 3.02 percent, sufficiently close to the reference point to assuage critics and opponents of EMU. The figures on national debt were less impressive, with Belgium, Italy, and Greece coming in well above 100 percent (the reference point being 60 percent).

In their respective convergence reports, published in March 1998, the EMI and the Commission drew attention to these large debts and adjured governments to accelerate economic reform and restructuring. In particular, the institute warned that "decisive and sustained corrective policies of a structural nature" were necessary in most countries. Nevertheless, both reports recommended that eleven member states begin Stage III in January 1999.[15] At the same time, the Commission's spring economic forecast predicted strong economic growth throughout the EU despite the possible impact of the Asian economic crisis.[16]

The recommendations of the Commission and EMI, obligatory under the terms of the Maastricht Treaty, made it inevitable that the European Council, meeting in May 1998, would formally select the same eleven countries for participation in Stage III. Only twelve months earlier, the Brussels summit had been expected to be contentious because of the possibility that the participants would have to decide on the composition of the eurozone by qualified majority vote. By early 1998, however, consensus on the composition of the eurozone threatened to rob the summit of all drama. In the event, the Brussels summit was highly memorable because of a drama of a different kind: a fierce row between Chirac and Kohl over the presidency of the ECB that overshadowed the formal selection of the single-currency countries.

At issue was Chirac's insistence that the first president of the ECB be French. This put Chirac at odds with the other national leaders, who supported Wim Duisenberg, a former head of the Dutch central bank. In effect, Chirac sought a Franco-German trade-off: a German location for the ECB (already decided) and a French president for the ECB (not yet decided). To everyone's surprise, Chirac doggedly pursued this demand, compromising only to the extent that Duisenberg could begin the ECB presidency's first eight-year term but would have to step down for Jean-Claude Trichet, governor of the Bank of France, halfway through. After ten hours of negotiation, which Kohl described as among the most difficult in his lengthy EU experience, Chirac accepted a decision by Duisenberg, supposedly reached "of my own free will . . . and not under pressure from anyone," to step down sometime in midterm.[17] The European Council agreed that Trichet would then succeed Duisenberg for a full eight-year term. (Duisenberg eventually resigned in November 2003, when Trichet took over.)

The outcome of the Brussels summit suggested that the ECB's independence was compromised even before the bank came into being and that the French government would attempt to interfere in European monetary policymaking. Such concerns were largely allayed by Duisenberg's robust performance as ECB president and by the composition of the ECB's governing board, all of whose members were experienced, independent-minded central bankers. Nor should Chirac's conduct be dismissed as "typically French." Although the French are generally not self-conscious about advocating national interests, Chirac's definition of the national interest was unusually narrow in this case and his behavior clearly idiosyncratic.

■ The Balkan Imbroglio

The petty dispute over the ECB's first president and weightier questions concerning the practicability and timing of EMU took place against the background of war in the Western Balkans throughout the 1990s. The Maastricht

Treaty was still being negotiated when Europe's first post–Cold War conflict erupted in Yugoslavia in June 1991. Initially the Yugoslav army, largely under Serb control, fought a short, unsuccessful war to prevent Slovenia from seceding from the Federal Republic of Yugoslavia. Later that summer, Serbia (Yugoslavia's dominant republic) launched a war against Croatia, which had also seceded from the federation. The new round of fighting unleashed a ferocity not seen in Europe since World War II. In April 1992 the war spread to Bosnia, where both Serbia and Croatia wanted to expand but where mutual hatred of Serbia turned Bosnian Muslims and Croatian nationalists into temporary allies. Although all sides committed atrocities, Serbia's ruthless siege of Sarajevo, Bosnia's capital, was especially callous. Nightly news film of maimed and murdered Bosnians, victims of Serb sniper and artillery attacks, sickened the outside world. Evidence of Serb "ethnic cleansing" in Bosnia recalled Europe's nightmare of World War II and made an even more compelling humanitarian case for intervention in the conflict.

Coincidentally, a meeting of the European Council had opened in Luxembourg on the same day that fighting first broke out in Yugoslavia. A delegation of foreign ministers went on a dramatic overnight peace mission to Belgrade, the Serbian (and Yugoslav) capital, returning to report to EC leaders before the summit's end. A remark by the Dutch foreign minister showed how confident the EC was of brokering a cease-fire: "When we went on this mission to Yugoslavia, I really had the feeling that the Yugoslav authorities thought that they were talking to Europe, not just to a country incidentally coming by but to an entity whose voice counts."[18]

What could the fledgling EU do? The instruments available to it included arbitration, inspection, diplomatic recognition or nonrecognition of the warring parties, and economic sanctions and inducements. The EU could neither take nor threaten to take military action, although individual member states and the Western European Union, a long-standing but largely dormant defense organization, could. In practice, deep divisions among national governments hampered the EU. Although many of them instinctively sympathized with Croatia and especially with Bosnia, both victims of Serb aggression, Greece sided with Serbia, with which it had close cultural and religious ties. Greece also blocked EU recognition of neighboring Macedonia unless the former Yugoslav republic, having stolen "a historically Greek name and feeding long-nourished appetites for Greek territory," changed its name.[19]

The most divisive row within the EU centered on Croatia as Germany, responding to mounting domestic pressure, began to press for EU recognition of the breakaway republic in the fall of 1991. A majority of member states doubted that the formal fragmentation of the Yugoslav federation would ultimately resolve the conflict and feared that diplomatic recognition would encourage, not discourage, Croatian and Serbian separatism. Matters came to a head at a meeting of the Council of Ministers in December. After ten hours of fierce debate, the foreign ministers drew up criteria for the recognition of new states in Yugoslavia and the former Soviet Union, which was then also coming apart, and agreed in effect to recognize Croatia's independence early in the new year.[20]

The EU's high hopes of mediation were an early victim of these and other disputes among governments over how best to respond to the conflict. Serbia's intransigence at the conference table and belligerence on the battlefield undermined the EU's efforts, which fared badly following the escalation of hostilities in Croatia and Bosnia. A strong public reaction against Serbian atrocities in Bosnia redoubled the EU's diplomatic offensive, culminating in a joint conference of the United Nations (UN) and the EU, which produced a peace plan for Bosnia in 1993.

This was the high point (or possibly the low point) of EU mediation in the conflict. Bosnian Muslims' unwillingness to accept a proposal that seemed to reward Serbian aggression, Bosnian Serbs' reluctance to cede control over any part of their recently acquired enclaves, and Croatia's determination to grab more territory in Bosnia doomed the painstakingly prepared peace plan. With its mediation effort in tatters, EU involvement was reduced to providing humanitarian assistance, although individual countries sent troops under UN auspices to protect so-called safe areas.

The wars of Yugoslav secession highlighted the inadequacy of the recently launched CFSP. This became obvious in April 1994 with the establishment of a Contact Group, consisting of Britain, France, Germany, Russia, and the United States, to "manage" the Yugoslav situation. Although the three EU countries in the group (later joined by Italy) supposedly represented the EU as a whole, in fact they were included because of their size and influence and represented only themselves. The establishment of the Contact Group and the lack of formal EU membership in it harked back to the old days of great-power politics and caused resentment among other member states, especially those (such as the Netherlands) with sizable contingents of troops in Bosnia.

The EU managed to act as one with the launch of a "joint action" (a CFSP procedure to undertake specific measures) in 1995 involving reconstruction and reconciliation in Mostar, a city in Bosnia bitterly divided between Croats and Muslims. This was the only time that the EU called upon the WEU to help implement a CFSP decision, although the operation was a civilian rather than a military one (the WEU provided a small police force). The EU action was successful only in the procedural sense; it failed to stop the fighting in Mostar or bring the divided communities any closer together.

The Bosnian war reached its denouement in the summer and fall of 1995, when Serbian atrocities in Sarajevo and Srebrenica finally compelled the United States to act militarily. Heavy NATO bombardment of Serbian positions in August 1995 brought the Serbs to their senses. The United States followed up diplomatically by convening a peace conference in Dayton, Ohio, at which a settlement was hammered out. In order to emphasize the transatlantic nature of the peace initiative, the so-called Dayton Accords were formally signed in Paris in November 1995. Yet this move could not disguise the predominantly US stamp on the peace process and the failure of EU efforts to end the fighting in the former Yugoslavia during the preceding four years.

Although unique in many respects, the Yugoslav wars provided a lesson in the limits of EU involvement in post–Cold War conflict resolution. The Balkans' history of instability, which had dragged the great powers into World War I and which, as German unification reminded everyone, cast a long shadow over twentieth-century Europe, complicated the EU's response to the collapse of Yugoslavia. Undoubtedly, Germany's support for Croatian independence in 1991 jogged memories of Nazi support for fascist Croatia fifty years previously. Similarly, France's instinctive sympathy for Serbia in 1991 echoed its support for Serbia during World War I. But the democratization of Germany (and Italy) since 1945, the demise of aggressive nationalism in Western Europe, and Western European solidarity during the Cold War—to which the process of European integration contributed—ensured that the Yugoslav war did not risk pitting EU member states against each other.

The impossibility of sending large numbers of German troops to Yugoslavia was a more pertinent legacy for the EU of recent Balkan and European history. Britain was extremely cautious about intervening militarily in Yugoslavia, apart from providing limited humanitarian assistance under UN auspices. Of the EU's three "great powers," only France appeared willing to take some form of military action, but not alone. The member states' reluctance to use force not only limited their policy options but also hindered the development of an EU "defense identity" during the early years of the CFSP's existence.

Developments in the Western Balkans in the 1990s therefore exposed deep foreign policy differences among member states and demonstrated the limits of EU international action. Moreover, the EU's ineffectual involvement in the conflict sapped popular support for European integration and for the nascent CFSP. The EU's performance had a similarly debilitating effect on opinion in the United States. A rash boast in early July 1991 by the foreign minister of Luxembourg, then in the Council presidency, that "this is the hour of Europe, not the hour of the Americans," gave explosive ammunition to critics of the EU, especially those in the US Congress.[21]

A new round of treaty reform in the mid-1990s, culminating in the Amsterdam Treaty, gave national governments an opportunity to draw on the lessons of Yugoslavia and strengthen the CFSP (see Chapter 17). Yet the EU would not necessarily have performed better had a stronger CFSP been in place earlier. The problem lay not simply in a lack of structure but rather in profound historical differences compounded by a radical contextual change following the end of the Cold War. The Yugoslav crisis was a salutary lesson in the limits of European integration, specifically in the difficulty of sharing sovereignty in the sensitive areas of security and defense.

It was precisely in the defense realm that the legacy of the Yugoslav conflict bore fruit at the end of the decade. As discussed in Chapter 17, British prime minister Tony Blair took the initiative in giving the EU the military capacity to tackle "future Bosnias," the necessity for which became all too apparent in early 1999, when Serbia took up its old tricks, this time in Kosovo. The EU did not yet have the military means to act against Serbia but seemed finally to have the political will to do so. Having watched Serbia start one Balkan war after another, EU leaders had little doubt about the need to stop Serbia from causing yet another humanitarian disaster. In NATO's name, the United States conducted an eleven-week air war against Serbian forces in Kosovo and against military and government targets in Serbia itself. Once again the EU was sidelined. Serbia's capitulation soon afterward removed the immediate possibility of another Balkan conflict. Nevertheless, the Kosovo crisis and NATO campaign strengthened Blair, Chirac, and other EU leaders in their determination to develop an EU military capability. The sophistication and power of the US military operation also showed how far the EU would need to go before having an effective joint force.[22]

■ The Amsterdam Treaty

The Maastricht Treaty mandated that a follow-on intergovernmental conference would take place in 1996 in order to adjust the treaty's new decisionmaking procedures, especially in the area of foreign and security policy.[23] By the mid-1990s, the institutional implications of the next round of enlargement overshadowed preparations for the new IGC. Even before the 1995 enlargement, the European Council had conceded the inevitability of further enlargement, but without specifying a timetable. A future EU of well over twenty member states seemed unworkable without major institutional reform. All the while, the cloud of war in not-too-distant Bosnia and the national governments' preoccupation with meeting the convergence criteria for EMU overshadowed the IGC.

Thanks to the lessons of the Maastricht ratification crisis, if anything the 1996–1997 IGC was overprepared. Among other things, EU leaders decided to establish the Reflection Group, a high-level committee to prepare the IGC, to which national governments appointed one representative each. The group also included a commissioner and two MEPs. The Reflection Group met for the first time in Messina, Sicily, in June 1995. The fact that the original Messina conference forty years earlier had paved the way for the Rome Treaty seemed auspicious for the group's deliberations. The group's remit was to draw up a manageable agenda for the conference and identify areas of likely agreement. Governments' different approaches and preferences were evident from the outset, with the more integration-minded countries (notably Belgium, Germany, Italy, Luxembourg, and the Netherlands) ranged against those less inclined toward supranational solutions, especially Britain. Indeed, the extreme Euroskepticism of Britain's Conservative government hobbled the group's work, just as it would hobble all but the final stage of the conference itself.

The Reflection Group sifted through the large number of institutional and policy issues that governments and other interested parties had raised in the run-up to the IGC. Without adopting specific recommendations, the group's report identified three main areas for reform: making the EU more relevant to its citizens (for example, by promoting human rights, internal security, employment, and environmental protection); improving the EU's efficiency and accountability (by reforming decisionmaking procedures and tackling the democratic deficit); and improving the EU's ability to act internationally (notably by strengthening the CFSP).[24]

The possibility of differentiated integration as a basic principle of European integration rather than an ad hoc arrangement emerged during the group's deliberations as an issue likely to dominate the IGC. Three main factors accounted for the timing and intensity of the debate over flexibility: British obstructionism, the likelihood that only a minority of member states would be able to participate in the final stage of EMU, and the prospect of Central and Eastern European enlargement. The budding debate burst into the open in September 1994, when the parties in Germany's conservative coalition government published a paper claiming that "the existing hard core of countries oriented to greater integration and closer cooperation must be further strengthened" and that "the further development of the EU's institutions must combine coherence and consistency with elasticity and flexibility." The authors identified the core group as Germany, France, Belgium, Luxembourg, and the Netherlands—in other words, the original EC member states minus Italy. As for Britain, the authors argued that "determined efforts to spur on the further development of Europe are the best means of exerting a positive influence on the clarification of Britain's relationship to Europe and on its willingness to participate in further steps toward integration."[25]

Already sensitive to criticism of its seeming inability to meet the EMU convergence criteria and embroiled in post–Cold War political upheavals, Italy was deeply offended. The smaller member states, even the three Benelux countries included in the putative hard core, shared Italy's fear of a possible Franco-German scheme to pursue closer political integration outside the EU system. Nor was the main thrust of the paper lost on the British government. For some time Prime Minister John Major had been talking cavalierly about flexibility, by which he meant an à la carte, pick-and-choose EU. In response to the German paper, Major rejected the idea of an EU "in which some (countries) would be more equal than others." By arguing against a two-tier EU and advocating instead a system in which countries could opt in and out of certain policies, Major drew one of the most important battle lines of the forthcoming IGC.[26]

National leaders launched the IGC at a special summit in March 1996.[27] France and Germany took a number of joint initiatives in the conference, notably on flexibility and foreign policy. But Franco-German leadership was noticeably weak in the mid-1990s as each country struggled with domestic and European problems. The few joint initiatives taken during the conference barely concealed the personal differences between President Chirac and Chancellor Kohl or disguised the fact that neither leader seemed particularly keen on the proceedings.

As for the other big countries, Britain had marginalized itself and lost all influence in EU affairs until the election of May 1997, when Labour swept the Conservatives from office. The change of government helped the IGC, allowing breakthroughs on a number of important issues. Italy's influence in the EU was minimal throughout, as the government focused its attention almost exclusively on the economic reforms necessary to adopt the euro. By contrast, Spain was unusually assertive under the leadership of José Maria Aznar, who had replaced Felipe González, one of the EU's most experienced statesmen, in January 1996.

With the British Conservatives out of power, monetary union seemingly set to start in January 1999 with a majority of member states, and Central and Eastern European enlargement looking likely to be staggered over a lengthy period, the question of flexibility lost its urgency in the run-up to the IGC. By the time the negotiations began, flexibility aroused more academic interest than political passion. Although some countries remained wary, a consensus emerged during the conference that, in principle, flexibility should be included in the treaty as long as it was limited, in practice, to precisely defined conditions that would not endanger the *acquis communautaire*.[28]

National governments eventually agreed to a compromise that included both general "enabling" clauses for countries wishing to cooperate more closely and particular provisions governing the use of flexibility in certain policy areas. One of these, which would allow any government to block the others from cooperating more closely by claiming that its "national interest" was at stake, harked back to the days of the Luxembourg Compromise. It also showed that Britain's Conservatives need not have been too concerned about the applicability of closer cooperation in the EU.

As for legislative decisionmaking, most governments favored the possibility of extending qualified majority voting (QMV) to additional policy areas. This issue became bound up with the technical but highly sensitive question of the reweighting of Council votes, which would dominate the debate on institutional reform for the next ten years. The big countries favored either an increase in the number of their votes or the introduction of a double majority, combining the traditional requirement of a qualified majority with a new demographic criterion. Without such a change, they argued, a qualified majority could be formed following the next round of enlargement by a group of countries that together did not represent a majority of the EU's population.

Negotiations about the reweighting of votes inevitably became enmeshed in another highly controversial issue: the size and composition of the Commission. Intellectually, nearly every government conceded that the Commission was too large; politically, few would countenance a Commission with fewer representatives than the total number of EU member states. Not least because large countries wanted to increase their relative weight in Council voting, small countries adamantly opposed the possible loss of "their" commissioner. With varying degrees of enthusiasm, large countries expressed a willingness to give up at least their second commissioner, but only in return for a reweighting of votes in the Council. France alone favored a radical reduction in the Commission's size, largely because it wanted to reduce the Commission's influence.

Meeting in Amsterdam in June 1997, the European Council negotiated far into the night, well beyond the summit's scheduled end, in an unsuccessful effort to reach a lasting agreement on institutional issues. EU leaders settled on a temporary solution: a protocol attached to the treaty stipulating that the Commission would comprise one representative per member state as soon as the next enlargement took place, provided that Council votes were reweighted in order to compensate the big countries for the loss of a second commissioner. The protocol also stated that at least one year before the EU enlarged to more than twenty member states, another conference would be convened "to carry out a comprehensive review of the provisions of the treaties on the composition and functioning of the institutions" (in order to decide, for instance, how to apportion twenty commissioners among more than twenty member states).

Issues relating to the EP—its size, location, and legislative powers— proved relatively easy to resolve. The conference accepted the EP's own proposal to set a ceiling of 700 members and agreed to enshrine in the treaty an earlier political agreement to hold the bulk of the EP's plenary session in Strasbourg (a persistent French demand). Following the change of government in Britain, the conference agreed to the EP's request that the number of legislative procedures be reduced to three: consultation, a simplified form of codecision, and assent. The extension and simplification of the codecision procedure would greatly enhance the EP's legislative power and political influence.

Judged by the main reason given by politicians for embarking on another IGC—the need to adapt the EU to meet the challenge of enlargement—the Amsterdam Treaty was a disappointment. Giving more power to the EP and extending the range of QMV were important changes but were unlikely to greatly enhance the EU's efficiency, credibility, or legitimacy. Instead, by deferring the hard institutional questions about the Commission's size and member states' weighted votes—the so-called Amsterdam leftovers—until another conference, the EU sent a negative signal to its own citizens and to the applicant states.

Nevertheless, the treaty was noteworthy for a number of important revisions, apart from strengthening the power of the EP. One was the inclusion of provisions for closer cooperation among like-minded member states. Hedged with qualifications and safeguards, however, flexibility would be difficult to put into practice. What emerged in the treaty was a far cry from what some countries favored and others feared: a two-tier EU. Yet most governments expressed satisfaction with the treaty's flexibility provisions. For the presumed hard core, having the principle of flexibility written into the treaty was a step forward; for the others, what mattered most was having a seat at the decisionmaking table if and when flexibility were ever invoked.

Another innovation in the Amsterdam Treaty helped clarify the character of the EU, largely in response to governments' concerns about the growing democratic deficit. Accordingly, the treaty included an important affirmation: "The Union is founded on the principles of liberty, democracy, respect for human rights and fundamental freedoms, and the rule of law, principles which are common to the member states." Whereas the EU and the communities that preceded it were political constructions, national governments had not explicitly imbued them with core political values. In the Amsterdam Treaty, by contrast, governments clearly stated what those values were.

The treaty also included a provision to sanction any member state that deviated from the EU's core values. Should it determine "the existence of a serious and persistent breach . . . of principles mentioned [in the treaty]," the European Council could decide by a qualified majority "to suspend certain of the rights deriving from the application of [the treaty] to the Member State in question, including the voting right of the government of that Member State in the Council." Governments drafted that provision with the Central and Eastern European applicants in mind. Indeed, it was one of the few provisions of the Amsterdam Treaty that owed its existence to impending enlargement.

Ironically, the possible suspension of membership rights became a pressing political issue soon afterward, not in relation to enlargement but because the Christian Democratic Party in Austria formed a coalition government in February 2000 with the far-right Freedom Party. To signal their displeasure, the other governments cited the Amsterdam Treaty and unofficially imposed mild sanctions against Austria, but backed down at the end of the year when the Austrian government threatened to call their bluff by holding a referendum on EU participation unless the sanctions were lifted. Sensing that the result of the referendum would have been a huge embarrassment to the EU, Austria's partners soon relented.[29]

Not surprisingly, given the origin of the IGC and the fact that the negotiations took place in the shadow of the Yugoslav debacle, the Amsterdam Treaty included significant changes in the CFSP. Rising public concern in the mid-

1990s about the internal security implications of external instability emboldened the Commission and national governments to strengthen treaty provisions
on justice and home affairs. The changes in the Amsterdam Treaty relating to
the CFSP and justice and home affairs (JHA) are explored in Chapter 17.

Despite these and other important reforms, the significance of the Amsterdam Treaty eluded most Europeans. With more than fifty pages of text,
including numerous references to existing provisions, the treaty was not easy
to understand. Ironically, a treaty intended to make the EU more intelligible to
its citizens was almost unintelligible even to experts. Overall, the Amsterdam
Treaty was a fitting testimonial to the impossibility of reconciling the complexity of EU governance with citizens' demands for greater simplicity and
comprehensibility, a difficulty that would become more acute in the years
ahead. Unlike the Maastricht Treaty before it, and the Nice and Lisbon treaties
to follow, at least the Amsterdam Treaty was easily ratified. In both Denmark
and Ireland, the only two countries to hold a referendum, large majorities
endorsed the treaty, which came into effect in May 1999.

Resignation of the Santer Commission

Implementation of the Amsterdam Treaty passed largely unnoticed in the EU.
Not so another development at the time, the Commission's enforced resignation. Here was a piece of political theater that drew massive media attention,
to the detriment of the Commission's image and generally that of the EU.[30]

The Commission is accountable to the EP, which may vote the college out
of office by a two-thirds majority of the total number of MEPs. Such a high
threshold reflects the seriousness of the censure procedure, long known as the
"nuclear option" in Parliament-Commission relations. In keeping with the doctrine of mutually assured destruction, the Commission presumed that the EP
would never press the button, although the EP occasionally threatened to do so.
Accordingly, the Commission was always somewhat high-handed in its
approach to the EP, which understandably resented the Commission's attitude.

The increasingly powerful EP was not spoiling for a fight with the Commission, but would not back down should a confrontation arise. The conflict
came in early 1999, following a series of skirmishes during the previous
twelve months. These began in March 1998 at a stormy plenary in Strasbourg
when MEPs, incensed by yet another report from the Court of Auditors that
was highly critical of the Commission's management of the budget, threatened
the Commission with censure. Parliament held its fire, but MEPs grew
increasingly annoyed throughout the year as additional allegations emerged of
fraud and financial mismanagement in the Commission.

Commission president Jacques Santer was never accused of financial
impropriety, but he failed to act decisively against the commissioners who

were. The most conspicuous case, although it involved a relatively small amount of money, concerned Edith Cresson, a former prime minister of France who allegedly awarded a contract to a friend who was unqualified to carry out the work. The EP demanded Cresson's resignation; Santer lacked the ability to dismiss Cresson, especially as the French government backed her to the end; and Cresson herself was haughty and unrepentant.

The prospect of a Commission-Parliament showdown kept Brussels in a tizzy. There was little public sympathy for either of the protagonists, although Parliament held the moral high ground against an apparently feckless and wasteful Commission. Lacking flair and largely unknown outside Brussels and his native Luxembourg, Santer was an easy target for media and public scorn. Cresson got off lightly in the court of public opinion—perhaps most people assumed that petty corruption was endemic in French politics.

Eager to avoid an interinstitutional confrontation, some national politicians urged their counterparts in the EP to drop the matter. Center-right politicians were especially concerned about the vulnerability of Santer, a Christian Democrat, to partisan attacks from the Party of European Socialists. By late 1998, however, the issue transcended party politics. Regardless of their party affiliation, most MEPs were too incensed to back down and wanted to put the Commission in its place.

Nevertheless, the Commission escaped censure in January 1999 when the EP failed to muster the necessary two-thirds majority. The EP decided instead, with the Commission's agreement, to establish a committee of independent experts to investigate the allegations. The committee's report, published in March 1999, was damning. One widely reported sentence could not have been more injurious: "It is becoming difficult to find anyone [in the Commission] who has even the slightest sense of responsibility."[31] Once the Parliament made it clear that a Commission that still included Cresson would not survive another censure motion, the Commission accepted the inevitable and resigned as a body.

Far from being the result of a calculated parliamentary maneuver, the Commission's collapse was the culmination of a series of mistakes and misjudgments in both institutions. But the widespread perception was that the EP had finally come of age and asserted its authority over an arrogant and corrupt Commission. As perception shapes political reality, the events of early 1999 therefore represented a major institutional advance for the EP, although its assertion of accountability did not so much tip an institutional imbalance as redress one. In principle, the Commission was always accountable to Parliament; in practice, it now had to behave accordingly.

The Commission's forced resignation has gone down in history as one of a series of events in the coming-of-age of the EP, on a par with the first direct elections or the introduction of the codecision procedure for legislative decisionmaking.[32] Undoubtedly it illustrated Parliament's growing political assertiveness and fed many MEPs' image of themselves as guardians of the public interest, despite their own reputation for extravagant pay and expenses. By contrast, the dramatic events of March 1999 dealt a further blow to the Commission's influence and morale, from which it has yet to recover. Ironically for a president genuinely interested in reform, Santer is best known for failing to tackle corruption and maladministration in the Commission.

Subsequently, national governments sought to strengthen the president's power within the college in order to prevent a recalcitrant commissioner from bringing down the entire body. Accordingly, the Nice Treaty of 2001, negotiated in the wake of the Commission resignation scandal, included a provision allowing the president to demand a commissioner's resignation, subject to the Commission's approval.

Despite being called the "Commission resignation crisis," the drama of March 1999 was not a crisis at all. It was a showdown between two institutions, from which the Parliament emerged stronger and the Commission weaker. There was no danger of mutual destruction because, compared to the EP, the Commission was unarmed. Strictly speaking, the EP was unable to fire its weapon in January 1999, when the necessary supermajority of MEPs failed to materialize, and needed only to threaten to fire in March 1999 when the Commission, realizing that the EP now had the necessary supermajority, resigned before being voted out.

Overall, the confrontation between the Commission and the EP may have strengthened the political system by striking a new institutional balance and forcing the Commission to undertake serious internal reform. Yet it weakened public support for the EU as a whole. At a time when Europeans were preoccupied with events in Kosovo, interinstitutional squabbles in Brussels and Strasbourg must have seemed trivial and irrelevant. Certainly, the EP did not reap the reward for its victory that it most craved: a large turnout in the June 1999 elections. On the contrary, turnout continued its decline since the first elections twenty years earlier.

▨ Notes

1. See Finn Laursen, "The Community's Policy Toward EFTA: Regime Formation in the European Economic Space," *Journal of Common Market Studies* 28, no. 4 (June 1990): 320–325, and Clive Church, "The Politics of Change," *Journal of Common Market Studies* 28, no. 4 (June 1990): 408–410.

2. Bulletin EC 5-1992, point 2.2.1.

3. European Commission, "Report on Enlargement," Bulletin EC S/3-1992, p. 13.

4. Lisbon European Council, "Presidency Conclusions," Bulletin EC 6-1992, points 1.3–1.4.

5. On the negotiations, see John Redmond, ed., *The 1995 Enlargement of the European Union* (Aldershot: Ashgate, 1997); Lee Miles, ed., *The European Union and the Nordic Countries* (New York: Routledge, 1996); and P. Luif, *On the Road to Brussels:*

The Political Dimension of Austria's, Finland's, and Sweden's Road to Accession to the European Union (Vienna: Austrian Institute for International Affairs, 1995).

6. Bulletin EC 3-1994, point 1.3.27.

7. Debates of the European Parliament, 1994/1995 Session, "Report of Proceedings from May 2–6, 1994," *Official Journal of the European Communities* 3-448: 123–144, 157–166, 167–177.

8. On the 1992–1993 currency crisis, see Willem H. Buiter, Giancarlo Corsetti, and Paolo A. Pesenti, *Financial Markets and European Monetary Cooperation: The Lessons of the 1992–93 Exchange Rate Mechanism Crisis* (Cambridge: Cambridge University Press, 2001).

9. On the road to EMU in the 1990s, see Ottmar Issing, *The Birth of the Euro* (Cambridge: Cambridge University Press, 2008), pp. 13–51; and Peter B. Kenen, *Economic and Monetary Union in Europe: Moving Beyond Maastricht* (Cambridge: Cambridge University Press, 1995), pp. 124–149.

10. Desmond Dinan, *Ever Closer Union? An Introduction to the European Community* (Boulder: Lynne Rienner, 1994), p. 435.

11. European Commission, "Report on Convergence in the European Union in 1996," COM(96)560, November 1996; European Monetary Institute, *Progress Towards Convergence* (Frankfurt, November 1996).

12. European Commission, "Green Paper on Technical Preparations for the Single European Currency," COM(95)333, May 1995.

13. Amsterdam European Council, "Presidency Conclusions," Bulletin EC 6-1997, point 1.1.10.

14. European Commission, *European Economy*, supp. A, no. 10 (October 1997).

15. European Commission, *Euro 1999: Progress Towards Convergence* (Luxembourg: Office for Official Publications of the European Communities, 1999); and European Monetary Institute, *Convergence Report* (Frankfurt, 1998).

16. European Commission, *European Economy*, supp. A, nos. 3–4 (March–April 1998).

17. The statement is reproduced at http://ue.eu.int/uedocs/cms_data/docs/press data/en/ecofin/08170-r1.en8.htm.

18. Interview in *International Herald Tribune*, July 1, 1992, p. 2.

19. Embassy of Greece, "News from Greece," 16/92, November 10, 1992, p. 1.

20. See Michael Libal, *Limits of Persuasion: Germany and the Yugoslav Crisis, 1991–1992* (Westport: Praeger, 1997).

21. Quoted in *Financial Times*, July 1, 1991, p. 1.

22. See John Roper, "Keynote Article: Two Cheers for Mr. Blair? The Political Realities of European Defence Cooperation," *Journal of Common Market Studies* 38, *Annual Review of the EU 1999/2000* (September 2000): 7–24.

23. See Philip Lynch, Nanette Neuwahl, and G. Wyn Rees, eds., *Reforming the European Union: From Maastricht to Amsterdam* (London: Longman, 2000).

24. Report of the Reflection Group, "A Strategy for Europe: An Annotated Agenda," Brussels, December 5, 1995.

25. Christian Democratic Union–Christian Social Union Group in the German Lower House, "Reflections on European Policy," Bonn, September 1, 1994.

26. John Major, "Europe: A Future That Works," William and Mary Lecture, Leiden University, September 7, 1994.

27. On the IGC and its outcome, see Geoffrey Edwards and Alfred Pijpers, eds., *The Politics of European Treaty Reform: The 1996 Intergovernmental Conference and Beyond* (London: Pinter, 1997); and Finn Laursen, ed., *The Amsterdam Treaty:*

National Preference Formation, Interstate Bargaining, and Outcome (Odense, Denmark: Odense University Press, 2002).

28. See Alexander Stubb, *Negotiating Flexibility in the European Union: Amsterdam, Nice, and Beyond* (Basingstoke: Palgrave Macmillan, 2003), pp. 58–105.

29. On the Austrian situation, see Gerda Falkner, "The EU14's 'Sanctions' Against Austria: Sense and Nonsense," *ECSA Review* 14, no. 1 (Winter 2001): 14–15.

30. See Desmond Dinan, "Governance and Institutions 1999: Resignation, Reform, and Renewal," *Journal of Common Market Studies* 38, *Annual Review of the EU 1999/2000* (September 2000): 27–30.

31. Committee of Independent Experts, "First Report on Allegations Regarding Fraud, Mismanagement, and Nepotism in the European Commission," Brussels, March 1999, point 1.6.2.

32. Julian Priestley, *Six Battles That Shaped Europe's Parliament* (London: John Harper, 2008).

6 The Unsettled European Union, 2000–2010

Two of the most momentous events in the history of European integration occurred in the early years of the new century. The changeover to euro notes and coins in January 2002, for the eleven countries then in the eurozone, completed the process of monetary union, the European Union's most ambitious policy innovation ever. The accession of ten member states in 2004 and two more in 2007 was an even greater accomplishment, the culmination of a long effort to heal the divisions of the Cold War. After lengthy and sometimes painful preparation, within three years the EU grew in membership from fifteen to twenty-seven countries and in population from 380 million to 500 million. The EU became a strikingly different entity: more diverse, fractious, and multifaceted than ever before.

Partly because of enlargement, for much of the new decade the EU was preoccupied with the politically fraught process of treaty reform. Initially national governments took a minimalist approach, sticking mostly to institutional fine-tuning. Consequently, the Nice Treaty of 2001 was narrow in focus and limited in impact. Dissatisfaction with the Nice Treaty led to the Convention on the Future of Europe, an experiment from which the Constitutional Treaty and its successor, the Lisbon Treaty, emerged.

The tortuous process of treaty reform in the first decade of the twenty-first century included rejection of the Constitutional Treaty by French and Dutch voters in 2005 and rejection of the Lisbon Treaty by Irish voters in 2008 (Irish voters endorsed the treaty in a second referendum in 2009). The results of the French, Dutch, and first Irish referendums were a stunning rebuke of the EU. Far from reassuring public opinion, each new treaty spurred growing Euroskepticism. The referendum results confirmed widespread dissatisfaction with the EU well beyond the three countries in question.

Few EU leaders were inclined to dwell on the EU's deep unpopularity. Most were more interested in rescuing a treaty in which they had invested considerable time and effort, and believed would improve the effectiveness of the EU, thereby making it more appealing to its citizens. Nevertheless many of

133

them must have wondered whether the long and arduous road to ratification of the Lisbon Treaty had been worthwhile.

The Lisbon Treaty undoubtedly improves the EU's institutional arrangements, democratic foundations, and overall effectiveness. Despite the claims of many Euroskeptics, it is far from a founding text for a European federation or superstate. Rather, it represents a consolidation of the existing treaties, with some useful institutional innovations and an extension of EU competence. Given the nature of the EU and the difficulties inherent in negotiating treaty reform, the Lisbon Treaty is hardly ideal. Yet under the circumstances, it is arguably the best possible outcome.

The EU's self-absorption with the Lisbon Treaty in late 2007 coincided with the onset of the global economic crisis. What unfolded over the next three years posed a severe test for EU solidarity, the single market, and the eurozone. As the crisis deepened, economic nationalism surfaced in the EU, with governments moving to protect vulnerable banks and industries. Fissures opened throughout the EU: among the big member states; between old and new member states, eurozone members and nonmembers. At first the crisis seemed to expose the fragility of European integration. Ultimately, it demonstrated the resilience of the EU and the member states' appreciation of both the importance of the single market and the value of the common currency. Governments realized that their prospects were vastly better in maintaining European integration than in undermining the EU through unilateral action. As the crisis eased toward the end of 2009, and the Lisbon Treaty was finally implemented, the state and fate of the EU began to look decidedly better, notwithstanding the impact of the Greek debt crisis (see Box 6.1).

■ Enlargement Unlike Any Other: From Fifteen to Twenty-Seven

The unexpected end of the Cold War triggered an avalanche of applications from the newly independent countries of Central and Eastern Europe. This round of EU enlargement would be unprecedented. The Central and Eastern European applicants were poorer than even the poorest of the EU15. All had been cut off from Western Europe for four decades, either by incorporation into the Soviet Union or by Soviet occupation and domination. The end of the Cold War and disintegration of the Soviet Union therefore presented a historic opportunity to restore Europe culturally, politically, and economically.[1]

The Central and Eastern European countries looked to the EU not only for financial support, market access, and technical assistance but also for recognition of their "Europeanness." The EU now had an opportunity to promote genuinely pan-European integration. In order to succeed, the EU would have to see the potential and not just the pitfalls of eastward enlargement; to look out-

Box 6.1   Chronology, 2000–2010

2000	February	Accession negotiations with Bulgaria, Latvia, Lithuania, Malta, Romania, and Slovakia begin; intergovernmental conference (IGC) begins
	March	Proclamation of Lisbon strategy
	December	IGC ends at Nice summit
2001	January	Greece adopts the euro
	February	Nice Treaty signed
	June	Irish reject Nice Treaty in referendum
2002	January	Changeover to euro notes and coins
	February	Convention on the Future of Europe begins
	October	Irish approve Nice Treaty in second referendum
	December	Accession negotiations with Cyprus, Czech Republic, Estonia, Hungary, Latvia, Lithuania, Malta, Poland, Slovakia, and Slovenia end
2003	April	Accession treaties with Cyprus, Czech Republic, Estonia, Hungary, Latvia, Lithuania, Malta, Poland, Slovakia, and Slovenia signed in Athens
	July	Convention on the Future of Europe approves Draft Constitutional Treaty
	October	IGC begins
2004	May	Cyprus, Czech Republic, Estonia, Hungary, Latvia, Lithuania, Malta, Poland, Slovakia, and Slovenia join the EU
	June	IGC ends with agreement on Constitutional Treaty; elections to the European Parliament (EP)
	October	Constitutional Treaty signed in Rome
	December	European Council agrees to open accession negotiations with Turkey in October 2005
2005	April	Accession treaties with Bulgaria and Romania signed in Luxembourg
	May–June	French and Dutch voters reject Constitutional Treaty in referendums
	June	European Council begins "period of reflection" on Constitutional Treaty
	October	Accession negotiations with Turkey and Croatia begin
2006	June	End of "period of reflection" on Constitutional Treaty
2007	January	Bulgaria and Romania join the EU; Slovenia adopts the euro
	June	European Council agrees on detailed mandate for new IGC
	July	IGC begins
	October	IGC ends at Lisbon summit
	December	Treaty of Lisbon signed
2008	January	Cyprus and Malta adopt the euro
	June	Irish reject Lisbon Treaty in a referendum
	December	European Council adopts Economic Recovery Plan
2009	January	Slovakia adopts the euro
	June	Elections to the EP
	October	Irish approve Lisbon Treaty in second referendum
	December	Lisbon Treaty comes into effect
2010	January	Greece has difficulty refinancing its public debt
	March	Eurozone finance ministers agree on an interim financial mechanism to help Greece
	April	EU reveals that Greece's 2009 budget deficit is 13.6 percent of GDP
	May	Following violent protests in Athens, EU leaders approve emergency funding together with the IMF, worth up to €750 billion, to ameliorate the Greek crisis

ward at a time of introspection; to overcome vested interests threatened by Central and Eastern European imports in sensitive sectors like agriculture, steel, and textiles; to restructure its institutions and policies to accommodate a diverse group of new member states; and to rethink Europe's future in the post–Cold War world.

These were immense challenges. Inevitably the EU could not meet all of them in a timely, effective, and generous fashion. Under the circumstances, it is remarkable that the EU succeeded so well. In 1989 the Commission launched the PHARE aid program to support reform in Central and Eastern Europe, and soon concluded trade and cooperation agreements with the countries in the region. In addition, the EU helped launch the European Bank for Reconstruction and Development (EBRD).[2]

Impressive though it was, the EU's initial response had been improvised and understandably ad hoc. The rapid pace of events made it difficult for the EU to devise a coherent strategy. The obstacles to Central and Eastern enlargement were formidable. Forty years of communist rule had left an appalling legacy. In order to move from command to free market economies, and therefore meet a basic requirement for EU membership, the Central and Eastern Europeans faced a daunting array of reforms, including the introduction of property rights and a code of business law, the development of banking and financial services, and the privatization of most state-owned companies. They needed to overhaul outmoded infrastructures, begin large-scale agricultural and industrial modernization, attract foreign investment, and address massive environmental degradation. Finally, people in Central and Eastern Europe would have to acquire the kinds of basic skills and attitudes taken for granted in the West.

As the cost and extent of reform became apparent, even enthusiasts of early accession realized that further EU enlargement was improbable in the near future. Eleven years had elapsed before Portugal and Spain joined the EC after the restoration of democracy in 1975. It seemed highly unlikely that any of the Central and Eastern European states would be ready to join the EU—an entity far more economically and politically integrated than that of 1986—within eleven years of the fall of the Berlin Wall. The EU therefore set about preparing the Central and Eastern European states for the long road to accession.

Preparation

The Council decided that the EU would offer "Europe agreements" to the prospective member states. But negotiation of the agreements pitted the member states' protectionist proclivities against their political rhetoric. When it came to granting liberal market access, a number of existing member states succumbed to domestic pressure and blocked generous terms. Only when Hungary and Poland threatened to walk out of the talks did the recalcitrant member states—notably France, Spain, and Portugal—come to their senses.

The EU eventually signed Europe agreements with most of the Central and Eastern European countries by the mid-1990s. These called for the eventual establishment of free trade areas, the gradual adoption by the associated states of EU legislation, and the launch of a political dialogue. Most important for the Central and Eastern Europeans was an acknowledgment that their "final objective" was to join the EU.

Criticism of the Europe agreements' limited trade concessions and the EU's self-absorption during the lengthy Maastricht Treaty ratification process prompted the European Council to spell out the conditions for eventual eastward enlargement, a prospect that remained controversial among the member states. Whereas Britain hoped that early accession would weaken political integration, most member states feared that an ill-prepared enlargement could turn the EU into a glorified free trade area. Eager to fill the strategic void on its eastern border, Germany wanted to bring the Czech Republic and Poland into the EU as soon as possible. Otherwise, Germany seemed lukewarm about enlargement. France fretted about the economic implications and about a potential German sphere of influence in the enlarged EU. Spain, Portugal, Greece, and Ireland worried about having to compete for regional development funds with new, poorer member states.

Mounting political pressure led the EU formally to acknowledge the inevitable and set out the conditions under which applicant countries could join. As approved by the European Council in June 1993, candidates would be judged for accession based on the "Copenhagen criteria":

- Stability of institutions guaranteeing democracy, rule of law, human rights, and respect for and protection of minorities.
- Existence of a functioning market economy and the capacity to cope with competitive pressure and market forces within the EU.
- Ability to take on the obligations of membership, including adherence to the aims of political, economic, and monetary union.

The European Council also stipulated that "the Union's capacity to absorb new members, while maintaining the momentum of European integration, [would be] an important consideration" in the accession process.[3]

In December 1994 the European Council launched a "structured dialogue" between the soon-to-be EU15 and the Central and Eastern European countries, most of which had just applied or were about to apply for membership.[4] The structured dialogue involved regular ministerial-level meetings as well as annual meetings of the leaders of the EU and of the applicant countries. Impatient to begin entry negotiations, most of the applicants dismissed the structured dialogue as a public relations exercise.

More important, perhaps, was a Commission white paper on the steps that the applicants would need to take in order to participate in the internal market.[5]

The conditions set out in the white paper were daunting for countries with low levels of economic development, little experience of free market economics, and inadequate administrative structures. Because the challenges were so great, the Commission reformed the PHARE program to focus on such mundane but essential objectives as establishing competent regulatory and bureaucratic structures in the recipient countries.

Guided by the Copenhagen criteria, the Europe agreements, and various Commission initiatives, the applicants set about overcoming the high economic and regulatory barriers to membership. Most adopted detailed plans, including quantifiable measurements of progress toward adopting the *acquis communautaire* (body of EU legislation). At the same time, the Commission drafted opinions on all the membership applications and a comprehensive report on the likely impact of enlargement on the EU itself. Collectively, the opinions and report made up Agenda 2000, which reached the following conclusions about the applicants' suitability for EU membership:

- *Democracy and the rule of law:* All applicants except Slovakia had adequate constitutional and institutional arrangements.
- *Functioning market economy, competitive pressures, and market forces:* All applicants had made good progress, but structural reforms were far from complete, especially in the banking and financial sectors and in social security.
- *The acquis communautaire:* All applicants had begun to incorporate EU rules and regulations into national law, but still had a long way to go.[6]

The Commission recommended that the EU begin accession negotiations in early 1998 with the Czech Republic, Hungary, Poland, Estonia, and Slovenia (plus Cyprus). The Commission's selection of the Czech Republic, Hungary, and Poland was not surprising; it chose Estonia and Slovenia largely because NATO had just announced that those three would be invited to join in 1999. The Commission did not want to be seen as endorsing for EU membership the same three countries tapped to join NATO, lest Russia claim that the EU and NATO were drawing a new dividing line in Europe.

The European Council approved the Commission's recommendation in December 1997, and called for individual partnerships between the EU and the five "fast-track" applicants to plan, assist, and assess their path to accession.[7] The accession partnerships, constituting a detailed map for each of the fast-track applicants on the road to EU accession, were later extended to the other candidates as well.

Negotiation
Accession negotiations began ceremoniously in Brussels in March 1998, marking the culmination of nearly ten years of preparatory work. Yet there

were no illusions about the difficulties that lay ahead. The first stage consisted of a screening exercise to assess the extent to which each of the candidates met the rules and obligations of membership and to identify difficult issues likely to arise later in the negotiations. Substantive negotiations began in November 1998 on seven of thirty-one chapters or issue areas. As the negotiations progressed, officials checked the chapters off using an accession scorecard.

Fears that differentiation would demoralize the slow-track candidates were unfounded. Indeed, the five countries that had not begun negotiations accelerated reforms in an effort to catch up. So successful were the supposed laggards that in October 1999 the Commission recommended opening negotiations with them as well. With war in Kosovo as an unnerving backdrop to the EU's deliberations, the European Council endorsed the Commission's recommendations, paving the way for the opening of negotiations with Latvia, Lithuania, Slovakia, Bulgaria, and Romania in 2000.

Despite their late start, the second group soon caught up with the first group. Although the EU negotiated separately with each country, the relative transparency of the process and publication of the negotiation scorecard pressured the candidates to make progress (none of them wanted to top the list of incomplete chapters). By the end of 2002 only the most contentious issues, such as agriculture and the budget, remained unresolved.

In a key report on enlargement in October 2002, the Commission recommended accession by 2004 for eight of the Central and Eastern European candidates, but not Bulgaria and Romania. While most of the candidates had problems meeting all of the EU's membership requirements, the Commission was optimistic that the negotiations would end soon. An agreement on funding the Common Agricultural Policy during the next budgetary cycle (2007–2013), reached by the European Council in October 2002, removed the last obstacle on the EU's side to a successful conclusion of the negotiations.

The negotiations—really a series of *diktats* by the EU—left some ill feeling on both sides. Poland, the largest of the applicant states, behaved at times as if the EU wanted to join it rather than the other way around. Hungary, by contrast, tended to go along with whatever the EU offered. The other candidates, lacking experience and influence in Brussels, were hardly in a position to make a strong case for themselves. The Poles and other applicants were particularly disgruntled with some of the blatantly discriminatory terms on offer. For example, the EU15 (led by Austria and Germany) insisted on retaining the right to prevent citizens of the new member states from working in the old member states for up to seven years after enlargement.

A last-minute row over agricultural subsidies nearly delayed enlargement, as the Poles and others resisted an EU offer of substantially smaller subsidies than farmers in the EU15 would receive. The rationale for the EU's position was that a sudden influx of agricultural subsidies as high as those in Western Europe would cause massive economic dislocation and social resentment in the new member states. That may have been a legitimate concern, but the EU simply did not have enough money to subsidize farmers in the new member states at the level to which Western European farmers had become accustomed.

After the Danish government managed to get a little extra EU money for Central and Eastern European farmers, negotiations with the eight candidates came to an end at the Copenhagen summit in December 2002.[8] Except for Bulgaria and Romania, this closed off enlargement "from Copenhagen to Copenhagen": from the announcement of the accession criteria in June 1993 to the conclusion of the negotiations ten years later. The EU and the initial group of successful candidates signed the accession treaties in a splendid ceremony in Athens in April 2003. All of the Central and Eastern European countries ratified the treaties by referendum. Although the turnout and the margin of victory varied significantly, the referendum results amounted to an impressive endorsement of accession.

Cyprus and Malta. Cyprus and Malta were a case apart. The Commission's main concern over Cyprus was the division of the island into the Greek Cypriot south and the self-styled Turkish Cypriot north, a separate entity backed by Turkey. The Turkish Cypriot government hotly disputed the right of the (Greek) Cypriot government to seek EU membership on behalf of the entire island. Thus, Turkish and Cypriot membership in the EU became bound up with each other and with the historical enmity between Greece and Turkey.

The EU invited Cyprus to begin accession negotiations in March 1998. Apart from partition, the EU's main concern was to reform Cyprus's banking laws, which had attracted a large influx of money of questionable provenance. The negotiations went well, although Turkey occasionally threatened to block the reunification of the island unless the EU promised to expedite Turkey's own application for membership.[9]

The EU's willingness to admit Cyprus without reunification robbed Turkey of some leverage. It also robbed the EU of its ability to pressure the Greek Cypriots, a large majority of whom rejected an admittedly imperfect United Nations plan for reunification, which a small majority of Turkish Cypriots accepted in an islandwide referendum in April 2004. Having already signed an accession treaty with Cyprus, the EU could do little except denounce the Greek Cypriot government for its intransigence and offer sympathy and economic support to the Turkish Cypriots. A partitioned Cyprus therefore joined the EU in May 2004 and promptly threatened to block further progress on Turkey's application.

The prospect of EU membership was deeply divisive in Malta in the 1990s, with the Conservative Party in favor and the Labour Party against. The only worrisome issue for the EU was Malta's size: the EU did not relish having another member state as small as Luxembourg but without Luxembourg's international standing or tradition of European integration.[10] Nevertheless

Malta easily completed its accession negotiations at the end of 2002. Although a majority in Malta approved membership in a referendum in March 2003, the fiercely anti-EU Labour Party insisted that the issue be decided in a general election held the following month. The governing Conservatives easily won reelection and brought Malta into the EU in May 2004.

Bulgaria and Romania. As expected, Bulgaria and Romania failed to make the cut for accession in 2004, primarily because of rampant corruption, weak administrative capacity, and dubious judicial independence. The transformative power of possible EU membership seemed less effective in Bulgaria and Romania than in the other Central and Eastern European countries. The temporary solution was to delay their membership in the EU.

The EU could have kept the two countries out indefinitely, but that would have weakened its leverage and tarnished the international image of the EU's enlargement policy. Instead, the EU included in the accession agreement provisions to sanction the two countries should they fail to carry through administrative and legal reforms or stop the fight against corruption and organized crime. In particular, the Commission could halt financial transfers, notably agricultural subsidies and regional development funds. The Commission could also suspend EU-wide recognition of court judgments in Bulgaria and Romania, which would greatly impair their participation in the single market.

Despite these precautions, there was little enthusiasm in Brussels and throughout the EU for Bulgarian and Romanian accession. Bowing to the inevitable, the European Council decided in December 2004 to conclude negotiations with both countries. The signing ceremony for the accession treaties, held in Luxembourg in April 2005, was decidedly less glamorous than the ceremony for the other Central and Eastern European countries.

Most Bulgarians and Romanians could hardly wait to join. The vote in the Romanian parliament on ratification of the accession treaty was unanimous. In the equivalent vote in the Bulgarian parliament, only one member voted against. National parliaments within the EU were decidedly less enthusiastic, but none blocked Bulgarian or Romanian accession. That paved the way for the two countries to join the EU in January 2007.[11]

Accession

The brief description of Central and Eastern European enlargement fails to convey the extraordinary transformation in the region. The prospect of joining the EU undoubtedly helped most of the applicants undertake painful political and economic reforms. The EU was hugely influential in strengthening democracy and fundamental rights throughout the region. Without EU conditionality, Central and Eastern Europe would be far less stable today.[12]

Nevertheless, success came at a cost: the long road to membership had produced "enlargement fatigue" well before the first group of countries joined.

Public opinion in the EU and the candidate countries (apart from Bulgaria and Romania) lost whatever enthusiasm for enlargement it had originally possessed. Indeed, opposition to enlargement accounted in part for the resurgence of the far right in Western Europe. Ireland's rejection of the Nice Treaty in June 2001 looked like a manifestation of anti-enlargement feeling, although the referendum was not about enlargement. France's rejection of the Constitutional Treaty in the May 2005 referendum owed much to resentment of alleged unemployment due to the "nearshoring" of jobs to the new member states and an influx of cheap labor from the east. Opinion in Central and Eastern Europe, where many people associated EU accession with economic hardships triggered by the collapse of communism, seemed equally skittish and helped strengthen populist parties throughout the region, notably in Hungary and Poland.

The likely consequences of enlargement for the institutions, policies, and politics of the EU had gradually sunk in among the existing member states. Clearly, enlargement would have a major impact on institutional arrangements and decisionmaking procedures, hence the EU's efforts, beginning with the Amsterdam Treaty, to prepare the EU institutionally for enlargement. These efforts were patently inadequate. With the 2002–2003 Convention on the Future of Europe, in which the candidate countries participated, the EU finally attempted seriously to meet the institutional challenges of enlargement. Subsequent rounds of reform, resulting first in the Constitutional Treaty and later in the Lisbon Treaty, underscored the need for far-reaching change. Yet existing arrangements, notably those for qualified majority voting that came into effect under the Nice Treaty, worked much better than expected; post-enlargement legislative gridlock in Brussels failed to materialize.

Nor, in the legislative arena, did a split emerge between the old and the new member states. Coalitions remained fluid, their membership depending on the issue. A more noticeable divide emerged on external relations, with the new countries generally advocating a harsher approach toward Russia and a friendlier approach toward the United States. On economic policy, the new members tended to be more liberal than France, Germany, and Italy. Membership or nonmembership in the eurozone is arguably the most significant fault line within the enlarged EU. The majority of non-eurozone countries are new Central and Eastern European member states, many of which feel that the criteria for membership are being applied more strictly now than when the eurozone was launched in 1999. Given the advantages of eurozone membership, especially at a time of global financial turmoil, some of the new member states feel deliberately excluded from the EU's inner sanctum.

Enlargement has had an obvious impact on specific EU policies. Agriculture and cohesion, core policies that account for the bulk of EU expenditure, come to mind. Concerns about the porousness of the Central and Eastern European countries' eastern borders triggered an acceleration of cooperation on justice and home affairs. Similarly, concern about the impact of enlargement on relations between the EU and its new neighbors in Eastern Europe, and concern in the Southern Mediterranean about the EU's apparent neglect of the region, led the EU to launch the European Neighborhood Policy. (The implications of enlargement for various EU policies are examined in Part 3.)

Politically, the EU's adaptation to enlargement was strained. It was difficult for some of the old members, none more so than France, to adjust to the new reality. In February 2003, for example, after a special summit to discuss the EU's response to the imminent war in Iraq, President Jacques Chirac lambasted the Central and Eastern European countries for supporting the United States and for not following France's lead.

Managing the impact of enlargement within the EU's institutions was bound to be difficult, not least because of the profusion of official languages. Politicians and officials, accustomed to the relative coziness of the EU15, were inclined to look down on their counterparts from Central and Eastern Europe. Undoubtedly some officials from the EU15 feared the impact of enlargement on their promotion prospects, given that officials from the new member states would have to be accommodated at all levels in the Brussels bureaucracy. By the time enlargement finally took place, thousands of Central and Eastern European officials had become thoroughly familiar with the functioning of EU institutions (as students, many had served internships in Brussels). As with previous enlargement, however, it took some time for officials from the new countries to settle into their posts.

■ Treaty Reform: From Nice to Lisbon

Having failed in the Amsterdam Treaty to tackle the contentious questions of voting weights and the composition of the Commission, national governments were obliged to try again before enlargement took place. They did so in a conference beginning in February 2000, in which governments also decided the number of seats and votes for the prospective new member states, issues that ordinarily would have been included in the accession negotiations.

There was little opportunity within this narrow agenda for side bargains or trade-offs among participants. No sooner had the IGC begun than prominent national politicians started to outline visions for the enlarged EU that went well beyond the scope of the negotiations. Foremost among them was Joschka Fischer, Germany's foreign minister and a leading proponent of a more federal EU.[13] What became known as the post-Nice debate on Europe's future began well before the Nice summit of December 2000, where the IGC ended, suggesting that for many national leaders the Nice Treaty was never intended to be more than a stopgap.

The negotiations on voting weights in the Council and the Commission's size opened a can of worms. These issues were all about the power of national governments to shape EU decisions. Not surprisingly, a split emerged between the big countries (Britain, France, Germany, Italy, and Spain) and the others, with the big countries wanting to increase their share of Council votes and reduce the size of the Commission, and the small countries mostly wanting to keep their share of Council votes and maintain national representation in the Commission.

A spectacular row broke out among EU leaders at an informal summit in October 2000, their first detailed discussion of institutional issues since the rancorous Amsterdam summit in June 1997. President Chirac irritated many of his counterparts by proposing a radical reduction in the size of the Commission while promising a system for the selection of a smaller group of commissioners that would ensure equality among member states. The small countries were unimpressed, distrusting France and fearing that the big countries would skew the proposed new system against them. Chirac claimed that the sharp exchange over the Commission's size cleared the air in the IGC. In fact, it led the small countries to dig in their heels and set the stage for a bruising battle at the Nice summit in December 2000.

The discussion of voting weights was equally acrimonious. France was determined to keep the same number of Council votes as Germany, a far more populous country. Chirac, a Gaullist, even cited Jean Monnet, the founding father of the European Community, to bolster his claim that equality between France and Germany was an inviolable part of the original Franco-German bargain. Chancellor Gerhard Schröder, participating in his first IGC, conceded the point in return for the addition of a demographic criterion for QMV. As for the small countries, the Netherlands infuriated Belgium, its less populous neighbor, by demanding more Council votes, thereby ending the traditional parity between the two countries.

When they convened in Nice, EU leaders were far apart on the main agenda items. After spending two days on other EU business, the European Council spent two more days concluding the IGC, making the Nice summit the longest in EU history. Yet the length of the summit hardly justified the effort. EU leaders haggled until the final minutes over the reallocation of Council votes. Still refusing to accept fewer votes than the Netherlands, Belgium was finally bought off with the promise of hosting all meetings of the European Council in Brussels. France managed to keep parity with Germany (both got twenty-nine votes), but the addition of a demographic criterion gave Germany extra voting weight. The final bargain struck in the IGC on Council decision-making was especially inglorious. Far from making voting simpler and easier to understand, it changed the system in a way that seemed unnecessarily convoluted (see Chapter 8).

As for the future of the Commission, the agreement called for the big member states to give up their second commissioner when the next Commission took office, and for the number of commissioners to be reduced to fewer than the number of member states when the EU reached twenty-seven members (a number based on the existing fifteen plus the twelve candidates). At that time, national governments would rotate Commission appointments according to a system yet to be worked out.

Signed without much fanfare in February 2001, the Nice Treaty barely succeeded in preparing the EU institutionally for enlargement. One of its most important provisions was to relax the criteria under which flexibility (closer cooperation among like-minded member states) could be used, as governments had agreed to remove the national veto on its use and reduce the number of member states allowed to initiate the procedure.

The Nice Treaty brought the EU and the process of treaty reform into disrepute. When Irish voters rejected the treaty in June 2001, it was difficult to regret the result. The European Council announced only a week later that the EU would enlarge regardless, probably in early 2004. Pressed by other governments and by the Commission, the Irish government badgered voters to approve the treaty in a second referendum in October 2002. Meanwhile, the Convention on the Future of Europe, intended to prepare a more far-reaching round of treaty reform, was meeting in Brussels. As the purpose of the convention was to help reform the EU in light of enlargement, it was hard to understand why the EU put such emphasis on the Nice Treaty. To the relief of the EU establishment and the candidate countries, the Irish endorsed the treaty in the second attempt, thanks to a much higher turnout.

The political legacy of Nice was more enduring than the treaty's institutional provisions. The conduct of the conference soured people's appetite for negotiations of treaty reform using the traditional IGC method. Small member states resented what they saw as the emergence of a more intergovernmental EU dominated by the big member states. Further reform, through necessary, would be difficult to achieve.[14]

The Constitutional Convention
Anticipating the inadequacy of the Nice Treaty, EU leaders included in it a declaration calling for yet another IGC, starting in 2004, to deal with a range of issues such as the democratic deficit, the effectiveness of particular policies, and the status of the Charter of Fundamental Rights, a nonbinding document that EU leaders had endorsed at the Nice summit in December 2000. In December 2001, the European Council decided not only to widen the agenda of the IGC but also to approach it in a different way. Drawing on the method used to draft the Charter of Fundamental Rights, representatives of various national and EU institutions would meet in a convention to prepare the IGC "as broadly and openly as possible." The adoption of the convention method reflected a consensus on the need to diversify participation in the process of treaty reform. The candidate countries would participate, but without a decisionmaking role.[15]

Chirac announced that the chairman would have to be French and proposed Valéry Giscard d'Estaing, the former president. The small countries remembered Giscard's lack of interest in them and dislike of the Commission when he had dominated the European Council in the 1970s, but felt powerless to block his appointment. And so the septuagenarian Giscard, an archdefender of the interests of big countries, came to personify the future of Europe.

The convention, which opened in Brussels in February 2002, soon became known as the Constitutional Convention because of Giscard's intention to draft not simply a new treaty but a constitution for the EU. In reality, the convention could only propose a constitutional treaty (an agreement among sovereign states with constitutional characteristics). The decision to draft a constitutional treaty was mainly symbolic, given that the Court of Justice already interpreted the existing treaties as constitutional texts. Drafting a constitutional treaty was far more than a mere tidying up of the existing treaties, however. For instance, incorporating the Charter of Fundamental Rights would give the EU the equivalent of a Bill of Rights, an important constitutional attribute.

Plenary sessions of the convention were large and unwieldy affairs. Their most striking feature was a palpable sense of Euro-enthusiasm. Delegates drafted hundreds of proposals and amendments. National governments nonetheless made most of the running. Although the purpose of the convention was partly to curb governments' monopoly of treaty reform, discussions in the plenary sessions and in the presidium (the convention's governing body) increasingly reflected national positions as the deadline approached.

The big country–small country divide was bound to resurface in the Constitutional Convention, especially when it addressed contentious institutional questions. Other EU developments in 2003 exacerbated tension between the big and small countries, none more so than the outbreak of the war in Iraq. To add fuel to the fire, French and German disregard for the Stability and Growth Pact, which supposedly underpinned Economic and Monetary Union, alienated many of the other countries in the eurozone.

A joint proposal by France and Germany in January 2003, submitted on the fortieth anniversary of the Franco-German Elysée Treaty, brought the big country–small country divide starkly to the fore, by endorsing a call already made by Britain, France, and Spain for a standing president of the European Council to replace the rotating presidency. Many of the small member states (plus the Commission) immediately cried foul. They feared that the standing president would always come from a big country and that the proposed new position would undermine the influence of the Commission president, traditionally a champion of the small countries.

There was general agreement among all governments that an EU foreign minister should combine and enhance the positions of High Representative for Common Foreign and Security Policy and commissioner for external relations. The same person would chair meetings of a newly configured Foreign Affairs Council and coordinate the Commission's external relations responsibilities. The advent of the elected European Council president and the EU foreign minister would downgrade the rotating presidency, which would be restricted to chairing the General Affairs Council and the sectoral councils.

In return, many of the small countries mounted a fierce rearguard action to scrap the provision in the Nice Treaty that broke the link between the number of member states and the number of commissioners, asserting their right always to nominate a commissioner. With the support of the big countries, however, Giscard pushed through a provision for a college of thirteen commissioners, selected on the basis of equal rotation among member states, plus the Commission president and the combined position of EU foreign minister and Commission vice president. The defenders of one commissioner per member state resolved to fight on in the ensuing IGC.

One of the most heated issues in the Constitutional Convention concerned the modalities of QMV in the Council. Keenly aware of their relative loss of power as a result of enlargement, which had brought and would bring into the EU many more small member states, France and Germany pressed for a new system based on the double majority principle. In future, half the number of member states representing at least 60 percent of the EU's total population would constitute a qualified majority. Such a proposal, coming so soon after the redistribution of votes agreed to at the Nice summit, was further evidence of deep dissatisfaction with the Nice Treaty's institutional reforms. Using their considerable powers of political persuasion, France and Germany succeeded in having the new voting formula included in the convention's Draft Constitutional Treaty.

As the convention proceeded, a noticeable divide emerged between the original Six (the founding member states) and the rest, particularly those about to join in 2004. French and German representatives worked closely together in the convention, giving the appearance of a concerted Franco-German drive, despite differences on a range of issues. Although often on the defensive, the British government's representative was rarely isolated. Nevertheless, Britain stuck rigidly to a number of positions, such as utterly rejecting the use of the word "federal" in the draft treaty. One of the most striking innovations was the inclusion of an "exit clause," an elaborate procedure for a country to withdraw from the EU, intended to nullify the Euroskeptical argument that the EU was a prison from which there was no escape.

Institutional issues were by no means the only sticking points. The question of EU competences preoccupied delegates in early 2003 and demonstrated the difficulty of demarcating EU-level and national powers in a process as politically and historically muddled as European integration. The convention eventually agreed on a short list of exclusive responsibilities (such as monetary policy and trade policy) and a long but not exclusive list of shared responsibilities (ranging from agricultural policy to economic and social cohesion). The EU could take supporting, coordinating, or complementary action in areas such as industry, culture, and civil protection. The limits of EU competences were governed by the principle of conferral by the member states, and the use of competences was governed by the principles of subsidiarity and proportionality.

Reaching agreement on the values and objectives of the EU was relatively easy, apart from an impassioned discussion about whether and how to recognize the EU's religious heritage. It did not go unnoticed that mention of an explicit Christian heritage would hinder (if not prevent) Turkish accession to the EU. In the end, the preamble merely included a reference to Europe's religious "inheritance." Membership in the EU would be open to all European states that respected the EU's values and were committed to promoting them together—hardly clear-cut criteria, either geographically or normatively.

Most delegates wanted to include the Charter of Fundamental Rights in the Constitutional Treaty in order to emphasize the EU's values and possibly increase the EU's appeal to citizens. The British and Irish governments were unenthusiastic, doubting that it would have any effect on public opinion (except perhaps to provide more ammunition to Euroskeptics) and fearing that strict adherence to it would raise business costs.

Bringing the various bits and pieces together and concluding the draft document was a daunting task. Undoubtedly democratic, the convention method was unavoidably awkward. It needed strong leadership to succeed. Giscard was determined to produce a single draft text instead of alternative versions of controversial provisions. He could not hope for unanimity, only for majority support. By emphasizing the convention's historic importance as the deadline of June 2003 approached, Giscard won the approval, grudging or otherwise, of most of the delegates for the final text.

The convention succeeded in producing a single, reasonably understandable (although long) Draft Constitutional Treaty. In one important respect, however, it was a failure: ordinary Europeans seemed to know little and care less about it. Media coverage was sparse, apart from a flurry of alarming articles in the British tabloid press. Even under the best of circumstances, it would have been difficult to interest most citizens in the vagaries of majority voting or other arcane institutional issues. If anything, the convention reinforced a widespread public perception that European integration was driven entirely by elites, for elites.

The Constitutional Treaty

The Constitutional Convention had been convened because of dissatisfaction with the traditional method of treaty reform. Yet under the terms of the existing treaties, governments had to convene an IGC in order to reform the treaties. Far from merely rubber-stamping the Draft Constitutional Treaty, most governments were determined to use the IGC to get a better deal in the definitive treaty. For many small countries, especially those about to join the EU, the IGC was a chance to reclaim the right to representation in the Commission. For Spain and Poland, it was a chance to try to preserve the Nice agreement on voting weights, which was extremely advantageous to them. For their part, France and Germany were determined to scrap the Nice arrangement in favor of the proposed new double majority system.

The IGC began in late 2003. However, the depth of French and Spanish feelings—on opposite sides of the issue—with respect to QMV, together with poor chairmanship of the Council presidency under Italy, caused a breakdown of negotiations in December 2003. Threats by France and Germany to link the outcome of the IGC to the upcoming budget negotiations (by implication cutting funds to Spain and Poland) and to forge ahead with a "core" or "pioneer" group of member states (by implication excluding Spain and Poland) were not helpful.

The incoming Irish presidency lost little time in early 2004 quietly getting the negotiations going again. Changes of government in Spain and Poland (for reasons unrelated to the IGC) improved the chances of success. Wanting to signal a more accommodating policy toward the EU, the two countries' new governments were willing to reach a compromise on the proposed new voting system. Although other issues remained on the table, an agreement on the Constitutional Treaty seemed possible by June 2004.

Altogether, the IGC approved eighty amendments to the Draft Constitutional Treaty. The small countries eventually agreed to a Commission reduced in size, but beginning in 2014. The new double majority was set at 55 percent of the member states and 65 percent of the population, making it easier for countries to form a blocking minority but without allowing the three biggest to do so alone. Overall, the Constitutional Treaty looked much like the convention's draft document, though advocates of deeper integration complained that many of the changes were retrograde steps.

Given the strength of Euroskepticism, or simply of indifference toward the EU, the fate of the Constitutional Treaty was highly uncertain. Ratification by each member state, especially by those countries holding referendums, could not be taken for granted. Not that the EU was in danger of falling apart without it. Strictly speaking, the Constitutional Treaty was desirable but not essential. Even with the Constitutional Treaty in place, strong national interests, a willful EP, and a weak Commission would continue to impair the EU's effectiveness.

France could have ratified the treaty on the basis of a vote in parliament, but Chirac called for a nonbinding yet politically crucial referendum, which took place in May 2005. French fears of economic integration, seen by many as a form of globalization, fueled opposition. French workers fretted about an influx of cheap labor from the new member states, personified by the mythical

Polish plumber. Nor did the possibility of eventual Turkish accession, hugely unpopular in France, help the treaty's chances. Not surprisingly, a majority of voters (55 percent) rejected the treaty.

The outcome of the referendum in the Netherlands four days later was 62 percent against. Opposition in Holland, which had never held a national referendum on any issue, had crystallized around the unpopularity of the government, resentment of the country's large contribution to the EU budget, and concerns about the loss of national identity. In Holland as in France, most of the dissatisfaction had little to do with the treaty itself. Clearly, the referendums had provided an opportunity for voters to express deep dissatisfaction with developments in their own countries and in the EU.

Although Spain had already ratified by means of a referendum, and several other countries had gone ahead with ratification mostly by means of votes in national parliament, the French and Dutch results were devastating. Instead of wrapping up EU-wide ratification by the end of 2006, the European Council agreed in June 2005 to consign the Constitutional Treaty to a yearlong "period of reflection."[16]

Despite the fate of the Constitutional Treaty and despite statements by politicians to the contrary, the EU was hardly in crisis. Day-to-day decision-making continued unabated. Contrary to prevailing expectations, British prime minister Tony Blair, then in the Council presidency, secured agreement in December 2005 for a new financial framework. The EU and the process of European integration were nonetheless in the doldrums. Yet the results of the referendums were a symptom, not a cause, of the malaise. The underlying problem was growing public dissatisfaction with the EU, compounded by national governments that were apt to exonerate themselves and blame the Commission, the European Court of Justice, and "Brussels" generally for everything from the constraints of the Stability and Growth Pact to tough competition policy rules, regardless of the reasons for those measures. To the extent that the EU was handicapped operationally in 2005 and might remain so for the foreseeable future, the underlying cause was political posturing on the part of national governments rather than institutional sclerosis.

The Lisbon Treaty

As the referendum campaigns receded, public opinion throughout the EU was supremely indifferent to the fate of the Constitutional Treaty. By contrast, most politicians and officials involved in EU affairs were loath to let the matter drop. Some national leaders reiterated oft-heard calls for a "core group," a "pioneer group," or an "avant-garde" of member states to press ahead in areas such as internal security, foreign policy, and defense. The impracticability of such proposals and opposition from most of the newer member states, as well as from Germany, raised the temperature of the constitutional debate.

The best hope for supporters of the treaty was to put old wine in a new bottle. First they would need to call the Constitutional Treaty something else. For

Finland's foreign minister, changing the name would be a "minor point," as "everyone agrees it was a mistake to call it a constitution."[17] Germany's foreign minister pointed out that his country's constitution was called the "Basic Law"; perhaps the EU's constitution could be called the "Fundamental Treaty"?

The European Council agreed in June 2006 to adopt a "twin track" approach: on the one hand, using existing opportunities to deliver a "Europe of results"; on the other, exploring the possibility of saving parts of the Constitutional Treaty, under a new name.[18] Hopes for a successful second track rose toward the end of 2006, thanks to German chancellor Angela Merkel's devotion to the issue and promise to make it a centerpiece of her country's Council presidency in the first half of 2007.

Despite some national leaders' serious misgivings about the Constitutional Treaty, no government stood in the way of relaunching the negotiations on treaty reform. Moreover, all agreed that the requisite IGC should be as short and swift as possible. To that end, Germany decided in effect to conduct the bulk of the negotiations during its Council presidency, before the IGC proper would begin later in the year under the Portuguese presidency.

Apart from diplomatic heft, the key to Germany's success was secrecy and speed. German officials sounded out opinion in other national capitals and ascertained the limits of each country's negotiating position. At the same time, Merkel held bilateral meetings with fellow leaders, hoping to reach agreement on a mandate for the IGC, leaving the IGC proper to wrap up the technical details.

The British, Dutch, and French governments wanted to change the Constitutional Treaty only in ways that would avoid having to hold new referendums. The British and Dutch found the solution: the new IGC would amend the existing treaties on the basis of most of the changes introduced in the Constitutional Treaty, not replace them with a new treaty. Governments could therefore claim that a referendum was unnecessary, given that changes to the existing treaties had happened in the past without recourse to a referendum.

In view of the virulence of Euroskepticism in the United Kingdom, Blair felt it necessary to declare a number of "red lines" or unalterable demands. These included removing the Charter of Fundamental Rights from the treaty text; dropping the title "foreign minister" from the proposed new Council/ Commission position; and retaining national control of foreign policy, defense policy, social security, and civil law. In general, Britain wanted the revised treaties to give the EU as unconstitutional and unstatelike an appearance as possible.

The presidential election campaign in France coincided with the beginning of the informal treaty renegotiations. Nicolas Sarkozy, the leading contender in the race, declared that he would not put a revised treaty to a second referendum. Elected in May 2007, Sarkozy signaled a vigorous approach to the constitutional question and to a variety of policy issues, announcing in his first speech as president-elect that "France is back in Europe."[19]

By contrast, Prime Minister Jarosław Kaczyński and President Lech Kaczyński of Poland insisted on reopening the "double majority" formula for QMV contained in the Constitutional Treaty. Understandably, Poland wanted to retain the Nice arrangement whereby Poland's share of the total number of Council votes almost equaled Germany's.

The German presidency circulated a working paper covering all the proposed changes days before the June 2007 summit opened. The remaining unresolved issues included "European symbols" (whether the new treaty should retain references to the EU flag and anthem, and celebration of Schuman Day); acknowledgment of the primacy of EC law, which Britain found objectionable but most other governments thought commonplace; where to put the Charter of Fundamental Rights; precise language on the delimitation of competences; and the exact role of national parliaments. The presidency set the question of QMV to one side as a particularly tricky issue. As expected, the presidency also proposed replacing the Constitutional Treaty with a new treaty that would amend the existing treaties—the Treaty on European Union and the Treaty Establishing the European Community, which would be renamed the Treaty on the Functioning of the European Union.

The June 2007 summit—Blair's last, after ten years in office—was a fractious affair. Those countries that had ratified the Constitutional Treaty tried to hold the line; the referendum-constrained countries pushed for cosmetic more than substantive changes; and Poland stuck to its guns on majority voting. Defenders of the Constitutional Treaty made many concessions to accommodate the other member states, including protecting Britain's red lines with a number of formal opt-outs. By the end of the second day, only the issue of QMV remained unresolved. Under intense pressure from almost every national leader, the Kaczyński brothers finally dropped their opposition to the double majority system in return for an agreement to delay its entry into force until 2014.[20]

EU leaders were hugely relieved with the outcome. It seemed as if all the contentious questions had been resolved and that the ensuing IGC would entail merely producing a legally clean text. Other than in Ireland, whose constitution mandates a referendum on EU treaty change, there would not be any referendums. Although the outcome of the referendum in Ireland could not be guaranteed, EU leaders were confident of success. The long constitutional saga was nearly over.

Procedurally, the 2007 intergovernmental conference appeared to resemble any other. In fact, it was unprecedented in that the work of the IGC fell mostly on the shoulders of a technical group of legal experts, who went through the presidency's draft treaty article by article, line by line, eventually producing a definitive version. Their work was uncontroversial but highly complicated, especially because of the need to accommodate various opt-outs and opt-ins.

Nevertheless, a summit held in October 2007 to conclude the IGC was not without drama. A number of touchy issues had arisen since the previous summit.

Foremost among them was yet another Polish demand for clarification of the provisions on QMV. Eventually the European Council found a form of words with which everyone could live.[21] With an election scheduled for the weekend of the summit, and public opinion turning strongly against the antics of the Kaczyński brothers, the Polish government was disinclined to put up its usual fight. Fundamentally, Poland was and would remain deeply attached to the EU. "Solidarity," a word with special resonance in Polish history, had become a code-word used by EU politicians and officials to alert Warsaw to the danger of alienating other member states. The resounding victory in the election of the opposition Civic Platform, which stood largely on a pro-EU ticket, bears out the point.

National leaders signed the new treaty in Lisbon in December 2007. Much to their dismay, the result of the Irish referendum, held in June 2008, was 54 percent against. Post-referendum opinion polls identified several reasons for the outcome, including lack of knowledge or understanding of the treaty, nebulous concerns about Irish identity, apprehension that the alleged militarization of the EU would put an end to Irish neutrality, and fear that the EU would somehow undermine Ireland's constitutional prohibition of abortion. Another concern was loss of influence and representation in Brussels because of a reduction in the Commission's size—a reduction already mandated by the Nice Treaty. Underlying everything was the government's unpopularity. Moreover, it was far harder to argue for than against the Lisbon Treaty, especially in short sound-bites. Under the circumstances, "If in doubt, vote no" seemed like good advice.[22]

For most EU leaders, the Irish result was yet another obstacle to a treaty reform that they were determined to see through. They would have to find a way to remove the Irish obstacle; prevent contagion to other "high-risk" countries, such as Britain, the Czech Republic, and Poland; and ensure implementation of the treaty as soon as possible. EU leaders were careful to say that they would not press the Irish government to find a solution, but behind the scenes the Irish government faced unrelenting pressure.

A growing realization among political and business elites that the June 2008 referendum result was a disaster for Ireland helped concentrate the government's mind. Spurious though many of the arguments against Lisbon appeared to be, the Irish government had no choice but to attempt to change the opinions of as many naysayers as possible by getting binding guarantees from the EU to allay their concerns. If the European Council would agree to legally binding language and agree also to retain one commissioner per member state, the government would hold a second referendum.

The "roadmap" involved a series of carefully choreographed steps. Thus the European Council in December 2008 agreed that it would decide in due course, "provided the Lisbon Treaty enters into force," to retain the Commission's size at one commissioner from each member state. The European Council also "carefully note[d] the other concerns of the Irish people" and, provided the Irish government committed itself to "seeking ratification of the Treaty of Lisbon by the end of the term of the current Commission [October 2009]," agreed that those concerns would "be addressed to the mutual satisfaction of Ireland and the other Member States."[23] Details of the special protocol for Ireland, a largely meaningless form of words intended to facilitate holding a second referendum—and ensure a successful outcome—were agreed to by the European Council in June 2009.[24] Soon afterward, the Irish government announced that the referendum would take place in October 2009.

By that time, prospects for a favorable outcome had improved considerably, thanks to the global economic crisis, which hit Ireland particularly hard. Although ratifying the Lisbon Treaty would not make a material difference to Ireland's economic plight, it would provide some comfort by affirming the country's good fortune to be in a relatively safe port—the eurozone—during a fierce financial storm. As expected, this time around the Lisbon Treaty passed by a majority of 67 percent, with a 59 percent turnout.

Ireland was not the only country not to have ratified the treaty before the end of 2009. Despite parliamentary approval, the Czech Republic was stymied by the refusal of its president, Václav Klaus, an ardent Euroskeptic, to sign the instrument of ratification until the last possible moment. Klaus raised an implausible eleventh-hour concern that the treaty could open the way for property claims by ethnic Germans expelled from Czechoslovakia after World War II. EU leaders appeased Klaus by giving the Czech Republic an opt-out from the Charter of Fundamental Rights. Having milked the ratification procedure for all it was worth, Klaus finally signed in November 2009, allowing the treaty to come into effect in December.

Germany's parliament had voted in good time to ratify the treaty, but the president was unable to sign the instrument of ratification pending a ruling by the country's constitutional court on the compatibility of the treaty with Germany's Basic Law. The court finally ruled in June 2009 that the Lisbon Treaty was indeed compatible, subject to a change in German law on the role of parliament in EU decisionmaking. Although proponents of the treaty breathed a sigh of relief, a closer look at the lengthy court ruling revealed that it raised several red flags about the direction of European integration. In particular, the court emphasized the limits of EU competence and the existence of a "structured democratic deficit" that only national parliaments, not the EP, could possibly close.[25] If anything, the ruling should have reassured Euroskeptics as to the limits of the Lisbon Treaty and the process of European integration.

Significance of the Lisbon Treaty and the Treaty Reform Process

Although the founding treaties, as amended by the Lisbon Treaty, are long, complicated, and difficult to read, the EU that they describe is, in many respects, more coherent and comprehensible than the old EU. The treaty unequivocally states that the EU is rooted in democracy, the rule of law, and respect for human rights and fundamental freedoms; its organizing principles are conferred powers, subsidiarity, proportionality, and loyal cooperation among member states; and its competences vis-à-vis national competences—exclusive, shared, or supporting—are clearly spelled out. The pillar structure is gone, but different decisionmaking procedures remain for foreign and security policy. The confusing distinction between "Union" and "Community" is abolished, with the former word replacing the latter throughout the new text. The EU finally acquired legal personality.

Overall, the Lisbon Treaty strikes a reasonable balance between institutional efficiency and democratic legitimacy. The double majority system for QMV is more equitable than its predecessor, which was based on a relatively arbitrary allocation of votes per member state. The EP, the EU's only directly elected body, has additional budgetary authority and a greater legislative role. Keeping the size of the Commission at one commissioner per member state—a late revision brought about by Ireland's initial rejection of the treaty—is arguably good for the EU. Better to have a Commission in which every country is represented than a smaller Commission from which, at any given time, some countries are bound to feel alienated.

The institutional innovations in the treaty portend an improvement in the effectiveness of EU policy, especially in external relations and JHA. The treaty recasts the balance among the institutions, with the European Council clearly in the ascendant. Apart from being given responsibility for decisionmaking in specific, politically sensitive areas other than lawmaking, the creation of the new office of standing president, elected by the European Council's members for a period of up to five years, is particularly significant for the institution's future. Although the treaty says little about the powers or prerogatives of the new office, experience suggests that it will evolve into a politically important post. In the long run, it could overshadow the Commission presidency, to the detriment of the Commission as a whole. Overall, the Lisbon Treaty maintains and reinforces the recent trend within the EU toward the emergence of a commanding European Council, a confident Council and Parliament sharing legislative responsibility, and a politically constrained Commission.

Valuable though many of the treaty reforms may be, they have further soured public sentiment on the EU. It seems fair to ask whether the Constitutional Treaty and its successor were worth the trials and tribulations of the prolonged reform process. What did the Constitutional Convention contribute? Undoubtedly it provided a wider diversity of views and greater institutional representation than is the case with IGCs. Yet the content of the Constitutional Treaty could perhaps have been negotiated as easily and more expeditiously in a conference of the kind that resulted in previous treaty reforms. Had a wholesale replacement of the existing treaties been negotiated in 2002–2003 exclusively in an IGC rather than first discussed in the convention, national governments might never have included in their version of a new, post-Nice treaty the words and symbols that many Europeans found so objectionable in the Constitutional Treaty.

It is debatable whether the convention provided more legitimacy for the treaty reform process.[26] Undoubtedly, it failed to generate any public interest or support. If anything, reaction to the Constitutional Treaty confirmed the impression that the permissive consensus in public attitudes toward the EU is long gone. When asked about European integration in opinion polls, Europeans were generally indifferent or, at best, mildly supportive. In a referendum, however, Euroskeptics could easily exploit general dissatisfaction with the EU to derail the proposed amendments.

Despite numerous elections in the EU during the commotion over the Constitutional and Lisbon treaties, only in Britain (where an election was not held, but where a change of leadership took place on 2007) and in Poland (where the EU became a major issue in the October 2007 election) did the issue of treaty reform resonate domestically. Governments in other countries were not as sensitive to, and therefore not as constrained by, domestic opinion on EU issues. Nevertheless, each government assessed the proposed treaty changes on the basis of their likely domestic impact; national influence, power, and prestige; and the legitimacy and efficiency of the EU. The outcome (the Lisbon Treaty) had to be positive-sum—beneficial for the EU as well as for each member state. At the very least it had to be presented, by the EU and its member states, as mutually beneficial.

Whatever else, the treaty text, including the numerous protocols, declarations, and statements attached to it, testifies to the convoluted nature of European integration. Every step in the process of building the EU has required concessions and compromises on the part of national governments responsive to domestic pressures and eager to nudge the European project in a preferred direction. Like every preceding treaty, the Lisbon Treaty reflects the art of the possible at a particular moment in EU history. Unlike previous treaty changes, it will have to last for a long time: national governments have lost their appetites and European publics have lost their patience for further treaty reform.

■ The Financial Crisis and Recession

In the summer of 2007, as EU leaders grappled with the future of the Constitutional Treaty, the EU economy seemed to be in fine shape. Economic performance varied greatly from country to country, ranging from tigerlike growth in Ireland and Estonia, to solid growth in Sweden, to respectable growth in Germany. In general, productivity was rising, GDP growing, and unemployment falling throughout the EU. Much to the delight of many Europeans, the combined economic growth of the eurozone was set to surpass that of the United States.

The financial news from across the Atlantic, where severe problems with mortgage-backed securities were beginning to cause major anxieties in money and credit markets, added to the sense of satisfaction enveloping many Europeans. So-called sub-prime mortgages—property loans given to applicants with little or no creditworthiness—were at the heart of the looming US crisis. Most Europeans considered such loans reckless and quintessentially American. The prevailing European attitude is best described by the German word *Schadenfreude:* malicious pleasure in someone else's misfortune.

Given the interconnectedness of global financial markets, however, Europe could hardly emerge unscathed from developments in the United States. Even if American "casino capitalism" was squarely to blame and European banks were beyond reproach, the EU was bound to suffer some side effects. In fact, many European banks had also been handing out easy loans and had participated enthusiastically in the global market for mortgage-backed securities. German banks, it soon transpired, were among the worst offenders.

Impact on the EU

The first major manifestation in Europe of the global crisis came in September 2007, in Britain, whose economic model resembled that of the United States more closely than those of continental European countries. Finance ministers first discussed the situation at a meeting of Ecofin in October. National leaders discussed it in the European Council in December, where they concluded optimistically "that macroeconomic fundamentals in the EU are strong and that sustained economic growth is expected."[27] In fact, EU leaders were far from sanguine. Chafing at the constraints of having to sit around the table with all twenty-seven national leaders plus the Commission president, British prime minister Gordon Brown called for a mini-summit of the Group of Four (G4: Britain, France, Italy, and Germany) at the end of January 2008.

As the mini-summit revealed, opinions among the G4 differed over how to respond to the crisis. President Nicolas Sarkozy wanted coordinated government intervention in EU financial markets, with better regulation and stronger supervision of financial institutions. He also wanted the EU's leading member states to take the lead in reshaping the international financial architecture. Brown acknowledged the need for greater intervention and supervision, but not to the extent that Sarkozy desired. Angela Merkel seemed uncertain of herself and, believing that Germany could weather the storm, was disinclined to adopt an ambitious agenda.

There was no coordinated follow-up to the mini-summit. Instead, as the crisis intensified in the United States and continued to spread throughout

Europe, national governments acted alone. For the eurozone countries, monetary policy was in the hands of the European Central Bank, which kept interest rates high, fearing inflation more than economic recession. In the other member states, central banks were independent or shadowed the ECB. The main instruments available to governments, therefore, were bank bailouts, recapitalization schemes, and fiscal stimulus packages. All were expensive and, if implemented separately in a space as tightly integrated as the EU, were unlikely to be fully effective. There was a glaring need for coordination, which the Commission seemed unwilling and the Council presidency (Slovenia in the first half of 2008) unable to provide.

Complacency finally gave way to alarm in summer 2008, as the extent of the damage in Europe became more apparent. Britain, with a large, lightly regulated financial sector and a recent housing boom, was in dire economic straits. The housing bubbles had burst in Ireland, Latvia, and Spain. Hungary, burdened by a big budget deficit, was another early victim. Even Germany, known for its prudence and fiscal rectitude, was not immune from the global crisis. German banks had invested heavily in risky sub-prime products, while German manufacturers were losing export orders. As exports rather than domestic consumption drove the German economy, which in turn drove the combined eurozone economy, this was a potentially disastrous development. France, by contrast, with a relatively small export sector, strong banks, and robust domestic demand, was doing quite well.

The enormity of the crisis became fully apparent in September 2008 with the sudden collapse of Lehman Brothers, the giant US-based global financial services firm. Its fall spread a wave of panic and a drastic drop in the value of stocks that reached far beyond Wall Street. European governments' piecemeal approach to the escalating crisis, now spreading rapidly into the "real economy," was unsustainable. The French presidency and the Commission finally began to act.

Sarkozy was in his element. Here was a chance to restructure the EU's financial framework, showcase the French economic model, and put France (and himself) at the forefront of international affairs. What followed was the most intensive period of high-level diplomacy in the history of the EU, with a host of summits among various combinations of national leaders, plus an informal EU-US summit, in the month of October alone. The summits showed clearly that the differences between the EU's top three national leaders (Brown, Merkel, and Sarkozy), which had come to light at the beginning of the year, were still unresolved.

Sarkozy wanted a European fund to rescue failing banks; Merkel was skeptical, knowing that Germany would be expected to foot the bill. Sarkozy wanted the ECB to lower interest rates (a matter over which national governments have no control) and reiterated his fondness for some form of economic government for the eurozone; Merkel preferred high interest rates if the alternative risked stoking inflation, but respected the independence of the ECB. Sarkozy again emphasized the importance of tough regulation of financial markets; Brown conceded that regulations would have to be tightened but wanted national bodies, not European institutions, to do the tightening.

Regardless of these differences, everyone agreed that there were two related fronts in the fight for financial stability and economic recovery, one regional (within the EU) and the other global, under the auspices of the Group of 20 (G20), a broader, more representative grouping of countries from around the world than the Group of Eight (G8). Merkel agreed to the idea, but held out against a specific EU fund to ensure liquidity for financial institutions. Officials from the eurozone finance ministries, the Commission, and the ECB worked out the details. At a eurozone summit on October 12, EU leaders adopted the plan and pledged "to act together in a decisive and comprehensive way in order to restore confidence and proper functioning of the financial system, aiming at restoring appropriate and efficient financing conditions for the economy."[28] The European Council endorsed the plan at its meeting in Brussels a week later.

Prodded by Sarkozy, who remained firmly in charge of the EU's recovery efforts, the Commission finally swung into action. José Manuel Barroso became the other public face of the concerted European response. By virtue of having responsibility for policing the single market, largely through competition policy and threats of taking member states to court, and for monitoring the Stability and Growth Pact, the mechanism for fiscal policy coordination among eurozone members, the Commission wanted to hold the line against national governments that might be tempted to skirt the rules. Yet by sticking to the letter of the law, the Commission risked alienating national governments that were disregarding competition policy rules or running an excessive budget deficit because of dire economic circumstances. The Commission had to strike a balance between enforcement and leniency, compassion and credibility. In other words, it had to be flexible.

Availing of the consensus among national governments on the need to improve financial controls and banking supervision in the EU, the Commission proposed a number of new measures, such as strengthening bank capital requirements and regulating credit rating agencies. The Commission also looked into the activities of hedge funds and private equity, which were being demonized for their alleged contributions to the crisis. Barroso established a high-level group to review the crisis more broadly and recommend more effective European and global supervision for financial institutions.

These steps did not mollify critics, notably on the left, who complained that the Commission was doing too little, too late. A self-professed neoliberal, at least until the crisis struck, Barroso became a lightning rod for criticism of the Commission's alleged ineffectualness. The fact that Barroso was known to be courting a second term as president put him at a disadvantage. Partly to bolster his image and restore confidence in the Commission, Barroso coordinated work on an economic recovery plan for growth and jobs. Announced in late November 2008, the plan was really a repackaging of existing EU measures, such as more lending, especially to small and medium-sized businesses, by the European Investment Bank and quicker disbursement to the poorer member states of social policy and regional policy funds, together with a list of national stimulus spending, which the Commission promised to view leniently with regard to conformity with various EU rules. Together, the existing and anticipated measures would amount to 1.5 percent of the member states' combined GDP over a two-year period (about €200 billion). This was a substantial sum of money by any standard, but far less than US stimulus spending (5.5 percent of GDP).

Three issues dominated the December 2008 European Council: the proposed Economic Recovery Plan, the ongoing discussions with Ireland about ratification of the Lisbon Treaty, and a complicated package of measures on energy and climate change. The recovery plan was the least contentious, with Sarkozy and Merkel having endorsed it in a joint letter published in two of the leading French and German newspapers. Nevertheless, the two leaders continued to disagree on responses to the deepening economic crisis. Sarkozy was unhappy with Germany's modest stimulus spending and with Merkel's refusal to reduce Germany's rate of value-added tax. Merkel thought Sarkozy profligate and insufficiently alert to the danger of deep budget deficits. Nevertheless, they overcame their differences and ushered the plan through the European Council.

While national leaders made an impressive display of unity in the European Council, internationally the crisis gave them an opportunity to cast the EU as a leader of the global reform effort and a savior of the rickety financial system. In global financial circles, Brown was better known and regarded than Sarkozy. Indeed, Brown had already become a key participant in discussions about global financial reform. Being in the Council presidency, however, Sarkozy had a powerful platform from which to project himself. Immediately after the meeting of the European Council in mid-October 2008, Sarkozy, with Barroso in tow, went to the United States to confer with President George W. Bush on resolving the global crisis and redesigning the international financial system. Reporting to the EP on his return, an exuberant Sarkozy described his visit as a triumph for the EU and as evidence of the EU's ability to shape the international system: "Europe must uphold the idea of recasting international capitalism. . . . The world needs Europe to be proactive. If it has things to say, it should say so."[29]

The international track of the EU's reform efforts bore fruit in November 2008 in the first meeting of the Group of 20, representing the world's major economies, at the level of heads of state and government. Going beyond the G8, which included only the developed countries, the G20 encompassed important emerging economies such as China and India and included the EU as an entity, represented by the Commission president. Leaders of the EU's G4, plus the Commission president, would therefore participate in the G20. Although EU attendance at the G20 belies the EU's self-image as a unitary actor on the international stage, at least the EU deserves credit for promoting a truly global dialogue on financial and economic problems of concern to every country with a stake in the system.

By the end of 2008, the launch of the Economic Recovery Plan and, to a lesser extent, the G20 process seemed to indicate the effectiveness of the EU in the face of a withering financial crisis. Yet the EU was by no means out of the woods. The extent of the downturn became fully apparent in early 2009 and put EU solidarity sorely to the test. Hard-hit countries in Central and Eastern Europe, with little money to spend on economic recovery and no prospect in the near future of entering the eurozone, felt increasingly resentful. Sarkozy's threat to support French car-makers only on condition that they repatriate their manufacturing plants from the Czech Republic was such an egregious example of economic nationalism that even Barroso felt obliged to complain.

Acutely aware of the rising resentment among the new member states, the Polish prime minister invited the leaders of the Central and Eastern European countries to meet just before the opening of yet another extraordinary EU summit, on March 1, to discuss the deteriorating financial and economic situation. This was the only time during the crisis that the Central and Eastern European countries met as a bloc in the EU. They quickly realized that they had little in common. Some, like Poland and the Czech Republic, were faring relatively well in the economic crisis; others were floundering (by March 2009 the danger of financial collapse in Hungary and Latvia was acute). It was not in the interests of the better-off countries to be lumped into a bloc with the worst cases.

At the extraordinary summit of the EU27 later that day, national leaders once again pledged "to act together in a coordinated manner, within the framework of the single market and EMU."[30] In other words, governments should avoid protectionism and respect the strictures of the Stability and Growth Pact. In the name of EU solidarity, Hungary called for massive financial assistance to recapitalize banks in Central and Eastern Europe and reschedule foreign currency debt. Merkel was not amused. Rather than establish a new EU fund to help countries in trouble partly because of their own irresponsibility, she favored intervention by the International Monetary Fund (IMF) and using an existing EU instrument to provide balance-of-payments support on a case-by-case basis to eligible non-eurozone countries.

EU leaders met again two weeks later at their regular March summit, which traditionally addresses mostly economic issues. There they agreed to contribute an additional €75 billion to the IMF, increase to €50 billion the size of the EU instrument for balance-of-payments support, and allocate an additional €5 billion from unused money in the current EU budget to energy and infrastructure projects. The decision to spend the unused €5 billion, instead of returning it to the member states, did not sit easily with the net contributors to the EU budget, including Germany. This was further evidence of the bitterness of budgetary discussions within the EU as well as the parsimoniousness of Germany and other wealthy states when it came to helping less well-off countries during the economic downturn.

Disputes over unilateral responses to the crisis arose spectacularly in spring 2009 when US car-maker General Motors, facing imminent bankruptcy, sought to divest itself of Opel, its European subsidiary. Opel had operations in several countries, including four factories in Germany. This prompted the German government, through generous provision of state subsidies, to ensure that the new owner of Opel would protect jobs in Germany. The Belgian government, which was equally concerned about keeping Opel jobs in Belgium but which lacked Germany's clout and deep pockets, was incensed; the prime minister went so far as to accuse Germany of breaking EU law.

It looked again as if the EU were in considerable disarray. In fact, the worst appeared to be over, at least until the acceleration of the Greek sovereign debt crisis in early 2010. By summer 2009 the financial system was stabilizing and the rate of economic decline slowing, although unemployment would remain stubbornly high for many months ahead.

With the economic clouds still dark but not as ominous as three months earlier, national leaders made a special effort at the June 2009 summit to present a united front. It helped that they were able to endorse a report on financial supervision in the EU that had been released in February. The report called for a new regulatory agenda, stronger supervision, and effective crisis management procedures. The devil, of course, was in the details. For instance, the report called for two new bodies at the EU level, the European Systemic Risk Council, to be set up under the auspices and with the logistical support of the ECB, and the European System of Financial Supervisors. National leaders were happy to approve these recommendations, but Brown, highly protective of national prerogatives in the areas of banking and finance, made it clear that detailed plans to flesh out the new bodies could be difficult to agree on.

Nevertheless, toward the end of 2009, national leaders were closer together on the broad outlines of the financial and economic challenges facing the EU than at any time in the previous two years. They had also overcome a rift with the United States. In the run-up to the second G20 summit, in London in April 2009, US officials complained that the EU was not doing enough to end the global recession, specifically through stimulus spending. EU officials countered that although their Economic Recovery Plan amounted to only half of all US stimulus spending, it did not include so-called automatic stabilizers— unemployment and other benefits that cushion the effects of sudden shock. Such benefits are far more generous in Europe than in the United States—

amounting to about €200 billion. Barack Obama and Angela Merkel, one of the few European leaders not to have fallen for the new US president's charm, became the leading protagonists of this transatlantic spat. Sarkozy swung behind Merkel, mostly because he wanted to ensure her support at the G20 in pushing for better global regulation of financial services. Obama and Merkel agreed to disagree at the G20 summit and this moment of EU-US friction passed, at least on the question of fighting the economic recession.

Implications for the EU

Given the different characteristics and performances of Europe's economies, it is not surprising that the effect of the crisis was so variable, ranging from the sudden demise of Ireland's Celtic Tiger, to near–financial collapse in Latvia and Hungary, to a relatively mild shock in France. The crisis exposed serious vulnerabilities in Germany, notably the weakness of the Landesbanken (independent state banks) and overreliance on exports for economic growth.

The crisis also demonstrated the fragility of the single market and EMU. The tendency on the part of national governments to protect their own banks and industries threatened to pull the single market apart. Similarly, the rapid deterioration of public finances in the eurozone undermined the credibility of the Stability and Growth Pact, the fiscal foundation of EMU. The fact that the value of the euro continued to rise against the dollar until November 2009, when fallout from Greece's precarious financial situation upset the markets, reflected global concerns about the long-term weakness of the US economy rather than confidence in the long-term strength of the eurozone economies.

Yet governments' behavior reflects the political realities in Europe. People look to their national capitals, not to Brussels, for solutions to pressing socioeconomic problems. Politicians would have been foolhardy to dismiss calls for national action by claiming that their hands were tied by EU competition policy or the budget deficit threshold of the Stability and Growth Pact. They had to meet pressing national needs within an EU structure that is little liked or understood by citizens, despite the tangible benefits of the single market and the obvious convenience of the single currency. Under the circumstances, most governments managed to strike a reasonable balance between national and European interests, or at least did not blame Brussels unduly for constraining their freedom of maneuver. The high and varied number of summits during the crisis demonstrated national leaders' appreciation of the importance of EU cooperation while also giving them an opportunity to let off steam.

Politicians always keep an eye on the next election. The most important looming election during the crisis was in Germany, where Merkel's Christian Democratic Party was locked in a coalition government with its Social Democratic rivals. The EP elections of June 2009 were seen in Germany as a forerunner of the September 2009 federal election and were an opportunity everywhere in the EU to gauge voters' reactions to governments' handling of the crisis. The results showed that voters punished governing parties deemed to have contributed to or mishandled the crisis, regardless of a party's ideological hue. In Germany, a majority of voters preferred the Christian Democrats' stewardship of the economy.

The way in which the crisis played out politically underscores the point that national governments are the decisive actors. The EU does not have responsibility for fiscal policy. Stimulus packages, whether in the form of subsidies or automatic stabilizers, can come only from national budgets. Of course national governments try to coordinate such decisions within the EU and especially in the eurozone. But the institutions that manage fiscal policy coordination in the EU—Ecofin (the council of finance ministers), the Eurogroup (finance ministers of countries in the eurozone), and the European Council—influence the direction of national policy without dictating it. When times are tough, governments will not put policy coordination ahead of political survival and national recovery.

Apart from the ECB, whose role is examined in Chapter 13, the EU institutions most directly involved in the crisis were the European Council and the Commission. Once again, the crisis showed that when the political stakes are high, only the European Council, which brings national leaders together, is able to move the EU forward. The European Council was well served by the French presidency in the second half of 2008 because Sarkozy appreciated the importance of the EU dimension to the crisis and, as president of a big, resourceful member state, was able to get things done. The succeeding Czech presidency was not only hobbled by domestic politics but also lacked the clout necessary to lead the European Council. The variable performance of Council presidencies during the crisis may have strengthened the appeal of a standing European Council president, as called for in the Lisbon Treaty. But had the Lisbon Treaty been in effect at the time, would Sarkozy—the egomaniacal leader of a powerful member state—have allowed himself to be upstaged by Herman Van Rompuy, the first elected president of the European Council?

The crisis also showed the difficulty of running the European Council effectively in an EU of twenty-seven member states. On a number of occasions, a few national leaders got together in smaller summits, notably of the G4, sometimes with Spain and the Netherlands and always with the Commission president. Having worked out a common position, these leaders were able to foist their views onto the other national leaders at the next meeting of the European Council. In theory, all countries are equal in the EU; in practice, when it comes to economics and finance, not to mention security and defense, the big countries remain more equal than the others.

Among the big countries, France and Germany predominate. The crisis was another test of their relationship and another opportunity for observers to lament the demise of the Franco-German tandem. Yet once again, despite personal differences (Merkel and Sarkozy could hardly have been less alike) and policy preferences (Germany is deeply averse to deficit spending, while France is comfortable with public borrowing), the two countries pulled together and nudged the EU in the direction of their choice. The effectiveness of the Franco-German partnership may have diminished in the enlarged EU, especially in the absence of a project as compelling as the single market or monetary union, but it remains a formidable force.

What more could the Commission have done and what could it have done better? Much of the criticism of the Commission focused on Barroso, who seemed curiously inactive as the crisis unfolded. He was not the only EU leader to underestimate the severity of the crisis, however. Merkel was similarly detached at the outset. Once roused to action, Barroso led a robust response within the constraints that the Commission faces with respect to fiscal and macroeconomic policy. In truth, the Commission president's most useful role is to push for concerted national action, using the bully pulpit of the presidency and participation in the European Council. Barroso could hardly have taken center stage from Sarkozy, especially when the French president was also president of the European Council.

The crisis left the EU economically weaker. Growth stumbled and in some countries went into reverse; unemployment—a persistent curse in EU member states—increased dramatically; and public finances deteriorated sharply, especially in Greece, Portugal, and Spain. By late 2009 even France had lost some of its appetite for deficit spending and Germany had passed a constitutional amendment in effect requiring a balanced budget by 2016. One cost of the crisis was an erosion of public and political support for the kinds of reforms, such as labor market liberalization in some countries, necessary to underpin sustained growth and employment. Many EU countries are facing an equally grave but less dramatic demographic challenge, which is driving demand for expensive entitlements, such as health care and pensions, while diminishing the supply of revenue needed to fund them. The fallout from the financial crisis makes it even less likely that national governments will respond adequately to the need for structural reform.

Joschka Fischer, who launched the debate on the future of Europe at the beginning of the decade, lamented in March 2009 that "the global economic crisis is relentlessly laying bare the EU's flaws and limitations. Indeed, what Europe lost, first and foremost, with the rejection of the Constitutional Treaty is now obvious: its faith in itself and its common future. . . . [Europe] threatens to revert to the national egoism and protectionism of the past."[31] Fischer's alarm may reflect his bitterness with what eventually emerged from the treaty reform process. Undoubtedly, European integration has a long way to go—if the destination is a federal Europe. A more realistic appraisal of the EU and of its response to the financial crisis is that European integration has already come a long way, given the resilience of nation-states in the global political system and the immense difficulty of pooling sovereignty in supranational organizations.

■ **Notes**

1. See Michael Baun, *A Wider Europe: The Process and Politics of European Union Enlargement* (Lanham: Rowman and Littlefield, 2000); Marise Cremona, ed., *The Enlargement of the European Union* (Oxford: Oxford University Press, 2003); and Wade Jacoby, *The Enlargement of the European Union and NATO: Ordering from the Menu in Central Europe* (Cambridge: Cambridge University Press, 2006).

2. See John Pinder, *The European Community and Eastern Europe* (London: Royal Institute of International Affairs, 1991), pp. 87–88.

3. Copenhagen European Council, "Presidency Conclusions," Bulletin EC 6-1993, point 1.4.

4. Essen European Council, "Presidency Conclusions," Bulletin EC 12-1994, point 1.1.10.

5. European Commission, "White Paper: Preparation of the Associated Countries of Central and Eastern Europe for Integration into the Internal Market of the Union," COM(95)163 final, May 1995.

6. European Commission, "Agenda 2000: For a Stronger and Wider Europe," COM(97)2000 final, July 1997.

7. Luxembourg European Council, "Presidency Conclusions," Bulletin EC 12-1993, points 1.3–1.4.

8. Copenhagen European Council, "Presidency Conclusions," Bulletin EU 12-2002.

9. See A. Theophanous, "The Cyprus Problem: Accession to the EU and Broader Implications," *Mediterranean Quarterly* 14 (February 1, 2003): 42–67.

10. See Pace Roderick, "A Small State and the European Union: Malta's EU Accession Experience," *South European Society and Politics* 7 (Summer 2002): 24–43.

11. On Romania's accession, see D. Papadimitriou, *Romania and the European Union: From Marginalization to Membership* (London: Routledge, 2008); on Bulgaria's accession, see *EurActiv,* "EU-Bulgaria Relations," http://www.euractiv.com/en/enlargement/eu-bulgaria-relations-archived/article-129603.

12. On the impact of EU conditionality, see Heather Grabbe, *The EU's Transformative Power: Europeanization Through Conditionality in Central and Eastern Europe* (Basingstoke: Palgrave Macmillan, 2006); and Milada Anna Vachudova, *Europe Undivided: Democracy, Leverage, and Integration After Communism* (Oxford: Oxford University Press, 2005).

13. See Joschka Fischer, "From Confederacy to Federation: Thoughts on the Finality of European Integration," speech at Humboldt University, Berlin, May 12, 2000.

14. On the significance of the Nice Treaty, see M. Andenas and J. A. Usher, *The Treaty of Nice and Beyond: Enlargement and Constitutional Reform* (Portland: Hart, 2003); D. Galloway, *The Treaty of Nice and Beyond: Reality and Illusions of Power in the EU* (Sheffield: Sheffield Academic, 2001); and Finn Laursen, ed., *The Treaty of Nice: Actor Preferences, Bargaining, and Institutional Choice* (Leiden: Brill, 2006).

15. On the conduct and outcome of the convention, see Erik Oddvar Eriksen, John Erik Fossum, and Agustín José Meníndez, eds., *Developing a Constitution for Europe* (London: Routledge, 2004); Finn Laursen, ed., *The Rise and Fall of the EU's Constitutional Treaty* (Leiden: Brill, 2008); and Peter Norman, *Accidental Constitution: The Making of Europe's Constitutional Treaty,* 2nd ed. (Brussels: EuroComment, 2005).

16. Brussels European Council, "Presidency Conclusions," June 16–17, 2005.

17. *Financial Times,* May 29, 2006, p. 4.

18. Brussels European Council, "Presidency Conclusions," June 15–16, 2006.

19. Nicolas Sarkozy, "Je serai le président de tous les Français," Paris, May 6, 2007, http://www.u-m-p.org/site/index.php/ump/s_informer/discours/je_serai_le_president_de_tous_les_francais.

20. Brussels European Council, "Presidency Conclusions," June 21–22, 2007.

21. "EU Summit: Leaders Strike Treaty Deal," *EurActiv,* October 19, 2007.

22. See Institute of International and European Affairs, *Ireland's Future After Lisbon: Issues, Options, Implications* (Dublin, 2008), pp. 32–49.

23. Brussels European Council, "Presidency Conclusions," December 11–12, 2008.

24. Brussels European Council, "Presidency Conclusions," June 18–19, 2009.

25. Constitutional Court of Germany, press release, 72/2009, and judgment, June 30, 2009, http://www.bundesverfassungsgericht.de/en/press/bvg09-072en.html.

26. Thomas Risse and Mareike Kleine, "Assessing the Legitimacy of the EU's Treaty Revision Methods," *Journal of Common Market Studies* 45, no. 1 (2007): 69–80.

27. Brussels European Council, "Presidency Conclusions," December 14, 2007.

28. "Declaration on a Concerted European Action Plan of the Euro Area Countries," Summit of the Euro Area Countries, Paris, October 12, 2008.

29. Quoted in *Europolitics,* October 22, 2008.

30. "European Summit: Meeting Reaffirms Principles but Short on Actions," *Europolitics,* March 3, 2009.

31. Joschka Fischer, "Europe in Reverse," *Project Syndicate,* March 9, 2009, http://www.project-syndicate.org/commentary/fischer36.

PART 2

Institutions

7

The Commission

The European Union has a singular governmental structure.
Superficially, it looks like a national system of government, with a council, a parliament, and a court of justice resembling the familiar executive, legislative, and judicial branches. Yet the similarity is misleading. The Council of Ministers, made up of government ministers, shares legislative authority with the European Parliament, which, unlike most national parliaments in Europe, does not determine the composition of the government (not least because the EU does not have a government analogous to a national government). Only the Court of Justice, consisting of judges appointed by the member states, approximates its national counterparts.

The EU has another institution—the European Commission—with no equivalent in national governmental systems. The Commission refers to the college of commissioners (the members of the Commission) as well as collectively to the commissioners and civil servants who work for the institution. Either way, the Commission epitomizes supranationalism and lies at the center of the EU political system. Not surprisingly, the Commission is synonymous with the EU itself.[1]

The Commission's fortunes have changed over time. Since the glory days of Jacques Delors's presidency (1985–1995), the Commission's political influence has been waning. The Commission owes its apparent decline primarily to more assertive national leadership and a powerful EP, which no longer sees the Commission as an ally in interinstitutional relations but as a junior partner in its dealings with the Council. In addition, the Commission suffers more than any other institution from the EU's perceived democratic deficit. Unlike the Council, whose members are elected nationally, and the EP, whose members are directly elected, members of the Commission are essentially unelected—they are appointed by the European Council and approved by the Parliament. As a result, the institution's democratic legitimacy is constantly in question.

Compounding its weak legitimacy, the Commission is unpopular. Europeans generally perceive the Commission as power-hungry, insensitive to their concerns, and subversive of national political systems. Undoubtedly the Commission's efforts to promote deeper integration have occasionally been heavy-handed. Undoubtedly also the Commission is highly bureaucratic and somewhat out of touch. But its faults are magnified by negative media coverage and the tendency of national politicians to blame it for unpopular policies, whether those policies emanate from Brussels or not.

José Manuel Barroso, who became Commission president in 2004 and was reappointed in 2009, has tried to restore the institution's prominence and sense of purpose. If not resurgent, the Commission under Barroso is as influential as it could possibly be under extremely difficult circumstances. Barroso is adept at presiding over a fractious Commission of twenty-seven members (one per member state). Under his presidency, the Commission has become more accountable and open, and more responsive to the needs of citizens. Under Barroso the Commission has been pragmatic in highlighting selective policy objectives. Aware of the constraints facing the Commission, Barroso is not inclined to tilt at windmills and challenge the predominance of national capitals. Supranationalists are disappointed with what they see as Barroso's subservience to national leaders and unwillingness to reassert the Commission's authority. A more evenhanded assessment is that Barroso is doing as much as he can at a time of resurgent intergovernmentalism, compounded by economic uncertainty and grandstanding by the EP.

■ The Once Powerful Presidency

The Commission president is "first among equals" in the college of commissioners. The president sets the tone for the Commission's term in office. Not surprisingly, each Commission is generally known by the name of its president, for example the Barroso Commission. Apart from personifying the Commission and the EU itself, the president has various formal and informal duties:

- Deciding on the internal organization of the Commission.
- Ensuring that the Commission acts consistently and efficiently.
- Mediating disputes and forging agreement among commissioners.
- Announcing to the EP in January each year the Commission's Annual Policy Strategy (work program).
- Launching policy initiatives.
- Representing the Commission in meetings of the European Council.
- Representing the Commission in key international forums, notably the annual G8 summits, occasional G20 summits, and regular EU-US summits.

A president's performance of these and other tasks depends on a variety of personal, political, and economic circumstances, such as individual experience, expertise, and acumen; relations with other commissioners and with national government leaders; prevailing political support for further integration; and current economic conditions. Presidential performance has varied widely over the years, and presidents have generally been judged by the perceived strength or weakness of their political leadership (see Box 7.1).

Profile and Selection

When he became Commission president, Barroso fit the profile of previous incumbents: all were male, middle-aged, and thoroughly immersed in the political processes of their countries. Although unusual because he emerged apparently out of nowhere to take the top job, Barroso's original appointment serves as a useful guide to the abstruse politics of choosing a Commission president.

Box 7.1 Commission Presidents

Name (years served)	Member State	Highest Prior Position in National Government	Political Influence
Walter Hallstein (1958–1967)	Germany	State secretary, German foreign ministry	Strong (1958–1965) Weak (1966–1967)
Jean Rey (1967–1970)	Belgium	Minister of economic affairs	Weak
Franco Malfatti (1970–1972)	Italy	Minister for posts and telecommunications	Weak
Sicco Mansholt (1972)	Netherlands	Minister of agriculture	Weak
François-Xavier Ortoli (1973–1977)	France	Minister of finance	Weak
Roy Jenkins (1977–1981)	United Kingdom	Chancellor of the exchequer	Moderate
Gaston Thorn (1981–1985)	Luxembourg	Prime minister	Weak
Jacques Delors (1985–1995)	France	Minister for economy, finance, and budget	Strong (1985–1992) Moderate (1993–1995)
Jacques Santer (1995–1999)	Luxembourg	Prime minister	Weak
Manuel Marin (1999)	Spain	State secretary, Spanish foreign ministry	Weak
Romano Prodi (1999–2004)	Italy	Prime minister	Weak
José Manuel Barroso (2004–)	Portugal	Prime minister	Moderate

National leaders select the Commission president-designate. Since the Nice Treaty, they have been able to do so by qualified majority voting. Given the political sensitivity of choosing a new president, national leaders prefer to seek consensus. Nevertheless, as in other areas of EU decisionmaking, the possibility of taking a vote helps them to reach agreement.

The European Council had difficulty selecting a Commission president in 2004, before finally settling on Barroso. According to the unofficial rotation, it was the turn of a right-of-center candidate from a small member state to succeed Romano Prodi, a left-of-center former prime minister of Italy. Belgian prime minister Guy Verhofstadt was the firm favorite. But other national leaders resented his close ties to French president Jacques Chirac and German chancellor Gerhard Schröder. In the face of strong British and Italian opposition, Verhofstadt withdrew from the race. The European Council could not agree on any of the other candidates. The Irish prime minister, in the European Council presidency, searched about for another candidate and suggested Barroso, who at the time was prime minister of Portugal.

Barroso's relative obscurity was an advantage, although his qualified support for the war in Iraq seemed likely to incur Chirac's wrath. Perhaps because there were no other obvious candidates left, and because Barroso satisfied the key French criterion that the new president-designate come from a country within the eurozone, Chirac relented (Barroso also speaks excellent French). Moreover, Chirac was pleased with the concurrent reappointment of Pierre de Boissieu as de facto head of the Council secretariat—an indication of where France thinks institutional power in the EU lies. Chirac's acquiescence allowed the European Council, meeting in a special session in June 2004, to put Barroso forward for the job.

Once nominated, Barroso had to be approved by the EP. This was by no means a formality. The EP had shown nearly ten years previously that it could not be taken for granted when it endorsed Jacques Santer by only a narrow margin. Although dissatisfied with the method of Barroso's selection, most members of the European Parliament were willing to support Barroso, who was a member of the European People's Party (EPP), the political group to which a majority of MEPs belonged. Accordingly, in one of its first votes, the newly elected Parliament approved Barroso's nomination by a large margin in July 2004.

Despite this resounding endorsement by the EP, the nature of Barroso's nomination and appointment raised questions about his legitimacy as Commission president as well as the legitimacy of the Commission as a whole. At least Barroso had held the most powerful elected office in his native country. For all his positive attributes, by contrast, Delors had never been elected to high office in France. This became a liability toward the end of Delors's presidency, when concerns about the Commission's legitimacy came to the fore.

As part of its mandate to address the democratic deficit, the Convention on the Future of Europe (2002–2003) considered various ways to boost the Commission's legitimacy. One idea was to hold a presidential election throughout the EU every five years, at the same time as the EP elections. The hope was that Europeans would become more interested in EU politics and turn out in higher numbers for elections to the EP. Aware that a presidential election would be difficult to conduct—how could candidates appeal to voters in so many different countries using so many different languages?—and might not generate voter interest, the convention concluded that the president should be elected by the EP after having been proposed by the European Council. Accordingly, national leaders agreed in the Lisbon Treaty that the European Council would choose a candidate for Commission president, if necessary by qualified majority vote, and that the Parliament would then elect the candidate by a majority of its members, not simply a majority of the votes cast, as under the Nice Treaty rules. This procedure, they hoped, would strengthen the democratic credentials of the president while bolstering his or her position within the Commission and in interinstitutional relations.

When selecting the Commission president and the other top EU positions— the European Council president and the combined position of High Representative and Commission vice president—the European Council would have to strike a balance based on geography, nationality, ideology, and gender. In other words, the holders of these posts should not all be from the same political party and the same country or cluster of countries. Moreover, the Lisbon Treaty requires the European Council to take "into account" the outcome of the elections to the EP and to hold "appropriate consultations" between the two institutions before designating the candidate for Commission president.

The Lisbon Treaty was not yet in force when a new Commission president was selected in 2009. Nevertheless, the EP pressed the European Council for a political agreement to abide by the rules of the treaty. Given that the EPP, to which Barroso belonged, had won the largest number of seats in the June 2009 EP elections, the European Council could fairly claim to be taking into account this outcome, as stipulated in the treaty.

This did not satisfy some MEPs, especially the Socialists and Greens, who despised Barroso for his neoliberal economic philosophy and his alleged coziness with big business. Though the Socialists were then in the process of divvying up the presidency of the EP with the European People's Party (each would fill the office for half of the five-year mandate), they claimed that pushing through Barroso's candidacy without due consultation with the EP was a violation of democratic principles. Barroso duly met with MEPs in each of the political groups and made his case for reappointment. The Socialists were split along national lines. For instance, the Portuguese delegation generally supported Barroso. In the event, Barroso convincingly won the vote in September 2009 on his reappointment, although by a smaller margin than in 2004.

Performance

When they first appointed and then reappointed Barroso, national leaders were looking primarily for someone who could run the Commission well, not for another Delors who would aggressively promote deeper integration. Delors had set the standard by which all Commission presidents, past and future, were measured. The early years of Delors's tenure had shown that in order to shine, a Commission president needed exceptional attributes and skills, shrewd political judgment, and a firm grasp of economics. Much depended as well on the caliber of Delors's close advisers, especially his *chef de cabinet*. It helped that Delors came from one of the EU's most important countries; was close to Chancellor Helmut Kohl, the EU's most influential national leader; and reportedly was interested in becoming a leading national politician after his stint in Brussels. The perception of Delors as a potential president of France, not merely president of the Commission, enhanced his stature immeasurably, especially at meetings of the European Council.

The lessons of the highly successful Delors presidency are clear: an assertive, self-assured leader with a sound political past, and ideally with good political prospects in a leading member state, is best suited to advance the Commission's interests and engineer deeper European integration. The existence of a compelling project, in which the Commission is a key player, greatly helps the Commission president's prospects. In the rough-and-tumble world of intra-EU bargaining, a Commission president needs to be forceful, authoritative, and direct. It is difficult for a Commission president to act decisively in the European Council and on the broader international stage without being equally decisive in the Commission itself.[2]

Coming from a small country, despite having been and possibly again becoming prime minister, Barroso had limited potential as Commission president. Nor does the EU in general and the Commission in particular have a grand project that Barroso could champion. He has enjoyed good but not close relations with the French president and German chancellor. As expected, Barroso has proved to be a good leader within the Commission but has not been able or willing to project leadership beyond the Commission itself. In his dealings with other commissioners, Barroso has benefited from treaty changes, some in response to the Commission's resignation in 1999, intended to strengthen the president's hand. The president now has greater authority to allocate and reshuffle portfolios, and under the terms of the Lisbon Treaty may oblige a commissioner to resign. Barroso has been adept at managing a large Commission partly by introducing procedural changes but largely by adopting a more presidential than collegial style.

Wolfgang Münchau, an influential but curmudgeonly *Financial Times* columnist, described Barroso as being "among the weakest Commission presidents ever, a vain man who lacks political courage."[3] Other prominent critics of Barroso have been kinder in their choice of words but no less fierce in their disparagement of him. Barroso has been widely but unfairly blamed for not having done enough to prevent voters from rejecting the Constitutional Treaty in 2005 and the Lisbon Treaty in 2008, as if he could have changed the minds of people who, often for irrational reasons, deeply disliked the EU and the Commission. More reasonably, Barroso is blamed for having responded slowly and inadequately to the financial crisis of 2007–2009. Barroso may indeed have failed to grasp the enormity of the crisis until late 2008, when he finally rallied the Commission and helped put together the Economic Recovery Plan. However, his initial underestimation of the extent of the crisis was no different from that of many national leaders, and his ability to respond as Commission president was limited by the nature of the office and the preponderance of national governments.

National leaders got what they wanted in Barroso as Commission president: a capable manager lacking the ability or ambition to push an agenda of deeper integration. As the "accidental president" who emerged after a host of other candidates had been rejected, as a politician from a small country, and as a president without a compelling project for which the Commission could provide indispensable leadership, Barroso has never had a chance of become a powerful presence on the EU stage. Instead, he has been a safe pair of hands, a good leader within the Commission, and an effective champion of key EU policies, notably on energy and climate change.

▪ The Uncollegial Commission

Platitudes about the Commission's collegiality notwithstanding, in reality commissioners are far from equal in influence and authority. The way commissioners are popularly known emphasizes the point. Rather than using names, commentators frequently refer to nationality: the "Dutch commissioner," the "Romanian commissioner," the "German commissioner," and so on. Because Germany is a far more powerful country than either the Netherlands or Romania, the German commissioner generally has more influence than his Dutch and Romanian counterparts. Yet hailing from a big country is not a precondition for success in the Commission; commissioners from small countries often fare well, especially if they have ideas, initiative, and a reasonably important portfolio. Commissioners' responsibilities include:

- Providing political direction to the Commission's directorates-general (departments) and services.
- Representing the Commission at meetings of the Council of Ministers.
- Accounting for the Commission's activities before the EP.

- Publicizing the Commission's work.
- Exchanging information and ideas between the Commission and the highest levels of national government.

The Commission's size, effectiveness, and collegiality are obviously related. The more commissioners there are, the more difficult it is for the Commission to act coherently or collegially. As Box 7.2 shows, the number of commissioners has grown over the years from nine to an unwieldy twenty-seven (there were thirty commissioners during an interim period in 2004, immediately after enlargement). Efforts to reduce the Commission's size by breaking the link between the number of commissioners and the number of member states have been unavailing. As discussed in Chapter 6, Ireland's insistence on keeping one commissioner per member state as a condition of holding a second referendum on the Lisbon Treaty overturned the agreement reached in the Constitutional Treaty whereby the Commission would be limited to a college corresponding to two-thirds of the number of member states.

Although controversy over the Commission's size has consumed much time and energy since the mid-1990s, radical reform was not necessarily in the Commission's interest. Arguably, it is more important for governments, citizens, and the Commission to have direct, high-level channels of communication via "national" commissioners than to go through the politically painful and potentially unrewarding exercise of drastically reducing the Commission's size. In other words, given that the Commission derives some legitimacy from the commissioners' connections to national governments, retaining one commissioner per member state may not be such a bad idea, regardless of the challenge it poses for the Commission's collegiality and manageability.

Selection

The Lisbon Treaty states that the Council and the Commission president-elect are responsible for selecting, by "common accord," the other commissioners. In practice, each national government nominates its commissioner, while informing but not necessarily consulting the Commission president-elect. Nominees were not subject to approval by the EP until the mid-1990s. As a result of treaty changes and political precedent since then, governments have lost some of their freedom with regard to nominating commissioners.

Governments generally announce their nominee three or four months before the current Commission's term expires. Domestic political considerations, rather than ability or merit, determine a government's choice of nominee for a lucrative and prestigious commissionership. It is hardly surprising that nominees rarely come from outside the government. Most are career politicians whose standing at home enhances their status and, ideally, their performance in Brussels. Indeed, prior holding of a senior elected office has

Box 7.2 Commissioners per Member State

Time Frame	Number of Member States	Number of Commissioners per Member State	Total Number of Commissioners
1967[a]–1972	6	France, Germany, Italy (2 each); Belgium, Netherlands, Luxembourg (1 each)	9
1973–1980	9	France, Germany, Italy, **Britain** (2 each); Belgium, Netherlands, Luxembourg, **Denmark**, **Ireland** (1 each)	13
1981–1985	10	France, Germany, Italy, Britain (2 each); Belgium, Netherlands, Luxembourg, Denmark, Ireland, **Greece** (1 each)	14
1986–1994	12	France, Germany, Italy, Britain, **Spain** (2 each); Belgium, Netherlands, Luxembourg, Denmark, Ireland, Greece, **Portugal** (1 each)	17
1995–2004	15	France, Germany, Italy, Britain, Spain (2 each); Belgium, Netherlands, Luxembourg, Denmark, Ireland, Greece, Portugal, **Austria**, **Finland**, **Sweden** (1 each)	20
May–November 2004	25	France, Germany, Italy, Britain, Spain (2 each); Belgium, Netherlands, Luxembourg, Denmark, Ireland, Greece, Portugal, Austria, Finland, Sweden, **Cyprus**, **Czech Republic**, **Estonia**, **Hungary**, **Latvia**, **Lithuania**, **Malta**, **Poland**, **Slovakia**, **Slovenia** (1 each)	30
November 2004–December 2006	25	France, Germany, Italy, Britain, Spain, Belgium, Netherlands, Luxembourg, Denmark, Ireland, Greece, Portugal, Austria, Finland, Sweden, Cyprus, Czech Republic, Estonia, Hungary, Latvia, Lithuania, Malta, Poland, Slovakia, Slovenia (1 each)	25
2007–	27	France, Germany, Italy, Britain, Spain, Belgium, Netherlands, Luxembourg, Denmark, Ireland, Greece, Portugal, Austria, Finland, Sweden, Cyprus, Czech Republic, Estonia, Hungary, Latvia, Lithuania, Malta, Poland, Slovakia, Slovenia, **Bulgaria**, **Romania** (1 each)	27

Note: a. Under the terms of the Merger Treaty, which came into effect on July 1, 1967, the ECSC High Authority combined with the EEC and Euratom commissions to form the Commission of the European Communities. Subsequent changes resulted from the accession of new member states (identified in bold) and from implementation of the Nice Treaty (with respect to the Commission formed in November 2004).

become an informal prerequisite for appointment to the Commission, in order to enhance vicariously the Commission's democratic credentials.

There was not much consultation between national governments and Barroso on the composition of his first Commission, although he asked that at least eight of the twenty-four nominees (he was the twenty-fifth) be women, a minimum threshold that he attained. Reflecting the rising political prominence of Commission nominees despite the Commission's declining influence, Barroso's first Commission-designate included three former prime ministers, five former foreign ministers, and three former finance ministers.

Governments began to announce their nominees for the second Barroso Commission in mid-2009. Perhaps the biggest surprise was Angela Merkel's choice of Günther Oettinger, the minister-president of Baden-Württemberg, the third largest state in Germany, as her country's commissioner. Until his selection, Oettinger was mostly unknown outside Germany and had little experience of the EU. Presumably Merkel chose him for domestic political reasons. Given his background, Oettinger would likely be a staunch defender of German interests in Brussels. By contrast, Nicolas Sarkozy chose someone with a prominent international profile and considerable EU experience: Michel Barnier, a former foreign minister and a commissioner for regional policy in the Prodi Commission (1999–2004).

An unprecedented aspect of the selection process for the second Barroso Commission was that, under the terms of the Lisbon Treaty, which came into effect in December 2009, one of the Commission vice presidents would also be the High Representative for Foreign Affairs and Security, a position that would be allocated on the basis of intensive intergovernmental bargaining. The selection of a Briton, Catherine Ashton, for the position took care of Britain's nomination of a commissioner-designate.

Fourteen of the new commissioners-designate were holdovers from the first Barroso Commission. The second Barroso Commission includes nine women. Commissioners come from different political groups, or "families." Reflecting the composition of most national governments at the time of their selection, a majority of the new commissioners are from the center-right of the political spectrum.

Appointments to the Commission are much sought after. The pay, privileges, and professional satisfaction (depending on the individual and the portfolio) are considerable. Yet being a commissioner is generally not preferable to being a senior minister in a national government. Romano Prodi, prime minister of Italy before he became Commission president in 1999, made no secret of his desire to return to Italian politics, which he did, again as prime minister, for a brief period after leaving Brussels in 2004. Peter Mandelson, trade commissioner in Barroso's first administration, surprised everyone by leaving Brussels in October 2008 in order to become (once again) a senior British government minister. Other departures from the first Barroso Commission—admittedly as its term in office was drawing toward a close—included the Cypriot and Greek commissioners, who became foreign ministers in their respective countries, and the Lithuanian commissioner, who was elected president of her country.

Commissioners may be reappointed any number of times. It is not unusual for them to serve two full terms (now ten years); Viviane Reding, from Luxembourg, has been a commissioner in three successive Commissions (beginning in 1999). Commissioners may resign from office but may not be recalled by the government of their home country. Nor must they step down if the government that appointed them loses an election or otherwise leaves office. When a commissioner resigns, his or her home country simply nominates a substitute, who usually receives the same portfolio. Barroso broke with precedent in May 2008 when the Italian Franco Frattini, commissioner for justice, freedom, and security, stepped down from the Commission. Rather than give that sensitive portfolio to Frattini's successor, a member of the right-wing Forza Italia party, and risk the wrath of the EP, Barroso switched portfolios between the Italian and French commissioners: the new Italian commissioner acquired the transport portfolio and the French commissioner acquired the more important justice, freedom, and security portfolio. The switch demonstrated Barroso's political savvy not only by avoiding a row with the EP but also by pleasing Sarkozy, who was happy France now had a more important portfolio, regardless of the portfolio itself.

Allocation of Portfolios

In principle, the Commission president is solely responsible for allocating portfolios; in practice, national governments are constantly interfering. Ever since the first enlargement, there have been more commissioners than substantial portfolios, resulting in too many commissioners chasing too few good jobs. Successive rounds of enlargement expanded the Commission's size at a greater rate than the increasing policy scope of the EU expanded the number of important portfolios.

Agriculture and trade policy have always been weighty portfolios. Various economic jobs became much more important as a result of the single market program in the late 1980s and the march toward monetary union in the 1990s. The environment became a desirable portfolio when the EC acquired competence for that policy area under the Single European Act of 1986, and shot up in importance with the emergence of climate change as a key issue in the mid-2000s. Indeed, Barroso carved a new portfolio, climate action, out of the environment portfolio when he put his second administration together. Similarly, regional policy became a politically significant portfolio following the reforms of the structural funds (including a generous appropriation of money) in the late 1980s. Under the Lisbon Treaty, the external relations portfolio has been merged with the office of High Representative for Foreign Affairs and Security, and its holder designated a Commission vice president, making it one of the most desirable jobs in the EU.

The widening gap between the number of commissioners and the number of worthwhile portfolios, despite the EU's growing policy remit, has forced national governments to compete fiercely for particular portfolios, regardless of the Commission president's formal responsibility for deciding who does what. The scramble for portfolios in the run-up to each new Commission demonstrates the seriousness with which governments view Commission appointments and suggests that commissioners are not "completely independent in the performance of their duties," as the Lisbon Treaty claims they should be and as commissioners swear they will be.

Sarkozy made no secret in 2009 of his determination that France's next commissioner be allocated the internal market and services portfolio, thereby ensuring that it not go to an economic liberal and especially a Briton (for Sarkozy the two are synonymous). Given the dearth of weighty portfolios, Barroso could have split internal market and services into two jobs. Instead, he surrendered to Sarkozy and handed the portfolio to the new French commissioner. Germany would appear to have lost out in the second Barroso Commission, as its commissioner secured the energy portfolio, an important responsibility but not a high-profile Commission job. Barroso juggled the portfolios in his new Commission so that none of the returning commissioners kept their original portfolios. Apart from climate action, Barroso reconfigured existing responsibilities to create two new portfolios, one for home affairs, the other for justice, fundamental rights, and citizenship (see Box 7.3).

Despite blatant jockeying for portfolios by national governments, new commissioners, once they take up their positions in Brussels, generally strike a reasonable balance between national and EU interests. There is a big difference between recognizing and upholding a national interest, and taking instructions from a national government. The Commission functions best when commissioners thrash out proposals from their own ideological, political, and national perspectives as well as on the abstract basis of what is best for the EU.

Organization of the College

Commissioners often use their cabinets (groups of private advisers) to absorb excessive national pressure and conduct domestic public relations campaigns. The cabinet system reflects a strong French influence on the EU's administrative apparatus. Over the years, cabinets have grown larger and more powerful. Most commissioners have a seven-member cabinet that includes career Eurocrats and appointees who come to Brussels with the commissioner. At least two members of the cabinet must be women, and at least three must come from a country other than the commissioner's. A good cabinet can boost the standing of an otherwise poor commissioner, and a poor cabinet can pull down an otherwise good commissioner. It is no coincidence that the most effective commissioners have the best-staffed and best-organized cabinets.

Box 7.3   The Second Barroso Commission

Commissioner	Country of Origin	Portfolio
José Manuel Barroso	Portugal	President
Catherine Ashton	United Kingdom	High Representative for Foreign Affairs and Security Policy (vice president)
Viviane Reding	Luxembourg	Justice, Fundamental Rights, and Citizenship (vice president)
Joaquín Almunia	Spain	Competition (vice president)
Siim Kallas	Estonia	Transport (vice president)
Neelie Kroes	Netherlands	Digital Agenda (vice president)
Antonio Tajani	Italy	Industry and Entrepreneurship (vice president)
Maroš Šefčovič	Slovakia	Inter-Institutional Relations and Administration (vice president)
Janez Potočnik	Slovenia	Environment
Olli Rehn	Finland	Economic and Monetary Affairs
Andris Piebalgs	Latvia	Development
Michel Barnier	France	Internal Market and Services
Androulla Vassiliou	Cyprus	Education, Culture, Multilingualism, and Youth
Algirdas Šemeta	Lithuania	Taxation and Customs Union, Audit and Anti-Fraud
Karel De Gucht	Belgium	Trade
John Dalli	Malta	Health and Consumer Policy
Máire Geoghegan-Quinn	Ireland	Research, Innovation, and Science
Janusz Lewandowski	Poland	Financial Programming and Budget
Maria Damanaki	Greece	Maritime Affairs and Fisheries
Kristalina Georgieva	Bulgaria	International Cooperation, Humanitarian Aid, and Crisis Response
Günther Oettinger	Germany	Energy
Johannes Hahn	Austria	Regional Policy
Connie Hedegaard	Denmark	Climate Action
Štefan Füle	Czech Republic	Enlargement and European Neighborhood Policy
László Andor	Hungary	Employment, Social Affairs, and Inclusion
Cecilia Malmström	Sweden	Home Affairs
Dacian Cioloş	Romania	Agriculture and Rural Development

Commissioners meet every Wednesday in Brussels, or in Strasbourg if the EP is in plenary session there. The president sets the agenda, which includes important policy initiatives and legislative proposals. Despite the large number of participants, meetings of the Barroso Commission tend to be short. Usually the president gets his way, although meetings sometimes become bruising battles that the president does not always win. The most notable struggles have been over competition policy, trade, and agriculture—policy areas that are highly sensitive politically in the member states. Under the Commission's rules of procedure, a simple majority vote may decide an issue, but commissioners rarely vote. For less pressing or politically important business, the Commission may make decisions using a written procedure. The increasing uncollegiality of the Commission does not always work to the president's advantage. Just as the president has a lot of discretionary power, a headstrong commissioner may also act independently and become a thorn in the president's side. Commissioners occasionally make speeches or release statements that are intended to annoy the president or score domestic political points rather than elucidate Commission policy.

■ The Unloved Civil Service

The Commission's civil service is surprisingly small. Despite the picture that Euroskeptics paint of a vast bureaucracy extending its reach throughout the EU, the Commission has a staff of about 25,000, including more than 3,000 personnel of the Joint Research Center and several thousand interpreters and translators (the EU has twenty-three official languages). The Commission comprises about forty directorates-general and services, corresponding roughly to its activities, responsibilities, and organizational needs (see Box 7.4).[4] For instance, reflecting the growing political salience of energy policy, Barroso established a new energy directorate-general (DG) in 2009 (previously energy was part of a combined energy and transport directorate-general).

Neither the number nor the responsibilities of the directorates-general and services correspond to the number or the portfolios of the commissioners. Thus a commissioner may have more than one directorate-general in his or her portfolio, and the responsibilities of a directorate-general may be spread over the portfolios of more than one commissioner.

The secretariat-general is one of the most important bodies in the Commission. It is first and foremost the commissioners' own secretariat. For that reason, the secretary-general is one of a handful of noncommissioners allowed to participate in the Commission's formal meetings (apart from a head of cabinet standing in for a commissioner). The secretary-general also presides over the regular Monday morning meetings of heads of cabinet and the regular Thursday morning meetings of directors-general. Under Barroso, the secretary-general and the secretariat-general have become more powerful, a development that has helped the president to manage such a large and diverse Commission.

Physically, the Commission is quite spread out. Most of its officials work in Brussels, but some are based in Luxembourg. A small number of Commission officials work in liaison offices in the national capitals and EU delegations (embassies) throughout the world. In Brussels itself, the Commission is dispersed in dozens of buildings rented from or through the Belgian government. The Commission's headquarters is in the Berlaymont, a large, star-shaped glass

Box 7.4   Commission Directorates-General and Services

Policies
Agriculture and Rural Development
Climate Action
Competition
Economic and Financial Affairs
Education and Culture
Employment, Social Affairs, and Equal Opportunities
Energy
Enterprise and Industry
Environment
Executive Agencies
Health and Consumers
Information Society and Media
Internal Market and Services
Justice, Freedom, and Security
Maritime Affairs and Fisheries
Mobility and Transport
Regional Policy
Research
Taxation and Customs Union

External Relations
Development
Enlargement
EuropeAid–Co-operation Office
External Relations
Humanitarian Aid
Trade

General Services
Communication
European Anti-Fraud Office
Eurostat
Joint Research Centre
Publications Office
Secretariat-General

Internal Services
Budget
Bureau of European Policy Advisers
European Commission Data Protection Officer
Human Resources and Security
Informatics
Infrastructures and Logistics–Brussels
Infrastructures and Logistics–Luxembourg
Internal Audit Service
Interpretation
Legal Service
Office for Administration and Payment of Individual Entitlements
Translation

and concrete building in the heart of the "European Quarter." The Berlaymont's closure during the 1990s for a floor-to-ceiling renovation was a painful reminder of the Commission's waning influence. During the more than decade-long renovation, the Commission president, his cabinet, and the secretariat-general moved to the nearby Breydel building, a short walk from the larger and more imposing Council and Parliament buildings. In order to denote decentralization and connect the commissioners directly with their staff, Commission president Romano Prodi moved the other commissioners and their cabinets out of the Breydel and into the buildings of the key directorates-general. The inconvenience of having the commissioners spread all over Brussels may have outweighed the presumed public relations and internal organizational advantages of this move. The Berlaymont's prolonged and expensive renovation came to an end in 2004, just in time for Barroso and his team of commissioners to move into the building at the beginning of their term in office. Bright and airy on the inside and gleaming on the outside, the renovated Berlaymont symbolized Barroso's hopes for an institutional renaissance.

Recruitment and Promotion

Commission staff work at either the professional (so-called administrative) or the service (so-called assistant) level. The Commission recruits civil servants for its administrative cadre through a highly competitive, EU-wide selection process (the *concours*) for university graduates. The small number of successful candidates who pass the aptitude tests, written examinations, interviews, and language proficiency tests begin work mostly at the lower end of the administrative scale. Some may already have gained experience in the Commission as *stagiaires* (paid student interns). Based on previous experience or personal predilection, new recruits may ask to work in a particular directorate-general or service but do not always get the assignments of their choice.

From the beginning of their careers, Commission civil servants enter a world of unstated but finely balanced national quotas, or what the Commission euphemistically calls "respect for geographical balance." Because the Commission's staff needs to reflect the population distribution and size of the EU's member states, the intake of new recruits and their promotion through the ranks are subject to an unofficial allocation of positions among each country's nationals at each rung of the ladder. Enlargement requires these quotas to be recalculated, as nationals of new member states need to be accommodated at all levels of the correspondingly expanded civil service.

Women are poorly represented in the Commission's administrative cadre, especially at the senior levels, but figure prominently as assistants. To rectify this situation, the Commission introduced a policy in the mid-1990s of discriminating in favor of women at the administrative level, although with different targets for two groups of member states. For the fiercely egalitarian Nordic countries (Denmark, Finland, and Sweden), the Commission aimed to achieve parity among men and women at the top levels. For the rest, the Commission set a less ambitious but more challenging goal of 25 percent women in the top positions. Progress has been slow, reflecting pervasive ambivalence in much of Europe about equal opportunity for women in the workplace.

What motivates people to join the Commission? Money may be the deciding factor. Commission civil servants are extremely well paid and enjoy many fringe benefits unavailable to their national counterparts. This probably explains why over 30,000 people routinely compete for a few hundred positions in the Brussels bureaucracy. Idealism may also play a part, although the Commission is not necessarily a hotbed of Eurofederalism. The prospect of living and working in a multilingual, multicultural environment is undoubtedly appealing. Brussels is by no means Europe's most beautiful city, but the parts of it colonized by people who work for and with the EU institutions are highly urbane. High regard for public service could also point toward a Commission career. Yet there are greater opportunities for advancement and for assorted assignments in national bureaucracies, and some countries with strong bureaucratic traditions, such as Britain and France, encourage their brightest people to eschew the Commission in favor of the national civil service.

Promotion through the junior and midcareer grades is generally predictable and uncontroversial. However, entry into the senior grades is highly politicized and extremely difficult. Not only is there a smaller number of jobs available than at lower levels, but national civil servants and others who "parachute" into the senior ranks of the Commission—for instance, as part of a commissioner's cabinet—reduce the availability of senior jobs for career officials. Despite a Court of Justice ruling as long ago as 1993 that the Commission was breaking EU rules by using national quotas rather than merit to recruit high-ranking officials, an informal quota system still applies at the higher levels. As part of a wide-ranging internal reform, Barroso mandated that the senior-most officials (directors-general and deputy directors-general and their equivalent) serve for two to five years, and not more than seven, in any particular post. As a result, every year or so the Commission implements a "mobility package" for top officials, which is painstakingly negotiated by the commissioners, their *chefs de cabinet,* and the heads of the directorates-general, with barely concealed interference from national governments via their permanent representations in Brussels.

The difficulty of progressing to the highest levels engenders a lot of frustration and resentment at the midcareer level of the Commission. The politicized nature of promotion and an obsession with national quotas mean that competence and merit, while still important, are not sufficient to reach the top. The president's inability to get rid of poor performers, who are often shielded by national governments, and the stranglehold that governments have on certain senior positions expose some of the Commission's serious administrative weaknesses.

Although the Commission is generally portrayed as a unitary actor, inevitably its officials have varying outlooks, ideological orientations, and policy preferences. It is hardly surprising that Commission officials are less nationalist and more cosmopolitan than most Europeans, or that they generally favor greater EU-level involvement in a range of public policy issues. Nevertheless, their political views and policy preferences cover a wide spectrum. Institutionally, orientations and preferences vary from directorate-general to directorate-general. For example, DG Competition inevitably attracts officials who have a commitment to, or at least a predisposition toward, neoliberal principles, whereas the ethos and culture of DG Regional Policy are less enamored of the free market and more inclined toward state intervention.

Reform

The Commission has struggled with the challenge of internal reform for more than thirty years. The famous Spierenburg Report pointed out many of the problems relating to national quotas and limited promotion prospects as early as 1979, but many of its recommendations remain unimplemented to this day. The Commission suffers from poor lateral as well as upward mobility. Over the years, commissioners and directors-general have understandably stuck to existing staff levels even as the Commission's priorities have shifted dramatically. Thus the Commission itself is far from overstaffed, but certain parts of it have become bloated while others, notably the directorates-general for external relations and competition, have remained seriously understaffed. Nor have governments been willing to approve a sizable increase in the civil service, especially at a time of budget cutbacks and public hostility toward European institutions.

Delors's success as president in the late 1980s raised the Commission's morale, yet by the end of the decade many officials identified Delors himself as part of the Commission's problem. Delors's disregard for fellow commissioners, disdain for many directors-general, and aggrandizement of power in his cabinet fueled resentment within the ranks. With the sudden rise in the Commission's responsibilities in the early 1990s and no commensurate increase in its size or efficiency, many officials feared that the institution would self-destruct. During the Maastricht ratification crisis, when the Commission unfairly came under widespread attack, the institution's morale reached rock bottom.

The Commission's structural and managerial problems were rooted in the national governments' determination to retain as much control as possible over the Commission and were compounded by successive enlargements, the proliferation of portfolios, and the excessive power of the cabinets. Staff policy was underused as an instrument of internal reform, new management techniques were rarely introduced, and a decentralization initiative launched in the early 1990s had only mixed results. Delors made a belated effort to streamline the Commission, but his management style made matters worse. As a result, Jacques Santer, Delors's successor, put internal reform at the top of his presidential agenda.

Santer launched a three-pronged reform effort. The first was development of "sound and efficient management," aimed at improving financial affairs by separating operational and financial management structures within the directorates-general. By the late 1990s the program had increased but not necessarily improved financial control in the Commission, often at a cost of additional bureaucratization and delays in payments to contractors. The second prong was to modernize administration and personnel policy, by means of decentralization, rationalization, and simplification. Easier said than done, its implementation was uneven and aroused the hostility of Commission officials and their unions, who were resentful of what they saw as yet another top-down management initiative with little serious input from the staff itself. The third prong, an ambitious initiative called "The Commission of Tomorrow," dealt with more politically sensitive issues, such as strengthening the Commission presidency, consolidating and reducing the number of portfolios, curbing the power of the cabinets, and basing promotion into the Commission's senior ranks on merit rather than country of origin.

Ironically for a president genuinely interested in internal reform, Santer will forever be remembered for the corruption and maladministration that triggered the Commission's resignation in March 1999 (see Chapter 5). In the wake of the resignation scandal, Romano Prodi, Santer's successor, redoubled the reform effort: he strengthened the recently approved codes of conduct for commissioners and senior officials, launched a major shakeup of the directorates-general, and radically reorganized the commissioners' portfolios. One seemingly unimportant but highly symbolic change was that the directorates-general, instead of being known by number as had been the case throughout the EU's history, henceforth became known by function (thus "DG VI" became "DG Agriculture," for example). Although difficult for old EU hands to learn, the new nomenclature helped to demystify the Commission.

Prodi chose Neil Kinnock, incongruously a holdover from the disgraced Santer Commission, to head a new reform portfolio. Kinnock, a loquacious former leader of the British Labour Party, threw himself into a difficult and thankless task. Following consultations with MEPs, other commissioners and commission officials, and representatives of national governments, Kinnock released a white paper on administrative reform in March 2000, on the basis of which the Commission adopted a detailed "roadmap."[5] Based on the roadmap, the Commission introduced a number of changes, including new methods of auditing and financial control; a system of activity-based management (intended to match responsibilities and resources); and new recruitment, promotion, and disciplinary procedures. In general, the Prodi reforms drew heavily on British and Scandinavian models of public administration, in contrast to the French model on which the Commission had largely been built.

In a related development, Prodi issued a white paper on governance in July 2001, following more than a year of consultations with politicians, officials, and representatives of civil society.[6] Whereas the white paper on administrative reform attempted to shake up the Commission, the white paper on governance sought to reassert the Commission's centrality in the EU system. It was therefore somewhat defensive in tone, while also advocating innovations in the policy instruments, methods, and systems of EU governance that were not necessarily in the Commission's best interest, such as soft regulation, the open method of coordination (a new framework for cooperation among member states in challenging policy areas), and the role of executive agencies. By the time the white paper appeared, the "post-Nice" debate on the future of the EU had already begun. The white paper was soon swamped by the contributions of leading national politicians. Ultimately, it was too vague and insubstantial to have an impact on the post-Nice debate.

Prodi's efforts to reform the Commission were urgent and important, but not entirely successful. Although they moved the Commission in the right direction, the Prodi reforms faced several entrenched obstacles. One was the inertia and even outright opposition of some parts of the bureaucracy. Prodi and Kinnock dared to question the generous pay and pensions of EU officials, and to link remuneration to performance. That stirred up a hornets' nest and provoked a number of work stoppages and strikes. Another, more serious consideration was the national governments' reluctance to give up their stranglehold on key aspects of the Commission's structure and staff policy. Despite rhetorical flourishes to the contrary, governments jealously guarded what they saw as their right to influence the appointment of senior officials, a not-so-subtle way of pushing national interests in the EU.

Barroso has continued the reform effort, which has become a permanent feature of life in the Commission and is more difficult to manage with so many more nationalities represented in the institution and so many more governments trying to meddle in its internal operations. As a singular institution in a singular political structure, the Commission clearly faces major organizational challenges. The difficulty for Barroso, as for Prodi and Santer before him, is to enhance the Commission's efficiency to the maximum extent possible within the limits set by the institution's multinational, multicultural, and multilingual character, and by the nature of the EU system in which the Commission is embedded. In the face of widespread public disgruntlement, heightened national sensitiveness, an ever assertive EP, and an unfavorable economic climate, Barroso faces an unenviable and almost impossible task.

■ The Commission's Roles and Responsibilities

The Commission is sometimes called the "motor" of European integration, not only because of its almost exclusive right to initiate legislation in socioeconomic policy areas but also because of its history, composition, culture, and European rather than national outlook. Indeed, according to the Lisbon Treaty, the Commission is obliged to promote "the general interest of the Union." In addition, the Commission upholds EU law and traditionally looks out for the small member states. As stipulated in the treaties and developed over time, the Commission's primary responsibilities include:

- Proposing and shaping legislation.
- Financial planning; initiating and managing the budget.
- Executing and implementing policy.
- Policing EU law.
- Conducting external relations.
- Contributing to enlargement and treaty reform.
- Monitoring and reporting on major EU developments.
- Pointing the way forward.

Upon coming into office, each Commission produces an overarching set of strategic objectives for the next five years. More concretely, each February the Commission sets out its main priorities for the next calendar year in a document called the Annual Policy Strategy. Later in the year (usually in October), following a "structured dialogue" (in-depth consultation) with the Council and the EP, the Commission adopts a legislative agenda (known as the Work Program) that fleshes out the Annual Policy Strategy and explains the practical steps necessary to achieve its priorities. The Annual Policy Strategy and follow-up Work Program are indispensable guides to the Commission's activities and objectives.

Legislative Role

It is an old axiom that "the Commission proposes [legislation] and the Council disposes," but this view omits the EP's role as codecisionmaker with the Council. The treaty authorizes the Commission to flesh out the treaty's skeletal framework by making recommendations, delivering opinions, and proposing legislation. Most of the Commission's legislative proposals have a clear legal base in the treaties. Others flow from legislation already adopted under the treaties or from judgments of the Court of Justice. National governments sometimes dispute the legal base of a Commission proposal either due to genuine difference of interpretation or for political reasons: they may not want the EU to involve itself in certain matters or may not want a legal base that involves QMV in the Council.

The volume of Commission proposals diminished in the aftermath of the single market program's heavy legislative schedule and in the post-Maastricht climate of suspicion toward the EU. Capitalizing on prevailing anti-EU sentiment, some national governments invoke subsidiarity (the principle that decisions should be taken at the lowest level practicable) in order to prevent the enactment of legislation at the European level and the implementation of EU legislation at the national level. By the same token, the Commission often invokes subsidiarity to dispel the popular perception that it has an insatiable appetite for new legislation.

Reacting to the popular and political mood, Santer vowed during his presidency (1995–1999) that the EU would legislate less and legislate better. In other words, the Commission would produce fewer legislative proposals, and the proposals that it did produce would be of a higher quality. Prodi went a step further, promising to cut back drastically the 14,000 or so legal acts that make up the *acquis communautaire*. The Commission launched a plan to that effect in February 2003, proposing to reduce the volume of EU law by one-third before the end of 2005. That was easier said than done. As the Commission admitted in a progress report in October 2003, it is difficult to agree on which laws should be repealed, simplified, and consolidated, and almost impossible to find the resources necessary to implement the plan.

As part of a "better regulation" initiative, in June 2002 the Commission established a new, integrated procedure to assess the likely impact of major proposals and improve the quality and coherence of the policymaking process. The Commission now uses impact assessments to analyze the possible economic, social, and environmental consequences of major proposals in the context of sustainable development (an overarching EU objective), and also with regard to subsidiarity and proportionality.

Apart from the Commission's own efforts to reduce the quantity of EU legislation, the member states' preference for soft law rather than hard regulation in pursuit of the so-called Lisbon strategy for economic modernization and reform has diminished the Commission's traditional legislative role. By endorsing the open method of coordination in a range of policy areas intended to make the EU a more dynamic and successful regional economy, the European Council explicitly relegated the Commission to a lesser role. Despite poor progress in implementing the Lisbon strategy, governments have shown little inclination to revert to the traditional Community method of legislative decisionmaking to achieve the Lisbon goals, although the Commission has managed to insinuate itself into the open method of coordination in a way that has restored some of its authority.

Barroso was one of the original proponents of the Lisbon strategy when he was prime minister of Portugal. He has remained enamored of it as Commission president, despite charges that its preference for "soft law" over EU legislation is relatively disadvantageous to the Commission. Barroso has also adhered to the Santer and Prodi mantras of fewer but better legislative proposals. His first Commission was notable for introducing fewer proposals for new legislation but more proposals for legislation intended to amend, reduce, or otherwise tidy up existing laws and regulations, and for producing numerous communications and other advisory documents.[7]

Regardless of the politics of subsidiarity and the vogue for introducing fewer proposals for new legislation, the Commission jealously guards its right to propose legislation where legislation is warranted, based on the principle that the Commission alone can best articulate and defend the EU's collective interest. Since the introduction of direct elections in 1979, the increasingly assertive EP has occasionally attempted to win for itself a similar right of initiative. Although the Commission has successfully resisted these efforts, the Parliament and the Council may request that the Commission submit a proposal. So too, according to the Lisbon Treaty, may EU citizens invite the Commission to initiate legislation, as long as they muster at least 1 million signatures and come from "a significant number of Member States." The Commission has a shared right of initiative in the Common Foreign and Security Policy, which under the Lisbon Treaty remains predominantly an intergovernmental undertaking, and has gradually extended its right of initiative, either exclusive or shared, in the area of justice and home affairs, also traditionally an intergovernmental sphere.

Apart from a request from the Council or Parliament for the Commission to initiate legislation, proposals may originate in a number of ways. A zealous Commission president, commissioner, director-general, or head of section might ask his or her subordinates to prepare legislation, or an ambitious and energetic midlevel Commission official could send his or her superiors suggestions for draft proposals. Similarly, a proposal could come as a result of a widely perceived need to develop EU policy in a certain area, or in response to the suggestion of a government or an interest group.

However they originate, proposals must work their way through the Commission bureaucracy. A network of internal and external committees assists the Commission's work. Internal committees are mostly ad hoc and are convened to ensure coordination among various parts of the Commission if a proposal cuts across departmental boundaries. The secretariat-general plays a key role, as do the commissioners' cabinets. Of course, there is frequent informal coordination among commissioners, members of their cabinets, and other senior Commission officials, which may take place casually in a corridor, at lunch, or over coffee.

Outside committees, most of which are chaired and serviced by the Commission, consist of experts from a wide variety of backgrounds and cover a wide variety of subjects. Examples include the Scientific Committee on Animal Health and Animal Welfare and the Scientific Committee on Consumer Products. Such committees are important not only because they provide invaluable technical advice but also because some of the national officials who sit on them may also sit in the working groups that will evaluate the proposal when the Commission formally submits it to the Council. Because they draw as well on interest groups and professional associations, outside committees help the Commission keep in tune with the real world of business and commerce.

In an effort to improve transparency and shore up public trust, the Commission has attempted to disseminate information about impending proposals as widely as possible and to solicit the views of all interested parties. To that end, the Commission publishes a large number of green papers, which outline the Commission's ideas about possible legislative proposals. Green papers trigger responses from interest groups, nongovernmental organizations (NGOs), and the general public. They often form the basis for white papers, which sometimes contain specific legislative proposals.

The consultation and proposal-drafting stage is an opportune time for interested parties to try to modify the shape and content of the contemplated legislation. The Commission is a relatively open organization; its officials are easily contacted and are susceptible to outside influence. This is also the stage when small countries, whose influence in the Council is relatively limited, make a sustained lobbying effort, often including contacts between government ministers and "national" commissioners.

Ideally, the college of the Commission would discuss and approve proposals before formally submitting them to the Council and the Parliament. But the pressure of other business makes that impossible. To expedite the process and cut down on the commissioners' workloads, draft proposals deemed uncontroversial are circulated among the commissioners and, if not objected to within a short time, are adopted by default. Alternatively, a subgroup of commissioners may agree to deal with routine proposals on behalf of their colleagues. Either way, the commissioners' cabinets play a decisive role.

Stakeholder input, as well as the political astuteness of most of the commissioners and their cabinets, usually ensures that the Commission does not submit a proposal that the Council or Parliament would be likely to reject outright. The Commission is reluctant to alienate the Council and Parliament and risk paralyzing the legislative process. But the Commission is not servile or afraid to introduce controversial proposals. While not wanting to isolate or embarrass national governments or political groups, the Commission appreciates that, inevitably, certain key players are likely to oppose certain proposals. Overall, the Commission has to weigh prevailing political realities against treaty obligations and the general European interest.

The Commission's role in shaping legislation as a proposal works its way through the decisionmaking process is discussed in Chapter 11.

Financial Planning and the Budget

The Commission launches the process for the annual budget and the multiannual financial framework, covering a five-year period (since implementation of the Lisbon Treaty), within which the annual budget is decided. The negotiation of financial frameworks has become a major political event in the life of the EU. Although it is essentially an intergovernmental process, the Commission is centrally involved in it. The current framework covers the years 2007–2013.

Submitting Proposals. The Commission starts the lengthy process of deciding the next financial framework nearly three years before that framework begins. The Commission's opening gambit is a communication to the Council and Parliament that is more political than technical, setting out the challenges likely to face the EU in the years ahead. The Commission follows up with another communication laying out the measures necessary to meet those challenges—and what they would cost. The purpose is to start a debate about the EU's policy goals and instruments over the coming years, before the national governments get down to the hard bargaining on anticipated expenditures. Although partly a negotiating ploy, the Commission's initial proposal tends to reflect its traditional extravagance and understandable preference for a bigger EU budget.

As for the annual budget, with much less fanfare the Commission prepares early each year a preliminary draft budget for the coming year (the financial year coincides with the calendar year), consisting of estimates of expenditure drawn up by each institution, except the European Central Bank. The Commission submits the preliminary draft budget, including estimates of expenditure as well as revenue, to the Council and Parliament (the combined budgetary authority) in May or June. As in the case of the financial framework, the Commission tends to propose a more generous annual budget that the Council and Parliament eventually agree to. The Commission may amend the draft budget at any time until the Council and Parliament reach agreement, usually in December.

Overseeing Revenue and Expenditure. The Commission has some obligations on the revenue side—namely overseeing the collection of the EU's own resources and national contributions—but its responsibilities lie primarily on the expenditure side. These include administering appropriations for:

- *Competitiveness and cohesion:* Includes the structural funds—comprising the European Social Fund, the European Regional Development Fund, and the European Agricultural Fund for Rural Development—and accounts for approximately 44 percent of expenditure in the 2007–2013 financial framework.
- *Natural resources:* Includes the European Agricultural Guarantee Fund (the main mechanism for financing agricultural policy) and accounts for approximately 43 percent of expenditure.
- *The EU as a global partner:* Covers the cost of external activities, including development and humanitarian assistance, and accounts for approximately 9 percent of expenditure.

The Commission prepares a monthly report for the Council and the Parliament on the status of revenue received and expenditure incurred. Expenditure is listed under general headings, such as "citizenship, freedom, security, and justice," and detailed categories, such as "agriculture and rural development."

As already noted, the Commission has a poor record of financial management and a reputation for profligacy. Given that payments for EU policies and programs are made by national authorities on the EU's behalf, most fraud takes place at the national level. Nevertheless, a number of Commission officials have been implicated. Frequent censure of the Commission by the Court of Auditors, the EU's accounting watchdog, fuels unfavorable media coverage and persistent parliamentary inquiry.

In order to fight fraud involving EU funds, the EU established the European Anti-Fraud Office (known by its French acronym, OLAF) in 1999, with independent investigative authority.

Executive Responsibilities

The Commission is often described as the EU's executive body, yet it has only limited executive power. The Commission conspicuously lacks the ability to implement EU policy "on the ground." The EU lacks the services necessary to give real effect to its legislation, such as customs, immigration, veterinary affairs, and myriad others. Instead, the Commission depends heavily on the member states' civil services. Without assistance from the national agriculture departments, for instance, the Commission could not possibly make the Common Agricultural Policy work. At the level where EU legislation should matter most—on farms, in factories, at airports and docks—the Commission depends almost entirely on national officials. Yet national officials can be notoriously recalcitrant when it comes to implementing EU legislation, either because they resent interference from Brussels or because they genuinely misunderstand the latest Commission regulation.

The Commission's executive powers therefore refer not to ground-level implementation but to the enactment of innumerable rules and regulations necessary to give EU legislation (as decided by the Council and the Parliament) practical effect. Thus the Commission issues several thousand directives, regulations, and decisions annually (these are qualitatively different from legislative acts emanating from the Council and the Parliament bearing the same name), dealing mostly with highly technical aspects of common policies. The increasing encroachment of Commission regulations, directives, and decisions into everyday life in the EU is a major reason for growing public hostility toward the Brussels bureaucracy. The Commission is too easily caricatured and reviled for its real or supposed rules on such arcane issues as the length of a British sausage, the local environmental impact of a public works project, or the size and shape of potted plants. Despite its apparent addiction to overregulation, the Commission lacks a free hand in implementing EU policy thanks to the complex "comitology" procedure, which is explained in Chapter 11.

The Commission alone is responsible for implementing EU competition policy, which includes measures to curb excessive state subsidies and abuse by companies of a dominant position in the marketplace. Because a vigorous competition policy is essential for the proper functioning of a single market, the Commission fought tenaciously after the launch of the single market program to win sole authority to approve or block large mergers and acquisitions that could distort the marketplace. The Commission has a large merger task force, whose relatively expeditious handling of many complicated and sensitive cases has generally won the respect of European companies and national competition watchdogs, although some governments have expressed annoyance with the task force's methods and recommendations. Despite political pressure from governments in particular cases, the Commission (as a college) invariably supports the task force. Some governments have threatened to try to take merger control at the EU level away from the Commission and give it instead to an independent agency, but have not yet succeeded in doing so. (Competition policy is discussed in detail in Chapter 13.)

The Commission helps to administer EU policy in a number of other ways. For example, it is an important player in the treaty-mandated "multilateral surveillance" of governments' economic and budgetary policies. In particular, the Commission encourages governments to maintain fiscal discipline and undertake economic reforms to ensure the success of Economic and Monetary Union and implementation of the Lisbon strategy. Each year, the Commission assesses governments' stability programs (for eurozone members) and convergence programs (for eurozone nonmembers) and makes recommendations for improvement. More generally, the Commission drafts the Broad Economic Policy Guidelines, a key document for economic policy coordination in the EU. First issued in May 1998, shortly after the decision to launch the final stage of EMU, the guidelines consist of both general and country-specific recommendations and now cover a three-year period. The Commission follows up with an annual implementation report to see how well governments are following the guidelines.

Policing Community Law

The Commission is sometimes grandiloquently called the "guardian" of the treaties. This means that the Commission may bring a member state before the Court of Justice for alleged nonfulfillment of treaty obligations. Governments generally respect the treaties; otherwise the EU would cease to function. Most national violations result from genuine misunderstandings or misinterpretations or from delays in transposing Community legislation into national law. Deliberate noncompliance nonetheless exists, notably in the areas of competition policy, the internal market, and the environment. For political and public relations reasons, governments and the Commission are reluctant to pursue cases all the way to the Court, and most disputes are resolved at an early stage.

The Commission may become aware of a possible infringement for any number of reasons. An individual, an enterprise, or a government may complain, or an investigation by Commission officials could uncover possible violations. If the Commission decides to take action, it first sends a "letter of formal notice" asking the government concerned to explain the alleged breach. The government in question has about two months to reply. If it fails to reply or does not provide a satisfactory explanation, the Commission issues a "reasoned opinion" outlining why it considers the country to be in violation of the treaty. Again, the Commission usually gives the government two months to comply. Most cases end with a letter of formal notice or a reasoned opinion.

Compliance with Community law is a sensitive political issue for governments and the Commission alike. Governments resent being taken to court, and the Commission is reluctant to risk antagonizing them. Although the Commission realizes that noncompliance by one country is unfair to the others and that the EU's credibility may be at stake, cases of political deals between the Commission and national governments abound. For example, in 2007, Austria linked reaching agreement on the Lisbon Treaty to resolving a long-standing dispute with the Commission over limits on the number of Austrian university seats available to foreigners, something that the Commission claimed was contrary to Community law (based on a 2005 Court ruling on university quotas) and that Austria claimed was essential to prevent medical faculties from being overrun by Germans. The problem was solved just before a crucial summit to work out final details of the Lisbon Treaty, when the Commission announced its willingness temporarily to suspend infringement proceedings against Austria. The Commission was sensitive to the likely negative impact on Austrian public opinion of infringement proceedings and, more to the point, the possibility that the dispute with Austria might derail the Lisbon Treaty. Discretion being the better part of valor, the Commission offered a five-year moratorium on taking legal action, hoping in the meantime to reach an acceptable agreement on the substance of the case itself.

As a rule, the Commission acts slowly and deliberately in dealing with infringement. Each year it publishes a report on its monitoring of the application of Community law. The Commission issues approximately 1,700 formal notices and 425 reasoned opinions annually, and refers about 200 cases each year to the Court of Justice. Greece, Italy, and Portugal are among the worst offenders; the new member states score rather well.[8]

External Relations Responsibilities

The Lisbon Treaty states that "with the exception of the [CFSP], and other cases provided for in the Treaties, [the Commission] shall ensure the Union's external representation." The Commission has always been an international actor, with its stature increasing significantly since the end of the Cold War, when it took responsibility for coordinating the Western assistance effort to the newly independent countries of Central and Eastern Europe. Despite being an area primarily of intergovernmental activity, the CFSP added a new dimension to the Commission's international involvement. Also in the 1990s, the Transatlantic Declaration and the New Transatlantic Agenda strengthened the Commission's role in US-EU relations, while the conclusion of the Uruguay Round of the General Agreement on Tariffs and Trade and the launch of the World Trade Organization (WTO) highlighted the Commission's importance as an international trade negotiator. The Commission conducts an ambitious development policy on behalf of the EU and participates in summits of the G8 and G20. Most so-called third countries (non-EU members) and international organizations have diplomatic relations with the EU, and the Commission is represented in the approximately 150 EU delegations (embassies) throughout the world.

Despite—or perhaps because of—its burgeoning responsibilities in this area, the Commission has had great difficulty adequately organizing its international relations portfolios and directorates-general. Each Commission president has organized things differently. The first Barroso Commission had a portfolio for external relations and European neighborhood policy, and separate portfolios for enlargement, trade, and development and humanitarian aid, areas that pertain directly to external relations. Moreover, many portfolios that do not deal specifically with external relations, such as competition, environment, justice, freedom, and security, had obvious external dimensions. In an effort to establish a formal coordinating mechanism, early in his first term Barroso established and led a working group of commissioners with major external relations responsibilities. Faced with other demands, Barroso did not devote much time to the group.[9] Clearly, successful coordination depended largely on informal dealings among the commissioners in question.

The establishment in 1999 of the office of High Representative for CFSP within the Council of Ministers institutionalized some friction between the Commission's external relations directorate-general and the High Representative's office. Fortunately for the EU, Javier Solana, the High Representative from 1999 to 2009, and the two commissioners in charge of external relations during that time had a good working relationship. The revamped office of High Representative, provided for in the Lisbon Treaty, combines the positions of High Representative and Commission vice president, thereby streamlining the process of EU foreign policy formulation and implementation. Despite being a joint position, the new office shifts the balance of EU external policymaking and representation away from the Commission and toward the Council, which is determined to keep a firm grip on EU foreign relations. Nor does it reduce the challenge of coordinating the work of commissioners with external relations responsibilities.

In his second Commission, Barroso divided the development and humanitarian aid portfolio (from his first Commission) into two, one for development alone and the second for international cooperation, humanitarian aid, and crisis response. He also separated European neighborhood policy from external relations and moved it to the enlargement portfolio, with external relations being subsumed into the responsibilities of the combined High Representative and Commission vice president position. Barroso kept a separate portfolio for trade. In his announcement of portfolios for the commissioners-designate in his second term, Barroso noted that the commissioners for enlargement and European neighborhood policy, development, international cooperation, humanitarian aid, and crisis response would work "in close cooperation with the High Representative/Vice-President in accordance with the treaties."[10] It will take some time to see how such cooperation works out in practice.

It also remains to be seen how Barroso, Ashton, and European Council president Herman Van Rompuy manage EU external representation among themselves. Barroso is the most eager to be in the limelight, in Europe or abroad. For that reason Barroso must have been pleased that the European Council chose such unassuming people as Van Rompuy and Ashton to be the first incumbents of the new, Lisbon Treaty positions. All three will, literally, be on the international stage together at press conferences following international summits. The fact that the EU has three external relations representatives demonstrates the peculiar nature of the EU itself.

Contributing to Enlargement and Treaty Reform

Enlargement and treaty reform, which often go hand in hand, change the EU's contours and character. Both are primarily intergovernmental processes. Indeed, accession negotiations with prospective member states are formally known as intergovernmental conferences. Accordingly, the Council is the lead institution in the enlargement process, with the Council presidency conducting the negotiations on behalf of the EU. Yet the Commission plays an important role as well. First, the Commission prepares an "opinion" on the suitability of an applicant country for EU membership. Accession negotiations cannot begin without the Commission's opinion, although the Council is not obliged to follow the Commission's advice.

The Commission prides itself on being an honest broker during the accession negotiations, telling each side—the existing and the prospective member state or states—the truth about the other. The Commission's annual monitoring reports on the candidate countries' preparedness for membership, issued every October or November, provide refreshingly frank assessments. Candidate countries eagerly await these progress reports, which form the basis for decisions by the Council on the pace and possible conclusion of the accession negotiations. Other aspects of the Commission's role in the enlargement process include conducting a screening exercise (assessing the compatibility of the candidates' laws with existing EU laws), publishing a scorecard on the state of play of the negotiations, implementing pre-accession aid programs, and helping the candidates meet the requirements of EU membership.

Treaty reform is another, more overtly intergovernmental process (the term "intergovernmental conference" is synonymous with it). Here again, the Commission helps to start the formal process by submitting a report on the advisability of holding an intergovernmental conference. Not being a government, however, the Commission cannot be a full participant in the conference itself. Instead, the Commission submits proposals and draft treaty changes, and Commission officials or commissioners attend meetings of the intergovernmental conference. The Commission often helps to broker an agreement in the conference but cannot block an agreement from being reached even if it strongly opposes the proposed changes.

The reform process culminating in the Constitutional Treaty, later amended to the Lisbon Treaty, was unusual in that a convention drawn from representatives of various national and European institutions, including the Commission, preceded the intergovernmental conference. Thus the Commission played a primary role in preparing the Draft Constitutional Treaty (although its influence was limited) but only a secondary role in the intergovernmental conference that followed. Given the controversy surrounding the Constitutional and Lisbon treaties, the days of grand treaty reform in the EU are probably over.

Depending on the political climate and the caliber of the commissioners involved (including the president), participation in the processes of enlargement and treaty reform affords the Commission an opportunity to assert itself politically vis-à-vis the Council and the Parliament. Yet enlargement, in particular, has imposed a considerable organizational burden on the Commission. Central and Eastern European enlargement was a dramatic case in point. In January 1999 the Commission established a major new unit, the Task Force for the Accession Negotiations, in anticipation of the formal opening of negotiations in March. Soon afterward the task force became a full-fledged directorate-general, drawing personnel and other scarce resources from elsewhere in the Commission. Although the EU still has a list of countries hoping to join, enlargement is no longer as pressing and demanding an issue as it was in the run-up to the accession of twelve new countries from 2004 to 2007. Accordingly, Barroso expanded the enlargement portfolio in his first Commission to include also European neighborhood policy in his second Commission.

Reporting on EU Developments

In order to carry out its various responsibilities, the Commission generates thousands of reports annually. Most of these are narrowly focused and rarely resonate outside the directorate-general or service in which they are written. However, the Commission also produces a number of reports on major EU developments that have a wider interest and readership. In some cases these are part of the Commission's regular responsibilities; in other cases they are the result of specific mandates from the European Council. Examples include:

- *The spring report on the Lisbon strategy for economic reform:* Produced for the meeting of the European Council in March each year and devoted primarily to reviewing progress on the Lisbon strategy. The spring report is a thorough examination of almost all of the EU's economic, social, and environmental activities.
- *Cohesion reports:* Published every three years, these examine progress made toward achieving economic, social, and territorial cohesion in the EU. Soon after releasing a cohesion report, the Commission holds a Cohesion Forum in Brussels, in which representatives of EU institutions, national governments, regional authorities, and nongovernmental organizations participate.

Pointing the Way Forward

One of the Commission's most important roles is unstated but historically important. As Jacques Delors put it during a celebration in Rome in March 1987 to mark the EC's thirtieth anniversary, the Commission has a "strategic authority" to "guarantee the continuity of the [integration] project despite the political or geopolitical hazards." Acting as a "custodian of European interests [and] as a repository of past achievements," Delors declared that the Commission has a cherished obligation to point "the way to the goal ahead."[11]

The history of the EU is replete with examples of the Commission pointing the way forward, especially during Delors's presidency. The single market program and EMU stand out. Since then, Commission presidents have had neither the aptitude nor the opportunity to lead the EU in quite the same way. The EU has a busy policy agenda, but is unlikely ever again to embrace a grand venture that could propel deeper integration under the leadership of a powerful Commission president or a national leader or leaders. There are few frontiers of European integration left to conquer, short of such politically improbable projects as fiscal federalism, the merging of national armies, or the establishment of a full-fledged federation. The Commission can no longer be in the vanguard of European integration because European integration, as a movement of fundamental economic and political change, has arguably run its course. Day-to-day European integration—implementing a range of EU policies and programs—is nonetheless a demanding and useful endeavor, in which the Commission will always be at center stage.

▨ Notes

1. See Gerhard Sabathil, Klemens Joos, and Bernd Kebler, *The European Commission: An Essential Guide to the Institution, the Procedures, and the Policies* (London: Kegan Page, 2008); and Andy Smith, ed., *Politics and the European Commission: Actors, Interdependence, Legitimacy* (London: Routledge, 2006).

2. On Delors's presidency, see Helen Drake, *Jacques Delors: Perspectives on a European Leader* (London: Routledge, 2000); Ken Endo, *The Presidency of the European Commission Under Jacques Delors: The Politics of Shared Leadership* (New York: St. Martin's, 1999); George Ross, *Jacques Delors and European Integration* (Oxford: Oxford University Press, 1995); Jacques Delors, *Mémoires* (Paris: Plon, 2004), pp. 171–430.

3. Wolfgang Münchau, "Like a Fish, Europe Is Rotting from the Head," *Financial Times*, May 11, 2009.

4. On the Commission's internal organization and staffing, see A. Stevens and H. Stevens, *Brussels Bureaucrats? The Administration of the European Union* (Basingstoke: Palgrave Macmillan, 2001). For an insider's account, see Derek-Jan Eppink, *Life of a European Mandarin: Inside the Commission* (Tielt: Lannoo, 2008).

5. European Commission, "Reforming the Commission: A White Paper," 2000, points 1–2.

6. European Commission, "European Governance: A White Paper," COM (2001)428 final, July 25, 2001.

7. See Sebastian Kurpas, Caroline Grøn, and Piotr Maciej Kaczyński, "The European Commission After Enlargement: Does More Add Up to Less?" CEPS Special Report, Brussels, February 2008, pp. 6–15.

8. See, for instance, European Commission, "25th Annual Report from the Commission on Monitoring the Application of Community Law (2007)," SEC(2008)2855, annex II, tab. 2.1, November 18, 2008.

9. See Kurpas, Grøn, and Kaczyński, *European Commission After Enlargement,* pp. 39–40.

10. *Europa,* "President Barroso Unveils His Team," Brussels, November 27, 2009, http://europa.eu/rapid/pressReleasesAction.do?reference=IP/09/1837&format=HTML&aged=0&language=EN&guiLanguage=en.

11. Jacques Delors, speech on the occasion of the thirtieth anniversary of the signing of the Treaty of Rome, March 25, 1987, Bulletin EC S/2-1987, p. 10.

8 The European Council and the Council of Ministers

The European Council and the Council of Ministers (generally known as the Council) are related but separate entities. The Council of Ministers consists of government ministers and a European commissioner who meet regularly to reconcile national positions and enact EU legislation (only the ministers may vote). By contrast, the European Council consists of each country's top political leader (head of state or government, depending on the country's political system), the elected European Council president, and the Commission president. The purpose of the European Council is to resolve intractable problems and to lead the European Union at the highest political level.

The history of the EU bears out the political importance of summit meetings. Without regular working sessions of government leaders, the European Community might not have survived Eurosclerosis in the 1970s or successfully launched the single market program in the mid-1980s. Nor could the EU have adjusted, however haltingly, to the post–Cold War world and the challenge of globalization in the 1990s. Thus the European Council is far more than a glorified meeting of the Council of Ministers, although it sometimes runs the risk of merely doing the latter's work.

The Council of Ministers combines elements of intergovernmentalism and supranationalism; its members (government ministers) in most cases make decisions on the basis of qualified majority voting. The European Council is more avowedly intergovernmental, despite the Commission president's participation within it. Ardent Eurofederalists often lament the European Council's ascendancy. Yet the emergence of the European Council in the 1970s contributed to a gradual strengthening, rather than weakening, of supranationalism. Aware of the intergovernmentalism inherent in regular summitry, national leaders agreed when they launched the European Council in 1975 to organize direct elections to the European Parliament in an effort to shore up supranationalism. EU leaders took other steps to strengthen supranationalism, such as expanding the EP's powers and extending the scope of voting in the Council, at subsequent

EU summits. Thus, the European Council's emergence generated a dynamic interrelationship between intergovernmentalism and supranationalism that contributed to the EU's transformation in the post–Cold War period and continues to this day.

▪ Europe's Most Exclusive Club

In a press conference at the end of the December 1974 Paris summit, French president Valéry Giscard d'Estaing declared with a rhetorical flourish that "the European Summit is dead, long live the European Council."[1] The EC's leaders had just decided to replace their ad hoc meetings with regular get-togethers. Nevertheless, the newly formed European Council did not become an official institution on a par with the Council of Ministers, the Commission, or the Parliament. The Single European Act merely recognized the European Council's existence and importance, whereas the Maastricht Treaty codified its composition and number of annual meetings. The Maastricht Treaty also specified that "the European Council shall provide the Union with the necessary impetus for its development and shall define the general guidelines thereof." Only with the Lisbon Treaty did the European Council become a formal institution, charged with defining "the general political directions and priorities" of the EU.

It seems odd that EU leaders waited so long to formalize the European Council's status. Yet national governments were reluctant to tip the constitutional balance by formally institutionalizing the European Council and implicitly reinforcing intergovernmentalism in the EU system. Only during the constitutional debate in the early 2000s, by which time it was obvious that the European Council had become politically the most important body in the EU and that its prominence had not weakened supranationalism, was the European Council given formal institutional status in the Lisbon Treaty.

The Lisbon Treaty specifies that the European Council "shall meet twice every six months, convened by its President." The European Council was already meeting four times a year, at the end of each Council presidency (in June and December) and midsemester in March and October or November. EU leaders decided at the Lisbon summit in March 2000, when they launched the Lisbon strategy for economic reform, that they would devote their annual spring meeting to economic affairs. Often, more immediate issues intrude on the agenda of a meeting of the European Council. Instead of discussing the Europe 2020 strategy in March 2010, for example, the European Council found itself embroiled in a discussion about the Greek debt crisis.

Development
In its early years, the European Council dealt less with urgent matters than with chronic economic and political problems. With decisionmaking in the

Council thrown into low gear by the Luxembourg Compromise and member states suffering from stagflation, the European Council helped keep the Community together. During the years 1979–1984, when the European Council was bogged down in the British budgetary question, national leaders found themselves debating the minutiae of agricultural prices and countries' financial contributions.

Resolution of the budgetary dispute in June 1984 finally allowed the European Council to revert to its original role as a forum for discussion of the Community's overall political and economic direction. Immediately thereafter, the European Council became "the decisive actor, the final arbiter, in the development of the internal market."[2] It was in the late 1980s that Jacques Delors imposed his stamp on the European Council, putting the Commission presidency at the center of the institution's affairs. Reflecting the changing nature and rising political stakes of European integration, national leaders and Commission presidents immersed themselves thereafter in detailed negotiations during the concluding summits of successive rounds of treaty reform and enlargement.

The inequality inherent in such an ostensibly egalitarian body as the European Council is evident in the attention paid to the leaders of the big member states. The leaders of France and Germany always dominate. Individual British leaders have been effective in the European Council, but British influence is diminished by the country's Euroskepticism and nonmembership in the eurozone. Italy's influence has been undermined in recent years by national leadership that was either weak (Prime Minister Romano Prodi) or highly idiosyncratic (Prime Minister Silvio Berlusconi).

From the outset, informality and spontaneity have characterized the European Council and contributed to its effectiveness. Although meetings of the European Council have unavoidably become more methodical, structured, and stylized over the years, their relative freedom from legal rules and regulations is a key ingredient of their success. Inevitably, the EU's growing size has robbed the European Council of its closeness, with many more national leaders and foreign ministers sitting around the table, until the foreign ministers' automatic attendance ended with implementation of the Lisbon Treaty. Nevertheless, with so many countries in the EU and frequent changes of national leadership, the composition of the European Council is constantly churning.

Roles and Responsibilities

Apart from specific functions, such as making appointments to key positions or deciding if a member state qualifies for adoption of the euro, the European Council's primary purpose is to provide strategic direction by considering the EU's and the member states' policies and priorities as an organic whole rather than as separate and competing ingredients. Other roles and responsibilities that have either existed from the outset or developed over time include:

- Acquainting the heads of state and government with each other and with each other's views on economic, social, and political issues.
- Discussing current global developments and issuing important foreign policy statements and declarations.
- Reconciling differences between the EU's external economic relations and the member states' foreign policies.
- Reaching agreement on the multiannual financial framework.
- Setting the agenda for further integration.
- Negotiating key treaty revisions during intergovernmental conferences.

Because of their political sensitivity, these tasks are peculiar to the European Council and could not be performed by any other EU body. But the European Council serves another purpose that possibly reduces its effectiveness and weakens the EU system. By acting as a "court of appeal" for the Council of Ministers, the European Council undermines its own and the Council of Ministers' efficiency. Although the European Council must take ultimate responsibility, too often it becomes involved in deciding issues that should have been settled at a lower level. The increasing use of qualified majority voting in the Council of Ministers since the early 1980s reduced some of the pressure on the European Council to replicate the ministers' work, but the culture of consensus and the continuing need for unanimity on certain issues ensure that to some extent the European Council will always be the final decision-making authority.

Conduct and Procedures

Until the early 2000s, regular meetings of the European Council took place in the country holding the presidency, and key outcomes were known by the location of the meeting. However, for reasons of security (antiglobalization protesters began to target meetings of the European Council) and as a side-payment to Belgium for accepting fewer Council votes than the neighboring Netherlands, EU leaders agreed in the Nice Treaty to centralize European Council meetings in Brussels. The Résidence Palace, an imposing Art Deco apartment block in the middle of the EU district, was refurbished to become the permanent meeting place of the European Council.

National civil servants, Commission officials, and officials of the Council secretariat under the direction of the European Council president prepare the European Council's agenda. An informal agenda and a draft set of summit conclusions begin to take shape at meetings of the Committee of Permanent Representatives and other special committees and are discussed at length by foreign ministers in the General Affairs Council (GAC) about two weeks before each summit. At the same time, the European Council president, accompanied by the head of the Council secretariat, visits some or all of the national capitals to discuss the imminent meeting. A few days before the European Council, the president writes to the other summit participants, outlining the principal themes and agenda items for the meeting. In keeping with the European Council's supposed informality, participants decide the final agenda themselves at the opening session.

The European Council's format remained largely unchanged until implementation of the Lisbon Treaty in December 2009. Most summits are still two-day affairs, usually beginning with lunch on day one and ending on the afternoon of day two. Extraordinary or informal summits, convened by the president to discuss specific issues or developments (such as the informal meeting of EU leaders in early March 2009 to discuss the European Economic Recovery Plan), tend to be shorter, lasting no more than a day or even a single evening. Foreign ministers once attended all sessions of the European Council. As the Lisbon Treaty came into effect, however, the presidency restricted participation in the European Council to the principals only, plus the High Representative for Foreign Affairs and Security, the latter of whom, under the terms of the treaty, "shall take part in [the European Council's] work." Government ministers and commissioners (other than the president and the combined position of High Representative and Commission vice president) are invited to attend sessions of the European Council dealing with specialized issues. The spring European Council, devoted to the economic reform, is preceded by the tripartite social summit, a meeting between EU leaders and representatives of the social partners (employers and private- and public-sector workers).

Dinner at the end of day one is restricted to the principals. Depending on the length of the preceding session, dinner can begin late and end in the early hours of the morning. Time permitting, it is usually followed by the traditional "fireside chat," when EU leaders are supposedly at their most relaxed and informal. The halcyon days of the fireside chat were in the late 1970s, when the EC had only nine member states. Since then, EU leaders have often canceled these intimate sessions in order to continue regular business.

Day two starts with the so-called family photo. The president of the EP then makes a statement before the morning session (but does not attend the European Council proper), setting forth Parliament's views on the various agenda items. In the course of the European Council, the president may break for "confessionals" (one-on-one meetings with participants) or for a meeting of several participants together. Most summits officially end with a press conference called by the European Council president and the Commission president after the morning session on day two. Since December 1994, EU leaders have invited their counterparts from the candidate countries or other guests to join them for the concluding lunch at one European Council annually. Occasionally summits run late into the afternoon or evening of day two. In exceptional cases, they have continued to day three (such events are called "three-shirt summits").

Although the principals meet in a relatively small group, an army of advisers and handlers is never far away. Government ministers, permanent representatives, members of other special committees, and numerous high-level officials cluster in groups in adjoining rooms, furiously drafting bits of the conclusions that, piece by piece, come before the European Council for adoption. The Council secretariat provides note-takers, whose most important function is unofficial: after their fifteen-minute spells with the EU leaders, they immediately tell accompanying officials what transpired in the meeting. Including interpreters, a relatively small number of people are privy to the European Council's deliberations.

The European Council operates almost exclusively on the basis of consensus—whenever national leaders are able to agree. For a long time, national leaders presumed that voting would sour the atmosphere and alter the dynamics of their cozy Euroclub. Only rarely has the presidency called for a vote in the European Council. Yet recent treaty changes have provided for decision-making by qualified majority vote in the European Council on a range of non-legislative issues, notably key EU appointments and whether to sanction member states that deviate from the EU's core values. Given its large size and the growing number of items coming onto its agenda, decisionmaking in the European Council may well switch from consensus to voting in the near future.

Personalities, Politics, and Publicity

Personalities are important in politics, especially at the rarified level of the European Council. EU leaders meet often and get to know each other well. They rarely miss a summit. EU leaders also participate in a dense network of other multilateral and bilateral meetings. Some are EU-related, others are not. EU-related examples include summits of European political-party leaders and Franco-German summits held under the auspices of the 1963 Elysée Treaty. Non-EU-related examples include NATO summits, G8 summits, and G20 summits.

Despite personal and political differences, national leaders have a powerful common denominator: all have been elected to their country's highest office. Well aware of the perils and pitfalls of political life, knowing each other extremely well, and enjoying membership in Europe's most exclusive club, they are careful never to do or say anything that could weaken their colleagues' domestic positions. Yet the strength of the European Council—regular, close encounters of the EU's leading politicians—is sometimes also its weakness. Highly successful, headstrong national politicians, accustomed to getting their own way at home, often grate on each other in the European Council, with unfortunate results.

The conduct of the European Council since the early 2000s has been unusually fractious. British prime minister Tony Blair and French president Jacques Chirac were at loggerheads over economic policy and the war in Iraq.

Many national leaders resented the preponderance of Chirac and German chancellor Gerhard Schröder, who seemed disdainful of the new member states. The IGC on the Constitutional Treaty broke down in December 2003 because of political disagreements between the Spanish and Polish prime ministers on one side, and Chirac and Schröder on the other, compounded by deep personal animosities. Poland's elections in October and November 2005 brought to power a prime minister and president (the Euroskeptical Kaczyński twins) who were uncongenial to most other leaders.

The situation improved when Donald Tusk replaced Jaroslaw Kaczyński as prime minister of Poland in November 2007. Chirac's departure the previous May also helped, although Nicolas Sarkozy, his successor, is notoriously impulsive, frequently interrupting other leaders, notably those from small member states. Angela Merkel, who replaced Schröder in October 2005, brought a welcome breath of fresh air to the European Council. Calm, unassuming, and unflappable, Merkel is a rock of stability in the sometimes tumultuous European Council. Representing a powerful member state, she is also a highly effective mediator and deal-maker.

Being astute politicians, EU leaders appreciate the European Council's publicity value. As one observer noted early in the history of the European Council, "all summit meetings are to a greater or lesser degree public relations exercises."[3] Since then, European Councils have turned into huge media events, with over 1,500 journalists covering important summits. Although intimate and supposedly private, summit deliberations are far from confidential. Even as discussions continue, the note-takers' reports to officials quickly make their way to waiting journalists and into news bulletins. During session breaks and immediately after a summit, ministers and officials brief journalists—especially journalists from their own countries—on what transpired.

■ The Council of Ministers

The Rome Treaty stipulated that "each government shall delegate to [the Council] one of its members." The Maastricht Treaty used a new form of words, describing the Council as consisting of "representatives of each member state at ministerial level authorized to commit the government of that member state." The reason for the change was to accommodate federations, such as Germany and Belgium, where members of regional governments had insisted on representation in the Council when the Council discussed issues that, in their own countries, were the responsibility of regional rather than federal government. Thus, members of subnational as well as national governments occasionally sit around the Council table.

The Council meets in Brussels, except during the months of April, June, and October, when it meets in Luxembourg. Meetings of the Council are numbered sequentially, beginning with the first meeting in January 1958. The Council's headquarters in Brussels is the cavernous Justus Lipsius Building, directly opposite the Commission's headquarters (the Berlaymont) in the sprawling European district. Despite its imposing size, Justus Lipsius was too small to accommodate the Council work of the enlarged EU, leading to the construction of the nearby Lex Building, which opened in 2006.

Although legally there is only one Council, in practice there are various Council formations organized along horizontal lines (for example, foreign affairs, finance) and sectoral lines (for example, agriculture, competitiveness). All are technically equal, but some are more equal than others. Because of the EU's expanding competence, the number of Council formations grew steadily over the years to more than twenty in the late 1990s. The multiplication of formations supposedly increased efficiency by allowing government ministers to decide issues in their particular areas of expertise and also to distribute responsibility for EU decisionmaking among a wider circle of cabinet colleagues. In fact, too many Council formations impeded the EU's effectiveness.

In particular, the GAC, consisting of foreign ministers, became increasingly sclerotic, especially with the onset of the Common Foreign and Security Policy. Foreign ministers were unable to devote adequate time to preparing meetings of the European Council, coordinating the work of the other Council formations, and managing the EU's external relations. Matters came to a head in 2002 when Javier Solana, clearly overwhelmed in his role as secretary-general of the Council secretariat as well as High Representative for CFSP, tried to lighten the load by improving the way the Council operates. Working closely with the Spanish presidency in the first part of the year, Solana drafted a report on Council reform, which the European Council endorsed at its Seville summit in June 2002.

The Seville reforms included recasting the GAC as the General Affairs and External Relations Council, authorized to hold separate meetings on successive days for its two areas of activity, including separate agendas and conclusions. In effect, the General Affairs and External Relations Council became two councils in one. Meeting under the rubric of general affairs, its members prepared EU summits, coordinated the work of other councils, and took legislative decisions in a range of policy areas (on the ground that foreign ministers possess a broad political and economic perspective on European integration that other ministers lack). The agenda of meetings on general affairs included "high political issues" that cut across sectoral lines as well as issues that the sectoral councils could not decide. Here the general affairs meetings ran the same risk as meetings of the European Council: issues that should have been settled at a lower level were pushed up to a higher level. The tendency of the general affairs meetings to become a glorified sectoral council or even a glorified Coreper diminished their effectiveness and tended to increase absenteeism. Foreign ministers' heavy travel schedules also explain why they sometimes missed regular meetings of the General Affairs and External Relations Council, or at least the parts that dealt with general affairs, with junior ministers or the Brussels-based permanent representatives often substituting instead.

In a renewed effort to tackle these problems, the Lisbon Treaty broke up the General Affairs and External Relations Council into two separate councils—the General Affairs Council (chaired by the rotating presidency) and the Foreign Affairs Council (chaired by the High Representative for Foreign Affairs and Security)—and allowed for the European Council to establish additional formations along sectoral lines (also chaired by the rotating presidency). According to the Lisbon Treaty, "the General Affairs Council shall ensure consistency in the work of the different Council configurations. It shall prepare and ensure the follow-up to meetings of the European Council, in liaison with the President of the European Council and the Commission." By contrast, "the Foreign Affairs Council shall elaborate the Union's external action on the basis of strategic guidelines laid down by the European Council and ensure that the Union's action is consistent."

In addition to attending numerous bilateral and multilateral meetings under the EU's auspices, foreign ministers participate in a host of other meetings—for instance, meetings of the United Nations, the Organization for Security and Cooperation in Europe (OSCE), and NATO. At these gatherings, foreign ministers have additional opportunities to conduct EU business and get to know each other better (personal factors and political empathy are as important in the General Affairs and Foreign Affairs councils as in the European Council). Although they see each other often, foreign ministers have far less intimate meetings in the General Affairs and Foreign Affairs councils than their bosses have in the European Council.

Whereas attendance at the European Council is strictly limited, General Affairs and Foreign Affairs councils include large numbers of officials. Each delegation has three seats at the council table and six seats behind, although sometimes as many as ten additional advisers accompany each delegation's top three (the foreign minister, the senior-most foreign ministry adviser, and the permanent representative). The Council president can limit the number present by calling for a restricted session—usually "inner table only," occasionally ministers and commissioner only. Lunch affords an opportunity for a restricted gathering of the meeting's principals. Anticipating the impact of the accession of ten new member states on the work of the Council, the Irish presidency called in early 2004 for better preparation of its meetings, improved coordination by the secretariat-general, and shorter speeches by the ministers themselves (politicians, like professors, are rarely succinct).

Once every six months, the foreign ministers, the High Representative, the European Council president, and the European Commission president escape with a few aides for an informal discussion of foreign and security policy. The first such event, involving only foreign ministers, was at Schloss Gymnich during Germany's presidency in early 1974. These biannual retreats are now known as "Gymnich-type" meetings and always take place in lavish settings and surroundings. Most are memorable for their cuisine and conviviality rather than for serious work.

Although the launch of the General Affairs and External Relations Council in 2002 amounted to fashioning two Council formations within one, another Seville reform reduced the overall number of Council formations to nine. Since implementation of the Lisbon Treaty and the breakup of the General Affairs and External Relations Council, the number of Council formations has increased to ten, still better than the situation before 2002 (see Box 8.1).

Box 8.1   Council Formations

Formation	Responsibilities	Preparatory Committees
General Affairs	General EU affairs; cohesion, enlargement, financial perspectives	Coreper
Foreign Affairs	Foreign and security policy, trade, development	Political and Security Committee
Economic and Financial Affairs	Economic and fiscal policy coordination; budget	Economic and Financial Committee
Eurogroup[a]	Economic coordination	Economic and Financial Committee
Justice and Home Affairs	External border control, visas, asylum, police cooperation, judicial cooperation	Coreper; Coordinating Committee
Employment, Social Policy, Health, and Consumer Affairs	Employment, working conditions, public health, consumer protection	Coreper
Competitiveness	Internal market, industry, research	Coreper
Transport, Telecommunications, and Energy	Transport, telecommunications, energy	Coreper
Agriculture and Fisheries	Common Agricultural Policy, Common Fisheries Policy, food safety	Special Committee on Agriculture
Environment	Environment, sustainable development	Coreper
Education, Youth, and Culture	Education, vocational training, cultural protection	Coreper

Note: a. This is an unofficial Council formation restricted to member states that have adopted the euro.

Yet having fewer Council formations has not necessarily resulted in fewer ministers coming to Brussels or Luxembourg, as several ministers from the same government, holding related portfolios, attend the same Council meeting. Moreover, in a new development in 2002, defense ministers began to attend the external relations part of Council meetings. Defense ministers also hold an informal Council meeting of their own, despite efforts by governments to reduce the number of informal Council configurations.

The number of Council meetings held annually depends on the scope and intensity of EU business and on the political momentum behind a particular issue. Most Council formations meet monthly. Regardless of which sector or issue it covers, a council has supreme decisionmaking authority. It is also empowered to make decisions relating to issues beyond its particular area of expertise. A council automatically approves any "A" points on its agenda—items already agreed to at a lower level that Coreper has identified for formal approval—whether or not those points pertain to that council's area of responsibility. A council may also approve, without a vote (although usually after considerable discussion), some of the "B" points—items thoroughly discussed at a lower level but on which Coreper was unable to reach agreement—or may send some of them back to Coreper for further deliberation. Occasionally the president will call for an "indicative vote" on contentious "B" points to see where each country stands. Depending on the outcome, the president may resume discussion and try to reach consensus, call for a definitive vote, or postpone the issue until another meeting.

Despite the official pretense of equality, there is an unwritten hierarchy of Council formations based on political and economic importance. The GAC is still at the top, despite the foreign ministers' exclusion from full participation in meetings of the European Council. This placement harks back to the early days of European integration when countries saw EC membership fundamentally as a foreign policy concern. As European integration covered more and more policy areas, however, it became impossible to distinguish between the foreign and domestic implications of EU membership. Accordingly, finance and economics ministers, who make up the Economic and Financial Affairs Council, demanded a greater say in EU affairs and, in national governments, challenged their foreign affairs colleagues for preeminence in domestic interministerial coordination. National bureaucratic rivalry over policymaking toward Brussels, and over decisionmaking in Brussels itself, remains endemic. EMU and the 2008–2010 financial crisis have greatly enhanced Ecofin's prominence in Brussels and finance ministers' influence in the coordination of national policy toward the EU. Moreover, EMU gave rise to a highly influential, albeit informal, Council configuration: the Eurogroup, comprising finance ministers whose countries have adopted the single currency. As a result of the prominence of Ecofin and the rise of the Eurogroup, foreign ministers are struggling to retain their bureaucratic ascendancy in EU affairs.

Apart from the GAC, Foreign Affairs, and Ecofin, the most influential Council formations are probably Agriculture and Competitiveness. Despite the steady decline in EU spending on agriculture (relative to the size of the EU budget), it would be wrong to think that the Agriculture Council's importance has greatly diminished. Ongoing debate about agricultural policy reform, especially in the context of global trade negotiations, has maintained the Agriculture Council's political prominence. The Competitiveness Council began life in 1983 as the Internal Market Council, which was charged with helping to remove nontariff barriers to intra-Community trade and was instrumental in launching and sustaining the single market program. It became the Competitiveness Council following the launch of the Lisbon strategy for economic modernization and reform.

Coreper and Other Subcommittees

The Committee of Permanent Representatives plays a vital part in preparing Council meetings and in behind-the-scenes EU decisionmaking. The European Commission has traditionally looked askance at Coreper, a highly influential committee of the member states' senior-most civil servants. Ironically, however, as the Commission's own position revived in the mid-1980s, relations with Coreper improved. Indeed, the harmonious Coreper-Commission relationship—specifically the relationship between Coreper and the Commission's secretariat-general—was a key ingredient of the Community's transformation in the late 1980s and early 1990s.

Countries' permanent representations (embassies) to the EU include national bureaucrats from a range of government departments on assignment in Brussels. Member states rank permanent representation in Brussels among their most important diplomatic missions. The caliber and effectiveness of permanent representation officials determine to a great extent how countries fare in the EU. As for the officials themselves, it may be more prestigious to serve in Washington, D.C., or in the capital of another member state (notably London, Paris, or Berlin), but a posting to permanent representation in Brussels is a sound career move.

Coreper's huge workload has resulted in two configurations of the committee: Coreper I, consisting of the deputy permanent representatives, and Coreper II, consisting of the permanent representatives themselves. There is a strict separation of responsibilities between the two: once a subject is given to Coreper I, Coreper II has nothing more to do with it. The division between one list of subjects and another is rigid.

Coreper's job is to prepare the agendas of the various councils, to decide what issues go to which council, and to set up and monitor legislative working groups of national officials who are based either at the permanent representation mission in Brussels or at home in their government ministries (about ten such groups meet on a given workday in Brussels). Each configuration of

Coreper meets at least once a week. The permanent representatives also brief visiting ministers and other dignitaries and report regularly to their national capitals on developments in the EU. Like their ministerial bosses, permanent representatives become well acquainted with each other, although enlargement has lessened the committee's sense of intimacy and camaraderie. Also like their senior ministers, the permanent representatives enjoy biannual retreats at the expense of the Council presidency.

The Special Committee on Agriculture substitutes for Coreper by preparing meetings of the Agriculture Council, although Coreper continues to deal with the political implications of agricultural issues (such as Common Agricultural Policy reform or international trade agreements) on behalf of the GAC. The Political and Security Committee assists Coreper with foreign and security policy–related issues that come before the Foreign Affairs Council. Whereas Coreper prepares a number of Ecofin agenda items, a separate Economic and Financial Committee, made up of officials from national governments, the European Commission, and the European Central Bank, advises Ecofin on monetary policy issues without reference to Coreper. Unlike other Council subcommittees, which adhere to the Council presidency rotation, the Economic and Financial Committee elects its president for a renewable period of two and a half years.

Coreper escaped criticism during and after the Maastricht Treaty ratification crisis because its existence and functions were little known outside Brussels. Yet Coreper is extremely powerful and relatively secretive. Coreper's ability to shape the Council's agenda and influence decisionmaking by categorizing items as either ready for automatic approval ("A" items) or for discussion and decision ("B" items) illustrates the committee's importance and suggests that, in certain cases, Coreper is the EU's real decisionmaker. Coreper's lack of accountability to the electorate and inaccessibility to the public are key elements in the EU's perceived democratic deficit. Yet Coreper's obscurity continues to shield it from public criticism, while its professionalism ensures generally favorable media coverage.[4]

Transparency

Transparency is a key characteristic of good governance. Lack of transparency in the Council's work has long undermined public confidence in the EU and was a major cause of the democratic deficit. The Council's deliberations were rarely disclosed to the public before the upheaval caused by the Maastricht ratification crisis in the early 1990s. Government ministers were never shy about publicizing their achievements in the Council, but usually did so in a way that increased the perception of its remoteness from national political life. In a bid to regain public confidence after the Danish rejection of the Maastricht Treaty, EU leaders promised to open up the work of the Council and other institutions. In its defense, the Council could legitimately claim that it was not only the

EU's co-legislator but also an intergovernmental negotiating forum. Critics pointed out that the Council was the only legislature in the Western world that severely curtailed public access to its deliberations; the Council contended that its diplomatic nature precluded full disclosure of its activities.

Pressure from some national governments, from the public, and from other institutions (notably the European Parliament) for transparency in EU decision-making unnerved Coreper, the Council secretariat, and many of the ministers themselves. As far as most national and Council civil servants were (and still are) concerned, public involvement would distract decisionmakers and impair the Council's effectiveness. As for the ministers, the confidentiality of Council deliberations was a welcome alternative to the intrusive media and public attention that generally pervades domestic political decisionmaking. Given that neither body wanted to open its doors, it is ironic that the Council charged Coreper with finding ways to implement the EU leaders' promise of greater transparency. Nor is it surprising that Coreper's recommendations and the Council's actions initially were so timid, until growing public disillusionment with the EU forced national governments to take bolder measures.

Responding in part to widespread public perception of a yawning democratic deficit, the debate on the future of Europe in the early 2000s included frequent references to the importance of openness in the Council's deliberations and access to Council documents, as did the Commission's landmark 2001 white paper on governance.[5] As a result, the work of the Council has become much more transparent. In 2006, the Council implemented new rules of procedure on legislative decisionmaking that open to the public, by video streaming on the Council's website, the presentation of Commission proposals and the Council's subsequent deliberations (but not the lengthy preparatory discussions in subcommittees and working groups). The Council also makes votes and explanations of votes public, and holds public debates on its operational program and the Commission's annual work program. Acknowledging existing practice and sharpening the distinction between the Council's legislative and diplomatic character, the Lisbon Treaty stipulates that "the Council shall meet in public when it deliberates and votes on a draft legislative act. To this end, each Council meeting shall be divided into two parts, dealing respectively with deliberations on Union legislative acts and non-legislative activities."

What some ministers see as an assault on their privacy has led them to seek refuge in a sacred Brussels institution: the working lunch. Not only are ministers free of cameras at lunchtime, they are also free of the hordes of officials who attend them in meetings. This dual freedom allows ministers to be unusually frank with each other and to make concessions that they might not otherwise make. Sometimes even the senior-most officials are absent from the detailed discussions that take place in this setting. Apart from complicating the officials' work (minutes of the lunchtime discussions need to be constructed from the ministers' often unreliable memories), the ministers' lunchtime seclusion means that officials cannot brief reporters on the course of the discussions (an indirect way of broadcasting Council meetings).

Just as public access to Council meetings has become more open, Council documents have become far more widely available since the early 1990s. By a declaration annexed to the Maastricht Treaty and by a decision of December 1993 on public access to its documents, the Council established a limited right of access to information and a procedure for those wanting to exercise that right. Following a ruling by the Court of Justice in 1995 that the Council had failed to strike a balance between the public's need for access and the Council's need for confidentiality, the Council revised and relaxed its policy toward transparency. Under further public pressure and also under internal pressure from the more transparency-minded member states, notably Finland, the Netherlands, and Sweden, governments included a "transparency clause" in the Amsterdam Treaty of 1997. This stipulated that "any citizen of the Union . . . shall have a right of access to European Parliament, Council or Commission documents" subject to certain principles and conditions. A separate treaty article clarified this clause with reference to the Council's dual nature as a legislative and a diplomatic body: "The Council shall define the cases in which it is to be regarded as acting in its legislative capacity, with a view to allowing greater access to documents in those cases, while at the same time preserving the effectiveness of its decision-making process."

The Commission duly tabled a draft regulation in January 2000. Intensive negotiations on the Commission's proposal revealed stark differences in approach to openness and access to documents among member states. In contrast to the countries advocating greater transparency, France and Spain were the most restrictive, whereas Austria and Germany did not even have domestic legislation on access to documents. Such differences made it difficult for the Council to reach a common position, although Sweden, in the presidency in early 2001, finally brokered an agreement. Following interaction with the EP under the codecision procedure, the Council enacted the landmark Regulation 1049, giving each institution six months to decide its own rules of procedure on implementation of public access to documents. The ensuing revision of the Council's rules of procedure greatly increased transparency—a public register of Council documents is available on the Council's website—although culturally the Council seems to be incapable of opening up entirely.

Legislative Decisionmaking

Depending on its base in EU treaty law and its stage in the legislative process, a proposal before the Council may be subject to a simple majority vote, a qualified majority vote, or unanimity. As a result of successive treaty changes, QMV has become the norm.

Qualified majority voting is one of the most distinctive features of supranationalism, which in turn is the most distinctive feature of the EU. As an instrument of supranationalism, QMV raises questions of principle, prestige, parity, and power, all of which are highly sensitive for national governments. It also touches directly on domestic politics and parliamentary prerogatives. Not surprisingly, national governments have fought bruising battles throughout EU history over the modalities of QMV—either the weighting of votes for each member state and the threshold for a qualified majority or, more recently, the threshold for the double majority (member states and population)—as well as over the scope of its application to policies under the EU's umbrella. Accession treaties for new member states and intergovernmental conferences for treaty reform have been the major battlegrounds.

Governments have fought over the appropriateness of using QMV even when provided for in the treaties. According to the Luxembourg Compromise of 1966, which ended the most serious political crisis in the history of the EU, a government could exercise a veto in the Council, even when the rules allowed for the use of QMV, if a "very important" issue was at stake. As a result, decisionmaking slowed to a snail's pace as succeeding presidencies generally refrained from calling for a vote in the Council, especially following the British accession. The situation improved gradually in the early 1980s as political pressure mounted to complete the single market. In the Single European Act, governments not only committed themselves to achieving a single market by the end of 1992 but also agreed to do so largely through QMV in the Council. By implication, this was the end of the Luxembourg Compromise. Subsequent treaty changes extended the applicability of QMV in Council decisionmaking, leaving fewer and fewer policy areas subject to unanimity.

The political salience of QMV grew with each round of treaty reform and enlargement, coming to a head in the IGC that preceded the Nice Treaty. The big member states were concerned about the impact on their decisionmaking power of the imminent accession of numerous small countries, ranging in size from Malta to Hungary. Accordingly, the Nice Treaty radically reweighted the number of votes for each existing member state and allocated votes to the prospective member states. The total number of Council votes increased from 87 to 321 after implementation of the Nice Treaty in November 2004 in the EU25, and to 345 after Bulgaria and Romania joined in 2007 (see Box 8.2). The four biggest member states maintained parity, with 29 votes each. Poland and Spain were also on a par, but with an astonishing 27 votes each, only 2 votes fewer than the biggest member states.[6]

The Nice Treaty introduced two additional criteria for a qualified majority:

- At least half (and in some cases two-thirds) of the member states
- At least 62 percent of the total population of the EU (if a member state seeks such confirmation)

Box 8.2   Weighted Votes in the Council

	Population (in millions)	Votes Before May 2004	Votes from May to October 2004[a]	Votes After November 2004[b]	Votes After January 2007[c]
Germany	82	10	10	29	29
Britain	60	10	10	29	29
France	60	10	10	29	29
Italy	58	10	10	29	29
Spain	42.5	8	8	27	27
Poland	38	—	8	27	27
Romania	22	—	—	—	14
Netherlands	16	5	5	13	13
Greece	11	5	5	12	12
Portugal	10.5	5	5	12	12
Belgium	10	5	5	12	12
Czech Republic	10	—	5	12	12
Hungary	10	—	5	12	12
Sweden	9	4	4	10	10
Bulgaria	8	—	—	—	10
Austria	8	4	4	10	10
Denmark	5	3	3	7	7
Finland	5	3	3	7	7
Slovakia	5	—	3	7	7
Ireland	4	3	3	7	7
Lithuania	3	—	3	7	7
Latvia	2	—	2	4	4
Slovenia	2	—	2	4	4
Estonia	1	—	2	4	4
Cyprus	0.8	—	2	4	4
Luxembourg	0.5	2	2	4	4
Malta	0.4	—	1	3	3
Total	483.7	87	120	321	345
Qualified majority		62	87	232	255
Blocking minority		26	34	90	91

Notes: a. Following EU enlargement.
b. Following entry into force of Nice provisions for qualified majority voting.
c. Following EU enlargement.

The apparent complexity of the Nice arrangements threw the Council voting system and the procedure for treaty change into public disrepute. Yet few people understand voting systems in most legislative arenas and the Nice system has proved remarkably efficient. Far from paralyzing Council decision-making, implementation of the Nice arrangements in the enlarged EU has not had a detrimental impact on the Council's legislative output.[7]

Nevertheless, political pressure to simplify the voting system by moving to a double majority of member states and population intensified in the aftermath of the Nice negotiations. Reflections on Council voting inevitably became bound up in the Convention on the Future of Europe, culminating in the Draft Constitutional Treaty in June 2003. National governments used the opportunity of the ensuing IGC to try to change parts of the draft treaty that they saw as detrimental to their interests. The most controversial issue, which caused a fierce row in 2003–2004 at the IGC that preceded the Constitutional Treaty and flared up again in 2007 during the short IGC that preceded the Lisbon Treaty, was QMV (see Chapter 6).

After much acrimony, the Constitutional Treaty and the follow-on Lisbon Treaty stipulated the following criteria for a qualified majority vote:

- At least 55 percent of the member states (casting one vote each)
- At least 65 percent of the total population of the EU
- At least fifteen member states

Moreover, a blocking minority must be formed by at least four member states, thereby preventing the three biggest member states alone from doing so.

These changes mean that the provisions for Council voting in the Lisbon Treaty are more complicated and are also less congenial to the big member states than the original proposal. On the one hand, it would be harder for the big countries to form winning coalitions; on the other, it would be harder for them to form blocking minorities. Yet compared to the traditional system of weighted votes, the four most populous countries (France, Germany, Britain, and Italy) would clearly be better off.

Availing of the opportunity for renegotiation of the Constitutional Treaty following the French and Dutch referendums in 2005, Poland won a delay in the entry into force of the double majority system until 2014, with the possibility thereafter of a safeguard clause for countries coming close to but not quite forming a blocking minority (this harked back to the Ioannina Compromise, a similar agreement reached in 1994 to accommodate British concerns about changes in QMV as a result of the 1995 enlargement). As in past disputes over QMV, the disputes surrounding the Constitutional Treaty and the Lisbon Treaty combined elements of principle, policy, politics, and personality.

Not only the Ioannina Compromise but also a variant of the older and more nefarious Luxembourg Compromise emerged in the post-Maastricht period of treaty reform. A decade after the SEA apparently buried the Luxembourg Compromise, a similar mechanism found its way into the Amsterdam Treaty with respect to the possible use of closer cooperation (flexible integration) among member states. According to the new provision, a government could, "for important and stated reasons of national policy," prevent a vote from being taken in the Council on whether to allow closer cooperation to take place. The inclusion of a quasi-veto with respect to flexibility, and elsewhere in the treaty with respect to "constructive abstention" in foreign and security policy decisionmaking, demonstrated the supreme sensitivity of these issues for most member states. Similarly, the Lisbon Treaty included so-called emergency brakes that governments could pull on grounds of alleged endangerment of the national interest in certain policy areas. The spectre of the Luxembourg Compromise hovering over the contemporary EU demonstrates the degree of national touchiness surrounding the question of QMV.

The Vagaries of Council Voting

The general demise of the Luxembourg Compromise since the launch of the single market program and the applicability of QMV to a wide range of policy areas as a result of successive treaty changes have not necessarily resulted in many more items being put to a vote. In other words, since the late 1980s there has been greater use of QMV in principle rather than in practice. National governments agree to abide by majority decisions but, ever sympathetic to political sensitivities and imbued with a deep-rooted culture of consensus, which soon pervades the new member states, they usually prefer that a formal vote not take place. The Council president may call for a vote, but voting does not always follow. Instead, the country or countries in the minority often accept the inevitable and acquiesce in the majority's position.

In keeping with the vogue for transparency, after each meeting the Council issues a press release that lists the legislation just enacted (if any) and also reveals how member states voted (if a formal vote took place). Journalists and other observers reconstruct what happened in the Council by viewing the webcast of Council deliberations and piecing together information from national delegations, the Commission's spokesperson, and the Council press office (the Council president and the relevant commissioner usually give a press conference after each Council meeting). Based on the available evidence, it seems that voting is relatively infrequent and that consensus remains the preferred path for decisionmaking in the Council. By all accounts, QMV is important in facilitating decisionmaking because of the so-called shadow of the vote and not necessarily because of actual voting.[8] There is little reason to think that things will change dramatically since implementation of the Lisbon Treaty.

Whether or not voting takes place in the vast range of policy areas not subject to an "emergency brake" or the vestigial Luxembourg Compromise, contentious items often become part of a package deal that accumulates during a number of Council meetings. Shortly after becoming Commission president in 1985, Jacques Delors deplored what he called "linkage diplomacy": the member states' tendency to link issues in an effort to negotiate the best deal possible.[9] Despite Delors's denunciation of it, linkage diplomacy flourished during the single market program. Indeed, the inherent give-and-take of legislative package-dealing facilitated rapid progress toward the 1992 target date and has since become a standard feature of EU policymaking.

Paradoxically, the use of QMV can deepen the democratic deficit. Although majority voting in the Council is inherently democratic, it weakens the already tenuous ties between governments and national parliaments on EU issues. By renouncing the national veto, governments reduce their parliaments' already poor leverage over EU legislation. After all, a national parliament could try to punish its government for not vetoing controversial legislation if the government were able to impose a veto. But a national parliament can hardly hold its government accountable for being outvoted.

■ The Presidency

The rotating presidency of the Council of Ministers is one of the EU's most distinctive features. Until implementation of the Lisbon Treaty's provisions for the European Council and the Council of Ministers in January 2010, a different country would take responsibility every six months for presiding over the two bodies. As originally constituted, the rotating presidency was a powerful symbol of equality among member states. It also brought home to each government the full responsibilities of EU membership. Yet the system was inherently inefficient: some small countries had great difficulty managing a successful presidency, six months was arguably too short to pursue a particular agenda, and frequent rotation impeded the continuity of some EU activities.

It was the imminence of Central and Eastern European enlargement that finally focused attention on reform of the rotating presidency. Accordingly, governments agreed in the Lisbon Treaty to end the rotating presidency in the European Council. Instead, national leaders would elect a president of the European Council for a once-renewable term of two and a half years. Governments also decided in the Lisbon Treaty to establish a separate Foreign Affairs Council under the chairmanship of the High Representative. These changes were among the most significant institutional innovations of the Lisbon Treaty.

The European Council
In 2002, British prime minister Tony Blair and his Spanish counterpart, José Maria Aznar, castigated the inefficiency of the rotating presidency of the European Council and led the charge for a radical change. Pushed by Britain and Spain with the support of France and Germany, other governments grudgingly agreed in the Constitutional Treaty to do away with the rotating presidency of the European Council by establishing instead the office of European Council president, which national leaders would fill by electing an individual for a once-renewable term of two and a half years. The leaders of many small countries, already alarmed by what they saw in the Constitutional Treaty as a tilt in the political balance toward big countries, feared that Britain, France, and Germany would dominate the position of European Council president.

Establishing a position of European Council president came to be seen as one of the most important aspects of the Constitutional Treaty and survived without objection in the Lisbon Treaty. Although the original proponents of the position were out of office by the time of the Lisbon negotiations, their successors enthusiastically supported the new position. President Nicolas Sarkozy, in particular, championed the need for a standing European Council president, even during France's successful presidency in late 2008. Whereas many of Sarkozy's accomplishments at that time, notably interceding with Russia over the Georgia war and prompting US president George W. Bush to convene the first G20 summit in Washington, D.C., in response to the financial crisis, owed as much (if not more) to his position as the powerful leader of a prominent European country as to his temporary presidency of the European Council, Sarkozy cited these and other developments as compelling proof of the need for a standing European Council president. Similarly, Sarkozy reveled in the ineffectualness of the succeeding Czech presidency, citing its poor performance as additional evidence of the need for change. Never mind that the Swedish presidency in late 2009 quickly picked up the pieces and provided a stellar example of the strengths of the rotating presidency of the European Council.

Allegedly, Blair wanted to establish the standing presidency partly because of his interest in the job. When he first proposed the position, Blair might have imagined himself stepping down as British prime minister and becoming the first elected European Council president. Such a scenario was blown off course by the collapse of the Constitutional Treaty and by the hostility of President Chirac and Chancellor Schröder toward Blair because of his support for the United States in the Iraq War. The travails of the Constitutional Treaty and the delay in ratifying the Lisbon Treaty seemed to boost Blair's chances of getting the job. Chirac and Schröder were gone, replaced by Sarkozy and Merkel, who bore no animosity toward Blair. Ultimately, however, the legacy of the Iraq War hobbled Blair, as did the fact that he was so prominent internationally. What should have been an asset—international prominence—in a candidate for the new position of European Council president turned out to be a liability, as Sarkozy and Merkel decided that the inaugural office holder should be a less forceful and less famous person. They opted instead for Herman Van Rompuy, the little-known, unassuming prime minister of Belgium. The other national leaders followed the Franco-German lead; Van Rompuy was elected by acclaim in November 2009.

The choice of Van Rompuy greatly disappointed those who saw in the existence of the new position an opportunity for the EU to assert itself internationally through the election of a high-profile European Council president. Such hopes were probably misplaced, given that the treaty merely gives the new president responsibility for preparing and chairing summit meetings, reporting to the EP afterward, and "driving forward" the work of the European Council. The new president would not have his or her own staff (apart from a cabinet or private office), but would be assisted by the Council secretariat. Nevertheless, EU history shows that influential positions can emerge from modest treaty provisions and that much depends on the acumen and ability of the office holder.

It seems safe to say, however, that Van Rompuy has no intention of turning the European Council presidency into a platform for forceful EU leadership, otherwise Sarkozy and Merkel would not have tapped him for the job. Instead, Van Rompuy has focused on improving the European Council procedurally by tightening its agenda, restricting participation in its meetings to the principals and inviting government ministers only on an ad hoc basis, shortening and sharpening summit conclusions, and ensuring better follow-through. He is not averse to convening special summits, in addition to the four annual summits called for in the Lisbon Treaty. The first special summit, on modifying the Lisbon strategy for economic reform—a topic at the top of Van Rompuy's agenda for the European Council—took place in February 2010.

National leaders undoubtedly miss the rotating European Council presidency. The leaders of small countries, in particular, enjoyed representing the EU in summits with other world leaders and generally being in the international limelight. The leaders of big member states will remain prominent globally and are unlikely to defer to a standing president of the European Council, especially during international crises or on issues of particular importance nationally. Organizationally, the reconfigured European Council presidency certainly makes sense. As for the EU's international representation, however, the advantages of the new arrangement are less clear-cut. Global partners may seek out Van Rompuy, but they will also deal with the Commission president and the High Representative, as well as national leaders—especially those of the big member states.

The Foreign Affairs Council

Before implementation of the Lisbon Treaty, the rotating presidency was responsible for coordinating foreign, security, and defense policy. As part of an effort to strengthen the EU's international effectiveness, governments established the position of High Representative for CFSP in the Amsterdam Treaty of 1997. Javier Solana, who became the EU's first High Representative in October 1999, provided a welcome degree of continuity in foreign and security policy, regardless of the rotating presidency, although at the risk of occasional friction with the foreign minister of the presidency country. Despite being a servant of the Council and therefore of the presidency, Solana often upstaged the president in office when they traveled together outside the EU.

Notwithstanding the existence of the High Representative, the rotating presidency's prominence in security and defense policy was burdensome for small countries and highlighted some disadvantages of the rotational system. The large number of foreign policy working groups called for a sizable pool of competent chairpersons, which small countries had difficulty providing. In addition, the presidency's responsibility to represent the EU internationally was sometimes detrimental to the EU's status and influence when a small country was in the chair. That being said, it was advantageous to the EU to have had France in the presidency when war broke out between Georgia and Russia in 2008.

In view of the representational and organizational challenges facing the Council presidency in the areas of foreign, security, and defense policy, EU leaders decided in the Lisbon Treaty not only to establish foreign affairs as a separate Council formation but also to give the High Representative responsibility for chairing the Foreign Affairs Council. Catherine Ashton, the new High Representative, began to chair meetings of the Foreign Affairs Council in January 2010. Moreover, members of the High Representative's office assumed responsibility for chairing meetings of the Political and Security Committee, which prepares meetings of the Foreign Affairs Council, and of the foreign affairs working groups.

This new arrangement deprived national foreign ministers of the opportunity to represent the EU internationally with regard to foreign and security policy, and deprived national foreign ministries of the opportunity to chair the Political and Security Committee and a host of related working groups. The transition has not been easy for national governments, especially for the Spanish and Belgian governments in 2010, when the innovations were introduced. Nevertheless, the benefits of the new arrangement, in terms of continuity and consistency of EU foreign, security, and defense policy, are manifest and welcome.

The General Affairs and Specialized Councils

Despite changes in the Lisbon Treaty with respect to the presidency of the European Council and chairmanship of the Foreign Affairs Council, the presidency of the other Council formations continues to change every six months, on the first of January and July each year. The six-monthly rotation has been reconfigured a number of times to ensure a sequence of big and small, old and new member states and to ensure that the presidency's workload is distributed evenly among member states. Because Brussels virtually closes down during the sacrosanct summer holidays in August and EU work accelerates rapidly at other times of the year according to a fixed legislative calendar in key areas, it would be unfair for the same countries always to be in the presidency either in the first or the second half of the year. (See Box 8.3 for the 2010–2020 Council presidency rotation.)

Accommodating the presidential rotation to the vagaries of the EU's legislative calendar suggests that the president's work is preordained, and to a certain extent it is. Particular EU business must be transacted at definite times of the year—for instance, farm price negotiations (each spring) and a budget agreement (each fall). Also, specific EU programs (such as completing the single market in the late 1980s and the three-stage EMU process in the 1990s) have relatively rigid timetables regardless of the country in the Council presidency.

Yet for three main reasons it can matter a great deal which country holds the presidency at any particular time. First, each country's approach to even

---

Box 8.3   The Council Presidency Rotation, 2010–2020

Spain	January–June 2010
Belgium	July–December 2010
Hungary	January–June 2011
Poland	July–December 2011
Denmark	January–June 2012
Cyprus	July–December 2012
Ireland	January–June 2013
Lithuania	July–December 2013
Greece	January–June 2014
Italy	July–December 2014
Latvia	January–June 2015
Luxembourg	July–December 2015
Netherlands	January–June 2016
Slovakia	July–December 2016
Malta	January–June 2017
United Kingdom	July–December 2017
Estonia	January–June 2018
Bulgaria	July–December 2018
Austria	January–June 2019
Romania	July–December 2019
Finland	January–June 2020

---

the most routine and uncontroversial EU business is bound to be slightly idiosyncratic. Second, countries have preferences for certain EU policies, programs, or activities. Third, changing circumstances inside and outside the EU sometimes confront a presidency with unexpected challenges that call for quick responses. Accordingly, the variables most likely to determine a country's presidential performance are size and resources, diplomatic experience and tradition, familiarity with the EU system, degree of commitment to European integration, and domestic political circumstances.[10]

The rotating presidency's importance has grown steadily over time because of a number of related developments: the progressive deepening of European integration, the profusion of technical or sectoral councils, the corresponding expansion of the influence and authority of Coreper, the proliferation of Council working groups, and the impact of intergovernmental cooperation in the fields of foreign and security policy on the one hand and justice and home affairs on the other. As a result, the rotating presidency's roles and responsibilities have expanded over the years and now include:

- Presenting a presidency program and subsequently reporting on the conduct of the presidency to the EP.
- Preparing and chairing meetings of the Council and its subcommittees—Coreper, various special committees, and a large number of standing or ad hoc working groups.

- Brokering deals in the Council in order to reach agreement on a particular legislative proposal or on a package of legislative proposals.
- Launching policy initiatives.
- Acting as an EU spokesperson.

In the Chair. In Eurospeak, the terms "presidency" and "chair" are often synonymous, because the foremost responsibility of a country in the rotating presidency is to chair the GAC, the specialized Council formations, and the Council's numerous subcommittees. The Council's rules of procedure for the presidency include such routine functions as planning its six-month calendar, convening meetings, preparing agendas and minutes, and drafting conclusions. Member states judge presidential performance primarily by how a country manages hundreds of meetings during its six months in the chair.

Running a good meeting is not purely procedural but also involves crafting compromise agreements and steering participants toward a decision. A country may organize meetings well, but unless it knows the issues thoroughly, understands other countries' points of view, appreciates how a discussion is developing, and judges properly when to call for breaks, adjournments, or decisions, even the best-prepared meetings can end inconclusively or disastrously. Brokering not just a single agreement but a whole package of agreements is an indispensable task of the presidency.

Countries in the presidency play a dual role in Council meetings and have a split personality. They seek both to advance their own positions and to act as impartial arbiters; they are biased and neutral at the same time. That dichotomy is formally recognized in the seating arrangements for Council meetings, where the country in the presidency not only sits at the head of the table but also maintains a separate national representative who sits next to the president, on the right-hand side of the table.

Yet the difference between a country's national and presidential roles should not be exaggerated. Of the two representatives present, the senior-most minister or official always wears the presidency hat, and countries generally see presidential service as being in their national interest. As part of their preparations for holding the presidency, countries coordinate interministerially in order to reconcile national and presidential interests, and if necessary subsume national under presidential interests. Thus, in areas subject to qualified majority voting, it is rare for countries in the presidency to vote in their own interest in order to produce the required majority. Nevertheless, without compromising its neutrality or credibility, the presidency can influence the conduct of EU business in a number of ways. Organizing the Council's agenda and chairing Council meetings afford the presidency a degree of control over the pace of legislation. Much depends on the competence and skill of a particular chairperson.

Responsibility for organizing, chairing, and running so many meetings during a Council presidency puts huge pressure on the country in question.

Large countries have an obvious advantage: their big bureaucracies provide solid infrastructural support. By contrast, it is sometimes difficult for small countries to find enough qualified people to chair all the meetings that take place during a six-month period. Most small countries, such as Portugal in late 2007 and Slovenia in early 2008, radically reorganize their bureaucracies in order to absorb the shock of the presidency, often at the cost of diminishing domestic government service. Despite the strain that holding the presidency puts on small countries, it is commonly conceded that small countries make more of an effort and generally run better presidencies than do big countries.

Agenda, Initiatives, and Representation. Governments outline their presidential priorities in a document circulated at the beginning of the presidency and in an inaugural address by the prime minister or foreign minister to the EP. In an effort to improve coordination among succeeding presidencies, each country in the presidency develops a specific six-month work program within the framework of an eighteen-month work program drawn up by a "trio" of successive presidency countries. Spain, the first country to hold the presidency following implementation of the Lisbon Treaty, formed a presidency trio with its successors, Belgium and Hungary. The three countries published a draft program in June 2009 of the "Spanish-Belgian-Hungarian trio presidency," covering the eighteen-month period from January 2010 to June 2011.[11]

Each country coming into the presidency makes predictable promises about strengthening European integration while outlining what it hopes to achieve during its six months in office. Spain, in the presidency in early 2010, had an ambitious, all-encompassing program: "consolidating Europe's social agenda; paying special attention to gender equality and the fight against domestic violence; promoting a People's Europe; getting out of the economic crisis; [promoting] energy security and the fight against climate change; enabling Europe to speak with its own voice on the international scene and promoting its common values, peace and well-being."[12] Of course, there is no guarantee that the presidency's goals, and especially its specific legislative objectives, will ever be realized. Much depends on prevailing political and economic circumstances and on the prestige, popularity, and skill of the politicians and officials of the country in the presidency.

Whether in speeches to the EP or elsewhere, the Council president may also launch strategic initiatives, a prerogative shared with the Commission president. Just as some Commission presidents are more active than others, some countries are more likely to launch major initiatives than others, and prominent politicians in a particular country inevitably differ in their degrees of interest in and enthusiasm for the EU. The coincidence of a dynamic Commission president, a country in the Council presidency with a reputation for promoting European integration, and effective leaders in that country can benefit the EU greatly.

The Politics of the Presidency. The rotating presidency can easily be turned to domestic political advantage either by distracting attention from pressing problems or by enhancing the government's prestige and popularity. The country in the presidency hosts numerous events during a six-month term, including up to five informal Council meetings. By distributing these spoils throughout the country, the government can score valuable political points. Presidencies also have an important educational function, especially in Euroskeptical countries, allowing governments to use the occasion of the presidency to try to enlighten the public about the benefits of EU membership.

Politically, the presidency can hold a crumbling coalition together. But such was not the case in March 2009, when the shaky coalition government in the Czech Republic collapsed during the country's Council presidency. The situation was exceptional, however, in that Czech president Václav Klaus, a virulent Euroskeptic, engineered the government's fall in order to embarrass the prime minister and undermine prospects for ratification of the Lisbon Treaty. The political shenanigans in Prague—a new, interim government took over only in May—greatly weakened the credibility and effectiveness of the Czech presidency and convinced many people of the wisdom of switching to the Lisbon Treaty arrangements for the European Council and the Foreign Affairs Council.

In their eagerness to trumpet presidential achievements, governments take credit for agreements reached during their term in office even if the necessary preparatory work took place during a previous presidency. Countries about to assume the presidency may be tempted to obstruct decisionmaking during the dying days of their predecessors' presidencies in order to delay agreement until they themselves are sitting in the Council chair. However, the risks are great that such behavior could rebound on the incoming presidency. As a result, governments almost always play by the unwritten rules. Also for domestic political reasons, the government in the presidency is more likely than other governments to make concessions in order to increase its presidency's productivity and prestige.

Experience suggests that big countries have a mixed record in the Council presidency. For instance, France under Jacques Chirac ran a notoriously poor presidency in late 2000, which contributed in part to the unsatisfactory nature of the Nice Treaty. Yet Nicolas Sarkozy led France enthusiastically in the Council presidency in late 2008, scoring a number of successes for the EU. Britain, at least, has a well-deserved reputation for running good meetings. Under Tony Blair, Britain conducted a workmanlike presidency in late 2005, managing to reach agreement on a new financial framework and begin accession negotiations with Turkey.

Like Britain, Germany takes a down-to-earth approach to running the presidency, but unlike Britain, is regarded as wholeheartedly in favor of European integration. The combination of a large, sophisticated bureaucracy, positive experience of previous presidencies, and overall support for further integration stood Germany in good stead when it took over the European Council presidency in January 2007. Although relatively new to the chancellorship at the time, Angela Merkel drew on her own abilities and her country's strengths to win political agreement on the Lisbon Treaty, leaving only a handful of issues for the incoming Portuguese presidency to resolve.

Despite or perhaps because of the obvious disadvantages owing to their size, small countries usually make a prodigious effort to run a successful presidency. In contrast to the mixed records of the big member states, small-country presidencies generally receive favorable reviews. The Czech Republic, hobbled in early 2009 by pervasive Euroskepticism and domestic political difficulties, stands out as the exception to the rule that small countries run good presidencies.

The Council Secretariat

The Council secretariat is a powerful, behind-the-scenes body in Brussels. The secretariat sees itself as being at the service of the Council presidency, helping it to solve problems, reach compromises, and coordinate work. Indeed, the presidency is the presidency plus the Council secretariat. What is involved is much more than close cooperation; it is a form of common action or symbiosis in regard to preparing and carrying out the presidency program. A member of the secretariat always accompanies the president unless a particular bilateral issue is being discussed.

Small countries in the presidency depend heavily on the Council secretariat for logistical support. With a staff of approximately 2,500 people, nearly two-thirds of whom are translators and interpreters, the Council secretariat assists the presidency by helping to draft the six-month work program, providing legal advice, briefing ministers on current EU issues, preparing the agenda for Council meetings, and drafting the meetings' minutes. The Council secretariat is divided into a legal service and eight directorates-general, covering the full range of EU activities.

The legal service represents the Council before the Court of Justice, ensures that all texts adopted are in order, and advises the Council at all levels. Indeed, a representative of the legal service sits to the right of the president during Council meetings and often intervenes, especially during discussions on intergovernmental policy areas. Given the presidency's importance in the process of treaty reform, the Council's legal service plays a critical role on such momentous occasions. For instance, the Council's legal service helped draft the statement on the issues of concern to Ireland following the rejection of the Lisbon Treaty in June 2008, making it possible for the Irish government to hold a second referendum in October 2009.

The Council secretariat has acquired a higher political profile since the deepening of European integration in the late 1980s. The Council secretariat successfully took on new tasks during successive rounds of negotiations on treaty reform, acting in support of the Council presidency. Insofar as the European Council president and the rotating presidency treat the secretary-general as a preferred adviser, the Commission president and his colleagues often charge that the secretary-general is exercising undue influence, not least when the European Council and the Council of Ministers decide not to follow the Commission's advice. The Commission also resents the Council secretariat's higher institutional profile since implementation of the Maastricht Treaty, which included a reference to the Council secretariat for the first time in one of the founding treaties.

The Amsterdam Treaty changed the role of the Council secretary-general in an important respect. Previously, the secretary-general simply ran the Council secretariat. After Amsterdam, the new position of High Representative for CFSP was combined with the existing position of Council secretary-general, and the deputy secretary-general assumed responsibility for running the general secretariat on a day-to-day basis. As High Representative, the secretary-general soon assumed a representational and political role much greater than that of previous secretaries-general.

As part of the Lisbon Treaty's institutional reforms, the newly configured High Representative is no longer head of the Council secretariat. The Council secretary-general nonetheless remains as important as ever, not least because of the secretariat's role in assisting the European Council president and the High Representative. In an indication of where it thinks power in the EU lies, France pushed hard in 1999 to have Pierre de Boissieu, formerly the country's permanent representative in Brussels, appointed deputy secretary-general to Javier Solana. De Boissieu became secretary-general following implementation of the Amsterdam Treaty. The European Council agreed in December 2009 that de Boissieu, who became secretary-general at that time, would step down in June 2011, when Uwe Corsepius, a close adviser to Angela Merkel, would take over. This is a good example of a Franco-German deal on a top-level EU appointment, which the other governments felt that they had no choice but to accept.

■ **Notes**

1. Quoted in *Agence Europe*, December 17, 1974, p. 4.
2. David Cameron, "The 1992 Initiative: Causes and Consequences," in Alberta Sbragia, ed., *Euro-Politics: Institutions and Policymaking in the "New" European Community* (Washington, DC: Brookings Institution, 1992), p. 63.
3. Annette Morgan, *From Summit to Council: Evolution in the EEC* (London: Chatham, 1976), p. 56.
4. For an assessment of Coreper's importance, see David Bostock, "Coreper Revisited," *Journal of Common Market Studies* 40, no. 2 (June 2002): 215–235.

234 final, July 25, 2001.

5. European Commission, "European Governance: A White Paper," COM(2001) 428 final, July 25, 2001.

6. See J. A. Usher, "Assessment of the Treaty of Nice: Goals and Institutional Reform," in M. Andenas and J. A. Usher, *The Treaty of Nice and Beyond: Enlargement and Constitutional Reform* (Portland: Hart, 2003), pp. 183–206.

7. S. Hagemann and J. De Clerck-Sachsse, "Decision-Making in the Enlarged Council of Ministers: Evaluating the Facts," CEPS Policy Brief no. 119, Brussels, 2007.

8. See Fiona Hayes-Renshaw and Helen Wallace, *The Council of Ministers,* 2nd ed. (Basingstoke: Palgrave Macmillan, 2006), pp. 277–297; D. Heisenberg, "The Institution of 'Consensus' in the European Union: Formal Versus Informal Decision-Making in the Council," *European Journal of Political Research* 44, no. 1 (2005): 65–90; and D. Naurin and Helen Wallace, eds., *Unveiling the Council of the European Union: Games Governments Play in Brussels* (Basingstoke: Palgrave Macmillan, 2008), pp. 23–80.

9. Jacques Delors, speech to the European Parliament, March 12, 1985, Bulletin EC S/4-1985, p. 6.

10. On the significance of the presidency, see K. Kollman, "The Rotating Presidency of the European Council as a Search for Good Policies," *European Union Politics* 4 (March 1, 2003): 51–75; and Jonas Tallberg, "The Power of the Presidency: Brokerage, Efficiency, and Distribution in EU Negotiations," *Journal of Common Market Studies* 42, no. 5 (December 2004): 869–1110.

11. "Spanish-Belgian-Hungarian Trio Presidency of the Council of the European Union, 2020–2011 Operational Program," http://www.europolitics.info/pdf/gratuit_en/ 259687-en.pdf.

12. Spanish presidency website, http://www.eutrio.es/en/presidencia/programapol/.

9   The European Parliament

The European Parliament is a fascinating institution. It is the largest democratically elected assembly in the world. Yet it is not a state or national assembly, but the directly elected parliament of a supranational entity. It has budgetary, legislative, and supervisory responsibilities analogous to those of national parliaments but, unlike most national parliaments in the EU, is not responsible for putting or keeping a government in power.[1]

As one would expect in a body consisting of over 700 politicians drawn from almost thirty countries and scores of political parties, the EP includes a wide spectrum of opinion. Nevertheless, the EP has a distinctive ethos, identity, and set of interests. Simply stated, the EP seeks to gain as much authority as possible and to maximize its political influence vis-à-vis the European Commission, the Council of Ministers, and the European Council. Not every member of the European Parliament subscribes to those objectives, which nonetheless define the nature and character of the institution. Indeed, the history of the EP is a history of relentless efforts by its leadership to increase their institution's power. Julian Priestley, who rose during a lifelong career in the EP to become the institution's secretary-general, identified six key battles in the EP's unrelenting "struggle not only to expand its formal institutional powers . . . but also to command respect and recognition from the other European institutions":[2]

- Budgetary authority.
- Entry into key decisionmaking forums, such as the European Council and intergovernmental conferences.
- Election of the Commission president and approval of the entire college.
- Internal reform (still being waged).
- Achievement of coequal status with the Council in legislative decisionmaking (which Priestley called "taking over").
- Overthrow of the Santer Commission (which demonstrated the EP's determination to hold the Commission to account).

235

The EP has used the perceived democratic deficit as a potent weapon to fight these battles, claiming that the EU's weak legitimacy could be strengthened solely, or primarily, by giving more power to the only institution that is directly elected at the European level. With the indispensable assistance of genuinely sympathetic or guilt-ridden governments, the EP has succeeded since the mid-1980s in obtaining substantially greater budgetary, legislative, and supervisory authority during successive rounds of treaty reform. Paradoxically, greater power for the EP has not resulted in a higher turnout in direct elections.

Partly as a consequence of the low voter turnout, the EP is strikingly out of tune with national governments, other EU institutions, and public opinion on the overarching issue of deeper European integration. The EP's reaction to the rejection of the Constitutional Treaty in 2005 and the Lisbon Treaty in 2008 is a case in point. While striving to save as much as possible of the Constitutional Treaty and wanting Ireland to hold a second referendum on the Lisbon Treaty, most EU and national leaders understood that they had to tread cautiously because of deep public dissatisfaction in many member states with the EU and with the process of treaty reform.

The European Commission, precisely because it is unelected and its legitimacy constantly questioned, is ultra-sensitive to the perception that it is out of touch with public opinion. Accordingly, the Commission responded cautiously to the referendum results. By contrast, the EP is an elected body. A majority of its members might therefore be expected to refrain from making extravagant statements in support of the treaties and passing resolutions calling for their immediate ratification. Yet some MEPs, especially those in leadership positions, in their rhetoric and in the language of relevant EP resolutions, were unequivocal in their support for the Constitutional Treaty and condemnation of the allegedly retrograde changes in the Lisbon Treaty.[3]

These incidents suggest that most MEPs need not take public opinion into account to the same extent that their counterparts in national and subnational parliaments must. This is one of the consequences of the consistently declining turnout in elections to the EP, which is a consequence of the public's underappreciation of the role of the EP and indifference to the work of its members. Extravagant statements and resolutions in the EP in support of the treaties generally went unreported in the national media. Even if reported on and taken note of by Europeans, such declarations most likely would have confirmed the widespread impression that MEPs live in a world of their own, divorced from reality.

A curious arrangement whereby the EP meets in both Brussels and Strasbourg, cities over three hours apart by road or rail, adds to the institution's poor public standing. MEPs spend three weeks each month in Brussels attending committee and political-group meetings and the other week in Strasbourg attending regular plenary sessions. A large part of the EP's secretariat is located in Luxembourg, approximately halfway between Brussels and Strasbourg. The cost and inconvenience of constantly transporting MEPs, officials, and innumerable boxes of papers in a 600-mile circuit every month, and of maintaining two sets of almost identical facilities (in Brussels and Strasbourg) and a smaller office complex in Luxembourg, seriously damage the EP's image and credibility.

In their defense, MEPs say that they would prefer to move entirely to Brussels, but that national governments are responsible for the institution's peripatetic existence. Over the years the governments of France and Luxembourg have gone to great lengths, including taking legal action and blocking decisions about where to locate new EU institutions and agencies, to prevent the EP's plenary sessions and secretariat from moving permanently to Brussels. Nevertheless, the Belgian government built a lavish facility in Brussels in an effort to lure all of the EP's activities there. Not to be outdone, the French government built an equally lavish facility in Strasbourg, where the EP had previously shared facilities with the Council of Europe.

After intense bargaining, governments added a protocol to the Amsterdam Treaty, now incorporated into the Lisbon Treaty, settling the matter: "The [EP] shall have its seat in Strasbourg where the twelve periods of monthly plenary sessions, including the budget session, shall be held. The periods of additional plenary sessions shall be held in Brussels. The committees of the [EP] shall meet in Brussels. The General Secretariat of the [EP] and its departments shall remain in Luxembourg."

Although MEPs can legitimately claim that the decision to stay in Strasbourg is beyond their control, they continue to bear the political brunt of the EP's monthly migration. MEPs' generous allowances and seemingly lavish lifestyles, as well as the institution's peculiar procedures, linguistic muddle (most of the EU's twenty-three official languages are used), and poorly attended plenary sessions, contribute to low public esteem for the institution. They also generate an endless supply of silly stories, even in the serious media, causing the institution severe political damage.

Undoubtedly many MEPs are hardworking, dedicated, and sensitive to popular cynicism about parliamentarians in general and MEPs in particular. But until the EP ends its monthly travels, simplifies its procedures, and reins in its members' spendthrift ways, simply giving the EP more power will not strengthen the EU's legitimacy and close the democratic deficit. After all, the democratic deficit is based on popular perception as much as political reality, and Europeans tend to see the EP as part of the problem.

▪ Size and Composition

The EP has grown in size with each round of enlargement as more seats have been allocated to new member states. Plenary sessions, which are rarely fully attended, need to be able to accommodate over 700 members. Accordingly, the EP's plenary chambers ("hemicycles") are huge, imposing edifices. Along with the proliferation of MEPs has come the proliferation of official languages. One of the most striking features of the hemicycle is the array of interpreters' booths lining the sides.

The size and composition of the EP have been a subject of intense intergovernmental bargaining. Since the beginning of the European Community, governments have distributed seats on the basis of "digressive proportionality," meaning that small countries have been relatively overrepresented and large countries relatively underrepresented. Without questioning that principle, the apportionment of seats among member states has always been contentious. For instance, the EP had 626 seats for the EU15. In anticipation of the accession of numerous new member states, national governments agreed in the Amsterdam Treaty to limit the number of MEPs to a maximum of 700. No sooner was the Amsterdam Treaty implemented in 1999 than governments reopened the issue during the intergovernmental conference that resulted in the Nice Treaty of 2001, setting a new size of 732 seats.

Ineligible to participate directly in the pre-Nice IGC, the applicant countries furiously lobbied the governments of the EU15 for as large a parliamentary representation as possible. At the same time, the EU15 fought among themselves either to maintain their current level of representation or to minimize the extent of its reduction. Even countries that traditionally disliked the EP, such as Britain and France, argued tenaciously for the largest possible national representation, suggesting that the size of a parliamentary delegation is a matter of both national pride and political advantage.

Given its large population and political influence, Germany won an increase in the size of its delegation from 96 to 99 MEPs, the largest national delegation in the EP. Most other countries saw their delegations shrink appreciably. Thus the allocation of seats for Britain, France, and Italy, the three next largest member states, dropped from 87 to 72; the allocation for Ireland, a much smaller country, dropped from 15 to 12. Just before enlargement in 2004, national governments decided to apportion the seats already allocated to Bulgaria and Romania, which were not due to join until 2007, among the EU25. That led to another round of bargaining, as a result of which many existing and soon-to-be member states received additional seats, albeit temporarily. The allocation for Britain, France, and Italy rose to 78 each; Ireland's increased to 13.

When Bulgaria and Romania joined the EU in 2007, the size of the EP increased temporarily to 785 to accommodate the new MEPs. Meanwhile, national governments agreed in the Constitutional Treaty that the size of the EP would in future be limited to 750. This time governments did not decide on the allocation of seats per member state (although they set a minimum limit of 6 seats and a maximum of 96 per country), but authorized the EP to do so, subject to European Council approval. In the short IGC of 2007 that concluded the Lisbon Treaty, Italy, for domestic political reasons, insisted on getting an additional seat. In a typical European Council concession, national leaders agreed to Italy's demand but, rather than officially increase the size of the EP above the 750-seat limit, decided that the EP would have 750 seats plus one for the institution's president—with Italy getting the extra seat (though the president would not necessarily be Italian).

The delay in implementing the Lisbon Treaty meant that the elections of 2009 took place under the rules of the Nice Treaty, as amended by the accession treaties of Bulgaria and Romania, thereby limiting the EP's size to 736 seats. Implementation of the Lisbon Treaty should have brought the EP finally to 751 members, as governments whose countries were entitled to extra seats nominated elected representatives to top up their national delegations. In fact the EP expanded to 754 seats in 2010, as Germany was allowed to maintain its outsized representation of 99 seats until the next elections, in June 2014, when the total number of seats would be fixed at 751, as mandated in the Lisbon Treaty (see Box 9.1).

This account of the fluctuating size of the EP over the past decade or so illustrates the perplexing politics of institutional representation in the EU. It also begs an obvious question: How large is too large? What is the optimal size of the EP in an EU of approximately 500 million people? Is it 785 seats (in June 2009), 736 (2009–2010), 754 (2010–2014), or 751 (after 2014)? By way of comparison, India's Lok Sabha (House of the People) has 543 members representing a population of about 1.2 billion; New Hampshire's House of Representatives has 400 members representing a population of about 1.3 million. India is a federation; New Hampshire is a state within a federation; the EU is an association of sovereign states within a supranational framework. Depending on the nature of the political entity, and therefore on the institution's roles and responsibilities, the main challenges with regard to parliamentary size are efficiency and manageability. Political scientists have long mulled over the ideal dimension of a democratically elected parliament. Not surprisingly, they have yet to reach a consensus. Absolute size is only part of the equation; the other is the ratio of elected representatives to overall population, which raises issues of fairness and proportionality.

Regardless of the number of MEPs, throughout the EU's history the distribution of seats among member states has resulted in striking differences in the ratio of parliamentarians to population from one country to another. In 2010, the ratio was approximately 1 to 860,000 in Germany and 1 to 66,000 in Malta. Even in a system of digressive proportionality, the disparity seems preposterous. Egon Klepsch, EP president from 1992 to 1994, proposed to the European Council in December 1992 a new scheme for the allocation of seats in the EP as a result of German unification, which increased the country's population by 17 million. As a result of Klepsch's intervention, united Germany

Box 9.1 Allocation of Seats in the European Parliament, 2009–2019[a]

Member State	Population (in millions)[b]	Percentage of the EU	Seats at End of 2004–2009 Mandate	Seats at Start of 2009–2014 Mandate (Nice)	Transitional Arrangement, 2010–2014	2014–2019 Mandate (Lisbon)
Germany	82.438	16.73	99	99	99	96
France	62.886	12.76	78	72	74	74
United Kingdom	60.422	12.26	78	72	73	73
Italy	58.752	11.92	78	72	73	73
Spain	43.758	8.88	54	50	54	54
Poland	38.157	7.74	54	50	51	51
Romania	21.61	4.38	35	33	33	33
Netherlands	16.334	3.31	27	25	26	26
Greece	11.125	2.26	24	22	22	22
Portugal	10.57	2.14	24	22	22	22
Belgium	10.511	2.13	24	22	22	22
Czech Republic	10.251	2.08	24	22	22	22
Hungary	10.077	2.04	24	22	22	22
Sweden	9.048	1.84	19	18	20	20
Austria	8.266	1.68	18	17	19	19
Bulgaria	7.719	1.57	18	17	18	18
Denmark	5.428	1.10	14	13	13	13
Slovakia	5.389	1.09	14	13	13	13
Finland	5.256	1.07	14	13	13	13
Ireland	4.209	0.85	13	12	12	12
Lithuania	3.403	0.69	13	12	12	12
Latvia	2.295	0.47	9	8	9	9
Slovenia	2.003	0.41	7	7	8	8
Estonia	1.344	0.27	6	6	6	6
Cyprus	0.766	0.16	6	6	6	6
Luxembourg	0.46	0.09	6	6	6	6
Malta	0.404	0.08	5	5	6	6
EU27	492.881	100.00	785	736	754	751

Sources: European Parliament, "Composition of the European Parliament After European Elections in June 2009," *Institutions*, December 10, 2007, http://www .europarl.europa.eu/news/expert/infopress_page/008-11449-283-10-41-901-2007 1008IPR11353-10-10-2007-2007-false/default_en.htm; European Parliament, "Background: Parliament's 18 Additional Seats," February 23, 2010, http://www.europarl .europa.eu/news/expert/background_page/008-69361-053-02-09-901-20100223BKG 69359-22-02-2010-2010-false/default_en.htm.

Notes: a. For the EU27, not taking into account post-2010 enlargement.

b. Population figures as officially established on November 7, 2006, by the Commission in Doc. 15124/06 on the basis of Eurostat figures.

got three extra seats. Klepsch proudly proclaimed that the new allocation "was based more accurately on the size of the [country]—as democracy demands."[4] Yet the ratio for Germany changed from 1 to 984,000 only to 1 to 805,000, hardly a huge improvement.

In its highly influential ruling of June 2009 on the Lisbon Treaty, the German constitutional court castigated the appropriation of seats in the EP. "Measured against requirements placed on democracy in states," the court wrote, elections do "not take due account of equality, and [the EP] is not competent to take authoritative decisions on political direction in the context of the supranational balancing of interest between the states."[5] In other words, the fact that the EU is not a federation undermines the EP's claim to democratic legitimacy, and even if the EU were a federation, a disparity such as 1 MEP to 66,000 in Malta and 1 MEP to 860,000 in Germany (following implementation of the Lisbon Treaty) would be democratically unsustainable.

The EU is in a dilemma. If national governments were to abandon the principle of digressive proportionality and simply divide the number of seats in the EP among the entire population, Germany's delegation would completely dominate the EU and some small countries would have no representation at all. Based on such an allocation, the possibility of Turkey—a country almost as populous as Germany—joining the EU would be even more worrisome for most member states. The current arrangement for the distribution of seats in the EP is far from ideal but is politically sustainable—as long as the EP does not continue to argue that it is the epitome of representative democracy in the EU and that giving it more power is the answer to the EU's democratic deficit. The German constitutional court demolished that argument, but the EP is unlikely to cease its political posturing.

▓ Elections

The adjective "direct" distinguishes the current system for electing members of the EP from the "indirect" system in operation before 1979. Originally, national parliaments nominated a number of their members to sit also as MEPs. The composition of each national delegation depended on the distribution of seats among political parties in the national parliaments.

The Rome Treaty called for the Assembly (as the EP was then known) to draw up a proposal "for elections by direct universal suffrage in accordance with a uniform procedure in all Member States." The EP did so in 1961 and again in 1963 and 1969, but the Council of Ministers never acted. Efforts to move from "indirect" to "direct" elections fell victim to the pervasive struggle between supranationalism and intergovernmentalism in the EU system. Supranationalists hoped, and intergovernmentalists feared, that direct elections would strengthen the EP's legitimacy and power and thereby weaken the Council's authority.

It was only in 1975, following the launch of the European Council (an avowedly intergovernmental initiative), that national leaders agreed finally to hold direct elections to the EP (a nod to supranationalism). After much arguing about the size and composition of the directly elected EP and over other organizational issues, the Council finally agreed, in September 1976, that direct elections would take place every five years. The inaugural elections were held in June 1979.

From the outset, the EP electoral system has varied from country to country. Differences include the way that candidates are nominated, order of names on voting papers, campaign rules, validation of election results, filling of vacant seats, and choice of election day (within a three- or four-day period in June). The most important differences concern:

- *The electoral system:* For a long time, Britain, with its "first-past-the-post system" (except in Northern Ireland), was the odd country out in elections to the EP; all the other member states used various forms of proportional representation. The British system was notorious for causing overrepresentation or underrepresentation of political parties in the national parliament and to a lesser extent in the EP. In theory, a small swing in electoral support could have resulted in a large gain or loss of seats for a particular party, which in turn could have determined which political group (coalition of national political parties) formed a majority in the EP. Thanks to the change of government in Britain in 1997, when the Labour Party came to power, EU governments agreed in the Amsterdam Treaty to allow the EP to draw up a proposal for direct elections in accordance with "principles common to all Member States," thereby paving the way for a common, EU-wide electoral system involving some form of proportional representation. The EP duly drafted an electoral act, which the Council approved in 2002. Reflecting the difficulty of harmonization among member states, however, the act left plenty of room for national variations in a supposedly common electoral system. In the 2009 elections, for example, all twenty-seven countries used proportional representation, but not the same form of it.
- *Eligibility to vote and stand for elections:* Most member states have the same minimum voting age (eighteen); in Austria it is sixteen. In other respects, voting rights differ greatly throughout the EU. Some countries allow absentee voting without restrictions; others extend it only to citizens resident elsewhere in the EU. The minimum age to stand as a candidate varies from eighteen to twenty-five. More significantly, for a long time nationality and residency requirements differed from country to country, with some restricting the right to vote to their own nationals and others extending it to residents from elsewhere in the EU. Accordingly, the Maastricht Treaty stipulated that the Council had to

arrange, by the end of December 1993, to allow "Union citizens" to vote and stand as candidates in elections to the EP regardless of where they resided in the EU. Aware of the political sensitivity of voting rights and acknowledging the unlikelihood of establishing a uniform system, the treaty permitted derogations "where warranted by problems specific to a Member State." Inevitably, such derogations meant that many EU citizens resident in a member state other than their own could not vote in the 1994 elections (the first ones after implementation of the Maastricht Treaty). Since then, most countries have abided by the requirement that nonnational residents from EU members be allowed to vote in elections in their country of residence, although some countries simply disregard it.

• *Demarcation of constituency boundaries:* In some member states the whole country forms a single constituency (electoral district); in others the country is divided into a number of regional constituencies that do not necessarily correspond to the constituencies used in national elections. A drawback of countrywide constituencies is the difficulty of developing close relations between constituents and MEPs, unless the country is relatively small. For that reason, the EP is attempting to make regional constituencies obligatory in large and medium-sized member states.

Although the EP's profile and power have increased greatly since the first elections in 1979, the experience of direct elections themselves—in terms of political-party behavior and voter turnout—has been hugely disappointing. The EU-wide turnout has declined consistently over time (see Box 9.2). European voters seem unaware of or unimpressed by the EP's undoubted importance in

---

Box 9.2   Turnout in European Parliament Elections, 1979–2009

	Voter Turnout (percentage)	Number of Member States
1979	61.99	9
1984	58.98	10
1989	58.41	12
1994	56.67	12
1999	49.51	15
2004	45.47	25
2009	43.00	27

Source: European Parliament, "Turnout at the European Parliament Elections (1979–2009)," http://www.europarl.europa.eu/parliament/archive/staticDisplay.do?language=EN&id=211.

the EU system. Much to the dismay of EU leaders, most voters view elections for the EP as second-order or even third-order contests, being less salient than national or regional elections.

The turnout in the 2009 elections was a mere 43 percent. Although high by the standards of midterm US congressional elections, a point that Europeans like to make, it is low by the standards of national elections in EU member states. The result was especially disappointing because of the Commission's and the EP's efforts to generate voter interest, especially in light of the fate of the Constitutional and Lisbon treaties. More than anything else, the EP wanted to turn the tide of declining turnout and, if possible, break the 50 percent threshold. To that end, the EP launched a public relations campaign in 2008 to apprise voters of the institution's relevance. At the same time, leaders of the two main political groups, the European People's Party (EPP) and the Party of European Socialists (PES), sharpened their attacks against each other in order to generate interest among the electorate. In a further effort to woo voters, the EP highlighted its major accomplishments since the previous elections, notably the enactment of complex legislation on the control of chemical substances, an issue of great environmental and commercial concern; laws making cell phone calls cheaper by capping roaming charges; and an ambitious energy–climate change package. The EP clearly failed to excite electors.

Whereas most candidates campaigned to some extent on EU issues and proclaimed their political-group affiliation, national political parties and issues predominated during the 2009 elections, as in elections past. In most countries the European elections became informal referendums on the performance of the national government, especially in coping with the financial crisis and economic recession. Accordingly, the governing parties in France and Poland did well; those in Britain, Greece, Hungary, Ireland, and Spain did not. Germans used the European elections to indicate how they would vote in the forthcoming national elections, due three months later (they favored the Christian Democratic Party of Chancellor Angela Merkel). Just as they dominate the European election campaigns, national political parties also dominated the selection of the approximately 9,000 candidates in the 2009 elections.

Candidates (and consequently MEPs) tend to fall into one of the following categories:

- Politicians with or without a background in local, regional, or national politics who choose to make careers in the EP.
- Aspiring politicians who failed to win selection as candidates for national elections.
- Aspiring politicians who won selection as candidates for national elections but subsequently lost the election.
- Established politicians who are temporarily out of national office or have retired from national politics (this category includes a number of

former senior government ministers and even a former president of France).

- Successful regional or local politicians who want to become MEPs either as an end in itself or as a stepping-stone to national political office.
- Prominent trade unionists and farmers' leaders who have worked extensively on EU issues.
- Former officials of EU institutions and, in a few cases, former commissioners.
- Celebrities eager to exploit their fame by winning a seat in Strasbourg.

Regardless of why they stand for election, an increasing number of MEPs (though arguably still a minority) take their work seriously. The secret of the EP's extraordinary success is that only committed and competent MEPs make their way into leadership positions.

MEPs are no longer allowed to hold the "dual mandate," that is, be members of both their national parliament and the EP. The dual mandate had the advantage of personifying a close relationship between national parliaments and the EP, but the demands of being a member of both bodies made it difficult for someone to hold the two positions simultaneously. Because holders of the dual mandate tended to devote more time to national politics, they unwittingly reinforced a negative stereotype of the EP as a publicly supported leisure center. Accordingly, at the EP's behest, national governments banned the dual mandate as of the 2004 election, although some MEPs were grandfathered into the new regime until 2009.

■ Political Groups and Transnational Parties

The EP's rules of procedure and allocation of resources strongly encourage members to join transnational political groups. The rules governing the formation of political groups have changed over the years, in keeping with the changing size and composition of the EP. After the 2009 elections, the minimum number of MEPs needed to form a political group was twenty-five, from at least seven member states. MEPs join a particular group for reasons of political affinity, shared interest, or convenience (the definition of "political affinity" is notoriously vague).

Many groups in the Parliament belong to transnational political parties whose membership extends beyond the EU. For example, the EPP group, largest in the Parliament following the 2009 elections, belongs to the transnational European People's Party, which according to its website has seventy-four constituent parties from thirty-eight countries, includes twenty government leaders and most members of the European Commission (including its president), and "is the leading political force on the continent."[6]

The EU has deliberately fostered the emergence of transnational political parties. National governments wrote into the Maastricht Treaty a statement that "political parties at the European level are important as a factor for integration within the Union. They contribute to forming a European awareness and to expressing the political will of the citizens of the Union." This statement reflected the view, especially among the more integration-minded governments, that pan-European party organizations would inculcate a sense of belonging and identity in the emerging EU. The encouragement of transnational party formation was linked to other aspects of the Maastricht Treaty, such as the concept of Union citizenship and the extension of voting rights in local and EP elections to Union citizens resident in a member state other than their own. Presumably, party activity at the European level would make it easier for citizens throughout the EU, regardless of their national origin, to participate in direct elections.[7]

The number and composition of political groups have varied greatly over time. Following the 2009 elections, there were seven groups in the EP, embracing members of over a hundred national and regional political parties, plus almost thirty unattached MEPs (see Box 9.3). From the beginning of the political-group system, three generic groupings (or "families," as they like to call

---

Box 9.3   Results of the 2009 European Parliament Elections

Political Group	Abbreviation	Number of Seats
Group of the European People's Party (Christian Democrats)	EPP	265
Group of the Progressive Alliance of Socialists and Democrats in the European Parliament	S&D	184
Group of the Alliance of Liberals and Democrats for Europe	ALDE	84
Group of the Greens/European Free Alliance	Greens/EFA	55
European Conservatives and Reformists Group	ECR	55
Confederal Group of the European United Left–Nordic Green Left	GUE–NGL	35
Europe of Freedom and Democracy Group	EFD	32
Nonattached	NA	26
Total		736

Source: Europa, the European Parliament, http://europa.eu/institutions/inst/parliament/index_en.htm.

Note: The EP's rules of procedure and allocation of resources strongly encourage members to join transnational political groups. The rules governing the formation of political groups have changed over the years, in keeping with the changing size and composition of the EP. After the 2009 elections, the minimum number of MEPs allowed to form a political group was twenty-five, from at least seven member states.

themselves) have eclipsed all others in the EP. These are the Socialists, Christian Democrats, and Liberals. Since the third direct election in 1989, the Socialists and Christian Democrats have predominated: both were the only groups to include political parties or individual politicians from each member state (since the 2004 elections, the Christian Democrats alone hold that distinction).

The Big Two: Christian Democrats and Socialists

The center-left Social Democrats and the center-right Christian Democrats benefited greatly from successive enlargements. From the inaugural elections in 1979 until the elections in 1999, the Socialists were the largest group in the EP. Dominated by large contingents of the British Labour Party and German Social Democratic Party, the Socialists benefited more than other groups from Spanish and Portuguese accession in 1986 and from the accession of Finland and Sweden—two countries with strong Social Democratic traditions—in 1995. In a postscript to the end of the Cold War, in January 1993 twenty Communists (mostly Italians) abandoned their sinking ship and joined the Socialists.

Following the EU's first enlargement in 1973, the Christian Democrats did not enjoy an influx of British and Danish Conservatives, who instead set up their own group, the European Conservatives, which later changed its name to the European Democratic Group. With the EP growing in importance as a result of the Single European Act, the European Democratic Group requested affiliation with the Christian Democratic Group immediately after the 1989 elections. However, concern among Christian Democrats about the strength of Euroskepticism among the British and Danish Conservatives delayed an alliance between the two groups until 1992.

Long before that, the Socialist and Christian Democratic groups in the EP had become branches of transnational Socialist and Christian Democratic parties. The Christian Democrats were first to form a transnational party, the European People's Party, in 1976. As a result, Christian Democrats in the EP became the EPP Group. In the early 1990s, with implementation of the single market program and the conclusion of the Maastricht Treaty, constituent national parties of the EPP, including their members in the EP, made a serious effort to turn the EPP into a real transnational party rather than a mere umbrella organization.

European Socialist parties also organized transnationally in the Party of European Socialists. Accordingly, the Socialists in the EP became the PES Group. Like the EPP, the PES developed into a well-organized transnational party, using similar methods to influence European integration in a Social Democratic direction.

Once they affiliated within the EP, the Christian Democrats and the European Democratic Group became the Group of the EPP-ED. The newly formed group had little success mobilizing participation in direct elections but quickly became more cohesive and effective in the EP than the preceding loose association of Christian Democrats and Conservatives. At the same time, constituent national parties and the EPP-ED began working closely together in the transnational party to try to influence EU policymaking in a variety of ways, notably by organizing summits of Christian Democratic and Conservative party leaders in the run-up to meetings of the European Council.

Both parliamentary groups (the EPP-ED and PES) benefited from EU enlargement in 2004 and 2007, with a large influx of new members from the Central and Eastern European countries where, since the collapse of communism, political parties were organized along the same lines as in Western Europe. During the heady days of the 2002–2003 Constitutional Convention, and later during the intensive intergovernmental conferences that led to the Constitutional and Lisbon treaties, the EPP-ED and PES sought to influence the outcome of these events by submitting position papers and lobbying national leaders, most of whom were members of one or another of the groups' transnational parties.

The EPP-ED went into the 2009 elections as the largest group in the Parliament, with 288 MEPs. Regardless of the vagaries of electoral politics, they were bound to come out of the election with fewer seats for the simple reason that the British Conservatives, the main party in the European Democratic wing of the EPP-ED, had decided beforehand to pull out of the combined political group. The decision was driven by domestic politics: strongly Euroskeptical, the Conservatives sought to distinguish themselves from the governing Labour Party by opposing most things European and by leaving a political group whose largest component, the Christian Democrats, was avowedly Eurofederal. The departure of the British and other Conservatives after the 2009 election robbed the EPP-ED of its European Democratic wing. With barely disguised relief, the Christian Democrats reverted simply to the EPP Group. Moreover, they emerged from the election with the largest number of seats in Parliament (265).

The PES fared poorly in the 2009 elections, which were really a set of separate national elections. The PES failed to turn voters' concerns about the dire economic situation into strong electoral support. To be more precise, they failed to convince voters that their Christian Democratic rivals, being economically more liberal and mostly dominant in government throughout Europe, were to blame for the financial crisis and should not be trusted to put Europe back on its feet. Instead, the Christian Democrats turned the tables by convincing voters that the Socialists lacked the experience and ability to right the economy and by casting themselves as best able to defend the much cherished European social model. Having gone into the elections with 217 MEPs, the PES came out with only 161, albeit in a Parliament with fewer seats to contest (785 in the old Parliament, 736 in the new). Nonetheless, the PES was buoyed by the decision of Italy's Democratic Party, with 21 MEPs, to join forces with it. As a result of the merger, the PES changed its name to the Group of the Progressive Alliance of Socialists and Democrats (known as the Socialists and Democrats, or S&D).

It is difficult for groups such as the EPP and the S&D, consisting of diverse parties from almost every member state, to adopt coherent electoral platforms and policy positions. Nonetheless, despite the apparent attenuation of ideological differences in European politics since the 1990s, the two groups differ in their approach to key issues such as the single market, social policy, and aspects of Economic and Monetary Union. Both support deeper economic integration but disagree over specific policy prescriptions. In general, the EPP Group is more economically liberal (free market–oriented), while the S&D Group is more interventionist. Notwithstanding the fallout from the financial crisis, the PES Group is less enamored than the EPP Group with the Lisbon strategy for economic reform and more concerned about protecting workers' rights and strengthening social welfare. Each group faces the challenge in the EP of reconciling its constituent parties to particular amendments and positions as draft legislation on a range of socioeconomic, environmental, and other issues passes through the committees and the plenary sessions.

Other Groups

Liberals have long been the third largest group in the EP. After the 2009 elections the Liberals had about one-third as many members as the EPP and half as many as the S&D. Previously called the Group of the European Liberal, Democratic, and Reformist Party, they reinvented themselves after the 2004 elections as the Alliance of Liberals and Democrats for Europe (ALDE). As a relatively small group, the Liberals were unable to win elections to top leadership positions in the EP until they allied themselves with the Socialists during the 1999–2004 parliamentary term, in the second half of which one of their members became president of the EP. The Liberals are liberal in the economic sense—they support deregulation and private enterprise—although their social policies are certainly also liberal, as are those of most groups in the EP. The ALDE group fared better in the 2009 elections than they expected, given the prevailing economic crisis, winning eighty-four seats. MEPs in the ALDE group come from nineteen member states. The group's leader is Guy Verhofstadt, a former prime minister of Belgium and an ardent Eurofederalist.

The Greens–European Free Alliance came into existence after the 2004 elections when MEPs representing "two separate and progressive European political families"—the environmentalist Greens and the European Free Alliance, consisting of "representatives of stateless nations and disadvantaged minorities"—merged to form a single group.[8] It is uncertain why members of regional and separatist parties in Europe, such as the Scottish Nationalist Party and the Republican Left of Catalonia, plus a stray Latvian, are presumed to be progressive. Clearly, the group is a marriage of convenience. The Greens are by far the largest component, having the lion's share of its fifty-five members following the 2009 election, in which the Greens fared extremely well (the European Free Alliance won only seven seats). Among the Greens is a member of Sweden's Pirate Party, whose sole interest is Internet freedom and which came into existence in 2005 to oppose a proposed EU software patent law. Being ultra–politically correct, the Greens have "two co-Presidents, and gender balance is always guaranteed."[9] The male co-leader is Daniel Cohn-Bendit, a colorful former student radical and a persistent critic of Commission president José Manuel Barroso.

A new group, the European Conservatives and Reformists (ECR), came into existence after the 2009 elections, consisting mostly of disaffected conservatives (the former European Democrats) who abandoned the EPP-ED. The British Conservative Party has by far the largest contingent (twenty-five members) in the ECR group. Other parties in the group include two notorious populist parties, Poland's Law and Justice Party and the Czech Republic's Civic Democrats. The ECR opposes Eurofederalism and wants fundamental reform of the EU "to make it more accountable, transparent and responsive to the needs of the people."[10] Being in such an openly Euroskeptical group as the ECR demonstrates how far the British Conservatives have veered from mainstream European political opinion. It was difficult for the Conservatives to be allied with the Christian Democrats, who openly espouse a federal Europe, but it is striking that they have relegated themselves to a small group that includes parties noted for political intolerance and extreme nationalism.

The European United Left–Nordic Green Left (GUE–NGL) calls itself a "confederal group" in order to emphasize the autonomy of its constituent national parties (although parties in the other groups have considerable independence as well). It is an odd collection of far-leftists who oppose the way in which mainstream European politics, society, and economics are organized and who, in some cases, are nostalgic for the good old days of communism in Central and Eastern Europe, with central economic planning, full (under)employment, and universal (but sometimes shoddy) social welfare. The largest constituent party, with eight members, is Germany's Die Linke, which includes the remnants of the Communist Party of East Germany.

Two parliamentary groups could not sustain themselves after the 2009 elections: the Independence-Democracy Group and the Union for Europe of the Nations Group. Many of the remnants of these groups decided to come together in a new formation, the Europe of Freedom and Democracy (EFD) Group. Despite its innocuous name, the group consists largely of virulent Euroskeptics, who want their countries to leave the EU or who want the EU to cease to exist. Its members are in the unusual position of serving in a Parliament whose legitimacy they reject. The largest and most striking contingent in the group is the UK Independence Party, which won thirteen seats in the 2009 elections, beating the governing Labour Party into third place in Britain (the Conservatives came in first).

The EP after the 2009 elections also had twenty-seven independent MEPs, mostly individuals or a handful of party members whose far-right, racist views were so objectionable that none of the groups would have them. The independents included MEPs from such notorious parties as Britain's National Party, France's National Front, and Hungary's Jobbik. Due to their status as independents, however, these MEPs have limited access to parliamentary funds and other resources, and can never attain leadership positions.

The Breadth and Diversity of Political Groups

MEPs cover the spectrum of European politics—a much broader spectrum than exists in the United States—from the far left to the far right. The European United Left–Nordic Green Left and unattached neo-Fascists are at the opposite extremes. The Socialists and Democrats and the Greens are left of center; the free market Liberals, the Christian Democratic European People's Party, the Conservatives and Reformists, and the strongly Euroskeptical Europe of Freedom and Democracy Group are right of center. In terms of ideological diversity yet concentration of MEPs on the center-right and center-left, the political-group system in the EP resembles the political-party system in national parliaments. Nevertheless, ideological rivalry is less intense in the EP, and the political-group system is by no means rigidly bipolar. Compared to national parties, the political groups in the EP are undisciplined, as the diversity of their composition suggests. Moreover, unlike their national counterparts, political groups are not responsible for forming governments or keeping them in power. This strengthens the mutual interest of the mainstream groups in working closely together to promote the EP's institutional agenda and secure the necessary majorities in order to have as big an impact as possible on the legislative process.

Although organized into political groups, MEPs remain acutely aware of their national identity and allegiance to national political parties.[11] MEPs caucus in national delegations within their respective groups. Obviously, some national delegations are larger and more influential than others. German MEPs constitute the largest national delegations in five of the EP's political groups. They are especially preponderant in the EPP, S&D, and Liberal groups. Britain is not represented at all in the EP's largest group, the EPP, and is poorly represented in the second largest group, the S&D, having only 13 of the group's 184 seats (this reflects the poor showing of Britain's ruling Labour Party in the 2009 elections). Most national delegations are concentrated in the EPP and S&D groups, but some are more diffused than others. Spain's is an example of a highly concentrated delegation: of its fifty members, twenty-three are in the EPP and twenty-one are in the S&D. By contrast, the Dutch delegation (twenty-five members) is spread out in all seven groups, and even includes four independents (this reflects the fragmentation of Dutch politics on EU issues).

One of the most intriguing questions about the European Parliament is whether MEPs vote along national or political-group lines. In other words, do they tend to support national positions? MEPs who come from the same country, thereby constituting national delegations, generally have views that span the political spectrum and disagree fundamentally among themselves on a range of policy issues. On any particular legislative or other issue, a national position is really the position adopted by the government of a particular member state. Opposition parties in that member state are likely to have a contending idea of what the national position should be. Given that national delegations in the EP consist of members coming from parties that are in government and opposition at home, it is highly doubtful that such a collection of MEPs could reach a consensus on a national position. For example, French Socialist MEPs are unlikely to adopt the position of the center-right government in Paris simply because it is the official French position. Just as Socialists at home take positions contrary to the center-right government, French Socialists in the EP take positions that are contrary to the center-right government and consistent with the principles and philosophy of Parliament's S&D Group. Voting along national lines would mean voting as a national block in order to support the official position of the national government, something that MEPs who belong to parties outside the government are unlikely to do.

MEPs' positions on policy issues depend largely on the positions taken by the political groups, not by the governments in their own member states. The political groups form their positions on the basis of consultations and discussions among group members, and if necessary by taking a vote. For that reason the size of a national delegation has a considerable impact within political groups. Moreover, political groups allocate leadership positions proportionately among national delegations. The larger a national delegation within a particular group, the more leadership positions this delegation will have and the more influential it will be in shaping the group's agenda. As national delegations in the EP coordinate closely with national political parties, either through direct contact with each other or indirectly within the pan-European parties to which most national parties and political groups belong, there is a strong national influence on positions adopted by the political groups. But such national influence is not necessarily government influence; rather it is the influence of national political parties that may be in government or opposition.

■ Parliament's Roles and Responsibilities

Whatever else may be said of it, the EP cannot be dismissed as a "windy debating chamber." MEPs spend only one week—in effect, three days—each month in full plenary session. Plenary sessions include agenda setting; voting; question time, with or without debate; speeches by commissioners, the Council presidency, or visiting dignitaries; discussions of emergency issues; and debates on general topics. Speaking time is carefully parceled out to political groups and independent members and strictly controlled—usually by the simple stratagem of turning off the microphone. MEPs rarely have an opportunity to prattle on. This may not be a bad thing, and some continental political cultures discourage intense parliamentary exchanges. British MEPs, whose domestic political system thrives on fierce debate, find debates in the EP disappointingly tame.

Apart from procedural problems and cultural differences, language is another obstacle to purposeful debate. Not all parliamentarians are fluent in a second EU language. Thus, most of the EU's twenty-three official languages are always in use (Irish, an official EU language since 2007, is seldom spoken in Brussels or Strasbourg). The costs of interpreting and translating are exorbitant, accounting for nearly one-third of the EP's total staff and about 30 percent of its annual budget.

Despite those constraints, debates provide the EP an opportunity to try to raise awareness and consciousness of certain important issues throughout the EU. For example, the EP prides itself on its advocacy of human rights, often an area selected each month for urgent debate in plenary session. The Subcommittee on Human Rights of the EP's influential Committee on Foreign Affairs monitors human rights in nonmember countries with the assistance of a special human rights unit. The committee's annual report forms the basis of a major parliamentary debate, which generates considerable media coverage.

Apart from raising awareness of important political, economic, and humanitarian issues, the EP has a number of well-defined roles and responsibilities in the EU covering the budget, the legislative process, scrutiny and oversight, and external relations.

The Budget

In the 1970s, when national governments agreed to fund the Community budget via "own resources," they agreed as well that, for reasons of democratic accountability, the EP should have some say in how the budget was spent. Governments made the necessary arrangements in two treaty reforms (1970 and 1975), but did not give the EP any responsibility for raising revenue, which remained the Council's responsibility.

Until implementation of the Lisbon Treaty, EU expenditure was divided into two categories: compulsory and noncompulsory. The important distinction between the two was that the EP could amend noncompulsory expenditure but could propose only modifications to compulsory expenditure. Not surprisingly, the EP sought over the years to expand its budgetary authority specifically by increasing the size of noncompulsory expenditure and, eventually, abolishing the distinction between noncompulsory and compulsory expenditure, thereby winning the right to make amendments in all areas of EU spending. The compulsory-noncompulsory distinction was difficult to justify on rational grounds; its sole purpose was to limit the EP's budgetary reach. Given growing pressure since the 1980s for greater democratic accountability in the EU—including accountability for the budget—and a widespread desire to simplify procedures, governments agreed in the Lisbon Treaty to abolish the compulsory-noncompulsory distinction and establish a new procedure for deciding the annual budget, covering all types of expenditure, that would put the EP and the Council of Ministers on an equal footing. The EP also won the right to approve the multiannual financial framework, within which the annual budget is set.

The EP has long had exclusive authority to grant a "discharge" of the general budget. The purpose of granting a discharge is to verify the accuracy of the Commission's budgetary management and to determine precise revenue and expenditure for a given year. The discharge procedure is arduous and time-consuming and involves close cooperation with the Court of Auditors. The EP usually votes on whether to grant a discharge two years after the annual budget in question.

The EP's exclusive power to grant a discharge has considerable political implications, especially in relations between the EP and the Commission, as was seen in the run-up to the Commission's resignation in 1999. More broadly, as in other policy areas, the EP has attempted over the years to use its budgetary authority to raise its political profile and enhance its institutional standing. This point is explored in greater detail in Chapter 11, which covers interinstitutional relations.

Legislative Decisionmaking

In the legislative field even more than the budgetary field, the EP has acquired greater powers over the years. Initially, its legislative role was limited to consultation with the Council of Ministers. The SEA enhanced the EP's legislative role by introducing the cooperation procedure and requiring parliamentary assent in a small number of cases. The cooperation procedure gave the EP the right to a second reading of certain draft legislation. Originally it applied to ten treaty articles, most dealing with the single market. The new procedure revolutionized the EP's role in legislative decisionmaking and had a profound impact on the behavior of the political groups, as only they could muster the required number of votes—an absolute majority of MEPs—to amend or reject the Council's position at the end of the first stage of the procedure.

The cooperation procedure resulted as well in a profusion of lobbying directed at parliamentary committee meetings in Brussels and plenary sessions in Strasbourg. Before the SEA, lobbyists had little reason to cultivate MEPs. Afterward, lobbyists lost little time trying to shape legislation passing through the EP under the cooperation procedure. In many cases lobbyists alerted MEPs to the procedure's potential and provided them with information about draft legislation that MEPs' small staffs were often otherwise unable to obtain.

The Maastricht Treaty extended the cooperation procedure to other policy areas and, more important, introduced the codecision procedure, whereby the EP and the Council could adopt legislation jointly in specified policy areas. The form of codecision introduced by the Maastricht Treaty dissatisfied the EP, which received only a limited right of rejection rather than a positive right of approval. The new procedure was also extremely complicated. Nevertheless, the EP's management of the codecision procedure belied those critics (especially in the Council secretariat) who claimed that the procedure was too awkward to work efficiently and expeditiously. Experience with the cooperation procedure should have shown that the EP would also master codecision, which it did.

The Amsterdam Treaty virtually abolished the cooperation procedure in favor of a revised codecision procedure that gave the EP far greater legislative power, putting it on a par with the Council in legislative decisionmaking. The treaty also increased to thirty-eight the number of issue areas subject to codecision, which the Nice Treaty further extended to forty-three. The Lisbon Treaty extended codecision to a total of about eighty policy areas, accounting for most EU legislation. In order to emphasize that codecision had become the norm, the Lisbon Treaty changed the name of the codecision procedure to the "ordinary legislative procedure."

Most participants and observers agree that codecision has greatly enhanced the EP's authority. The EP has generally succeeded in having its legislative amendments accepted by the Commission and the Council. Unsuccessful efforts by unfriendly governments to block the extension of codecision suggest that the procedure has indeed been politically advantageous to the EP. Without doubt, the EP is now a powerful player in legislative decisionmaking, the political dynamics of which are examined in Chapter 11.

In addition to its other institutional innovations, the SEA introduced an "assent" procedure covering a small number of policy areas. Under this procedure the EP may not delay or amend proposals, only accept or reject them. As in the case of codecision, the scope of the assent procedure has increased markedly, especially in the area of external relations, as a result of successive treaty changes. Between the codecision and assent procedures, there are few EU policy areas in which the EP does not play a decisive role.[12]

The EP does not have the right to initiate legislation, although the Maastricht Treaty formally gave it the same authority as the Council to request that the Commission submit legislative proposals. Such requests do not oblige the Commission to act; however, the Commission has agreed to take the greatest possible account of them. In collusion with the Council, the EP may also pressure the Commission to initiate legislation by linking agreement in a codecision case to calls for the Commission to introduce specific proposals, a practice that the Commission strongly resists.

Scrutiny and Supervision

The EP has a number of ways to scrutinize the work of the Commission and the Council and to approve the appointment of the Commission president and the college of commissioners. MEPs may submit written and oral questions as a means of making the Council and Commission answerable to them. Additional supervisory powers range from the innocuous (discussion of the Commission's annual General Report) to the vigorous (ability to force the Commission to resign as a body by a two-thirds majority). The EP uses its powers of scrutiny and supervision not only to improve the quality of EU governance but also to maneuver itself into the classic role of a legislature holding the executive to account. The Maastricht Treaty confirmed another supervisory practice that the EP had already developed: convening temporary committees of inquiry. At the request of one-quarter of its members, the EP may appoint such a committee to investigate "alleged contraventions or maladministration in the implementation of Community law." Because of the impact of these methods of scrutiny and supervision on interinstitutional relations, the EP's exercise of them is examined in Chapter 11.

Other tools in the EP's supervisory arsenal aim to assist EU citizens suffering directly from alleged maladministration of EU law. One is an EU citizen's right to petition the EP "on a subject which comes within the Community's fields of activity and which affects him directly."[13] Another is the office of the ombudsman, elected by MEPs for a renewable five-year period. The ombudsman may "receive and investigate complaints from EU citizens, businesses and organizations, and from anyone residing or having their registered office in an EU country."[14] Upon receiving a complaint, the ombudsman investigates and makes a report to the EP and the institution concerned. The ombudsman receives a large number of complaints annually (usually over 3,000), although not all of them are admissible. About three-quarters of the complaints come from individual citizens, the rest from companies and associations. The ombudsman helps in most cases, either by opening an inquiry; transferring the complaint to a competent body, such as a national regional ombudsman in a member state; or directing complainants to other appropriate bodies. The ombudsman's two biggest problems are lack of resources and the difficulty of defining "maladministration." Nevertheless, the work of the ombudsman has helped to improve the quality of EU administration from the citizen's point of view.[15]

External Relations

The prominence of its Committee on Foreign Affairs, including the Subcommittee on Security and Defense, suggests that the EP is centrally involved in an important area of EU activity: the Common Foreign and Security Policy. In fact, governments are often reluctant to involve parliaments in foreign affairs, and EU governments have been particularly reluctant to involve the Parliament in the CFSP, let alone in an emerging defense policy, in any meaningful way.

The Maastricht Treaty limited the Parliament's involvement in the emerging CFSP to being consulted and kept regularly informed by the Council presidency and the Commission, being allowed to ask questions of the Council and make recommendations to it, and holding an annual, pro forma debate on foreign and security policy. The EP's role in this regard remained largely unchanged following subsequent treaty reforms, although the Lisbon Treaty gives the EP the opportunity to hold an investiture hearing for the High Representative for Foreign Affairs and Security, because that position is combined with a Commission vice presidency. Moreover, the High Representative must "regularly consult" the EP on the main aspects of the CFSP and also "ensure that the views of the European Parliament are regularly taken into account"— although it is unclear exactly what this means. Despite its limited formal role in the CFSP, the Parliament is able to influence foreign and security policy through its control of the budget, notably for the office of the European Council president and the High Representative, and for the EU's external delegations and new External Action Service.

Surprisingly, given that it lies squarely within the EU's economic realm, the EP's role in the common commercial policy was virtually nonexistent until the Lisbon Treaty. The EP's Committee on International Trade would monitor the conduct of EU trade policy, but the EP as a whole was not required to approve or reject agreements negotiated by the Commission. National governments, which decide the Commission's mandate and approve final agreements, were reluctant to share responsibility for trade policy with the EP. Nevertheless, they agreed in the Lisbon Treaty to give the EP a more prominent role. First, the Commission must consult the EP on the conduct of negotiations. Second, the EP must give its consent, on an up or down basis, to proposed trade agreements. Third, legislation on implementing trade policy is subject to the ordinary legislative procedure, in which the EP is coequal with the Council.

By contrast, the EP plays a decisive role in another important foreign policy sphere: EU enlargement and association with third countries. Under the assent procedure introduced by the SEA, an absolute majority of parliamentarians must approve accession and association agreements. Initially this provision seemed insignificant: in 1986, after the third enlargement, the EU's boundaries appeared unlikely to change for a long time to come. Yet the success of the single market program and the sudden end of the Cold War gave rise to new rounds of accession negotiations and association agreements. Moreover, the assent procedure covers revisions or additions to existing association agreements, such as financial protocols. The EP has repeatedly used the assent procedure to leverage respect for human rights in countries that have or want association agreements with the EU. The assent procedure covers all international agreements that establish institutions, have major financial implications, or require legislation under the ordinary procedure.

Internal Organization

The EP carries out its budgetary, legislative, supervisory, and other responsibilities through an elaborate leadership structure involving the work of the political groups, a strong committee system, and frenzied plenary sessions. A large, full-time staff assists MEPs with their work.

Leadership Structure

The EP's leadership structure and responsibilities are as follows:

- *President:* Presides over plenary sessions, chairs meetings of the Bureau and the Conference of Presidents, represents the EP at interinstitutional meetings, and signs the budget into law.
- *Vice presidents:* Fourteen vice presidents preside over plenary sessions when the president is absent and represent the EP in the conciliation committee.
- *Bureau:* Comprises the president and vice presidents of the EP, and makes key budgetary, procedural, and personnel decisions.
- *Conference of Presidents:* Comprises the president of the EP and heads of the political groups, and decides the agenda for plenary sessions; discusses the annual legislative program, interinstitutional relations, and relations with non-EU institutions; and manages the committee system.
- *Quaestors:* Five ordinary MEPs make necessary day-to-day administrative decisions.

The Bureau, Conference of Presidents, and quaestors meet approximately twice a month—in Strasbourg during plenary sessions and in Brussels during committee or political-group meetings.

All are elected positions; elections take place every two and a half years, at the beginning and in the middle of the EP's five-year term. Since 1989, the Christian Democrats and Socialists, who together have commanded an absolute majority of seats in the EP, have shared the presidency between them. Members of other groups have denounced this as undemocratic and damaging to the EP's image and credibility. The pact broke down during the 1999–2004 term, when the Christian Democrats collaborated with the Liberals against the Socialists, resulting in the election of a Liberal as president for the period January 2002–July 2004. The Socialists and the Christian Democrats reverted to their old ways after the 2004 and 2009 elections, however. In July 2009, as part of the pact between the two biggest groups, a member of the EPP was elected president until December 2011, with a Socialist to follow until June 2014. It was up to the EPP to decide which of its members to put forward for the post. There were two contenders, an Italian and a Pole, both strongly supported by their national governments. Eventually the Italian withdrew, and the Pole, Jerzy Buzek, a former prime minister, was elected president. Buzek's election, which for the first time placed someone from Central and Eastern Europe in a top EU leadership position, was hailed as a breakthrough. Yet it came about as a result of deal-making between the EPP and the Socialists and backroom bargaining among national leaders.

Regardless of the circumstances of their election, recent presidents have worked hard to raise the EP's political profile both inside and outside the EU. The president's presentation of the EP's views at the beginning of each meeting of the European Council testifies to the institution's growing influence and to the importance for the EP of having a politically weighty president. In that regard, being a former prime minister is certainly to Buzek's advantage.

The outcome of the presidential election determines the outcome of the elections for other leadership positions (except for political-group leaders, who are elected by political-group members). Although other leadership elections are supposedly open, the political groups decide among themselves who gets what. The leadership's composition generally reflects the distribution of seats by political group and national delegation.

Committee System

The EP could not manage its burgeoning budgetary, legislative, and nonlegislative agenda without an adequate committee system. The committee system evolved along with the EU, changing over the years to reflect the EU's increasing competence and the EP's growing assertiveness and responsibility. For instance, in response to the Maastricht Treaty, the EP revamped its Political Affairs Committee and renamed it the Committee on Foreign Affairs, which has two subcommittees, one addressing human rights and the other security and defense. It also established a new Committee on Civil Liberties and Internal Affairs (now the Committee on Civil Liberties, Justice and Home Affairs). The EP has twenty standing committees covering every facet of EU activity (see Box 9.4).

Clearly, some committees are more influential than others. The Committee on the Environment, Public Health and Food Safety and the Committee on Budgetary Control are influential because the EP exercises considerable power in those areas. The importance of the Committee on Budgets (as distinct from the Committee on Budgetary Control) is undiminished despite the existence of an interinstitutional arrangement for medium-term financial planning. Other

Box 9.4   European Parliament Standing Committees

Foreign Affairs
  Human Rights
  Security and Defense
Development
International Trade
Budgets
Budgetary Control
Economic and Monetary Affairs
Employment and Social Affairs
Environment, Public Health and Food Safety
Industry, Research and Energy
Internal Market and Consumer Protection
Transport and Tourism
Regional Development
Agriculture and Rural Development
Fisheries
Culture and Education
Legal Affairs
Civil Liberties, Justice and Home Affairs
Constitutional Affairs
Women's Rights and Gender Equality
Petitions

Source: European Parliament, "Committees," http://www.europarl.europa.eu/
activities/committees/committeesList.do.

committees, such as the Committee on Transport and Tourism, have always been less important, although much sought after by MEPs who like to travel (which means, in effect, all of them).

Thus, a committee's popularity among MEPs is not necessarily related to its inherent importance, although popularity can enhance a committee's influence. The Committee on the Environment, Public Health and Food Safety, one of the largest in the EP, is popular with MEPs not only because of the EP's legislative authority in that area but also because environmental issues have growing political and economic salience throughout the EU (and beyond). By contrast, the Committee on Budgetary Control, one of the most powerful in the EP, deals with a complicated and colorless issue (discharge of the budget) and has a correspondingly small membership. Foreign and security policy is as fashionable as environmental policy. Accordingly, the Committee on Foreign Affairs is as large as the Committee on the Environment, Public Health and Food Safety and has an equally powerful chairman but only limited power. The Committee on Constitutional Affairs has no real power either, yet it attracts prominent MEPs because of its reputation as a driving force in the process of European integration.

The EP's leadership allocates committee seats among political groups according to their strength in the EP, using a system of proportional representation called the d'Hondt rule. The groups in turn allocate seats to their members based on seniority, personal preference, and nationality. Certain political groups and nationalities have strong preferences for particular committee assignments. Obvious examples are the Greens (environment, energy) and the Poles (agriculture, regional development). Committee assignments are reallocated every two and a half years; there is no time limit on an MEP's committee service.

The EP designates two weeks of each month for committee meetings. The frequency of each committee's meetings depends on the business before it; most meet at least monthly. Committee meetings take place in the EP's labyrinthine Brussels building, a complex of offices and conference rooms near Schuman Circle. Most meetings last the equivalent of one full day. MEPs' attendance is often sporadic. Meetings may also be attended by officials from the Council and Commission and occasionally by commissioners, government ministers (especially from the country in the presidency), and the European Council president.

Given their smaller size and less formal nature, committee meetings are less beset by language problems than are plenary sessions. Nevertheless, interpreters not only provide the essential service of making people mutually intelligible but also, because of the costs involved, ensure that meetings do not run over the allotted time. Apart from paying for simultaneous interpretation, committees run up extra costs by producing documents in many languages, at each step of the legislative process. The most striking sight on entering a committee meeting, regardless of the committee's size, is the mountain of documents immediately inside the door. The committee leadership structure replicates the EP's leadership structure: each committee has a chair and up to three vice chairs, who form the committee's bureau. The political group members within each committee appoint coordinators for their respective groups, whose role is to keep the other group members informed of developments and ready for key votes. Committees appoint rapporteurs (writers) from among their members for each of their reports (parliamentary reports are commonly known by the names of their rapporteurs).

In the case of legislative proposals, committees do the preliminary work, on which the EP as a whole bases its decisions during plenary sessions. Before examining proposals in detail, committees verify the legal base in consultation with the Committee on Legal Affairs. For proposals subject to the ordinary legislative procedure, rapporteurs follow the draft legislation's progress through the Council's working groups, through Coreper, and through the Council itself. Committee preparation of draft amendments gives interested parties an opportunity to influence legislation. Certain committees are a target of intense lobbying. As well as its twenty standing committees, the EP may establish special committees. For instance, in October 2009 the EP established a special committee to assess the cause of the financial, social, and economic crisis and its impact on the member states. The committee had a twelve-month mandate and produced recommendations in a midterm and end-of-term report.

Plenary Sessions

Plenaries are the most visible and least flattering part of the EP's existence. For a week each month (in reality, from Monday afternoon until the following Friday morning, although most members leave on Thursday evening), MEPs participate in a full session of the entire body. The most striking aspect of the plenaries is how few MEPs are present at any one time, although most manage to sign in for their daily allowance.

Plenaries include debates; speeches by commissioners, the European Council president, and the Council of Ministers president; question time; and most important, votes on legislative amendments and other resolutions. A legislative resolution constitutes the EP's opinion on draft legislation, indicating whether the EP approves, rejects, or amends the relevant proposal. Near the chamber or hemicycle itself, within the cavernous building where plenaries take place (in Brussels or Strasbourg), MEPs hold political-group and occasional committee meetings, entertain constituents, and parry lobbyists (a corner of the concourse near the entrance to the Strasbourg hemicycle is appropriately called the "lobbyists' bench").

Too much happens during plenaries in too short a time. Voting alone can occupy several hours, despite a change of rules reducing the number of amendments (previously about a thousand per session) that reach the hemicycle. The pressure of voting and the difficulty of knowing what each vote means are so great that many MEPs simply stay away. Because amendments require at least a majority of the whole house to pass, rampant absenteeism sometimes causes important amendments to fail. Presidents constantly urge MEPs to deal with technicalities in committee and use the plenaries to debate big issues.

Staff

MEPs have an allowance to hire staff (they often hire their own family members), and rely for policy and legislative assistance on the political groups' staff. Each group may hire a staff commensurate with the size of its membership. Committees have small staffs of their own (drawn from the EP's secretariat) to help rapporteurs draft and write reports; large national delegations also have separate staffs funded by national parties or the transnational political parties to which they are affiliated. The EP's secretariat—a permanent civil service with about 4,500 positions, similar to the Council secretariat and Commission civil service—provides the institution with support ranging from research to public relations to translation and interpretation. As in other branches of the EU's civil service, promotion in the upper echelons of the EP's secretariat is highly political and depends on ideological affinity as well as nationality.

■ More Power to Parliament?

The formal power and informal influence of the EP have increased dramatically in the past two decades. Despite its considerable budgetary and legislative authority, the EP craves more power, ostensibly in order to close the EU's democratic deficit, which it sees as the gap between the powers of the Commission and Council, on the one hand, and those of the EP, on the other. National governments' introduction of the cooperation procedure in the SEA and extension of it in the Maastricht Treaty, and their introduction of the codecision procedure in the Maastricht Treaty and extension of it in the Amsterdam and Lisbon treaties, went some way to meet the EP's demands, but not far enough. Fundamentally, the EP resents having to share legislative authority with the Commission (which initiates proposals) and the Council (which codecides).

The Commission and the Council acknowledge that the perception of a democratic deficit poses a serious problem for the EU but do not necessarily agree that the solution lies in giving more power to the EP. After all, the EU is not a state, and its institutional framework and political system will never correspond to those of a classic liberal democracy, centered on the legislature. Similarly, the Commission will never acquire the characteristics of a national executive. Instead, the EU is a singular system with singular institutions; conventional views of the democratic deficit and conventional proposals for its solution overlook that fact. Undoubtedly the EP is an essential ingredient of political accountability and representation in the EU, but it is not the sole source of legitimacy, as the German constitutional court pointed out in June 2009 (see Chapter 6). Tackling the democratic deficit therefore requires an imaginative blend of public representation and participation at the regional, national, and European levels, involving parliamentary and other bodies from all three spheres.

Most Europeans, if they think about the EU at all, more than likely would doubt that giving more power to the EP would help to close the democratic deficit. Indeed, few people outside the EP consider the institution capable of providing a solution to the EU's problem of weak legitimacy. MEPs are marginal figures at the national level, regardless of their political influence at the European level. Far from clamoring for a transfer of sovereignty to Strasbourg, most Europeans do not bother to vote in direct elections. Indeed, the consistently low turnout (by European standards) in direct elections seriously weakens the EP's image and undermines MEPs' arguments in favor of greater institutional power.

■ Notes

1. Richard Corbett, Francis Jacobs, and Michael Shackleton, *The European Parliament*, 7th ed. (London: Harper, 2007); David Judge and David Earnshaw, *The European Parliament*, 2nd ed. (Basingstoke: Palgrave Macmillan, 2008); and Berthold Rittberger, *Building Europe's Parliament: Democratic Representation Beyond the Nation State* (Oxford: Oxford University Press, 2007).

2. Julian Priestley, *Six Battles That Shaped Europe's Parliament* (London: John Harper, 2008).

3. See, for instance, European Parliament, Resolution A6-0197/2007, June 7, 2007, on the roadmap for the Union's constitutional process; and European Parliament, Resolution A6-0279/2007, July 11, 2007, on the convening of the IGC on the European Parliament's opinion.

4. "Reflections of Former Presidents of the European Parliament," *Agence Europe*, March 20, 2008.

5. Constitutional Court of Germany, press release, 72/2009, and judgment, June 30, 2009.

6. See http://www.epp.eu/hoofdpagina.php?hoofdmenuID=1.

7. On the composition and development of the political groups and the transnational party system, see Amie Kreppel, *The European Parliament and Supranational Party System: A Study in Institutional Development* (Cambridge: Cambridge University Press, 2002).

8. Greens–European Free Alliance website, http://www.greens-efa.org/cms/default/rubrik/6/6270.htm.

9. Greens–European Free Alliance website, http://www.greens-fa.org/cms/default/rubrik/6/6563.bureau.htm.

10. European Conservatives and Reformists website, http://www.ecrgroup.eu/.

11. See Roger Scully, *Becoming Europeans? Attitudes, Behaviour, and Socialization in the European Parliament* (Oxford: Oxford University Press, 2005).

12. See Andreas Maurer, "The European Parliament After Lisbon: Policy-Making and Control," April 25, 2008, http://www.eu-consent.net/library/deliverables/d19.pdf.

13. European Parliament's "Petitions" website, http://www.europarl.europa.eu/parliament/public/staticdisplay.do?id=49.

14. European Parliament's "European Ombudsman" website, http://europa.eu/institutions/others/ombudsman/index_en.htm.

15. See Roy Gregory and Philip Giddings, "Citizenship, Rights, and the EU Ombudsman," in Richard Bellamy and Alex Warleigh, eds., *Citizenship and Governance in the European Union* (London: Continuum, 2001), pp. 73–92.

10 Other Institutions and Bodies

The European Council, the Council of Ministers, the European Commission, and the European Parliament are the European Union's core decisionmaking institutions. In addition, the EU has a judicial branch, comprising the Court of Justice, the General Court, and the Civil Service Tribunal. It has a Court of Auditors, which examines the EU's financial affairs, and two advisory bodies, the European Economic and Social Committee and the Committee of the Regions. This chapter examines these institutions and bodies as well as the European Investment Bank (an autonomous lending institution) and a growing and diverse group of "Community agencies." It also looks at the role of national parliaments in the EU system. The European System of Central Banks and the European Central Bank—key institutions for the management of monetary union—are examined in Chapter 13.

■ The Court of Justice

The European Court of Justice (ECJ) is the primary EU court. For much of its existence the ECJ was the EU's least-known institution. Located in Luxembourg, far from the political fray in Brussels and Strasbourg, the Court initially received little outside attention as it waded through a growing number of arcane and seemingly unimportant cases. Only gradually did the significance of the Court's rulings become apparent to the nonlegal world. In the 1970s, while the European Community seemed to languish, the ECJ persevered and produced an impressive amount of case law that maintained the momentum for deeper integration. In doing so, the Court not only defined and shaped a new legal order but also contributed to the revival of European integration in the 1980s.[1] Inevitably, critics accuse the Court of judicial activism, testimony to its huge impact on the EU's political development. Sensitive to such criticism, especially from countries usually thought to favor deeper integration, arguably the Court has grown noticeably less adventurous in recent years.

The Court's principal purpose, unchanged since the launch of the EU and reiterated in the Lisbon Treaty, is "to ensure that in the interpretation and application of [the treaties] the law is observed." EU law, a distinct body of law that is binding on the member states, comprises three related types of legislation:

- *Primary legislation:* Original treaties, the treaties of accession, and the various treaty amendments.
- *Secondary legislation:* Laws (notably regulations, directives, and decisions) made by EU institutions in accordance with the treaties.
- *Case law:* Judgments of the EU courts.

From the outset the ECJ has seen the original treaties not simply as narrow international agreements but, because of the member states' far-reaching decision to share sovereignty, as the basis of a constitutional framework for the EU. "If one were asked to synthesize the direction in which the case law produced in Luxembourg has moved since 1957," Federico Mancini, a member of the Court, wrote as long ago as 1991, more than a decade before the debate about the Constitutional Treaty, "one would have to say that it coincides with the making of a constitution for Europe."[2] In a succession of cases, the ECJ held that the EU's "constitution" is based on custom and on shared values as well as on EU primary and secondary legislation. The Court first referred explicitly to the EC treaty as "the basic constitutional charter" of the Community in a 1986 ruling.[3] One of the most compelling stories in the history of European integration is how the ECJ "fundamentally transformed the nature of the bargain struck between the Member States: [changing the EU] from an interstate organization founded on the basis of an international treaty, to a supranational legal order constructed upon a *constitutional* framework."[4]

Fundamental human rights—an essential ingredient of any liberal, constitutional democracy—underpin EU law. Although the original treaties made no mention of human rights, the preamble of the Single European Act acknowledged the Court's repeated emphasis on the issue by declaring the member states' determination "to work together to promote democracy on the basis of the fundamental rights recognized in the constitutions and laws of the Member States, in the Convention for the Protection of Human Rights and Fundamental Freedoms and the European Social Charter, notably freedom, equality and social justice." The Maastricht Treaty did not institute a charter of fundamental rights and freedoms, as the EP had wanted it to, but it did include a new article explicitly stating that "the Union shall respect fundamental rights, as guaranteed by the European Convention for the Protection of Human Rights and Fundamental Freedoms [ECHR] . . . and as they result from the constitutional traditions common to the Member States, as general principles of Community law."

Despite its use of the ECHR, which dates from 1950, as a source for upholding the fundamental rights of individuals under EU law, the Court ruled in March 1996 that the EC could not, without a treaty amendment, accede to the ECHR.[5] Moreover, the Court expressed concerns about incorporating a separate international legal order into the EU legal system. Based partly on the Court's misgivings, member states decided during the 1996–1997 negotiations on treaty reform that the EU should not accede to the ECHR, although the member states themselves are all signatories to the convention. The solution adopted was to confirm that Community law was subject to the European Convention, but as applied by the ECJ.

The EU finally developed its own Charter of Fundamental Rights—a catalog of civil, economic, and social rights—in the run-up to Central and Eastern European enlargement. Proposed by the German government in 1999, negotiations on the Charter, involving representatives of various national and EU bodies, proceeded swiftly in 2000. In what could "rightly [be] counted as among the Union's legal response to enlargement," EU leaders "solemnly proclaimed" the Charter at their summit in Nice in December 2000 but did not include it in the treaties, deferring further discussion of it until the next intergovernmental conference.[6]

The British government and some business leaders objected to the inclusion in the Charter of social rights that could increase labor costs and possibly reduce Europe's global competitiveness. A more subtle critique came from those, such as prominent EU law scholar Joseph Weiler, who questioned the wisdom of enumerating rights in a charter, for possible inclusion in the treaty. Far from protecting European citizens, Weiler argued, the impact of the Charter could be counterproductive if, for instance, "each time an innovative concept were argued before the European Court, it would be pointed out that a proposal to that effect was considered in the drafting of the Charter and failed."[7]

Pending the Charter's incorporation into the treaties or into a new EU treaty, how would the Court respond to it? No sooner was it proclaimed than applicants before the Court and advocates-general (senior officers of the Court) began citing the terms of the Charter in a number of cases. The Court itself began referring in 2002 to the Charter in its decisions. Yet the Court seemed reluctant to cite it copiously until the Charter was given legally binding status as a result of a new treaty reform. A big step in that direction was incorporation of the Charter into the Draft Constitutional Treaty of 2003. National governments agreed in the ensuing IGC to keep the Charter in the Constitutional Treaty, as well as a provision giving the EU the right to accede to the ECHR.

As part of the renegotiation of the Constitutional Treaty, the British government sought to appease Euroskeptics by insisting, among other things, that the Charter be removed from what became the Lisbon Treaty. As a result, the Lisbon Treaty does not include the Charter, but contains a reference to it, making it legally binding. This has greatly strengthened the human rights component and constitutional character of the EU. Nevertheless, for domestic political reasons, Britain, Poland, and the Czech Republic have secured opt-outs from the Charter.

The impact on EU law of the Charter's de facto incorporation into the Lisbon Treaty remains to be seen, but is likely to be formidable. As a long-standing champion of fundamental rights in the EU, the Court undoubtedly sees the elaboration of the Charter as an important step forward. Moreover, the Court is surely pleased that the Lisbon Treaty gives further substance to EU citizenship, especially as the Court developed this concept before member states included it in the Maastricht Treaty.

Basic Rules of EU Law

Apart from identifying the sources of EU law and endowing the treaties with the attributes of a constitution, the Court also developed two essential rules on which the new legal order rests: direct effect and supremacy. These twin pillars emerged in a series of cases early in the EU's history and clarified the working relationship between the national and EU legal orders.

Direct Effect. The Court first ruled on the direct effect of primary legislation in a case that, though technical, raised a fundamental principle of EU law. In *Van Gend en Loos* (1963), a Dutch transport firm brought a complaint against Dutch customs for increasing the duty on a product imported from Germany. Citing the "direct effect" of EU law, the firm argued that the Dutch authorities had breached the article of the Rome Treaty that prohibited member states from introducing new duties or increasing existing duties in the common market.

The Court agreed. In a landmark judgment it ruled that the article in question had direct effect because it contained a "clear and unconditional prohibition." Determined to make its mark, the Court declared that any similar treaty provision, being "self-sufficient and legally complete," did not require further intervention at the national or European level and therefore applied directly to individuals. Not mincing its words, the Court stated that "the Community constitutes a new legal order . . . the subjects of which comprise not only the member states but also their nationals. Independently of the legislation of member states, Community law not only imposes obligations on individuals but . . . also confers rights upon them. These rights arise not only where they are expressly granted by the Treaty, but also by reason of obligations which the Treaty of Rome imposes in a clearly defined way upon individuals as well as upon member states and upon the institutions of the Community."[8]

The Court continued to push the principle of direct effect in cases involving directives (addressed to member states) as well as regulations (addressed to individuals). The Court delivered a landmark judgment in *Grad v. Finanzamt Traunstein* (1970) when it ruled that a directive had direct effect if it contained a clear and unconditional obligation on a member state and had not been implemented by that state within the period prescribed in the directive.[9]

Supremacy of EU Law. The principle of direct effect would have had little impact if EU law did not supersede national law. Otherwise governments would simply ignore EU rules that conflicted with national rules. Although the Rome Treaty was unclear on the issue, the Court had no hesitation in asserting the supremacy of EU law over national law. The Court's first chance to do so came in *Costa v. ENEL* (1964), only a year after *Van Gend en Loos,* when the Court pointed out that member states had definitively transferred sovereign rights to the Community and that Community law could not be overridden by domestic legal provisions without the legal basis of the Community itself being called into question.[10] The Court expanded on the primacy of EU law in *Simmenthal v. Commission* (1978) when it ruled that "every national court must . . . apply Community law in its entirety . . . and must accordingly set aside any provisions of national law which may conflict with it."[11]

The *Costa, Van Gend en Loos,* and *Simmenthal* cases established the twin principles of direct effect and primacy of EU law, taking the national courts by surprise. Some national courts reacted strongly against what they saw as the encroachment of a new legal order. A major challenge came in the late 1960s when the constitutional courts of Italy and Germany hinted that because EU law arguably guaranteed a lower standard of fundamental rights than national law, the validity of EU law could be called into question at the national level. In a move that not only developed the EU's human rights case law but also warded off a potentially serious threat from national courts, the ECJ held in *Nold v. Commission* (1974) that "fundamental rights form an integral part of the general principles of [EU] law."[12]

Types of Cases
Cases before the Court originate in one of three ways:

1. Requests from national courts for a "preliminary ruling" on points of EU law.
2. Actions brought directly to the Court by other institutions, member states, or natural and legal persons (although individuals have only a limited ability to come before the Court to challenge EU legislation).
3. Appeals against judgments of the General Court, the ECJ's "lower court."

The bulk of ECJ cases, and the most important in terms of developing the body of EU law, arise out of requests for preliminary rulings and direct actions.[13]

Requests for Preliminary Rulings. Under Article 267 of the Treaty on the Functioning of the European Union, if an individual argues before a national court that a national law or policy conflicts with EU law, and if the court is unable or unwilling to resolve the dispute itself based on previous EU case law, the court may seek "authoritative guidance" from the ECJ by making a preliminary ruling reference (request). The parties involved, as well as EU institutions and national governments, may submit legal arguments to the ECJ. Based on its assessment of the arguments, relevant case law, and relevant treaty provisions, the ECJ issues a ruling, which the national court then applies to the case in question. Requests for preliminary rulings came slowly at first but accelerated in the 1970s and 1980s. In recent years, there have been approximately 250 requests for preliminary rulings annually.

Clearly, the success of EU law depends to a great extent on the willingness of national courts to seek preliminary rulings and abide by them. Under Article 267, lower national courts may seek guidance from the Court in cases involving EU law, but the highest national courts *must* do so. The general complicity of national courts in consolidating EU law is all the more striking because, in most cases, landmark Court judgments have come in response to requests from national courts for preliminary rulings. The original intent of Article 267 was to ensure uniform interpretation and application of EU law in each member state. Almost immediately, however, Article 267 became a powerful tool with which the Court could strengthen EU law and the Court's own role within the EU system. It also became a device that citizens could use to ascertain the compatibility of national and EU law.

The increasing rate of preliminary ruling requests from national courts has enhanced the stature of the Court, effectively giving it the power to review national law and thereby turning it into a supreme court. Increasingly, the Court has reformulated national courts' questions in order to elucidate what it considers to be the most important points at issue. This allows the Court to address essential points of law that otherwise might not come before it. In so doing, Article 267 has gradually undermined the authority of the highest national courts.

Why do so many lower national court judges apply for preliminary rulings "given that such judges must attend to their career prospects within hierarchically organized national judicial systems"?[14] The answer may be simply that the concept of EU law is naturally attractive to all judges (just as the concept of European Monetary Union is naturally attractive to all central bankers). Whatever the reason, Article 267 has brought about a special relationship, indeed a close partnership, between national courts and the ECJ. As a result, national judges have become the upholder of EU law in their own member states.

Direct Actions. References for preliminary rulings constitute one branch of EU case law; direct actions make up the other. Direct actions usually take one of the following forms:

- Cases brought mostly by the Commission against a member state or, rarely, by a member state against another member state for failing to fulfill a legal obligation. The number of such cases has increased steadily over the years and now averages about 200 annually.

- Cases against the Commission, Council, Parliament, or European Central Bank concerning the legality of a particular regulation. These are called "proceedings for annulment," because the Court may annul a particular act. Grounds for annulment include lack of competence, infringement of an essential procedural requirement, infringement of the treaties or of any rules relating to their application, and misuse of powers. The famous *Isoglucose* (1980) ruling, in which the Court annulled a regulation because the Council had acted before the EP had delivered an opinion under the terms of the consultation procedure for legislative decisionmaking, thereby infringing a key treaty provision, falls into this category.[15]

- Cases brought by member states or other institutions against the Commission, Council, or Parliament for failure to act. One of the most famous cases of that kind was *Parliament v. Council* (1985), in which the Parliament brought the Council to court for failing to lay the foundation of a common transport policy (the EP was only partially successful).[16]

- Cases for damages against the EU for the wrongful act of an EU institution or an EU servant, known as "actions to establish liability."

- Cases brought by EU officials for unfair dismissal, unlawful failure to promote, and the like. These are heard by the Civil Service Tribunal.

Composition and Procedures

The treaties stipulate the role, composition, location, procedure, jurisdiction, and powers of the ECJ. The Court's size—one judge per member state—has increased over time to reflect the EU's enlargement. The principle of one judge per member state is an important factor in the evolution of EU law and in the acceptance of the Court's rulings by the member states.

The Treaty on European Union stipulates that judges and advocates-general "shall be chosen from persons whose independence is beyond doubt." The president—elected by the members of the Court for a period of three years (renewable)—never asks a judge to be rapporteur for a case involving that judge's member state (the rapporteur is responsible for writing the "report for the hearing"—a summary setting out the facts, procedural history, and arguments of the case—for use by the Court as a whole). As the Court's impact on the EU's development became more conspicuous, there were suggestions that the judges' independence would need to be safeguarded. A government's most obvious means to pressure or influence "its" judge is to threaten not to renew the judge's six-year term. With that in mind, some judges have suggested that their terms should be lengthened to twelve years. The EP has also proposed having a say in judicial appointments, supposedly as a way of strengthening the judiciary's independence. However, the manner of appointing judges and the length of their terms in office have not changed over the years.

Judges come from the upper levels of national judiciaries, from the legal profession, and from academia. Eight advocates-general, who have backgrounds similar to those of the judges, complete the Court's membership. Advocates-general consider cases and give opinions for the Court's guidance at the end of the oral procedure. Judges are free to reject an advocate-general's opinion, but in most cases they accept it.

Britain, France, Germany, Italy, and Spain appoint one advocate-general each; the three others come from the smaller member states, based on a rotation system. Only weeks before the October 2007 summit at which national leaders were to have wrapped up the Lisbon Treaty, Poland raised a new concern about the number of advocates-general. As a "big" member state, Poland not unreasonably—but unreasonably late in the treaty negotiations— demanded the right to appoint an advocate-general. Whereas other last-minute issues proved difficult to resolve, Poland's demand concerning the ECJ was easily settled. The European Council agreed to allow the ECJ to request an increase in the number of advocates-general from eight to eleven—a request that the Court is more than likely to make. In that event, one of the advocates-general would always be Polish, and other new member states would have a better chance of occasionally appointing an advocate-general. Although advocates-general do not act along national lines and presumably share common European values, the discussion at the October 2007 summit of their number and nationality demonstrates the extreme sensitivity, for reasons of legitimacy, influence, and prestige, surrounding the appointment of senior EU officials.

By majority vote, after consulting the advocates-general the judges select a registrar for a renewable six-year term. As the Court's secretary-general, the registrar is responsible for conducting proceedings before the Court, maintaining records, publishing the Court's judgments, and administering the Court. The registrar meets regularly with members of the Court to schedule cases and decide procedural aspects. The Court has a relatively small staff of about a thousand officials to provide research, language, and administrative support.

The Court meets either in plenary session (with a quorum of fifteen members) or, more commonly, in chambers. The number and composition of chambers have changed over the years, reflecting the Court's increasing caseload. Chambers now consist of three or five judges each; there is also a grand chamber of thirteen judges, which hears unusually complex and important cases. The Court hears cases two days a week and has an administrative session every two weeks.

The Court gives requests for preliminary rulings a higher priority than direct action cases because national courts must await a result before proceeding with the case in question. Indeed, the Lisbon Treaty includes an "urgent preliminary ruling procedure" in the event that the question referred to the

Court concerns a case pending before a national court with regard to a person in custody (such cases come within the purview of cooperation on justice and home affairs). Direct action cases involve written proceedings, an investigation or preparatory inquiry, oral proceedings, and the judgment. Requests for preliminary rulings are not contentious and have a less cumbersome procedure than direct actions, although the original parties may submit written observations to the Court and may attend the oral hearing. Cases are heard in the EU's official languages, but French is the Court's working language.

Each judge has a small cabinet of legal secretaries, although most judges draft opinions without assistance after internal deliberations limited exclusively to the judiciary. Judges neither prepare nor issue minority opinions, nor do they indicate how many of them supported a decision, which the Court always announces as unanimous. Legal scholars complain that this makes it difficult to track the influence of individual judges' preferences and philosophies on the Court's judgments, but much can be divined from occasional speeches and articles by judges, and interviews with them.

Impact of Case Law

Apart from establishing the principles of direct effect and supremacy, EU case law has greatly advanced the objectives of the treaties and been decisive in helping to achieve the EU's fundamental economic and social goals. To a great extent, case law is the glue that holds the EU together. It has had a profound impact in the following areas:

- Protection of individual rights.
- Delineation of competences; development of the powers of the EU and its institutions; interinstitutional relations.
- Development of the principles of substantive EU law, such as the free movement of capital, people, goods, and services; equal treatment (issues of pay, pensions, training, promotions, part-time work, and so forth); competition policy; environmental policy; and consumer protection.
- Enforcement and protection of EU law.

Court rulings occasionally stir up a hornets' nest in particular member states. For instance, there was a national furor when the Court for the first time overruled a British act of parliament. In *The Queen v. Secretary of State for Transport, ex parte Factortame,* the Court ruled that the 1988 Merchant Shipping Act, which stated that 75 percent of directors and shareholders in companies operating fishing vessels in United Kingdom waters must be British, contravened EU law. Basing its ruling on the freedom of establishment and freedom to provide services, the Court declared that Britain could not demand strict residence and nationality requirements from owners and crews before granting their vessels British registration.[17]

There was a similar reaction in Austria in July 2005 when the Court ruled that legislation to limit the number of university places available to foreigners constituted indirect discrimination on grounds of nationality, and therefore was contrary to EU law.[18] At issue was the Austrian government's effort, strongly supported by the public, to prevent medical faculties from being overrun by German students. The Austrian government cleverly exploited the negotiations on the Lisbon Treaty in 2007 to get the Commission temporarily to suspend infringement proceedings against it for disregarding the ECJ ruling.

Despite the wide-ranging impact of EU case law, Court rulings rarely attract much attention throughout the EU as a whole. The 1995 *Bosman* case, which radically affected nationality and transfer rules in European soccer clubs, was an obvious exception, as was the Court's rejection of the rules requiring soccer clubs to field teams with only a limited number of professional players who were nationals of other member states (except for international matches).[19] The Court found that the existing rules constituted an obstacle to the free movement of workers.

Enforcement

Although national courts and governments accept the principles of direct effect and supremacy of EU law, the problem of enforcement remains acute. The worst areas of noncompliance are environmental policy, the single market, and agriculture; the worst offenders tend to be France, Italy, and Spain (the Central and Eastern European member states have relatively good implementation records).

The Court is well aware that inability or refusal to implement EU rules and regulations uniformly in each member state will erode public confidence in Community law. In *Johnson v. RUC* (1984), the Court declared that the right to a judicial remedy is a general principle of EC law and continued its assault on the enforcement problem in a series of cases in the early 1990s.[20] The most important of these was *Francovich and Bonifaci v. Italy* (1991), in which the Court held that in certain circumstances, individuals are entitled to sue governments for damages sustained as a result of the government's failure to implement a directive within the prescribed period.[21] In a series of subsequent cases, the Court spelled out what these circumstances were: where the rule of law infringed is intended to confer rights on individuals, where there has been a sufficiently serious breach of that rule of law, and where there is a direct causal link between the breach of the obligation resting on the member state and the damage sustained by the injured party. The Court extended the scope of *Francovich*-type liability to public law bodies, legally independent of the state, and later ruled that individuals were entitled to compensation in cases where the highest national courts had not sought a preliminary ruling or had disregarded the Court's interpretation in a preliminary ruling.

Aware of the growing problem of enforcement, governments agreed during the 1991 intergovernmental conference on treaty reform to give the Court some direct enforcement power. As a result, the Maastricht Treaty included a provision allowing the Court to fine a government for refusing to act on a Court ruling that it failed to fulfill its obligations under the treaties. The Lisbon Treaty improved the system for fining national governments.

Relations with Other Institutions and with National Governments

Because of the far-reaching nature of its rulings, the Court has a unique relationship with the Council, Commission, Parliament, and national governments, all of which are frequent litigants in Court cases. Although the Court has often ruled against the Commission (especially in cases where the Commission has attempted to extend its competence in the field of external economic relations), the Commission is nonetheless an obvious ally; after all, as "guardian of the treaties" the Commission prosecutes many Court cases. The Commission and the Court work closely together to promote economic integration, particularly through the use of infringement proceedings and competition policy instruments.

Similarly, the Court and the EP share a common supranational outlook. Indeed, the Court has generally promoted the Parliament's institutional interests, most notably in the *Isoglucose* case. The Court also corrected the anomaly whereby, under the original Rome Treaty, the Parliament could not bring proceedings for judicial review of Community acts, a provision that seemed especially incongruous after the Parliament won greater legislative power under the SEA. Accordingly, in 1990 the Court ruled that in order to ensure institutional equilibrium, the Parliament should have the right to take action against the Council and the Commission in cases involving parliamentary prerogatives.[22] Despite some governments' criticism of the Court's assertiveness, negotiators in the 1991 IGC incorporated the operative part of the Court's judgment almost verbatim into the Maastricht Treaty. The Nice Treaty further extended Parliament's right of recourse before the Court.

Following implementation of the SEA, the Maastricht Treaty, and the Amsterdam Treaty, the Court was inundated with cases concerning the Council and Parliament squabbling over the correct legal base for legislation (the issue being the extent of parliamentary involvement in the legislative process). The issue became largely redundant following implementation of the Lisbon Treaty, which extended the ordinary legislative procedure to the vast majority of EU policy areas. Nevertheless, in the interinstitutional battles over the correct legal base, the Court did not always side with Parliament.

Regardless of how the Court acts, the Council and its members (the national governments) generally regard the Court as favoring the Commission and the Parliament, in keeping with the Court's integrationist outlook. Indeed, the Court's relationship with the Council, and especially with certain governments, can be strained. Institutionally, the Council upholds national interests in the EU system, whereas the Court upholds the broader EU interest. Some observers see in the Court's rulings an institutional bias toward deeper economic and political integration. Particular Court rulings in politically charged cases under media scrutiny have angered national governments, including governments that tend to see themselves as favoring further integration. The Court is not insensitive to such reactions. Aware of governments' likely response to being fined by the ECJ, the Court has been reluctant to make use of that sanction.

The ECJ and Treaty Reform

The *Factortame* and a number of later judgments led the British government to propose, during the 1996–1997 IGC, several measures to curb the Court's effectiveness and to establish a right of appeal against the Court's decisions. Combined with other countries' criticism of the Court, this proposal fueled speculation that the Court's prerogatives would be seriously curtailed in the ensuing Amsterdam Treaty, and even that the provision for preliminary rulings might be repealed. For its part, the Court recommended that the new treaty include a number of changes in the Court's composition and operations and an extension of judicial review to the EU's two intergovernmental pillars (covering internal and external security).

In the event, most governments were too appreciative of the Court's overall importance to reduce its role in the EU system, and there were no fundamental challenges to the basic tenets of EU law. Moreover, the Labour government that came to power in Britain in 1997 lacked its predecessor's reforming zeal. If anything, the Court emerged from the Amsterdam Treaty slightly better off than before: the treaty brought much of the old third pillar (covering justice and home affairs) into the first pillar, where the Court is fully involved, and extended judicial review to what remained of the third pillar (subject to certain conditions). However, the treaty did not extend judicial review to the Common Foreign and Security Policy.

In response to persistent pressure from the Court to relieve its workload (the Court faced a huge backlog of cases), governments agreed in the 2000 IGC to amend the treaty in order to allow the Court of First Instance, later called the General Court, to take on more cases. Nevertheless, the ECJ's workload remains unrelenting, and the duration of proceedings continues to increase. A long-overdue change to the Court's rules of procedure in 2000, introducing the possibility of an expedited procedure for urgent cases, was used for the first time in 2001. The Court is very sparing in its use of this provision, however, not wanting to disrupt other, ongoing work, which would then take even longer to complete. The Nice Treaty also allowed national governments to make changes to the Court's rules of procedure by qualified majority voting instead of unanimity in the Council, thereby facilitating greater adaptability by the Court to changing circumstances (not least the challenge of enlargement and the unceasing pressure of new cases). Going a step beyond that, the Lisbon Treaty made changes in the Court's operating procedures subject to the ordinary legislative procedure, thereby involving the EP fully in such decisions.

▨ The General Court

For more than thirty-five years the EU had only one court—the ECJ—responsible for hearing cases involving everything from important issues of EU law to relatively trivial matters of staff promotion and dismissal. Apart from its wide jurisdiction, the Court's rapidly increasing caseload threatened to become unmanageable. Only in 1985, during the negotiations that resulted in the SEA, did the Court successfully raise the issue of judicial reform. Accordingly, governments agreed in the SEA to empower the Council, acting unanimously on a proposal from the Court, to establish a Court of First Instance (CFI). Thus the SEA gave rise to "a hierarchy of judicial institutions at the Community level."[23]

Following the statutory request by the ECJ, the Council finally decided in October 1988 on the CFI's composition and jurisdiction. The new court began operating in October 1989 and delivered its first judgment in January 1990.

Jurisdiction

The CFI's initially narrow jurisdiction reflected the Council's difficulty in deciding which of the ECJ's cases, apart from staff cases, the CFI should hear. As it was, the SEA denied the CFI any jurisdiction over cases brought by member states or EU institutions or over questions referred for a preliminary ruling. Thus the CFI could hear only "certain classes of action or proceedings brought by natural or legal persons." The Council's October 1988 decision gave the CFI even narrower jurisdiction, encompassing:

- *Competition cases:* Generally actions by firms contesting fines imposed by the Commission under the EU's competition policy.
- *European Coal and Steel Community cases:* Mostly stemming from the system of production quotas imposed on the steel industry in an effort to deal with recession and overcapacity; the demise of the ECSC in 2002 removed a particular category of cases before the CFI.
- *Staff cases:* Ranging from unfair dismissal to failure to win a promotion.
- *Claims for damages:* Brought by natural or legal persons where the damage allegedly arises from an action or failure to act that falls into one of the three previous categories.

According to the original Council decision that established the CFI, the court's purpose was to hear cases that require "an examination of complex facts," such as highly technical competition policy cases. Thus, a useful way to understand the original difference between the Court of Justice and the CFI is that "the Court of First Instance is the judge of factual matters, while the Court of Justice is in principle the judge of points of law."[24] Although this is still helpful, changes in the jurisdiction of the CFI, giving it competence for all direct actions (especially requests for annulments and damages and claims of failure to act), have blurred the jurisdictional demarcation between the two courts.

The CFI, established to ease the burden of the ECJ, was itself soon over-burdened. Its productivity seemed much lower than that of the Court of Justice. Apart from staff cases, on average the CFI took nearly thirty months to deal with cases, leaving it with 624 cases in hand at the end of 1997. By contrast, the ECJ took an average of twenty-one months to deal with preliminary rulings—the most complicated category of its cases—and had 683 cases in hand at the end of 1997 (not an unusually high amount for the ECJ).[25]

Concerned that its workload was becoming unmanageable, the CFI requested, in the run-up to the Amsterdam Treaty, that the Council appoint more judges to it and that certain cases be heard by one judge sitting alone. But many governments (and many lawyers who appear before the CFI) disliked the idea of single-judge rulings, and no national government relished the prospect of fighting with other governments over the selection of a handful of new CFI judges. As a result, the Amsterdam Treaty did not incorporate the CFI's recommendations. Under the unrelenting pressure of more new cases, however, national governments changed the CFI's rules of procedure in May 1999 to allow for single-judge rulings in certain types of cases that hitherto had been assigned to three-judge chambers.

Finally, in November 2004, in an effort to alleviate the workload of the CFI, the Council decided to establish a special tribunal to hear staff cases. The Civil Service Tribunal came into operation in 2007. Composed of seven judges appointed by the Council for a six-year, renewable term, the tribunal allows the CFI to focus on more substantive cases affecting the EU as a whole. In the meantime, despite the CFI's existence, the ECJ continues to bear a heavy workload. Of course, if the CFI did not exist, the ECJ would have the additional burden of hearing all the cases that currently come before the lower court (as it is, the ECJ hears about 20 percent of them on appeal).

Governments agreed in the negotiations leading to the Lisbon Treaty to change the name "Court of First Instance" to "General Court." This was in keeping with one of the objectives of the ill-fated Constitutional Treaty, which was to simplify the EU, streamline its operations, and demystify the process of European integration.

Composition and Procedures

Like the main court, the General Court consists of one judge per member state appointed for renewable six-year terms. It has no advocates-general, but any judge may be asked to perform the task of advocate-general for a particular case. As with their counterparts on the ECJ, judges on the General Court must be independent of national governments. In view of the highly technical work they sometimes perform, General Court judges need not come from the legal profession, although in practice almost all of them do. The General Court meets in chambers of three or five judges. Judges may also hear cases singly, and in exceptional cases the General Court meets in plenary session. The judges elect one of their members to serve as president for a renewable three-year term; they also appoint a registrar, who serves in a capacity similar to that of the main court's registrar.

In providing for the original CFI, the SEA included a right of appeal to the ECJ. However, litigants may appeal to the ECJ on a point of law only, such as the General Court's lack of competence to hear the original case, breach of procedure, or infringement of EU law. An appeal must be lodged within two months of notification of the decision.

Significance of the General Court

The CFI's first president remarked at the court's official launch in September 1989 that "this moment does not mark the end of an era in European judicial history, but rather a stage along the road towards the ultimate maturity of the judicial system of the Communities."[26] Since then there have been several rounds of treaty reform, none of which radically revised the EU judicial system. Instead, governments have tinkered with the lower court's composition and jurisdiction in an effort to alleviate the ECJ's workload. Yet the establishment of a lower court has been more significant than merely relieving pressure from the ECJ. Far from being a shrinking violet, what is now the General Court is "growing in stature, gaining in confidence and developing its own distinctive voice—yet at the same time being reminded of, and responding to, the ECJ's 'senior role.'"[27]

■ The Court of Auditors

The Court of Auditors (ECA) is not a judicial court; its responsibility lies solely in examining the EU's financial affairs. The problem of inadequate control over EU finances is as old as the EU itself. In an effort to rectify the situation, and as a corollary to the granting of budgetary authority to the EP, the 1975 budget treaty replaced the old Auditor Board with the new ECA. The court's authority covers all bodies created by the EU and all payments made before the year's accounts are closed; the court has complete administrative and budgetary autonomy.

National governments agreed in the Maastricht Treaty to elevate the ECA to the institutional status of the Council, Commission, Parliament, and ECJ. The ECA's higher stature and significance reflected not only a substantial increase in the EU's revenue and expenditure since the late 1980s but also growing public and political concern about fraud, waste, and mismanagement of EU resources. Indeed, the court sees its role in alleviating such concern as a fundamental contribution to strengthening democracy in the EU by providing greater accountability and transparency.

The court's scrutiny of EU spending has provided telling evidence to substantiate anecdotal accounts of squandering and financial incompetence. By exposing financial irregularities in the EU, the court can exert considerable pressure for reform, especially of the Commission, which is legally responsible for EU spending. Paradoxically, because management of EU spending is highly decentralized, governments themselves are responsible on a day-to-day basis for most EU expenditure, and most fraud takes place at the national or subnational—not the European—level.

The Court of Auditors consists of one member per member state, appointed for renewable six-year terms. Membership in the court is staggered, so that the court's composition does not change completely at any one time. Members of the court must have experience with the control of public funds in their own countries. Each government nominates a suitably qualified member of the court; the Council then appoints the members unanimously, after consulting the EP. Here, as elsewhere, the EP has attempted to extend its authority by insisting on a right of approval. The EP has occasionally rejected nominees on the grounds of their alleged lack of auditing experience; a government once changed its nominee as a result. The EP routinely complains about the appointment procedure, accusing the Council of not providing adequate information about the nominees.

The court elects one of its members as president to serve a renewable three-year term. The president is first among equals, represents the court externally—for instance, every February the president presents the ECA's annual work program to the EP's Committee on Budgetary Control—and is responsible for managing the court's activities. A change of president is followed by a general change of portfolios; each member of the court sits in one of five groups organized on thematic lines (see Box 10.1). The court is located in Luxembourg and has a staff of about 750. It is supposed to be completely independent of national governments.

The court publishes an annual report on each year's budget, in November of the following year, and also publishes special reports and opinions. All are adopted by a majority vote of the court's members. The annual report consists mostly of a financial management assessment, which involves comparing the

Box 10.1 Court of Auditors

Unit	Responsibilities
Presidency	Supervision of the court's work performance; relations with the other institutions and international audit organizations
Audit Group I	Preservation and management of natural resources
Audit Group II	Structural policies, transport, research, energy
Audit Group III	External relations
Audit Group IV	Revenue, banking activities, administrative expenditure, institutions and bodies of the EU, internal policies
CEAD Group	Coordination, communication, evaluation, assurance, development
Administrative Committee	All administrative questions requiring a court decision
Secretariat General	Human resources, finance and support, information technology, translation

general goals and specific targets of EU policies and programs with the results obtained. Another innovation in the Maastricht Treaty was its requirement for the ECA to provide the Council and the EP "with a statement of assurance as to the reliability of the accounts and the legality and regularity of the underlying transactions." To date, the court's statements of assurance have been far from reassuring, with the court noting too many errors with respect to EU payments to give a positive assurance of their legality or regularity. Special reports allow the court more flexibility than do annual reports, and their highly critical assessments of EU policies and programs often attract media attention. The court's opinions are fewer than its special reports but are not necessarily less spirited.

The ECA's interaction with the Commission, Council, and Parliament in financial management and the budget discharge procedure is examined in Chapter 11. Other EU institutions, any bodies managing revenue or expenditure on behalf of the EU, and national audit bodies or government departments must provide the ECA with documents on request. If necessary, according to the treaty, the court may examine these "on the spot in the other institutions of the Union, on the premises of any body, office or agency which manages revenue or expenditure on behalf of the Union and in the Member States, including on the premises of any natural or legal person in receipt of payments from the budget." The court works directly with its national counterparts when carrying out investigations in member states. Special liaison officers ensure that the court and the national audit bodies collaborate closely. The liaison officers meet in Luxembourg at least once a year, and the president of the court meets annually with presidents of the respective national bodies either in Luxembourg or in a national capital. The Lisbon Treaty reiterates the importance of cooperation between the ECA and national audit bodies.

Under the leadership of Vitor Caldeira, who became president in January 2008, the Court of Auditors has accelerated a reform process begun in 2006 to increase its effectiveness and raise its profile far beyond Brussels and Luxembourg. First, the court developed an audit strategy for 2009–2012 that set priorities and identified a number of policy developments and management issues for particular attention. These include growth and jobs, climate change and sustainable development, and management and control measures at the national level. Second, the court asked representatives of four national audit authorities, including two from outside the EU (Canada and Norway), to undertake an independent peer review of its operations. Conducted in 2008, the review was generally favorable, but identified a few areas for improvement, the most notable and challenging of which is the importance of developing a culture of unity in a court consisting of members drawn from countries with different audit practices and traditions. Third, in 2008 the court launched its inaugural annual activity report. Aimed at a general audience, the annual report presents the court's work in a readable and even interesting way. Nevertheless, the ECA faces a steep uphill task in acquainting Europeans with its undoubtedly important role in strengthening accountability and financial control in the EU.

■ Consultative Bodies

The EU has two bodies that advise it in the legislative process: the Economic and Social Committee (ESC), established when the European Community was founded, and the Committee of the Regions (CoR), of more recent vintage. They have an uneasy relationship with each other. The ESC views the CoR as an upstart; the CoR views the ESC as an anachronism and resents being treated condescendingly. Most members of the CoR took exception to a protocol attached to the Maastricht Treaty stating that the two committees "shall have a common organizational structure." Both have the same number of members, drawn in the same numbers from all member states (see Box 10.2). They also share facilities and administrative support.

Within two years of the establishment of the CoR, relations between the two bodies were so strained that the ESC's staff staged a strike against the new committee, which promptly moved out of the ESC's premises into another building. The two bodies patched up their differences and now again share facilities in a building that once belonged to the EP. The two committees share a common core of departments and about 520 staff, although each also has a small staff (of about 100) of its own.

The Economic and Social Committee
The ESC consists of 344 representatives of workers, employers, and professional and consumer organizations, appointed for four years by the Council on

Box 10.2   **Membership in the Economic and Social Committee and the Committee of the Regions**

Country	Number of Members
Germany, Britain, France, Italy	24 each
Spain, Poland	21 each
Romania	15
Austria, Belgium, Bulgaria, Czech Republic, Greece, Hungary, Netherlands, Portugal, Sweden	12 each
Denmark, Finland, Ireland, Lithuania, Slovakia	9 each
Estonia, Latvia, Slovenia	7 each
Cyprus, Luxembourg	6 each
Malta	5
Total	344

the recommendation of national governments. The Lisbon Treaty extends the members' terms to five years, in line with the mandate of the Commission and the EP. Committee members meet in plenary session nine times a year, more frequently in smaller sections. The committee's purpose is to advise the Commission, Council, and Parliament on social and economic issues, but none of those institutions is obligated to heed the committee's advice. More often than not, the committee's opinions sit, unread, in Council meetings; in that way the Council fulfills its legal responsibility to solicit the committee's views on certain kinds of legislative proposals.

The committee is modeled on national systems for institutionalizing interest-group participation in policymaking. The committee's raison d'être is to increase democratic accountability, make EU decisionmaking more transparent, and familiarize the economic and social sectors with the EU's legislative output. Originally the committee had almost the same political stature as the EP, but the EP soon became far more powerful and prominent.

Members represent a wide variety of social and economic interests in the EU and form three distinct groups of approximately equal size:

- Group I comprises employers (from industry and the service sector).
- Group II comprises employees (mostly from national trade unions).
- Group III comprises various interests (farmers, environmentalists, consumers, professionals, etc.).

Committee members are unpaid but are reimbursed for expenses. Although the committee has little clout, its members enjoy occasional trips to Brussels and the prestige of being involved in EU affairs. National governments look upon the committee as a means of dispensing patronage.

Despite its relative insignificance, the committee generally produces readable and relevant reports, either in response to a Commission request or on its own initiative. The treaties stipulate that the Council and Commission must consult the committee on specific issues, notably social policy, the environment, the single market, cohesion, and employment policy. The Maastricht Treaty made the committee more independent of the Council, in particular with regard to adopting its rules of procedure, and gave the committee authority to meet on its own initiative. The Amsterdam Treaty gave the committee the right to be consulted by the EP, but disappointed the committee by not granting it the status of an EU institution, which it still lacks.

The committee elects a president every two years (extended to two and a half years in the Lisbon Treaty) to represent it in relations with EU institutions, member states, nonmember states, and interest groups, and with national economic and social councils and similar national bodies. A leadership bureau consisting of the president, two vice presidents, and thirty-seven other members assigns ESC members to one of six sections, each comprising a mix of nationalities and groups:

- Agriculture, rural development, and the environment
- Economic and Monetary Union and economic and social cohesion
- Employment, social affairs, and citizenship
- External relations
- The single market, production, and consumption
- Transport, energy, infrastructure, and information society

Study groups of about twelve members each draft opinions on behalf of the sections, usually soliciting expert advice on technical matters. Opinions and reports are adopted by a simple majority in the plenary sessions. Needless to say, consensus is almost impossible to achieve in such a diverse body, and committee opinions and reports often include dissenting points of view. The committee adopts about 170 opinions and reports a year, about 25 of which are reports issued on its own initiative.

The ESC looks to the European Commission for political support. Relations between the committee and the Commission grew especially close under Commission president Jacques Delors (1985–1995), a trade unionist with a strong interest in social policy. Delors presented the Commission's annual program at a plenary session of the ESC early each year and insisted that commissioners with relevant portfolios attend at least one plenary session annually, which they still do. The Council politely ignores the committee, although a representative of the Council presidency—usually a junior minister—outlines the presidency's six-month program at a plenary session. For its part, the EP no longer sees the committee as any kind of threat.

Despite its marginal role, the ESC serves some useful functions. It brings to Brussels representatives of influential social and economic interests and provides a forum for them to hold regular and systematic exchanges of views on important issues. The ESC also acts as a conduit for information from Brussels to the member states and alerts interest groups to the implications of social and economic policy. Although it aspires to a greater role in EU policymaking, the combination of a powerful EP and a highly organized lobby of interest groups in Brussels leaves little room for the committee to assert itself.

Even after the establishment of the ESC in 1958, the Consultative Committee of the European Coal and Steel Community—a body analogous to the ESC—continued to function. When the Coal and Steel Community came to an end in 2002, national governments decided to incorporate a new Consultative Commission on Industrial Change, representing steel producers, workers, consumers, and retailers, into the ESC's structure. The Consultative Commission brings together forty-eight members of the ESC and an equal number of nonmembers.

The Committee of the Regions

"Europe of the Regions" is a popular catchphrase. It describes an EU that is more inclusive and democratically accountable because of the involvement of local and regional representatives in its policymaking process. In the 1980s, individual regions came together on their own initiative and formed the Assembly of European Regions, a pan-European body that sought a formal role in EU affairs. Partly for reasons of democratic legitimacy and partly because it sees regionalism as integral to federalism, the Commission supported the assembly's efforts to give regions and localities a greater voice in the Community system. But the assembly itself was too large and unwieldy to play such a role, and some of its constituent regions were not even within the EU. Accordingly, in 1991 the Commission floated the idea of a Committee of the Regions to advise the Council and itself on relevant policy issues, notably economic and social cohesion. National governments concurred and included in the Maastricht Treaty a provision to that effect. The CoR held its inaugural session in 1994.

The Commission clearly intended that the committee's members hold elective office, but the Maastricht Treaty merely stipulated that the CoR consist of "representatives of regional and local bodies." The Council decided in June 1992 that it was up to each government, using its own criteria, to nominate people to represent regional and local communities (formally, the Council appoints CoR members "acting unanimously on proposals from the respective member states"). Most governments duly nominated elected representatives, but the question of the CoR's composition became a vexing issue in Britain, then under Conservative rule. The British government opposed the Commission's proposal to establish the committee but reluctantly went along with the idea in the Maastricht Treaty. Moreover, because Britain was then a highly centralized state, there were no elected representatives to designate from mainland Britain's three constituent nations (England, Scotland, and Wales). Understandably perhaps, the government tried to buy off Scottish and Welsh nationalists by overrepresenting Scotland and Wales in Britain's CoR delegation.

The Labour government, elected in May 1997, launched a constitutional revolution that included holding successful referendums to establish separate parliaments in Scotland and Wales, thereby bringing Britain more into line with the internal organization of large EU member states. Nevertheless, a fundamental problem with the CoR continues to be the great disparity between the size and political power of regions in the EU and the fact that smaller countries themselves constitute single regions. Thus, a relatively small, unitary state such as the Netherlands has little or no interest in the CoR. By contrast, regions in the EU's three federal member states (Austria, Belgium, and Germany), and especially in member states where there is a strong movement in favor of federalism (such as Italy and Spain), see the CoR as a vehicle to assert their independence vis-à-vis the central government—much to the discomfiture of the governments concerned.

Many members of the CoR therefore have a double agenda: to carry out their functions as stipulated in the treaties and to advance regionalism in their own countries and throughout the EU. Potentially, the committee provides a platform for propagating regional autonomy or even independence within the framework of pan-European market integration and security cooperation. Thus, regionalism and supranationalism complement rather than conflict with each other. Indeed, supranational institutions and regional authorities share a mutual suspicion of national governments, their natural political adversaries.

Role, Structure, and Ethos. The size and composition of the CoR are identical to those of the Economic and Social Committee (see Box 10.2). Also like the ESC, members of the CoR are appointed for four years and elect a president for a two-year term (changed in the Lisbon Treaty to five years and two and a half years, respectively). Unlike the ESC, the CoR has a "first" vice president and twenty-seven other vice presidents (one from each of the national delegations). The CoR also has a much larger bureau (sixty members) than does the Economic and Social Committee. The CoR holds five plenary sessions a year.

The Maastricht Treaty tasked the CoR with providing advice to the Commission and the Council in five policy areas that have a direct bearing on local and regional government: cohesion, transport, public health, education and youth, and culture. The Amsterdam Treaty extended the committee's consultative role to five other areas: employment, social policy, the environment, vocational training, and transport. The committee's members are distributed among commissions that correspond to its areas of interest:

- Territorial cohesion
- Economic and social policy
- Sustainable development
- Culture, education, and research
- Constitutional affairs, European governance, and the area of freedom, security and justice
- External relations and decentralized cooperation

The Maastricht Treaty gave the CoR authority to issue opinions on its own initiative, which it frequently does. Like the ESC's opinions, the CoR's opinions are useful and informative. As expected, they always reflect regional and local perspectives and emphasize especially the importance of the subsidiarity principle. Also like the ESC's opinions, they go mostly unread in the Council. All opinions, whether issued on its own initiative or mandated by the treaty, are approved by a majority in plenary session.

The CoR had pushed hard in recent intergovernmental conferences to enhance its political profile and influence. Among other things, the committee has requested that the principle of subsidiarity be redefined in order to refer explicitly to subnational levels of government, that it be allowed to bring subsidiarity cases before the Court of Justice, and that it be designated an EU institution. No sooner was the CoR established than the usually sympathetic Commission criticized it for "running the risk of casting its net too wide" by making excessive demands and for straying outside the bounds of its mandate in issuing opinions on its initiative.[28] Subsequent treaty reforms have strengthened the CoR's position, but not as much as the committee would like. Apart from extending the committee's consultative role to new areas, the Amsterdam Treaty enhanced the independence of the CoR by allowing it to adopt its own rules without reference to the Council and by repealing the protocol in the Maastricht Treaty that called for a common organizational structure for the EU's two consultative bodies. Only in the Lisbon Treaty did the committee win the right to bring subsidiarity cases before the Court of Justice.

In a series of written questions in 1992 and early 1993 on the eve of the CoR's establishment, members of the European Parliament expressed concern about the committee's relationship with their own institution. In reply, the Council reassured them that the CoR "will have no direct dealings with the Parliament" and will not duplicate Parliament's role in any way.[29] Fears that the CoR might undermine the EP indeed proved unfounded, although MEPs have a reasonable point when they complain that the CoR is redundant because MEPs are elected to represent local, regional, and national interests (the same is true for the Economic and Social Committee because MEPs also represent employers, workers, and other interests). The Amsterdam Treaty gave the CoR the right to be consulted by the EP, while stipulating that "no member of the committee may also be [an MEP]."

In September 2004 the committee voted by a large margin for its members to sit in political groups rather than in alphabetical order, as they had since the first plenary session in 1994. The decision reflects the determination of a majority of the committee's members to raise the political profile of their institution. Committee members now sit in four political groups similar to those in the EP—the European People's Party, the Party of European Socialists (the CoR group has not changed its name, as has the group in the EP), the Alliance of Liberals and Democrats for Europe, and the Union for Europe of the Nations–European Alliance. The committee's inferiority complex vis-à-vis the EP arose during the debate on the new seating arrangements, with some of those who advocated a change arguing that by organizing in political groups, CoR members would be more effective and be taken more seriously by the EP. Some of those against the proposal argued that the committee should not try to replicate the EP, in form or substance.

■ The European Investment Bank

The European Investment Bank (EIB) is one of three financial bodies of the EU. The others are the European Central Bank (examined in Chapter 13) and the European Investment Fund (EIF), which specializes in risk-financing of small and medium-sized enterprises (SMEs) and is largely owned by the EIB (the bank and the fund together constitute the EIB Group). Established in 1958 under the terms of the Rome Treaty, the EIB seeks to promote economic development in the EU by offering loans to the public and private sectors, guaranteeing loans from other financial institutions, and putting financial packages together. The Commission and the recipient country's government must confirm that an EIB loan would help to meet national and EU objectives. A sizable number of EIB loans (about 10 percent of the total) are also directed outside the EU in pursuit of the EU's external relations objectives.

EU member states are the EIB's shareholders, with the size of their subscriptions depending on their economic weight. Thus Britain, France, Germany, and Italy each subscribe about 16 percent of the EIB's capital, whereas Malta subscribes only 0.04 percent. Before the 2004 and 2007 enlargement, the bank's capital base was €150 billion; after enlargement it rose to €163.7 billion. The new member states account for about 4.6 percent of the subscribed capital, which is guarantee capital; only 5 percent is actually paid in. The bank's statute stipulates that aggregate loans and guarantees may not exceed 250 percent of subscribed capital.

The EIB raises almost all funds necessary to finance its lending operations by borrowing on capital markets, mainly through public bond issues quoted on the world's major stock exchanges. The bank's enviable record and reputable shareholders give it a triple-A credit rating. This allows it to mobilize extensive resources without burdening national budgets and to channel resources in an economically efficient way to regions and sectors in need of support. The EIB borrows more than any other international financing institution, including the World Bank. It borrows and lends in several currencies, the most important of which is the euro.

The EIB makes long- and medium-term loans (usually worth about €45 billion a year, but as much as €70 billion in 2009 because of the economic crisis). But the EIB is not a normal bank: it waits for projects to be brought to it and expects them to be largely financed commercially first. The bank can contribute up to 50 percent of a project's cost but typically lends only about 25 percent. The bank's lending rates are highly competitive because of its excellent credit rating and nonprofit status. As well as offering loans, the bank finds cofinanciers and increasingly issues guarantees to commercial banks to encourage them to lend rather than lending directly itself.

The bank is located in Luxembourg and has a staff of about a thousand. National governments, as they do with other high-level EU positions, vie with each other for the privilege of having one of their nationals appointed president of the bank, a highly desirable and lucrative position. Philippe Maystadt, a former finance minister of Belgium, was reappointed president of the bank for a second six-year term in January 2006. The EIB has its own legal personality and a unique administrative structure:

- *Board of governors:* One representative (usually the finance minister) per member state; provides general directives on credit policy; approves the balance sheet and annual report; decides on capital increases; appoints members of the board of directors, management committee, and audit committee.
- *Board of directors:* One representative (usually a senior finance ministry official) per member state plus a Commission representative; five-year terms; decides on loans and guarantees, fundraising, and lending rates; decisions may be taken by majority, but the majority must represent at least one-third of the board and at least 50 percent of subscribed capital; meets on average ten times a year with the bank's president as chair.
- *Management committee:* The bank's permanent executive body; based in Luxembourg; nine members (the bank's president and eight vice

presidents); six-year terms; controls all current operations; recommends decisions to the directors and then carries them out.

- *Audit committee:* Three members; three-year terms; verifies that the bank has carried out its operations and kept its books in order.

Like other EU institutions and bodies, the EIB is responding to growing demands, in this case from nongovernmental organizations, to open itself to scrutiny and generally improve transparency. Criticism of alleged secrecy and conflicts of interest prompted EU finance ministers to oblige the bank to explain and publish its governing principles, which it did for the first time in September 2004.

A number of developments in the late 1980s and early 1990s greatly enhanced the EIB's stature and importance. First, the single market program increased demand for EIB loans to improve the EU's infrastructure and expand industrial competitiveness. Second, the concomitant emphasis on economic and social cohesion, and the subsequent reform of the EU's structural funds, led to massive EIB financing for projects located in regional development areas. Third, German unification further fueled demand for EIB financing, especially for environmental programs. Fourth, the Commission's leadership of the Central and Eastern European assistance effort extended the bank's financing activities in that direction. Between 1990 and 2004, the EIB lent €27 billion to what became the new Central and Eastern European member states, sometimes through cofinancing projects with the European Bank for Reconstruction and Development.

The Maastricht Treaty confirmed the EIB's centrality in the EU system and essential role in financing European integration. Like the articles concerning the Court of Auditors, the articles concerning the EIB were moved to the section on institutions (although the EIB was not designated an EU institution). The treaty reaffirmed that the bank's main task is to provide funding for investment in underdeveloped regions and included a new paragraph instructing the bank to "facilitate the financing of investment programs in conjunction with assistance from the structural funds and other Community financial instruments." The Maastricht Treaty also called for greater EU involvement in areas in which the bank was already heavily committed: trans-European transport, telecommunications, and energy supply networks; industrial competitiveness; environmental protection; and development cooperation with third countries. Regional development remains the EIB's top priority and accounts for most EIB lending, notably to projects in the EU's less well-off rural regions (in Portugal, Greece, Spain, Italy, and all of the Central and Eastern European member states) and in declining industrial areas, notably in Britain, France, and the Netherlands.

The EIB's activities within the EU can be broken down into the following major categories:

- *Improving transport and telecommunications infrastructure:* The Channel tunnel, the undersea rail link between Britain and France (also known as the Chunnel), was the EIB's largest-ever single project. As the EIB's president pointed out during the project itself, "financing the tunnel fits the EIB's task of furthering the development and integration of the EC. It forms a key element in the development of the transport infrastructure necessary to meet the challenges of the single market."[30] Infrastructural projects, which include highways, airports, railways, and communications networks, account for about 45 percent of the bank's lending activity in the EU.
- *Protecting the environment:* Even before the Maastricht Treaty emphasized the need for environmental protection, the bank had identified this as a priority area. The EIB assesses the environmental impact of all projects under consideration. More recently, the bank has focused on projects to mitigate the effects of climate change.
- *Strengthening EU competitiveness and promoting cross-border collaboration:* The bank helps EU industry adjust to structural change and promotes enterprise and innovation. The bank is especially active in support of small and medium-sized enterprises, particularly through the European Investment Fund.

The vast majority of the EIB's lending activity takes place within the EU (including the EU's overseas countries and territories). Outside the EU, the bank provides assistance under various financial agreements, mainly with four groups of countries:

1. *Candidate countries and other countries in southeastern Europe:* The EIB has been active for several years in the EU candidate countries of southeastern Europe (Croatia, Macedonia, and Turkey) and in other countries in the region, and is progressively increasing its technical assistance and long-term lending in the region.
2. *European Neighborhood countries:* The EIB provides loans to countries that are partner to the European Neighborhood Policy, largely through the Facility for Euro-Mediterranean Investment and Partnership, a body that includes a ministerial committee comprising the economics and finance ministers of the EU and the participating states. It forms an essential ingredient of the Euro-Mediterranean Partnership, relaunched in 2008 as the Union for the Mediterranean, and focuses on private-sector development and support for small and medium-sized enterprises.
3. *African, Caribbean, and Pacific countries:* Under the Cotonou Convention, the EIB offers subsidized loans and risk capital assistance to

African, Caribbean, and Pacific countries for industrial, agricultural, tourism, telecommunications, and transportation programs.

4. *Asian and Latin American countries:* The EIB lends to countries in Asia and Latin America with which the EU has cooperation agreements.

As part of a package to try to stimulate economic growth in the early 1990s, the European Council asked the EIB to manage a new, supposedly temporary lending facility to help boost investment in the EU and accelerate the financing of capital infrastructure projects.[31] Accordingly, the EIB and the Commission worked with other financial institutions to establish the European Investment Fund (EIF). The EIB is the major shareholder, subscribing 60.5 percent of the fund's capital; the Commission subscribes 30 percent; European banks and financial institutions subscribe 9.5 percent. The fund was launched in 1995, with the president of the EIB acting as chair of its supervisory board.

In November 2000, as part of the Lisbon strategy to boost competitiveness and employment, EU finance ministers designated the EIF as the specialist financial institution for small and medium-sized enterprises, with responsibility for providing venture capital and guarantee investment. The fund does not invest directly in such enterprises but channels money to them mostly through "global loans" concluded with intermediary institutions.

The EIB received another new mandate in December 2003 when the European Council endorsed the so-called Growth Initiative (officially the European Action for Growth). This originated in a proposal from the Commission, in cooperation with the EIB, for an initiative to spur growth by increasing overall investment and private-sector involvement in trans-European networks (transport, energy, and telecommunications) and research and development.

More recently, the EIB has been pressed into service to help the EU cope with the global economic crisis. In December 2008, the EIB committed itself to increase its overall lending in 2009 by 30 percent, or €15 billion, as part of the Economic Recovery Plan; six months later, the bank agreed to raise its lending target to €70 billion. The bank also teamed up with the World Bank and the European Bank for Reconstruction and Development to provide a €25 billion aid package for Central and Eastern European countries, both inside and outside the EU.

In addition to providing more money to projects within the EU, the bank took on greater levels of risk and expedited the process of lending to businesses. This did not satisfy everyone. In particular, the European car industry, reeling from the economic downturn, complained that the €7 billion in EIB loans that it received in 2009, up from €2 billion annually, was far less than the €40 billion needed to help the sector. EIB president Maystadt was unapologetic, pointing out that the automotive industry already accounted for 10 percent of the bank's annual lending and that there were limits to the bank's activities in terms of sector concentration.

Overall, the president was pleased with the bank's response to the economic crisis, saying that it gave his institution "a new lease on life"—not that the EIB had been moribund. Nevertheless, Maystadt was suitably modest about the bank's role: "the EIB cannot bail out companies in difficulties, nor provide short-term liquidity, nor substitute for structural reforms that might be needed in some industries. . . . What we can do—and what we are doing—is to support viable, good quality projects that are in line with EU policy objectives, from the fight against climate change to supporting poorer regions of the Union, or fostering the small businesses that are the bedrock of the European economy. We are doing so by increasing the volume of our lending and by taking all the necessary risk, in a controlled manner, for more value added."[32]

■ Agencies

One of the most striking features of the EU in recent years is the profusion of independent agencies charged with assisting the Commission by undertaking a variety of technical, scientific, or managerial tasks.[33] EU agencies (variously called agencies, authorities, centers, foundations, and offices) appeared in three distinct waves. The first generation, few in number and limited in scope, date from the 1970s. The second generation, more numerous and specific in their policy function, appeared in the early 1990s in response to the single market program. The third generation, equally numerous and policy-specific, began to appear in the early 2000s as the EU broadened its reach from traditional socioeconomic areas to include foreign policy, internal and external security, and defense. One of the best-known European agencies—the European Space Agency—is not an EU agency; it is a separate intergovernmental organization whose members include non-EU countries. There are nearly forty EU agencies, employing approximately 7,500 people, spread throughout the member states.[34]

To some extent the existence of EU agencies reflects trends at the national level, where there has been a proliferation of independent agencies to promote decentralization and help regulate economic and social policy. The Commission acknowledged this point in its 2001 white paper on governance, which described the emergence of independent agencies as evidence of the maturation of the EU system and as a means of increasing the credibility, efficiency, and transparency of the policymaking process.[35] A subsequent communication from the Commission on the role, organization, and political relevance of EU agencies attempted to provide further rationalization, but failed to dispel the impression that, at the European level, agencies have emerged largely in an ad hoc, unplanned, and opportunistic way.[36]

EU agencies range in their roles and responsibilities from think tanks (such as the European Center for the Development of Vocational Training) to a public health information provider (the European Monitoring Center for Drugs and Drug Addiction) to a functional service provider (the Translation Center for the Bodies of the European Union). Following the acceleration of European integration in the late 1980s, a large number of EU agencies acquired regulatory responsibilities.[37] Examples include the European Environment Agency and the European Medicines Agency. The relative paucity of powerful EU agencies—only a handful have the authority to take decisions that are legally binding on third parties—reflects the reluctance of governments and the Commission to confer extensive rulemaking and enforcement power on independent EU bodies and the lack of an "agency culture" in Europe (in contrast to the United States, for instance). The Commission has been happy to delegate onerous and time-consuming technical tasks to specialized agencies, while maintaining overall responsibility for policy implementation. Establishing agencies is also a way for the Commission to mitigate the impact of strict limits, imposed by the Council, on the hiring of new Commission officials.

EU agencies have their own legal personalities, organizational arrangements, and governance structures. In general, each one has a director, an administrative or management board, and scientific, technical, or coordinating committees. The administrative or management boards usually include at least one representative per member state, plus a Commission official. With enlargement, agency boards have become too big and inefficient, a point made by the Commission in its 2008 communication. The Commission's proposed solution is to have smaller boards consisting of an equal number of national and Commission representatives, a prospect uncongenial to the member states. The scientific, technical, or coordinating committees bring together a wide array of experts across the EU, providing valuable networks underpinning EU policy and linking EU and national policy communities in dense, transnational webs.

Inevitably in an entity like the EU, the location of agencies and other bodies is a controversial and politically charged issue. Largely for reasons of prestige and patronage, each country wants a piece of the agency action. Such competition resulted in a major row in the early 1990s, during the second wave of agency creation, which held up a decision about the location of the European Central Bank and was resolved only at the highest political level: a meeting of the European Council in October 1993. As part of a package that included an agreement to locate the ECB in Frankfurt (an almost nonnegotiable German demand), the European Council decided to move the European Center for the Development of Vocational Training from Berlin (where it had resided since 1975) to Thessaloniki, Greece. The package also allowed the European Environment Agency to open its doors in Copenhagen (the aggressively Green Danish government coveted this agency) and removed a final obstacle to the functioning of the Trademark and Design Office in Alicante, Spain.

Tempers flared again ten years later over the location of a plethora of newly established agencies and bodies, temporarily located in Brussels. Finland and Italy locked horns over the permanent location of the European Food Safety Authority, a plum agency with a large budget and a staff of 250. Silvio Berlusconi, Italy's mercurial prime minister, insisted on locating the authority in Parma, renowned for its ham and cheese. Matti Vanhanen, Finland's phlegmatic prime minister, made the case for Helsinki. In a typical outburst, Berlusconi reportedly proclaimed at a European Council meeting in October 2003 that "the Finns don't even know what prosciutto is."[38] EU leaders finally resolved the row in December 2003 as part of a package deal on the location of several existing and planned agencies. Helsinki got the less charming European Chemicals Agency; the food agency went to Parma, a city that soon became synonymous not with good food but with corporate greed, following the collapse into bankruptcy of Parmalat, the Italian dairy-products group based nearby. EU leaders also agreed to give priority to the new member states in the distribution of the seats of agencies that might be set up in the future. As a result, an EU agency of some sort can be found in each member state.

The Lisbon Treaty introduced the phrase "institutions, bodies, offices, and agencies" to refer to the range of EU entities, and mentioned agencies specifically with regard to the key principles of transparency, personal data protection, financial probity, and judicial review.

■ National Parliaments

National parliaments are not EU institutions or bodies, but they are an increasingly important part of the EU system. Before direct elections, national parliaments delegated a certain number of members to sit in the EP. Such parliamentarians held the so-called dual mandate and personified the link between national parliaments and the European Parliament. Once that link was broken, national parliaments and the EP went their separate ways: the vast majority of MEPs had little involvement with their national counterparts, and the vast majority of national parliamentarians had little contact with their European counterparts. National parliamentarians generally disapproved of MEPs' lifestyles and political posturing, and MEPs resented not being taken seriously by their national counterparts.

Clearly, closer contact between the two groups was desirable not only to improve each institution's perception of the other but also to help close the democratic deficit, which widened in the late 1980s largely as a result of decisionmaking reforms introduced in the SEA. Whereas the new cooperation procedure for legislative decisionmaking increased the EP's authority, greater use of qualified majority voting in the Council undermined national parliaments' control over national governments. As mentioned in Chapter 8, as soon as governments subscribed to QMV, national parliaments could not reasonably hold them accountable for being outvoted in Brussels and abiding by a majority decision.

Before the increasing use of QMV, few national parliaments paid much attention to EU decisionmaking. Denmark's was an exception: the Folketing's powerful European Affairs Committee held government ministers strictly accountable for their behavior in the Council of Ministers and the European Council. Denmark's parliament disliked the antidemocratic implications of qualified majority voting and therefore voted down the SEA in 1986 (the notoriously Euroskeptical Danish electorate rescued the act in an ensuing referendum).

For its part, the EP was unhappy with the cooperation procedure's relatively narrow scope, especially with the existence after the SEA of a number of policy areas subject to QMV but not subject to the cooperation procedure. As the Council successfully implemented the single market program in the late 1980s, using QMV to great effect, national parliaments and the EP became increasingly alarmed by the widening democratic deficit but differed in their suggested solutions to it.

Nevertheless, a number of forums for formal contact between the EP and national parliaments emerged in the late 1980s. These now consist of:

- Conference of Speakers of the Parliaments of European Union Member States and the European Parliament (meets once a year).
- Conference of Community and European Affairs Committees of Parliaments of the European Union (known by its French acronym, COSAC; meets every six months; six members represent each parliament).
- Bilateral and multilateral meetings between specialized committees of national parliaments and the European Parliament to discuss legislative and other developments in the EU (no fixed schedule).

Concerned about the democratic deficit and about national parliaments' estrangement from the EU decisionmaking process, national governments attached a declaration to the Maastricht Treaty on the role of national parliaments. This promised that national governments would send to their own parliaments "proposals for [EU] legislation in good time for information or possible examination" and generally encouraged contact between MEPs and national parliamentarians. Such an anodyne declaration had little practical effect. Some national governments were more assiduous than others about informing their parliaments of impending EU legislation, and some national parliaments were more assiduous than others about insisting on such information.

Pressure from national parliaments for greater involvement in EU affairs intensified throughout the 1990s.[39] Germany's parliament had pressed the government successfully during the Maastricht Treaty ratification crisis for the right to evaluate draft EU legislation. In 1995, enlargement brought into the EU two Nordic countries (Finland and Sweden) whose parliaments were unwilling to cede control of EU legislation entirely to the Council and the EP. At the same time, the somewhat Euroskeptical British and Danish parliaments continued to press for more involvement in the EU legislative process.

Under the circumstances it was not surprising that the issue resurfaced during the 1996–1997 intergovernmental conference. There, governments agreed on the need to keep national parliaments better informed but could not agree on the feasibility or desirability of a new body to represent national parliaments at the European level. Finally, national governments attached a protocol to the Amsterdam Treaty outlining practical ways in which national parliaments would receive information on developments in the EU and encouraging the Conference of European Affairs committees of EU parliaments to "make any contribution it deems appropriate for the attention of the institutions of the EU."

The persistence in subsequent rounds of treaty reform of the question of national parliaments' formal involvement in the EU political system was due less to the agitation of national parliaments themselves than to the desire of government leaders to strengthen the EU's weak legitimacy. Most Europeans found the EU baffling and turned out for EP elections in ever smaller numbers. By contrast, they were familiar and comfortable with their own national parliaments, even though the turnout in national elections varied greatly from country to country and overall was also in decline. Engaging national parliaments more closely in the EU political process seemed vital if the EU was to close the democratic deficit. Accordingly, EU leaders agreed in the Laeken Declaration of December 2001, which mandated the Convention on the Future of Europe, to include the role of national parliaments in the convention's deliberations. Moreover, they agreed that national parliamentarians would be well represented in the convention itself (two parliamentarians from each member state).

Not surprisingly, the convention concluded that it was essential to increase the participation of national parliaments in EU affairs in order to increase citizens' links to the European level of governance. Valéry Giscard d'Estaing, chairman of the convention, wanted a new, joint national-EP assembly to act as subsidiarity watchdog, but encountered opposition on the grounds that the very citizens to whom it should appeal would balk at the establishment of yet another EU body. Instead of proposing a joint assembly, the Draft Constitutional Treaty recommended giving national parliaments themselves the right to veto Commission proposals for conformity with the principle of subsidiarity.

The Constitutional Treaty and its successor, the Lisbon Treaty, elaborated upon the role of national parliaments in the EU system. The most significant provision stipulates that the Commission must submit all legislative and other proposals simultaneously to national parliaments as well as to the Council and the EP. If, within eight weeks, at least one-third of the national parliaments object on the grounds that the proposal violates the principle of subsidiarity, the Commission must review the proposal, presumably with a view to amending or withdrawing it. In an effort to appease public opinion during the Lisbon ratification crisis, the Commission unilaterally implemented this provision even before full implementation of the treaty itself.

The June 2009 German constitutional court ruling on the compatibility of the Lisbon Treaty with Germany's Basic Law emphasized the centrality of national parliaments in the democratic life of the EU.[40] Lamenting the existence of a "structural democratic deficit" in the EU and the EP's inability to close the gap, the court admonished the two houses of Germany's parliament (the Bundestag and Bundesrat) for not being more directly involved with the government of the Federal Republic in the conduct of EU affairs. The court ruled not only that German law on parliamentary involvement in the EU would have to be strengthened before Germany could ratify the Lisbon Treaty, but also that the legitimization of the EU—an association of sovereign states—rested primarily on national parliaments. The ruling was nothing less than a call to arms to all national parliaments, while at the same time criticizing the inadequacy of the Lisbon Treaty provisions for national parliamentary involvement in EU affairs.

Yet the cultural and organizational diversity of national parliaments, as well as the difficulty of institutionalizing cooperation among them, makes it unlikely that they will ever become powerful players in the EU decisionmaking process. Moreover, giving national parliaments a formal right to object to Commission proposals adds another layer to the already cumbersome process of legislative decisionmaking. Nevertheless, the protracted discussion about the role of national parliaments in the EU system, culminating in the relevant provisions of the Lisbon Treaty and the German constitutional court ruling, raises the possibility of turning national parliaments into a locus of debate and lobbying on the EU, thereby stimulating greater citizen interest in what goes on in Brussels.

In the meantime, despite the difficulty of finding a formal role for national parliaments at the European level, national parliamentarians and MEPs have largely overcome their mutual suspicion and resentment. The most obvious sign of this rapprochement is close collaboration between both groups in transnational political parties such as the European People's Party and the Party of European Socialists. It is also through the work of these parties that national parliamentarians and MEPs, outside their respective institutions, are most successful in shaping EU policy.

■ Notes

1. See Anthony Arnull, *The European Union and Its Court of Justice,* 2nd ed. (Oxford: Oxford University Press, 2006); and Gráinne de Burca and J. H. H. Weiler, eds., *The European Court of Justice* (Oxford: Oxford University Press, 2002).

2. G. Federico Mancini, "The Making of a Constitution for Europe," in Robert O. Keohane and Stanley Hoffmann, eds., *The New European Community: Decision-Making and Institutional Change* (Boulder: Westview, 1991), p. 177.

3. *Les Verts v. Parliament* (1986), ECR 1339, at 1365.

4. Jo Hunt, "Legal Developments," in *The European Union: Annual Review 2002/2003* 41 (2003): 79 (emphasis in original).

5. Opinion 2/94 (accession by the EC to the ECHR), ECR I-1759.

6. George Bermann, "Law in an Enlarged European Union," *EUSA Review* 14, no. 3 (Summer 2001): 6.

7. Joseph Weiler, "Editorial: Does the EU Truly Need a Charter of Rights?" *European Law Review* 6, no. 2 (2000): 96.

8. *Van Gend en Loos* (1963), ECR 29-62.

9. *Grad v. Finanzamt Traunstein* (1970), ECR 825.

10. *Costa v. ENEL* (1964), ECR 6-64.

11. *Simmenthal v. Commission* (1978), ECR 777.

12. *Nold v. Commission* (1974), ECR 372.

13. See Paul Craig and Gráinne de Burca, *EU Law: Text, Cases, and Materials,* 4th ed. (Oxford: Oxford University Press, 2008).

14. Martin Shapiro, "The European Court of Justice," in Alberta Sbragia, ed., *Euro-Politics: Institutions and Policymaking in the "New" European Community* (Washington, DC: Brookings Institution, 1992), p. 127.

15. *Isoglucose* (1980), Cases 138 and 139/79.

16. *Parliament v. Council* (1985), Case 13/83.

17. *The Queen v. Secretary of State for Transport, ex parte Factortame* (1989), ECR 213.

18. *European Commission v. Republic of Austria* (2005), Case C-147/03.

19. *Union Royale Belge des Sociétés de Football Association ASBL & Others v. Jean-Marc Bosman* (1985), *Case C-415/93.*

20. *Johnson v. RUC* (1984), Case 222/84.

21. *Francovich and Bonifaci v. Italy* (1991), Cases 6/90 and 9/90.

22. *European Parliament v. Council* (1990), Case 70/88.

23. Phil Fennell, "The Court of First Instance," *European Access* 1 (February 1990): 11.

24. Spiros A. Pappas, *The Court of First Instance of the European Communities* (Maastricht: European Institute for Public Administration, 1990), p. xii.

25. European Court of Justice, *1997 Annual Report* (Luxembourg: Office for the Official Publications of the European Communities, 1998), pp. 130–131.

26. José Luis da Cruz Vilaca, speech at the official launch of the CFI, September 25, 1989, reproduced in Pappas, *Court of First Instance,* p. 10.

27. Hunt, "Legal Developments," p. 95.

28. European Commission, "Report on the Operation of the Treaty on European Union," SEC(95)731 final, May 10, 1995, p. 15.

29. Written question no. 1250/92, OJ C 247, vol. 35, September 24, 1992, p. 53; and written question no. 1206/92, OJ C 6, vol. 36, January 11, 1993, pp. 10–11.

30. Hans-Gunther Bröder (EIB president), interview in *Europe Magazine,* November 1991, p. 20.

31. Edinburgh European Council, "Presidency Conclusions," Bulletin EC 12-1992, point 1.30.

32. European Investment Bank, "Statement by Mr. Philippe Maystadt, President, to the Annual Meeting of the Board of Governors," Luxembourg, June 9, 2009, http://www.eib.org/attachments/general/events/bg_2009_statement_en.pdf.

33. See Sami Andoura and Peter Timmerman, "Governance of the EU: The Reform Debate on European Agencies Reignited," CEPS and EPIN working paper, October 2008; and M. Egeberg, ed., *Multilevel Union Administration: The Transformation of Executive Politics in Europe* (Basingstoke: Palgrave Macmillan, 2006).

34. See Europa, "Agencies of the EU," http://europa.eu/agencies/index_en.htm.

35. European Commission, "European Governance: A White Paper," COM(2001) 428 final, July 25, 2001.

36. European Commission, "European Agencies: The Way Forward," March 11, 2008, http://shop.ceps.eu/bookdetail.php?item_id=1736.

37. See Giandomenico Majone, *Regulating Europe* (London: Routledge, 1996).

38. Quoted in the *Financial Times,* October 31, 2003, p. 1.

39. On the role of national parliaments in the EU, see John O'Brennan and Tapio Raunio, eds., *National Parliaments Within the Enlarged European Union: From Victims of Integration to Competitive Actors?* (London: Routledge, 2007).

40. Constitutional Court of Germany, press release, 72/2009, and judgment, June 30, 2009, http://www.bundesverfassungsgericht.de/pressemitteilungen/bvg09-072en.html.

11 Interinstitutional Dynamics

Brussels is a hive of political and policymaking activity. Most of the action takes place in the sprawling European Quarter of the city, in the meeting rooms and corridors of the European Commission, Council of Ministers, and European Parliament. Restaurants and coffee shops in the warren of nearby squares and streets cater to officials, politicians, lobbyists, journalists, interns, and even the occasional academic, all of whom participate to some extent or other in the EU policymaking process. But Brussels, Luxembourg, and Strasbourg (the other seats of EU institutions) are not the only places where EU business takes place. The country in the Council presidency hosts hundreds of meetings, conferences, and seminars. Officials, politicians, lobbyists, and others involved in EU affairs are constantly traveling on business throughout the EU, and the Commission and Parliament have offices in each national capital. Think tanks in Brussels and elsewhere try to influence policy, however indirectly, by analyzing issues, hatching ideas, and disseminating information.

Players in the EU game have particular perspectives, shaped by personal, national, cultural, institutional, ideological, political, and professional considerations. National interests, by contrast, are really the interests of the governments that happen to be in power at any given time. It is those interests that government ministers and officials defend and promote in the EU, notably in the European Council and the Council of Ministers (including various subcommittees and preparatory bodies) and in dealings with the Commission, Parliament, and other bodies. The Council of Ministers likes to think of itself as having a realistic perspective on EU affairs, in contrast to what it sees as the Commission's Euro-optimism and the EP's unbridled ambition.

As the institutional embodiment of supranationalism, the Commission as a whole has a federalist ethos that exceeds most governments' view of what the EU is or should become. Constitutionally, the Commission is the guardian of the treaties. Politically, it is the guardian of the "Community method," which is both a legislative principle that gives the right of initiative to the

301

Commission and, more fundamentally, an assumption that the Commission is at the heart of a historically unprecedented, supranational polity moving inexorably toward ever closer union. Individual commissioners may eschew the idea of deeper integration upon their arrival in Brussels, but by the end of their tenure it is remarkable how many of them subscribe to the Commission's traditional ethos.

The EP generally shares the Commission's perspective on the historical importance of the EU. But having been an institutional orphan in the early years of European integration, and having had to struggle to get where it is today, the EP is a radical institution constantly agitating for change. As a directly elected assembly in a protofederal system, it wants to acquire the authority that it believes it deserves. Individual members of the European Parliament do not necessarily think that way, but the institution as a whole has a power-hungry culture.

Politicians and officials of the Commission, European Council, Council of Ministers, and EP interact with each other all the time. The EU's advisory bodies, national parliamentarians, lobbyists, and diplomats from nonmember states contribute to the mix. The weekly meetings of the Commission, quarterly meetings of the European Council, monthly meetings of the Council of Ministers, and monthly plenary sessions of the EP are the tip of the iceberg. Beneath the surface, the bulk of institutional interaction takes place in hundreds of formal and informal meetings of Council working groups, EP committees, Council-Parliament conciliation committees, and the like.

Given the nature of the decisionmaking process, interinstitutional dynamics are particularly important. It is by virtue of their institutional roles, after all, that individuals make decisions and shape policy in the EU. Such decisions range from the annual budget and multiannual financial framework to treaty change to enlargement. Most decisions, however, are of a legislative nature. It is in the legislative arena, in particular, that the Commission, Council, and EP are permanently and intensively engaged.

It is also in the legislative arena that interest groups are most active. There are an estimated 15,000 lobbyists in Brussels—the precise number is unknown because lobbyists do not need to register with the Commission or the Parliament. Nor is the word "lobbyist," with its connotation of Washington-style influence peddling, much liked in Brussels. Most lobbyists work independently as "European affairs consultants"; many work for the 3,000 or so interest groups that have offices in and around the European Quarter. These range from small, boutique operations; to sectoral associations, such as the European Automobile Manufacturers Association; to BusinessEurope, a powerful confederation of industry associations; to the regional divisions of multinational public-interest groups, such as Greenpeace. Complementing the Brussels-based corps are an indeterminate number of lobbyists working on EU issues in the national capitals.

■ Legislative Decisionmaking

In the everyday world of legislative decisionmaking, the Commission, Council, and Parliament are closely engaged with each other. The Commission and the Council have a special relationship, symbolized by the Commission's presence at the other end of the rectangular table from the Council presidency at all levels, beginning with the Council working groups, continuing through the Committee of Permanent Representatives, and ending with the decisive meeting of the Council of Ministers itself. Accordingly, the Commission learns the national governments' positions and the possibilities for maneuvering and compromise (the Commission is supposed to act as a mediator between the Council and the Parliament).

At the beginning of each Council presidency, virtually the entire college of the Commission and the entire government of the country in the presidency meet for a full day to discuss the legislative agenda. During the six months of the presidency itself, officials from the Commission and the country in the presidency are in constant contact, while the presidency foreign minister and the European Council president, on one side, and the Commission president and relevant commissioners, on the other, usually get together before each meeting of the General Affairs Council. Indeed, a successful presidency involves continuous contact with officials at all levels of the Commission and requires especially close cooperation between the Council secretariat and the Commission's secretariat-general.

Even under the best of circumstances, however, Council-Commission relations are prone to occasional outbursts on either side. Sporadic battles break out not only in committee meeting rooms but also in the public domain, at press conferences, and at other media events. Sensitive to public concern about excessive EU intrusion into everyday life, national governments instinctively blame the Commission for unpopular legislation, even though they are responsible, together with the EP, for enacting EU laws. Some governments use subsidiarity, the principle that decisions should be taken at the European level only if the objective cannot be achieved at the national level, as a weapon against the Commission.

Personal chemistry and political differences among government ministers and commissioners also matter. The perceived political weakness of successive presidents since the mid-1990s has not helped the Commission in its dealings with the Council of Ministers, let alone the European Council. Nevertheless, many individual commissioners have been highly competent and forceful in their dealings with the Council. Particular Council formations often have an affinity with the relevant commissioner because of a shared policy interest and expertise.

National and commission officials interact closely in legislative decisionmaking. Commission officials and the staffs of the member states' permanent representations in Brussels are the main points of contact. As career officials, they share an interest in moving decisionmaking along, although they are often fiercely competitive. Deeply immersed in the minutiae of specific policy areas, they haggle over the choice of words or placement of punctuation. For some, telling the story of a particular legislative act is akin to reminiscing about a good soccer match or round of golf.

The EP is a relative latecomer in the legislative game. For much of the EU's history the Council was the sole decisionmaking body. The EP could only give an opinion on a Commission proposal, which the Council could—and usually did—ignore. That changed in the late 1980s with the introduction of the cooperation procedure, which gave the EP the right to amend the Council's position and established a high threshold (unanimity) for the Council to reject the EP's objections. The crucial turning point in Council-Parliament relations came with the introduction, subsequent reform, and growing scope of the codecision procedure, as a result of which the Council and Parliament have become coequal legislators for most EU policies.

The adjustment to legislative equality was not easy for the Council. The Council secretariat long resented the EP's intrusion into what it saw as national governments' preserve, even though the intent was to strengthen democracy in the EU. National ministers and officials bridled at having to take proposed EP amendments into account. Many ministers and officials were sure that the cooperation and codecision procedures would not work, that the EP was too cumbersome to manage the procedures expeditiously, and that efficiency was being sacrificed for the sake of democracy. Partly to prove its critics wrong, the EP adjusted rapidly to the new and revised procedure. To be precise, the EP's leaders—the president and vice presidents, the heads of the political groups, and the secretary-general—made the necessary changes and dragged the rest of the institution along.

The paradox of the codecision procedure, renamed the ordinary legislative procedure in the Lisbon Treaty, is the apparent ease with which it operates despite its complexity. The procedure looks like an infernal but well-oiled machine. Its parts consist of innumerable meetings within and among the institutions; informal get-togethers; minutes and memorandums; and phone calls, text messages, and e-mails. The outcome is legislation on a range of socioeconomic issues that, once implemented in the member states, affect the everyday lives of millions of Europeans. Like any legislative procedure in any political system, the EU's procedure is arcane and difficult to explain. Because of its unusual origin, development, and impact, however, it is particularly interesting to follow.

From Cooperation to Codecision

It is essential to understand the profound impact that the cooperation procedure had on the EP's development and on interinstitutional relations. The new procedure had two stages (first and second reading) and strict time limits. The EP would issue an opinion in its first reading, which could include amendments to the Commission's proposal. Based on that opinion, the Council would adopt a "common position," either accepting or rejecting some or all of the EP's proposed amendments, by a qualified majority vote. The common position formed the basis for deliberations in the next stage of the procedure.

In the second reading, the EP could adopt the Council's common position by a majority of MEPs present in the plenary session (usually a low number). It could also suggest amendments to or reject the common position, but only by an absolute majority of its members (a much higher threshold). If the EP rejected the common position, the Council could proceed with the second reading only on the basis of a difficult-to-achieve unanimous decision. The Commission could withdraw its proposal or include some or all of the EP's amendments. The Council could then (1) do nothing—in effect abandoning the proposed legislation; (2) adopt the revised proposal, by qualified majority vote; (3) amend the revised proposal, by unanimity; or (4) adopt the Parliament's amendments that were not included in the Commission's revised proposal, also by unanimity.

The EP radically revised its internal rules so that committees and plenary sessions could meet the demands of the cooperation procedure, and quickly learned to exploit the opportunity to become a powerful player in the legislative process by building coalitions of political groups in order to form the majorities needed to amend, or possibly reject, common positions. Faced with an ambitious, well-organized EP, the Council sought to avoid major amendments and, especially, the EP's outright rejection of its common position. The importance of the cooperation procedure instilled in political groups a greater sense of identity and cohesion as well as encouraging coalition building.

Nevertheless, discipline is lax in the EP by the standards of national parliaments, where a government's survival often depends on party loyalty. The heterogeneity and cultural diversity of political groups militate against strict control of members' behavior. On ideological issues, either the Socialists or the Christian Democrats would try to form the core of a parliamentary majority, vying for the support of other groups. When issues were not contested along ideological lines, the two major political groups often collaborated to amend or reject a common position in order to assert their institution's authority.

The EP regarded the cooperation procedure as a stepping-stone to genuine power-sharing with the Council. By introducing a new legislative procedure—codecision—for a number of policy areas, the Maastricht Treaty went a long way toward meeting the EP's goal. The most important innovation was the provision for a conciliation committee, consisting of representatives of the Council and Parliament, to work out a joint text (if necessary) at the end of the second reading. The joint text would then be subject to approval by the Council and Parliament in a third reading.

Once again, the EP confounded its critics, notably in the Council secretariat, by quickly mastering the codecision procedure. Yet the original (Maastricht) version of the codecision procedure did not put the EP on par with the Council in legislative decisionmaking. Most galling to the EP was the fact that the Council could disregard the outcome of the conciliation committee and adopt its original common position, which it had agreed upon by qualified majority vote, as the final legislative text. It could only do so, however, on the basis of unanimity, which was increasingly difficult to achieve in an enlarging EU. Nevertheless, this possibility gave the Council greater power than Parliament in the new procedure.

Supported by governments that strongly supported the EP's equal involvement in EU decisionmaking as a means of addressing the democratic deficit, the EP achieved its goal of "genuine codecision" in the 1997 Amsterdam Treaty. The most significant change with respect to codecision was a revision of the third-reading stage. The Council would have to approve or reject the joint text agreed upon with the EP in the conciliation committee; it could no longer enact its earlier common position, even by unanimity. Reforming the one-sided third reading put the EP on an equal legislative footing with the Council and increased the incentive for the Council to reach agreement with the EP earlier in the procedure. Another change to the codecision procedure was the possibility of reaching a decision at the end of the first reading, giving the Council and Parliament an incentive to cooperate closely.

These and other procedural changes, together with the extension of codecision in the Amsterdam Treaty to more policy areas, further intensified interaction among the Commission, Council, and Parliament in legislative decisionmaking. In particular, dealings between the Council and Parliament became much more frequent and intricate. The Nice Treaty extended codecision to yet more policy areas. The Lisbon Treaty made only small procedural changes to the codecision procedure and extended its policy scope even further. As noted earlier, the Lisbon Treaty also changed the name of codecision to "ordinary legislative procedure," recognizing it as the norm.[1]

The Politics of the Ordinary Legislative Procedure

Jean-Paul Jacqué, former director in the Council's Legal Service, noted that "the [ordinary legislative procedure] works well in general and has proven the adaptability of the EU institutions." The secret of its success lies in part in the dedication and expertise of a relatively small number of MEPs, commissioners, government ministers, and officials from the EP, Commission, Council secretariat, and national permanent representations in Brussels, who are the high priesthood of EU decisionmaking. They are masters of procedural rules and possibilities, and have formed dense professional and personal networks that cut across the three institutions. As Jacqué observed, people who become deeply immersed in EU lawmaking share the overriding objective "of reaching agreement and avoiding failures."[2]

Nevertheless, failures sometimes occur. Differences within the Council (among national governments) and the EP (among political groups), or between the Council and Parliament, may be unbridgeable. In the case of interinstitutional disagreement, the procedure rarely progresses beyond the first-reading stage. The EP has rejected only a handful of joint texts in the third-reading stage, usually in order to make a political point.

A number of interinstitutional arrangements have emerged over the years to facilitate the smooth operation of legislative decisionmaking, including legislative programming, an interinstitutional agreement on lawmaking, a common approach to impact assessment, joint declaration on the codecision procedure, and trilogues.

Legislative Programming. The Commission first suggested developing an annual legislative program with the EP in the late 1980s, following introduction of the cooperation procedure and launch of the single market program. The Commission, Parliament, and Council agreed in 1992 that legislative programming was indispensable for EU decisionmaking to function effectively. In the early 2000s, the Commission took up the cause of better regulation, urging the Council and the EP to formalize interinstitutional programming. In October 2002 the Commission adopted its first legislative and work program, soliciting input from the Council and Parliament. Soon thereafter the Commission began to draft its work program in a "structured dialogue" with the two other institutions.

Interinstitutional Agreement on Better Lawmaking. In June 2002 the European Council requested the Council of Ministers, Commission, and Parliament to adopt an interinstitutional agreement on improving all aspects of EU lawmaking. This was easier said than done: the Council was wary of reopening a debate on rules governing the Commission's executive authority, while the EP was concerned about the possible use (or abuse) of so-called soft regulation, such as codes of conduct and sector-specific agreements among economic actors, which were becoming increasingly prevalent in the EU. The Commission, Council, and Parliament finally concluded the Interinstitutional Agreement on Better Lawmaking at the end of 2003. In it, they outlined ways of working closely together for the sake of better legislation, such as making greater use of impact assessment, sharing more information at all stages, and having members of the Council and Commission attend all parliamentary plenary sessions and committee meetings.[3]

Common Approach to Impact Assessment. Following implementation of the Maastricht Treaty, the Commission had to conduct impact assessments of certain legislative proposals with respect to subsidiarity, and the Council and Parliament had to conduct similar impact assessments when amending such proposals. By the early 2000s the scope of impact assessments had broadened to include social, environmental, and economic aspects of proposed legislation. Accordingly, in November 2005 the three institutions agreed on a common approach, covering methodologies, content, and timing, with the Commission's impact assessment being the starting point for the other institutions' contributions.[4]

Joint Declaration on Practical Arrangements for the Codecision Procedure. The first joint declaration, in 1999, dealt with arrangements for managing codecision following the Amsterdam Treaty. Subsequent changes in the functioning of codecision, notably the tendency to reach agreement on a legislative proposal in the first or second reading, prompted the Conference of Presidents of the European Parliament to revise the joint declaration. Their work complemented those parts of the Interinstitutional Agreement on Better Lawmaking that dealt specifically with the codecision procedure. The new joint declaration, signed by the presidents of the Commission, Council, and Parliament in June 2007, explains each institution's responsibilities at every stage, clarifies widely used but not always well-understood terms, and elaborates on the final steps of the procedure (between reaching a political agreement and publishing the joint text in the Official Journal).[5]

Trilogues. Trilogues are meetings among representatives of the Commission, Council, and Parliament intended to move the legislative procedure along by resolving differences among the institutions and helping to reach agreement on a draft legislative act. Informal trilogues of key players in the process—parliamentary rapporteurs, chairs of Council working groups, and midlevel Commission officials—have become standard throughout the ordinary legislative procedure, especially in the first-reading stage. Formal trilogues begin in the second-reading stage, at the level of the chair of the EP's responsible committee, the permanent representative or deputy permanent representative of the country in the presidency, and the relevant Commission director-general. Formal trilogues play an important part in the conciliation stage, where they are organized at the highest negotiating level (an EP vice president, minister of the Council presidency, and commissioner).

　　These interinstitutional arrangements provide a structure within which the ordinary legislative procedure operates. The trend toward reaching agreement in the first stage or early in the second stage is striking. During the EP's 2004–2009 term, 72 percent of codecision cases ended with an agreement at first reading and a further 11 percent at early second reading.[6] The reasons for such a high success rate include:

1. Greater familiarity with the codecision procedure in all three institutions.
2. More intensive preparation (through evaluation of the Commission's impact assessment, systematic evidence-gathering, studies, public hearings, etc.).
3. The possibility of concluding an agreement in first reading by a simple majority vote in the EP.
4. Better contacts between the institutions, whose representatives start talking to each other routinely early in the procedure.
5. A higher number of uncontroversial, technical proposals.
6. Greater difficulty for the Council, as a result of enlargement, to reach a common position, thereby giving the EP an opening to act as the Council's internal consensus building and forge a first-reading agreement.
7. Eagerness of Council presidencies to close codecision files during their terms in office, especially in first reading, where arrangements are more flexible than in later stages of the procedure.

The preponderance of agreements reached in first reading is testimony to the efficiency of the procedure. Ironically, it is now so efficient that MEPs complain that it is undemocratic. The speed and specialization of decision-making leave little time for scrutiny by anyone outside the small circle of key participants. Many MEPs who want to track EU legislation feel shut out of the process and fear that the EP may be sacrificing its ability to evaluate proposals carefully for the sake of maximizing efficiency and political leverage over the Commission and the Council.

The landmark energy-climate package of December 2008, discussed in Chapter 15, is an extreme example of how the EP's leaders and the Council presidency sometimes collaborate to push through important legislation, arguably at the expense of proper scrutiny and better lawmaking. The Commission introduced the proposals in January 2008, with a view to wrapping up the package within a year. Steering such a far-reaching, momentous, and potentially divisive set of proposals to completion in such a short time was a Herculean task. It could only have happened because the Commission, Council, and Parliament had decided to fast-track the legislative process. In particular, the Council presidency looked to the EP for swift adoption of the package at the first-reading stage.

Needless to say, the institutions engaged in numerous trilogues throughout the year, culminating in a final meeting immediately after the December European Council at which national leaders had approved the package. The EP's leadership worked out an agreement among the political groups in support of the legislation, which the MEPs approved in late December. Regardless of where they stood on the final package, many MEPs expressed concern about the way in which the European Council, led by an aggressive French presidency, together with the EP's leadership and eager for a headline-grabbing agreement, appeared to have hijacked the codecision procedure. As Avril Doyle, rapporteur for one of the draft directives, complained, there should be "no question of [the EP] accepting a European Council diktat. . . . There is no legal provision for heads of state to be involved in the co-decision process. . . . [T]his high-level consultation was exceptional and should not in any way be seen as setting a precedent for any other co-decision issue."[7]

The Future of the Procedure

Misgivings on the part of some MEPs and outside observers are unlikely to change the way in which the ordinary legislative procedure operates. The EP's leadership puts a premium on efficiency (quick decisionmaking) and credibility (its ability to deliver on time). The big question about the future concerns the role of national parliaments, which under the terms of the Lisbon Treaty may use an "early warning system" to object to proposed legislation. Will they muster enough reasoned opinions to wave a warning card? Would the Commission withdraw a proposal in the face of national parliamentary objections? Would the Council or Parliament—or both—vote to kill a Commission proposal?

The Conference of Community and European Affairs Committees of Parliaments of the European Union undertook a number of exercises before implementation of the Lisbon Treaty to see how national parliaments might avail of the early warning system. In each case, several parliaments drafted reasoned opinions, but in no case would these have been sufficient to trigger the early warning system.[8] Based partly on the COSAC exercises, but largely on differences in the way that national parliaments approach EU affairs, it seems unlikely that they will become the gatekeepers of the ordinary legislative procedure.

■ Comitology

The Commission, the EU's executive branch, implements EU legislation. Implementation generally requires a spate of regulatory measures to flesh out and follow through on the original legislation. The Commission makes about 2,500 implementing rules and regulations annually. Its authority derives from powers delegated to it by the Council and the Parliament, the EU's legislators. But the Commission is not entirely free in the conduct of its executive responsibilities. Jealous of their prerogatives and wary of the Commission exceeding its authority, first the Council and then the EP acquired oversight of the Commission's implementing powers. The result has been the emergence of a system called "comitology," one of the ugliest words in the glossary of European integration, denoting one of the most arcane activities in the EU.

From the outset, the Council insisted that the Commission draft its legislative acts in collaboration with national officials in formal committees. It did so because governments feared that the Commission would exceed its remit and possibly alter the Council's acts with its own implementing acts. In any case, the Commission did not have either the country-specific knowledge or the administrative capacity to regulate without assistance from national officials. Over the years, as the scope of EU policymaking broadened, these committees developed into the elaborate system of comitology, the purpose of which is to supervise (some would say constrain) the Commission's executive powers.

National governments reiterated in the Single European Act that, in general, EU legislation should confer implementing powers on the Commission. Yet governments had difficulty agreeing on a set of principles and rules to define the exercise of those powers. Finally, in July 1987, the Council stipulated that the Commission would exercise powers of implementation either alone or through one of three types of comitology committees.

Comitology was a source of wounded pride for the Commission, which sparred with the Council over the appropriate implementing procedure for each legislative act. Yet the Council-Commission dispute was more ritualistic than real. In effect, the Commission enjoyed a considerable degree of autonomy; the culture of the Commission in any case stressed the importance of legislative initiation rather than implementation; and the efficiency of the various procedures was never an issue (although the variety of procedures available often resulted in protracted and theoretical discussions about which one to use, thereby slowing down the legislative process). Thus the Commission reached the logical but politically surprising conclusion in a preparatory report for the 1996–1997 intergovernmental conference that, in general, "the implementing procedures operate satisfactorily and present no major obstacles to actual implementation." The Commission also provided a compelling statistic: of the thousands of decisions by comitology committees since 1992, only six had been referred back to the Council, which had then made a decision in each case.[9]

If comitology were still restricted to Council-Commission relations, it would appear only in the lifeless pages of the Official Journal and the Commission's annual General Report. But by giving the EP real legislative powers through the codecision procedure, the Maastricht Treaty added a new twist to an already complicated story. The EP had always taken a keen interest in comitology and had long complained about a lack of transparency in the process. Until the Maastricht Treaty came into effect, however, the EP did not have a reason to become directly involved in comitology. Thereafter the EP could argue that it should have equal rights with the Council to monitor implementation by the Commission of legislation enacted jointly with the Council (through codecision). Most national governments were aghast at the idea of parliamentary involvement in comitology and claimed that the Council's and Parliament's roles were not comparable in that respect.

The president of the EP warned the Council in July 1994 "not to try to use comitology to deprive Parliament of co-decision rights [to which] it is entitled . . . under the Maastricht Treaty."[10] The intensity of parliamentary feeling became clear shortly afterward when Parliament caused the conciliation phase of the new codecision procedure to fail for the first time (in legislation on voice telephony) because of the Council's refusal to make concessions on comitology.

An interinstitutional agreement in December 1994 committed the parties to settle the matter definitively at the next intergovernmental conference. Although favoring an extension and revision of codecision in order to enhance Parliament's role, the Commission did not advocate parliamentary involvement in comitology but sought instead to devise simple procedures with minimum interference either from the Council or the Parliament. In the event, governments agreed in the 1997 Amsterdam Treaty to strengthen the EP's legislative powers by radically revising the codecision procedure. They also called for a new comitology decision to replace that of 1987.

The ensuing comitology battle was fought not between the Council and the Commission or the Council and the Parliament but between the Commission and the Parliament. Rather than advocating a complete overhaul of the system, the Commission merely proposed keeping the EP better informed of developments in comitology. The EP pressed for a bigger role and warned that it would be on the lookout for significant changes to legislation introduced under the guise of implementing measures. The EP backed up its demands by putting funds for comitology meetings in a reserve, thereby bringing the system to a standstill. In its new comitology decision, enacted in June 1999, the Council agreed to involve Parliament more fully in the implementation of acts adopted by codecision, to simplify procedures largely by sticking to the three types of committees (dropping the variations and safeguard measures introduced in 1987), and to provide more public information on comitology.

Given its interest in the matter and agitation for change, it is surprising that the EP settled for the 1999 decision, which still gave the Council the upper hand in comitology. Whereas the EP could scrutinize implementing measures and pass nonbinding resolutions if it considered that the Commission had exceeded its authority, the Council could intervene directly. Perhaps the EP was preoccupied with making the most of the revised codecision procedure, a much more visible and politically salient activity than comitology. The EP seemed driven more by determination to enhance its power than by concern about the quality of implementing acts. As two scholars of comitology observed, "On the whole it seems fair to say that the European Parliament has been selective in making use of its scrutiny rights specifically in areas in which it also has a political interest in voicing its opinion, rather than systematically scrutinizing all incoming implementing measures transmitted to it by the Commission."[11]

It was only a matter of time before the EP returned to the fray. Matters came to a head in 2001 when the EP objected to an aspect of the Financial Services Action Plan, a Commission initiative to accelerate integration in the financial services sector. In particular, the EP objected to the proposed establishment of a powerful European Securities Committee, consisting of representatives of the Commission and the national governments, which would fast-track implementation of financial services legislation and greatly reduce the EP's right of scrutiny.

Aware of the damage bound to be caused to European securities markets by continuing uncertainty over the fate of the action plan, the EP relented in 2002. It did so in the knowledge that it would have a golden opportunity in the Convention on the Future of Europe, due to begin later in the year, to open a wide-ranging discussion on the future of comitology.

As expected, the Convention's report—the Draft Constitutional Treaty—included provisions with potentially far-reaching implications for comitology. First, the rules of comitology would in future be made on the basis of the ordinary legislative procedure, thereby greatly boosting the EP's ability to reshape the system. Second, the Draft Constitutional Treaty made a distinction between legislation enacted by the ordinary or special legislative procedures and measures necessary to implement those acts, over which the EP would have greater oversight. National governments incorporated these changes into the Constitutional Treaty and, later, the Lisbon Treaty.

Pending implementation of the Lisbon Treaty, the EP pressed for revision of the Council's 1999 decision on comitology. The Commission, Council, and Parliament concluded an interinstitutional agreement in June 2006, paving the way for a new Council decision on comitology in July (see Box 11.1).

The 2006 reform introduced a number of innovations. One was a distinction between quasi-legislative and other implementing measures, with a new "regulatory procedure with scrutiny" applicable to quasi-legislative measures used to implement laws enacted by codecision. "Quasi-legislative" is difficult to define, but according to new rules on comitology it refers to measures having a significant impact that may nonetheless be delegated to the Commission rather than having to be enacted by the ordinary or special legislative procedures. In the case of quasi-legislative measures emanating from codecision, the Commission submits draft implementing measures to the Council and Parliament as well as to a new type of committee, the "regulatory committee with scrutiny." Regardless of the committee's decision, the Council (acting by qualified majority) or Parliament (acting by absolute majority) may block the implementing measure and send it back to the Commission. The EP may take such action if it believes that the measure exceeds the implementing powers provided for in the basic legislation, is not compatible with the aim or the

---

Box 11.1   Comitology

Comitology is "the system of . . . committees that control the Commission in the execution of delegated powers." There are four types of committees: advisory, managerial, regulatory, and regulatory with scrutiny. They cover almost every aspect of EU policy. There are about 250 committees in all, bringing together thousands of national civil servants for occasional meetings in Brussels, which the Commission chairs. The legislative authority (usually the Council and Parliament acting together) designates the type of committee to assist the Commission with policy implementation. Advisory committees merely counsel the Commission on rulemaking. Management and regulatory committees may oblige the Commission to send proposed measures to the Council for review. Management committees usually oversee policies with budgetary implications, notably agricultural and cohesion; regulatory committees usually oversee other policy areas. The newly established regulatory committees with scrutiny are assuming responsibility for legislation enacted under the ordinary legislative procedure. Parliament may send back to the Commission any implementing measures that go through these committees. Comitology is being revised following implementation of the Lisbon Treaty.

Note: Comitology definition quoted from Thomas Christiansen and Beatrice Vaccari, "The 2006 Reform of Comitology: Problem Solved or Dispute Postponed?" *EIPASCOPE* 3 (2006): 9.

---

content of the basic legislation, or does not respect the principles of subsidiarity or proportionality.

The EP itself was quick to appreciate the change, claiming that the 2006 decision "has started to remove the democratic deficit that comitology created, as it allows Parliament, as colegislator, to effectively monitor the measures adopted to implement European legislation. . . . Comitology is becoming a major aspect of European integration, and creating a major role for Parliament. It is an issue which is constantly evolving, and Parliament will need to continue to adapt its working methods to future changes."[12]

Nevertheless, the concrete impact of the 2006 reform has been slow to manifest itself. The Commission began an alignment exercise in late 2006 to bring existing legislation into conformity with the new procedure, beginning with the most urgent legislative acts (priority alignment) and continuing in 2007 for the whole of the *acquis communautaire* (general alignment). The regulatory procedure with scrutiny was finally implemented only in 2008. An early assessment concluded that "so far, Parliament has been moderate in the number of objections it has tried to raise, although it is not clear to what extent this is due to the fact that the vast majority of regulatory procedures with scrutiny measures are still to come in the future; to [MEPs] not yet being familiar enough with the new procedure and its full potential; to the non-controversial nature of the draft measures; or because it is not easy to find a voting majority for resolutions."[13]

The Lisbon Treaty distinguished among three types of legal acts: legislative, delegated, and implementing. Only the Council and Parliament have the authority to pass legislative acts; the Commission is responsible for delegated and implementing acts. Delegated acts refer to what the 2006 comitology decision identified as quasi-legislative measures, to be dealt with in a procedure along the lines of the existing regulatory procedure with scrutiny. Implementing acts cover routine administrative matters, to be dealt with in committees similar to the old comitology committees.

Even before implementation of the Lisbon Treaty, the EP called on the Commission in November 2008 to submit, once the treaty entered into force, a proposal for a regulation of the Council and Parliament laying down the general rules and principles governing comitology. Pending the entry into force of the new comitology regulation, the provisions of the 2006 decision, with which the institutions were still coming to terms, would apply.[14]

As a result of the lengthy implementation of the 2006 Council decision and dragged-out ratification of the Lisbon Treaty, the inherently complicated comitology system remained in flux in 2010. Despite the vast effort devoted to reforming procedures for implementing EU legislation, comitology has received little media or public attention. Clearly, comitology lacks the visibility and drama of legislative decisionmaking. Yet it is no less important in terms of interinstitutional relations and, especially, its impact on everyday life in Europe. Given its complexity, however, it may be just as well that comitology is largely unknown outside Brussels: the EU already has enough trouble explaining itself to skeptical citizens.

▨ The Budget

The Council and Parliament are the two branches of the EU's budgetary authority. The Commission also plays a part: its proposals get the process going. The Commission and the EP tend to aim high in their budgetary requests; the Council tries to rein them in. After all, most of the EU's revenue comes in the form of a percentage of the member states' gross national income (GNI). The percentage in question—1.24—is small, but the amounts of money involved are large, although governments get some money back in the form of EU expenditure. In general, the Commission and the EP want the EU to move in a more federal direction, with an appropriately large budget. Few national governments want the EU's budget to grow substantially.

There are two related budget procedures. One is for the multiannual financial framework or perspective, within which the other procedure—deciding the annual budget—is embedded. The idea of a multiannual financial framework came about in the late 1980s in the wake of the SEA, as spending rose substantially. EU leaders hoped that the annual negotiations would become less contentious and more manageable within a long-term framework.

Because of the likelihood of interinstitutional disputes over the annual budget, the Council and Parliament established a conciliation procedure specifically for the budget as long ago as 1971. This evolved into biannual meetings of the Council, Parliament, and Commission, first when the Council prepared to adopt the draft budget and later when the Council was about to decide on the EP's proposed amendments. In addition, high-level representatives of the Council presidency, the EP, and the Commission held "budgetary cooperation meetings" in December during the plenary session at which the EP adopts the budget.

These arrangements for conciliation and cooperation did not prevent the Council and Parliament from clashing repeatedly. Most often at issue were the EP's efforts to increase the size of "noncompulsory" expenditure, notably on regional policy, for which it had the power to propose amendments, and indirectly to curb agricultural expenditure, the main item of "compulsory" expenditure, for which it could only suggest modifications. Even the newly elected and more assertive EP rejected the budget in 1979. According to Julian Priestley, a member of the EP's secretariat at the time, the EP's fateful decision to reject the budget, which shocked the Council, "was an act of affirmation . . . a defining lesson for member states that at least on the budget they had to take Parliament seriously. And when they moved . . . to a multiannual approach on the budget, they knew they had to bring the Parliament on board."[15]

The situation improved following agreement among national governments in February 1998 on the first multiannual financial framework (the so-called Delors I package) and ensuing interinstitutional agreement on implementing the framework and maintaining budgetary discipline. The Council and Parliament completed the 1989 budget on time, without a major dispute. Nevertheless, the Council and Parliament continued to squabble over the distinction between compulsory and noncompulsory expenditure—a squabble that led the Court of Justice to declare the 1995 budget illegal because the EP had changed some of the classifications. The EP pressed for the issue to be included in the 1996–1997 intergovernmental conference, but, apart from financing the Common Foreign and Security Policy, budget issues were almost wholly absent from the negotiations that led to the Amsterdam Treaty. Several years later, national governments agreed to abolish the distinction between compulsory and noncompulsory expenditure. This and related provisions of the failed Constitutional Treaty, incorporated into the Lisbon Treaty, greatly strengthened the budgetary powers of the EP.

The multiannual financial framework translates the EU's political priorities into appropriations for broad policy areas, with upper limits on revenue and expenditure. The Commission submits a proposal, which national governments argue intensively over before reaching agreement in the European Council. An interinstitutional agreement, including procedures for revision and technical adjustments, complements the process of multiannual budget planning.

The necessity for an interinstitutional agreement to implement the multiannual financial framework gives the EP considerable leverage over the European Council. In December 2005, for example, British prime minister Tony Blair's intransigence on the question of his country's annual rebate, a legacy of the bitter budget disputes of the early 1980s, threatened to thwart agreement on the new financial framework. A forceful speech by EP president Josep Borrell, days before the make-or-break European Council, on the unreasonableness of Britain's position may have prompted Blair to make a better offer. Immediately after the successful summit, Blair, in his capacity as Council president, had to report on the outcome to the EP. As Andrew Duff, a leading MEP, observed, "For Blair it was much more than a public relations outing because the parliament has the power [by not concluding an interinstitutional agreement] to approve or reject the package proposed by the European Council and, within certain parameters, to adjust figures between headings." Blair's presentation, "which skillfully mixed confidence and contrition," aimed to mollify the EP in the run-up to the interinstitutional negotiations.[16]

In the event, the EP dug in its heels and, in a vote in January 2006, overwhelmingly rejected the Commission's proposal for an intergovernmental agreement based on the financial framework concluded by the European Council. The EP's main complaint was the nature of the budget itself, which allocated too much spending on agriculture and too little on policies that could have a broader economic impact and boost European competitiveness. Although the EP was not in a position to revise the financial framework radically, it pressed for a promise by national leaders to conduct a far-reaching midterm review of the budget. The Commission, Council, and Parliament finally reached an agreement in April 2006 that called for the Commission "to undertake a full, wide ranging review covering all aspects of EU spending, including the [agricultural policy], and of resources, including the UK rebate," in 2008–2009. The EP would be fully involved in the review, which would include an assessment of the functioning of the interinstitutional agreement. The Council and Parliament separately approved the interinstitutional agreement on budgetary discipline and sound financial management in May 2006, allowing the current financial framework to come into effect in January 2007.[17]

Apart from the midterm review, the interinstitutional agreement has been revised occasionally since January 2007. For example, in May 2009 the Council and Parliament amended the agreement in order to finance the Economic Recovery Plan.[18] Because the Lisbon Treaty fixed the length of the financial framework at five years, the EP has called for an extension of the term of the current framework until the end of 2016 or 2017 (instead of 2013), so that the EP elected in June 2014 and the Commission taking office in November 2014 would be involved in concluding the new framework and negotiating the concomitant interinstitutional agreement.

The Lisbon Treaty introduced another significant change to the multiannual financial framework. In future, the Council and Parliament would jointly conclude the financial framework in the form of a regulation, using a special legislative procedure. In a report on the institutional implications of the Lisbon Treaty, the EP welcomed this development but regretted that the treaty kept the requirement that the Council act unanimously when adopting the framework, thereby "rendering the decision-making procedure very difficult and encouraging negotiations on the basis of the 'lowest common denominator.'" The EP also regretted that under the new procedure it has only a right of approval rather than the power of codecision. By calling on the Council to engage in "a structured political dialogue . . . in order to take full account of [the EP's] priorities" whenever it adopts a financial framework, the EP once again signaled its determination to wring the most politically out of the Lisbon Treaty's innovations.

The Annual Budget. The Lisbon Treaty simplifies the procedure for adopting the annual budget, reducing it to one reading each for the Council and Parliament, followed, if necessary, by a conciliation stage (see Box 11.2). The treaty also does away with the distinction between compulsory and noncompulsory expenditure, thereby putting the Council and Parliament on an equal footing with respect to all types of EU spending.

The new, simpler budgetary procedure requires considerable adaptation within the Council and Parliament. Without the luxury of a second reading, the two institutions must prepare more intensively before the first reading and hold numerous meetings in the preparatory, first-reading, and conciliation stages. In a resolution of May 2009 on financial aspects of the Lisbon Treaty, the EP noted that "the introduction of informal arrangements for dialogue between the institutions is crucial to facilitating agreement before the procedure starts and then throughout its duration," and that the EP will need to equip itself "with the means to manage effectively both the tighter timetable and the greater need to plan ahead thoroughly which will result from the introduction of the new procedure."[19]

Financial Control and Budget Discharge. As noted in Chapter 10, the Court of Auditors prepares a "statement of assurance" annually for the Commission and the EP regarding EU expenditure, for which the Commission has responsibility. So far, since preparing the first statement of assurance in 1995, the court has been unable to verify "the legality and regularity of the underlying transactions" and, therefore, give the Commission a clean bill of health. The EU engages in so many transactions that the court, which bases its judgment on a sample of them, is bound to find some irregularities. Although its qualified statements of assurance are an embarrassment to the Commission and a boon to Euroskeptics, the court has never questioned the reliability of the Commission's accounts.

Before adopting its annual and other reports, the court and the Commission engage in what is called the *procedure contradictoire,* whereby the Com-

---

Box 11.2   The Annual Budgetary Procedure

The budgetary procedure takes place in the year preceding budget implementation (Year $N - 1$).

1. *Commission proposal:* The Commission draws up a preliminary draft budget (see Chapter 7).
2. *Council's first reading:* The Council adopts a position on the draft budget and forwards it to Parliament no later than October 1, along with an explanation of its position.
3. *Parliament's first reading:* Within forty-five-days:
   - Parliament may adopt the Council's position or do nothing, in which case the budget can be adopted.
   - Parliament may propose amendments (by an absolute majority of its members). If so, Parliament sends its amendments to the Commission and the Council. This triggers the conciliation stage, unless the Council approves Parliament's amendments within ten days, in which case the budget can be adopted.
4. *Conciliation:* The conciliation committee has twenty-one days to produce a joint text. If it fails to do so, the procedure ends and the Commission must submit a new proposal. If it succeeds, then within fourteen days the budget can be adopted if:
   - The Council (acting by a qualified majority) and the Parliament (acting by an absolute majority) approve the joint text.
   - One of the institutions approves the joint text and the other one fails to act.
   - Parliament approves the joint text and, if the Council rejects it, Parliament confirms its amendments with a supermajority vote—an absolute majority of MEPs and at least three-fifths of the votes cast. (For example, in a Parliament of 736 members, an absolute majority is 369; confirming its amendments by this minimum acceptable number of votes and thereby overriding the Council's rejection of the joint text would require at least 615 MEPs to have voted. Given the problem of low attendance at plenary sessions, this is a very high number of votes for the Parliament to muster.)
   The joint text cannot be adopted if:
   - Both institutions reject it or fail to act.
   - One institution rejects it and the other fails to act.
   - The Council approves the joint text but Parliament rejects it by an absolute majority.
5. *Signing into law:* The budget is formally adopted when the presidents of the Council and the Parliament sign it into law, usually at a ceremony in Strasbourg in December.
6. *"Provisional twelfths":* If the institutions fail to agree on a budget before the beginning of the year in which it is to be implemented (Year N), the EU operates on a month-to-month basis under a system called "provisional twelfths"— the monthly budget being one-twelfth of the previous year's budget—until a new budget is agreed on and comes into operation.

---

mission tries to tone down the court's criticisms. Every court publication includes the Commission's reply to the court's findings, which are often politically sensitive. Indeed, the Commission generally objects to what it sees as the court's tendency to make critical political judgments. Siim Kallas, budget commissioner in José Manuel Barroso's first administration, rashly promised that he would win an unqualified statement of assurance from the court by the time he left office in 2009. He failed to do so.

Notwithstanding Parliament's own problems of financial management, the EP and the court are allies in the battle to improve financial management in the EU. The court has helped indirectly to increase the EP's budgetary authority, and the EP has helped to boost the court's institutional standing.[20] The court went so far, in January 2009, as to award Hans-Gert Pöttering, EP president at the time, a special distinction "in recognition of the cooperation between the two institutions" and of Parliament's "commitment to implement the court's reports and opinions."[21]

The EP is the court's natural ally because the EP has the sole authority to approve (grant discharge to) the Commission's annual financial statement of accounts (see Box 11.3). As in other areas of responsibility, the EP often uses that authority to enhance its institutional power, although arguably to the detriment of the budgetary and accounting aspects of the discharge function. As long ago as July 1979, the budget commissioner opined that refusal to grant a discharge would be "a political sanction . . . an event of exceptional seriousness [that] would have to lead to the dismissal of the existing [Commission] team. I venture to think that we shall never reach that point."[22] Yet five years later, in November 1984, the EP refused a discharge of the 1982 budget as a means of censuring the Commission. A political crisis was averted only by the expiration

---

Box 11.3   The Budget Discharge Procedure

The discharge procedure for the budget of any given year (Year *N*) begins late in the following year (Year *N* + 1) and ends early in the year after that (Year *N* + 2).

Year N + 1
First Step: The Commission prepares a summary report on expenditures, which it submits to the Court of Auditors and, in September, to Parliament's budget control committee.
November: The president of the Court of Auditors presents the court's report on the budget in question first to Parliament's budget control committee, then to a plenary session of Parliament.
December: The president of the Court of Auditors presents the court's report to the Economic and Financial Affairs Council (Ecofin). The Council asks the Committee of Permanent Representatives (Coreper) to examine the report and draft a recommendation to Parliament on whether to grant discharge to the Commission.

Year N + 2
February: The Council adopts a recommendation, based on Coreper's draft, and sends it to Parliament.
March: Parliament's budget control committee votes on whether to grant discharge to the Commission, taking into account the Council's recommendation.
April: Parliament votes in plenary session on whether to grant discharge to the Commission, guided by the budget control committee's earlier vote.

of the Commission's term in office (the EP finally granted a discharge for the 1982 budget in March 1985). In 1998 the EP delayed discharge of the 1996 budget to protest the Commission's poor management of successive budgets, based on highly critical reports by the Court of Auditors. As discussed in Chapter 5, this action triggered the events that culminated in the resignation of the Santer Commission in March 1999, a development that greatly weakened the political authority of the Commission and enhanced that of the EP.

The EP's power to approve (grant discharge to) the Commission for its management of the annual budget does not extend to approving Council expenditure, as the Commission has overall responsibility for managing the EU budget. Nevertheless, the EP has become highly critical of the way in which the Council spends money on the CFSP and has sought to institute a separate budget discharge procedure for the Council. The EP held a debate on the issue in April 2009, which the Council presidency chose not to attend. Some MEPs were highly critical of the Council and of the CFSP. For example, a Christian Democrat MEP asked if it was really necessary for CFSP High Representative Javier Solana "to travel to the four corners of the earth for this, that and everything," as taxpayers "would find it hard to understand such expenses." The chairman of the EP's security and defense subcommittee was more conciliatory, pointing out that members of the subcommittee and of Solana's services frequently exchange information.[23] The debate highlighted Parliament's irritation with the Council and eagerness to hold it to account.

▩ Political Accountability

The EP is accountable to an EU-wide electorate. To whom are the other institutions accountable? Governments are accountable to national electorates, but the Council of Ministers and the European Council—made up of government ministers and national leaders—are not directly accountable within the European system. The EP tries to increase the accountability of both institutions by engaging the Council presidency in discussions and debates, but this is a weak mechanism.

By contrast, the EP holds the Commission accountable in many ways, not least by having the authority to dismiss the Commission with a vote of censure, which requires the support of at least two-thirds of the total number of MEPs. José Maria Gil Robles, a former president of the EP (1997–1999), thinks that because "the two-thirds majority is an anachronism, a relic from the time when the Commission was appointed by the [national] governments alone," a vote of no confidence by a simple parliamentary majority "must mean the end of the Commission."[24] Although the Commission would disagree with Gil Robles, the EP's rising political influence and the Commission's declining fortunes suggest that his assessment may well be correct.

Temporary committees of inquiry are another instrument that the EP uses to hold the Commission to account. For example, it was a highly critical report issued by a temporary committee of inquiry that led the EP to adopt a nonbinding resolution of "conditional censure" to pressure the Commission to implement the EP's recommendations for administrative improvements in the wake of the Commission's mishandling of an outbreak of bovine spongiform encephalopathy (BSE, or "mad cow disease") in 1996.[25]

Although the Rome Treaty did not give it a role in appointing the Commission, since 1981 the EP has voted on the investiture of each new Commission. The Maastricht Treaty formalized that practice by mandating that the newly nominated president and other members of the Commission "shall be subject as a body to a vote of approval by the European Parliament." The EP carried out this new responsibility for the first time in July 1994 when it voted on Jacques Santer's nomination as Commission president. Reacting against the manner of his selection, the EP endorsed Santer by only a narrow majority. Then, to the dismay of the Commission and some national governments, the EP successfully interpreted the investiture procedure to require not only that it vote on the Commission-designate (as a college) but also that it hold hearings on each of the commissioners-designate. Klaus Hänsch, president of the EP at the time, reminisced that "there was no basis in the Treaties for [individual hearings]. What was then a coup has now become established procedure. . . . This success showed me that it is more important for the European Parliament to exert the influence it does have, right down to the last detail, rather than bemoaning its lack of powers."[26]

The EP uses the investiture procedure to explore the suitability of the Commission president and the commissioners for their jobs and to assert its right to hold the Commission accountable. In general, the hearings have contributed to the changing dynamics of Commission-Parliament relations, which are becoming more confrontational. Matters came to a head in October 2004 when the EP's Social Affairs Committee narrowly voted not to approve commissioner-designate Rocco Buttiglioni, a conservative Catholic who made objectionable remarks about women and gays. This presented Commission president-designate Barroso with a quandary: should he appease the EP by sacrificing the commissioner in question, or insist that the EP vote on his entire college, as stipulated in the treaty? When it became clear that a majority of MEPs would vote against the Commission, Barroso withdrew his support from the embattled commissioner-designate. Fortunately for Barroso, Italian prime minister Silvio Berlusconi withdrew Buttiglioni's nomination. Similarly, Bulgaria's commissioner-designate withdrew her nomination in January 2010 in the face of withering allegations from MEPs about her financial interests and about her husband's business dealings.

As part of a framework agreement negotiated in 2005 to govern Commission-Parliament relations for the remainder of Barroso's mandate, the

EP wanted the right to hold a hearing and take a binding vote on the appointment of replacement or new commissioners during the lifetime of the Barroso Commission. The Commission countered that midterm appointments were entirely the prerogative of the national governments. Nevertheless, the Commission agreed that a hearing and vote could take place, and that the outcome would be politically significant. But it would be up to the government in question to withdraw its politically handicapped new commissioner.

The issue was not academic. In anticipation of their countries' accession to the EU in January 2007, Bulgaria and Romania nominated commissioners-designate in late 2006. Barroso was unhappy with the Romania nominee, who was tainted by allegations of corruption and links with the communist-era secret police. Apart from personally disliking the individual, the last thing that Barroso wanted was a row with the EP over the candidate's credentials. In the event, the Romanian government withdrew its first choice and nominated instead an uncontroversial replacement. The EP chose to vote in December 2006 only on the suitability of the two nominees, not on the entire college, basing its actions on Bulgaria's and Romania's accession treaties rather than on the Nice Treaty, which provided for the EP to approve the college as a whole. The relevant committees easily approved the new commissioners in November, and a majority of MEPs endorsed them wholeheartedly in the December plenary session. The EP held advisory votes, without political incident, on the numerous replacement commissioners in the final year of Barroso's first administration.

The EP does not have the right to censure and therefore dismiss individual commissioners. Yet former EP president Gil Robles claims to have had an agreement with Commission president Romano Prodi "that would enable [the EP] to demand the resignation of any commissioner who had lost [its] confidence," and interpreted the EP's success in preventing Buttiglioni's appointment as evidence of the EP's ability to dismiss individual commissioners.[27] The EP's insistence on getting rid of an individual commissioner in the face of strong opposition from a national government or from the Council, regardless of the Commission president's preference, would likely ignite a fierce interinstitutional battle.

Apart from the investiture proceedings, regular appearances by commissioners before plenary sessions and committees give the EP frequent opportunities to hold the Commission to account. Yet these occasions often turn into efforts by MEPs to score political points. Martin Schulz, leader of the Socialist group in the Parliament, was a bitter critic of Barroso, especially early in Barroso's first administration when the Commission president hewed more closely to a neoliberal line. Schulz's dogged criticism of Barroso succeeded in raising the profile of the Socialist group (and with it the group's leader) and introducing a sharp political edge into the EP's proceedings.

Whereas Barroso was relatively passive in response to such attacks, commissioners do not always play the EP's game. Charlie McCreevy, commissioner for the internal market during Barroso's first term, was notoriously dismissive of the EP. That led three leading Socialist MEPs to complain at the height of the financial crisis in December 2008 that "Commissioner McCreevy's action [in not regulating hedge funds and private equity] shows a total absence of respect for the European Parliament and appears to be more appropriate for a paid lobbyist of the finance industry than a European commissioner."[28] McCreevy's notorious tactlessness toward the EP and others in Brussels was beyond Barroso's control.

Apart from attempting to score political points or needle individual commissioners, MEPs use debates, questions, and committee meetings to try to shape the Commission's agenda and direction. Jerzy Buzek, elected EP president in July 2009, stated shortly before taking office that the EP should "meet with the European Commission president every month" so that it could "influence" the Commission's work.[29] Julian Priestley, a former secretary-general of the EP, thinks that Commission-Parliament relations may have tilted too much in the EP's favor. Looking back at the collapse of the Santer Commission, Priestley wondered whether forcing the Commission out "was really in the Parliament's long-term interest because a weaker Commission is not necessarily best for the Parliament."[30]

The EP has much less leverage over the Council of Ministers, let alone the European Council. Nevertheless, the EP acts unofficially as a Council watchdog. The Council president reports to the EP after each summit and at the beginning and end of each presidential rotation, giving MEPs an opportunity to debate the presidency's performance and priorities. Some national leaders get a better reception than others.

A final aspect of institutional accountability is worth mentioning: the EP's unofficial oversight of the European Central Bank. The ECB is an independent institution, whose president is appointed by the European Council for a nonrenewable term of eight years. The EP has the right to consider the European Council's nominee, without being able to block the appointment. The EP exercised this right for the first time in 1998, when the European Council chose Wim Duisenberg as the inaugural ECB president. The controversial nature of Duisenberg's appointment, which caused a bitter row between France and Germany, gave the EP an opportunity to win a commitment from the ECB president to appear regularly before the EP to report on the bank's progress. As a result, the ECB president appears quarterly before Parliament's Committee on Economic and Monetary Affairs.

By virtue of these "dialogues," the EP sees itself as the ECB's main institutional interlocutor and seeks to strengthen the bank's legitimacy by increasing the transparency of its decisionmaking procedures. The EP is not entirely happy with the ECB's responsiveness. As a close observer of the ECB noted in 2009, for years the Economic and Monetary Affairs Committee has expressed "concerns about the ECB's lack of procedural transparency . . .

[and] pressed unsuccessfully for details about the decision-making process, without being able to engage the ECB president or other bank officials 'in serious discussion.'"[31] Experience in other areas of oversight suggests that, eventually, the EP may well get its way.

■ Notes

1. For a diagram of how the ordinary legislative procedure works, see European Parliament, *Codecision and Conciliation: A Guide to How the Parliament Co-legislates Under the Treaty of Lisbon*, Annex F: Presentation of the Ordinary Legislative Procedure (Article 294 TFEU), http://www.europarl.europa.eu/code/information/guide _en.pdf.

2. *Codecision News: Newsletter from the European Parliament Conciliations and Codecision Secretariat* no. 1 (October 2008).

3. See European Commission, "Better Regulation," http://ec.europa.eu/governance/better_regulation/ii_coord_en.htm.

4. European Commission, "Inter-Institutional Common Approach to Impact Assessment," November 2005.

5. European Parliament, Council, and European Commission, "Joint Declaration on Practical Arrangements for the Codecision Procedure," *Official Journal of the European Union,* C145/4, June 30, 2007.

6. See European Parliament, "Conciliation and Codecision Activity Report: July 2004–May 2009," pp. 11–12, http://www.europarl.europa.eu/code/information/activity _reports/activity_report_2004_2009_en.pdf.

7. Quoted in "Agreement for Energy–Climate Change Package Is Victory for Climate but Not for Democratic Procedures, Says Parliament," *Europolitics,* December 18, 2008. See also Avril Doyle, MEP, rapporteur for the European Parliament, "Carbon Emissions Trading Report Agreed," EPP-ED Group in the European Parliament, press release, December 13, 2008.

8. European Commission, "Report from the Commission on Subsidiarity and Proportionality (15th Report on Better Lawmaking 2007)," COM(2008)586 final, September 26, 2008, pp. 6–7.

9. European Commission, "Report on the Operation of the Treaty on European Union," SEC(95)731 final, May 10, 1995, p. 22.

10. Debates of the European Parliament, OJ 4-449, July 19–22, 1994, p. 13.

11. Thomas Christiansen and Beatrice Vaccari, "The 2006 Reform of Comitology: Problem Solved or Dispute Postponed?" *EIPASCOPE* 3 (2006): 11.

12. European Parliament, Conference of Committee Chairs, *Comitology Handbook: The European Parliament's Work in the Field of Comitology,* March 2009, p. 2.

13. Alan Hardacre and Mario Damen, "The European Parliament and Comitology: PRAC in Practice," *EIPASCOPE* 1 (2009): 17.

14. József Szájer, rapporteur for the European Parliament, "Follow-Up to the European Parliament Resolution with Recommendations to the Commission on the Alignment of Legal Acts to the New Comitology Decision, Adopted by the Commission on November 18, 2008," A6-0345/2008/P6_TA-PROV(2008)0424, September 23, 2008.

15. Julian Priestley, *Six Battles That Shaped Europe's Parliament* (London: John Harper, 2008), quoted in an interview in *Europolitics,* March 19, 2008.

16. Andrew Duff, "The British Presidency," www.ft.com, January 29, 2006.

17. European Parliament, Council, Commission, "Interinstitutional Agreement Between the European Parliament, the Council, and the Commission on Budgetary Discipline and Sound Financial Management," *Official Journal of the European Union*, 2006/C 139/01.

18. "Decision of the European Parliament and of the Council of 6 May 2009 Amending the Interinstitutional Agreement of 17 May 2006 on Budgetary Discipline and Sound Financial Management as Regards the Multiannual Financial Framework (2007 to 2013)."

19. European Parliament, Resolution of May 7, 2009, on financial aspects of the Lisbon Treaty, http://www.europarl.europa.eu/sides/getDoc.do?type=TA&language=EN&reference=P6-TA-2009-0374.

20. See Brigid Laffan, "Auditing and Accountability in the European Union," *Journal of European Public Policy* 10, no. 5 (October 2003): 762–778.

21. See "Pöttering Strikes Gold," *European Vice*, February 5, 2009.

22. Quoted in Daniel Strasser, *The Finances of Europe*, 7th ed. (Luxembourg: Office for Official Publications of the European Communities, 1992), p. 290.

23. "2007 Budget: Parliament Postpones Council's Discharge Due to Lack of Clarity," *Europolitics*, April 24, 2009.

24. *Agence Europe*, "Reflections of Former Presidents of the European Parliament," part 2, March 20, 2008.

25. See Martin Westlake, "'Mad Cows and Englishmen': The Institutional Consequences of the BSE Crisis," *Journal of Common Market Studies, European Union: Annual Review of Activities* 35 (1997): 11–36.

26. *Agence Europe*, "Reflections of Former Presidents of the European Parliament," part 2, March 20, 2008.

27. Ibid.

28. Quoted in "Three Members of PES Group Denounce McCreevy's Attitude Regarding Hedge Funds and Private Equity," *Europolitics*, December 18, 2008.

29. "EU Parliament Has 'Equal Power' to Member States," *EUObserver*, July 9, 2009.

30. Interview with Julian Priestley, *Europolitics*, March 19, 2008.

31. Anne Sibert, "What Role Should the ECB Play in Financial Market Supervision?" briefing paper prepared for the Committee on Economic and Monetary Affairs of the European Parliament for the quarterly dialogue with the president of the European Central Bank, March 2009, p. 4, n. 6, http://www.europarl.europa.eu/document/activities/cont/200903/20090312att51660/20090312att51660en.pdf.

PART 3
Policies

12 Agriculture and Cohesion

Agriculture and cohesion (efforts to reduce socioeconomic disparities among regions) are highly distinctive areas of European Union policy. The Common Agricultural Policy was put in place in the 1960s. Although it has changed markedly since then, its original rationale remains the same: the CAP is a welfare program intended to give farmers an income comparable to that of workers in other sectors, which requires substantial financial transfers to the agricultural sector from the EU budget. For a long time the CAP was the largest item of EU expenditure; its declining share of spending is due not to cutbacks in payments to farmers but to higher spending on cohesion, the other main category of EU outlay.

EU agricultural subsidies are visible (and welcome) to the farmers who get the checks, but are hardly perceptible to the population of the EU as a whole. By contrast, the impact of the structural funds (the instruments for promoting cohesion) is readily apparent. Travelers throughout the EU, but especially in the less developed areas (notably in Central and Eastern Europe), frequently encounter road and rail improvements paid for in part—as the blue signs with gold stars proudly proclaim—by EU structural funds. Workers in transition and the unemployed are also aware that their vocational training courses are paid for to some extent by the structural funds. Apart from monetary union, which puts a common currency in people's pockets, no other EU policy has such high visibility.

■ The Common Agricultural Policy

The CAP is one of the oldest and most controversial EU policies.[1] It covers almost every aspect of farming life in an EU that, with successive enlargements, has acquired an ever more diverse agriculture sector, incorporating small family farms and large factory farms, farms in the plains of Poland and the highlands of Scotland, farms in the frozen north of Finland and the sweltering south of

329

Spain. The variety of agricultural products is as diverse as EU farm size and type, ranging from cereals, beef, milk, olive oil, fruit, and vegetables to tobacco and reindeer meat. Agriculture in the EU employs 8 million people (5.3 percent of the working population), and agricultural exports account for 8 percent of total EU exports.

Critics of the CAP denounce it as expensive, wasteful, ecologically unsound, and trade-distorting. It accounts for approximately 45 percent of annual EU spending, has caused food surpluses warehoused throughout the EU or dumped in foreign markets, and contributes to land and river pollution through farmers' excessive use of fertilizers and pesticides. Because of its complexity, the CAP is difficult to manage; because of its largesse, it is prey to massive fraud. The CAP is a source of friction in the EU's external economic relations by virtue of its import restrictions and export subsidies. Farmers, who depend on it for their livelihoods, are ambivalent about the CAP. Most welcome the generous financial support that it provides but resent what they see as excessive bureaucratization and unfavorable reforms, which they ascribe to pressure from the consumer, environmental, and global development lobbies.

Despite its obvious failings, the CAP remains a cherished icon of European integration, and especially of Franco-German accord. It evokes the heady days of the late 1950s, when Germany supposedly agreed to European subsidization of France's large agricultural sector in return for French acceptance of a common market in industrial goods. The truth was less clear-cut, but French leaders habitually evoke the myth of the EU's constitutive bargain to deflect pressure for far-reaching CAP reform. German leaders invariably perpetuate the CAP for its own sake and for the sake of harmonious relations with France.

Nevertheless, the CAP is changing in significant ways. Since the early 1990s, the CAP has been in a process of almost continuous reform. The EU has largely moved away from the system of price supports that had caused overproduction to a system of direct income support for farmers, and has been linking payments to the requirement that farmers meet environmental and animal welfare obligations. But the EU is not about to abandon large-scale subsidization of agriculture. At French prompting, the EU rationalized farm subsidies in the late 1990s on the grounds that agriculture in the EU is different from agriculture anywhere else in the world; that the "European model of agriculture" with its mixture of social, environmental, and economic elements requires a high degree of government intervention and support.[2]

Although the phrase "European model of agriculture" is no longer in vogue, the sentiment that it encapsulates persists among EU elites, who continue to see agriculture as a singular sector in need of large-scale subsidization. Undoubtedly agriculture is a case apart—food is a basic need, rural life has a special appeal, and farms have a romanticism about them that factories and offices do not. Nevertheless, the vast majority of Europeans, who are not involved in agriculture and who are far more exposed to global competition, restructuring, and job losses, are less indulgent of their compatriots on the land and more resentful of the money—their money—being lavished on farmers.

Looked at purely from an economic perspective, the CAP does not make sense. But it cannot be understood only from an economic point of view. Rather, comprehending the CAP requires some knowledge of the history and politics of European integration, in which agricultural policy is deeply interwoven. History and politics favor what has become the status quo—continuous reform but maintenance of the CAP's underlying characteristics—rather than a radical overhaul. Although agricultural policy is undergoing considerable change, the CAP will likely endure forever as an emblem of European integration and an instrument of support for a privileged socioeconomic sector.

Characteristics and Unintended Consequences

The objectives of the CAP have remained remarkably consistent over time. Originally outlined in the Rome Treaty of 1957, they are essentially unchanged in the Lisbon Treaty of 2007:

- Increase agricultural productivity.
- Ensure a fair standard of living for farmers.
- Stabilize agricultural markets.
- Guarantee regular supplies of food.
- Ensure reasonable prices for consumers.

Similarly, member states remain committed to replacing various "national organizations" of agricultural markets with a "European market organization" that has at its disposal such interventionist measures as "regulation of prices, aids for the production and marketing of the various products, storage and carryover arrangements and common machinery for stabilizing imports or exports."

The guiding principles for the CAP, first elaborated by the European Commission in 1958, are as valid today as they were when the policy came into being:

- *Single market:* Agricultural produce should be able to move freely throughout the EU.
- *Community preference:* Priority should be given to produce originating within the EU over that of other countries.
- *Financial solidarity:* The cost of the policy should be borne by the common EU budget rather than by individual member states.

Based on Commission proposals, the Council of Ministers fleshed out the CAP in the 1960s by replacing national systems of customs duties, import quotas, and minimum prices with harmonized price supports throughout the European Community, unrestricted intra-Community trade in agricultural products, and common protection vis-à-vis nonmember countries. National governments agreed to establish the European Agricultural Guarantee and Guidance Fund (EAGGF) to underwrite the entire operation. The guarantee section (accounting for the bulk of the fund) would cover the costs of market intervention; the guidance section would pay for structural improvements. The Council agreed to finance the EAGGF by national contributions only for the first three years, after which a new arrangement would have to be made. Commission proposals to finance the EAGGF after July 1965 by using the EC's own resources sparked the infamous "empty chair" crisis; it was only in 1970, as part of a wide-ranging budgetary agreement, that the EC finally switched to paying for the CAP through its own resources.

Beginning in the 1960s, national governments negotiated separate regimes, known as Common Market Organizations (CMOs), for key agricultural commodities within the CAP. Each CMO had a guaranteed price for a particular commodity; an intervention system to guarantee the sale of produce regardless of market demand; an entry price that protected the EU market from cheap imports; and an export subsidy that enabled farmers to sell their products on the world market, given that the EU's guaranteed minimum price was generally higher than prevailing world prices. Over time, the number of CMOs grew to twenty-one (as part of the Commission's better-regulation initiative, there is now only a single CMO covering all agricultural products).

Annual farm price negotiations in the Agriculture Council (agriculture ministers) were one of the most distinctive features of the CAP. The process began in January of each year with a set of Commission proposals. The Special Committee for Agriculture, rather than the Committee of Permanent Representatives as in most other EU policy areas, considered the proposals during the next two or three months. The special committee and the agriculture ministers would try to reach agreement on the price package during the Council's monthly meeting in April or May, but negotiations sometimes continued into June or even into the beginning of a new Council presidency in July.

This brief description belies the monumental effort involved in concluding the annual package of farm prices, a staple of the EU until national governments introduced reforms in the early 2000s, in anticipation of Central and Eastern European enlargement, that reduced the annual negotiations to only a few sectors, and robbed them of much of their drama. Indeed, the effort was so great that the rotating Council presidency was organized so that a country in the presidency for the first half of the year (and therefore responsible for managing the agriculture negotiations) assumed the presidency for the second half when its turn next came around. In the latter stages of the price-setting process, negotiations could last several days, taxing the patience and stamina of the negotiators. Price packages sometimes contained fifty or sixty regulations that included not only monetary amounts but also complex changes to already complicated market mechanisms.

The European farmers' lobby—notably the powerful Committee of Professional Agricultural Organizations (COPA)—is active in all stages of CAP policymaking, contacting the Commission, the European Parliament, agriculture ministers, and national officials (especially the senior officials on the Special Committee for Agriculture). National governments are highly susceptible to pressure from farmers. Despite the popular notion that France is the CAP's most tenacious defender, Germany has proved equally obdurate in perpetuating price-driven support and blocking meaningful reform, thanks largely to the Bavarian farm lobby's sway over the Christian Social Union, a small but nationally influential political party.

The CAP's market-regulating mechanisms—target prices, intervention, levies, and export subsidies—ensured a number of positive outcomes: agricultural production increased greatly, farmers enjoyed a better standard of living, agricultural markets were stabilized, and food security was ensured. However, consumers clearly lost out as high prices in shops and supermarkets reflected high target prices for farm products and high duties on imported foodstuffs.

Although the CAP could be judged a success on the basis of its stated objectives, the policy's market-regulating mechanisms caused serious unintended consequences:

- Guaranteed prices bore no relation to demand and encouraged colossal overproduction.
- Surplus produce had to be stored in "intervention" (warehoused) throughout the EU at considerable cost to taxpayers (these were the infamous butter mountains, wine lakes, and the like).
- "Big" farmers (those with large farms) produced more and thereby earned more money, whereas small farmers, who most needed assistance, earned less.
- In order to increase output from their already overworked fields, farmers used excessive amounts of herbicides, pesticides, and artificial fertilizers, exacerbating the EC's acute environmental problems and diminishing biodiversity.
- The maintenance of quotas, levies, and tariffs in agricultural trade angered exporters to the EU and contrasted unfavorably with the EU's efforts to promote global market liberalization in other sectors.
- Export price supports distorted world prices and undercut non-EU producers, hampering global development and triggering trade disputes.

The 1973 enlargement made matters worse by bringing into the EC two small countries (Denmark and Ireland) with large agricultural sectors, and a large country (Britain) with a small agricultural sector but many big farmers.

Britain had traditionally pursued an agricultural policy that was the antithesis of the CAP (it was even called the "cheap food" policy). Not since the beginning of the Industrial Revolution had Britain attempted to be self-sufficient in food production. Britain's population was too large and its amount of arable land too small to feed everyone on the island solely from homegrown stocks. Accordingly, Britain imported food from the empire and, as the empire shrank, from Commonwealth countries and other inexpensive suppliers—hence Commonwealth concerns about Britain's entry into the EC; hence also Britain's instinctive antipathy toward the CAP.

By the time that Britain joined the EC, vested agribusiness and rural interests had a firm grip on the CAP and could successfully resist major reform. Farmers maximized political support for the CAP by lobbying effectively and by portraying themselves as a disadvantaged and beleaguered group providing a vital service to society. Despite paying high prices over the counter, the nonfarming sector had relatively little information about or interest in the CAP and failed to appreciate the program's pernicious economic impact. Thus, politicians could win farmers' votes without alienating other social groups and political constituencies. As a result, not just agriculture ministers but also foreign ministers and national leaders aggressively advocated farmers' interests, often invoking the national veto to do so.

The idiosyncratic nature of the Agriculture Council compounded the problem. Apart from convening more often than most other Council formations and being served by the Special Committee for Agriculture rather than by Coreper, the Agriculture Council consists mostly of ministers with strong ties to the rural community and a strong personal and political awareness of the CAP's importance. Similarly, until the dramatic increase in the pace and scope of European integration in the late 1980s, the Commission's identity was bound up almost entirely in the CAP, the Community's most important and expensive policy. Within the Commission, Directorate-General VI, now DG Agriculture and Rural Development, was the largest and most influential unit, staffed by officials who saw the CAP as an essential building block for the powerful EU to which they aspired. For nearly four decades, the head of DG Agriculture was always French and, needless to say, always a stout defender of the old-fashioned CAP (the Commissioner was never French, but always came from a farming background).

Obscene levels of overproduction in the late 1970s intensified calls for CAP reform. In 1979 the Council introduced a modest change in the system of price guarantees and imposed a "coresponsibility" levy on dairy farmers to help meet the cost of storage and subsidized sales of surplus produce. When the levy failed to curb output, the Commission proposed a production quota. After an intensive series of negotiations at the highest level, which at one point saw the Irish prime minister walk out of a summit meeting, EC leaders agreed in March 1984 on a quota system for milk production.[3]

The milk quota was an inadequate response to the problem of overproduction and did little to reduce spending on the CAP (which by 1984 accounted for over 70 percent of the EU budget). The possibility of bankruptcy and impending Mediterranean enlargement, together with Britain's insistence on budgetary reform, intensified pressure for reform. Indeed, as part of the budgetary package agreed to at the June 1984 Fontainebleau summit, the European Council resolved to curtail the growth of CAP expenditure. At the same time, however, it agreed to increase the Community's own resources, thereby eliminating the most compelling reason for far-reaching CAP reform: the threat of running out of money.

Budgetary pressure again brought the question of CAP reform to the top of the EC's agenda in 1987 and 1988. As part of the Delors I package for the first multiannual financial framework, introduced in 1987 in the wake of the Single European Act, the Commission proposed a mix of measures to prevent overproduction, limit expenditure, diversify support for farmers, and promote rural development. Germany's fragile government was unwilling to countenance reform until after crucial local elections (curtailing agricultural spending was unpopular with farmers and could have cost the government valuable votes). Once the elections were out of the way, negotiations on the Delors I package came to a conclusion at an extraordinary summit in Brussels in February 1988.

Like previous reform efforts, the 1988 package proved only moderately successful. Pressure for more far-reaching reform continued to build not only because of the CAP's exorbitant cost but also because the CAP encouraged unfavorable international comment on the recently launched single market program. Although the single market program was popular within the EC itself, it raised fears abroad about the possible emergence of a "fortress Europe." Undoubtedly, the CAP's abominable international image fueled concern in nonmember countries about the single market's consequences. If the protectionist and trade-distorting CAP was an example of a common policy in action, the single market would hardly help the rest of the world. Thus, the EC's vigorous efforts to combat pessimistic prognoses about the single market's external impact intensified internal pressure for agricultural reform. At the same time, efforts to complete the Uruguay Round negotiations of the General Agreement on Tariffs and Trade, which involved agricultural issues, threw another harsh light on the CAP.

CAP Reform

There have been three rounds of major CAP reform—in 1992, 1999 (when EU leaders reached agreement on Agenda 2000 reforms), and 2003—plus a "health check" (minor reform) in 2008. The CAP is poised for another major reform before the end of the current multiannual financial framework in 2013, or possibly later if the framework is extended by a few years (see Chapter 11).

The MacSharry Reform (1992). Agriculture commissioner Ray MacSharry was the architect and prime political mover of the CAP's first major reform, which set the direction of subsequent reforms. As Ireland's first-ever agriculture commissioner, MacSharry seemed more suited to keeping things as they were, but the extent of the CAP's propensity for overproduction genuinely appalled him. MacSharry was just as concerned about the inequitable distribution of price supports between big and small farmers, not least because his political roots lay in the poor western part of Ireland. Driven by MacSharry's deep commitment to reform, in July 1991 the Commission for the first time adopted a proposal to break the automatic link between price support and volume of food production.

To balance the deepest price cuts ever contemplated by the Community, the Commission proposed full compensation for small farmers and scaled compensation for big farmers, subject to big farmers' removal of large tracts of land from production (so-called set-asides). The idea of replacing the system of guaranteed prices with a program of direct income support for farmers was radical and politically difficult. Farmers like to pretend that they operate in a free market system; direct payments reveal the truth. Nor would it be easy to target assistance to those farmers who needed it most. Accordingly, although the MacSharry Plan included a shift toward direct income support, it did not propose to abolish guaranteed prices.

Predictably, agriculture ministers and farmers' organizations almost uniformly opposed the MacSharry Plan. Initially MacSharry appeared to lack even the Commission's support. Fearful of alienating French political opinion, Commission president Jacques Delors never backed MacSharry completely. Only after intensive discussion did the Commission eventually approve the plan and forward it to the Council, where discussion of it proved more contentious. British, Dutch, and Danish ministers complained that the plan discriminated against large producers; Spanish, Greek, Portuguese, and Irish ministers complained that it did not compensate small farmers adequately; and the French government opposed reform of any kind. Unusually, the German government, hoping to conclude the GATT negotiations as soon as possible and apprehensive about the impact of German unification on farm policy, supported the MacSharry Plan (there were no elections in Germany at the time).

The agreement finally reached by the Agriculture Council in May 1992, after a classic fifty-hour meeting, was a triumph for MacSharry and for the Portuguese presidency, which got the package through by qualified majority vote.[4] Although smaller than the cuts in the original proposal, the price reductions approved by the Council were nonetheless substantial. As a concession to the French and British governments, the compensation offered to big farmers was substantially higher than MacSharry's original offer.

Paradoxically, the generous compensation package agreed to by the Agriculture Council made the reformed CAP more expensive than the unreformed

CAP. But by cutting guaranteed prices and taking land out of production, the reform helped reduce the EU's ruinous agricultural surpluses. At the same time, farmers did not experience the drops in income predicted by their leaders; on the contrary, farm incomes across the board rose steadily in the following years.

Enlargement and Agenda 2000. In the late 1990s the EU began to confront the challenge of imminent enlargement to the east. In agriculture as in other policy areas, Central and Eastern European enlargement was qualitatively different from previous enlargements: the accession of all ten countries in the region would result in a doubling of the farm labor force and a 50 percent increase in agricultural land in the EU. Moreover, agricultural prices in Central and Eastern Europe were much lower than in Western Europe. Thus, extending the CAP to the new member states would necessitate either a big increase in the EU's budget, major cuts in price supports throughout the enlarged EU, or lower subsidies for the new member states than those paid to farmers in the existing member states. Raising the EU budget and cutting the level of subsidies in the existing member states were political impossibilities. The only option left was to subsidize Central and Eastern European farmers at a lower level than their Western European counterparts. This difference would be justified on the grounds that a huge infusion of money into economies lacking the capacity to absorb it would be socially and economically catastrophic.

The impetus of enlargement, together with growing environmental and consumer concerns about the CAP, underlay the proposals for reform in Agenda 2000, the Commission's strategy "for strengthening and widening the Union in the early years of the 21st century."[5] Released in July 1997, Agenda 2000 included revised policy objectives for the CAP that revealed the influence on agricultural policy of new social movements and economic trends and showed how far the EU had changed in the four decades since the launch of the EC in 1958. The revised goals for the CAP included:

- Improving the EU's global competitiveness through lower prices.
- Guaranteeing the safety and quality of food to consumers.
- Ensuring stable incomes and a fair standard of living for the agricultural community.
- Making agricultural production methods environmentally friendly and respectful of animal welfare.
- Integrating environmental goals into CAP instruments.
- Seeking and creating alternative income and employment opportunities for farmers and their families.

In essence, Agenda 2000 proposed that the EU continue the MacSharry reforms by shifting agricultural subsidies from price supports to direct payments. The Commission suggested large cuts in guaranteed prices for a range of agricultural products; farmers would be compensated with direct payments of one kind or another. Indeed, the Commission estimated that the cost of the compensatory payments would exceed the savings from reduced price supports by €6 billion annually. However, expected increases in EU revenue (linked to projected annual economic growth) meant that CAP spending would remain within existing guidelines and continue to shrink as a percentage of overall EU spending.

Agenda 2000 paid particular attention to the environment and the increasing use of the countryside for recreation. Accordingly, the package proposed making rural development the second pillar of the CAP, with price and market policy (the CMOs) being the first. Improving CAP management was another major thrust of the proposed reform, which emphasized the desirability of giving national and regional governments more responsibility for implementation of EU agricultural policy. However, the Commission sought to balance the vogue for decentralization and subsidiarity against the risk of renationalizing the CAP.

Farmers' reactions to the Commission's calls for cuts in guaranteed prices were predictably negative. Most national governments also reacted negatively, but not necessarily for the same reasons. For countries critical of the CAP, such as Britain, the proposals did not go far enough to reduce price supports; for others, such as France, they went too far. As on so many occasions in the past, Germany's reaction was moderated by Bavarian farmers' unequivocal rejection of Agenda 2000. With federal elections looming, the German government was not willing to risk alienating the farmer-friendly Bavarian Conservatives' vote by wholeheartedly endorsing Agenda 2000.

The Commission followed up the broad outlines of Agenda 2000 with precise legislative proposals in March 1998. Sensitive to the general perception that many farmers were bilking the system, the Commission also proposed a ceiling on the amount of direct aid that a farm could receive under various support schemes. As was the case with all proposals for agricultural legislation, the Commission's reform proposals were chewed over by the Agriculture Council and its special committee. Early in the process, agriculture ministers signaled their concerns about the extent of the proposed cuts and complained that the various compensatory schemes were inadequate. However, given the overall political importance of Agenda 2000, the General Affairs Council (foreign affairs ministers) staked a claim to oversee the legislative program for CAP reform. Despite deep differences among governments on specific parts of the proposals, foreign ministers were more likely than their agricultural counterparts to take a broader view of things. Moreover, the change of government in Germany in October 1998 augured well for the fate of Agenda 2000. With the farmer-friendly Bavarian Conservatives out of the coalition government and the environmentally conscious Greens in, Germany was more inclined toward CAP reform.

The political salience of both CAP reform and a new financial framework for the period 2000–2006—the other key component of Agenda 2000—meant that a final decision would have to be taken by the European Council. Meeting in March 1999, EU leaders reached agreement on the entire package. On agriculture, French president Jacques Chirac, a tenacious defender of the unreconstructed CAP, led the charge against large-scale price cuts. Chirac prevailed over Gerhard Schröder, the inexperienced German chancellor, who may have been more accommodating because Germany was in the Council presidency. Unwilling to stand up to the farmers' lobby, the other EU leaders went along with Chirac and Schröder. As a result, despite some cuts in guaranteed prices and in direct payments to big farmers, the cost of the CAP would remain largely unchanged.

Overall, the Agenda 2000 CAP reform was extremely modest, involving as it did neither a radical shift from a price support system nor a major reduction of spending on agriculture. At least the elevation of rural development to a separate pillar of the CAP signaled a new emphasis on environmental standards in European agriculture. Yet the overall package did not adequately address the affordability of the CAP in the post-enlargement period. It seemed as if enlargement, the ostensible reason for further CAP reform, hardly intruded on the Agenda 2000 agreement.

Instead, EU leaders dealt specifically with the question of the CAP and enlargement some years later as the accession negotiations drew to a close. They agreed at their summit in October 2002 to phase in direct payments for the new member states, starting at 25 percent of the level of support available for Western European farmers and ending at 40 percent in 2007, when a new financial framework would begin. Far from accepting a fait accompli, the candidate countries pressed for larger allocations in the run-up to the next meeting of the European Council, in December 2002, when a final decision on enlargement was due to be made. As anticipated, agriculture therefore became the most contentious and longest-lasting issue in the accession negotiations. The summit ended successfully when the Danish presidency managed to eke out some more money for farmers in the new member states, thus paving the way for enlargement to take place in May 2004. But the entire affair embittered the acceding countries, which resented the second-class citizenship inherent in the CAP agreement.

The Fischler Reform (2003). Agenda 2000 mandated a review of the EU budget in 2003, halfway through the 2000–2006 financial framework. The net contributors to the EU budget, led by a now more experienced Schröder, anticipated the midterm review with a call for additional CAP reform. So did Franz Fischler, the agriculture commissioner, who sought to revisit the Agenda 2000 debate and push agricultural policy further in the direction of the MacSharry reform. Defending the status quo, France led a group of countries, including Greece, Ireland, Portugal, and Spain, that benefited greatly from the existing

CAP. Britain, traditionally in the forefront of the reform campaign, was in a difficult position as both sides took aim at its budget rebate, negotiated by Prime Minister Margaret Thatcher in 1984 and considered sacrosanct by subsequent British governments, regardless of their political stripe.

The Commission's proposals for the midterm review sought to strike a balance between the contending French and German positions, between maintaining the status quo and reducing the cost and complexity of the CAP. In keeping with the direction of CAP reform in recent years, the Commission's proposals linked direct payments to environmental, forestation, and animal welfare measures (so-called cross-compliance), thereby advancing the broader social and environmental objectives of EU agricultural policy. Also in keeping with previous reform efforts, France and Germany overcame their differences and reached a common position, in this case in the form of a deal between Chirac and Schröder just before the EU summit in October 2002 to freeze annual expenditure on agriculture in the forthcoming financial perspective (2007–2013) at the 2006 level of approximately €45 billion, with a 1 percent increase for inflation. Much to the consternation of the reform-minded countries, Chirac and Schröder pushed this agreement through at the summit itself. Once again, Schröder chose Franco-German harmony over discord, perhaps fearing that without a guarantee of continued agricultural largesse, France would delay a final agreement on enlargement.[6]

The European Council's agreement on agricultural expenditure for the next ten years postponed difficult decisions about the amount of agricultural spending until at least 2013, when a new financial perspective would have to be completed and the existing pie divided among many more member states. In the meantime, there was ample room for changing the modalities, if not the munificence, of the CAP. The Fischler reform, eventually concluded by agriculture ministers in June 2003, included the following elements:

- Further decoupling of subsidies from production with a single payment for EU farmers regardless of how much they produce (the Single Payment Scheme was introduced in 2005–2006; nearly 90 percent of direct support to farmers is now decoupled).
- Renewed emphasis on cross-compliance (respect of environmental, food safety, and animal welfare standards).
- Shift of resources to rural development (pillar two).
- More equitable distribution of payments from big to small farmers.
- Reduction of prices in some hitherto unreconstructed agricultural sectors.

Essentially, the 2003 reform was a continuation of the MacSharry reform of 1992. Its most noteworthy achievement was the extent of decoupling (ending production-linked payments) and the introduction of the Single Payment

Scheme. Given the history of the CAP, it represented a series of small steps rather than a giant leap toward a more rational, efficient, and cost-effective agricultural policy. In keeping with previous reform efforts, it included a patchwork of compromises and concessions to obstinate member states—the usual suspects being France and Spain.

As part of the Fischler reform, the Council agreed in June 2005 to divide the fund for the CAP into two separate funds: the European Agricultural Guarantee Fund (EAGF) and the European Agricultural Fund for Rural Development (EAFRD). The establishment of a free-standing fund for rural development emphasized the growing importance of this activity for the CAP.

The Health Check (2008). As part of the agreement reached in December 2005 on a new multiannual financial framework, the European Council decided to conduct a "health check" of the CAP in 2007–2008. The choice of words suggests that leaders had in mind a number of adjustments rather than a radical overhaul. The Commission got the process going with a set of proposals in November 2007 that aimed at ending the link between payments and production, continuing the shift in resources from the first pillar of the CAP (direct payments) to the second (rural development), phasing out milk quotas, further limiting the size of direct payments, and doing away with set-asides (compulsory fallow land). On this occasion the agriculture commissioner was Mariann Fischer Boel, a Danish farmer who, like MacSharry and Fischler before her, sought to protect the CAP by moving it in new directions while safeguarding the interests of farmers and rural communities. Her goal was to continue in the direction of the MacSharry and Fischler reforms rather than embark on a thorough overhaul of the CAP.

The Commission's proposals set off a lengthy period of consultation, during which national governments, farmers' organizations, and other interest groups, notably the environmental lobby, staked out their positions. The Commission followed up with legislative proposals for policy changes in May 2008. The EP delivered a nonbinding opinion, paving the way for agriculture ministers to reach a political agreement in November 2008, during France's Council presidency. The yearlong process, overshadowed by the Lisbon Treaty's delayed ratification, entailed behind-the-scenes intervention from national leaders as the negotiations drew to a close. The outcome was not as far-reaching as the Commission had hoped, but the changes to the CAP were nonetheless significant:

- Ending most remaining production-based subsidies and shifting assistance for producers to the Single Payment Scheme.
- Phasing out milk quotas by 2015 at the latest.
- Transferring more money from direct support to rural development, but not as much as the Commission had initially called for.

- Putting a special emphasis in pillar two (rural development) on pressing issues such as climate change, renewable energy, water management, and biodiversity.
- Abolishing set-asides.
- Simplifying and improving the implementation of cross-compliance.
- Giving greater flexibility to national governments to offer assistance from funds allocated to pillar one (direct payments) to sectors with special problems.

Reasons for Reform

A number of factors have driven—and continue to drive—CAP reform. Some of them, such as financial pressure, have been prevalent almost since the beginning; others, such as public unease with the CAP and dissatisfaction with the EU, are more recent but no less potent. Climate change is an example of a new issue that is bound to have an effect on agricultural policy and that is helping to shape CAP reform.

Trade and Development. The EU's main trading partners, notably the United States, have long claimed that the CAP is a major impediment to global trade in agricultural products and especially to the conclusion of multilateral trade agreements. Developing countries, many of which have large but poor agricultural sectors, complain about the ruinous domestic effect of EU agricultural export subsidies as well as the difficulty they have in accessing the lucrative EU market. Nonagricultural business associations within the EU have pressured national governments and the Commission to reform the trade-distorting aspects of the CAP, while the development lobby has highlighted the double standard inherent in EU trade and development policy (undermining the agricultural sectors of poor countries while at the same time trying to promote their economic growth).

So far, trade rather than development policy has been a major driver of CAP reform. Indeed, it was pressure to complete the Uruguay Round of the GATT that pushed the EU to adopt the MacSharry reform. The MacSharry reform, in turn, gave a decisive boost to the Uruguay Round, which finally came to an end in December 1993. The agreement on agriculture, which set limits on levels of domestic support, export subsidies, and market access, provided the framework for global trade in agriculture under the auspices of the World Trade Organization's Committee on Agriculture. The agreement also called for new negotiations to continue the process of liberalizing agricultural trade.

The negotiations on agriculture became part of the next major initiative for global trade negotiations, the Doha Round. Even more than in the early 1990s, the EU's trading partners targeted the CAP as an obstacle to the success of this ambitious effort to liberalize global trade and investment. Moreover, because the new round was specifically linked to global development, the EU faced added pressure to change the CAP so that farmers in the developing world would not be disadvantaged by it.

Growing WTO-related pressure gave the EU a strong incentive to continue CAP reform. For its part, the EU hoped that the 2003 Fischler reform would facilitate a breakthrough in the Doha Round in general and the negotiations on agriculture in particular. Switching income support for farmers from production subsidies to direct payments reduced the scope for food surpluses, import levies, and export subsidies, thereby lessening the trade-distorting impact of the CAP. Nevertheless, the EU's trading partners remained skeptical, preferring to see concrete proposals for agricultural trade liberalization in the WTO negotiations themselves.

In August 2003, the United States and the EU, hitherto highly critical of the impact of each other's agricultural policies on the prospects for a Doha Round agreement, came together and presented a "joint approach" to agricultural, dealing with domestic support, export subsidies, and market access. It used to be that a transatlantic initiative in the WTO was analogous to a Franco-German initiative in the EU: when the two leading players took the lead, the others often had little choice but to follow. On this occasion, however, the US-EU initiative was insufficient to ensure progress.

With the WTO having missed the deadline of January 2005 for completion of the Doha Round, in part because of dissatisfaction among developing countries with the Europeans' and Americans' offers of agricultural trade liberalization, the EU came under additional pressure to reform the CAP. The European Council had already agreed on the size of the CAP budget for 2007–2013, the period of the new financial framework, but not on how to allocate agricultural expenditure among a considerably enlarged EU. Yet WTO-related pressure for CAP reform was considerably less intense than it had been in 2003, or than GATT-related pressure for CAP reform had been in the early 1990s. The changeover to direct payments, accelerated under the CAP health check, effectively removed subsidies as a stumbling block to a global trade accord. EU tariffs and quotas on agricultural imports continued to irritate US and other major agricultural producers, but for other reasons the Doha Round remained far from completion. Despite ritualistic exhortations by global leaders in forums such as the G8 and G20 for completion of the round, governments lacked the appetite for making the kinds of concessions across a range of sectors that were necessary to reach an agreement. As a result, trade policy has declined in intensity as a driver of CAP reform.

The Environment. As environmental policy grew in political salience for the EU, inevitably it became a factor propelling CAP reform. Environmentalists were aghast in the 1970s and 1980s at the high levels of land and water pollution and the extensive ecological damage caused by intensive farming, which seemed driven by the CAP's financial incentives for overproduction. The first mention of environmental policy in the treaties, in the SEA, had no direct impact on the CAP but served notice of the increasing importance of environmental issues in the EU. The Maastricht Treaty went considerably further by including respect for the environment as a basic objective of the EU, and the Amsterdam Treaty went further again by declaring that "environmental protection requirements must be integrated into the definition and implementation of the Community policies and activities . . . with a view to promoting sustainable development."

As a result, environmental concerns have had a major impact on CAP reform since 1999, notably in the shift away from production-linked subsidies; the emphasis on cross-compliance (obliging farmers to satisfy basic environmental and ecological standards); and the launch and growth of the rural development pillar, which provides support to farmers specifically for projects tied to protecting the environment and the ecosystem. Within the Commission, Directorate-General Environment has emerged as a counterweight to the traditionally powerful DG Agriculture. Even within DG Agriculture, environmental interests are now well represented. Similarly within the Council, environment ministers hold considerable sway over the formulation of agricultural policy. Sensitive to the power of the environmental lobby, farmers and their political allies have tried to recast themselves as champions of environmental protection, while the EU lists this as a key policy objective for the CAP. Most environmental groups seem unconvinced and remain fiercely critical of the CAP.

Food Safety. Consumers first became concerned about the CAP not because of high prices but because of food safety. Whereas food security (meaning self-sufficiency in food production) was one of the CAP's original objectives, for most of the CAP's history, farmers and agricultural officials paid little or no attention to food safety (meaning the quality and healthfulness of food). By contrast, consumers gradually grew more concerned about food safety in the 1980s and 1990s, largely as a spin-off of the environmental movement. European farmers and agricultural officials happily jumped on the bandwagon when it involved issues such as hormones in beef and genetically modified organisms (GMOs); because such practices were prevalent in the United States rather than in Europe, opposing them was a useful way primarily to oppose beef and cereal imports into the EU. Yet consumer concerns about hormones in beef and GMOs paled in comparison with concerns about bovine spongiform encephalopathy ("mad cow disease"), which first appeared in Britain in the 1980s.

An announcement by the British government in March 1996 of a possible link between bovine spongiform encephalopathy (BSE) and Creutzfeld-Jakob disease (CJD), a human brain condition that affects mostly young people and can be fatal, caused widespread panic throughout the EU. Here was an indigenous food safety crisis; no one could blame the Americans (the United States was BSE-free). Moreover, European officials had been aware for the previous decade of BSE's existence but had done little to control or eradicate the disease. The Commission now leaped into action, banning all exports of beef from Britain. A major political crisis followed, as the EP blamed the Commission for mishandling the whole affair.[7]

The British announcement caused an immediate public health scare and depressed the European beef market overnight. Consumers questioned not only the safety of beef but also the safety of other products of a system (the CAP) that emphasized mass production and paid little attention to product quality. Although farmers in other countries fell over themselves to present their products as safe for human consumption, it was too late to put the genie of consumer criticism back into the bottle. As a result of the BSE and several subsequent food safety scares, such as a pork dioxin crisis in Ireland in December 2008 caused by contaminated animal feed, the CAP has become a target for persistent consumer complaints, forcing farmers and officials to incorporate food safety into CAP reform and portray European agriculture in a health-conscious light.

Animal Welfare. Animal welfare relates to environmentalism and food safety, but is an important issue in its own right. Many advocates of animal welfare decry the consumption of animal products and advocate vegetarianism. Farmers engaged in animal husbandry are well aware of the political force of the animal welfare movement. So are politicians, who have included a reference to animal welfare in the Lisbon Treaty and incorporated animal welfare provisions into the CAP in a number of recent reforms.

Cost. With the shift in agricultural subsidies from production to direct support for farmers, the cost of the reformed CAP is less apparent to consumers today, although high tariff barriers push up the price of agricultural imports. Nevertheless, the cost of the CAP—about €45 billion annually—is exorbitant and represents a considerable outlay for taxpayers in the EU. Defenders of the CAP like to point out that the policy accounts for a smaller portion of the EU budget now than it did in the past, but they are referring to the CAP's relative rather than absolute cost.

Clearly, budgetary pressure has been a major driver of CAP reform. Yet successive reforms have changed the modalities of the CAP without reducing its overall cost. With governments showing little inclination in recent years to increase the size of the EU budget, the CAP imposed a huge opportunity as well as a real cost. Every euro spent on agriculture is one euro less that could be spent on more beneficial measures for the broader European economy. A group of outside experts, asked by the Commission to study the EU budget, called in 2003 for a major cut in agricultural spending in order to finance more important priorities such as education and research.[8] EU leaders did not do so in 2005, when they reached agreement on the current financial framework. Yet the cost of the CAP is likely to be a much bigger issue in the negotiations for the next financial framework, not least because of the lingering impact of the 2008–2009 economic recession.

Inequality and Inefficiency. The CAP is notoriously inefficient and unequal in its allocation of resources. Direct income support goes to landowners, who are not necessarily the farmers who work the land. Big farmers continue to fare better than small farmers, and rich Western European countries fare better than poor Southern or Eastern European countries. The glaring east-west divide in CAP support is unlikely to survive the next round of budget negotiations.

Public Opinion. The permissive consensus that characterized the early decades of European integration gave way long ago to public dissatisfaction and rampant Euroskepticism. Such feelings pertain generally to the EU and its institutions rather than specifically to EU policies. Given its unrelentingly negative image, however, especially for financial, environmental, and food safety reasons, the CAP is becoming a target for popular ire and opposition. Nonfarmers are understandably resentful of the generous subsidies that farmers receive, subsidies that go far beyond the welfare benefits available to workers in the nonagricultural sectors. In that regard the economic recession of 2008–2009 was salutary, with government cutbacks of unemployment and other benefits contrasting sharply with high levels of income support for farmers under the CAP.

Transparency. Growing awareness of the CAP's many failings is driving public opposition to the policy. Such awareness is due to detailed information about who gets what from the CAP, which the Commission and national governments have recently made available, under pressure from journalists, critics of the CAP, and advocates of better governance. The Commission, itself a champion of openness and transparency, could hardly object to throwing light on the CAP. National governments were reluctant to identify the recipients and the amounts of CAP support, knowing that the system was deeply flawed. Nevertheless, the Council agreed in 2005 that governments would have to publish, on the Internet, the identities of CAP fund recipients and the amounts received, in order "to enhance transparency regarding the use of the Funds and improve their sound financial management."[9] Some governments dragged their feet in complying with the new regulation, which came into effect in 2008, and have made the websites containing the information difficult to navigate. As expected, the information has been an eye-opener for Europeans, few of whom have searched for it themselves but many of whom are aware of it through extensive media coverage. Analysis of the data shows that, over the years, large CAP payments have gone to rich investors, wealthy aristocrats, and large conglomerates, and have funded golf courses, theme parks, and the like.

The Future of the CAP

The forces of CAP reform seem inexorable. Under the circumstances, it is hard to imagine that funding for the CAP will not be reduced in the next financial perspective, and that more fundamental reforms are not also in the offing. One of the great unknowns about the future of the CAP concerns the influence of the European Parliament. Historically, the EP has been excluded from CAP decisionmaking. With the abolition in the Lisbon Treaty of the distinction between compulsory and noncompulsory expenditure, however, and the extension of the ordinary legislative procedure to almost every EU policy area, the EP is becoming involved in everyday CAP decisionmaking. The impact of these changes is likely to be mixed. Most members of the EP's agriculture committee are highly sympathetic to the farming community (many of them are farmers), and are unlikely to want to change the status quo. By contrast, the EP as a whole is less interested in agriculture and is less beholden than national parliaments and governments to agricultural interests. On fundamental issues such as the allocation for agriculture in the multiannual financial framework, the EP may well be inclined to support major reform. Nevertheless the CAP is likely to remain an iconic and predominant EU policy area for many years to come.

■ Cohesion Policy

Regional policy aims to achieve economic, social, and territorial cohesion, a fundamental objective of the EU. "Cohesion policy," a term used interchangeably with "regional policy," is unabashedly interventionist: it presumes that market mechanisms are insufficient to reduce economic and social disparities between richer and poorer regions and may even exacerbate them. Only by intervening with a range of policy instruments—and a large infusion of public money—can the EU hope to achieve more equitable levels of wealth, living standards, and opportunities across a vast geographical area.

The Emergence of Cohesion Policy

The development of regional policy is inextricably linked with EU enlargement and with the deepening of European integration since the late 1980s. The preamble of the Rome Treaty mentioned the need to reduce regional disparities, but the treaty itself included few references to regional policy. The European Social Fund and the European Investment Bank, established by the treaty, were not intended primarily to promote what later became known as cohesion, but were nonetheless expected to help the EU's poorer regions. Similarly, the treaty declared that national subsidies (aid to states) were compatible with the common market as long as they promoted "the economic development of areas where the standard of living is abnormally low or where there is serious underemployment."

Apart from those concessions, the prevailing attitude in the late 1950s, encapsulated in the Rome Treaty, was that the common market would of its own accord "promote throughout the Community a harmonious development of economic activities" and thereby lessen disparities among regions. After all, the treaty was a package deal to distribute losses and gains among member states, not to redistribute resources between rich and poor regions. In any case, with the notable exception of the south of Italy (the Mezzogiorno), regional disparities in the EC of six member states were not as striking as in the enlarged Community of nine, ten, and twelve member states, let alone in the EU of nearly thirty member states.

Successive enlargements increased regional disparities with regard to income, employment, education and training, productivity, and infrastructure. The EC's growing regional differences manifested themselves in a north-south divide, with Ireland included in the southern camp. The spatial characteristics of the EC's regional imbalance conformed to the core-periphery concept used by social scientists to analyze inequalities between or among regions. As a result, the EU built its cohesion policy in the late 1980s and early 1990s largely on the assumption of a poor periphery (Scotland, Ireland, Portugal, central and southern Spain, Corsica, the Mezzogiorno, Greece, and—after 1990—eastern Germany) and a rich core (southern England, northeastern France, the Benelux countries, northwestern Germany, and northern Italy).

A protocol attached to Ireland's accession treaty emphasized the need to end regional disparities in the EC, but the European Regional Development Fund was established only in 1975, largely to compensate Britain for its poor return from the CAP. The EC began coordinating national governments' regional aid schemes in the late 1970s, although its own regional aid policy remained rudimentary. The extent of the EC's failure to redress regional imbalances became more apparent after Greece's accession in 1981 and in the run-up to Spain's and Portugal's accession in 1986. All three countries were economically underdeveloped and lagged far behind the existing member states (except Ireland) in per capita GDP.

Economic, political, and moral arguments underpinned the Commission's efforts to promote cohesion at the time of the Mediterranean enlargement. Commission president Jacques Delors had long been aware of a growing rich-poor divide in the EC, which the accession of Spain and Portugal would greatly exacerbate. Delors warned the EP in March 1985 that the enlargement negotiations had "revealed a tension in Europe which is, let's face it, a tension between north and south. It stems not only from financial problems but from a lack of understanding, from a clash of culture, which seems to be promoting certain countries to turn their backs on the solidarity pact that should be one of the cornerstones of the Community."[10]

The contemporaneous emergence of the single market (1992) program greatly boosted the Commission's and the poorer countries' leverage for a well-funded cohesion policy. The gradual worsening of regional disparities since the 1960s suggested that market liberalization would not necessarily narrow the rich-poor divide. Advocates of a stronger regional policy exploited uncertainty about the distributional consequences of the single market program to press their claims for cohesion. Fear that market integration would make rich regions richer and poor regions poorer and that the dynamic of liberalization would intensify existing disparities led to an explicit link between cohesion policy and the single market program.

Delors used an influential report by Italian economist Tommaso Padoa-Schioppa to make a compelling case for a massive increase in spending on regional policy. Published in April 1987, the report assessed the "implications for the economic system of the Community of . . . [the] adoption of the internal market program and the latest enlargement." One of its major conclusions pointed out "the serious risks of aggravated regional imbalances in the course of market liberalization" and, in a memorable phrase, warned that "any easy extrapolation of 'invisible hand' ideas into the real world of regional economics in the process of market opening would be unwarranted in the light of economic history and theory."[11] This was grist to Delors's mill and strengthened the southern countries' determination to win a sizable redistribution of resources in conjunction with the single market program.

Apart from vague notions of solidarity and precise projections of the likely economic impact of greater regional disequilibrium, the politics of the single market program strengthened the case for cohesion. The single market might never be implemented if poorer countries, resentful of their situation, blocked legislation in the Council of Ministers necessary to complete the 1992 program. Accordingly, in the run-up to the SEA, the Commission advocated a substantial redistribution of resources to the EC's less prosperous regions. Although one of the attractions of the single market program for a financially strapped EC was its relative lack of cost, the Commission's emphasis on cohesion raised the prospect of a hefty increase in the budget. National governments deferred until later a decision about the amount of money involved, but committed themselves in the SEA to reducing "disparities between the various regions and the backwardness of the least favored nations," and to reforming the so-called structural funds—notably the European Regional Development Fund and the European Social Fund—within a year of the act's implementation.

The Structural Funds. Reform of the structural funds in 1988–1989 and the introduction of the European Cohesion Fund in 1992 were key events in the development of cohesion policy. Both were linked to the new system of multiannual financial programming, begun in 1988 with the Delors I package. As a staunch economic liberal, British prime minister Margaret Thatcher opposed regional policy and rejected the idea of guiding the "invisible hand." In her view, market liberalization would hasten rather than hinder economic development in the poorer member states. Despite Thatcher's misgivings, the rich countries' endorsement of the new financial framework demonstrated their acceptance of redistributional solidarity as part of the single market program. A delighted Delors called the decision to double the structural funds by 1993 "a second Marshall Plan" for Europe.[12]

Apart from increasing the size of the structural funds, the Council reformed cohesion policy later in 1988 in order to improve the funds' effectiveness. In particular, the Council sought to weld regional development policy and aspects of social policy into a powerful means of narrowing the north-south divide.

The 1988 reform radically recast cohesion policy by introducing a number of new principles and procedures and strengthening existing ones:

- *Additionality:* Structural funds must add to, not substitute for, national public expenditure.
- *Partnership:* The partnership principle was the key to involving regions, not just national governments, in formulating and implementing structural policy. Because EU projects would complement national measures, there would have to be close consultation and cooperation among the Commission, national governments, and regional or local bodies at all stages of a structural program. Eligible national plans for regional assistance would be incorporated into Community Support Frameworks, which were contractual agreements between the Commission and national and regional authorities. The Community Support Frameworks set out the program's priorities, type of aid, methods of financing, and so on.
- *Programming:* The reform of structural funds involved a major switch from project-related assistance to program assistance and decentralized management, putting the emphasis on planning and continuity rather than on ad hoc activities. Under the old system the Commission dealt with thousands of separate projects; under the new system the Commission would oversee a much smaller number of Community Support Frameworks.
- *Concentration:* Instead of spreading the EC's financial resources widely and ineffectively, structural funds would be concentrated on a few major objectives. Functional and geographic concentration would restrict assistance to five priorities or objectives, the most important of which (Objective 1) was assistance to "regions whose development is

lagging behind," that is, regions with a per capita GDP of less than 75 percent of the EC average (all of Greece, Ireland, and Portugal; large parts of Spain; and southern Italy, Corsica, and the French overseas departments). Almost 80 percent of the Regional Development Fund (by far the largest structural fund) was allocated to Objective 1 projects. Other objectives sought to promote economic conversion and modernization in declining industrial areas, integrate young people into the workforce, assist "regions dependent on fishing," and support certain "rural areas."

The 1988 reform and the ensuing centrality of cohesion policy in the EU had political as well as financial implications. The structural funds now accounted for about 35 percent of a substantially larger EU budget, a close second to agricultural policy in terms of EU expenditure. Politically, the rise of cohesion policy raised the profile and influence of the Commission, and within it of the commissioner and directorate-general for regional policy. Moreover, the principles of concentration and partnership allowed the Commission to work closely with regional authorities as well as national governments, thereby extending its reach throughout the EU. The Commission used these contacts "to act as a lever for regions that are not yet traditionally recognized" and to promote the emergence of new "Euroregions" straddling national frontiers.[13] Most regions opened offices in Brussels and became active in the Assembly of European Regions, a Brussels-based interest group. Thus the formulation and implementation of cohesion policy strengthened regionalism in Europe and contributed to the emergence of multilevel governance both in the day-to-day operations of the EU and as a way of conceptualizing European integration.[14] It also contributed to the inclusion in the Maastricht Treaty of a provision calling for the establishment of the Committee of the Regions, an EU advisory body that came into existence in 1994.

Moves toward monetary union raised concerns among the poorer countries similar to those prevalent at the outset of the single market program. The 1989 Delors Report, which set the stage for monetary union, pointed out that because monetary union would deprive countries of their ability to devalue, it could worsen the balance-of-payments difficulties of poorer countries. Indeed, the need for countries to harmonize their budgetary policies in a monetary union, coupled with a loss of exchange rate flexibility, portended serious problems for the less developed member states.[15]

During the negotiations leading to the Maastricht Treaty, Ireland, Spain, and Portugal attached the highest priority to strengthening cohesion policy. Using arguments honed during the Delors I debate, they claimed that failure to meet their demands would impair prospects for monetary union and undermine the EU. From their point of view, the outcome of the negotiations was highly satisfactory. The Maastricht Treaty provided a framework for extending and deepening EU policies and actions to promote cohesion in parallel with the achievement of monetary union. It also identified cohesion as one of the EU's main goals and listed rural development as an objective of structural policy. Of more immediate importance, the treaty stipulated that the Council could set up a cohesion fund by the end of December 1993. The purpose of the fund was to help poorer countries reconcile the apparent contradiction in the treaty between the budgetary rigor necessary to achieve economic convergence (a prerequisite for monetary union) and the budgetary flexibility necessary to promote cohesion (a key EU objective).

In February 1992 the Commission sent the Council a proposal (Delors II) for a new financial framework for the years 1993–1999. It included a large increase in the EU budget, including a higher allocation for the structural funds. An EU-wide economic recession, together with Germany's effort to meet the costs of unification, made it difficult to reach an agreement on the Delors II package. Ironically, the Maastricht ratification crisis—another gloomy development—may have helped. Battered by a year of economic and political blows, national leaders wanted to demonstrate their ability to act decisively in the EU's interest. The Delors II package was a good way to show that redistributional solidarity had survived the year's setbacks. The new financial framework, which the European Council concluded in December 1992, more than doubled EU spending on cohesion in Ireland, Greece, Portugal, and Spain.

The Impact of Central and Eastern European Enlargement. The 1995 enlargement had little effect on cohesion policy, apart from leading to the creation of a new objective "for the development of regions with very low population densities." This was a sop to Finland and Sweden, net contributors to the EU budget that would otherwise not get much from the structural funds. Austria, another net contributor, would benefit from some of the existing objectives, at least enough to give the appearance of a fair return for its money.

In its impact on cohesion policy, however, the 1995 enlargement paled in comparison with what was on the horizon. The countries of Central and Eastern Europe were underdeveloped compared to the EU's Mediterranean countries, let alone the EU's more affluent members. Their accession would dramatically change the face of the EU. All of the Central and Eastern European states would qualify for Objective 1 funding. Meeting the organizational challenges and the high cost of Central and Eastern European enlargement would test the EU to the limit (see Box 12.1).

The initial response came in the Commission's proposals for Agenda 2000, including a financial framework covering the period 2000–2006. The Commission recommended keeping funding for cohesion policy at 0.46 percent of the EU's GDP, amounting to €275 billion over the seven-year period. Of that amount, €45 billion would be earmarked for the new member states,

---

Box 12.1   The New Central and Eastern European Member States (2004)

- Had an average per capita GDP less than half the average in the EU15.
- Only 56 percent of those of working age were employed, compared to 64 percent in the EU15.
- As much as 92 percent of their populations lived in regions with a per capita GDP below 75 percent of the average per capita GDP in the EU25, making those regions eligible for the highest possible level of support from the structural and cohesion funds.
- Accounted for just under 5 percent of the EU's GDP but almost 20 percent of the EU's population, thereby reducing the average per capita GDP in the EU25 by about 12 percent from what it had been in the EU15.
- Had a poor administrative capacity, making it difficult to manage allocated funds in the run-up to accession and in the early years of membership.

Source: European Commission, *A New Partnership for Cohesion: Third Report on Economic and Social Cohesion* (Luxembourg: Office for Official Publications of the European Union, 2004).

---

which were likely to join toward the end of the financial perspective, plus €22 billion in pre-accession aid. The Commission proposed as well reducing the structural fund objectives from six to three and making some badly needed administrative and managerial improvements.

Although the Commission's budgetary proposals were modest by the standards of other estimates of the likely cost of enlargement, Agenda 2000 generated controversy in existing and prospective member states. Net contributors to the EU budget wanted to pay less, recipients of large-scale transfers from the structural and cohesion funds wanted to maintain or increase their share, and prospective member states wanted more than the Commission offered. The inevitable row over cohesion funding began in earnest in March 1998 when the Commission followed up with precise legislative proposals for the new financial framework. Almost every country—not only the poorer ones—pleaded for special treatment. Despite hard bargaining in the ensuing negotiations, the final agreement stuck closely to the Commission's proposal.

At the same time, Agenda 2000 included some important procedural reforms. Given the stronger institutional capacity of many formerly disadvantaged regions and the Commission's administrative overreach, the reforms gave more responsibility for the management of cohesion policy to the national governments and regional authorities concerned, and reduced the Commission's responsibility for implementing, monitoring, and evaluating programs. Instead, the Commission assumed greater financial control. To encourage better management, the Commission introduced a financial incentive in the form of a performance reserve for allocation in 2004 to countries that achieved their program targets set at the beginning of the financial perspective in 2000.

The Commission's next set of proposals for cohesion policy came in July 2004, shortly after enlargement and in the run-up to the negotiations for a new financial framework for the period 2007–2013.[16] The fact that the EU now included eight Central and Eastern European states, with two more (Bulgaria and Romania) expected to join in the near future, overshadowed the budget negotiations. So did the fact that the net contributors, notably Germany and the Netherlands, strongly opposed increasing the size of the EU budget and resented the idea of generous financial transfers going to countries (like Ireland) that were doing well economically or (like Greece) that allegedly squandered regional development assistance. Nor did it help that France wanted to increase spending on the CAP and Britain wanted to protect its cherished budget rebate.

Under the circumstances, the negotiations for the new financial framework were extremely fraught. The agreement reached in December 2005 included an allocation of 35.7 percent of the budget—€347.41 billion—to cohesion policy, the bulk of it for the new member states. Because those countries were so poor, none of the EU15 would qualify any longer for Objective 1 funding, the most generous source of cohesion support. For reasons of fairness and political expediency, EU leaders decided that any of the older member states that would have qualified for Objective 1 funding in the EU15 but did not qualify in the EU25 (because of the so-called statistical effect) would continue to receive Objective 1 support until 2013.

The launch in March 2000 of the Lisbon strategy for economic modernization and reform had an important impact on cohesion policy. The neoliberal language of the Lisbon strategy soon pervaded most policy areas, including cohesion policy. Accordingly, negotiations in 2004 and 2005 on the future of cohesion policy during the next financial framework were laced with references to private enterprise, greater innovation, more competitiveness, and higher productivity, with a view to stimulating growth and employment, cohesion's traditional objectives. A neoliberal approach did not sit well with a policy built upon government intervention. Nevertheless, the imprint of the Lisbon strategy was evident in the legislative package enacted in 2006 to regulate cohesion policy for the period 2007–2013.

Under this legislation, three headings replaced the existing policy objectives:

- *Convergence:* Supporting growth and job creation in the least developed member states (formerly Objective 1 regions) by modernizing infrastructure and strengthening economic foundations, with a particular emphasis on areas such as transport, research and technological development, information society, and entrepreneurship.
- *Competitiveness and employment:* Helping regions in the other member states to innovate and adjust to particular challenges.

- *Territorial cooperation:* Encouraging cross-border cooperation, including cooperation across borders between member states and non-member states.

The Future of Cohesion Policy

Over the years, the EU has spent hundreds of billions of euros on cohesion policy and plans to continue doing so well into the future. Is the money well spent? How effective is cohesion policy? Economists disagree sharply in their answers to these questions.[17] Disregarding serious problems with the management of structural and other cohesion funds, empirical evidence of the utility of cohesion policy is difficult to distill because of the multifaceted nature of economic growth and decline. It is hard to imagine that large-scale financial flows into poor countries and regions would not have a beneficial effect, although on economic grounds alone such a rationalization of cohesion policy (or global development policy) is surely unconvincing.

Not surprisingly, the Commission claims that the north-south economic divide within the EU is closing, yet with enlargement a new east-west gap has opened. In general, economic differences between rich and poor regions are widening, not narrowing, in the enlarged (and enlarging) EU. Some of the biggest beneficiaries of cohesion funding in the EU15 have performed well economically; others have not. Similarly, some of the biggest beneficiaries of cohesion funding in the new member states are performing well economically, despite the 2008–2009 recession; others are not. What role, exactly, does cohesion policy play?

Ireland and Poland are instructive examples. Ireland is generally seen as the classic success story of cohesion policy, despite its spectacular economic fall in 2008–2009. Thanks to annual growth rates well in excess of 5 percent, Ireland's per capita GDP rose from 63.6 percent of the EU average in 1983 to 89.9 percent in 1995, at a time when the country received huge financial transfers from Brussels. Despite no longer being eligible for Objective 1 funding, Ireland continued to grow economically; by 2004, it had the second highest per capita GDP in the EU. Yet Ireland's economic takeoff was not due solely, or even largely, to cohesion funding. Massive foreign direct investment, major economic reforms, and a national consensus on moving the country forward and using cohesion funding wisely were essential for Ireland's success. By contrast, Portugal and Spain fared less well, and Greece remained in an economic rut despite receiving generous cohesion funding. As well as attracting relatively little inward investment (less than 1 percent of its GDP, compared to about 21 percent in Ireland) and failing to undertake macroeconomic policy reforms, Greece reputedly squandered much of its cohesion funding through fraud and mismanagement.

Poland's experience bears out the point that the key to economic development in the poorer member states is a combination of sensible macroeconomic policies, large-scale inward investment, sound management of cohesion funding, and closer coordination in the formulation and implementation of regional policy at the European, national, and subnational levels. Despite the downturn that began in 2008, Poland continued to attract a substantial share of global investment, thanks to its EU membership and, no doubt, to infrastructural and other improvements undertaken through cohesion policy. Like Ireland in the 1990s and early 2000s, Poland in the late 2000s owed its success to inflows of foreign investment as well as or even more than cohesion funding—and the adoption of sound public policies. Other Central and Eastern countries have been both less fortunate in their particular circumstances and less sensible in their policy choices.

Net contributors to the EU budget continue to complain that their contributions are too large and their direct return, notably in agricultural and cohesion transfers, too small. The economic recession has increased the frequency and loudness of such complaints. For their part, the main beneficiaries of cohesion funding have used the recession to strengthen their case for large-scale financial transfers, arguing that convergence is more urgent yet more difficult at a time of economic downturn. They (and the Commission) also point out that the net contributors benefit from extra public works contracts and other business in the poorer member states.

A bruising budgetary battle looms for the next financial framework. Although the EU budget is unlikely to grow, cohesion policy will probably maintain its share of approximately 35 percent. Unlike agricultural policy, which faces a severe legitimacy crisis, cohesion policy generally enjoys public support or at least does not face entrenched opposition. Thousands of cofinanced projects scattered throughout the EU, ranging in scale from small business start-ups to large-scale infrastructural development, have generated considerable goodwill toward cohesion policy.

The moral, political, and economic justifications for cohesion remain strong. If anything, they are more compelling in the aftermath of enlargement, as glaring economic gaps have opened up in the EU. Most of the older member states acknowledge that the Central and Eastern European countries have a lot of catching up to do and need generous assistance along the way.

Doubtless the modalities of cohesion policy will continue to change over time. Yet the underlying goal remains the same: to help regions with poor infrastructure, labor skills, and social capital to develop more rapidly than they otherwise would, or at least to prevent them from regressing further than they otherwise might. Despite neoliberal critiques of the effectiveness of cohesion policy, most politicians are wedded to what has become an iconic EU policy area. Like social welfare within member states, cohesion policy rests on cherished principles of fairness and solidarity. Also like social welfare, however, the costs of cohesion policy are high and may prove untenable, pitting pragmatism against principle in the years ahead, especially if the EU ever embraces Turkey, an impoverished European country for which few other Europeans appear to have much sympathy or to show much solidarity.

■ Notes

1. See Isabelle Garzon, *Reforming the Common Agricultural Policy: History of a Paradigm Change* (Basingstoke: Palgrave Macmillan, 2007); and Berkeley Hill and Sophia Davidova, *Understanding the Common Agricultural Policy* (Earthscan, 2010).

2. See Luxembourg European Council, "Presidency Conclusions," Bulletin EC 12-1997, point 1.5.11.

3. See Michel Petit et al., *Agricultural Policy Formation in the European Community: The Birth of Milk Quotas and CAP Reform* (Amsterdam: Elsevier, 1987).

4. Council of Ministers, Press Release 6539/92, May 18–21, 1992, 1579th Council meeting (Agriculture).

5. European Commission, "Agenda 2000: For a Stronger and Wider Europe," COM(97)2000 final, July 16, 1997.

6. Christilla Roederer-Rynning, "Impregnable Citadel or Leaning Tower? Europe's Common Agricultural Policy at Forty," *SAIS Review* 23, no. 1 (Winter–Spring 2003): 133–151.

7. See Martin Westlake, "'Mad Cows and Englishmen': The Institutional Consequences of the BSE Crisis," *Journal of Common Market Studies, European Union: Annual Review of Activities* 35 (1997): 11–36.

8. André Sapir, *Agenda for a Growing Europe: Report of an Independent High-Level Group* (Brussels: European Commission, July 2003).

9. European Commission, "Member State Websites Providing Information on Beneficiaries of CAP Payments," http://ec.europa.eu/agriculture/funding/index_en.htm.

10. Bulletin EC S/4-1985, p. 5.

11. Tommaso Padoa-Schioppa, *Efficiency, Stability, and Equity: A Strategy for the Evolution of the Economic System of the European Community* (Oxford: Oxford University Press, 1987), pp. 3–4, 10.

12. Quoted in *The Economist,* February 27, 1988, p. 41.

13. European Commission, *Reform of the Structural Funds: A Tool to Promote Economic and Social Cohesion* (Luxembourg: Office for Official Publications of the European Communities, 1992), p. 18.

14. See Liesbet Hooghe, ed., *Cohesion Policy and European Integration: Building Multi-Level Governance* (Oxford: Oxford University Press, 1996).

15. Jacques Delors, *Report of the Committee for the Study of Economic and Monetary Union* (Luxembourg: Office for Official Publications of the European Communities, 1989).

16. European Commission, *A New Partnership for Cohesion: Convergence, Competitiveness, Cooperation* (Luxembourg: Office for Official Publications of the European Communities, 2004).

17. For a positive assessment, see Robert Leonardi, *Cohesion Policy in the European Union: The Building of Europe* (Basingstoke: Palgrave Macmillan, 2005).

13 The Internal Market and Monetary Union

The internal market—an area in which goods, capital, services, and people move freely across national frontiers—is one of the European Union's greatest achievements. Although envisioned in the Rome Treaty of 1957, it began to take shape only in the 1990s, following implementation of the single market program. The internal market remains a work in progress. Even with the best political will in the world, it can never be entirely complete. New technologies, business practices, judicial rulings, and policy preferences call for the constant review and occasional revision of internal market legislation. Moreover, there is bound to be political resistance to some liberalizing measures. National governments may appreciate the advantages of market integration but often succumb to political pressure to protect vested interests. Even if a perfect internal market existed, ingrained personal biases and language barriers would inhibit cross-border economic activity to some extent.

Competition policy buttresses the internal market by ensuring that governments, cartels, and large companies do not distort economic activity, disadvantage other actors, and shortchange consumers. EU competition policy developed in tandem with efforts to put the internal market in place. Only by policing the internal market from Brussels can the European Commission hope to ensure a level playing field throughout the EU. National governments see the logic of that argument but cannot resist providing state subsidies and supporting national champions, often in contravention of EU law. Similarly, companies are likely to engage in anticompetitive practices in the absence of a vigilant EU competition authority.

The launch of the euro in 1999 was an achievement even greater than the construction of the internal market. Countries agree to share sovereignty in monetary policymaking and adopt a common currency only in exceptional circumstances. For founding members of the eurozone, those circumstances included a high level of economic integration, the intensifying pressure of globalization, and the geopolitical upheavals in the aftermath of the Cold War. Most academic economists were dubious about the soundness of monetary union, pointing out that the EU is not an optimal currency area. Nevertheless, the euro exists and has survived for well over a decade, notwithstanding the global financial crisis and the Greek debt crisis of 2010.

The fact that a number of member states have not adopted the euro, and perhaps never will, suggests that monetary union is not essential for the success of the single market. Nevertheless, monetary union helps to consolidate market integration, while the single market, in turn, provides an economic rationale for monetary union. The convenience and savings of using a common currency in an internal market are indisputable, as any person traveling or conducting business in the eurozone will attest. The Commission tends to exaggerate the benefits of monetary union, but it would be churlish to dispute its claim that "the euro has proved an anchor of stability and a driving force for the single market process that has benefited the EU economy as a whole, not only the euro area."[1]

▪ The Internal Market

The internal market is so successful that most people take it for granted. Young people cannot remember a time when border controls existed between most member states; older people cannot imagine them existing again. Precisely because they vividly remember border controls, citizens of the new Central and Eastern European member states revel in the personal and economic freedom provided by the single market, despite some residual restrictions on the movement of workers into the EU15. Like their counterparts in the west, EU citizens in the east presume that the single market is permanent and immutable, unlikely ever to disappear.

Yet a single market among sovereign states is an extraordinary accomplishment. It requires a high degree of trust, political will, and administrative capacity on the part of participating countries. To put the EU's achievement in perspective, consider that the United States, which came into existence in the late eighteenth century, completed the process of market integration only in the early twentieth century. Or, to take a contemporary example, consider how far the United States and Canada, neighboring countries with highly developed economies, are from establishing a true single market. Far from achieving closer economic integration, Canada, Mexico, and the United States have only an elementary free trade regime that lacks strong popular and political support.

Europeans were reminded during the 2008–2009 economic recession of how far European integration had come and also how politically fragile it could be. Under pressure from falling demand and rising unemployment, governments reverted to the rhetoric of economic nationalism at the height of the recession. Politicians throughout the EU criticized "Brussels" for sticking rigidly to the single market rulebook, allegedly to the detriment of national economic recovery. The German chancellor sought to protect Opel car factories in Germany at the expense of those in Belgium; the French president wanted French car manufacturers to repatriate plants and jobs from the Czech Republic; the British prime minister spoke of British jobs for British workers.

In the event, national leaders did not pursue blatantly protectionist policies, as they had done in the 1970s during a protracted recession. Perhaps mindful of the ruinous consequences of economic nationalism, politicians restricted themselves largely to making protectionist noises. Nevertheless, their rhetoric was a salutary reminder that a fully functioning single market requires constant vigilance and strong political support.

The second referendum in Ireland on the Lisbon Treaty caused a prominent Euroskeptic to rally in defense of the single market. Michael O'Leary, the founder and director of Ryanair, Europe's largest budget airline, had clashed with the Commission over state subsidies for Charleroi airport outside Brussels, from which Ryanair benefited, and over arrangements for booking flights on the Web, which the Commission insisted that Ryanair make more transparent and consumer-friendly. But Ryanair could not have existed without the Commission's push to liberalize air transportation in the 1990s. The prospect of a second rejection of the Lisbon Treaty, and therefore of serious political damage to the EU, especially at a time of rising economic nationalism, led O'Leary to overcome his antipathy toward the Commission and spearhead the campaign in Ireland in support of the Lisbon Treaty.

Cheap air travel is one of the clearest manifestations for many people of the single market; reduced roaming charges for cell phone calls across national borders are another. Yet people are also reminded daily of how incomplete the single market remains. Wolfgang Münchau, a *Financial Times* columnist, gave a telling example about an experience of his in 2008: "As a resident of Belgium, I tried to make an online purchase of a computer in Germany—where some IT equipment costs about 50 percent less—but my efforts were eventually frustrated. Half the German online retailers do not accept any international means of payment, such as credit cards: the other half does not deliver abroad."[2] Clearly, the single market is still weak with regard to services—especially financial services. Many of the advantages of complete market integration have yet to be realized in Europe.

The Single Market Program, 1992

The Rome Treaty saw the internal market as the apotheosis of economic integration. The customs union, put in place in 1968 to remove tariff barriers among member states, was an essential first step. Yet national governments failed to complete the single market in the following years because of political setbacks, institutional rigidities, and economic recession. If anything, the European market became more fragmented as governments failed to remove non-tariff barriers to trade and even put new ones in place. Eventually, confronted by intense international competition in the early 1980s, EU leaders committed themselves in the Single European Act to completing the single market by the target date of 1992 (see Chapter 4).

The Commission's famous white paper of June 1985 contained the detailed legislative blueprint for implementing the single market program and meeting the 1992 deadline. Some of the directives tabled in the white paper were intended to tidy up previously enacted single market legislation; others came in response to changing technology or new social and environmental priorities. Completion of the single market also required measures to remove quotas and other trade restrictions imposed by member states in order to protect their markets from nonmember imports. Finally, the success of the single market program spurred efforts to liberalize energy and telecommunications, two sectors initially excluded from the program.

The white paper specified almost 300 measures necessary to complete the single market, grouped into three categories of barriers to integration: physical, technical, and fiscal. The following description of the single market program conveys the intricacy and scale of the operation.

Physical Barriers. Physical barriers—customs and immigration posts at border crossings between member states—were the most tangible obstacles to a single market. Border posts impeded the movement of goods (due to delays for assessing duties and inspection) and of people (due to passport controls and residence restrictions). Accordingly, the Commission sought unequivocally "to eliminate in their entirety . . . internal frontier barriers and controls . . . by 1992."[3]

Movement of goods. Ending costly delays at border crossings proved politically uncontroversial. Measures included the eventual abolition of paperwork needed at frontier posts and a new statistical system for tracking trade among member states once border posts disappeared. The Council and Parliament duly adopted all the necessary legislation. The removal of physical barriers had a direct bearing on agriculture, as border checks ensured compliance with a wide array of plant and animal health and food safety requirements. Sixty-three of the white paper's proposals covered disease control and livestock trade generally, as well as trade in food products. Another eighteen covered plant health and similar measures. Of the eighty-one measures in these two categories, only three remained outstanding at the end of 1992.

Movement of people. Barriers to the movement of people proved the biggest challenge of the 1992 program. Passport and visa requirements remained the exclusive preserve of governments, some of which agreed to eliminate all border formalities under the auspices of the so-called Schengen regime, outside the treaty framework. Although signed in 1985 by France, Germany, and the

Benelux countries, the Schengen Agreement came into effect only in the late 1990s. The legally complicated and politically contentious question of free movement of people became bound up with the provisions of the Maastricht Treaty for intergovernmental cooperation on justice and home affairs, which are examined in Chapter 17.

Technical Barriers. The white paper used the term "technical barriers" almost as a catchall: proposals under this heading covered product standards, testing, and certification; movement of capital; public procurement; free movement of labor and the professions; free movement of financial services; transport; new technologies; company law; intellectual property; and company taxation. Not surprisingly, it was by far the largest category of white-paper measures.

Standards, testing, and certification. The use of different product standards, testing, and certification in each country traditionally posed major barriers to intra-European trade. A key treaty provision called on the Council to develop harmonized standards in cases where national standards differed. However, the arduous and politically sensitive process of harmonization led to a huge backlog of cases by the mid-1980s.

To end the backlog and remove a major obstacle to the free movement of goods, the Commission developed the principle of mutual recognition of national regulations and standards. Instead of trying to harmonize a potentially limitless number of product standards throughout the Community, member states would recognize and accept each other's standards as long as those standards satisfied certain health and safety concerns. Mutual recognition rests squarely on the outcome of the famous Cassis de Dijon (1979) case, in which the European Court of Justice overruled a ban imposed by German authorities on the importation of cassis, a French liqueur, because it failed to meet Germany's alcohol-content standards.[4]

Building on the Cassis de Dijon judgment, the white paper proclaimed that "subject to certain important constraints . . . if a product is lawfully manufactured and marketed in one member state, there is no reason why it should not be sold freely throughout the Community." By emphasizing mutual recognition on the basis of treaty obligations and EU case law, the Commission hoped to drop numerous stalled harmonization proposals stuck in the Council decision-making machinery. The Commission also hoped that a combination of self-interest, common sense, goodwill, and peer pressure would reduce recourse to the escape clause allowing governments to impose their own product standards for reasons of health and safety. Yet there could be no question of member states' forsaking legitimate health and safety concerns about specific products manufactured elsewhere in the Community. The white paper sought to maximize mutual recognition, not to abolish harmonization. Where harmonization remained essential, the white paper proposed a two-track strategy: (1) a "new approach" approved by the Council in May 1985, while the white paper was still being drafted; and (2) the old approach of sectoral harmonization.

The new approach consisted of two parts. The first limited legislative harmonization to the establishment of essential health and safety requirements. Governments would transpose those fundamental requirements into national regulations but could not impose further regulatory requirements on the products in question. The white paper included "new approach" directives on a wide range of products such as toys, machinery, and implantable medical devices. Because manufacturers might have problems proving that their products met fundamental requirements without the aid of further technical specification, the second part of the new approach required the Commission to contract with European standards organizations to develop voluntary European standards, so-called European Norms. Manufacturers adhering to those standards would be presumed to be in compliance with the essential requirements, and their products would be assured free circulation throughout the Community.

For the system to work, governments had to agree not only on the essential requirements, but also on the level of proof needed to demonstrate compliance. They did so in December 1989 by adopting a "global approach" that described a set of standard "modules" for testing and certification of products, in most cases offering manufacturers some degree of choice. The options ranged from the least burdensome—in which a manufacturer could simply declare that a product met essential requirements—to the most burdensome, where, for instance, a third party (such as a nationally approved laboratory) would test and evaluate the product.

Another option involved a "quality systems" approach, in which a manufacturer's consistent application of quality-control measures from design through production would be certified by an outside body. The rigor of the requirements specified in the "new approach" directives—the modules that manufacturers are required to follow—varied according to the perceived risk attached to the product. Where required, "notified bodies"—laboratories or other institutions nominated by governments—would perform third-party tests or certification. Governments were required to allow free circulation of goods certified by the notified bodies of other member states.

The European Conformity (CE) mark, applied either by the manufacturer or by the notified body certifying the product, would play a key part. Conformity marks were intended primarily to show customs and regulatory authorities that products complied with essential requirements (they are not quality marks such as those awarded by other national bodies).

Although "new approach" directives covering a wide range of products were largely completed by the end of 1992, application of the system ran into trouble. European standards bodies, bureaucratic and slow, soon lagged behind in developing the necessary norms. Some requirements turned out to be inconsistent and in some cases incompatible. In April 1993, the Council eventually approved a directive on the CE mark retroactively harmonizing existing directives and laying down a single set of rules.

The continuing delay in the development of European Norms was a more serious problem. A 1989 Commission recommendation on ways to remove bottlenecks met with a frosty response from the leadership of the European standards bodies, which agreed to streamline procedures as much as possible.

Recognizing that the new approach could not be applied to all sectors, the Commission kept the old approach of working toward total sectoral harmonization—developing a single, detailed set of technical specifications for a given product that all member states would have to accept—in a number of key areas traditionally subject to intensive member state regulation because of safety risks and public concern. In the white paper, the Commission advocated the old approach for motor vehicles, food, pharmaceuticals, chemicals, construction, and a number of other items.

In the case of pharmaceuticals, where the European market was highly fragmented, the white paper included fifteen directives addressing common testing rules, price transparency, patient information, advertising, and above all, centralized approval of new drugs. The Commission envisioned a European-level agency that would eventually take responsibility for all new drug approvals. Member states finally decided in 1992 to establish the European Medicines Agency, with responsibility for approving all medicines based on biotechnology and all veterinary medicines based on their likelihood of improving the productivity of farm animals.

Movement of capital. Since the 1960s, the Community had achieved considerable liberalization of the initially tight postwar restrictions on capital flows. As member states became richer, many lifted restrictions unilaterally. Three white-paper directives aimed to complete the process by obliging governments to lift all restrictions on capital movements except measures to ensure the liquidity of local banks or temporary restrictions during major disruptions in foreign exchange markets. The Commission saw these measures as a final step on the road to "an effective and stable Community financial system"—a prerequisite for monetary union.

Public procurement. Public procurement, which accounted for as much as 15 percent of Community GDP, remained overwhelmingly the preserve of national suppliers at the beginning of the single market program. The Commission correctly characterized such a distortion of competition as "anachronistic" and contrary to the spirit of European integration. The Commission had a particular concern about the telecommunications sector, fearing that closed public markets and a cozy relationship between public authorities and cosseted but internationally weak "national champions" would hinder the development of a European telecommunications industry capable of competing in the harsher world market.

The white paper proposed seven directives to eliminate distortions caused by local procurement bias, covering open bidding system, penalties for violations, use of common standards, and procedures for award of public contracts. The directives also extended those rules to cover nearly all public procurement above certain thresholds.

The most important of these directives was the so-called utilities, or excluded-sectors, directive, extending EU public procurement rules to enterprises offering public services in the water, energy, transport, and telecommunications sectors. As well as setting out minimum thresholds for application of its rules and procedures to ensure transparency, the directive required public authorities to evaluate bids on objective and nondiscriminatory criteria. Other procurement directives covered supply of services and public works, such as construction and similar projects, and developed remedies for violations. All were adopted by the spring of 1993.

Free movement of labor and the professions. The white paper included proposals for putting into practice the right, enshrined in the Rome Treaty, of citizens to live and work in other member states. In order to facilitate the movement of workers, the Commission took on the task of establishing equivalencies among national professional and vocational regimes and of removing old rules that prevented members of regulated professions, such as doctors and lawyers, from offering their services in other member states. The Council eventually adopted two directives on the recognition of diplomas.

Free movement of financial services. The Commission followed three principles to permit free movement for financial services: harmonization of essential standards; mutual recognition among supervisory authorities; and home-country control, that is, making a financial institution's branches the responsibility of the member state in which the institution's head office is located. The white paper proposed eight directives intended to allow banks incorporated in one member state to operate across national borders without having to seek authorization from national regulatory authorities in each member state. The Commission based its approach to creating a single market for insurance services on the principles used in the banking sector. Nine white-paper directives built on an existing body of EC legislation on insurance. Another directive set out the system for a single authorizing procedure, reciprocity with third countries, common prudential rules, cooperation among supervisory authorities, and other necessary elements in the area of investment services. Not all of these financial services directives had been formally adopted when the single market supposedly became operational at the end of 1992.

Transport. Opening up the EU's highly regulated transport markets required twelve directives covering a number of sectors. While most international air transport markets are regulated by government agreements that usually inhibit competition, the situation in Europe was a particularly egregious example, combining a number of relatively small markets with national champions (frequently government-owned) that were protected through market-sharing arrangements, fixed fares, and occasional massive subsidies—all governed by 200 bilateral agreements covering twenty-two countries. Not surprisingly, the result was high consumer costs. The Commission tackled the morass in three stages, with the Council adopting aviation packages in 1987, 1990, and 1992 that gradually liberalized the market in areas such as competition in fares, sharing of passenger capacity, access to routes for all operators, application of Community competition rules, and the right to carry passengers between two locations inside another member state (cabotage) for European airlines, starting in January 1997. It was this package of measures that made possible the rise of Ryanair and other low-cost carriers.

Before the single market program, road haulage between member states was generally subject to quotas that restricted rights to carry cargo on the return leg of any cross-border journey. As a result, hordes of empty trucks trundled through the EU, adding to congestion and pollution and raising transport costs. In addition, trucks were subject to different and often incompatible work rules or technical specifications. The Commission approached the problem with three initiatives: harmonization to the extent possible of technical specifications and work rules, abolition of all quotas on road haulage between member states, and the gradual introduction of cabotage. As a result, road haulage in the EU was liberalized by June 1993.

New technologies. The 1985 white paper included five directives on "new technologies," focusing on opening markets in areas such as cable and satellite broadcasting. These included the infamous "television without frontiers" directive, which liberalized national television markets by prohibiting discrimination against works from other member states (with the exception of some language quotas). The directive also harmonized advertising standards, including prohibiting tobacco advertising, and obliged broadcasters to encourage European culture by showing a majority of EU-origin programming where practicable (a requirement that sparked fierce opposition from the United States). Related directives covered mobile telephones, a European code of conduct for electronic payment systems, radio frequencies, data protection, and standards for high-definition television.

Company law. The white paper went beyond existing efforts to maximize freedom of movement for enterprises by calling for an EU-wide framework for cross-border corporate activity. The Commission revived a stalled proposal for the European Company Statute, intended to allow enterprises to establish themselves in one place in the EU with one set of rules and a unified management and reporting system, thereby becoming "European companies" subject primarily to EU law. The white paper also included a regulation defining the European Economic Interest Grouping, a legal entity created to accommodate firms or other entities wanting to pool their resources for a common goal, but not wanting to merge. Perhaps the best-known example was Airbus Industrie before it became a limited company in 1999. The Commission enjoyed only limited success with these measures. After years of blockage, it made some of the proposals—notably those dealing with corporate structure and voting rights, cross-border mergers, and harmonization of rules on takeover bids—"nonpriority" for the creation of the single market. In a triumph of hope over experience, however, the Commission declared that the European Company Statute remained a top priority for completion of the single market.

Intellectual property. Also under the general heading of removing technical barriers, the Commission proposed nine directives dealing with intellectual property rights, only four of which were adopted by the end of 1992. The major disappointment in this area was the legislation establishing the Community Trademark Office, which was thoroughly derailed by nonsubstantive but unresolvable disputes over the location of the office itself and the working languages to be used.

Fiscal Barriers. The white paper included an ambitious set of initiatives for harmonizing taxation—a prerequisite not only for eliminating borders (where many taxes were assessed) but also for reducing distortion and segmentation of the single market through disparate tax practices. To take one of the more extreme examples, consumer groups calculated that the cost of a car varied as much as 100 percent across Europe because of value-added, excise, and other tax differentials.

Value-added tax. Of the wide variety of indirect taxes assessed on European goods, value-added tax (VAT) is the most visible and important. The white paper called on countries to harmonize their disparate VAT rates and develop a system for charging VAT on cross-border sales once border posts had been eliminated.

Because VAT revenues were in many cases the mainstay of national social welfare systems, high-VAT countries resisted harmonization downward, even into the broad bands proposed by the Commission. Governments feared having to explain to voters why they were cutting back on prized social security programs for the sake of the single market. Elimination of such local exceptions to VAT as food or children's clothing was equally certain to create political fallout. The alternative, proposed by some countries such as Britain, was to leave VAT unharmonized and let the market force member states align their VAT rates with those of their neighbors, if need be. This was a prospect only an island nation could face with equanimity; others feared that masses of consumers, streaming across borders to get the best tax deal, would bankrupt local retailers and cut into the revenues of high-tax states.

Governments eventually adopted a general framework, stipulating a standard rate of 15 percent or above in each country as of January 1993. The Council also agreed on rules for who should pay VAT and where. The Commission had proposed a straightforward system: VAT was to be paid in the country of sale. However, governments insisted on adopting an ungainly "transitional" system in which VAT on cross-border trade must be paid in the country of destination. To make the system work, sellers and buyers were required to declare their cross-border transactions regularly to tax authorities, including such information as the VAT registration number of the buyer, and pay the VAT applicable in their own country on imports from other member states (firms whose cross-border transactions fell below a threshold were exempt from regular reporting). Private consumers shopping in other member states, by contrast, paid VAT in the country of sale—except on mail-order purchases and on cars, for which VAT was payable at registration.

Excise tax. The second aspect of the indirect taxation dossier concerned excise taxes—internal taxes levied mainly on fuels, liquor, and tobacco. In March 1991, the Council adopted a harmonized structure and rates for excise duties. At the end of 1992, the Council decided to eliminate restrictions on cross-border purchases by consumers of items subject to excise taxes. The logical consequence of removing fiscal frontiers should have been an end to duty-free shops in airports and on ferries. However, politics overcame logic in this case, as many airports and ferry operators gathered a large part of their operating revenues from highly profitable duty-free sales, to which travelers seemed addicted. Accordingly, the Council decided to put off the demise of duty-free shopping until 1999.

Related Measures. In order to eliminate internal borders, the Commission also had to address quotas and other restraints imposed by individual member states under the Rome Treaty. Nearly a thousand such measures, including over a hundred restrictive quotas, were in place by the late 1980s. Using its power to deny quotas, the Commission managed to phase out all but six of them by 1992.

For exporters to the EC of certain products—notably textiles, bananas, and Japanese cars—the promise of 1992 was unfulfilled. For instance, responding to French and Italian consternation at the prospect of losing their harsh import restrictions and the potentially disastrous consequences for their sluggish national champions, the Commission negotiated a voluntary-restraint agreement with Japan that allowed Japanese car imports a steadily increasing market share, reaching a ceiling of 15.2 percent of the European auto market by 1999, when the EU was expected to lift all restrictions. Although production of Japanese-brand cars in Europe, so-called transplants, was not to be counted as part of the overall ceiling, the agreement effectively protected European producers for most of the decade.

One of the bitterest, if more risible, rows erupted over banana quotas. Seeking to protect the market share of high-cost bananas from former colonies in the Caribbean (as well as even more inefficient growers in the Spanish Canary Islands), France, Britain, Spain, and Portugal imposed on an indignant Germany and the Netherlands a restrictive tariff quota limiting imports of so-called dollar bananas from Latin America. Outvoted in the Council, Germany, whose per capita banana consumption had hitherto been the highest in Europe, threatened to bring a case to the Court of Justice, and the Latin Americans initiated a challenge in the General Agreement on Tariffs and Trade to the EU's banana regime. The World Trade Organization subsequently concluded that the European system was in violation of world trade rules. Efforts by the Commission to devise a system that preserved protection for Caribbean producers while technically falling within the WTO ruling elicited both internal and external criticism.

Significance of the Single Market Program. The official unveiling of the single market on January 1, 1993, happened at an inauspicious time. The European economy was in the doldrums, with parts of it, including Britain, in a deep recession. The brisk economic growth of the late 1980s, which had lent credence to extravagant claims for the single market, had suddenly stopped. It seemed unlikely that merely announcing the existence of the single market would get the economy going again.

Sensing public skepticism and even hostility during the Maastricht ratification crisis, the Commission kept the celebrations low-key. Aside from sponsoring a chain of bonfires across Europe and a fireworks display in Brussels, the Commission's main response was to issue reams of information keyed to perceived citizen concerns about such issues as conditions for transporting horses or the fate of unemployed customs agents. Thus, the long-awaited advent of the single market was an anticlimax. As the bonfires smoldered, the griping began. Businessmen complained vociferously about the computerized VAT reporting system, with smaller firms threatening to stop shipping across European borders. Members of the EP were irate when asked for their passports in the Strasbourg airport, and journalists tried to provoke border guards by walking through border posts carrying armloads of bananas. The only conspicuously happy constituency was the horde of Britons reboarding ferries at Calais with cars full of cheap French wine.

Amid all the bluster were some real grounds for criticism: transition periods and derogations stretching toward the end of the century meant that the single market program was far from being entirely in place. The highly visible failure to abolish border checks on people was bound to tarnish the image of the single market, already under fire from environmental and social groups characterizing it as a heartless sellout to business interests. Manufacturers of products covered by "new approach" directives faced uncertainty and disruption over the pace at which European standards could be developed and introduced. Taxation policies and exemptions from competition rules that prevent cross-border price shopping meant that customers would benefit little from lowered manufacturers' costs brought about by harmonization. Consumer banking charges, especially in the foreign exchange area, remained opaque and disparate. The double-barreled VAT system became a fertile source of confusion.

Nevertheless, the single market program brought tangible economic improvement and was an undoubted political success. Notwithstanding a lack of perfection and logic—inevitable in any political process—the 1985 white paper functioned largely as intended. By tying so many elements to a coherent and attractive vision, the Commission managed over the years to push the Council and Parliament into adopting proposals that would not otherwise have engendered much political enthusiasm. There was always a risk that the Commission would become a victim of its own publicity success, that failure to "complete" the single market precisely on time would deal a crushing political blow to the Commission's credibility. In the event, public reaction was favorable and the Council and Parliament continued to adopt the remaining proposals at a respectable pace.

The main achievement of the 1992 initiative may well have been psychological. It created a climate in which individuals as well as firms could begin to identify themselves as European and look for opportunities beyond their own borders. It also created an atmosphere in which national governments could contemplate sharing further sovereignty. Despite the political setback of the Maastricht ratification crisis and lingering citizen anxieties about cultural identity and economic competition, those attitudinal and psychological changes have persisted. The single market program, and the Commission's drive in pushing it through, restored the image of the EU as a vital and modern entity and paved the way for the successful launch of the single currency.

Beyond 1992

The single market program was never an end in itself. Market integration was a continuing process that would require the enforcement of existing rules and the occasional enactment of new ones. Threats would come from a variety of sources, such as poor implementation of directives, the slow pace of standards development, and lack of mutual recognition. New regulations, such as environmental measures, that could hinder the free circulation of goods were an additional concern.

The regional and global context of the single market changed dramatically in the years after 1992. Enlargement in 1995 extended the single market to three countries—Austria, Finland, and Sweden—that had little difficulty adopting the EU's rules and regulations. The next enlargement was a different matter, however. The countries of Central and Eastern Europe lagged far behind the EU15 in economic development as well as administrative and legal capacity. For them, the long road to EU accession included putting in place the vast amount of legislation and regulation necessary to participate in the single market. The advantages for these countries of becoming part of a large, vibrant, integrated market were great; so too were the costs of compliance.

The single market program had been a response to incipient "globalization," a term not widely used until the mid-1990s. Its purpose was not only to promote economic growth and generate new jobs but also to strengthen the EU's ability to withstand intense global competition and avail of greater global opportunities. Concern about the EU's performance led the European Council in March 2000 to proclaim the Lisbon strategy for economic reform, of which the single market was a cornerstone. Far from detracting from the single market, the launch of the Lisbon strategy refocused attention on the need to intensify market integration in the EU.

The commissioners for the internal market during the period of EU enlargement and accelerating globalization—Frits Bolkestein (1999–2004) and Charlie McCreevy (2004–2009)—were staunch neoliberals who aggressively espoused greater integration and liberalization. Both believed that a single market was the essence of European integration and that the 1992 program represented only a beginning. During their terms in office, the Commission undertook various initiatives to complete and perfect the single market, sometimes in the face of internal resistance and frequently with only lukewarm support—or outright opposition—from powerful national governments.

The Commission's efforts to bolster the single market focused on the following:

- Enactment of unfinished proposals still on the table at the end of 1992 and of new proposals necessitated by social, economic, and technological changes.
- Complete liberalization of the energy and telecommunications sectors, which were largely excluded from the single market program.
- Completion of the single market for general services, which account for the bulk of economic activity in the EU.
- Completion of the single market for financial services, without which the economy could not reach its full potential.
- Refining the new approach to technical harmonization and standards.
- Transposition of directives into national law and prevention of new trade barriers.

Unfinished Business. The EU pressed ahead with completion of the single market program well into the 1990s. Examples of the most important legislative developments in the post-1992 period involving preexisting and new proposals include company law, intellectual property rights, and value-added tax.

Company law. In February 1996 the Commission proposed a new directive on public takeover bids in the EU, replacing a moribund proposal long before the Council. Thus began an epic saga of EU legislative decisionmaking characterized by bitter disputes within the Council and between the Council and the Parliament over various aspects of the proposal. At issue was the Commission's effort to facilitate takeovers by removing existing barriers, thereby encouraging corporate restructuring and promoting economic growth. Not all takeovers improve efficiency and add value, however. Moreover, the rights of minority shareholders and employees need to be protected. The directive eventually adopted in 2004, the culmination of nearly twenty years of interinstitutional wrangling, included provisions for a company to inform its employees about all the companies involved in a takeover bid and for the employees or their representatives to draft an opinion on it. The outcome was a disappointment for the Commission, as the directive's main provisions, intended to restrict the ability of companies to defend themselves against bidders, were not mandatory. Indeed, many governments availed of the options and exemptions provided for in the directive, thereby maintaining—or even strengthening—a company's defenses against a hostile bidder. A frustrated Commissioner McCreevy complained in 2007 that "too many Member States are reluctant to lift existing barriers, and some are even giving companies yet more power to thwart bids. The protectionist attitude of a few seems to have had a knock-on effect on others. If this trend continues, then there is a real risk that companies launching a takeover bid will face more barriers, not fewer. That goes completely against the whole idea of the Directive."[5]

The proposal for the European Company Statute was another long-standing issue that remained doggedly beyond reach of agreement. The Commission had inserted the proposal into the 1985 white paper in the hope that the single market euphoria would carry it through. In the event, it foundered yet again because of fundamental disagreements among governments over the issues of worker rights and provision for a European works council comprising union representatives of multinational firms operating under the statute. The proposal sprang back to life in the late 1990s. Pushed aggressively by Bolkestein in a more favorable political climate (the Labour Party had come to power in Britain), the proposal was finally enacted in 2001. The European Company Statute finally became available for use in October 2004, over thirty years after the Commission had first proposed it. Yet the final agreement represented a compromise that, from the Commission's perspective, was far from satisfactory: establishing a European company would require complicated negotiations on the involvement of employees in the company's management. Should such negotiations end without agreement, a set of standard principles would apply, depending on the nature of worker participation in the company concerned before the European company was set up. As a result, the European Company Statute has not been very popular or successful.

Intellectual property rights. In 1998 the Council adopted a directive on the legal protection of biotechnological inventions, after the Parliament had rejected a previous proposal because of ethical concerns related to animal welfare. Legislation establishing the Community Trademark Office (CTMO) was finally unblocked following a political package deal in October 1993 on the location of EU institutions and agencies. The CTMO opened in Alicante, Spain, in January 1996, allowing companies to file for a single Community trademark for products and services marketed in the EU.

Value-added tax. Whereas other single market program leftovers were eventually agreed upon, value-added tax remained impervious to agreement, with some national governments refusing to go beyond the supposedly interim 1993 accord. A VAT system based on payment in the country of origin remains elusive.

Energy and Telecommunications. The Commission turned its attention in the 1990s to liberalizing energy and telecommunications, two sectors excluded from the 1992 program except with respect to procurement and, in the case of telecommunications, measures relating to new technologies. The energy sector, because of its relationship with environmental policy, is examined in Chapter 15. Like the energy sector, the telecommunications sector in Europe was traditionally the preserve of national monopolies and resulted in such anomalies as telephone calls between countries often costing twice as much as calls of equivalent distance within a country. Unlike in the energy sector, however, the impetus to liberalize telecommunications received an additional boost from rapid technological changes with huge commercial implications, such as the development of the Internet. In October 1994 the Commission recommended full liberalization for voice-telephone services by January 1998 (countries with less developed networks had until 2003 to adjust). The Council adopted the Commission's proposed timetable in June 1994 but could not agree on early liberalization of "alternative networks," such as those owned by railways and utilities.

The Commission then tackled key issues such as interconnection and interoperability; licensing of telecommunications infrastructures, networks, and services; and the provision of universal service and third-country reciprocity. It recommended an EU framework within which national regulators would operate.

Building on widespread support among stakeholders, the Commission pushed through much of the legislation under the Rome Treaty's competition policy provisions, including directives to liberalize the mobile telephone sector (the fastest-growing in the EU) by January 1996, lift restrictions on the use of alternative infrastructures for telecommunications services, and implement full competition in the EU telecommunications market by January 1998.

The single telecommunications market began as planned in 1998, although Greece, Ireland, and Portugal received temporary exceptions. Thus, in principle, any telephone company could offer callers in most countries a local or long-distance service. Like the success of the single market program, the success of the single telecommunications market would depend on Commission vigilance and national compliance. It would depend as well on the ability of new national regulatory authorities to enforce directives in a sector still overshadowed by powerful former monopolies.

General Services. The single market program had mostly facilitated the free movement of goods throughout the EU; general services, which account for about 70 percent of economic activity, were largely unaffected by it. Although the Rome Treaty includes the rights of movement and establishment, meaning that service providers in one member state should be able freely to set up shop or travel across frontiers to work in another member state, the reality after decades of European integration was that a plethora of national rules and administrative hurdles remained firmly in place. The EU had tackled services before, during, and after the 1992 program, but on a piecemeal and sector-specific basis.

Following a renewed push to consolidate the single market, notably with the 1997 single market action plan and 1999 strategy paper, the Commission broadened its approach to services from the sector-specific to the general. The launch of the Lisbon strategy, with its emphasis on the service economy, emboldened the Commission to introduce a far-reaching legislative proposal. Bolkestein, an avid free-marketeer, enthusiastically spearheaded the Commission's effort.

The gist of the proposal was that companies providing services in any particular member state should be allowed to operate freely in another member state, and that individual service providers should be able to work in another member state, subject to the law in their home member state (the "country of origin" principle). Thus, an Italian travel agency should be able to open an office in London, or an electrician licensed in Spain should be able to take a job wiring a house in France. The Commission's sweeping approach seemed to go beyond what some of its interlocutors had advised. Nevertheless, the Commission was confident of success, not least because of its estimates of the economic advantages, in terms of lower costs and greater choice, of such legislation.

The so-called Bolkestein directive soon hit a wall of opposition from unions and politicians on the left, who saw it as an attempt to undermine the European social model by hiring lower-paid service workers from Southern and Eastern Europe in high-cost Western European countries. Already fearful of the impact of globalization on wages and welfare provision, opponents of the services directive complained about the prospect of "social dumping"—an influx of cheap labor from east to west in the EU—should the directive become law. Unions organized massive protests against the proposal. Emerging on the eve of enlargement, the issue revealed a deep aversion on the part of organized labor in Western Europe toward workers in Central and Eastern Europe.

As it wound its way through the codecision procedure, the proposal became bound up in the controversy in France over ratification of the Constitutional Treaty. Opponents of the treaty cited the Bolkestein directive as evidence of a neoliberal bias in the EU. If the Constitutional Treaty were ever implemented, its opponents warned, France would be awash in low-skilled and poorly paid Eastern European service providers. Fearful that hostility to the Bolkestein directive was turning opinion against the Constitutional Treaty in the run-up to the 2005 referendum, French president Jacques Chirac demanded a radical revision of the directive. In the event, a majority of French voters rejected the Constitutional Treaty. Chirac's strident opposition nonetheless ensured that the directive, in its current form, would not be enacted.

The Commission introduced a new proposal in April 2006, without the contentious "country of origin" clause and with several other changes that blunted its likely economic advantage. In the less heated post-referendum atmosphere—the Lisbon Treaty was not yet on the agenda—the revised directive passed in December 2006, with full implementation set for December 2009. By that time Bolkestein had left the Commission, although McCreevy, his successor, was no less combative in defense of the original proposal.[6]

Financial Services. Bolkestein was more successful in liberalizing financial services (notably banking, insurance, and securities). In 1997, the Commission proposed a directive tightening supervision of EU insurance groups, complementing existing single market legislation in the insurance sector. Nevertheless, key financial services directives remained on the table, delaying completion of an integrated European capital market. Accordingly, the Commission adopted the Financial Services Action Plan (FSAP) in May 1999. The purpose of the plan was to generate political momentum to enact forty-two measures that the Commission deemed essential to integrating the capital and financial services markets. The Commission proposed a deadline of 2004 for implementation of the plan.

The European Council endorsed the FSAP in March 2000, incorporating it into the Lisbon strategy, and later asked Alexandre Lamfalussy, a retired Belgian banker and former head of the European Monetary Institute, to chair a group of "wise men" to report on aspects of the plan pertaining to securities markets. The Lamfalussy Report, presented in February 2001, highlighted three fundamental weaknesses of the legislative and regulatory process: it was too slow, did not allow swift adjustment to a fluid market environment, and produced poor regulation. The report urged faster, better legislation for the securities markets and recommended that the EU institutions maintain continuous, transparent consultation with investors, issuers, and financial intermediaries throughout the legislative process.

Lamfalussy proposed that the EU establish two new committees: the European Securities Committee (senior representatives of the Commission and the national governments) and the European Securities Regulators Committee (national regulators). Based on input from market participants, end-users, and consumers, the European Securities Regulators Committee would advise the Commission on technical implementing measures. The Commission, in turn, would seek approval from the European Securities Committee before adopting the measure. The European Parliament could adopt a nonbinding resolution if the proposed measure exceeded the Commission's mandate.

The EP's hostility to the Lamfalussy Report sparked a lengthy controversy about procedural issues that threw a revealing light on the interaction among EU institutions. Specifically, the EP protested the likely impact of the proposed changes with respect to comitology, the committee system for overseeing EU policy implementation. By proposing changes in executive decisionmaking and the establishment of a powerful European Securities Committee, the Lamfalussy Report opened a procedural Pandora's box. At first the EP insisted on the right to a "call-back" (in effect, veto) of any Commission proposal to the European Securities Committee, which the Commission saw as a threat to its executive authority. By endorsing the Lamfalussy Report in March 2001, the European Council implicitly supported the Commission against the EP.

The Commission went ahead and established the European Securities Regulators Committee in May 2001. Pending EP approval, however, the Lamfalussy reforms were in limbo. In a report in January 2002, the EP's Committee on Constitutional Affairs dropped the call-back demand but insisted on various other safeguards. The EP's relative acquiescence permitted full implementation of the Lamfalussy Report almost a year after its publication. The EP's more conciliatory mood reflected awareness of the potential damage to European securities markets from continuous bickering. Nevertheless, the EP insisted that comitology procedures be included on the agenda of the next intergovernmental conference on treaty change (see Chapter 11).

Once the procedural issue was resolved, the Commission pushed the FSAP vigorously. The momentum of the Lisbon strategy carried most of the measures forward. The contemporaneous controversy over the Bolkestein directives may have helped by deflecting possible criticism away from the highly technical financial services directives.

Biannual progress reports on the FSAP, published by the Commission, kept up the pressure for adoption of the proposed directives. The final progress report, published in June 2004, noted with satisfaction that thirty-nine of the original forty-two measures had been adopted by the Council and Parliament, a remarkable legislative achievement.[7]

McCreevy, who succeeded Bolkestein soon after completion of the FSAP, had a particular interest in financial markets. He soon pushed a further five measures that were drafted in response to wider market developments. McCreevy was also vigilant about national implementation of the financial services directives, launching a publicly available Internet database in July 2006. Such openness fit well into the Commission's "better regulation" initiative and pressured recalcitrant national governments.

In December 2005, the Commission published a white paper on financial services, setting out its objectives for the next five years. In addition to implementing the FSAP directives at the national level, the white paper called for greater supervisory convergence; more competition between service providers, especially at the retail level; and expansion of the EU's influence in globalizing capital markets.

Revisiting the New Approach. In November 2005, the Commission celebrated the twentieth anniversary of the new approach to technical harmonization and standards, the backbone of the single market program. At a conference in Brussels, Heinz Zourek, a senior Commission official, hailed the success of the new approach, which he described as "a regulatory technique whereby product legislation is restricted to the requirements necessary to protect the public goals of health and safety, at the service of our strategy to complete the internal market and implement the Lisbon objective of better regulation."[8] Günther Verheugen, commissioner for enterprise and industry, was equally upbeat. The new approach, he pointed out, "has the immense advantage of better balancing the burdens of the legislative process between the operators and public authorities, and thus avoiding unnecessary excessive administrative and legislative requirements. It is *the* example of co-regulation."[9]

So successful was the new approach that Verheugen recommended extending its use to other sectors and policy areas, such as the environment, workplace safety, and services. Nevertheless, he appreciated that the new approach was not without problems. The Commission was increasingly alarmed by reports of unequal implementation of the new approach in member states, erratic market interventions (such as product recalls), abuses of safeguard mechanisms, and loss of consumer confidence in the European Conformity labeling due to a number of product safety scares. The Commission sought to address these problems primarily by improving market surveillance and strengthening the conformity assessment bodies.

To that end, in February 2007 the Commission proposed a package of measures, the first since inception of the single market program, aimed at increasing intra-EU trade in industrial goods. The most significant were a proposal for a regulation (enacted in 2008) to strengthen rules to protect consumers from unsafe products, including imports (it was unstated that such imports came primarily from China), and a proposal for a common legal framework for industrial products, which among other things would clarify the role and meaning of conformity labeling.[10]

The package also included an "interpretative communication" on purchasing cars in one member state for use in another member state, an issue that resonated with many Europeans. The single market should have made it possible for people to purchase cars wherever they wished in the EU, and the common currency highlighted price differentials in the eurozone. Yet problems abound when people try to register a foreign-bought car in their home country. As the Commission pointed out, "this remains the source of many complaints, in particular due to burdensome approval requirements and registration procedures. As a result many people do not buy a car from another Member State, due to the hassle and extra cost it can involve." The purpose of the communication was to ease cross-border car purchases by explaining how the existing rules should be applied.[11]

Problems of Transposition and Enforcement. Enactment of directives is only the first step in establishing a single market. The next step involves transposing those directives into national law. Without transposition, a single market could not work. Transposition rates vary from country to country and from sector to sector. In some cases, governments deliberately delay transposition in order to gain a temporary competitive advantage or for fear of aggravating domestic constituencies; in most cases, delays are the result of the technical complexity of legislation and procedural hurdles in the member states themselves.

In the aftermath of the single market program, the Commission was publicly circumspect on transposition, with the internal market commissioner even suggesting that gentle encouragement was the best means of moving forward. In private the Commission took a tougher line, backed up with the threat of legal action. As "guardian of the treaties," the Commission could begin infringement proceedings against governments for nonimplementation of single market measures.

Over the years, the Commission has issued a seemingly interminable series of communications, papers, and reports adjuring national administrations to transpose single market legislation more quickly and effectively. Ritualistic calls by the Council of Ministers for greater national compliance are another staple feature of efforts to fine-tune the single market.

The final step necessary to make a success of the single market is for governments to enforce the national law into which they have transposed EU directives. Successful enforcement depends on the quality and clarity of the legislation (claims that transposed directives are vague or unreasonable sometimes give member states a good excuse to avoid enforcement). It also depends on national courts, which in turn requires that lawyers and judges be familiar with EU law. Effective enforcement benefits as well from networks through which national officials can compare notes and develop best practices.

The Commission's annual reports on the single market contain useful information about the enactment of directives and their transposition (or non-transposition) at the national level. These reports indicate a steady increase over the years in both enactment of single market legislation and transposition in the member states. Transposition has been consistently poor in insurance, intellectual property, and procurement, and Germany and France are often among the worst offenders. Scoreboards have regularly ranked governments on their level of implementation of directives in force, and the press has mulled over the occasional dramatic leaps registered by Italy or the irony that politically refractory Denmark consistently topped the charts. Yet these statistics yielded little real information on the state of the single market, as they failed to reflect the quality of legislation or the likelihood that national authorities would actually enforce it.

The 2004 and 2007 enlargements posed a new potential challenge as the new member states struggled to implement and enforce a raft of EU legislation. In fact, having prepared for many years to join the EU, the new member states have generally met their single market requirements.

Maintaining Political Momentum. The 1992 program looms large in the historical memory of the Commission: older officials look back on it nostalgically; younger officials are told about it reverentially. Unable to replicate the 1992 program, the Commission wants at least to keep up the political pressure for perfection of the single market. Over the years, the Commission has launched numerous initiatives to celebrate the single market and to press for new, fine-tuning measures.

Thus, in June 1997 the Commission launched the Action Plan for the Single Market, a concerted effort to accelerate implementation of the single market in parallel with progress on monetary union.[12] The European Council put its weight behind the action plan in December 1997, as did the incoming British presidency. Eager to make its mark in the EU and push a liberal economic agenda, the new Labour government was not averse to "naming and shaming" in order to improve its partners' compliance with single market legislation. The British presidency focused especially on better implementation, prodding other countries on mutual recognition and public procurement issues as well as enforcement. The British also sought to broaden the single market scoreboard to include market integration indices, such as price-level differentials and volumes of intra-EU trade, alongside the more legalistic yardstick published at the time.

Apart from the Financial Services Action Plan, the next big push for the single market came in 2003, when the EU celebrated "ten years without frontiers." In a publication marking the anniversary, the Commission credited the single market with having created about 2.5 million jobs and generated €877 billion in economic activity via new market opportunities and more foreign direct investment. Nevertheless, the Commission cautioned that the single market was still a work in progress, requiring "constant effort, vigilance, and up-dating of the legal framework."[13]

In April 2006 the Commission launched a public consultation and report on the single market that focused on five areas for attention: market entry and innovation, better regulation, implementation and enforcement, the global context, and information and communication. The consultation and report were part of a Commission initiative, driven by defeat of the Constitutional Treaty, called "A Citizens' Agenda: Delivering Results for Europe." By highlighting the advantages of market integration, the Commission hoped to connect with European citizens and enhance the EU's output legitimacy.[14]

A follow-on review of the single market led to a package of initiatives in November 2007 intended to "ensure that the single market does even more to take advantage of globalization, empower consumers, open up for small businesses, stimulate innovation and help maintain high social and environmental standards." The lead document, "A Single Market for the 21st Century," sought to rekindle the old excitement of the 1992 program and offered concrete proposals, notably on implementation and enforcement of single market rules and on building upon the single market to enhance the EU's global economic influence.[15]

A progress report in December 2008, at the height of the financial crisis, reviewed how the Commission had implemented its vision for the single market of the twenty-first century and argued the relevance of market integration even at a time of economic downturn. In June 2009, at the height of the recession, the Commission went back to basics by urging national governments to defend the single market and strengthen the transposition and enforcement of EU directives.

The Commission's continuous emphasis on the importance of the single market reinforced similar statements by the European Council. When it revised the Lisbon strategy in December 2006, the European Council reiterated the significance of the single market for generating growth and jobs, and agreed that governments would include information on the functioning of the single market in their annual Lisbon strategy reports. Of course, national leaders say one thing at a European summit and another thing at home; the protectionist rhetoric of national leaders during the economic crisis was at variance with the content of European Council pronouncements. Even when inclined to bash the EU, however, few mainstream politicians seriously contemplated dismantling the single market.

■ Competition Policy

Without rigorous rules to police business practices, control state subsidies, and liberalize state-owned or state-sponsored industries, the single market could not function fairly or efficiently. The Rome Treaty therefore identified competition policy as a core area of Community activity and the Lisbon Treaty lists competition policy as one of only six areas of exclusive EU competence. An effective competition policy is an integral part of the EU's strategy for economic reform.[16]

EU competition policy comprises two main branches, one dealing with the activities of private enterprises, the other with the activities of governments and state-sponsored bodies. The first covers what is generally referred to in the United States as "antitrust," that is, the prevention of monopolistic behavior or collusion by private entities. The second pertains to the control of "state aid" (public subsidies to firms) and the liberalization of "regulated industries" (companies either owned by or having a special relationship with national governments).

The EU's antitrust efforts draw on the US experience. Indeed, US antitrust doctrine has exerted considerable influence over officials in the European Union. Unlike competition policy in the United States, however, competition policy in the EU deals not only with private-sector abuses but also with government assistance to national enterprises and to utilities—such as electricity, water, and telecommunications—which European governments have traditionally controlled. By including efforts to curb state subsidies to industry and to confront government monopolies, EU competition policy involves much more than antitrust.

As well as policing the marketplace, EU competition policy seeks to break down barriers between national markets, thereby promoting European integration. Speaking at the University of Chicago—famous for its scholarship on law and economics—Sir Leon Brittan, a former competition commissioner, jocosely described the "Brussels School" of competition policy: "It includes rules on state aids and on firms granted special or exclusive rights, and has special concerns to promote market [and European] integration."[17]

As the single market program gained momentum, the Commission focused on the closely related area of competition policy. Without the energetic application of competition rules, the elimination of national barriers could easily be nullified by price-fixing and market-sharing between firms, and by rampant government intervention. As a result, the EU implemented important competition policy reforms in the late 1980s and early 1990s.

The Commission launched a thorough review of competition policy a decade later, in anticipation of Central and Eastern European enlargement and in the context of the Lisbon strategy. The imminent accession of so many new member states, most of them unfamiliar with the concept of competition policy, prompted the Commission to reassess the conduct of EU competition policy. Officials from the candidate countries began working in Directorate-General Competition on a temporary basis well before enlargement took place. The new member states had to apply competition policy rules with only some transitional arrangements for state aid, although their economies were still very different from those of the existing member states. Enlargement increased the Commission's overall state aid workload by about 40 percent.

Apart from the possible impact of enlargement, the Commission attempted to hone competition policy as an instrument of economic reform. Under the forceful leadership of competition commissioner Mario Monti (1999–2004), the Commission recommended tightening competition rules and pressed governments to curtail the provision of state aid, especially to declining enterprises. Monti sought to ensure that competition policy was grounded in sound economics: instead of taking a legalistic approach to competition policy cases, the Commission would look at the likely impact of the activity on markets and consumers. To that end, the Commission established the new position of chief economist, assisted by a team of industrial economists, to provide independent economic analysis in individual antitrust, merger, and state aid cases throughout the investigation process. Describing herself as "an economist by training [and] . . . an antitrust enforcer by profession," competition commissioner Neelie Kroes (2004–2009), Monti's successor, continued to advocate competition policy based on sound economic assessment rather than abstract theory.[18]

Controversy over the future of competition policy arose in June 2007, during the negotiations in the European Council on the Lisbon Treaty, when newly elected French president Nicolas Sarkozy launched a tirade against what he saw as excessive liberalization in the EU. "Competition as an ideology, as a dogma," Sarkozy asked, "what has it done for Europe? It has only brought fewer and fewer people who vote in European elections and fewer and fewer people who believe in [the EU]." At Sarkozy's request, a reference to "free and undistorted competition" as an EU objective was moved from the body of the Lisbon Treaty and put into a protocol on the internal market. Sarkozy's outburst raised concerns about the application of competition policy under his presidency and under the Lisbon Treaty.[19]

Kroes allayed such concerns when she presented the Commission's annual report on competition policy shortly after the June 2007 summit, declaring that "the protocol to the treaty is a legally binding confirmation that the system of undistorted competition is part of the internal market. Of course, competition is not an end in itself, but it is one of the best means to create conditions for growth and jobs. Putting it in a protocol on the internal market clarifies that one cannot exist without the other. That is a fact, and the competition rules which have served citizens so well over the last fifty years remain in force, and the Commission will continue to enforce them firmly and fairly."[20]

During the 2008–2009 recession, Sarkozy and other national leaders complained that rigid adherence to competition policy rules was hindering economic recovery. The Commission was in an awkward position, trying to strike the right balance between enforcing competition policy and giving companies and countries some leeway in the difficult economic circumstances. In general, the Commission adopted a commonsensical approach. According to Kroes, "the Commission's actions in the field of competition [in 2008] were a determining factor in preserving the single market and the benefits of competition, while ensuring stability in the financial system. Strong cooperation between partners at European and national level has allowed us to tackle the crisis in an efficient and timely manner. But there has been no let up in other competition enforcement: the competition rules are even more vital to the economy in times of crisis, and the Commission's enforcement record remains extremely strong."[21]

Restrictive Practices and Abuse of Dominant Position
Articles 101 and 102 of the Treaty on the Functioning of the European Union (formerly Articles 81 and 82 of the Treaty Establishing the European Community) form the legal basis of EU antitrust policy:

- *Article 101:* Prohibits agreements and concerted practices that prevent, restrict, or distort competition and that affect trade between member states. This article generally refers to collusion between companies (in cartels) to fix prices or control production.
- *Article 102:* Prohibits abuse of practices of dominance that distort trade between member states. Such abuse could consist of predatory pricing (setting artificially low prices to drive competitors from the market), limiting production or markets, applying dissimilar conditions, and making the conclusion of contracts subject to acceptance of supplementary obligations. Dominance is presumed to mean more than 50 percent of market share, although increasingly the Commission relies more on economic effect than market share to determine whether a company dominates the market.

In 1962 the Council adopted a regulation obliging firms to notify the Commission of restrictive agreements and giving the Commission extensive powers of investigation, adjudication, and enforcement, including the power to grant individual or block exemptions under certain circumstances. Most companies under investigation cooperate with the Commission, however grudgingly. In the event that some would not, the regulation authorized Commission officials to arrive unannounced at businesses throughout the Community and conduct immediate, on-site investigations. Only after the launch of the single market program did DG Competition's "trustbusters" go on the offensive, with the enthusiastic support of successive competition commissioners.

Yet it would be misleading to imagine Commission officials conducting dramatic dawn raids. Unannounced on-site inspections take place during normal working hours, in the presence of national competition authorities, and are the exception, not the rule. However, the unexpected arrival of Commission officials usually yields otherwise unobtainable evidence of wrongdoing.

A new regulation that came into effect in May 2004 simplified the enforcement of the treaty's antitrust rules. In a major departure from past practice, firms no longer have to notify the Commission of restrictive agreements (notifications had become an unnecessary burden on firms and on the Commission, which was spending too much time simply processing them). Instead, the Commission prosecutes possible infringements on the basis of complaints and investigations undertaken on its own initiative. The new regulation also provided for joint enforcement by the Commission, national competition authorities, and national courts. The Commission and the national enforcement bodies—the so-called European Competition Network—work closely together in order to ensure consistent application of the rules.

The Commission resolves most antitrust cases informally. If the Commission decides to take formal action, it sends the firm in question a detailed statement of objections. Firms may respond in writing and present their case at a hearing. If it concludes that there is an infringement, the Commission may impose a fine of up to 10 percent of the firm's total global turnover. Although such large fines are rarely levied, the Commission routinely imposes penalties of tens of millions of euros (the money is paid into the EU budget).

The Commission has a leniency program to encourage companies with insider information about cartels to contact DG Competition. Firms that come forward may be granted total immunity from fines or a reduction in the amount of the fine. The leniency program has proved quite successful in resolving antitrust cases.

The "car glass" case is a good example of a successful antitrust action. Responding to an anonymous tip, the Commission conducted an investigation into four companies—Asahi, Pilkington, Saint-Gobain, and Soliver—that together controlled 90 percent of the glass used in cars, a market worth about €2 billion annually. In the course of its investigation, which included surprise inspections at several car glass makers, the Commission discovered that, from 1998 to 2003, the companies had violated the EU's ban on cartels and restrictive practices, notably by allocating market share and customers among themselves. In November 2008, the Commission imposed fines totaling €1.3 billion. The Commission increased the fines on Saint-Gobain by 60 percent because it was a repeat offender, and reduced the fine on Asahi by 50 percent under the leniency program. These are the highest cartel fines the Commission has ever imposed, both for an individual company and for a cartel as a whole.[22]

The Microsoft case is perhaps the most famous antitrust case prosecuted by the Commission. After an exhaustive investigation, the Commission found Microsoft guilty in 2004 of anticompetitive behavior because it refused to supply interoperability information and incorporated a software product, Windows

Media Player, into its operating system. In addition to demanding that Microsoft remove Windows Media Player from the version of its operating system sold in Europe, the Commission fined Microsoft €497 million, the largest fine ever imposed against an individual company. The case dragged on during an appeal by Microsoft and claims by the Commission that Microsoft was ignoring the original ruling. Microsoft lost its appeal in September 2007. In February 2008 the Commission fined Microsoft an additional €899 million for failure to comply with the original antitrust decision.

The Commission may investigate entire sectors and types of agreements across sectors. The Commission generally undertakes such investigations if it observes lack of cross-border trade in a particular sector, a paucity of new entrants in the market, price rigidities, or other indicators of restrictions or distortions.

Mergers. An extensive body of EU law has extended the scope of what is now Article 102 to include structural changes brought about by mergers and acquisitions. Initially, a firm was judged to have contravened Article 102 if it created or strengthened a dominant position by means of a takeover or merger. Yet the Community's limited merger control applied only to cases where a dominant market position had already been established. Although merger-control reform had been on the Community's agenda for years, little progress was made until a plethora of mergers and acquisitions took place in the late 1980s at the outset of the single market program.

The number, size, and speed of 1992-induced mergers gave the Commission an opportunity to press national governments to cede more regulatory authority to Brussels. Governments appreciated the threat that uncontrolled EU-wide mergers posed to the emerging single market and the advantage for businesses of dealing with a single European competition authority rather than several national ones. Nevertheless, governments disagreed on the criteria for Commission vetting and approval, with Germany and Britain—the countries with the strongest national competition authorities—putting up the most resistance. As a result, it was not until December 1989 that the Council adopted a regulation providing for the prior authorization of mergers, thus enabling the Commission to control the buildup of dominant firms. The 1989 merger regulation constituted a cornerstone of the EU's competition policy and single market program.

The regulation drew a clear distinction between mergers with an EU dimension, where the Commission had the power to intervene, and those that mainly affected a particular member state. An EU dimension existed when all of the following were true:

- The firms involved had an aggregate worldwide turnover of more than €5 billion.

- At least two of the firms had an aggregate EU-wide turnover of more than €250 million each.
- At least one of the firms had less than two-thirds of its aggregate EU-wide turnover within one particular member state (transnationality).

The crucial test for Commission scrutiny was dominant position, taking into account such factors as the structure of the markets concerned, actual or potential competition, the market position of the firms involved, the opportunities open to third parties, barriers to entry, the interests of consumers, and technical and economic progress. The regulation also included compulsory prior notification and a strict timetable for Commission decisionmaking. The Commission established a merger task force to implement the new regulation, which came into force in September 1990.

Of the hundreds of notifications that it receives annually, only a handful go to a full-scale, four-month, second-stage investigation. If the Commission considers that a proposed merger is incompatible with the single market, it may insist on "remedies," such as the sale of some production facilities or other assets. Otherwise, the Commission can block the merger. Companies that ignore the Commission's ruling can be fined up to 10 percent of their turnover (subject to appeal to the Court of Justice). Most of the mergers dealt with by the Commission are in dynamic business sectors such as telecommunications, financial services, pharmaceuticals, and the media.

From the outset, the Commission worked with industry, the legal profession, and national competition authorities to ensure that the landmark 1990 merger regulation worked well. Firms seemed pleased to deal with a single EU-level procedure, and most companies complied with the notification requirement. Indeed, many firms complained about the high thresholds triggering notification, as those whose mergers and acquisitions fell below these thresholds had to deal with a number of national authorities rather than the Commission's "one-stop shop."

In February 1996 the Commission suggested, in the face of considerable national opposition, that the thresholds be lowered. Over a year later, in May 1997, the Council agreed to change the merger regulation, but not by reducing the notification thresholds, as requested by the Commission. Too many national competition authorities, especially those in Britain and Germany, were jealous of the Commission's control over big competition cases. Nevertheless, the Council agreed to increase the Commission's role by giving it jurisdiction over mergers falling short of the turnover thresholds that required multiple notifications to national competition authorities. The Council's intent was to obviate the need for companies in certain merger cases to notify and await approval from multiple national authorities.

A more far-reaching change came in January 2004, when the Council decided on a new merger regulation. It specified that "a concentration [that] would significantly impede effective competition in the common market or in a substantial part of it, in particular [but not exclusively] as a result of the creation or strengthening of a dominant position, shall be declared incompatible with the common market." The Commission could therefore intervene against all anticompetitive mergers, not just those that met the old "dominance test." The reform promised greater transparency in merger investigations, including more interaction among regulators and businesses, giving firms an opportunity to respond to the Commission's concerns before a possible adverse ruling. The reform was also a response to the fact that the Court of First Instance overturned three important Commission merger rulings in 2002.

Examples of Commission disapproval or conditional approval of mergers include:

- In November 1994, a proposed joint venture known as MSG Media Service, among Bertelsmann, the Kirch Group, and Deutsche Telekom, became one of the first deals blocked by the Commission under the merger regulation. According to the Commission, the venture would have led to the creation or strengthening of a dominant position in three markets, including those for pay-television and cable networks. The Commission blocked another deal involving Bertelsmann and Kirch in 1998—a planned German digital pay-television venture— when Bertelsmann rejected a last-minute compromise proposed by DG Competition.
- In March 2003, following a lengthy investigation, the Commission authorized the takeover by Pfizer Incorporated of Pharmacia Corporation, creating the world's largest pharmaceutical company. Concerned about the impact of the acquisition on competition in the pharmaceutical sector and on the functioning of the single market, the Commission linked its approval to an agreement by the two firms to give up certain products in development and, unrelated to the single market, to address some animal welfare issues.
- In October 2007, in the financial sector, the Commission approved a merger between two banks, ABN Amro and Fortis, on condition that both would divest themselves of certain activities. After the Dutch government took over the banking and insurance activities of Fortis in the Netherlands, including Fortis's interest in ABN Amro, in October 2008 at the height of the financial crisis, the Commission agreed to extend until October 2009 the deadline for the divestitures to take place.

State Aid and State-Sponsored Bodies

Control of state aid such as subsidies, tax breaks, and public investments is even more politically sensitive than mergers. The treaties prohibit state aid, defined as an advantage in any form whatsoever conferred on a selective basis to undertakings by national public authorities. Nevertheless, governments have allowed themselves broad latitude under the exceptions included in the treaty—notably for aid to poorer regions—especially during economic recession and when facing political and social fallout from the precipitous decline of industries. Nor have they always informed the Commission in advance of plans to grant or alter aid. The mixed character of the European economy, where government ownership of industry is still considered an acceptable instrument of economic development, means that the precise level of state support is often difficult to determine.[23]

Old Article 88 of the Treaty Establishing the European Community (now Article 108 of the Treaty on the Functioning of the European Union) authorized the Commission, in cooperation with national governments, to monitor state aid closely. Old Article 89 (new Article 109) allowed the Council to adopt appropriate regulations to prohibit market-distorting public assistance. In 1983 the Commission notified national governments that it would require them to refund any aid granted without prior notification to the Commission or prior ruling by the Commission on the aid's compatibility with competition rules.

Strict control of state aid became as vital as the vigorous application of antitrust law for the success of the single market. By subsidizing companies in their own countries, national governments distorted competition throughout the Community and put nonsubsidized companies at an obvious disadvantage. The Commission began a comprehensive review of state aid policy to determine the real level of aid, taking on the most anticompetitive and wasteful subsidies and trying to roll back the general level of support. Based on case law, a more favorable political climate, and a number of specific actions, the Commission began to make an impression.

The Commission also launched a procedure to tackle the ongoing problem of aid granted without notification to the Commission. It called for governments to supply full details of the alleged aid within thirty days, sooner in urgent cases. If the government failed to reply or gave an unsatisfactory response, the Commission could make a provisional decision requiring the state to suspend application of the aid within fifteen days, and could initiate proceedings to make the government provide the necessary data. If the government still refused to comply, the Commission could adopt a final decision of incompatibility and require repayment of the amount of state aid allocated. Should the government ignore the Commission's decision, the Commission would refer the matter to the Court.

Despite the Commission's apparent feistiness, state aid remained ubiquitous in the EU, amounting to many billions of euros annually. The four biggest member states—Germany, France, Italy, and Britain—accounted for a growing share of state aid, most of which therefore went to the EU's better-off regions. The Commission received approximately 600 notifications annually of new aid schemes or amendments to existing aid schemes, and registered approximately 100 cases annually of unnotified schemes. Yet the Commission raised no objection to the vast majority of these, either because difficult economic circumstances appeared to warrant government assistance to firms in need of restructuring or because the assistance contributed to EU objectives in other areas such as social, regional, or environmental policy. Of the cases it pursued, the Commission rarely prohibited aid, although it occasionally attached conditions to approvals.

Aware of the incompatibility of indiscriminate state aid with the commitment to boost economic growth under the Lisbon strategy, the European Council agreed in March 2001 to reduce overall aid levels and to redirect what they provide to so-called horizontal objectives rather than to specific sectors. Horizontal objectives are areas that cannot function entirely on the basis of the free market, such as research and development (R&D), environmental improvement, energy saving, and support for small and medium-sized enterprises. At the same time, the Commission granted block exemptions covering state aid in five areas: aid to SMEs, research and development carried out by SMEs, aid for employment, aid for training, and regional aid. Subsidies under a block exemption do not require notification to the Commission.

The Commission began to tighten approval of state aid under competition commissioners Monti (1999–2004) and Kroes (2004–2009). Partly because of its tougher approach and partly because of the European Council's commitment, the overall amount of subsidies offered by national governments began to fall. The Commission also scored some significant successes, such as the removal of state guarantee from German regional banks, thereby allowing other institutions to compete fairly with them. As in other areas of competition policy, the Commission began to pay more attention to state aid that has a significant economic impact throughout the single market, for instance by focusing on aid to sectors producing tradable goods and services. The Commission especially opposes aid to large companies and is redoubling its efforts to recover aid illegally granted.

Enlargement in 2004 and 2007 posed a particular challenge for the EU's state aid regime. The countries of Central and Eastern Europe had emerged in the early 1990s from centrally planned economic systems characterized by state ownership of almost everything. Those countries then underwent wrenching reforms, including extensive privatization. Nevertheless, the state continued to support many economic activities on which millions of people depended for a living. Although the new member states had to adopt existing EU law, most were granted exemptions and transition periods with respect to state aid rules. In particular, the Commission tolerated existing aid (pre-accession) but prohibited new aid (post-accession).

Inevitably, friction arose as the new member states settled into the EU and state aid rules began to bite. The most striking example was a Commission campaign to clamp down on illegal state aid from the Polish government to three shipyards, including the iconic Gdansk shipyard from which the Solidarity movement had emerged nearly twenty years earlier. The Polish government's concessions to the Commission shocked public opinion and may have outweighed the positive impression created by the billions of euros flowing into the country from the EU.

The Commission adopted an action plan in June 2005 that included proposals to make the rules on state aid more transparent and less bureaucratic, and to consolidate and extend the existing block exemptions. The plan triggered a lengthy process of consultation and decisionmaking, which was still not complete when the impact of the financial crisis and economic recession took center stage.[24]

In an effort to shame governments into reducing public subsidies, the Commission maintains a state aid scoreboard. This shows that governments have been reducing and better targeting their state aid, which has fallen from over 2 percent of combined EU GDP in the 1980s to around 0.5 percent in 2008. About 80 percent of state aid now goes to horizontal objectives, compared with around 50 percent in the mid-1990s, with greater spending on R&D and the environment. However, there was a marked increase in state aid in 2008–2009, during the economic recession, with the share of rescue and restructuring aid rising dramatically.[25]

The Commission issued three communications in 2008 on the role of state aid policy in coping with the economic situation. The first provided guidance on the application of state aid rules to national assistance for financial institutions, based on a treaty provision that permits aid intended to remedy a serious disturbance in a country's economy. The second explained how governments could recapitalize banks in order to stabilize financial markets and ensure adequate levels of lending to the rest of the economy. The third outlined the circumstances in which governments could provide other forms of state aid to tackle the effects of the financial crisis on the real economy. All measures were limited to the end of 2010, at which time the Commission would evaluate the situation.[26]

There is a danger that governments will continue in the aftermath of the recession to provide exceptional levels of state aid. Even with a reduction in spending to pre-recession levels, the Commission would have its hands full trying to enforce state aid rules. For the Commission, the fight against unfair national subsidies is never-ending.

Regulated Industries. European governments have traditionally sheltered certain industries from competition because of those industries' fundamental economic importance. Telecommunications, energy (electricity and gas), banking, insurance, and transport have usually been highly regulated and in many cases government-owned. In close association with the single market program, the Commission began in the early 1990s to apply competition law to those sectors, often in the teeth of fierce national opposition.

Article 106 of the Treaty on the Functioning of the European Union (formerly Article 86 of the Treaty Establishing the European Community) provides for the full application of treaty rules, including those on competition and free movement of goods and services, to companies owned by or in a special relationship with national governments—except where the application of such rules would prevent the companies from carrying out their public service obligations. The Commission applies the treaty rules by adopting appropriate directives or decisions without Council approval. The Court has upheld the Commission's right to do so, spelling out in a number of important cases the extent to which governments may grant statutory monopolies or special rights. As a result, there is much less uncertainty about the competition rules for regulated industries.

The Politics of Competition Policy

As is obvious from many of the cases already mentioned, competition policy is an extremely sensitive subject for the Commission, which must balance concern for preventing market distortion with the need to avoid overreaching its own political (as distinct from legal) authority. Although striving for integrity, the Commission cannot divorce from politics the process of implementing antitrust law, merger policy, control of state aid, and liberalization of regulated industries. Decisions are taken by the full college of commissioners, who must consider political timing and the need to maintain the appearance of national and regional impartiality. Governments are quick to accuse the Commission of favoritism. Arguably the competition policy commissioner is the most powerful person in the Commission. In order to be effective, however, he or she must be able to stand up to forceful business interests and national governments, often without the support of the entire college of commissioners.

Since the original merger regulation entered into force in 1990, the Commission has blocked on average only one merger a year. Some critics contend that this low rejection rate is due to the Commission's susceptibility to political pressure. Whether or not the Commission is politically vulnerable, controversial mergers generate intense lobbying. Arguments inside the Commission often mirror contending national positions.

Critics of the Commission's alleged susceptibility to pressure cite the high merger approval rate as a reason to give responsibility for competition policy to a separate authority. A number of observers suggested before the negotiations in 1996–1997 on treaty reform that an independent EU competition authority, along the lines of Germany's Bundeskartellamt (federal competition office), should be established. Others accepted that idea in principle but argued that it should not be implemented until the EU's political development made it more likely that such an office could be fully independent, or at least manifestly more independent than DG Competition appeared to be. In the event, the idea was never pursued.

Those who criticize the Commission for being too vigorous in the application of competition policy have been unrelenting in their attacks. The French and German governments are among the Commission's harshest critics. France seems wedded to supporting national champions, while the federal and state governments in Germany are highly partial to state aid. Commissioner Monti's conviction that in order "to be able to keep some parts of its social model, [the EU] simply has to become more and more similar to the US in its own domestic economic structure . . . more liberal, more efficient, more productive, more competitive," found little sympathy in Paris or Berlin.[27] It is also the kind of rhetoric, typical of statements by recent competition commissioners, that fueled Sarkozy's outburst against competition policy and other "Anglo-Saxon" deviations.

Having a competition policy watchdog at the European level undoubtedly helps national economies. Without the Commission's vigilance, anticompetitive behavior would be far worse, and far costlier in its economic impact. Governments generally understand that subsidies are often expensive, wasteful, and frequently unavailing, but politically they find it difficult to risk electoral support by withdrawing them. The Commission's state aid authority can prove most useful to governments by allowing them to blame Brussels for having to cut back on public subsidies. In so doing, of course, governments risk eroding support for the Commission and for the EU as a whole. For the sake of domestic electoral support, however, it is a risk that governments seem more than willing to take.

The International Dimension

EU competition rules have an important global dimension, as they affect the activities of all companies operating in or having an impact on the EU market, regardless of where those firms are based. This situation can cause considerable friction in the EU's external relations, especially with the United States. Moreover, the EU includes competition policy provisions in many of its external relations agreements and has actively pushed the unpopular notion of competition rules in the WTO. The Commission is a strong supporter of the informal International Competition Network, a body that sets guiding principles and recommended practices for the control of multijurisdictional mergers, and of the OECD's global forum on competition.

US-EU friction over competition policy is a staple of the transatlantic relationship, with the US government and US companies highly critical of what they see as an EU competition policy that favors European companies. Although EU competition law is based on US practices and principles, US companies have a dim view of its partiality. US concerns came to the fore in the late 1990s when the Commission threatened to block a merger between Boeing and McDonnell Douglas despite the US Federal Trade Commission's unconditional approval. The Commission objected to the deal on the grounds that the new firm would dominate the European market for large airliners, that Boeing's civil business might enjoy defense spillovers, and that Boeing had exclusive twenty-year contracts with a number of US airlines. Boeing took steps to allay the Commission's first two concerns but argued that the third concern was beyond the scope of the merger and was not an issue for the US airlines involved in the contracts. Boeing pointed out that a challenge to its exclusive contracts was in the interests only of its archrival, Airbus.

"Airbus" is a dirty word in US aviation and government circles, where it is synonymous with EU protectionism and subsidization. The involvement of Airbus in the dispute, however indirectly, raised the political stakes. Despite intense pressure from Washington, including threats of a trade war, the Commission obstinately refused to approve the deal unless Boeing made extra concessions. Boeing did so at the last moment, agreeing not to sign any new exclusive contracts for ten years and not to enforce the deals it had signed. This concession paved the way for Commission approval of the merger, but at a cost of casting the Commission once again as an unswerving supporter of Airbus and endangering cooperation between the United States and the EU in competition policy.

The Commission's veto in 2001 of General Electric's $45 billion bid for Honeywell also caused consternation in the United States, whose competition authorities had already approved the deal. Clearly, the Commission's concerns about the consequences of the proposed deal for the aerospace industry reflected different assumptions on both sides of the Atlantic about the impact of mergers on competition and consumers, with the United States taking a more laissez-faire approach.

US antitrust authorities also vet mergers involving EU companies.[28] Because of their mutual interest in megamergers, the Commission and its US counterpart concluded an agreement as long ago as 1991 to consult on competition cases (the agreement came into effect in 1995 due to procedural delays on the EU side). Despite some spectacular exceptions, US-EU cooperation on competition policy has greatly improved. The two sides concluded a "Positive Comity Agreement" in 1998 and agreed on a set of best practices in reviewing mergers in 2002, thus establishing an advisory framework for interagency cooperation.

In February 2004, competition commissioner Monti described cooperation on competition policy as "one of the most important (and perhaps least heralded) success stories in EU-US relations in recent years" and praised the Commission's "quiet and business-like cooperation" with its US counterpart agencies (the Department of Justice and the Federal Trade Commission).[29] The merger later that year between Air France and KLM Royal Dutch Airlines is a good example of such quiet cooperation. Once the airlines offered to provide substantial remedies, neither the Commission nor the US Department of Justice challenged the deal. Similarly, in March 2008 the Commission approved

Google's $3.1 billion acquisition of the online advertising technology company DoubleClick, having concluded that the merger of these two US-based companies would be unlikely to have harmful effects on consumers. The US Federal Trade Commission had approved the merger the previous December.

■ Economic and Monetary Union

Of all the EU's policy innovations, Economic and Monetary Union is the boldest and most ambitious.[30] Yet EMU is a misnomer. The EU has a monetary union, but not full economic union. Economic integration in the EU has not reached a level analogous to a national economy. National governments control fiscal policy (taxation and spending), and the single market is still a work in progress. Indeed, conventional economic indicators are a reminder of how fragmented the European economy still is. Most economic indicators disaggregate the EU into its constituent member states, and the eurozone is rarely included as a separate entity.

Even without full economic integration, a monetary union among sovereign states is a vast undertaking. Few countries would ever be willing to exchange their currency and monetary policy independence for a common currency and common monetary policy. Why are EU countries so different in that regard? First, EMU was built upon decades of economic integration, during which time countries developed mutual trust and a long record of cooperating closely. Second, EMU would likely bring tangible benefits, such as price transparency, lower inflation, and the abolition of currency exchange costs, and could stimulate broader economic reform at a time of accelerating globalization. Third, EMU was a reaffirmation of the commitment to ever closer union, at a time of profound geopolitical change brought about by the end of the Cold War.

Not every member state was equally committed to EMU, and each country had a mix of motives for wanting to participate. Uninterested in ever closer union and unconvinced of the economic advantages of EMU, Britain chose not to participate in Stage III—the irrevocable fixing of exchange rates, adherence to a common monetary policy, and adoption of the euro. Denmark had decided at the time of the Maastricht Treaty that it would opt out of Stage III, and Sweden decided in 1999, when Stage III was launched, not to participate either. Of the remaining member states, only Greece was not an inaugural member of the eurozone, having failed to meet the convergence criteria for eligibility (see Box 13.1).

For a long time Germany was highly ambivalent about EMU, despite its stalwart support for European integration. Germans were deeply attached to their currency, the Deutschmark, which symbolized postwar recovery and respectability. Intensely fearful of inflation, Germans also saw the Deutschmark,

---

Box 13.1   The Three Stages of EMU and the Convergence Criteria

---

Stage I (1990): EU member states abolished all restrictions on capital movements within the EU.

Stage II (1994–1999): EU institutions and national governments made technical preparations for the launch of monetary union and established the European Monetary Institute (EMI), forerunner of the European Central Bank, which took over from the EMI toward the end of this stage.

Stage III (1999–): Launch of monetary union and the euro, with the European Central Bank assuming responsibility for monetary policy in the euro area (the zone of countries participating in Stage III).

The *convergence criteria* are standards that countries must meet before participating in Stage III of EMU. The purpose is to ensure a degree of economic convergence among participating countries, thereby strengthening the stability of the euro area. The five criteria are:

Price stability: The inflation rate should be no more than 1.5 percent above the previous year's rate for the three EU countries (regardless of their participation in the monetary union) with the lowest inflation.

Budget deficit: The national deficit should not be higher than 3 percent of GDP.

National debt: The national debt should not exceed 60 percent of GDP; if higher, the national debt should be falling steadily.

Interest rates: Long-term rates should be no more than 2 percentage points above the previous year's rate in the three EU countries (regardless of their participation in the monetary union) with the lowest interest rates.

Exchange rate stability: The national currency's exchange rate must have remained within the authorized fluctuation margin of ERM II (plus or minus 15 percent) for two years.

Source: Adapted from *EU Focus*, Issue No. 28, January 2009.

---

and the central bank (Bundesbank), as the epitome of price stability. Precisely because of lack of enthusiasm for EMU, the German government insisted that the European Central Bank be located in Frankfurt, home of the German central bank, and that the ECB, like the Bundesbank, focus almost exclusively on price stability (fighting inflation).

France, a proud and sovereignty-conscious country, willingly entered Stage III of EMU because, by that time, it had long been locked into a de facto Deutschmark zone. The exchange rate mechanism of the European Monetary System, launched in 1979, had evolved by the mid-1980s into an area of low inflation and monetary stability whose interest rates, in effect, were set by the Bundesbank. Rather than have the Bundesbank, acting entirely in Germany's interest, determine French monetary policy by default, the French reckoned that it would be better to have the ECB, acting in the interest of participating countries whose representatives would have a seat at the decisionmaking table, conduct monetary policy.

For Italy, the appeal of EMU was both symbolic (of its status as a founding member of the original European communities) and practical (notoriously undisciplined in managing its public finances, Italy hoped that EMU membership would impose a fiscal straitjacket on the country). Other member states had their own set of reasons for participating in Stage III.

Despite a poor economic climate in the mid-1990s and despite having missed the 1997 target date, a majority of member states (including France and Germany) indeed qualified for the 1999 deadline for the launch of Stage III. Altogether, eleven of the then fifteen member states participated in monetary union at the outset, in January 1999, when the ECB assumed responsibility for their common monetary policy and when their national currencies became denominations of the euro (still a virtual currency). Having met the convergence criteria in 2000, Greece became the twelfth country to participate in monetary union, in January 2001.

Managing Monetary Union

Would EMU work? The short answer is that it would have to, because politicians had invested so much in it and because Europeans gave it the benefit of the doubt. During the transition stages, governments displayed a determination to make it happen, new and existing administrative bodies demonstrated the necessary expertise to bring it about, and public opinion showed surprising compliance with it. Having concluded not only that EMU was feasible but also that the political and economic price of failure was unsustainable, politicians, technocrats, and ordinary Europeans alike were bound to conclude after the launch of Stage III that the costs of maintaining the single currency were considerably lower than the costs of its collapse.

Nevertheless, the challenges of managing monetary union were substantial. The first and most obvious challenge was to launch the euro itself, as a real currency (in people's pockets), in January 2002. The challenge was mostly logistical and informational. It involved printing euro notes (some €15 billion worth) and minting euro coins, distributing the new currency, withdrawing the old currencies, adjusting coin-operated machines and automated teller machines (ATMs), preventing possible counterfeiting, and alerting businesses and consumers to the changes about to take place. To prepare people for what lay ahead, retailers displayed prices in euros as well as in national currencies for at least two years before the changeover. In the meantime, the Commission launched a huge public information campaign ("Euro 2002"), and governments conducted similar campaigns nationally.

The transition to the new currency went remarkably well. As one commentator noted, "vending machines did not jam, ATMs did not melt, the plague of allergic reaction to the new coins' alloy did not stalk the land, and no great inflationary pyre lit the euro area's winter sky."[31] People seemed to enjoy the novelty of the notes and coins, although for years afterward most had to convert the euro mentally into what soon came to be called "old money." Participating countries had six months during which they could allow transactions in either the new or the old currencies. Most people switched immediately to the euro, and most governments concluded that the six-month transitional period was both unnecessary and undesirable.

More than any other event in the history of the EU, introduction of the euro brought home to people the extent and impact of European integration. Few people, even in Germany, mourned their national currencies: as long as the value of the euro was sound, people were willing to accept it. There were some allegations of price increases as a result of the changeover, with many businesses having conveniently rounded prices up or taken the opportunity to charge substantially more in euros for their products and services. There was keen competition in cross-border sales as shoppers in border regions reaped the reward of price transparency and the convenience (and savings) of not having to change money. Those who went on holidays in each other's countries immediately enjoyed the relief of being able to use the same currency while vacationing abroad.

The external value of the virtual euro dropped markedly in the first three years of its existence. The late 1990s was therefore a great time for Americans, for example, to vacation in the eurozone, but an expensive time for eurozone residents to travel to the United States. The big drop in the external value of the euro was due partly to the strength of the US economy and partly to uncertainty about the intentions of the ECB. Many European politicians and officials, who naively viewed the exchange rate of the euro as an indicator of the EU's virility, were disappointed with its early performance. Businesspeople had a more pragmatic outlook, appreciating the advantage of a weak euro for foreign sales. Exports from the eurozone enjoyed a considerable boost from 1999 until 2002 as a result of the euro's depreciation vis-à-vis the US dollar.

The situation reversed itself with a vengeance in the mid-2000s as the euro appreciated rapidly and the dollar declined precipitously. European politicians and officials who had lamented the weakness of the euro only a few years previously now complained bitterly about the impact of the strong euro on the competitiveness of eurozone exports. European businesspeople who had enjoyed the export advantages of a weak euro now paid the price (fewer foreign sales) of a strong euro. The value of the euro reflected the weakness of the US economy more than the strength or inherent attractiveness of the eurozone economy. Beginning in 2003, US politicians and officials seemingly talked down the value of the dollar in an effort to gain a competitive advantage for US exports, thereby introducing another bone of contention into the transatlantic relationship. For residents of the eurozone, at least, the reversal in the euro's fortunes had a silver lining: vacations and shopping expeditions in the United States became extremely affordable. Given the exchange rate between the euro and the dollar since the mid-2000s, it would be less expensive for Dutch skiers, for example, to go to the slopes in Colorado or Utah than in Austria or France. By contrast, US visitors to the eurozone experienced severe sticker shock.

Regardless of the fluctuating value of the euro, the ECB operated quietly and successfully in Frankfurt. Jean Claude Trichet, a former head of the French central bank, became its president in 2003. "A man who combines charm and steel in equal measures . . . [and is] by far the most experienced member of the ECB board . . . [Trichet] plays a commanding role in internal deliberations and in external policy utterances."[32] Although France insisted that the successor to Wim Duisenberg, the first ECB president, be French, Trichet is unquestionably independent of the French government.

There are five other members of the ECB's executive board, appointed by the European Council. The executive board is responsible for daily management and for implementing the decisions of the ECB's governing council, which consists of the members of the ECB's executive board and the governors of the national central banks in the eurozone. The governing council meets monthly to analyze economic developments in the eurozone, assess the risks to price stability, and decide the appropriate level for key interest rates. Since the onset of the global financial crisis in 2007, meetings of the governing council have become major media events, with reporters feverishly speculating about possible interest rate changes.

Together, the eurozone's national central banks and the European Central Bank make up the Eurosystem (see Box 13.2). The ECB focuses on policy formulation, and the national central banks focus on implementation. The ECB and the national central banks of all EU member states comprise the larger European System of Central Banks. The latter will become identical to the Eurosystem when, if ever, all EU member states participate fully in EMU.

From the outset, the ECB has pursued a monetary policy aimed primarily at maintaining price stability (defined as an inflation rate below but close to 2 percent). Initially, there was little inflationary pressure throughout the eurozone, apart from some hot spots such as Ireland. The disparity in economic performance and inflationary pressures between Ireland and Germany, the weightiest economy in the eurozone, highlighted a concern about EMU: the suitability of a "one-size-fits-all" monetary policy for national economies that in some respects seemed to be diverging rather than converging.

Box 13.2   Responsibilities of the European Central Bank and the Eurosystem

- Define and implement monetary policy for the euro area.
- Conduct foreign exchange operations.
- Hold and manage the official foreign reserves of participating member states.
- Promote the smooth operation of payment systems.
- Authorize the issue of euro banknotes and coins by national central banks in the euro area.
- Contribute to financial stability and supervision through monitoring, assessing, and advising national authorities.

Given such diversity, monetary tightening or loosening would obviously affect countries in different ways at different times. Managing the single currency, like preparing for it, imposes costs that are unevenly spread among participating states. In extreme cases, an economic shock in one country could prompt a response from the ECB that would disadvantage another country; alternatively, the ECB's refusal to respond to a regional economic shock could undermine support for the ECB. Without financial transfers to compensate those parts of the eurozone in recession, and with relatively little cross-border labor mobility and strong constraints on the use of national fiscal instruments, the ECB's likely response to asymmetrical shocks has assumed great political importance.

Apart from such extreme cases, precisely because of the difference in size between the Irish and German economies (to return to that example), the ECB was bound to pay much more attention to developments in Germany than in Ireland when formulating its monetary policy, inevitably giving rise to accusations of a pro-German bias. With the sluggish performance of the German economy and the boom in Ireland in the early 2000s, Germany could have benefited from lower interest rates and Ireland from higher ones. If anything, the ECB seemed divorced from the reality of economic circumstances in the eurozone, not least in Germany, the country in which it is located. Poor economic performance and high unemployment in Germany cried out for fiscal and monetary policy incentives as well as domestic structural reforms. Ideology and party politics limited the possibility of domestic reforms, the Stability and Growth Pact (SGP) constrained the government's fiscal policy options, and the ECB's independence and fixation on price stability meant that a loose monetary policy was unlikely.

Frustration boiled over in Germany soon after the launch of monetary union when Oskar Lafontaine, a populist Social Democrat and finance minister in the new Green–Social Democratic coalition government, publicly attacked the ECB for its tight monetary policy, which, he claimed, exacerbated unemployment. An old-fashioned socialist, Lafontaine broke the golden rule by publicly criticizing an independent institution, especially such a fragile institution as the new ECB. The ensuing scandal caused Lafontaine to resign and strengthened the credibility of the ECB, which had refused to cave in to political pressure.

Reflecting the credibility and maturity of both EMU and the ECB, governments and financial markets have become less sensitive over the years to public criticism of the bank. That explains the bank's studied indifference and the euro's continued strength in the face of calls by French president Nicolas Sarkozy, beginning in 2007, for a looser monetary policy (to stimulate economic activity and help generate jobs) and for stronger economic government in the eurozone (code for political interference in the bank's operations). However, the bank was less sanguine in June 2009 when German chancellor Angela

Merkel criticized it in response to the financial crisis. The bank took Merkel more seriously than it did Sarkozy because of the unprecedented nature of her criticism and because German support is crucial for the success of EMU. The fact that Merkel openly criticized the bank, as Sarkozy frequently did (although for very different reasons), at least suggested that the ECB was indeed acting independently of the eurozone's two most powerful governments.

Politicians and businesspeople who are unhappy with prevailing monetary policy tend to direct their anger at "Brussels" as well as "Frankfurt," thereby fueling Euroskepticism and calling the legitimacy of the ECB into question. This relates to a wider, long-standing problem of democratic accountability in the EU. The legitimacy of the ECB is especially touchy because its decisions have a profound impact throughout the eurozone. The European Parliament is the bank's official interlocutor at the European level. Regular meetings with the EP's Committee on Economic and Monetary Affairs have helped to build support for the ECB.

Concerns about the bank's legitimacy and policies have made it imperative for ECB board members to give frequent speeches, interviews, and press conferences about the bank's policy goals and instruments. ECB president Jean Claude Trichet has been a much more effective communicator than his predecessor. He is adept at signaling likely interest rate changes without alarming the markets. Trichet became a high-profile and reassuring media figure during the financial crisis, appearing often at international meetings alongside US Federal Reserve chairman Ben Bernanke.

The global financial crisis was a true test of the euro's acceptance and durability. Beyond that, the success of EMU could be gauged by the extent to which it helped to promote structural economic reform. Modest economic growth indeed followed the launch of Stage III, due to the abolition of currency conversion costs between participating countries and (after the launch of the euro) greater price transparency. Similarly, the removal of currency barriers stimulated some additional cross-border shopping. Yet proponents of EMU exaggerated the benefits to transnational trade. Business and consumer spending did not increase appreciably. Nor did prices converge in the eurozone, not least because of vastly different tax rates among member states.

A more significant issue was whether EMU would spur sustained economic growth and make a serious dent in unemployment. That would depend not only on global economic circumstances but also on whether EMU would trigger major economic and financial restructuring in participating states. The Lisbon strategy, launched in 2000 (a year after the launch of the euro), subsumed the reform potential of EMU under its broad umbrella. The fact that the EU launched the Lisbon strategy, however, implies a realization among national governments that major economic reform would not follow automatically in the wake of EMU, or that the single market and EMU alone were inadequate to bring about the desired results. Many governments, especially the French government, soon perceived EMU as hindering economic growth by restraining government spending. In particular, they resisted strict implementation of the Stability and Growth Pact.

The Stability and Growth Pact. The SGP imposes a political and legal obligation on members of the eurozone. Politically, they agree to participate in peer review (and therefore to accept peer pressure) through a budget surveillance process to help ensure that they do not run an excessive deficit (defined as greater than 3 percent of GDP). Eurozone governments submit annual stability programs, which Ecofin (the council of finance ministers) examines. Ecofin may trigger an "early warning mechanism" if it is concerned about a country's budgetary situation. In the event that a country exceeds the permissible percentage point, Ecofin may invoke the "excessive deficit procedure," which includes the possibility of fining errant member states.

When national leaders agreed to the SGP in 1997, they presumed that their countries' economic circumstances would improve after the launch of the euro. Most countries were in reasonably good shape by the late 1990s, but the economic downturn early in the new decade strained public finances. France and Germany (architect of the SGP) approached and soon exceeded the 3 percent limit (in Germany's case, reunification was still a huge economic drain).

Ireland, by contrast, had a budget surplus of no less than 4.6 percent of GDP. Yet the European Commission publicly rebuked Ireland in February 2001 for having loosened its fiscal policy. It seemed bizarre for the Commission to take the EU's best economic performer to task, but the incident suggested that the Commission would police the SGP vigilantly. Indeed, in July 2002 the Commission launched the excessive deficit procedure against Portugal for having run up a deficit of 4.2 percent the previous year. Portugal and Ireland were small, relatively uninfluential member states. Would the Commission act as aggressively against large member states? All eyes turned to France and Germany, whose deficits for 2002 were projected to exceed 3 percent of GDP.

As their budgetary situation deteriorated, France and Germany, traditionally in the vanguard of European integration, complained bitterly about the futility and illogicality of the SGP. They may have had a point: sticking rigidly to an arbitrarily chosen indicator for fiscal management ignored prevailing economic circumstances and could be counterproductive. The Germans also claimed that if their contribution to the EU budget were taken into consideration, they would comfortably come under the 3 percent limit. Other governments, especially those struggling to meet the limit, were unsympathetic; so was the ECB, which argued that the credibility of EMU rested on governments respecting the pact. The Commission as a whole was equally adamant, although Romano Prodi, its president, caused considerable embarrassment when he called the SGP "stupid."[33]

Prodi's dismissal of the SGP was less damaging than it could have been. If anything, the reaction to it strengthened the determination of the Commission to impose the SGP's rules. Matters came to a head in November 2003, the second successive year in which France and Germany exceeded the 3 percent limit, when the Commission tried to censure them at a meeting of Ecofin. France and Germany promptly marshaled the requisite number of Council votes to reject the Commission's proposal, whereupon the Commission brought the Council to the Court of Justice for exceeding its authority.

The Court ruled against the Council in July 2004. But it was a Pyrrhic victory for the Commission. With France and Germany unapologetic, although eager to restore their public finances to good health, in effect the SGP remained in abeyance. Revelations in November 2004 that Greece had misled the EU about the state of its public finances in 2000, when it had applied to participate in Stage III of EMU, cast further discredit on the eurozone's fiscal framework. The Commission agreed to revise the SGP, taking account of the need for countries to make credible commitments and the reality of the political and economic pressures that they face. The changes eventually approved by the European Council in March 2005 kept the 3 percent reference point for budget deficits but gave members of the eurozone ample room for maneuver. However, France's and Germany's disregard of the SGP had raised questions about the credibility and long-term viability of EMU.

Yet the budget trials of the early 2000s were nothing compared to the tribulations later in the decade. Ireland, a shining example of economic growth and fiscal responsibility as recently as 2006, was mired in recession and running up a double-digit deficit by 2009. The Commission's efforts to police the SGP assumed an air of unreality. As the Commission noted dryly in a statement in June 2009, for most member states "budgetary positions are estimated to deteriorate markedly, reflecting the ongoing recession and the economic stimulus packages adopted in line with the Economic Recovery Plan that called for timely and targeted fiscal measures in Member States with fiscal room for maneuver."[34]

The Commission could only wring its hands and hope that countries would come back into compliance with the SGP at the earliest possible moment. Economic and monetary affairs commissioner Joaquín Almunia was resigned to the situation, observing that "national budgetary positions in the EU and elsewhere have deteriorated considerably in the last year [2008] and will deteriorate even more this year on account of the recession and of the stimulus packages appropriately put in place. . . . To limit the costs of the debt for generations present and future, [however], it is crucial that governments devise an adjustment path whereby they commit to correct public deficits from the moment the economy starts to recover."[35] Almunia spoke well before the EU discovered that Greece's 2009 budget deficit was a whopping 13.6 percent of GDP.

The Commission was not alone in its concern. Germany grew increasingly alarmed about the precarious state of public finances in the eurozone as the recession deepened. Indeed, Germany passed a constitutional amendment in 2009 that, beginning in 2016, would generally prohibit the federal government from running a budget deficit above 0.35 percent of GDP over the economic cycle. In the meantime France, whose budget deficit had exceeded 3 percent for several years, seemed uninterested in making the sacrifices necessary to put its finances in order, especially during a severe economic downturn.

Enlarging the Eurozone

Notwithstanding the shenanigans over the Stability and Growth Pact, the eurozone seemed more likely to expand than to contract. No country would seriously contemplate leaving the eurozone—the costs, in terms of a possible default on euro-denominated debt, a currency devaluation, and the restoration of the old currency, were simply too high. Nor could any country be kicked out. Britain and Denmark always had the option of entering Stage III (presuming that they met the convergence criteria), and Sweden, never having officially opted out, was obliged to participate in Stage III whenever it met the criteria. Sweden avoided doing so by staying out of the original and modified versions of the exchange rate mechanism (see Box 13.3).

Denmark held a referendum in September 2000 on whether to adopt the euro; 53 percent voted against. As usual in such cases, the result reflected general dissatisfaction with the EU rather than specific concerns about EMU. The national debate before the referendum had as much to do with sovereignty, identity, the role of Germany, and possible cuts in social welfare as with the euro. Nevertheless, a majority of Danes simply did not want to give up their own currency, at least not until the financial crisis struck. By that time, Denmark's prime minister was pressing for a second referendum, citing concerns that Denmark had less influence in the EU because it was not a full EMU participant.

Box 13.3   The Revised Exchange Rate Mechanism

The revised exchange rate mechanism (ERM II) is the successor to the original exchange rate mechanism established in 1979 as part of the European Monetary System. Under ERM II, participating currencies may fluctuate within a specified margin (plus or minus 15 percent) around a stable but adjustable central rate. When necessary, a currency is supported by intervention (buying or selling) to maintain the exchange rate within those limits. ERM II aims both to ensure that exchange rate fluctuations between the euro and other EU currencies do not disrupt the single market and to help countries prepare to join the euro area. As of 2010, Denmark, Estonia, Latvia, and Lithuania had participated in ERM II.

Source: Adapted from *EU Focus*, Issue No. 28, January 2009.

The Swedish government was equally concerned about the political costs of staying outside the eurozone and arranged for a referendum on the issue in September 2003. The debate in Sweden was similar to that in Denmark. So was the result: 56 percent against. However, the government in Sweden seemed unmoved by the global financial turmoil at the end of the decade and still did not want to adopt the euro.

Tony Blair, prime minister when the euro was launched, made no secret of his preference for British participation in Stage III of EMU, but Gordon Brown, chancellor of the exchequer (finance minister) at the time, was skeptical. In order to put the question of Britain's eurozone membership on as objective a footing as possible, the government promised that Britain would not join without first holding a referendum based on a set of five economic tests for adopting the euro:

1. *Convergence:* Are British and eurozone business cycles and economic structures compatible? Could Britain live comfortably with euro interest rates?
2. *Flexibility:* If problems arose, would Britain be able to make quick economic adjustments?
3. *Investment:* Would joining the eurozone draw investment to Britain?
4. *Financial services:* Would joining the eurozone benefit Britain's financial services industry, particularly its wholesale markets?
5. *Employment and general economic performance:* Would joining the eurozone promote higher growth and more employment?

Regardless of the tests, public opinion in Britain is firmly against adopting the euro. A populist "Save the Pound" campaign feeds a virulent Euroskeptical movement. Not even the financial crisis helped to change British minds.

By contrast, most of the countries that joined the EU in 2004 and 2007 were eager to adopt the euro as soon as possible. Although there were marked variations in economic performance among the new member states, meeting the criteria for monetary union initially seemed possible in most cases: inflation rates were generally low, public finances were by and large sound, the margins of ERM II were generous (15 percent), and interest rates were converging. Familiarity with the euro in the new member states would undoubtedly help. But not all necessarily wanted to give up their own currency. As is the case in Britain, Denmark, and Sweden, many people in the new member states were concerned about national sovereignty and identity. Nevertheless, almost all of the countries that joined the EU in 2004 hoped to adopt the euro by 2010 at the latest.

Slovenia was the first to do so, in January 2007; Malta and Cyprus, the smallest of the new member states, followed suit in January 2008; and Slovakia joined the monetary union in January 2009 (see Box 13.4). The remaining new EU members, including Bulgaria and Romania, which joined in 2007, had difficulty meeting the convergence criteria, because of poor public finances, high inflation, or both. Lithuania was rebuffed for eurozone membership in 2006. Apart from Slovenia, the other Central and Eastern European countries still outside the eurozone did not push to join the monetary union. Although it has no bearing on their prospects for monetary union membership, Estonia, Latvia, Lithuania, and Bulgaria have pegged their currencies to the euro, in effect giving up monetary policy independence. (Although it has no bearing on their prospects for EU membership, Montenegro and Kosovo have simply adopted the euro as their currency.)

The onset of the financial crisis in 2007 increased the eagerness of the new Central and Eastern European member states to participate fully in EMU. Variously described as a port in a storm or a big ship in rough seas, the eurozone seemingly offered protection from speculative attacks and the corresponding need for high interest rates during the global financial crisis. Small countries, including Iceland—badly buffeted by the financial crisis and not even an EU member—desperately wanted to enter the relative safety of the eurozone.

Yet precisely because of the financial crisis, the EU was not about to relax the convergence criteria and facilitate quick entry for vulnerable countries. Iceland was not a serious contender unless it first joined the EU. Of the Central and Eastern European countries still outside the eurozone but wanting to get in, Latvia's hopes were dashed by a ballooning public deficit and economic collapse, leading to an IMF bailout in December 2008. Estonia and Lithuania struggled with financial and economic deterioration that pushed off the possibility of eurozone membership until 2012 at the earliest. Hungary was in bad shape throughout the 2000s because of serious economic mismanagement, which threw its public finances way out of line. Despite having fared relatively

---

Box 13.4   Slovakia Meets the Convergence Criteria and Adopts the Euro

The Commission and European Central Bank conducted a convergence assessment in May 2008 and recommended that Slovakia join the monetary union. The Council agreed in June 2008, paving the way for Slovakia's membership in January 2009.
According to the convergence assessment:

- Slovakia's twelve-month average rate of inflation was 2.2 percent, well below the 3.2 percent reference rate for the euro area.
- Slovakia's deficit of 2.2 percent of GDP, and debt of 24.9 percent of GDP, were well within acceptable limits.
- Slovakia's long-term interest rate over the previous year was 4.5 percent, below the reference rate of 6.5 percent.
- The Slovak koruna had participated successfully in ERM II since November 2005.

Source: Adopted from *EU Focus,* Issue No. 28, January 2009.

well during the downturn, Poland nonetheless increased public borrowing beyond the threshold for eurozone membership. Faced also with a difficult political situation—entry would require a constitutional amendment—the Polish government deferred until at least 2012 its planned adoption of the euro. Similarly, the financial crisis damaged the Czech Republic's prospects of participating in monetary union, although the country's economic fundamentals were quite sound. Bulgaria and Romania, late EU entrants, were not serious candidates for eurozone entry.

Despite their straitened circumstances, some of the Central and Eastern European outsiders were irate that the Commission held so rigidly to the convergence criteria, not least because the Commission was relaxing the rules on budget deficits for existing eurozone members. Moreover, the criteria seemed less and less relevant to the situation facing the EU in the late 2000s. Collectively, the aspiring members would add less than 10 percent to the GDP of the existing eurozone. Even with higher-than-average inflation rates, their participation in monetary union would not raise the eurozone average by much. Nor did it seem fair to base the inflation criterion on the performance of the three EU countries with the lowest rates, when some of those countries, such as Britain and Sweden, were outside the eurozone. In the event, inflation became less of a concern during the recession, whereas budget deficits assumed even greater importance. Despite (or perhaps because of) the poor state of public finances among existing eurozone members, the Commission insisted on holding the aspiring members strictly to the convergence criterion of a deficit no greater than 3 percent of GDP.

The Financial Crisis

The period 2007–2010 was an exciting time to be a central banker, as the financial crisis and ensuing economic recession posed a challenge not experienced since the Great Depression of the 1930s. The challenges were especially acute for the ECB, a new institution still establishing itself both regionally (within the eurozone) and globally. Moreover, unlike central banks outside the eurozone, the ECB did not operate in a system with a single government and a common fiscal policy. Whereas the ECB could act decisively in the area of monetary policy for the entire eurozone, national governments, prompted by the Commission, would have to coordinate fiscal measures to complement the ECB's actions. Slow and sometimes inadequate fiscal coordination hindered the eurozone's response to the crisis. By contrast, the ECB acted decisively and responsibly, and emerged from the crisis with its credibility and standing greatly enhanced.

At the onset of the crisis, in August 2007, the ECB injected almost €95 billion in overnight funds into the financial system in order to ease credit flows. The ECB's action caught other central banks by surprise and signaled an aggressive approach to combating the crisis. During the next two years, the

ECB's strategy of "enhanced credit support" provided additional liquidity by giving emergency help to eurozone banks rather than buying assets outright, as the US Federal Reserve and the Bank of England were doing. Nevertheless, the ECB also ventured into what its US and British counterparts called "quantitative easing," an unorthodox form of monetary policy that seeks to stimulate economic recovery by purchasing government bonds and other assets—a practice that critics decry as printing money.

Specifically, in May 2009 the bank decided to buy over €60 billion worth of covered bonds, high-quality securities that are a major source of mortgage finance in Europe. The move was controversial. Within the ECB, a number of governing council members, including the head of the German central bank, reportedly objected strenuously to what they saw as an unconventional operation that would inflate the money supply. The action brought a swift and highly unusual rebuke from Chancellor Merkel, who claimed that the ECB was caving in to international pressure and conforming to the irresponsible practices of the US Federal Reserve and the Bank of England. "We must return to independent and sensible monetary policies," Merkel proclaimed, "otherwise we will be back to where we are now in ten years' time."[36]

While flooding the financial system with liquidity, initially the ECB was slow to lower interest rates, a conventional way of dealing with an economic slowdown. In that respect, the bank also acted differently from its two main international counterparts. Concerned about inflation, which peaked at over 4 percent in mid-2008 (well above the 2 percent reference point and the highest in eurozone history), the ECB raised interest rates in July of that year—nearly twelve months after the onset of the financial crisis—to 4.25 percent. At a time when the rapidly deteriorating economic situation called for a substantial cut in interest rates, the ECB was moving in the opposite direction. Once again, critics claimed that the bank was blinded by its obsession with price stability.

The bank began cutting interest rates in October 2008; by May 2009 the main rate was 1 percent (after seven cuts in eight months). By that time also, inflation had fallen to zero. It turned negative—stoking fears of deflation—in July 2009. The bank held the line at 1 percent during the worst of the economic recession, deflation did not happen, and inflation gradually returned at a rate still below the 2 percent target.

The financial crisis was an inauspicious time to commemorate the tenth anniversary of the euro, in January 2009. Nevertheless, the ECB had much to celebrate. The bank was helping to relieve congested money markets, although the credit crunch was still acute. Falling interest rates were beginning to have a salutary economic effect. Perhaps most noteworthy of all, the financial crisis had not torn the eurozone apart, as some doomsayers had predicted or hoped that it would. Nevertheless, the crisis highlighted serious weaknesses in the common monetary policy.

One of the most striking of these is the fact that the eurozone has sixteen separate bond markets. As the crisis deepened, a large spread began to open between the yield on German government bonds, which the market perceived as safe, and those of less fiscally responsible eurozone countries, notably Italy, Greece, and Ireland. What would happen if one of those countries were unable to repay its debt? The ECB may not finance deficits, and countries may not assume the debts of others in the eurozone. Would Germany nonetheless intervene somehow in order to prevent a potentially disastrous financial collapse in a eurozone member? The question became urgent in early 2010 when Greece, running a budget deficit of over 13 percent of GDP and facing entrenched public resistance to government-imposed austerity measures, teetered on the brink of bankruptcy.

Clearly, there was no contingency for dealing with a sovereign default. That led to speculation about setting up a European Monetary Fund for the eurozone, analogous to the International Monetary Fund in the global system. There was talk also of having a common euro bond instead of separate national bonds. Both prospects seemed uncongenial to Germany, whose taxpayers would end up bearing a higher burden. Germany's seeming indifference to Greece's plight caused a deep rift among eurozone members and led to accusations that Germany's own economic model of export-led growth and relatively low domestic spending was a major cause of imbalance in the eurozone. EU leaders failed to respond adequately to the Greek crisis at an extraordinary summit in February 2010 but finally reached agreement at their regular spring summit a month later on a mechanism "to safeguard financial stability in the euro area as a whole" in the event of a possible national default. At Merkel's insistence, the mechanism, made up mostly of loans from eurozone members, would include some financing from the IMF. All agreed that the proposed mechanism was a temporary solution and recognized "the need to strengthen and complement the existing framework to ensure fiscal sustainability in the euro zone and enhance its capacity to act in times of crises."[37]

A positive outcome of the Greek crisis was a realization on the part of the less fiscally responsible governments that monetary union did not shield them from market pressures to bring their deficits and debts under control. The higher cost of issuing debt, or the prospect of no longer being able to borrow money, provided a powerful incentive to introduce fiscal reforms. The political price of cutting government expenditure, and therefore cutting welfare programs, would be hard to bear, but arguably was better than being outside the eurozone, where the costs of public borrowing for the countries in question would be much higher.

The Greek crisis raised anew the tricky issue of economic governance in the eurozone. The Eurogroup—the unofficial council of finance ministers of countries that participate in monetary union—is the main political body for coordinating policy in parallel with the activities of the ECB. Because it is not an official council, the presidency of the Eurogroup does not rotate, giving it an unusual degree of continuity.

The French have long been dissatisfied not with the existence of the Eurogroup but with the lack of a higher, more powerful body that would interact—or interfere—with the ECB. The financial crisis gave President Sarkozy an opportunity to reiterate that point. Speaking in the EP in October 2008, Sarkozy called for an economic government in the eurozone, to which the ECB would be answerable. "The [Eurogroup] is not up to the task," Sarkozy claimed; only the national leaders have the "democratic legitimacy . . . to form a government worthy of this name."[38] Sarkozy suggested that economic governance become the preserve of special summits of the leaders of countries in the eurozone, two of which took place during the financial crisis to deal with specific aspects of it.

Sarkozy's statement reflected the French tradition of political interference in monetary policymaking and long-standing French concerns that the ECB's conduct of monetary policy places undue emphasis on fighting inflation at the expense of economic growth. Other prominent supporters of stronger economic government are less interested in pressuring the ECB than in improving fiscal policy coordination and promoting economic reform. Thus Joschka Fischer, a former German foreign minister and prime mover of the defunct Constitutional Treaty, wrote during the financial crisis that "institutionally, there is no way around a 'European economic government' or 'enhanced economic coordination' (or whatever you want to call it), which in fact would be possible informally and thus without any treaty change."[39]

The German political establishment may share Fischer's opinion, but not Sarkozy's goal. Merkel has repeatedly distanced herself from Sarkozy's calls for better economic government, seeing in them a veiled attempt to assert political control over the ECB. Despite her criticism of the ECB during the financial crisis, in general Merkel respects the bank's anti-inflationary efforts and appreciates Trichet's behavior, which is more characteristic of a German than a French central banker. Nevertheless Merkel and others agree that members of the eurozone need to coordinate their fiscal policies more closely in order to prevent the kind of misalignment that occurred during the financial crisis.

The International Role of the Euro and Representation of the Eurozone

Despite the impact of the Greek crisis, which caused the euro to lose value against the dollar in late 2009 and early 2010, the euro remains one of the most stable currencies in the world. It is attractive globally because of the economic weight of the eurozone, the political stability of the EU, and the ECB's sound monetary policy. The euro is the world's second reserve currency, after the US dollar. Just as they view the external value of the dollar as a sign of the EU's strength, many EU politicians and officials relish the prospect of the euro one day displacing the dollar as the world's leading reserve currency. Such hopes may eventually be realized, but not in the near future. Despite the decline in its external value, the US dollar is still the currency that most countries prefer to hold. As long as the eurozone remains politically weak and economically fragmented, and as long as global commodity prices are denominated in dollars, the status quo is unlikely to change.

ECB president Jean Claude Trichet speaks authoritatively for the eurosystem both at home and abroad. Who speaks for the eurozone as an economic entity? The EU is overrepresented and misrepresented in most international organizations. For instance, the Commission president and European Council president represent the EU in the G20, but Britain, France, Germany, and Italy are members of the G20 as well. The big member states keep their seats at the table while having a major say in the EU's position, which is represented separately from them. As a result, the EU's voice on global economic issues is sometimes cacophonous and unclear.

The secretary of the US Treasury has multiple interlocutors in EU-US discussions on fiscal and economic policy, including the commissioner for economic and monetary affairs, the Eurogroup president, the Ecofin president, and various national finance ministers. In corresponding discussions dealing with monetary policy, by contrast, the chairman of the US Federal Reserve and the president of the ECB are the sole interlocutors. Similarly, in global forums on monetary policy, the ECB president speaks clearly and distinctly for the eurozone. On issues of substance and not just representation, the coherence of monetary policymaking in the eurozone contrasts strikingly with the inconsistency of financial and economic policymaking, arguably to the detriment of the EU's regional and global interests.

▓ Notes

1. European Commission, "A Single Market for the 21st Century," November 20, 2007, p. 1.

2. Wolfgang Münchau, "Time to Safeguard Europe's Single Market," *Financial Times,* June 1, 2009, p. 10.

3. European Commission, "Completing the Internal Market: White Paper from the Commission to the European Council," COM(85)210 final, June 14, 1985.

4. For an assessment of the wider implications of the case, see Karen Alter and Sophie Meunier-Aitsahalia, "Judicial Politics in the European Community: European Integration and the Pathbreaking Cassis de Dijon Decision," *Comparative Political Studies* 24, no. 4 (1996): 535–561.

5. European Commission, "Corporate Governance: Member States Reluctant to Give a Greater Say to Shareholders in the Context of Takeover Bids, Says Commission

Report," February 27, 2007, http://europa.eu/rapid/pressReleasesAction.do?reference=IP/07/251&format=HTML&aged=0&language=EN&guiLanguage=en.

6. Bruno de Witt, "Setting the Scene: How Did Services Get to Bolkestein and Why?" Law Working Paper no. 2007/20 (Florence: European University Institute, 2007).

7. European Commission, "Financial Services: Turning the Corner," 10th report, June 2, 2004, p. 1.

8. Heinz Zourek, director-general of DG Enterprise and Industry, speech on the occasion of the twentieth anniversary of the "New Approach," Brussels, November 30, 2005, http://ec.europa.eu/enterprise/newapproach/pdf/zourek_speech_anniversary_naga.pdf.

9. Günther Verheugen, commissioner for enterprise and industry, speech on the occasion of the twentieth anniversary of the "New Approach," Brussels, November 30, 2005, http://ec.europa.eu/enterprise/newapproach/pdf/verheugen_%20speech_%20anniversary_%20naga.pdf (emphasis in original).

10. See European Commission, "The Internal Market for Goods: A Cornerstone of Europe's Competitiveness," February 14, 2007, http://eur-lex.europa.eu/LexUriServ/site/en/com/2007/com2007_0035en01.pdf.

11. European Commission, "Interpretative Communication on Car Registration for Motor Vehicles Originating in Another Member State," SEC(2007)169 final, February 14, 2007, http://ec.europa.eu/enterprise/regulation/goods/car_registration/docs/sec_2007_169_en.pdf.

12. European Commission, "Action Plan for the Single Market," CSE(97)1, June 4, 1997.

13. European Commission, "The Internal Market: Ten Years Without Frontiers," January 2003, http://ec.europa.eu/internal_market/10years/docs/workingdoc/workingdoc_en.pdf.

14. European Commission, "A Citizens' Agenda: Delivering Results for Europe," May 10, 2006, http://eur-lex.europa.eu/LexUriServ/LexUriServ.do?uri=COM:2006:0211:FIN:EN:PDF.

15. See "Commission Unveils Its Vision for a Modern Single Market for All," November 20, 2007, http://europa.eu/rapid/pressReleasesAction.do?reference=IP/07/1728&format=HTML&aged=0&language=EN&guiLanguage=en.

16. See Michelle Cini and Lee McGowan, *Competition Policy in the European Union*, 2nd ed. (Basingstoke: Palgrave Macmillan, 2008).

17. Leon Brittan, "Competition Law: Its Importance to the European Community and to International Trade," speech at the University of Chicago Law School, April 24, 1992, p. 8.

18. Neelie Kroes, "Preliminary Thoughts on Policy Review of Article 82," speech at the Fordham Corporate Law Institute, New York, September 23, 2005, http://europa.eu/rapid/pressReleasesAction.do?reference=SPEECH/05/537.

19. Quoted in "Brussels Plays Down Competition Policy Fears," *EurActiv*, June 27, 2007, http://www.euractiv.com/en/competition/brussels-plays-eu-treaty-competition-fears/article-164974.

20. Neelie Kroes, "No Question of Downgrading Competition Policy," June 27, 2007, http://www.europarl.europa.eu/sides/getDoc.do?language=EN&type=IM-PRESS&reference=20070626IPR08389.

21. European Commission, "Competition: Commission Publishes 2008 Annual Report on Competition Policy," August 19, 2009, http://europa.eu/rapid/pressReleasesAction.do?reference=IP/09/1241&format=HTML&aged=0&language=EN&guiLanguage=en.

22. European Commission, "Antitrust: Commission Fines Car Glass Producers over €1.3 Billion for Market Sharing Cartel," November 12, 2008, http://europa.eu/rapid/pressReleasesAction.do?reference=IP/08/1685&guiLanguage=en.

23. See Kelyn Bacon, ed., *European Community Law of State Aid* (Oxford: Oxford University Press, 2009); and Conor Quigley, *European State Aid Law and Policy,* 2nd ed. (Portland: Hart, 2009).

24. See European Commission, "State Aid: Commission Launches Consultations on Simplified Rules for Block Exemptions," April 24, 2007.

25. See European Commission, "Report on Competition Policy 2008," COM(2009)374 final, July 23, 2009, pp. 9–10.

26. See ibid., pp. 9–11.

27. Quoted in *Financial Times,* July 26, 2004, p. 26.

28. See Mats A. Bergman, Malcolm B. Coate, Maria Jakobsson, and Shawn W. Ulrick, "Atlantic Divide or Gulf Stream Convergence: Merger Policies in the European Union and the United States," December 20, 2007, https://editorialexpress.com/cgi-bin/conference/download.cgi?db_name=IIOC2008&paper_id=341.

29. Mario Monti, "Convergence in EU-US Antitrust Policy Regarding Mergers and Acquisitions: An EU Perspective," speech at the University of California–Los Angeles, February 24, 2004, p. 2.

30. See Michele Chang. *Monetary Integration in the European Union* (Basingstoke: Palgrave Macmillan, 2009); Madeline O. Hosli, *The Euro: A Concise Introduction to European Monetary Integration* (Boulder: Lynne Rienner, 2005); Otmar Issing, *The Birth of the Euro* (Cambridge: Cambridge University Press, 2009); and David Marsh, *The Euro: The Politics of the New Global Currency* (New Haven: Yale University Press, 2009).

31. Massimo Beber, "'One Careful Driver from New': Earning the European Central Bank's No-Claims Bonus," *Journal of Common Market Studies* 40, *Annual Review* (September 2002): 75.

32. David Marsh, "Trichet Needs Help to Deliver the Bad News," *Financial Times,* May 5, 2009, p. 9.

33. Quoted in *Financial Times,* November 2, 2002. On the Stability and Growth Pact, see Marco Buti and Gabriele Giudice, "Maastricht's Fiscal Rules at Ten: An Assessment," *Journal of Common Market Studies* 40, no. 5 (December 2002): 823–848; Paul De Grauwe, "Challenges for Monetary Policy in Euroland," *Journal of Common Market Studies* 40, no. 4 (November 2002): 693–718.

34. European Commission, "Commission Assesses Remainder Stability and Convergence Programs," June 24, 2009, http://europa.eu/rapid/pressReleasesAction.do?reference=IP/09/990.

35. Ibid.

36. Quoted in *Financial Times,* June 3, 2009, p. 1.

37. Council of the European Union, "Statement by the Heads of State and Government of the Euro Area," Brussels, March 25, 2010.

38. Quoted in *Europolitics,* October 22, 2008.

39. Joschka Fischer, "Europe in Reverse," *Project Syndicate,* March 9, 2009, http://www.project-syndicate.org/commentary/fischer36.

14 Economic Performance: Growth and Jobs

The European Union is usually portrayed as a single economic entity, but there is no single European economic model. The nature of the market economy differs in Europe from country to country. Some European countries put greater emphasis on social equality, and some are more successful at achieving that goal. Despite these differences, the term "European social model" applies to a general preference among Europeans for generous welfare provision.

Europe's social model is expensive. Concerns about its affordability grew in the 1990s, a decade of intensifying globalization and generally sluggish economic performance. It was also a decade when the EU began to face a related demographic and economic challenge. Europe's population was falling, while average life expectancy was rising. Relatively high unemployment and earlier retirement increased the burden of dependency: those in the workforce had to support (through taxes) larger numbers of unemployed and retired people. In response, European political and business leaders sought to boost productivity in the hope that higher economic growth would translate into more and better jobs for European workers.

By contrast, productivity and employment surged in the United States in the 1990s. Eager to move in the same direction, EU leaders made a bold—some would say rash—commitment at a summit meeting in Lisbon in March 2000: within ten years they would transform the EU into "the most competitive and dynamic knowledge-based economy in the world, capable of sustainable economic growth and more and better jobs."[1]

Language of that sort was more familiar to American than European ears. Indeed, the Lisbon goal was a tacit acknowledgment that the EU had to adopt a more aggressive, US-style approach. Not surprisingly, it was the leaders of member states already in the throes of sweeping economic reform who advocated the so-called Lisbon strategy, hoping to push the EU as a whole toward greater market liberalization and less government intervention.

415

Yet the Lisbon strategy and its successor, Europe 2020, do not seek higher growth at any cost. They include the goal of "greater social cohesion," a concept alien to the United States but beloved in the EU, and a commitment to environmental sustainability. The Lisbon strategy rests on three pillars—economic, social, and environmental—and aims to fashion an EU that is prosperous, socially just, and environmentally sound.

Boosting economic growth and generating more and better jobs are easier said than done. Given that responsibility for pensions, health care, education, taxation, and the like rests with national governments, the EU's efforts to boost growth and employment depend greatly on the open method of coordination (OMC), an elaborate procedure that includes national reporting, multilateral surveillance, peer review, and guidelines for better performance. The OMC involves intensive interaction among the social partners (workers' and employers' representatives), the Commission, the European Parliament, EU advisory bodies, the Council of Ministers, and, at the apex of the system, the European Council.

Europe 2020 combines the OMC with a range of EU policy areas that directly affect economic performance. Foremost among these are the single market and monetary union, discussed in Chapter 13. Others include social policy and employment, enterprise and industry, research and development, and education and training. This chapter examines the nature and development of the Lisbon strategy and Europe 2020, before looking at each of these related policy areas.

◼ The Lisbon Strategy and Europe 2020

There was widespread agreement by the late 1990s that in order to sustain their high standards of living, EU member states would have to improve their economic performance and get many more people into the workforce. Although some EU countries performed extremely well, the EU as a whole continued to fall further behind the United States. Taking matters into their own hands, British prime minister Tony Blair and Spanish prime minister José Maria Aznar, leaders with a market-oriented, pro-business philosophy, urged Portugal, then in the Council presidency, to convene a special summit to inject new political life into economic integration. The summit took place in Lisbon in March 2000, and produced an overall goal for the EU, a set of targets, and a strategy for achieving them (see Box 14.1).

Achieving greater social cohesion, part of the Lisbon goal, would entail maintaining or even increasing welfare provision, which most EU countries could ill afford to do. Moreover, environmentally sustainable economic growth was an expensive objective. On the face of it, therefore, the Lisbon strategy was extremely audacious.

Box 14.1   The Lisbon Goal, Strategy, and Targets

Meeting in Lisbon in March 2000, the European Council set a goal for the EU *"to become the most competitive and dynamic knowledge-based economy in the world, capable of sustainable economic growth, with more and better jobs and greater social cohesion."* Meeting in Gothenburg in June 2001, the European Council expanded the Lisbon goal to include "sustainable development." Achieving this goal would require an overall strategy of three parts:

- Prepare the transition to a knowledge-based economy through better policies for the information society and research and development sector, accelerate the process of structural reform for competitiveness and innovation, and complete the internal market.
- Modernize the European social model, invest in people, and combat social exclusion.
- Sustain a healthy economic outlook and favorable growth prospects by applying an appropriate macroeconomic policy mix.

Specific targets for 2010 included:

- Annual economic growth of about 3 percent of GDP
- Creation of 20 million new jobs
- Overall employment rate of 70 percent
- Employment rate for women of over 60 percent
- Employment rate for older workers of 50 percent
- Overall spending on EU research and development approaching 3 percent of GDP, with two-thirds of it coming from the private sector (this target was set in March 2002)

Sources: Lisbon European Council, "Presidency Conclusions," March 2000; Gothenburg European Council, "Presidency Conclusions," June 2001; Barcelona European Council, "Presidency Conclusions," March 2002.

Yet the Lisbon targets were not necessarily new. Indeed, the summit conclusions were a patchwork of preexisting commitments in a variety of policy areas. The Lisbon strategy was part political exhortation and part procedural change. In order to keep up the pressure, EU leaders agreed to hold a special summit every spring to review progress, thereby putting the European Council at the institutional core of the Lisbon strategy.

Some of the Lisbon targets required EU legislation. The Lisbon summit and the follow-on summits were supposed to generate the political will necessary to overcome blocks in the decisionmaking process. The Lisbon strategy also included the OMC, a more flexible process involving benchmarking, best practices, and target-setting, in the hope that peer pressure would achieve progress in areas that did not fall within the EU's competence.

Business leaders strongly supported the Lisbon strategy but knew that EU summits tended to generate extravagant rhetoric. Moreover, the fact that French prime minister Lionel Jospin, a doctrinaire Socialist, had signed on to the strategy cannot have been reassuring. Nor was a statement by Nicole

Fontaine, president of the EP, warning EU leaders at the summit not to pursue "untrammeled capitalism and remorseless pursuit of profit at the expense of working men and women."[2]

The Commission enthusiastically endorsed the initiative, or at least internal market commissioner Frits Bolkestein did. An unabashed economic liberal, Bolkestein believed that "the best and probably the only way to raise our growth levels is to inject more competition into our markets and ensure that the most productive and innovative companies are generously rewarded."[3] Bolkestein and like-minded commissioners saw the Lisbon strategy as an opportunity to push their reform agenda. Thanks to their efforts, the Commission began to produce scorecards on the Lisbon strategy and played a vital part in the annual spring summits. In 2004, José Manuel Barroso made the success of the Lisbon strategy the leitmotif of his Commission presidency.

Barroso was quick to note that progress on reaching the Lisbon targets was decidedly mixed. France and Germany dragged their feet on energy and transportation liberalization, complained about the rigorous enforcement of competition policy, and turned toward old-fashioned industrial policy. Other member states, more comfortable with economic reform, became increasingly impatient. Business leaders, grateful for any progress, tried to maintain the momentum for change. Meanwhile, nearly every meeting of the European Council produced a ritualistic endorsement of either the Lisbon strategy as a whole or some aspect or another of the Lisbon goal. The gap between rhetoric and reality was glaring.

A high-level group under the leadership of former Dutch prime minister Wim Kok painted an unflattering picture. According to the group's report, the strategy was "too broad to be understood as an interconnected narrative. [It] is about everything and thus about nothing. Everybody is responsible and thus no one." The group decried the failure of the national governments "to act on the Lisbon strategy with sufficient urgency" and complained about the crowded agenda and poor coordination. The report concluded that "the task is to develop national policies in each Member State, supported by an appropriate European-wide framework . . . and then to act in a more concerted and determined way. . . . In the end, much of the Lisbon strategy depends on the progress made in national capitals. . . . Governments and especially their leaders must not duck their crucial responsibilities. Nothing less than the future prosperity of the European model is at stake."[4]

The report echoed a consensus in the Commission that a much smaller set of actions and priorities was in order. Many governments were eager to implement the Lisbon strategy, although none was blameless when it came to particular proposals. Nevertheless, France and Germany were a case apart, blithely promising to undertake domestic reforms but lacking the political will or ability to do so.

The Revised Lisbon Strategy

Drawing on the Kok Report, the Commission called for a radical overhaul of the Lisbon strategy in a scathing midterm review. The Commission urged "rigorous prioritization" of growth and employment through a new "Partnership for Growth and Jobs" between the EU and national levels. The partnership would be institutionalized through Integrated Policy Guidelines (proposed by the Commission and approved by the Council), consisting of the Community Lisbon Program (actions at the EU level) and the National Reform Programs (actions at the national level). The Commission also called on stakeholders— governments, employers, workers, nongovernmental organizations, consumers, and the like—to take "ownership" of the reform process.[5]

The European Council endorsed the Commission's review in March 2005, thereby relaunching the Lisbon strategy.[6] Realizing that the deadline for the original targets was largely unattainable, the European Council kept only two "headline targets" to be achieved by 2010:

- Overall employment rate of 70 percent
- Overall spending on research and development approaching 3 percent of GDP

At the same time, the European Council identified four priority areas for EU and national attention:

- Knowledge and innovation
- Business environment
- People and labor markets
- Energy and climate change

The EU dropped the inflated rhetoric of the original Lisbon declaration. As the Commission put it more modestly in 2005, "the key aim [of the revised Lisbon strategy] is getting into a rhythm of high sustainable annual growth and low unemployment by 2010." The Commission also downplayed the comparison with the United States, while nonetheless acknowledging the importance of closing "the competitive gap" across the Atlantic.[7]

The Commission soon produced the first Community Lisbon Program, in July 2005.[8] It consisted of fifty initiatives, grouped into eight "key measures":

- Support knowledge and innovation.
- Reform state aid policy.
- Simplify the regulatory framework.
- Complete the internal market for services.
- Complete the Doha Round of multilateral trade negotiations.

- Remove obstacles to physical, labor, and academic mobility.
- Develop a common approach to economic integration.
- Improve efforts to deal with the social effects of economic restructuring.

By repackaging a number of initiatives, the Commission hoped to generate political momentum within the Council and Parliament for their enactment or advancement by other means.

Later in 2005, the Council approved the first Integrated Policy Guidelines (2005–2007). The following year, governments produced their National Reform Programs, followed by annual reviews on implementation. The Commission also produced annual reviews on implementation of the Community Lisbon Program and the National Reform Programs, and a strategic report on the first cycle of the Integrated Policy Guidelines, which included recommendations for the next cycle (2008–2010). The Commission avoided identifying leaders and laggards in its press releases and published documents.

The gist of the annual reviews and the broader strategic review was that the revised Lisbon strategy was more effective than its predecessor; that governments were finally pursuing a reform agenda, but with varying levels of commitment; and that progress was being made at the EU level. Based on the Commission's reviews and other reports, the European Council assessed overall progress, issuing hortatory statements and providing a political push to areas in need of special attention.

The relaunch of the Lisbon strategy coincided with an economic improvement throughout the EU. Ireland and Spain continued to boom. Germany enjoyed higher economic growth, thanks to limited reforms implemented in the late 1990s and wage restraint. The new Central and Eastern European member states generally benefited from growing intra-EU trade and high foreign direct investment. The Commission claimed that "the Lisbon Strategy is contributing to the recent much improved performance of the EU economy. Structural reforms are starting to raise potential further growth, improving the long-term prospects for prosperity."[9] As a prominent economist observed, however, "countries continue to differ markedly in their enthusiasm for reform and it is far from clear that 'Lisbon' can take much credit for the . . . economic upturn."[10]

The subsequent economic downturn was less helpful. Not unexpectedly, by 2010 the EU had not achieved its two headline targets. Equally detrimental were widespread "reform fatigue," and specifically "Lisbon fatigue," throughout the EU. The Commission had tried to portray the Lisbon strategy in positive terms, as a chance to take advantage of the opportunities of globalization. The public was not reassured. For many Europeans, globalization has extremely negative connotations, which cynical politicians shamelessly exploited. Yet the same politicians had subscribed to the Lisbon strategy.

Europe 2020

Toward the end of his first term in office, Barroso seemed to back away from the Lisbon strategy. Yet his apparent change of heart may have had less to do with criticism from the left than from President Nicolas Sarkozy, who, despite his center-right ideology, grew increasingly reluctant to implement economic reform in France and highly critical of calls for economic reform in the EU. Barroso, who needed Sarkozy's support in order to be reappointed Commission president, saw which way the wind was blowing.

Even if it had enjoyed full public and political support, there was a limit to what the Lisbon strategy could have achieved. Arguably the strategy did not adequately address the complex relationship among competition, innovation, and growth, but merely presumed that collectively these three things would generate a virtuous circle and produce higher employment. A political economist studying the process concluded that "it is difficult to establish a direct and deterministic relationship between [the] market liberalization reforms of the Lisbon agenda and the targets for higher innovation, higher growth rates, and higher employment."[11]

Was the Lisbon strategy therefore a wasted effort? On the surface, the strategy was a caricature of how the EU works: endless meetings, studies, reviews, declarations, and exhortations, with few results. However, the process was relatively cost-free and probably politically worthwhile. It engaged EU and national officials in a continuous dialogue about best practices, benchmarks, goals, and targets; it applied peer pressure on poor performers to improve and adopt better procedures and processes; it drew attention to the gap between member states' economic potential and achievement; and it highlighted the need for higher productivity in the face of a shrinking population and a rising dependence ratio. Perhaps the most appropriate question to ask is how much worse off Europe would be without it.

A more confident Barroso promised after his reappointment as Commission president to pursue the Lisbon strategy more energetically. Yet the name "Lisbon strategy," with its connotation of neoliberalism and missed targets, was fatally compromised. EU leaders, reviewing the economic situation at their March 2010 summit, on the tenth anniversary of the summit at which the Lisbon strategy was launched, spoke instead of pursuing reform in the context of "Europe 2020," with a limited number of headline targets:

- An employment rate of 75 percent for men and women aged 20–64.
- A combined public and private investment of 3 percent of GDP in EU-wide research and development.
- A reduction in greenhouse gas emissions by 20 percent compared to 1990 levels, an increase to 20 percent in the share of renewables in final energy consumption, and a move toward a 20 percent increase in energy efficiency.

- An improvement in education levels, with the European Council subsequently to set a numerical rate.
- The promotion of social inclusion, in particular through the reduction of poverty.

With respect to Europe 2020, the overall objective and well-established procedures of the Lisbon strategy remained largely in place.[12]

Social Policy and Employment

The Rome Treaty contained a number of provisions pertaining to labor mobility (one of the prerequisites for a fully functioning internal market) and equal pay for equal work performed by men and women. It also called for the establishment of the European Social Fund to help achieve the EU's social policy objectives, which include improved living and working conditions and close cooperation among member states on labor issues.

The EU built the first phase of its social policy, in the 1960s, almost entirely on the treaty provisions for labor mobility. Broader aspects of social policy got a boost at the Hague summit in 1969, and leaders reiterated their commitment to a comprehensive and effective social policy at their next summit, in Paris in 1972. That led to the Community's first social action program, in 1974, which included wide-ranging measures intended to achieve full employment, better living and working conditions, worker participation in industrial decisionmaking, and equal treatment of men and women in the workplace.

A flurry of activity followed, but the legislative output was unimpressive. Successful measures included directives on workers' information and consultation rights and on equal pay and equal treatment for women. The Community established two institutions—the European Foundation for the Improvement of Living and Working Conditions, and the European Center for the Development of Vocational Training—to disseminate information and conduct research on social policy issues.

Fresh ideological winds in the late 1970s did not bode well for social policy in the EC, bringing a neoliberal reaction against excessive government intervention. Renewed economic recession and emerging market forces pushed social policy onto the back burner in the early 1980s. Nevertheless, the Single European Act affirmed in its preamble the need to "improve the [EC's] economic and social situation by extending common policies and pursuing new objectives."

The SEA also introduced qualified majority voting for legislation on "the health and safety of workers," which produced the largest and most important body of social policy legislation in the late 1980s and early 1990s and opened a loophole through which the Commission tried to enact other social policy measures. Moreover, a commitment in the SEA to economic and social cohesion led the European Council in 1988 to increase substantially the structural funds over time.

The SEA also obliged the Commission "to develop the dialogue between management and labor at Community level." This put the highest stamp of approval on the "Val Duchesse process," begun in 1985 when the Commission convened a meeting in Val Duchesse outside Brussels to encourage the social partners to develop a working relationship in order to provide informal input into the Community's legislative process. BusinessEurope, the new name for the European association of employer organizations, represents employers in the social partnership; the European Trade Union Confederation (ETUC) represents labor. BusinessEurope has always been more coherent, better organized, and generally more influential than ETUC. Indeed, the Commission has consistently bolstered ETUC in order to provide a counterweight on the labor side to BusinessEurope on the management side. In March 2003, in an effort to give new impetus to the social dialogue, EU leaders launched the Tripartite Social Summit for Growth and Employment. The summit is now an annual event, bringing together the Council presidency, Commission president, and representatives of the social partners on the eve of the spring European Council, which deals mainly with the Europe 2020 strategy.

The Social Charter

In an effort to counter criticism that the single market program of the late 1980s would benefit only business interests, Commission president Jacques Delors began what he called a "careful consideration of [the single market's] social consequences."[13] Most national leaders supported Delors. Some sympathized with the ideological underpinnings of a social dimension and saw Community-level action as a way to improve social policy at home without losing competitiveness abroad. They also feared "social dumping," the possibility that countries with higher labor costs would lose production to those with lower labor costs.

With the single market well on track and the economy booming, political support for an active social policy began to gather speed. In June 1988, the European Council agreed that "it was necessary to improve working conditions, living standards, protection of health and safety, access to vocational training, and dialogue between the two sides of industry."[14] Delors proposed the "Community Charter of the Fundamental Social Rights of Workers" (the Social Charter), which eleven of the EC's then-twelve national leaders endorsed in December 1989 (British prime minister Margaret Thatcher, a staunch economic liberal, was the lone dissenter).[15]

Following a preamble that outlined the development of social policy at the European level, the Social Charter listed twelve categories of fundamental social rights:

- Freedom of movement
- Employment and remuneration
- Improvement of living and working conditions
- Social protection
- Freedom of association and collective bargaining
- Vocational training
- Equal treatment for men and women
- Information, consultation, and participation for workers
- Health protection and safety in the workplace
- Protection of children and adolescents
- Protection of elderly persons
- Protection of disabled persons

Being entirely hortatory, the Social Charter lacked binding legal force. Nevertheless, it implied strong political support for an active social agenda. The charter also provided the basis for the social rights included in the Charter of Fundamental Rights, proclaimed by national leaders in Nice in December 2000 and later attached to the Lisbon Treaty.

The Social Charter's brief concluding section called on the Commission to submit proposals to implement those rights for which the Community had competence to enact legislation. In its ensuing "action program," the Commission, mindful of the subsidiarity principle, sought to strike a balance between what was desirable and what was feasible at the European level.[16]

Of the forty-seven proposed measures, only seventeen were new. Inevitably, familiar proposals dealing with industrial democracy, women's issues, and vocational training resurfaced; their proponents hoped that the momentum generated by the Social Charter would somehow carry them through. Aware of the huge stumbling block posed by the unanimity requirement for most social legislation, the Commission resorted in many cases to instruments other than legally binding directives or recommendations.

The Social Charter and the action program represented the high point of EU activism in the realm of traditional, legislation-based social policy. By the end of 1992 the Council had adopted only a handful of directives, concerned primarily with the less contentious question of health and safety at work. As the Commission coyly observed, "Discussions on most of the proposals for directives on important matters have not made sufficient progress to enable a final text to be adopted."[17] In other words, at least one country—usually but not always Britain—had prevented the Council from reaching agreement on draft directives covering such issues as the length of the workweek or European works councils.

The Social Protocol

Given the British Conservative government's intense opposition to the Social Charter, it was not surprising that the 1991 intergovernmental conference on treaty reform almost foundered on the social chapter, a package of social policy provisions that most countries wanted to include in the Maastricht Treaty but that Prime Minister John Major adamantly opposed. Realizing the extent of Major's intransigence, Delors suggested at the Maastricht summit in December 1991 that the social chapter be removed entirely and replaced with a protocol attached to the proposed new treaty. All twelve governments subsequently signed the social protocol, which authorized eleven of them (Britain being the exception) to proceed along the lines laid down in the Social Charter and to use the EU's institutions and decisionmaking procedures for that purpose. Britain would not take part, and legislation adopted via the social protocol would not apply to Britain. The social protocol included:

- Revised policy objectives, such as an emphasis on employment.
- Extension of QMV procedures to cover proposals on working conditions, consultation of workers, and equality between men and women with regard to labor market opportunities and treatment at work.
- Unanimous decisionmaking in areas such as social security, termination of employment, and third-country worker protection.
- Greater involvement of the social partners, including collective agreements at the European level.

Concern about the implications of Britain's exclusion from the social protocol dampened the Commission's ardor. Moreover, the Council enacted only two directives under the auspices of the social protocol, emphasizing the difficulty of legislating in the area of social policy. The Labour Party's victory in the May 1997 British general election heralded a breakthrough. Within days the new government announced its willingness to bring the social protocol into the Amsterdam Treaty, which governments were about to conclude, thereby ending both British exceptionalism and differentiated integration with respect to social policy.

The Amsterdam Treaty therefore represented considerable progress on social policy: the social protocol was incorporated into the treaty largely unchanged; equality between men and women was added to the list of Community objectives; a new provision of the treaty extended the scope of EU involvement to equal treatment more generally and to equal opportunities; and another new provision authorized the Council, acting unanimously, to take "appropriate action" to combat discrimination based not only on sex but also on race, ethnicity, religion, disability, age, or sexual orientation.

The Demise of Traditional Social Policy

The Labour government's embrace of the social protocol in 1997 implied a sea change in Britain's approach to a hitherto extremely touchy issue. Yet the government's position on the substance of social policy was not so new. Whereas the Conservatives opposed social policy on ideological grounds and had painted themselves into a corner politically, Labour took a pragmatic approach that did not necessarily favor new social policy legislation.

Other countries also took a more pragmatic approach to social policy. By the late 1990s, with unemployment moving to the top of the EU's agenda, there was little support anymore for old-fashioned social policy. The Commission lost much of its zeal even before Delors's departure, emphasizing instead flexibility with regard to social policy. The Amsterdam Treaty's new section on employment avoided "anything that might smack of a social approach to employment" and was "inserted next to [the title on] economic and monetary union, not social policy."[18]

A new direction was clearly evident in the Commission's 1994 white paper on social policy.[19] In keeping with prevailing concerns about competitiveness, the Commission argued rather defensively that social policy was not an obstacle to economic growth but rather was a key element of it. The white paper's main themes were job creation, labor mobility, equal opportunity, and the integration of social and economic policies. The Commission was careful not to propose a lengthy new legislative agenda. By relying less on legal instruments to protect and strengthen workers' rights and more on discussion and conciliation, the program signaled a shift in the direction of EU social policy and less reliance on regulation.

The last gasp of old-fashioned social policy came in the second half of 2000, during France's presidency of the Council. France's social affairs minister, none other than Martine Aubry, Jacques Delors's daughter, set her sights on "build[ing] a social Europe that works."[20] To that end, she attempted to tweak the Commission's social policy agenda in a more interventionist direction.

That was too much for most other governments. The French made predictable noises about the dangers of globalization and the need for better social protection but eventually gave in. At the Nice summit in December 2000, EU leaders endorsed a relatively restrained social policy agenda for the period 2000–2005. The agenda's key objectives illustrated the shift toward an emphasis on growth and employment:

- Accelerate development of the knowledge-based economy in order to produce more and better jobs.

- Achieve a new balance between flexibility and security ("flexicurity") in a changing work environment.
- Combat poverty, social exclusion, and discrimination.
- Modernize social protection systems.
- Promote equality between men and women.
- Reinforce the social dimension of enlargement and prepare candidate countries to meet the EU's standards.

Employment Policy

In the mid-1990s, even as many member states enjoyed respectable levels of economic growth, unemployment continued to hover around 11 percent of the workforce. A former secretary-general of the Commission estimated in December 1997 that unemployment benefits cost EU countries almost €200 billion a year, requiring high levels of taxation that drained the public purse.[21] Politically, double-digit unemployment undermined the EU's credibility— after all, the internal market and monetary union were supposed to deliver economic growth and jobs. Instead, the drive toward monetary union was widely seen as having exacerbated unemployment.

The Amsterdam Treaty's provisions on employment strengthened the EU's approach to the issue. The treaty modified the EU's objectives to include "a high level of employment" and affirmed the necessity for "coordination between national employment policies . . . with a view to enhancing their effectiveness by developing a coordinated strategy for employment." Competence for employment policy would remain at the national level, but the European Council would develop "common guidelines" based on input from various EU institutions and bodies. The Commission would monitor compliance with these guidelines, leaving it up to the European Council to take additional political steps. The Amsterdam Treaty also established an employment committee, comprising national and commission representatives, to conduct a continuous dialogue on employment and help prepare Council deliberations on the subject.

Concern about job losses had reached the top of the EU's political agenda by the time of the Amsterdam summit, as unemployment in France and Germany peaked at record levels for the postwar period. Both countries pursued economic policies that seemed almost to guarantee a high rate of structural unemployment. Labor market rigidities included high minimum wages, generous employment benefits that lasted for years, weak tests for claiming unemployment benefits, and strong trade union bargaining power. Industrial rigidities included an inability to grow small firms quickly into big ones and, at the other extreme, an inability to downsize quickly (by firing workers).

The cure for high unemployment in France, Germany, and elsewhere in the EU might therefore have been obvious: lower and shorter-term unemployment benefits, stricter tests for benefits, lower payroll taxes and other charges, greater wage flexibility, less job protection, and the provision of earned-income tax credits. Taken together, of course, these recommendations read like a recipe for what many Europeans decried as the callous Anglo-Saxon economic model, which a majority of EU countries were loath to embrace because of its supposed social consequences—growing income inequalities, the emergence of a "working poor" underclass, and the lack of a social safety net.

Most national governments hoped to find a middle way between the demonized US model and the idealized European model. The Netherlands seemed to have found that middle way, but what worked for a small country with a culture of consensus was more difficult for large countries such as France and Germany. The French government advocated a thirty-five-hour workweek and public-sector job creation, whereas the conservative German government failed to introduce potentially employment-enhancing tax reforms in 1997 and 1998 because of its weak hold on power (the new Social Democratic–Greens government was not inclined to revisit the issue).

Lack of EU competence for social security and related areas, as well as the political vagaries of the member states, precluded the adoption of the reforms necessary to translate economic growth into job creation. The EU had to rely instead on soft measures such as multilateral surveillance, benchmarking, and peer pressure. The latter evolved during the late 1990s into a highly choreographed and stylized process called the European Employment Strategy, launched at a special jobs summit in Luxembourg in November 1997, soon after the Amsterdam Treaty came into force.

Britain put employment at the top of its Council presidency agenda in early 1998, advocating a flexible approach. At the Cardiff summit in June 1998, the European Council discussed for the first time member states' annual employment action plans, based on assessments by the Commission and the Council of Ministers. As well as making general statements about the contents of the plans, the European Council adjured the relevant Council formations to "continue to work together to exchange best practice . . . [and] to develop peer group evaluation" of future plans.[22]

The European Employment Strategy received a major political boost when the European Council incorporated it into the broader Lisbon strategy in March 2000 and embraced the objective of raising the overall employment rate in the EU to 70 percent, and the employment rate for women to more than 60 percent, by 2010. The European Council sharpened these targets in March 2001, when it concluded that the overall rate should be increased to 67 percent (57 percent for women) by 2005 and added that the employment rate for older workers should be at least 50 percent by 2010.

Now in existence for well over ten years, the European Employment Strategy involves governments submitting national employment action plans for annual peer review. In March 2002, the EU streamlined its annual economic and employment policy coordination cycles (the centerpiece of economic coordination being the Broad Economic Policy Guidelines and the centerpiece of employment coordination being the European Employment Strategy). The main elements of the employment strategy and the annual sequencing of economic and employment policy coordination (a rolling program of yearly planning, examining, reporting, and monitoring) are illustrated in Box 14.2.

The European Employment Strategy is procedurally intricate and impressive. Like the Lisbon strategy more broadly, it is tempting to dismiss it as a classic example of EU excess. Yet the point of the employment strategy is to get countries to coordinate closely in policy areas that have traditionally been off the agenda of European integration but that have a profound effect on the

---

Box 14.2   The Annual Policy Coordination Cycle

January: Implementation Package. This contains:
- Broad Economic Policy Guidelines Implementation Report
- Internal Market Strategy Implementation Report
- Draft Joint Employment Report (prepared by the Commission and the Council, this is a synthesis of the member states' National Action Plans and comparative analysis of their implementation, as well as a progress report on the employment situation in the member states and collectively in the EU)

March: Spring Report. Prepared by the Commission, this report outlines the main agenda items for the Spring Summit and sets out the Commission's strategic priorities for the EU.

March: Spring Summit. This is the annual meeting of the European Council, supposedly devoted to reviewing the strategy for economic modernization and reform (other, more pressing business often intervenes). The European Council's conclusions provide general political orientation for the European Employment Strategy.

April: Guidelines Package. Based on general political orientations provided by the European Council, the Commission prepares:
- Broad Economic Policy Guidelines
- Employment Guidelines (containing specific policy objectives)
- Employment Recommendations

April–June: Input from the European Parliament and relevant Council formations into the Guidelines Package.

June: The European Council reaches political agreement on the Guidelines Package and issues conclusions.

June: Council of Ministers' Action. The relevant Council formations adopt (by qualified majority voting):
- Broad Economic Policy Guidelines
- Employment Guidelines
- Employment Recommendations

July–December: National Action Plans and Peer Review. Based on the Broad Economic Policy Guidelines, Employment Guidelines, and Employment Recommendations, member states adopt National Action Plans to implement the Employment Guidelines in specific national circumstances and contexts. This process includes a two-day presentation and critique of member states' National Action Plans.

EU's overall economic performance. Given the domestic political stakes, most governments are extremely wary of giving the EU competence for issues such as tax incentives and wage policy.

According to the Commission and others, the four-pillar structure of the employment strategy (employability, entrepreneurship, adaptability, and equal opportunity) is sound, although progress has been more pronounced on employability and entrepreneurship. Critics argue that the strategy favors quantity over quality when it comes to job creation, and that the traditional agenda of EU social policy has been sacrificed on the altar of Anglo-Saxon economic liberalism. The employment situation improved in Europe after the low point of 1997–1998. Between 1997 and 2004, over 10 million new jobs were created in the EU15.

Enlargement in 2004 and 2007 initially changed the employment situation for the worse. The average employment rate in the EU dropped by almost 1.5 percentage points as soon as the bulk of the new member states joined, in May 2004 (the long-term unemployment rate in the EU25 was 4 percent, compared to 3.3 percent in the EU15). Enlargement also encumbered the employment strategy, adding many more players to the process. Anticipating these difficulties, the Commission began preparing the candidate countries for participation in the employment strategy long before 2004, notably through joint assessment papers and employment policy reviews, promoting cooperation between civil society organizations from the EU and the candidate countries, and ensuring the successful participation of candidate countries in EU action programs.

Employment continued to rise in Europe in the middle of the decade, before dropping steeply after 2008 as a result of the recession. Progress may have had as much to do with the general economic situation, which improved markedly in the mid-2000s, as with the impact of the employment strategy. Many of the new jobs, however, were only part-time and low-quality. The EU therefore generated new jobs that were qualitatively similar to many of the new jobs generated in the United States, but it still lagged behind the United States in job creation numbers.

Undoubtedly the EU's labor markets and employment policies became more efficient and adaptable as a result of the employment strategy, although the rate of job creation was not enough to achieve the Lisbon targets. Hence the European Council's repeated emphasis on the importance of more labor market flexibility, higher investment in human capital (through education and training, and especially lifelong learning), and the need to keep older people in the workforce.

Even when the economy was buoyant, the solution to Europe's employment problems was not easy. Yet many governments seemed finally to be on the right track, especially those that introduced more wage and labor flexibility, however reluctantly. For most member states, monetary union imposed a constraint on job creation programs that might have increased the national deficit beyond 3 percent of GDP. The rising value of the euro, beginning in the mid-2000s, also made it harder for countries to boost exports outside the eurozone. Germany, a country with strong export-led growth, increased its competitiveness by boosting productivity and holding wages in check, thereby maintaining and even increasing export market share and enhancing employment. Nevertheless, Germany was a laggard when it came to labor market and other reforms, and did not score well in the joint (Commission-Council) employment report.

Social Inclusion and Protection

Social inclusion—ensuring that everyone has an opportunity to participate actively in society—is a feature of the European model. As part of the Lisbon strategy, in March 2000, EU leaders launched the Social Inclusion Process and set another ambitious goal and deadline: eradicating poverty by 2010. As with the employment strategy, the EU provides a framework for fighting social exclusion by means of policy coordination among the member states and by engaging nongovernmental organizations, the social partners, and local and regional authorities as well as national governments. Poverty may never be eradicated; much depends on the definition of poverty and the level of the officially recognized poverty line. More realistically, the EU has identified five key challenges, without target dates, for its program of social inclusion:

- Eradicate child poverty.
- Make labor markets truly inclusive.
- Ensure decent housing for everyone.
- Overcome discrimination and facilitate the social integration of disabled people, ethnic minorities, and immigrants.
- Tackle financial exclusion and overindebtedness.

Social protection systems, covering health care, unemployment benefits, and pensions, are highly developed in the EU. However, national governments jealously guard their responsibility for those systems, which account for the bulk of public spending and often determine the outcome of general elections. Nonetheless, social protection has an EU dimension, notably when people live and work in a member state other than their own; hence the need for EU legislation to coordinate national social security systems.

Beyond that, the EU and national governments use the open method of coordination to promote discussions among the member states on the modernization of social protection systems, especially in the areas of pensions and health care. The Commission and the Council conduct an annual joint analysis and assessment of national strategies for social inclusion and protection, which governments present each October.[23]

A Seamless Policy Area

Beginning in 2000, with the launch of the Lisbon strategy, the EU has radically broadened the scope of social policy to encompass employment, social inclusion and protection, and traditional social policy measures.[24] This all-encompassing approach was evident in the 2006–2010 social policy agenda, which developed two distinct tracks. The first of these, called "strengthening citizens' confidence," focused on measures aimed at reassuring people bewildered by the rapid pace of social, demographic, and economic change. To that end, the Commission reiterated the importance of adapting social protection systems, improving the integration of young people, and addressing the highly charged question of migration. A Commission plan to incorporate the European social model into external dialogue and measures was hardly likely to improve the confidence of the EU's international interlocutors.

The second track featured measures relating to employment and equal opportunities. The Commission's call for full employment was predictable. More interesting was a statement that "the creation of a genuine European labor market is essential." This implied removing the remaining barriers and drawing up policies to ensure that all concerned derive maximum benefit from the integrated European area. As for equal opportunities, the Commission proposed several actions to resolve such ongoing problems as the gender pay gap, women's access to and participation in the labor market, training, career advancement, and the reconciliation of family and working life.[25]

By the end of the decade, social policy seemed firmly embedded in the Lisbon strategy. Beginning in 2007, however, President Sarkozy resurrected the language of traditional social policy. Appealing to a domestic audience, Sarkozy spoke of the need to relaunch "social Europe" and make the EU "more protective," and complained that the Lisbon strategy focused unduly on growth at the expense of jobs and workers' rights. Those views set Sarkozy on a collision course with Prime Minister Blair and other economic liberals, especially in the run-up to France's Council presidency in the second half of 2008. The Commission carried out consultations in 2007–2008 with the social partners, and released a document at the beginning of the French presidency on the "renewed social agenda."

The renewed social agenda, which met all national concerns, simply repackaged the EU's existing approach to dealing with pressing economic and social challenges.[26] It also included a convenient overview of the different policy tools used at EU level to achieve social policy objectives:

- *Legislation:* Generate proposals to tackle discrimination outside the labor market, strengthen patients' rights in cross-border health care, and improve the functioning of European works councils.
- *Social dialogue:* Encourage representatives of workers and employers to make full use of the possibilities offered by the European social dialogue.

- *Cooperation:* Reinforce cooperation among member states on social protection and social inclusion.
- *Financial support:* Mobilize the EU's structural funds, the European Globalization Adjustment Fund, and the PROGRESS program (employment and social solidarity).
- *Partnership and communication:* Involve and consult nongovernmental organizations, regional and local authorities, and other stakeholders.
- *Screening new initiatives:* Ensure that all EU social and employment policies promote opportunities, access, and solidarity.

Enterprise and Industry

The Lisbon strategy aims to promote enterprise—entrepreneurial activity, business development, industrial growth—by fostering a competitive economic environment. On the face of it, the EU would seem well suited for such a strategy. After all, Europe is the cradle of the Industrial Revolution and home to many successful enterprises (big companies such as IKEA, Heineken, Michelin, Nokia, and Siemens come to mind).

Yet Europe has a reputation for being a difficult place in which to start or run a business, and entrepreneurship appears to be lagging, especially in comparison with the United States. Europeans are hardly less imaginative or innovative than Americans, but they seem more risk-averse when it comes to launching new businesses. European society is not particularly forgiving of failure; bankruptcy carries a large stigma and is legally onerous. Venture capital is not easily available and relatively few companies are listed on the stock market. The regulatory framework in many European countries is not conducive to starting or running a business, as anyone who has tried to shop in Germany on a Sunday can attest.

The full picture is more nuanced and varied. As far as competitiveness is concerned, Europe is not doing too badly. Indeed, the World Economic Forum's highly reputable Global Competitiveness Index (2009–2010) ranks five member states, including Germany, in the top ten (see Box 14.3).[27] The Nordic member states hold privileged positions in the rankings: Sweden, Finland, and Denmark are placed fourth through sixth. France is in sixteenth position. The United States, against which every country in the world measures itself, is second to Switzerland.

The EU collectively is not ranked in the Global Competitiveness Index, which shows how far the EU remains from being a single economic entity and also how difficult it is for traditional economic indicators to capture the EU. Disaggregating the EU by its member states, the range of rankings demonstrates the extent of differentiation among national economies. In contrast to the five member states in the top ten, the five lowest-ranking EU countries (out of

Box 14.3   Rankings for Competitiveness and Ease of Doing Business

Country	Global Competitiveness Index[a]	Ease of Doing Business Index[b]
Sweden	4	18
Denmark	5	6
Finland	6	16
Germany	7	25
Netherlands	10	30
United Kingdom	13	5
France	16	31
Austria	17	28
Belgium	18	22
Luxembourg	21	64
Ireland	25	7
Czech Republic	31	74
Spain	33	62
Cyprus	34	40
Estonia	35	24
Slovenia	37	53
Portugal	43	48
Poland	46	72
Slovakia	47	42
Italy	48	78
Malta	52	—
Lithuania	53	26
Hungary	58	47
Romania	64	45
Latvia	68	27
Greece	71	109
Bulgaria	76	44
For Comparison		
United States	2	4
China	29	89
India	49	133
Turkey	61	73

Sources: a. World Economic Forum, *Global Competitiveness Report, 2009–2010*, http://www.weforum.org/en/initiatives/gcp/Global%20Competitiveness%20Report/index.htm.
b. World Bank, *Doing Business 2010*, http://www.doingbusiness.org/Economy Rankings/.

133) are Bulgaria (76), Greece (71), Latvia (68), Romania (64), and Hungary (58). All except Greece are new Central and Eastern European member states, whose competitiveness might be expected to lag behind that of the EU15. Apart from Greece, the three lowest-ranking of the EU15 are Italy (48), Portugal (43), and Spain (33). Clearly, there are huge variations in member states' competitiveness, compounded by north-south and east-west economic divides.

The Global Competitiveness Index rests on twelve "pillars": institutions, infrastructure, macroeconomic stability, health and primary education, higher education and training, goods market efficiency, labor market efficiency, financial market sophistication, technological readiness, market size, business sophistication, and innovation. Accordingly, the index provides a well-rounded picture of the economic health of a country, but does not present a sharp image of the business environment there. From the point of view of enterprise alone, the World Bank's "doing business" index is far more useful. The index is based on a range of indicators that provide "a kind of cholesterol test for the regulatory environment for domestic businesses."[28] Its findings confirm anecdotal evidence that Europe is not especially business-friendly.

In 2010, three member states scored in the top ten: Britain (5), Denmark (6), and Ireland (7). Only one of these countries—Denmark—was also in the top ten of the Global Competitiveness Index. By contrast, the five lowest-ranking EU countries (out of 183) were Greece (109), Italy (78), the Czech Republic (74), Poland (72), and Luxembourg (64). In general, the picture is similar to that of the Global Competitiveness Index, with the Central and Eastern European and the Mediterranean member states (especially Greece) faring poorly. What is striking about the World Bank's index, however, is how badly the original EU member states scored. Italy's and Luxembourg's embarrassing rankings have already been noted. The other four founding member states ranked as follows: Belgium (22), Germany (25), Netherlands (30), and France (31).

The EU's contribution to competitiveness, as measured by the World Economic Forum, is multifaceted. It ranges from increasing the size of the market (through enlargement and consolidation of the internal market), to strengthening institutions (through bolstering democracy and building institutional capacity in the new member states), to enhancing macroeconomic stability (through Economic and Monetary Union, the Stability and Growth Pact, and the Broad Economic Policy Guidelines).

How does the EU promote enterprise and industrial development? The internal market and monetary union are part of the answer, but businesses complain that some internal market regulation, as well as environmental and other regulation, is excessive and imposes high costs. For a long time, traditional industrial policy in the EU protected national champions rather than fostering a business environment in which companies could grow and thrive without subsidies. Competition policy is the antithesis of traditional industrial policy and is much more conducive to dynamic economic development. Because of the Commission's association with old-fashioned industrial policy and its image as excessively interventionist and bureaucratic, the Commission had a difficult time fashioning a modern enterprise policy. Nor does the huge variation in member states' competitiveness and business environments make it easy for the Commission to achieve its goal.

Industrial Policy

When it came into being in 1958, the European Community inherited a strong interventionist ethos. Governments were used to underwriting specific enterprises or sectors whose success they deemed essential. The instruments of industrial policy include "soft" loans, grants, tax concessions, guaranteed procurement contracts, export assistance, and trade barriers. Industrial policy was driven by nationalism as much as by ideology. Even if they deliberately eschewed direct intervention, governments of all political persuasions have had a major impact on industrial planning and production. Public contracts and defense-related procurement are obvious ways in which governments intentionally or unintentionally assist national manufacturers.

Governments retained as much power as possible within the European Community over industrial sectors, including the right to nurture "national champions." Yet the Rome Treaty contained an industrial policy in that it mapped out a strategy for economic development through market integration and competition. In the recessionary 1970s, governments resorted instead to restrictive practices to protect national champions and encouraged the Commission to intervene directly to help ailing or dying industries, mostly in steel, shipbuilding, and textiles.[29]

The high-technology sector (including computers, consumer electronics, and telecommunications) was new—yet it was also in trouble, especially in the face of intense US competition. Compared to US industry's enterprise, scale, and international ambition, European firms seemed severely handicapped.

Throughout the 1970s, European governments responded to the US challenge largely by supporting national champions. Yet by the early 1980s the transatlantic technology gap had widened, and a new chasm was opening between Western Europe and Japan. Poor economic performance exacerbated Europe's predicament. With little economic growth, industries lacked incentive to invest in research and development. Nor did the limited size of their domestic markets encourage new initiatives.

At the same time, European companies undertook a number of collaborative ventures, notably in aircraft manufacturing and marketing. Concorde, the joint Anglo-French effort to produce a supersonic passenger plane, is the most obvious and expensive example. In the early 1960s, France and Britain also began to collaborate on Airbus, a project to produce short- to medium-range wide-bodied passenger aircraft in direct competition with Boeing. Germany joined the consortium in 1966, and Britain departed in 1968. Airbus began badly, with numerous cost and time overruns. Concorde was already in service by the late 1960s, but the first Airbus still remained on the drawing board. Only in the mid-1970s, when Airbus received its first non-European orders, did the venture really take off.

The EC did not participate in those collaborative projects, although the Commission strongly encouraged cross-border cooperation. Persistent industrial difficulties, the soaring cost of research and development, the increasing importance of new technologies—especially in microelectronics and semiconductors—as well as continuing global threats convinced many European manufacturers, politicians, and government officials that closer collaboration under the EC's auspices held the key to European industry's survival and success. The notion of national champions became increasingly outmoded.

The best approach seemed to be to end the fragmentation of Europe's own market by breaking down the plethora of nontariff barriers that impeded cross-border business and trade. Big business in Europe encouraged the Commission to promote liberalization, harmonization, and standardization. Far from interpreting industrial policy in an interventionist light, big business saw it in broader terms as a way to help level the playing field for manufacturers throughout the Community. The Commission argued vociferously that the competitive discipline of the internal market would be the best possible medicine for European manufacturers. In the sense that it opened up vast opportunities for European industry, not least by forcing many national champions to restructure radically, the single market program became the most important instrument of Community industrial policy by the early 1990s. The aggressive application of competition policy reinforced the point. As the Commission observed, "Maintaining effective competition is one of the key factors in ensuring that Community industry is successful."[30]

Many European firms nevertheless seemed unable to compete internationally. The problem was especially acute in the electronics sector, which encountered serious difficulties in the early 1990s despite market liberalization and considerable research funding from the EU budget. Lobbying by European electronics companies for the Commission to dispense old-fashioned industrial assistance began to grow.

In response, and in an effort to lay the ground rules for a post–single market industrial strategy, the Commission produced a key discussion document on competitiveness. Following a contentious internal debate, the Commission declined to offer any traditional industrial policy measures. Instead, it rejected sectoral policies as ineffective and stressed that the Community's role should be to maintain a competitive environment. The guidelines accomplished two important objectives: establishing a coherent philosophical framework to justify the Commission's policies and dashing expectations that the Community would act to support and protect a given sector, no matter how strategic.[31]

In the Commission's analysis, the role of government should be limited to providing, first, a competitive business climate and, second, "catalysts to encourage firms to adjust rapidly to changing circumstances." The Commission insisted that EU assistance would be "horizontal" rather than industry-specific and would consist largely of policing the marketplace. The Commission also reiterated the current conception of industrial policy as a combination of environmental, social, regional, and competition policies contributing to a level playing field as well as an aggressive trade policy to ensure that the international economic environment was as fair as possible.

The European electronics industry, battered by foreign competition and holding on to less than half of its own domestic market, provided the first testing ground for the Commission's noninterventionist stance. After a spirited tussle between the market-oriented DG Competition and the largely French-influenced (and therefore protectionist) DG Technology, the Commission produced a paper that blamed the feeble state of Europe's electronics industry on market fragmentation and high capital costs. It also advocated the development of the trans-European infrastructure networks, better training, more market-oriented research and development at the European level, and the pursuit of global trade liberalization as suitable approaches to resolving the industry's problems.[32]

A coalition of governments with no national champions to protect supported the Commission's position. Britain, Ireland, Spain, and Portugal feared that protection of European industry would hamper foreign investment in their countries, harm consumers, and divert scarce EU resources to giant firms in France, Germany, and the Benelux countries. Nor was it clear where new sectoral subsidies could come from, in either EU or national budgets.

Subsequent Commission papers met a much less stormy reception. Perhaps all sides had learned the pitfalls of trying to push an overtly interventionist policy in the EU context. The debate over electronics clearly demonstrated that conflicting national interests made it impossible to support sectoral initiatives at the EU level. Despite their panic at the thought of fully opening markets to the Japanese in 1999 (the long grace period was itself a concession to the need for structural adjustment among overprotected national champions), European automakers were unable to wring much more from the Commission than some modest worker-training proposals for firms in poorer regions. The Commission applied the same principles to other sectors with increasing confidence and decreasing backlash from firms and member states.

Reflecting the ongoing debate on industrial policy, the Maastricht Treaty contained a new section on the subject, calling on the EU and its member states "to ensure that the conditions needed to make Community industry competitive are met in a system of open and competitive markets." In order to achieve the objectives of structural change, a favorable business environment, and better exploitation of innovation and research, the treaty stipulated that the Council "may adopt specific measures in support of action taken by member states." However, the Council could act only unanimously.

Later Commission initiatives suggested that the debate had moved past the old interventionist arguments. Despite renewed recession in the late 1990s, a widening trade deficit with Japan, and growing economic nationalism on both sides of the Atlantic, ardent interventionists mostly failed to make their voices heard. The difficulty of designing a sectoral policy that could give real benefits to the affected sector without distorting competition, undermining cohesion, and drawing fire from member states whose industries would be disadvantaged was the most compelling reason for maintaining the horizontal approach. By the end of the 1990s there seemed to be a general consensus that a range of liberalizing measures aimed at boosting growth, prosperity, and jobs was the best industrial policy. Symbolizing that consensus, DG Industry changed its name to DG Enterprise and Industry.

The Lisbon strategy seemed to sound the death knell of traditional industrial policy. However, French and German leaders sometimes seem unable to resist the lure of old-fashioned industrial policy. The French are driven in part by an atavistic attraction to state intervention, the Germans by an inclination to follow the French lead.

The relentlessness of globalization, resulting in greater competition not only from the United States but also from China and India, has stirred protectionist impulses in the EU. Economic competition closer to home, from the low-wage Central and Eastern European countries, has aroused a similar reaction in the EU15, notably in France and Germany. At the time of the 2004 enlargement, politicians and business leaders in both countries warned of rapid deindustrialization in Western Europe as a result of "nearshoring" in Eastern Europe.

Due largely to French and German pressure, the Commission revisited the question of industrial policy, but reiterated the obvious point that without a globally competitive industry the EU could not achieve its economic and social goals. In a communication in April 2004 on industrial policy in an enlarged EU, the Commission argued that there was no evidence of a generalized process of deindustrialization and urged European industry to restructure in the face of global competition.[33]

Far from backing down, French and German leaders explored the possibility of formulating a Franco-German industrial policy. An opportunity to create a Franco-German champion arose in 2004 when Siemens of Germany was about to buy a large part of Alstom, the giant French engineering company. Instead, the French government bailed out Alstom with the Commission's approval. The French government's action discomfited Germany, as it signaled France's preference for a national champion (Alstom) rather than a Franco-German champion (an arrangement between Alstom and Siemens).

Regardless of the fate of Franco-German industrial collaboration, leading politicians in Paris and Berlin pressed for a new, supereconomic portfolio in the first Barroso Commission, presumably under a French or German commissioner, to direct industrial recovery in Europe. The implication was clear: both countries wanted to revive the old approach to industrial policy. Barroso failed to oblige, although he gave Günther Verheugen, Germany's commissioner, the enterprise and industry portfolio. Barroso added "industry" to the name of the portfolio "to reflect the renewed importance attached to our industrial heartland."[34] In fact, Verheugen was an economic liberal who strongly supported the Lisbon strategy.

The onset of the economic recession in 2008 prompted renewed calls in France and Germany for a return to an old-fashioned industrial policy in the EU, and the end of the first Barroso Commission in 2009 fueled speculation about the possible elevation of industrial policy in the second Barroso Commission. This time, the talk about an EU-wide industrial policy or a narrower Franco-German industrial policy was more ritualistic. Even in the economic crisis, protectionism had little genuine appeal.

Occasional Franco-German utterances about going back to the future with respect to industrial policy tend to elicit negative reactions from other governments and from the Commission. As Frits Bolkestein, the internal market commissioner, wrote scathingly shortly after the 2004 enlargement: "I cannot help feeling that I am in a time warp. I have to pinch myself to make sure that I am not back in the 1960s, 1970s, or 1980s. Or even under the mercantilist regime of Jean Baptiste Colbert in King Louis XIV's France. The defenders of vested interests and cozy corporatist arrangements rarely miss a trick when it comes to resisting the opening of markets. Warnings of deindustrialization are just the latest wheeze to try to stave off competition, notably from new member states, instead of making the most of enlargement's opportunities. . . . [T]o listen to recent statements by French and German politicians, you would think the [Lisbon] strategy had never existed."[35]

The Commission and its economically liberal allies in the Council have won the argument over industrial policy. Thus the Commission's website confidently proclaims that it is important

> to be clear what industrial competitive policy is *not:*
>
> • It is not about ad-hoc intervention, picking winners or bailing out losers, or similar concepts
> • It is not about more regulation or more state aid
>
> Instead it is about less but better regulation and about less but better focused state aid. . . . [It aims] to provide the right framework conditions for enterprises and to make the EU an attractive place for industrial development and job creation . . . [through an] integrated and non-interventionist approach.[36]

Enterprise Policy

Rather than intervening to support certain industries or sectors, EU enterprise policy seeks to foster innovation, entrepreneurship, and competitiveness by providing a business-friendly climate and a helpful regulatory environment. The health of European industry depends on a large number of factors, including its ability to innovate and adapt to the challenges of global competition.

Under the auspices of enterprise policy, the Commission produces a steady stream of industry- and sector-specific studies, reports, and recommendations.

Enterprise policy is not a stand-alone area of EU activity but overlaps generally with the internal market, competition, and trade policy. In certain sectors, such as chemicals and pharmaceuticals, it intersects with environmental and health policy. Enterprise and innovation are also closely related to research and development policy. For knowledge-intensive industries, such as biotechnology and life sciences, the emphasis is on research and product regulation, whereas for old-economy industries, global market access is a primary consideration.

The Commission sees small and medium-sized enterprises—independent businesses with fewer than 250 employees—as "the backbone of EU enterprise." There are more than 20 million SMEs in Europe; they represent 99 percent of businesses and provide most of Europe's private-sector jobs. In a typically extravagant gesture, the European Council approved the "European Charter for Small Enterprises" in June 2000, shortly after the launch of the Lisbon strategy. This called upon governments and the Commission to take concerted action to support SMEs in a number of key areas, including:

- Education and training for entrepreneurship
- Cheaper and faster start-up
- Better legislation and regulation
- Improved Internet access
- Help with taxation and financial matters
- Making the most of the single market
- Improved technological capacity for small enterprises

Following the launch of the single market program, the Commission funded a host of "Euro Info Centers," dotted throughout the EU (and beyond), to provide technical information and assistance to SMEs trying to comprehend EU rules and regulations. The centers became a core component of the Enterprise Europe Network. Launched in January 2008, the network links chambers of commerce, regional development authorities, and business incubators, providing information on EU legislation and funding opportunities, and assists in finding business partners and developing research capacities.

The Competitiveness and Innovation Framework Program is a bigger EU initiative to encourage the competitiveness primarily of SMEs. The program, which runs from 2007 to 2013 and has a budget of €3.621 billion, supports innovation activities, notably eco-innovation; provides better access to finance; and delivers business support services in less developed regions. Efforts to encourage wider and better use of information and communications technologies are a centerpiece of the program, as are efforts to promote renewable energies and energy efficiency.

In June 2008, the EU adopted the Small Business Act for Europe, a comprehensive SME policy framework that includes guidelines for initiatives at the European and national levels. The act aims to improve the administrative and legal environment throughout the EU.

Such initiatives are popular with SMEs, a diffuse but important business and political lobby. Although these efforts have produced some beneficial results, arguably the EU needs to focus not only on sustaining SMEs but also on growing them into large, globally competitive companies.

To that end, the EU is trying to provide a better economic and regulatory environment for entrepreneurship, focusing especially on opportunities for people to launch, sustain, and grow new businesses. Key policy areas, such as the internal market, environment, and energy, determine the overall regulatory framework in the EU. The Commission's "better regulation" initiative, an important component of enterprise policy, attempts to ensure that regulation adopted at the EU level, regardless of policy area, is as simple, comprehensible, and effective as possible. Accordingly, the Commission launched a "simplification program" in 2005 to review and overhaul the *acquis communautaire* (body of EU law), with a view to repealing, codifying, and recasting hundreds of legislative acts. The simplification program involves a continuous review of existing regulation. Other parts of the initiative involve scrutinizing legislative proposals to ensure that they are necessary, easily understandable, and enforceable.

■ Research and Development

Research and development—essential for innovation and economic growth—is a central plank of the Europe 2020 strategy. Although most R&D spending comes from the private sector, even the most ardent advocates of private enterprise concede that R&D is one of the few areas (along with education and infrastructure) in which government involvement is essential.

EU involvement in R&D originated in the Joint Research Center, established in Ispra, Italy, in 1958 under the auspices of the Atomic Energy Community. There are now seven institutes within the Joint Research Center system, conducting research on subjects such as the environment, climate change, food safety, nuclear measurement, advanced materials, informatics, and safety technology (see Box 14.4). The Joint Research Center is funded by the EU and accountable to the Commission.

The Commission established a directorate-general for science, research, and development in 1967 and issued calls for Community-level R&D programs in various industrial sectors during the 1970s. Thanks largely to Vice President Etienne Davignon, the Commission unveiled a proposal for the European Strategic Program for Research and Development in Information Technology, which the Council, already being lobbied by European industry, approved the follow-

---

Box 14.4   The Joint Research Center

The Directorate-General is located in Brussels.

The seven JRC institutes are located on five separate sites in Belgium, Germany, Italy, the Netherlands, and Spain. The institutes are:

> The Institute for Reference Materials and Measurements (IRMM)
> The Institute for Transuranium Elements (ITU)
> The Institute for Energy (IE)
> The Institute for the Protection and Security of the Citizen (IPSC)
> The Institute for Environment and Sustainability (IES)
> The Institute for Health and Consumer Protection (IHCP)
> The Institute for Prospective Technological Studies (IPTS)

Source: European Commission, Joint Research Center, http://ec.europa.eu/dgs/jrc/index.cfm?id=1440.

---

ing June. ESPRIT called for major European manufacturers, smaller firms, universities, and institutes throughout the Community to collaborate on "precompetitive" (basic) research. A pilot scheme of thirty-eight projects, funded jointly by the Community and the private sector, was launched in 1983.

Later in the 1980s the Community launched not only a full-fledged ESPRIT but also related research initiatives with catchy names such as RACE (advanced communications technologies), BRIDGE (biotechnology), FLAIR (agroindustry), and COMETT (education and training for technology). In 1985 the EC became a founding member of EUREKA, a French-led effort to develop European technology as a response to the US Strategic Defense Initiative.[37]

The SEA provided a new and explicit basis for R&D policy. With the aim of "strengthening the scientific and technological base of European industry and [encouraging] it to become more competitive at an international level," it stipulated that the Council should unanimously adopt "multiannual framework programs" to delineate the main scientific and technological objectives of R&D policy and define priorities. The only important change to R&D policy in the Maastricht Treaty concerned decisionmaking: henceforth framework programs would be adopted jointly by the Council and the Parliament using the codecision procedure. A further decisionmaking change in the Amsterdam Treaty dropped the unanimity requirement for the adoption of framework programs by the Council.

Activities under the umbrella of the framework programs range from the work of the Joint Research Center to work undertaken by research centers and universities where the EU covers between 25 percent and 100 percent of the cost. The essential prerequisites for EU funding are that the research be of a precompetitive nature and involve at least two organizations in two different member states. In practice, most projects involve about eight partners, with EU financing amounting to several million euros.

The seventh framework program, covering the period 2007–2013, consists of four strands corresponding to the main themes of European research policy:

- *Cooperation:* Research in areas such as health, food, biotechnology, information and communication technologies, the environment and climate change, and new production technologies.
- *Ideas:* The European Research Council, launched in Berlin in February 2007, is the principal activity under this strand. The council seeks to promote first-rate, investigator-driven fundamental research at the EU level and end the prevailing fragmentation of research efforts along national lines. The council's first call for proposals in April 2007 generated nearly 10,000 responses.
- *People:* Programs that provide scholarships, fellowships, and other opportunities for student and faculty exchange, including exchanges between industry and universities.
- *Capacities:* Efforts to strengthen research infrastructures, support R&D carried out by small and medium-sized enterprises, and promote science knowledge generally.

The sixth and seventh framework programs reflect a renewed emphasis on R&D since the launch of the Lisbon strategy, which included establishing by 2010 a "European Research Area" to allow the free movement of researchers, ideas, and new technologies. The so-called fifth freedom inherent in the putative research area was somewhat notional, as ideas know no borders and researchers may, literally, move freely around the EU. The point, however, was to promote close cooperation on issues pertaining to research, education, and innovation, and to involve all actors—governments (at the European, national, and subnational levels), universities, research institutes, businesses, and nongovernmental organizations—in the process.

As in other policy areas, enlargement in 2004 and 2007 posed a challenge for EU research and development policy. The new member states had less money to spend on R&D, and private investment on R&D was much lower as well. Interest in the putative European Research Area flagged in mid-decade. Slovenia, one of the new member states, made reviving the proposed research area a priority of its Council presidency in early 2008. At an informal meeting of the competitiveness council in April 2008, ministers launched what they called the Ljubljana Process to complete the European Research Area. In particular, they agreed to apply the open method of coordination to research and development policy by exchanging ideas, setting high common standards, and benchmarking progress.[38]

In December 2008 the Council adopted the European Research Area Vision 2020. In this case the year 2020 was a catchword rather than a deadline. The European Research Area envisioned by that time included "the unfettered circulation of researchers, knowledge and technology across the EU; attractive conditions for performing and investing in research; a focus on scientific competition and excellence; a degree of cooperation and coordination amongst policymakers that would make the best use of existing resources; and a focus on research responsive to the needs of society and capable of contributing effectively to the sustainable development and competitiveness of Europe."[39]

EU officials like to extol the "knowledge triangle"—the relationship among education, innovation, and research. Following the revival of the Lisbon strategy in 2005, Barroso became a leading proponent of a European institute of technology, a flagship European intuition for scientific research analogous to the world-renowned Massachusetts Institute of Technology. Inevitably, the proposal generated strong criticism from existing universities and research institutes that feared new competition for limited resources, and rivalry over where the new institution should be located. Nevertheless, the Council and Parliament agreed in March 2008 to establish the European Institute of Innovation and Technology, and the Council subsequently decided to locate the institute's headquarters in Budapest. The institute itself is more virtual than real. Rather than having its own faculty and student body, the institute facilitates networking and cooperation among researchers throughout and beyond the EU in "Knowledge and Innovation Communities."

Although it has not emerged quite as Barroso hoped that it would, the European Institute of Innovation and Technology symbolized the EU's commitment to R&D policy. The ITER reactor, under construction in Cadarache, France, is another such symbol. ITER is funded by a consortium that includes the EU, Japan, and the United States. Its purpose is to develop nuclear fusion, an environmentally friendly but technologically challenging alternative to nuclear fission. The EU won a bitter political struggle with a number of partner countries over the location of the first nuclear fusion device, which is expected to generate as much electricity as a normal power plant.

Space technology may be the final frontier for EU research and development policy. The European Space Agency is not an EU body but includes most EU member states (and a number of nonmember states as well). The EU collaborates with the space agency on projects, including communication by satellite, human spaceflight, and microgravity. Space received its own research for the first time in the seventh framework program. The EU is developing Galileo, its own global positioning system, a project driven as much by envy of the preexisting US system as by legitimate economic and security considerations. The costs of developing Galileo are formidable; the EU is having difficulty attracting private investment to match public funding for the project.

Money has been the biggest obstacle confronting the EU's research and development ambitions. National governments support EU-level R&D policy but want to limit spending. The Commission and Parliament inevitably push for a higher budget than the Council is willing to countenance.

EU spending through the framework program accounts for less than 10 percent of total EU-wide spending on civilian R&D, which is still far lower than in the United States. The EU missed its target of spending 3 percent of combined GDP on R&D by 2010. A Council presidency report in September 2009 pointed out that while overall R&D expenditure in Europe has increased by 14.4 percent since the target was set in 2002, national efforts vary greatly.[40]

Undaunted, the Commission is keeping up the pressure on European governments and industries to try to reach the 3 percent threshold, despite the impact of the economic recession. While appreciating the importance of R&D for innovation and economic growth, government ministers are wary of new targets. As the Czech presidency noted in May 2009, "concerning the setting of the post 2010 targets, it will be necessary to find the right balance between ambitions and credibility."[41]

The Commission has long urged greater coordination among national- and EU-sponsored R&D programs to ensure consistency and value for money. Following the drop in private investment in R&D as a result of the recession, the need for such coordination became more important than ever. Undoubtedly coordination among national R&D agencies and authorities is far better than in the recent past, but there is plenty of room for improvement.

The EU's involvement in R&D policy has had a major impact on the European research community and, to a lesser extent, on business and industry. Europe has some global leaders in the high-technology sector, and researchers in European institutes and universities are doing some highly advanced work. Yet on the whole, Europe continues to lag far behind the United States in scientific research and its commercial application. Although R&D policy was never intended as a panacea for Europe's high-technology sector or as a substitute for industry-wide restructuring, EU-sponsored projects have so far produced little commercially useful technology. As a pillar of the Europe 2020 strategy, R&D policy still has a long way to go.

■ Education and Training

Alongside innovation and research, education is a component of the "knowledge triangle" espoused by the EU. Despite its economic importance for the EU as a whole and its potential for inculcating a sense of "Europeanness," education remains predominantly the preserve of national and regional governments. Nevertheless, the Maastricht Treaty formally introduced education and youth programs as new areas of EU competence. Accordingly, the EU aims to support and supplement national action in areas such as cooperation between educational establishments, student and teacher mobility, youth exchanges, and language teaching.

Formal involvement in education policy came on the heels of highly successful educational and exchange programs organized by the EU since the late 1980s, including:

- *European Community Action Scheme for the Mobility of University Students (Erasmus):* Facilitates student and faculty exchange throughout the EU by offering grants to fund curriculum development and a badly needed course-credit transfer system.
- *Action Program to Promote Foreign Language Competence in the European Community (Lingua):* Provides financial support to encourage second- and third-language acquisition, thereby helping students and educators to exploit the full potential of Erasmus.
- *Trans-European Mobility Scheme for University Students (Tempus):* Links universities throughout Europe and the United States and funds joint research projects in a wide variety of disciplines.

Erasmus is the best known and most popular of these programs. The Commission estimates that by 2009, over 2 million students had studied in another country thanks to Erasmus.[42] In some cases these exchanges may have reinforced national prejudices and stereotypes, but in the vast majority of cases they have broken down barriers and helped students feel more European (they have also spawned innumerable transnational love affairs). In existence since 1987, Erasmus has generated a large network of former participants who are now in influential positions in government, industry, and the professions.

Between 1995 and 2006, Erasmus and other educational activities were organized and funded under the umbrella of the so-called Socrates program. Thereafter, the Commission integrated its various educational, training, and e-learning initiatives into the Lifelong Learning program, with a budget of almost €7 billion for the period 2007–2013.

Some of Lifelong Learning's programs sound like items from an IKEA catalog. They include Grundtvig, a program for adult education, and Comenius, a program for secondary school students and teachers. Nor are the EU's efforts confined to the territory of the EU. For example, Erasmus Mundus is an extension of the Erasmus program that offers financial support for institutions and scholarships for individuals involved in joint degree and other activities spanning EU and non-EU member states.

Complementing the Erasmus program, the Leonardo da Vinci program promotes vocational training exchanges. It dovetails with the work of the European Center for the Development of Vocational Training, an EU agency based in Thessaloniki, Greece, that provides information on and analysis of vocational training policy. In addition, the Commission is encouraging governments to converge toward common requirements and standards for vocational education in the EU.

The equivalency (or nonequivalency) of degrees remains one of the most formidable obstacles to the mobility of university graduates in the EU job market. How similar (or different) are master's degrees in Ireland and Estonia? What about bachelor's degrees in Scotland and Slovenia? Inevitably, the Commission wants to promote convergence and comparable qualifications in higher education.

The Commission and national education ministers participate in the Bologna Process, launched in 1999 with a view to bringing the requirements for bachelor's and master's degrees approximately into line. The Bologna Process, a pan-European and not an EU initiative, includes forty-six countries. Going well beyond degree equivalency, the process aims to create a European Higher Education Area in which degrees are organized in a three-cycle structure (bachelor, master, doctorate) with defined learning outcomes for each cycle, standards are ensured in accordance with common guidelines, and students and faculty participate easily in exchange programs.

Laudable though its goals are, the Bologna Process is not without controversy. Some national and subnational authorities resist what they see as unnecessary harmonization at the European level threatening deep-rooted national practices and traditions. Nor do all students, the most obvious beneficiaries of the process, support its ethos and objectives. Some of them, deeply skeptical of globalization in a way that overprivileged university students sometimes are, see the Bologna Process as a stalking horse for the Europe 2020 strategy, which in turn is a stalking horse for globalization.

Language is perhaps the biggest practical barrier to realizing the potential of the single market, let alone developing a common political culture. EU citizens may be free to work anywhere in the EU, but unless they are fluent in the language of their host country, they will be restricted to certain kinds of jobs. Apart from the Lingua program, the EU has launched a number of initiatives to promote the acquisition of other languages, especially less-used languages. The Commission's goal ("mother tongue plus two") is for EU citizens to know two EU languages in addition to their own. Many European professionals, especially from small countries in which English is not the first language, have already attained that goal. For most Europeans, however, it is probably unrealistic.

▉ Notes

1. Lisbon European Council, "Presidency Conclusions," March 23–24, 2000.
2. Quoted in *Financial Times,* March 24, 2000, p. 4.

3. Frits Bolkestein, speech at the informal meeting of the Competitiveness Council, Maastricht, July 2004, http://www.hi.org/news/europe/midex/2004/04-07-02.midex .html.

4. Wim Kok et al., *Facing the Challenge: The Lisbon Strategy for Growth and Enlargement: Report of the High Level Group* (Brussels: European Commission, 2004), pp. 6–7, 10, 18, 45.

5. European Commission, "Working Together for Growth and Jobs: A New Start for the Lisbon Strategy," COM(2005)24, February 2, 2005.

6. Brussels European Council, "Presidency Conclusions," March 22–23, 2005.

7. European Commission, "Working Together for Growth and Jobs."

8. European Commission, "Common Actions for Growth and Employment: The Community Lisbon Program," COM(2005)330 final, July 20, 2005.

9. European Commission, "The Renewed Lisbon Growth and Jobs Strategy Is Working, but the EU Must Reform Further to Succeed in a Globalised Age," December 11, 2007, http://europa.eu/rapid/pressReleasesAction.do?reference=IP/07/1892& format=HTML&aged=0&language=EN&guiLanguage=en.

10. Ian Begg, "Lisbon II, Two Years On: An Assessment of the Partnership for Growth and Jobs," CEPS Special Report, Brussels, July 2007, p. 1.

11. See Mehmet Uger, "Can Lisbon Deliver? Credibility and Ownership Issues," *EUSA Review* (Spring 2007): 14.

12. Brussels European Council, "Presidency Conclusions," March 25–26, 2010.

13. Jacques Delors, speech to the EP outlining the Commission's program for 1988, Bulletin EC S/1-1988, January 20, 1988, p. 12.

14. Hannover European Council, "Presidency Conclusions," June 27–28, 1988, Bulletin EC 6-1988, point 1.1.1.

15. Strasbourg European Council, "Presidency Conclusions," December 8–9, 1989, Bulletin EC 12-1989, point 1.1.10.

16. European Commission, "Communication from the Commission Concerning Its Action Programme Relating to the Implementation of the Community Charter of Basic Social Rights for Workers," COM(89)568 final, November 29, 1989.

17. European Commission, "Second Report from the Commission to the Council, the European Parliament and the Economic and Social Committee on the Application of the Community Charter of the Fundamental Social Rights of Workers," COM(92)562 final, December 23, 1992.

18. Michel Petite, "The Amsterdam Treaty," Harvard Jean Monnet Chair Working Paper no. 2/98, 1998, p. 18.

19. European Commission, "European Social Policy: A Way Forward for the Union," COM(94)333, July 27, 1994.

20. Quoted in *European Report,* September 27, 2000, p. 6.

21. David Williamson, "The European Union: New Money, New Treaty, New Members," *The European Union: Speeches,* December 9, 1997, http://www.eurunion .org/news/speeches/971211dw.htm.

22. Cardiff European Council, "Presidency Conclusions," June 15–16, 1998, Bulletin EC 6-1998, point 1.2.

23. On social protection and inclusion, see European Commission, "A More Cohesive Society for a Stronger Europe," http://ec.europa.eu/employment_social/spsi/ active_inclusion_en.htm.

24. See Linda Hantrais, *Social Policy in the European Union,* 3rd ed. (Basingstoke: Palgrave, 2007).

25. See European Commission, "Social Policy Agenda," http://europa.eu/legislation _summaries/employment_and_social_policy/social_agenda/c10127_en.htm.

26. European Commission, "Renewed Social Agenda: Opportunities, Access, and Solidarity in 21st Century Europe," July 2, 2008, http://eur-lex.europa.eu/LexUriServ/LexUriServ.do?uri=COM:2008:0412:FIN:EN:PDF.

27. World Economic Forum, "Global Competitiveness Index," http://www.weforum.org/en/initiatives/gcp/Global%20Competitiveness%20Report/index.htm.

28. World Bank, *Doing Business 2010*, http://www.doingbusiness.org/Economy Rankings/, p. vi; http://www.doingbusiness.org/Documents/DB10_About.pdf.

29. European Commission, *The European Community's Industrial Strategy* (Luxembourg: Office for Official Publications of the European Communities, 1983), p. 47.

30. European Commission, *21st Report on Competition Policy* (Luxembourg: Office for Official Publications of the European Communities, 1992), p. 22.

31. European Commission, "Industrial Policy in an Open and Competitive Environment: Guidelines for a Community Approach," COM(90)556 final, November 16, 1990.

32. European Commission, "The European Electronics and Information Technology Industry: State of Play, Issues at Stake and Proposals for Action," SEC(91)565, April 3, 1991.

33. European Commission, "Fostering Structural Change: An Industrial Policy for an Enlarged Europe," COM(2004)274 final, April 20, 2004.

34. José Manuel Barroso, portfolio assignment letter to Günther Verheugen, August 12, 2004, http://europa.eu.int/comm/commissioners/newcomm_pdf/pf_verheugen_en.pdf.

35. Frits Bolkestein, "Let the Market Choose Europe's Champions," *Financial Times,* June 14, 2004, p. 19.

36. European Commission, "Enterprise and Industry: Industrial Competitiveness," http://ec.europa.eu/enterprise/policies/industrial-competitiveness/industrial-policy/index_en.htm (emphasis in original).

37. See Margaret Sharp, "The Single Market and European Policies for Advanced Technologies," in Colin Crouch and David Marquand, eds., *The Politics of 1992: Beyond the Single European Market* (Oxford: Blackwell, 1990), pp. 100–120.

38. See Council Presidency, " Launch of 'Ljubljana Process' to Revive the European Research Area," April 15, 2008, http://www.eu2008.si/en/News_and_Documents/Press_Releases/April/0415MVZT_COMPET.html.

39. Council Presidency, "Discussion Note for the Ministerial Seminar Under the Swedish Presidency on 24 September 2009," September 11, 2009, http://register.consilium.europa.eu/pdf/en/09/st13/st13070.en09.pdf.

40. Ibid., p. 6.

41. Council Presidency, "European Research Area Vision 2020," status report in Council Presidency, "The First Steps Towards the Realization of the European Research Area Vision 2020," May 18, 2009, http://register.consilium.europa.eu/pdf/en/09/st09/st09956.en09.pdf.

42. European Commission, "Erasmus Reached the 2 Million Student Mark," July 30, 2009, http://ec.europa.eu/education/news/news1565_en.htm.

15 The Environment, Energy, and Climate Change

Support in Europe for strict environmental standards is rooted in history, geography, and political culture. Europeans have suffered from environmental degradation since the excesses of industrialization in the eighteenth and nineteenth centuries, compounded by the shortsightedness of central planning in Central and Eastern Europe under communist rule. Today, the environment in Europe is under enormous stress from the problems associated with affluence and high population density (the continent is relatively small and crowded), notably disposing of billions of tons of waste annually and curbing soaring levels of carbon dioxide (CO_2) emissions from homes and vehicles.

While not originally mentioned in the Rome Treaty, the environment has become one of the most politically important and active areas of European Union policy. Growing public concern about environmental degradation, the impact of a number of heavily publicized environmental disasters, and the politicization of the environmental movement in the 1970s and 1980s account for the EU's initial involvement in the area. At the same time, fearing that national environmental measures would distort Community-wide competition, governments strengthened EU environmental policy as a corollary to their efforts to complete the single market. A number of global concerns—climate change, depletion of the ozone layer, dwindling natural resources, and excessive pollution—increased the EU's involvement in international environmental affairs. As a result, environmental policy is at the top of the EU's political and policymaking agenda.[1]

Sustainable development, which "meets the needs of the present without compromising the ability of future generations to meet their own needs," enjoys strong public support in the EU and is listed in the Lisbon Treaty as an objective of European integration.[2] Most Europeans consider sustainable development environmentally essential and economically advantageous, although some manufacturers complain that environmental regulation increases costs and decreases international competitiveness. As climate change becomes ever more apparent,

451

as fossil fuels become scarcer and more difficult to extract, and as China—the world's most populous and most rapidly developing country—uses vast amounts of energy and pumps out huge quantities of greenhouse gases, demand for environmentally friendly technologies, manufacturing processes, and products is bound to grow. The EU believes that it is well placed to meet that demand, at home and abroad.

EU environmental policy is therefore highly pragmatic. Yet it has an ideological edge as well. Being a global environmental leader comports with the EU's self-image as an entity founded on principles and values that surpass narrow political and economic interests. The Lisbon Treaty states that "in its relations with the wider world, the Union shall . . . contribute to peace, security, [and] the sustainable development of the Earth." As much as anything else, a strong commitment to sustainable development distinguishes the EU as an international actor. The distinction is especially marked in relation to the United States, which, during the presidency of George W. Bush (2001–2009), renounced an international environmental role, leaving the EU to fill the void.

Not least because of concerns about climate change, environmental concerns have been extensively incorporated into EU energy policy. Indeed, environmental policy and energy policy are increasingly linked, as reflected in the parallel development of the EU's climate change and energy strategies. Although energy policy goes far beyond the environment and climate change, it is discussed in this chapter because of its centrality to both issues.

■ Environmental Policy

Early EU environmental legislation tended to be narrow and technical, justified either as an internal market measure or on the basis of a vague commitment in the preamble of the Rome Treaty to improve "living and working conditions" in Europe. As the environmental movement gathered momentum, national governments and the Commission developed a keen interest in environmental issues. Accordingly, at their summit in Paris in October 1972, national leaders called unequivocally for a Community environmental policy.

Within a year the Council adopted the first environmental action program. This and the second program (1977) listed measures that were essentially corrective; subsequent programs emphasized preventive measures. The third program (1982) advocated a European-level environmental impact assessment procedure and, for the first time, offered some Community financing for environmental projects.

Reflecting the growing importance of environmental policy, in 1981 the Commission established a separate directorate-general to deal with environmental issues. DG Environment quickly acquired a reputation for activism and as a main channel for environmental groups to pressure the EC to pursue "greener" policies. This reputation often put DG Environment at odds with its powerful counterparts engaged in economic and internal market activities. DG Environment has since grown in size and importance, and is now one of the most influential directorates-general in the Commission.

As the environment emerged onto the Community's agenda, the "green troika" of Denmark, Germany, and the Netherlands pushed hardest for legislation at the European level, and the poorer southern countries put up the most resistance.[3] The 1985 negotiations on treaty reform gave the green troika an opportunity to incorporate environmental policy into the treaty. Accordingly, the Single European Act devoted an entire section to environmental policy and included in its single market provisions a new article on environmental protection.

Whereas the SEA apparently gave the Community wide scope for environmental action, its provisions seemed to limit that scope by invoking, for the first time, the principle of subsidiarity. Moreover, the act's general environmental provisions and specific provision on environmental protection relating to the single market used different legislative procedures—consultation and cooperation—to achieve essentially the same result, thereby opening the door to disputes among national governments and between the Council and the European Parliament over the choice of legal base for environmental legislation.

Based on the SEA, the Community developed new environmental principles and measures in its fourth environmental action program (1987). References to environmental policy in successive European Council conclusions testified to growing political interest. Generally, the Commission tried to make environmental policy an integral part of all other policies—notably economic, industrial, transport, energy, agricultural, and social. Specifically, the Commission worked on priority areas such as air and marine pollution, waste management, biotechnology, and enforcement of environmental legislation, trying to keep disputes over the choice of legal base to a minimum.

The Maastricht and Amsterdam Treaties

The Maastricht Treaty reiterated the importance of taking environmental policy into account when formulating and implementing other EU policies. In addition, the treaty assuaged the concerns of poorer member states by allowing temporary derogations and authorizing the Cohesion Fund to compensate them for environmental measures with disproportionately high costs. However, the treaty's most important contribution may have been its clarification of the legislative process. In future, the cooperation procedure would be used for most environmental measures and the new codecision procedure for general action programs.

Written with the Maastricht Treaty in mind, the EC's fifth environmental action program, covering the period 1993–2000, noted a "slow but relentless deterioration . . . of the environment" despite two decades of Community action. The report called for such measures as waste reduction through reuse and recycling, lower energy use, a change of general consumption patterns, integrated pollution control measures, environmentally friendly transport, and industrial risk assessment. It identified five target sectors: industry, energy, transport, agriculture, and tourism. One of the report's most striking aspects was a shift in the EU's general approach from purely regulatory measures, such as emission limits, to an emphasis on economic and fiscal measures, including taxes, incentives, and subsidies through the structural funds.

At about the same time, the EU established the Financial Instrument for the Environment (LIFE) to help meet EU environmental objectives. Under the terms of the program, the EU cofinances environmental activities in member states and in nonmember states bordering the Mediterranean and the Baltic Sea. Its current iteration, LIFE+, came into effect in 2007. For 2010–2011, LIFE+ offered €250 million for cofinancing of projects under three headings: nature and biodiversity, environment policy and governance, and information and communication. Other sources of EU funding for the environment include the structural funds and the research framework program.

The 1995 enlargement brought into the EU two countries—Finland and Sweden—known for their commitment to environmental policy. The accession negotiations on environmental aspects of Finland's and Sweden's membership were especially contentious because standards were generally higher in those countries than elsewhere in the EU. Negotiators strove to reconcile the desire of the applicant states to maintain higher standards until EU standards reached an equivalent level, with the EU's desire to maintain free movement of goods in the single market. Under a compromise agreement, Finland and Sweden were allowed temporarily to maintain their higher standards. The agreement was reformulated in the Amsterdam Treaty; under its terms, member states could obtain exceptions to EU rules because of environmental considerations as long as proposed national measures were based on new scientific evidence and the problem was specific to the country proposing the exceptional measures. Nevertheless, the treaty explicitly gave the Commission the right to reject such measures even if they were not found to be a means of arbitrary discrimination or a disguised restriction on trade.

Due mostly to pressure from the original green troika plus Finland and Sweden, negotiations on environmental policy in the run-up to the Amsterdam Treaty focused more generally on extending the use of codecision and heightening environmental awareness by stressing the need for sustainable development. As expected, the new treaty extended the codecision procedure to almost all areas of environmental policy decisionmaking. It also enshrined the principle of sustainable development as one of the EU's aims and included a general stipulation that "environmental protection requirements must be integrated into the definition and implementation of . . . Community policies and activities . . . in particular with a view to promoting sustainable development."

The use of codecision for environmental policy decisionmaking empowered the EP, whose environment committee (now called the Environment, Public Health, and Food Safety Committee) became a key player, alongside the Commission's DG Environment and the Council presidency, in environmental policymaking. Given the highly technical nature of environment policy, the EP as a whole came to depend heavily on the committee's expertise. Lobbyists soon made the environment committee a target of their attention, and ambitious MEPs quickly saw the advantage of getting a seat on the committee.

Even before the Amsterdam Treaty came into effect, the European Council, meeting in Cardiff in June 1998, endorsed a Commission paper on integrating the environment into other policy areas. Accordingly, the Commission and the relevant Council formations developed an environmental dimension for most policy areas, not just the obvious ones such as agriculture and energy, through the so-called Cardiff Process. As part of a strategic approach to environmental policymaking, the sixth environmental action program, covering the period 2001–2012, called for renewed efforts to integrate environmental concerns into other policy areas and for developing policy in a new way, focusing on crosscutting themes rather than specific pollutants or economic activities, taking a longer-term perspective and setting clear environmental objectives, and identifying the most appropriate instruments to achieve policy goals efficiently and affordably.

Sustainable Development Strategy
Sweden, the leading proponent of environmental policy among the member states, pushed during its Council presidency in 2001 for adoption of a strategy for sustainable development with both an intra-EU and an external dimension. Margot Wallström, the environment commissioner at that time, was also Swedish. She and the Council presidency worked closely on devising a strategy for sustainable development, which the European Council endorsed in Gothenburg in June 2001. This strategy, renewed in 2006, provides a conceptual framework for environmental policymaking in the EU, highlighting key global challenges—such as climate change, conservation and management of natural resources, and demography and migration—in addition to the importance of crosscutting policies and activities as well as the need for better regulation and policy integration in the EU.

As part of the Gothenburg agreement on sustainable development, the environment became the third pillar, alongside the economic and social pillars, of the Lisbon strategy for modernization and reform, which the European Council had proclaimed in 2000. The European Council's annual spring meeting, devoted primarily to reviewing what is now called the Europe 2020 strategy, therefore includes also a review of the sustainable development process. However, the European Council has tended to focus on the economic rather than environmental aspects of the Lisbon strategy, with the review process for sustainable development being increasingly perfunctory.[4] At the behest of the European Council, the Commission issues progress reports on implementation of the sustainable development process that review developments in key policy areas, note the inevitable shortfalls, and suggest improvements (the Commission published its second report in June 2009).

Central and Eastern European Enlargement

The EU's emphasis on sustainable development coincided with the accession of the Central and Eastern European states, for whom EU environmental standards posed a major challenge. After decades of Soviet-style economic planning and performance, the environmental situation in Central and Eastern Europe in the early 1990s was truly abysmal. Although air and water pollution levels in the region dropped significantly during the decade, thanks to the collapse of heavy industry and mining, the Central and Eastern Europe countries had a long way to go to meet EU requirements. Nuclear contamination and unsafe nuclear plants were particularly worrisome and expensive to rectify.

The association agreements between the EU and the Central and Eastern European states stipulated that the associated countries' economic policies must be guided by the principle of sustainable development and take full account of environmental conditions. Beyond that, the Commission's proposals for integrating the applicant states into the internal market covered only a small fraction of the EU's environmental rulebook. In its opinions on the Central and Eastern European states' membership applications, the Commission included an assessment—often bleak—of the environmental situation in each of the applicant countries.[5]

Bringing the Central and Eastern European states up to Western European environmental standards required massive investment in everything from wastewater treatment to solid-waste management to air pollution reduction. It also required a huge improvement in the administrative capacities of the applicant countries. Without efficient regional and local environmental administrations, for instance, the Central and Eastern European states would not be capable of issuing a single permit to enterprises covering all types of emissions, as required by the integrated pollution prevention and control directive, a key piece of EU legislation.

Beginning in the mid-1990s, the EU provided financial assistance, partly under the LIFE program, to help bring the prospective new member states up to EU environmental standards. Later, in the run-up to enlargement, the EU provided specific pre-accession assistance for environmental improvements. This aid was sometimes conditional on the applicants taking certain steps, such as developing waste management plans, although the Commission had less leverage as the date of enlargement approached. In general, the Commission estimated that bringing Central and Eastern Europe fully up to Western

European environmental standards would require an investment of 2–3 percent of the new member states' GDP. Nevertheless, the accession countries did not receive any derogations or exemptions from EU environmental law, only some transitional periods for its implementation.

Just as the 2004–2007 enlargement caused a drop in the average per capita GDP in the EU, it also reduced the average level of environmental well-being in the EU. Clearly, it would take Central and Eastern Europe a long time to catch up to Western Europe environmentally as well as economically. Indeed, many Central and Eastern Europeans worried that the costs of environmental improvements would hold back their economic development. Not surprisingly, most of the new member states are far less aggressive in the pursuit of environmental policy than their Western European counterparts.

The Environment and the Economy

As the case of Central and Eastern European enlargement shows, there is an inherent tension between environmental policy and economic development. Environmental regulation is expensive; it imposes costs on businesses and raises concerns about competitiveness. Governments are sensitive to such concerns, especially during an economic downturn. Far from retreating in the face of fierce global competition and weak economic performance, however, advocates of high environmental standards in the EU have consistently argued that environmental policy and economic development complement rather than contradict each other.

As long ago as 1982, when the Community was struggling economically, the third environmental action program specifically called for environmental initiatives that would contribute to growth and job creation through the development of lower-polluting industries. More recently, with the acceleration of globalization, EU leaders have attempted to assuage concerns about the costs of regulation by highlighting opportunities for innovation and competitiveness through greater resource efficiency and new investment. Under the auspices of the Lisbon strategy, the EU identified energy-efficient technologies and processes as key ingredients of economic growth and job creation. The influential Kok Report of 2004 urged the EU to promote the development and diffusion of eco-innovations and build on its existing leadership in major eco-industry markets.[6] At the same time, the Commission adopted an action plan for environmental technologies to encourage small and medium-sized enterprises to develop eco-innovative products and processes.

The onset of the financial crisis in 2008 challenged the EU's assumptions about the economic benefits of environmental policy and could have jeopardized efforts to complete the energy-climate package, one of the most ambitious undertakings in EU environmental policymaking (discussed later in this chapter). While the sharp economic downturn complicated negotiations over the energy-climate package, it did not prevent the Commission and the French presidency from securing agreement in December 2008. If anything, the economic setbacks of 2008 and 2009 intensified the EU's propensity to cast environmental policy as a boon rather than a bane for innovation and entrepreneurship.

In particular, the Commission saw the economic crisis as "a crucial opportunity to 'green' our economy and lay the foundations for low-carbon and resource-efficient growth," arguing that "a stronger environment policy can help spark economic recovery and lasting EU competitiveness."[7] The Economic Recovery Plan, adopted by the Commission in November 2008, included an array of measures to improve energy efficiency, develop clean technologies, and accelerate the transition to an eco-efficient economy. Ministers in the environment and competitiveness councils met jointly in July 2009 to underscore that economic recovery was fully compatible with environmental protection.[8]

Just as it played a crucial role in promoting sustainable development during its 2001 Council presidency, Sweden again pushed environmental policy during its 2009 Council presidency. The message of the Swedish presidency was that the EU could emerge stronger from the economic crisis by investing in environmental infrastructure, energy and resource efficiency, and eco-innovation. The Commission and the Swedish presidency worked closely together to make the EU a world leader in economically viable eco-innovation.

As in other areas of EU activity, however, the rhetoric of policymakers often outpaces the reality of everyday life. European manufacturers are quick to jump on the green bandwagon without necessarily contributing much to a more livable world. Karl Falkenberg, director-general for environmental policy in the Commission, admitted as much when he said that "many programs are called 'green' but if you scratch the surface a bit you see that they have very limited benefits for the environment."[9] The EU risks promoting new technologies that are unsustainable without subsidies. Alternatively, EU and national subsidies may generate thousands of eco-industry jobs that are unlikely to stay in Europe once mass production begins in China and elsewhere. Similarly, including environmental costs in product prices could make European goods prohibitively expensive unless other countries take a similar tack. For that reason, devising an economically feasible environmental policy requires a global and not just a regional approach.

Key Environmental Initiatives and Legislation

The corpus of environmental legislation enacted at the EU level is vast. Beginning with some scattered pieces of legislation in the 1960s and 1970s, EU environmental legislation mushroomed in the 1980s and 1990s in response to changing norms and values, political pressures, interest-group lobbying, rulings of the European Court of Justice, and international agreements. Initially, EU environmental legislation developed unevenly, varying from measures on specific problems to directives on catchall issues. By the 1990s, EU environmental legislation developed along two main lines: (1) framework directives such as those on air and water quality, and (2) the consolidation or revision of existing directives such as those on the prevention of major accidents involving dangerous substances. The following discussion gives a flavor of the depth and scope of EU environmental initiatives and legislation by profiling developments in a number of key sectors and thematic areas.

General. In 1985 the Council adopted a directive requiring member states to demand environmental impact assessments before approving projects that by virtue of size, nature, or location are likely to have a significant impact on the environment. Assessments are mandatory for certain types of industrial and infrastructural projects; other types of activity may be subject to environmental impact assessments at the discretion of member states. The 1985 directive was amended in 1997 and 2003.

In December 1996 the Council adopted a directive on integrated pollution prevention and control, obliging governments to install regulatory systems that would issue a single permit to enterprises covering all types of emissions (including air, water, and soil), which the Council and EP updated in 2008. A Commission proposal to incorporate the revised directive with six other directives on aspects of industrial pollution was extremely controversial because of its likely impact on tens of thousands of industrial facilities throughout the EU. Disagreement within the EP and among governments centered on how to use the best available technologies to achieve better results by means of limiting emissions. A core group of governments—the environmental policy leaders—held out against efforts by the more cost-conscious member states, especially in Central and Eastern Europe, to set lower emission limits, secure derogations, and include lengthy transition periods in the directive. The EP concluded its first reading in March 2009 and the Council adopted a common position in February 2010. Detailed negotiations continued throughout 2010 within and between the two legislative decisionmakers on one of the most complex and consequential pieces of environmental legislation in EU history.

Accidents. Major accidents have given rise to several important legislative acts. For instance, an industrial disaster in Seveso, Italy, in 1977, resulted in a directive requiring that manufacturers using dangerous materials, as well as local authorities, have adequate contingency plans to limit the environmental impact of accidents. The directive was revised and updated in a 1996 directive (Seveso II), which in turn was amended in 2003. Two disastrous oil spills, one from the tanker *Erika* in Brittany in 2000 and the other from the tanker *Prestige* off the coast of Spain in 2002, led the EU to strengthen standards for maritime safety and pollution and establish the European Maritime Safety Agency.

Biodiversity and Habitats. The loss of biodiversity due to rampant economic development, land clearance, deforestation, loss of wetlands, and the spread of invasive species is a major global concern. The EU sees biodiversity and nature conservation as second only to climate change on the list of environmental challenges that it faces. The EU's efforts to halt the loss of biodiversity hinge on two major initiatives, a 1979 directive on the conservation of wild birds (frequently updated in response to scientific breakthroughs and enlargement) and a program for the protection of natural habitats, called "Natura 2000," that allows the EU to designate sites as special conservation areas. Between the directive on wild birds and Natura 2000, the EU has more than 25,000 protected sites, covering about 17 percent of its territory. The EU's Biodiversity Action Plan, a framework for efforts to halt biodiversity loss by 2010, has not been particularly effective. In late 2009, the Commission and the Swedish Council presidency started devising a new strategy for halting biodiversity loss. At the same time, they began developing the EU's position for the Conference of the Parties to the United Nations Biodiversity Convention in October 2010.

Air Quality. Well before climate change came onto the agenda, the EU sought to reduce pollution from cars, factories, and other sources. Beginning with a landmark directive in 1970, subsequently amended many times, car emissions have been reduced by 80–90 percent over the past four decades. Nevertheless, the far greater number of cars on European roads today, and high emissions from other sources, impel the EU to act. EU efforts to curb emissions now come under the auspices of the Clean Air for Europe program, which in turn shaped a thematic strategy for air quality. The so-called air quality directive, adopted by the Council and Parliament in 2008, was among the most significant initiatives undertaken as part of the thematic strategy.

The EU has long been involved in efforts to end the use of ozone-depleting substances. The Commission and the member states participated in the negotiation of the 1987 Montreal Protocol, which created a mechanism for phasing out ozone-depleting substances, and subsequent protocols tightening these restrictions and accelerating phaseout of some substances. Following the 2007 modifications to the Montreal Protocol, in 2009 the Council and Parliament adopted a new regulation on ozone-depleting substances.

Water Quality. The EU enacted most of its initial legislation on water quality in the 1970s and 1980s, and passed updated legislation thereafter. Major horizontal directives cover the quality of drinking water and bathing water, discharges to groundwater, quality of water containing freshwater fish and shellfish, quality of surface water for drinking, and treatment of urban wastewater. The landmark framework directive on water (2000) emerged out of a major initiative by the Commission to address the deteriorating quality of water. The EU enacted a number of specific directives, for example on standards for surface water and bathing water, over the next eight years in support of the directive.

Waste Management. The EU began regulating waste disposal (hazardous and nonhazardous) in 1975 with the adoption of a framework directive, followed by a series of directives dealing with specific areas of hazardous waste disposal. For instance, the EU has a system of compulsory prior notification and authorization for transport of hazardous wastes across national borders, including uniform documentation requirements. The EU made its first foray into the reduction of nonhazardous waste with a directive in 1985 requiring governments to draw up a four-year program to reduce the contribution of beverage containers to the waste stream. Thereafter the Commission introduced proposals covering multiple aspects of waste management, including civil liability for damage caused by waste, based on the "polluter pays" principle; uniform site design for landfills and standards for incineration of hazardous waste; and recycling of waste packaging.

The waste-packaging directive originated in response to German legislation requiring producers to take back, or guarantee recycling of, all packaging waste from consumer products sold in Germany—legislation that risked disrupting the single market. Initially, the Commission called for recycling 60 percent of each type of packaging waste as well as energy recovery (incineration) of a further 30 percent in each member state within ten years. The proposal also required extensive tracking of waste generation and disposal trends in the packaging area while leaving precise methods of implementing the targets to individual member states. The proposal provoked lively controversy, with some countries complaining that the directive was too lax and industry objecting that the targets were technologically unreachable for certain types of materials. The debate grew testy when it became clear that Germany was meeting its seemingly admirable recycling goals via massive exports of used packaging materials, threatening to destroy national recycling systems by driving prices below cost throughout Europe. Following intensive negotiations, the Council and Parliament adopted a much more modest directive in December 1994, with lower recovery and recycling levels to be attained by the first target date of 2001, with regularly upgraded targets thereafter. A 2004 amendment to the original directive proved uncontroversial.

The Commission's thematic strategy on waste prevention and recycling, adopted in December 2005, outlined a comprehensive approach to all aspects of waste management policy and set the scene for a revision in November 2008 of the landmark 1975 framework directive. The new directive incorporates national waste prevention programs and sets ambitious targets for household, construction, and other waste recycling to be achieved by 2020.

Soil Protection. A proposal from the Commission in September 2006 for a framework directive on soil protection met stiff resistance from a number of national governments because of its likely financial and administrative costs and because of the subsidiarity principle (the argument that legislation on soil protection was best left to the national level of governance). The proposed directive deals with the identification, management, and cleanup of contaminated sites.

Harmful Substances. The Commission adopted a thematic strategy in 2006 on the sustainable use of pesticides, accompanied by a proposed framework directive on the subject. The Council and Parliament adopted the directive in 2009, which requires member states, for example, to enforce regular inspection of pesticide application equipment and ban aerial spraying.

One of the most controversial and complicated pieces of EU environmental legislation ever passed falls into the realm of harmful substances: the Registration, Evaluation, Authorization, and Restriction of Chemicals (REACH) regulation, enacted in 2006 after a lengthy gestation period and finally implemented in 2007. REACH replaced a hodgepodge of existing legislation, dating from a 1967 directive on the classification and labeling of dangerous substances. The new, all-encompassing regulation originated in a request by the environment council in April 1998 for the Commission to review existing legislation in light of growing public concern about environmental, health, and safety issues relating to the manufacture and use of chemicals. Over the course of the next ten years, during which time the Commission published a white paper on future chemicals policy (2001) and made a legislative proposal (2003), the formulation and negotiation of REACH became a classic case study:

- *Relationship among regulation, innovation, and competitiveness:* Chemicals manufacturers argued that the cost of new regulation would smother innovation and make them less competitive globally. Environmentalists argued that REACH would stimulate research on greener technologies, processes, and substances and put EU manufacturers at the forefront of global eco-industry.
- *Intrainstitutional conflict:* Differences had to be handled between the environment and enterprise directorates-general in the Commission; differences among governments in the Council and between the Council's environment and competitiveness formations; differences among political groups and between the environment and the internal market committees of the EP.
- *Interinstitutional conflict:* The difficult and lengthy passage of REACH through the codecision procedure demonstrated the complexity and political salience of key EU legislation.

- *Role of EU agencies:* REACH included provision for a European Chemicals Agency to manage the highly intensive registration, evaluation, authorization, and restriction processes for chemical substances. Based in Helsinki as part of a package deal in the European Council on where to locate EU agencies, the Chemicals Agency began functioning in 2007 and was quickly overwhelmed by the enormity of the task it faced.
- *Lobbying in the EU:* Transnational environmental and business lobbies, ranging from the World Wildlife Fund to the European Chemical Industry Council, battled each other in the pre-proposal stage and during every step of the legislative procedure.
- *Global impact of EU regulation:* Non-EU chemicals manufacturers that export to Europe chafed at the foggy registration procedure and costs associated with REACH.

In general, under the terms of the legislation, companies must register with the European Chemicals Agency all chemical substances manufactured in or imported to the EU above a small threshold. The agency evaluates the registration data to determine if the substance should be authorized or restricted. Given the huge number of chemicals involved, the legislation includes various exceptions, exemptions, and deadlines spread over a ten-year period for registering certain substances. REACH is less burdensome than industry initially feared, while offering a lower level of environmental protection than activists initially sought. Nevertheless, REACH imposes considerable bureaucratic cost and sets high environmental standards for substances that are ubiquitous in everyday life.

Sustainable Consumption and Production. This is an overarching theme relating to environmentally conscious patterns of consumption and production whereby consumers can make more informed choices and manufacturers can promote products that meet high environmental standards. Aspects include a voluntary eco-management and audit scheme to certify the environmental performance of companies and organizations. The EU has revised and extended the use of the Ecolabel, which companies may display when they prove to national certification bodies that their products meet certain ecological and performance criteria (the Ecolabel is a badge of environmental approval that many European consumers look for). The EU has a set of compulsory eco-design requirements for manufacturers of energy-using products.

Access to Information, Public Participation, and Access to Justice. This is a relatively new area of environmental legislation, driven by principles of good governance and by the EU's adherence to an international agreement (the Aarhus Convention) on the subject. It includes 2003 directives on public access to environmental information and on facilitating public participation in the drawing up of certain plans and programs relating to the environment. A 2003 Commission proposal for a directive on granting public access to justice in environmental matters in the member states faced stiff national resistance and has made little progress.

Problems of Enforcement

Enforcement is a chronic problem in EU environmental policy. Differing legal regimes, economic concerns, degrees of public interest, and commitment among member states have contributed to uneven implementation of environmental rules. Until the European Environment Agency became fully operational in 1995, the Commission was hampered by a dearth of reliable data on the state of the environment in Europe. The Commission remains constrained by its reliance on national governments for the information needed to pursue some infringement proceedings.

The Commission generally paints a gloomy picture of enforcement of EU environmental rules by the member states; few countries—even the environmental leaders—ever escape criticism. Problems range from egregiously late transposal of EU measures into national law, to failure to conform to standards established in EU legislation, to nonsubmission of required reports. Calls for better implementation are a staple of the annual Commission reports on environmental policy. Indeed, fuller implementation and better enforcement of environmental policy obligations are priority objectives of the sixth environmental action program (2002–2012).

Economic actors often disregard the environmental impact assessment directive, a key piece of EU environmental legislation. Impact assessments are a fruitful source of conflict between the Commission and national governments, not least because the directive allows environmental organizations to appeal to another, highly visible authority against the action (or inaction) of their own governments. The Commission has brought infringement proceedings against a majority of member states. Even where the procedure laid down by the directive is formally followed, the Commission complains that impact studies are often of mediocre quality and almost always underestimate harm to the environment.

In areas covered by substantive legislation (air, water, waste, and the like), the Commission considers the situation to be least satisfactory where EU legislation lays down obligations to plan ahead. Water quality is a prime example: many countries, especially in Central and Eastern Europe, simply have not undertaken the massive public investment programs necessary to meet the standards to which they agreed in the Council. This failure is especially evident with respect to the directives on drinking and bathing water, in which concentrations of certain pollutants routinely exceed EU norms, sometimes with the explicit permission of national authorities. As of early 2010, the Commission had identified approximately 500 towns and cities in the EU whose wastewater treatment was not in compliance with EU law. Belgium still has not fulfilled all its obligations under the directive on urban wastewater treatment. There are a number of flagrant abuses in the area of air quality (Athens comes immediately to mind).

In addition to the usual plethora of disputes over conformity of implementing legislation, a key problem in the area of waste is violation of control and documentation rules by waste shippers and an increase in uncontrolled or illegal dumps or landfills. Italy is a persistent thorn in the EU's side, with thousands of illegal and uncontrolled waste disposal sites throughout the country.

In the area of nature protection, the Commission cites continual problems over member states' failure to designate adequate numbers of special preserves, as well as the persistence of hunting in violation of the directives on protection of birds and other wildlife. The Commission took Spain to task in 2009 for not having conducted an adequate assessment of the likely effects on two critically endangered species of allowing coal-mining inside a Natura 2000 site. The Commission scored a victory in 2009 when the Polish government decided not to continue construction of a highway bypass through an important wetland and forest ecosystem in the Rospuda valley in the northeast of the country.

The EU's Role in Global and Regional Environmental Affairs

Almost from the beginning, EU environmental policy acquired an international dimension. Realizing that pollution knew no bounds and that environmental degradation was a global problem, member states undertook as early as 1973 to coordinate their international positions on environmental issues. On that basis, the EU became increasingly involved in worldwide environmental affairs.

The SEA authorized the Community to enter into international agreements on environmental issues "with third countries and with . . . relevant international organizations," and the fourth environmental action program called on member states and the Community to participate actively on the international stage to protect the environment. As a result, the EU is now party to over thirty international conventions and agreements on the environment, covering issues such as acid rain, biodiversity, climate change and greenhouse gases, desertification, and protection of major rivers. The EU also participates in environmental activities with a range of international organizations. In addition, environmental criteria are integral to EU assistance to neighboring countries and to EU development policy (for instance, the Cotonou Convention provides for general environmental cooperation and includes a specific ban on exports of hazardous waste to the participating African, Caribbean, and Pacific countries).

The EC and the member states participated in the pathbreaking United Nations Conference on Environment and Development (the "Earth Summit") in Rio de Janeiro in June 1992, which adopted general principles relating to the environmental implications of economic development and a comprehensive work program covering virtually every aspect of environment and development. The EC and the member states signed the UN Framework Convention on Climate Change and the Convention on Biodiversity at the Rio Conference, both of which emerged from negotiations begun long before that, and set the stage for active EU involvement in global climate change and biodiversity negotiations in the decades ahead.

The Baltic Sea Strategy, announced by the Commission in June 2009 and promoted enthusiastically by the Swedish presidency in the second half of the year, is an example of a regional initiative involving (in this case) one non-EU member state—Russia. The other Baltic Sea Strategy countries are Denmark, Estonia, Finland, Germany, Latvia, Lithuania, and Poland. The strategy fits into a sea-basin approach to environmental policy developed in a Commission green paper (discussion document) on Integrated Maritime Policy and could be a precursor of similar strategies in the Mediterranean and the Black Sea. Priorities for the Baltic Sea Strategy include the marine environment, sustainable economic development, and security and safety. The EU would carry out most of the measures necessary in support of the strategy, with some assistance from Russia.

◼ Energy Policy

Russia looms large in EU energy policy, as do concerns about climate change.[10] Energy policy was initially at the forefront of European integration. Two of the original European communities—the European Coal and Steel Community and the European Atomic Energy Community—dealt with the provision of energy for the European economy. Yet energy soon receded in importance for the European communities. The ECSC served a diplomatic more than an economic purpose and in the 1960s oil replaced coal as the main source of energy in Europe. The ECSC came to an end in 2002; Euratom was never more than a footnote in the history of European integration. Today, the energy mix varies widely among member states, ranging from majority nuclear power generation in France and gas-heavy infrastructure in Germany, the United Kingdom, and the Netherlands to high dependence on coal in Poland and other new member states.

Even when the oil crises of the early and late 1970s crippled the European economy, national governments responded separately rather than together. Instead of forging a common energy policy to try to integrate energy markets, diversify energy sources, and reduce dependence on imported oil, national governments pursued individual policies often at each other's expense. Far from becoming more energy-independent, Western Europe in the 1980s added dependence on Russian gas to its decades-old dependence on Middle East oil. The United States warned Western Europe of the danger of depending on the Soviet Union for a large share of its energy needs, a danger that became fully apparent more than two decades later when Russia cut gas supplies to Ukraine, and thereby to other European users, partly for political reasons.

By the time of the Russian gas cuts in the late 2000s, energy had re-emerged on the EU's agenda for two main reasons. One was the success of the single market program, which focused attention on a number of areas omitted from the original plan, including the energy sector. Emboldened by the momentum generated by completion of the single market, the Commission began to break up national energy monopolies on competition policy grounds and to promote the liberalization and integration of energy markets in the EU. Thus began a long, arduous struggle for the Commission, battling against entrenched national, corporate, and regulatory interests. It is remarkable not that the Commission has failed so far fully to attain its objectives, but that it has achieved so much in the face of concerted opposition.

Climate change is the other reason why energy policy reappeared on the agenda of European integration. The EU has been regulating industrial and other emissions for a long time, largely for reasons of public health and environmental quality. As concern about global warming grew in the 1990s, the EU turned its attention squarely to combating climate change, which necessitates improving energy efficiency, reducing the use of fossil fuels, and developing alternative energy sources. In addition to market liberalization and integration, therefore, the Commission included climate change as a crucial rationalization for EU energy policy. Unlike energy market liberalization and integration, however, on climate change the Commission enjoyed the full support of most national governments and nongovernmental actors.

Liberalization and Integration

Traditionally in Europe, partly or wholly state-owned suppliers monopolized national energy markets because of governments' concerns about security of supply and related public service obligations of universal, uninterrupted provision. As result, energy—notably the supply of electricity and natural gas—was highly regulated at the national level and sheltered from competition. Efforts to establish a single energy market in the EU, even limited to electricity and natural gas, therefore required a fundamental change in attitude based on acceptance of the economic philosophy of liberalization and intra-European competition. The Commission sought to establish a competitive regime, with some necessary constraints to satisfy the requirement for safe, uninterrupted supply to all parts of the EU.

The Commission had an ally in Prime Minister Margaret Thatcher, who liberalized the energy market in Britain in the 1980s. By contrast, France and Germany remained skeptical of energy liberalization. Unable initially to obtain consensus among governments for market liberalization measures, the Commission decided instead to use competition policy rules to pry open the sector. Accordingly, the Commission decided in 1991 that an agreement concluded among a number of electricity companies violated Community competition policy rules by impeding imports by private industrial consumers. Beyond that, the Commission took a flexible and gradual approach to energy market liberalization, hoping that the 1992 momentum would push the electricity and gas monopolies into a more competitive environment.

Practical steps necessary to achieve a single energy market included the removal of numerous legal obstacles, the approximation of tax and pricing policies, the establishment of common norms and standards, and the setting of environmental and safety regulations. The Commission made completion of a single energy market a top priority in the mid-1990s. In 1995 the Commission published a long-awaited white paper on energy policy, which proposed a work program and timetable for liberalizing the energy sector.[11] The more market-oriented countries, such as Britain, criticized the Commission for not going far enough with its proposals; the more protectionist countries, such as France, criticized the Commission for going too far. These political differences were compounded by the existence of two separate systems of electricity market organization in the EU, one of which was peculiar to France. Partly by threatening to use its competition policy powers to break up national monopolies but largely because of pressure from influential industrial consumers of electricity, the Commission managed to erode national resistance to market liberalization. A breakthrough came in December 1996 when the Council passed a directive on the gradual creation of a single market for electricity that would allow industrial users to shop around for the lowest-cost EU provider. Efforts to open national gas markets were equally contentious but followed the same political and economic logic. Finally, in 1998 the Council adopted a directive on opening up the natural gas market, dealing with issues such as transmission, supply, storage, and distribution.

These directives constituted the first stage of the Commission's efforts to liberalize EU energy markets. The Commission returned to the fray soon after with proposals for further liberalization, culminating in new directives covering both sectors in 2003. By that time it was clear that vertically integrated companies—those engaged in production and supply as well as distribution and transmission—posed the greatest challenge to liberalization. Such companies prevented new producers and suppliers from using their distribution and transmission networks, thus thwarting competition. The ideal solution was ownership unbundling—breaking up the large incumbent energy suppliers that also owned the electricity and gas transmission networks. But that was a bridge too far for countries like France and Germany, dogged defenders of their national energy champions.

The 2003 directives nevertheless represented a major advance for the Commission and its liberalizing allies in the Council. The directives opened the market to more competition, called for national system operators to manage transmission and distribution facilities to which new suppliers could have access, specified public service obligations, and included measures for consumer protection. National regulatory authorities would oversee the new regime and would coordinate loosely in European regulatory groups. As in any directive of such magnitude and scope, the 2003 directives on electricity and gas liberalization contained safeguard clauses for national governments and numerous derogations. Nevertheless, the directives went a long way toward giving household and industrial consumers a choice of electricity and gas suppliers at competitive prices.

It soon became clear, however, that the legislation was unsatisfactory. Complaints from new suppliers about barriers to market entry and from consumers about difficulties in choosing suppliers led the Commission to conduct an inquiry into the operation of the gas and electricity markets. Published in 2007, the results of the inquiry confirmed that significant barriers to competition continued to exist. National regulators were weak; vertically integrated companies fiercely guarded access to transmission and distribution networks; and European regulatory groups were ineffective. Nothing less than complete unbundling, the Commission believed, would bring about the full liberalization of electricity and gas markets in the EU.

Earlier, the Commission had concluded that "in practice, the EU is still a long way from achieving its objective of a real internal market in which each consumer has the legal right to choose [an electricity and gas] supplier and exercise this right simply and effectively. . . . The legal and functional unbundling of system operators vertically connected to suppliers and producers has proven insufficient to guarantee equal access to the networks. The traditional operators thus maintain their dominant position and new companies wishing to enter the market encounter many problems caused by discriminatory access conditions, lack of available network capacity, a lack of transparent data on the network situation and poor investment. National regulators do not have the powers or independence necessary for succeeding in their mission."[12]

The Commission's proposed solution was a third internal energy market package of legislation (after the 1998 and 2003 packages). Its centerpiece would be a definitive separation between production or supply activities, on the one hand, and the operation of transmission systems, on the other. The separation could be based on either complete ownership unbundling or the introduction of a fully independent transmission system operator, should the system remain in the hands of the vertically integrated companies. As always, the Commission's preference was for complete ownership unbundling, which would not only "eliminate the different interests of system operators but also avoid the need for excessively detailed and complex regulations ensuring independence of vertically integrated system operators."[13]

The Commission introduced its new legislative package in November 2007. The proposals met predictable resistance from the French and German governments, which were still defending their national champions, and from large utilities companies, which complained about violation of property rights. Nevertheless, the Council and Parliament reached a compromise in March 2009 that allowed the vertically integrated energy companies to remain intact but obliged them to put their gas and electricity transmission networks under strict third-party control. Once again, this was less than the Commission wanted but represented a further step toward full energy market liberalization. A major innovation in the 2009 package was the establishment of two European networks of transmission system operators, one for electricity and the other for gas. These bodies help to manage the electricity and gas transmission networks and facilitate cross-border trade and supply for the EU and some connected countries.

The 2009 package most likely represents the last great EU energy liberalization effort. Like the single market generally, the internal energy market is not perfect, but is a far cry from the fragmentation along national lines that existed as recently as the early 2000s. The Commission will always need to apply competition policy rules in order to prevent abuse by large utility companies and unfair assistance from national governments. In the meantime, the Commission is pressing ahead with integrating energy networks throughout the EU and promoting energy security through greater efficiency, more use of renewables, and reduced dependence on Russian gas.

Integrated Energy Networks

Energy networks—electricity grids and gas pipelines—have developed historically along national lines. EU energy policy seeks to change that pattern by promoting interoperability, cross-border connections, and a comprehensive trans-European network. Member states agreed in the Maastricht Treaty on the establishment of trans-European networks (TENs) in a number of areas, including energy. Yet progress over the years has been slow and sporadic, not least because of the huge costs involved. In 1996 the EU adopted guidelines to define the general objectives and priorities for trans-European energy networks (TEN-Es). These were updated in 2003 and again in 2006, with an emphasis on sustainability, supply, and competitiveness. The idea is to encourage investment in infrastructure development and modernization throughout the enlarged EU. The 2006 guidelines list and rank projects in three categories:

- *Projects of common interest:* Economically viable electricity and gas networks that meet basic criteria for Community support relating to the environment, security of supply, and territorial cohesion.

- *Priority projects:* Selected from among the projects of common interest, these projects are likely to improve the functioning of the single market and considerably enhance security of supply, including the use of renewables. Such endeavors have priority over projects of common interest for Community funding.
- *Projects of European interest:* Selected from among the priority projects, these forty-two projects are exclusively of a cross-border nature and have the potential to improve trans-European transmission capacity greatly. Projects of European interest have the highest priority for Community funding under the TEN-E budget (about €20 million annually, mostly for feasibility studies) and the structural funds for regional development.[14]

The Commission provided additional momentum for the projects of European interest by presenting a priority plan for interconnection in 2007 and a green paper on integrated energy networks in 2008. Lamenting the underdevelopment of the trans-European networks due to insufficient national investment and the recalcitrance of large, vertically integrated companies, the Commission called again for a concerted effort to connect separate networks across the EU.

Given the importance of imports, which account for over 50 percent of supplies, the development of energy networks has an essential external dimension. The Commission's second strategic energy review, published in November 2008, suggested that security of supply could best be tackled by improving energy efficiency, keeping larger reserves of oil and gas in storage, and reducing the volume and diversifying the source of imports. Greater energy efficiency would help reduce demand for imports. As it happened, demand dropped markedly in 2009 due to ongoing efforts to improve efficiency and reduced economic activity during the recession.

Nevertheless, the EU remains highly dependent on energy imports. The main external sources of oil and gas for the EU are Russia, the Middle East, and North Africa. The external dimension of EU energy policy aims not only to improve access to oil and gas in those regions but also, specifically with regard to Russia, to reduce dependence on imports. Russian disputes with Ukraine, resulting in the disruption of supplies to the west, alarmed the EU. Yet the member states' initial response suggested that the EU was far from adopting a common position on the question of gas imports. Countries such as Germany and Italy preferred to deal separately with Russia, seeing security of supply primarily in national rather than regional terms. Yet persistent concerns about the unreliability of Russian gas supplies bolstered the Commission's efforts to forge a common EU position on the diversification of gas imports from the east.

In its 2008 strategic energy review, the Commission therefore proposed a new pipeline to bring gas to the EU from Azerbaijan through Turkey, thereby avoiding Russia. The so-called Nabucco pipeline could be extended under the

Caspian Sea to reach suppliers in Kazakhstan and Turkmenistan. The five transit countries for the pipeline—Turkey, Bulgaria, Romania, Hungary, and Austria (where it would link up with existing distribution networks)—signed an agreement in July 2009 to launch the project, which nevertheless faces formidable financial hurdles. The expected cost—about €8 billion—will be difficult to raise, notwithstanding a promised loan from the European Investment Bank of €2 billion. The Commission has committed €200 million of stimulus funding, largely as seed money.

Needless to say, Russia opposes the construction of the pipeline and is trying both to dissuade the EU from undertaking the project and to preempt western buyers by purchasing the gas from Central Asia and transshipping it to Europe. Russia prefers to deal separately with favored interlocutors in the EU, such as Germany and Italy, rather than collectively with the Commission and the Council of Ministers. The political and financial hurdles of the proposed Nabucco pipeline may be too high for the EU, and Russia may succeed in maintaining a near-monopoly of gas supplies from the east. The issue of the Nabucco pipeline therefore looms large in EU energy policy and in EU-Russia relations, despite its potentially modest contribution to total EU gas supply.

■ Climate Change

Given the extent of public concern about the effects of climate change and the influence of green parties within European coalition governments, it is hardly surprising that the EU has been one of the strongest voices in favor of a binding international agreement on climate change. Beginning with a 1990 commitment to stabilizing carbon dioxide emissions among member states, the Commission attempted to stake out a position for the EU as a global leader in reducing emissions of greenhouse gases and to exert moral pressure on others (mainly the United States) to follow the EU example. In practice, most member states found it impossible to halt emissions growth; the exception, Germany, was able to post impressive reductions after reunification led to the shutdown of most East German electricity-generating plants powered by highly polluting soft coal. The Commission's failure to persuade member states to adopt a Community-wide carbon dioxide tax in the early 1990s further widened the gap between rhetoric and results.

The Kyoto Protocol

The EU entered into the international negotiations that culminated in the Kyoto Protocol with the ambitious proposal that industrial countries reduce emissions of three greenhouse gases by 2010 to 15 percent below 1990 levels. However, the proposal imposed no targets on developing countries. The United States, which had some of the highest per capita emissions in the world, proposed stabilizing rather than reducing emissions and opposed the exclusion of developing countries from a global agreement. Indeed, the US Senate made clear that it would reject any deal that did not include developing-country commitments (the United States had China primarily in mind). Another contentious issue was the means by which countries could take credit for gains occurring elsewhere. The EU proposed allowing member states to take collective credit for any reductions within the EU; the United States pushed for "joint implementation" that would allow it to take credit for reductions achieved through US investment in Russia and other fuel-inefficient countries.

The negotiations ended in December 1997 when representatives of 160 countries, meeting in Kyoto, signed a protocol to the UN Framework Convention on Climate Change. The agreement, which eventually entered into force in 2005, committed developed countries to binding targets for reductions in greenhouse gas emissions from a 1990 baseline. The EU committed to an 8 percent cut, with separate targets for each of the then-fifteen member states under that umbrella.

For key EU members, the choice of 1990 as a baseline was a godsend: for Germany, 1990 baseline emissions included those from East German industries that shut down almost overnight following reunification; for the United Kingdom, they included reductions following the large-scale switch to natural gas and corresponding reduction of high-carbon coal consumption in the 1990s. As for Russia and the Central and Eastern European countries that experienced massive economic contractions in the 1990s, the Kyoto Protocol offered substantial room for increases in emissions as well as the sale of "hot air" (emission reductions on paper) to countries not equally favored by economic misfortune.

Kyoto's Clean Development Mechanism offered the opportunity for developed countries to fulfill their commitments at a lower cost by financing "offsets" in developing countries not bound by targets. Economically, this provision made sense: as greenhouse gases enter the atmosphere, irrespective of origin, taking the lowest-cost opportunities first both reduced total cost and provided useful infrastructure improvements for developing countries. Yet the system was bedeviled by problems of accountability and practicability.

Despite its drawbacks, the Kyoto Protocol was a notable diplomatic achievement for the EU. For the first time, an international agreement set globally binding targets for emission reductions, based on a reference year that fortuitously minimized compliance costs for most EU member states. In a magnanimous but costly gesture, the Kyoto Protocol exempted developing countries from taking any meaningful action, a clause that eventually led the United States to abandon the agreement, leaving the EU as the self-proclaimed leader of an idealistic but ultimately ineffective climate deal.

Although Kyoto was signed in 1997, EU implementation efforts began in earnest only in the new decade. The EU launched its first climate change program in 2000, an arrangement whereby the Commission proposed measures to fight climate change following interaction with industries and NGOs. Measures proposed under the first climate change program included an emission trading scheme, a directive on generating electricity from renewable energy sources, and a voluntary agreement with the auto industry to reduce CO_2 emissions from cars. The Commission launched a second climate change program in 2005, which reviewed what had been achieved under the inaugural program, explored the idea of carbon capture and storage, and sought to bring the transport sector into the emission trading scheme.

The emission trading scheme was the most ambitious and innovative policy approach to meeting, and possibly surpassing, the EU's Kyoto commitments. When it became operational in January 2005, the trading scheme allowed energy-intensive power-generating and industrial plants in all twenty-five member states to trade carbon dioxide pollution permits, based on an emission cap set according to a national allocation plan and approved by the Commission. Reductions in the discharge of greenhouse gases in Central and Eastern Europe, following improvements in the efficiency of coal-powered energy-producing methods, made power plants in the new member states attractive emission trading partners. Like all new schemes, however, the emission trading scheme was plagued by problems. Limited industrial coverage meant that the scheme included only about 40 percent of the EU's total CO_2 emissions, and a large number of key emitters were allocated free permits, essentially eliminating any incentive for them to invest in lower-carbon practices or technology. A thin market led to wild fluctuations in price, putting pressure on the Commission to issue new permits. The experience of the trading scheme provided further evidence for many economists, unconcerned by political realities, that a carbon tax would be a more efficient approach.

Aided to some extent by these implementation efforts, but largely by the choice of 1990 as the baseline and by low economic growth, the EU as a whole was able to claim emission reductions equivalent to 8.6 percent by 2005, exceeding its Kyoto commitment. Far from falling, however, EU emissions continued to rise. In October 2006, the European Environment Agency warned that only two member states (Sweden and the United Kingdom) would reach their targets, and that the EU15 would achieve only a 0.6 percent reduction by 2010 without credits from the Clean Development Mechanism and other offset mechanisms.[15]

The Energy-Climate Package
Concerned about the sluggish pace of its emission reductions and with an eye to the global negotiations for a successor to the Kyoto Protocol, due to expire at the end of 2012, the EU sharpened its focus on climate change in the late 2000s. Prompted by the European Council in March 2007, the Commission mulled over and finally introduced a raft of legislative proposals in January

2008 that aimed to reduce carbon dioxide emissions in the EU by 20 percent, increase renewable energy use by 20 percent, and improve energy efficiency by 20 percent by 2020.[16] The Commission, Council, and Parliament agreed to fast-track the legislative process with a view to wrapping up the "20-20-20" energy-climate package by December 2008. There was broad consensus within the EU on the goals of the package, but not on how best to achieve them. Given the dependence of Central and Eastern European countries on carbon-heavy coal for electricity generation and the steep price of conversion to cleaner fuel—not least the security cost of switching to Russian gas—the energy-climate package risked exacerbating the EU's east-west divide.

The French presidency took up the challenge in July 2008 of reaching an agreement by the end of the year, seizing the initiative from the Commission. Two groups of countries demanded concessions. Belgium, Italy, and Germany were primarily concerned about "carbon leakage"—the possible relocation of energy-intensive firms to countries with less onerous and less expensive climate change regulation. The second, the so-called Group of Nine Central and Eastern European countries, wanted free allocation of emissions permits for their largely coal-fired electricity generators. By threatening, or threatening to threaten, a veto, Poland succeeded at the October 2008 summit in getting inserted into the conclusions a commitment that the eventual deal would "[have] regard to each Member State's specific situation."[17]

President Nicolas Sarkozy spent considerable time and political capital in bilateral and multilateral meetings with fellow national leaders in the run-up to the December European Council, eventually producing a final package that, although undoubtedly important and hailed as historic, was riddled with concessions, exemptions, and transition periods, and irritated MEPs who felt that the Council presidency had hijacked the codecision procedure. In a departure from the "20" theme, the Council offered to commit to a 30 percent reduction by 2020 if other developed countries made "comparable" reductions in the ongoing negotiations to conclude a follow-on agreement to the Kyoto Protocol.

The EU's eagerness to be seen as the global leader on climate change, especially before a new, environmentally friendly US administration came into power, accounts in part for the speed and the mode of decisionmaking on the energy-climate package. So does Sarkozy's determination to reach an agreement during France's Council presidency and José Manuel Barroso's desire to reach an agreement well before the end of his Commission presidency, with a view to being reappointed for a second term. While undoubtedly a significant accomplishment, the final package might nonetheless have benefited from more time and reflection. The extent to which the quality of the package suffered from the haste and manner of its adoption would become apparent in due course, arguably to the detriment of the EU's credibility as a climate change leader.

The energy-climate agreement also has implications for all economic actors, including small-scale emitters in sectors such as transport, buildings, agriculture, and waste, which represent about 60 percent of total greenhouse gas emissions in the EU. By 2020, emissions from these areas are to be reduced by an average of 10 percent compared to 2005, shared among member states according to differences in per capita GDP. The agreement maintains the national targets for member states, together with a linear, legally binding trajectory for the period 2013–2020, including annual monitoring and compliance checks.

However, an improved emission trading scheme is the keystone of the energy-climate package. The new scheme aims to cover additional sectors and greenhouse gases, increasing the coverage of total EU emissions (currently about 40 percent), beginning in 2012. The number of allowances issued would decline each year to produce a 21 percent reduction by 2020. The system retains a number of loopholes, however, including transitional allowances for new member states and free allocations for energy-intensive industries "exposed to international competition," provided they invest in the "most efficient" technologies. The number of allowances actually auctioned (as opposed to being handed out free of charge) would rise gradually toward a goal of 50 percent of all allowances, starting in 2013, and reaching 100 percent in 2027. The new trading scheme would also continue to allow offset credits from outside the EU, notably from projects under Kyoto's Clean Development Mechanism, limited to "below half" of total EU emission reductions under the trading scheme. The EU hoped that the extended scheme, the world's largest greenhouse gas emission trading system, would serve as the nucleus of a much larger global carbon market.

In a break from international practice, the EU decided to include international aviation in the emission trading scheme. This measure was largely a political gesture to Europe's green lobby: aviation accounts for only 3 percent of EU emissions, and barring a technological breakthrough, emission reductions are likely to depend mainly on government efforts to improve air traffic control systems. The move irritated a number of EU trading partners, who argued that the International Civil Aviation Organization has sole jurisdiction over international aviation emissions and that the costs of curbing emissions would fall disproportionately on non-EU long-haul carriers.

In April 2009 the EU issued a regulation on emissions standards for new passenger cars. The regulation is an important tool to help countries meet their emission targets in those sectors that are not part of the emission trading scheme (cars account for about 12 percent of the EU's carbon emissions). The new legislation, along with complementary measures such as the fuel quality directive, sets binding targets to ensure that carbon dioxide emissions from the new car fleet are reduced to an average of 120 grams per kilometer by 2012 (a reduction of about 25 percent from 2008 levels), with a stringent long-term target of 95 grams per kilometer by 2020. The new standards are expected to contribute about one-third of the emission reductions required by 2020 from the sectors that are not part of the emission trading scheme. The fuel quality directive places an obligation on suppliers to reduce greenhouse gases from the entire fuel production chain by 6 percent by 2020. A review before then will consider increasing the level to 10 percent by 2020, possibly through the inclusion of international projects, the development of carbon capture and storage, and greater use of electricity-powered cars.

Carbon dioxide emissions from shipping account for 2–3 percent of global emissions and are growing by 3–4 percent annually. Although legislation to reduce shipping emissions was not included in the 2008 energy-climate package, the Commission plans to introduce it as part of its overall approach to combating climate change.[18]

The commitment in the energy-climate package to increase the share of renewable energy in the EU mix to 20 percent (10 percent in the transport sector) is probably optimistic. The commitment arose out of the obvious appeal of wind, water, solar, and biodegradable energy sources, coupled with strong political support among certain member states (especially Germany) and in the EP. Bright hopes for biofuels, popular with farming interests, appear unlikely to be realized. A boom in biofuel production in the EU, driven by subsidies in Germany and proposals for mandatory minimum shares in the energy mix, faltered as food prices skyrocketed in the global commodity boom of 2008 and as concerns rose about the effect of biofuel production on global food security. At the same time, disappointing estimates of actual life-cycle carbon savings, given the energy costs of transporting and processing bulky raw materials, diminished the appeal of biofuels. A provision in the fuel quality directive setting sustainability criteria for biofuels attempted to resolve the sustainability debate, but is unlikely to satisfy all parties. While emerging technologies promise to reduce the economic and carbon cost of biofuels, the promise remains a commercial dream. As a result, expectations for biofuels have been pared back at both the national and EU levels.

The energy-climate package did not address nuclear energy, the elephant in the room of EU climate change policy. The role of nuclear power in reducing carbon emissions is a highly charged issue in the EU, given profound, almost theological differences among national governments and interest groups. In France it appears to be a non-issue: about 70 percent of the country's electricity comes from nuclear plants, resulting in enviably low carbon intensity for a wealthy developed nation. By contrast, Germany and the United Kingdom, struggling to meet their Kyoto commitments, have bowed to antinuclear campaigners and ruled out further nuclear plants. In 2000, Germany's Social Democratic–Green coalition government announced its intention of phasing out nuclear power altogether by 2020, leaving an inconvenient 20 percent deficit in power generation that will have to be filled by other low-carbon technologies—or by gas from Russia—unless subsequent governments change course. As evidence of climate change mounts, soul-searching among stakeholders appears to be mounting as well, with some environmental activists apparently dropping their full-throated opposition to nuclear power.

From Kyoto to Copenhagen

Following adoption of the energy-climate package, the Commission turned its attention to developing an international negotiating position for the post-Kyoto regime consistent with its domestic targets, in a fundamentally altered international context. The conceptual flaws in the Kyoto framework had become ever more apparent. Overall emissions growth showed no signs of abating; any gains in developed countries were swallowed up by emissions growth in China, whose economic boom was fueled largely by coal. China had become the world's largest single CO_2 emitter, overtaking the United States. At the same time, rapidly rising goods imports from China sharpened EU industry concerns about "carbon leakage." Despite steadily rising emissions, the United States was no longer an outlier; its share of global emissions had declined from 36 percent in 1990 to about 20 percent in 2009.

The environmental stakes were rising even as the ability of the developed world to solve the problem was declining. The Intergovernmental Panel on Climate Change (IPCC) issued a report in 2008 warning that avoiding climate change was no longer possible and that keeping it merely below catastrophic limits would require developed countries to reduce emissions by 25–40 percent and developing countries to make substantial cuts as well. With the increasingly inadequate Kyoto Protocol due to expire in 2012 and the need for concerted international action fully apparent, parties to the UN Framework Convention on Climate Change, meeting in Poznan, Poland, in December 2008, committed themselves to achieving a new international agreement at a follow-on conference in Copenhagen in December 2009, with a view to the active participation of the new US administration of President Barack Obama.

In January 2009, the Commission released a communication proposing binding numerical targets for all developed countries, together with a new demand: a "significant contribution" on the order of a 15–30 percent decline in emissions growth below the "business as usual" projection for developing countries. The Commission also called for reform of the Kyoto Protocol's Clean Development Mechanism to phase out some countries and sectors and improve accountability, a global cap and trade system for emissions from aviation and shipping, and negotiations to link national emission trading systems. In addition, the Commission floated the idea of global funding to help cover the costs of "mitigation" (reduction of greenhouse gas emissions) and adaptation to climate change for developing countries. The environment council endorsed these goals, although finance ministers were more circumspect with regard to the proposed new fund.

In the run-up to the Copenhagen Conference, EU efforts to exert leadership quickly became entangled in multiple points of contention that slowed the global negotiations. The main issues were targets and finance, with other issues such as treatment of intellectual property rights in the diffusion of low-carbon technologies creating further friction. The EU faced growing resistance at home to new, ambitious targets; a new US administration promising action but unwilling to get too far ahead of Congress; and Chinese and Indian leaders resistant to accepting binding international commitments. Unable to leverage its position on the international front, the Commission made "comparable" action from other developed countries a main theme of its negotiating strategy, while dutifully pressing China and India to make some kind of commitment on emissions growth.

The Commission's proposal that some developing countries commit to restraining growth in emissions, a clear break with the paternalistic framework of the Kyoto Protocol, was clearly more acceptable to the developed than the developing countries. China and India denounced any effort to bind their emissions growth, even though both had begun to face the dire economic and environmental need to rein in fossil fuel consumption at home. Engaging with both countries became a key focus of EU diplomacy, but with mixed results. Presumably in response to domestic exigencies, US pressure, and EU efforts (in roughly that order), China announced in November 2009 an unprecedented, although exceedingly modest, offer to commit to a decrease in carbon intensity (emissions per unit of GDP growth). India, by contrast, reiterated its absolute refusal to make any commitments. Constrained by internal politics, the United States remained immune to repeated EU urgings to "do more" and eventually announced a target of 17 percent below 2005 levels, subject to uncertain congressional support. Going into the Copenhagen negotiations, the Swedish presidency nonetheless held out the hope that the EU might be able to up the ante to the 30 percent target mentioned in the December 2008 energy-climate package, under the right conditions.

The influential Stern Report on climate change, commissioned by the British government and released in October 2006, argued that investment in low-carbon technologies would ultimately pay off in sustainable economic growth, and also that the cost of inaction, in terms of droughts, floods, crop failure, and other climate change effects, would be far greater than the cost of timely action. All parties in the global negotiations agreed that the up-front cost of reducing greenhouse gas emissions worldwide would nonetheless be enormous and would be well beyond the means of most poor countries without disastrous effects on their economic development. Who would pay the piper—and how? Responses ranged from a call by developing countries for a fund made up of over 1 percent of global GDP annually, to which the developed countries would be the main contributors, to a proposal by British prime minister Gordon Brown for developed countries to provide up to $100 billion a year, starting in 2020. Other ideas included possible World Bank funding, international registries, and levies on global emission trading.

As the Copenhagen negotiations approached, ambitious financial commitments on the part of the EU seemed beyond the reach of member states buffeted by the recession and concerned about the competitiveness of domestic industry. Despite its undoubted commitment to tackling climate change, Germany showed signs of increasing discomfort over its role as designated paymaster. Poland, coal-dependent and unimpressed by the Commission's call to global leadership, insisted that financial contributions should be voluntary. At issue was both fast-start funding to help mitigation and adaptation efforts in developing countries between 2010 and 2012 and funding thereafter as part of the post-Kyoto regime.

It looked in October 2009, at an acrimonious meeting of the European Council, as if national leaders would fail to reach agreement on a generous EU contribution to the proposed climate change funds. The summit conclusions merely noted that "the EU and its member states are prepared to take on their . . . fair share of total international finance."[19] The Commission and the Swedish presidency returned to the charge at the December European Council, which took place as the climate change negotiations opened in Copenhagen. Undoubtedly moved by the momentousness of the Copenhagen Conference, and aided by the Polish government's concern about being seen as a spoiler, national leaders finally reached agreement on an EU contribution of €2.4 billion a year to the fast-start fund, based on voluntary national contributions. As expected, Britain, France, and Germany made the largest pledges.[20]

The breakthrough on fast-start funding at the December summit restored some of the EU's luster at the Copenhagen Conference. Climate change was an issue on which the EU had staked a global leadership role; the Copenhagen Conference was to have been a triumph for EU diplomacy. The generosity of the EU's commitment to fast-start funding, and the EU's willingness to increase to 30 percent its target for emission reduction if other developed countries agreed to make a similar effort, seemed to bode well for the EU's hopes of leading the conference participants to an ambitious post-Kyoto agreement, despite huge remaining differences among major players and demands verging on the delusional from small, developing countries.

In the event, EU leaders, having arrived in Copenhagen for the concluding session of a conference characterized by far too much intransigent rhetoric and operational chaos, were upstaged by their US and Chinese counterparts, who, together with the leaders of Brazil, India, and South Africa, reached a last-minute accord that recognized the need to prevent a global temperature rise of 2 degrees Celsius, but without setting either a peak year or a target for reducing overall emissions.[21] Although the accord was significant because of the willingness of China and the United States to reach an agreement and because it provides a framework for future action, its weakness was a bitter disappointment for those countries, including the EU and most of its member states, hoping for an ambitious outcome. The EU's acquiescence in a highly unsatisfactory deal was a bitter blow to Brussels's self-image of global leadership on climate change. If anything, it was a stark lesson in great-power politics and a reminder that international relations among sovereignty-conscious states are uncongenial to a self-consciously postnational entity such as the EU.

▪ Notes

1. See John McCormick, *Environmental Policy in the European Union* (Basingstoke: Palgrave, 2001).

2. European Commission, "Towards Sustainability: The European Community Program of Policy and Action in Relation to the Environment and Sustainable Development (Fifth Environmental Action Program)," 1993, p. 10.

3. See Alberta Sbragia, "The Push-Pull of Environmental Policy-Making," in Helen Wallace and William Wallace, eds., *Policy-Making in the European Union,* 3rd ed. (Oxford: Oxford University Press, 1996), pp. 235–256.

4. See Marc Pallemaerts, "The EU and Sustainable Development: An Ambiguous Relationship," in Marc Pallemaerts and Albena Azmanova, eds., *The European Union and Sustainable Development: Internal and External Dimensions* (Brussels: VUB, 2006), pp. 19–52.

5. European Commission, "Agenda 2000: For a Stronger and Wider Europe," COM(97)2000 final, July 16, 1997.

6. Wim Kok et al., *Facing the Challenge: The Lisbon Strategy for Growth and Enlargement: Report of the High Level Group* (Brussels: European Commission, 2004), pp. 35–38.

7. European Commission, *2008 Environment Policy Review* (Luxembourg: Office for Official Publications of the European Communities, 2009), p. 12.

8. See *Europolitics,* July 2009.

9. Interview with Karl Falkenberg, *Europolitics,* April 2009.

10. See David Buchan, *Energy and Climate Change: Europe at the Crossroads* (Oxford: Oxford University Press, 2009).

11. European Commission, "An Energy Policy for the European Union," COM (95)682, December 15, 1995.

12. European Commission, "Prospects for the Internal Electricity and Gas Market," January 10, 2007, http://europa.eu/legislation_summaries/energy/internal_energy_market/l27075_en.htm.

13. Ibid.

14. See Trans European Energy Networks, http://europa.eu/legislation_summaries/energy/internal_energy_market/l27066_en.htm.

15. See "EU Climate Change Policies," *EurActiv*, December 6, 2007, http://www.euractiv.com/en/sustainability/eu-climate-change-policies/article-117453.

16. European Commission, *2008 Environment Policy Review.*

17. Brussels European Council, "Presidency Conclusions," October 15–16, 2008.

18. See European Commission, *2008 Environment Policy Review,* p. 15.

19. Brussels European Council, "Presidency Conclusions," October 29–30, 2009.

20. Brussels European Council, "Presidency Conclusions," December 10–11, 2009.

21. UN Framework Convention on Climate Change, Copenhagen Accord, December 18, 2009, http://unfccc.int/files/meetings/cop_15/application/pdf/cop15_cph_auv.pdf.

16 Beyond the EU's Borders

By virtue of what it does internally, the EU has a big external footprint. In addition, the European Union has a number of policies that specifically address issues beyond its borders. Trade policy, development policy, and humanitarian aid are obvious examples examined in this chapter. The Common Foreign and Security Policy is a key component of the EU's external relations, but is examined in the next chapter, along with the EU's efforts to organize itself as an Area of Freedom, Security, and Justice.

The EU aims to promote abroad what it seeks at home: stability, security, democracy, and sustainable development. In pursuit of those goals, the EU has entered into a bewildering number and variety of highly institutionalized bilateral and multilateral arrangements. EU external action, as external relations are called in the Lisbon Treaty, gives the impression of intense busyness and procedural complexity. EU politicians and officials are constantly engaged with their non-EU counterparts in structured dialogues, ministerial and summit meetings, joint parliamentary committee meetings, and the like, spawning new initiatives, declarations, and communiqués. The power of word-processing becomes fully apparent when reviewing official EU documents in the realm of external action. In no other area of EU activity does procedure seem so much more important than substance.

Not that the EU is an ineffective international actor; rather its global impact is less than the combined weight of nearly thirty European countries would appear to warrant. Yet the EU is both more and less than the sum of its parts. EU competence for external action is exclusive in some areas (such as trade policy) and limited in others (such as security and defense policy). In an international system still dominated by power politics, the influence of the EU is inevitably constrained. Actual or aspiring superpowers such as China, India, and the United States see the EU as it is (a collection of countries with limited global power), not as the EU wants to be seen: a postnational entity capable of shaping global affairs on the basis of soft (nonmilitary) power.

The special nature of the EU has given rise to a branch of external action that is truly unique: enlargement policy. Chris Patten, a former external relations commissioner, has described enlargement as "the most successful foreign policy pursued by [the EU]."[1] The purpose of enlargement is to bring countries into the EU, after which those countries cease to be an object of EU foreign policy. Enlargement has been successful not just procedurally but substantively, in that it has helped to achieve the EU's core objectives—stability, security, democracy, and sustainable development—in the EU's immediate neighborhood, which has been incorporated into the EU proper.

Given the unusual nature of the EU, external action has always posed an internal organizational challenge. The Lisbon Treaty included numerous changes relating to external action, not least by upgrading the High Representative for CFSP (now the High Representative for Foreign Affairs and Security), combining the position with that of Commission vice president, and calling for the establishment of the External Action Service (see Chapter 17). Procedural changes in the Lisbon Treaty enhance the power of the European Parliament in a number of policy areas, including trade.

■ Enlargement

Enlargement—the accession of new member states—has been a permanent feature of European integration since the early 1960s (see Box 0.1). Countries have wanted to join the EU for a variety of reasons, such as better market access, more trade and investment opportunities, and eligibility for structural funding and agricultural subsidies. Security considerations have also been a factor. Why has the EU wanted to expand? The ethos of integration is inclusive: from the beginning, the EU has sought to promote prosperity and strengthen security by bringing European countries together. Enlargement enhances the EU's identity and sense of purpose. It also raises the EU's international image and potential policy impact. Finally, it brings economic benefits for the existing member states, in the form of a larger internal market with more intra-EU investment and trade.

Nevertheless, enlargement can be disruptive and costly, at least in the short term. Enlargement has also become a highly complicated process because of the mismatch between the growing policy scope and institutional complexity of the EU, on the one hand, and the relatively poor economic situation, weak administrative capacity, and shaky democratic foundation of many of the most recent new members—and of the remaining prospective members—on the other. Iceland, a sophisticated, stable, well-off country (despite the impact of the financial crisis), would have little difficulty meeting the demands of EU membership; Ukraine would have a tough time doing so, and would be much more difficult than Iceland for the EU to digest.

As seen in Chapter 6, the EU drew up the so-called Copenhagen criteria for membership in 1993. The criteria set out the general economic and political conditions that applicants must meet in order to join the EU: guarantees for democracy, rule of law, and human rights; a functioning market economy; and the ability to take on the obligations of membership in all policy areas. The Copenhagen criteria were drawn up for the newly independent Central and Eastern European countries whose transition to democracy and capitalism became synonymous with transition to EU membership.

The most obvious criterion for EU membership—a criterion stated in the EU's founding treaties—is that a country must be European. In the west, Europe begins (or ends) with Iceland and Greenland; in the north, with Norway and Russia; in the south, on the shores of the Mediterranean. But where does Europe begin or end in the east? With Russia, which stretches all the way to the Pacific Ocean? With Georgia, Armenia, and Azerbaijan in the southern Caucasus? With Turkey, only a small part of which lies on the western side of the Bosporus, traditionally the dividing line between Europe and Asia Minor?

The answer is political, not geographical. For the purpose of joining the EU, a country is European if EU leaders decide that it is. Many Europeans doubt that Turkey is European. Nevertheless, the Council of Ministers decided as long ago as 1963, when it approved an association agreement between the European Community and Turkey, that Turkey *is* European. More recently, in December 1999, the European Council recognized Turkey as a candidate for EU membership; in December 2004 it decided to open accession negotiations. Discussions about Turkey's "Europeanness" seem pointless, despite the fact that leaders such as Nicolas Sarkozy in France and Angela Merkel in Germany want to keep Turkey out or that the negotiations have stalled.

A majority of EU leaders would prefer that the EU's eventual eastern border remain uncertain, not necessarily because they want more countries to join but because they do not want to weaken the EU's ability to leverage economic and political reform (a process called conditionality) in prospective member states. The EU holds considerable sway over aspiring member states, whose prospects for membership depend on meeting the Copenhagen criteria. If a country knows that it has no prospect ever of joining the EU, it will be unlikely to respond well to EU efforts to influence its behavior.

The EU's enlargement strategy rests on three pillars: meeting its commitments to prospective members, applying fair and rigorous conditionality, and better communicating enlargement.[2] The EU omitted another key word: "credibility." How credible is the EU's commitment to extend membership to Turkey, given that prominent EU leaders have stated unequivocally that Turkey does not belong in the EU? How credible is the prospect of the EU acquiring new members in Eastern Europe, let alone the southern Caucasus, a far corner of Europe?

Opponents of further enlargement worry about the EU's "absorption capacity," an imprecise term suggesting that the EU's institutions and policies can cope only with a finite number of member states. It is impossible to say what that number *could* be, although some people have a definite idea of what it *should* be. Empirical evidence shows that the EU functioned surprisingly well with twenty-seven members, with or without the Lisbon Treaty. Undoubtedly, enlargement is awkward and messy; it alters the EU's institutional arrangements, complicates decisionmaking, and changes the EU's character. Such is the nature of ever closer union.

Advocates as well as opponents of admitting new members into the EU acknowledge "enlargement fatigue"—public weariness of the seemingly endless process of EU accession. Before 2004 and especially 2007, most people in the EU paid little attention to enlargement. The scale and impact of the 2004–2007 enlargement ended that obliviousness. Horror stories, real and imagined, of Romanian migrants in Italy; fears about Polish plumbers undercutting their competitors in France; and rumors about lawless Lithuanian migrants in Ireland brought enlargement to people's attention in a wholly negative way. Unease in Western Europe about the labor and social consequences of enlargement is magnified many times over when the country in question is Turkey. "Enlargement fatigue" really means concerns about jobs, migrants, and social disruption.

Apart from Turkey, the universe of possible new member states is quite large. It includes the countries of the Western Balkans, all of which are designated by the EU as either candidate or potential candidate countries; Russia (which is unlikely ever to want to or be allowed to join); Belarus, Moldova, and Ukraine; and the three countries of the southern Caucasus (Georgia, Armenia, and Azerbaijan). There are also a few prospective candidates in Western Europe, notably Iceland, Norway, and Switzerland.

The European Free Trade Area and the European Economic Area

Iceland, Liechtenstein, and Norway participate with the EU in the European Economic Area, which came into being in January 1994. Together with Switzerland, the three countries constitute the European Free Trade Association. Switzerland chose not to join the EEA after a referendum in December 1992. Despite the huge imbalance between its EU and EFTA members, the EEA is nevertheless the most highly institutionalized and integrated external economic arrangement involving the EU. Substantively, the EEA covers the single market, competition, and some other core economic policy areas. The EEA acquired ten new members—on the EU side—following enlargement in 2004 and 2007, making it easily the world's largest commercial bloc.

Norway and Switzerland are the only continental Western European countries neither in the EU nor actively seeking to join it. Norway and Switzerland have other similarities and some striking differences: both are highly national-istic and wealthy but differ markedly in their security policies, with Norway being in NATO and Switzerland doggedly neutral. Both are strongly Euro-skeptical, yet a near-majority of their populations and the vast majority of their governing and business elites advocate EU membership. Indeed, Norway has developed an unusually close relationship with the EU, even contributing to its budget and participating in a number of its policies.

Although Switzerland decided not to pursue EU membership, successive Swiss governments have pursued a policy of de facto European integration. As a result, no other country has as many agreements with the EU. These cover everything from free trade to Switzerland's participation in the Schengen regime. In view of Swiss people's concerns about being swallowed up by the EU behemoth, Switzerland and the EU have a touchy political relationship that is further complicated by EU criticism of the country's banking secrecy laws.

Iceland experienced a national trauma in 2008–2009 when its recently deregulated and globally integrated financial system collapsed and the IMF had to come to the rescue. Traditionally, Iceland has been uninterested in join-ing the EU, fearing the impact of membership on its identity and economy (Iceland does not want to lose control of its lucrative coastal fisheries). The shock of the financial crisis made EU membership, and especially euro area membership, much more appealing for Iceland. Nevertheless, the issue is politically contentious in the small island country.

Following the general election in May 2009, the new Icelandic govern-ment applied to join the EU. There are no real barriers to membership—Iceland has already incorporated many EU laws—but the government would like to negotiate an exemption or opt out from the Common Fisheries Policy, which the EU is unlikely to countenance. Apart from fish, Iceland's member-ship would give the EU access to the Arctic, an area of growing strategic importance. Even if Iceland and the EU conclude an accession agreement, a majority of Icelanders could well vote not to join the EU.

The Candidate Countries

As of early 2010, there were three candidate countries: Croatia, Macedonia, and Turkey. Croatia applied to join in February 2003; the European Council endorsed its application in June 2004, giving the country candidate status. Because of Croatia's relatively strong economy and solid democratic struc-tures, the accession process was reasonably smooth, the most difficult issue being the question of Croatia's relations with the International Criminal Tribu-nal for the former Yugoslavia (Croatia was allegedly sheltering a number of indicted war criminals). Under intense EU and US pressure, Croatia finally cooperated fully with the court.

In late 2008 a maritime border dispute with neighboring Slovenia sud-denly erupted and blocked progress on Croatia's accession. Having only a small coastline, Slovenia demanded use of part of a disputed bay so that it could access international waters. Slovenia's insinuation of a bilateral dispute into Croatia's accession negotiations irritated the other member states, which were powerless to end Slovenia's obstructionism. The dispute neared a resolution in November 2009 when the Croatian parliament approved a deal between the two countries to bring the issue before an impartial international mediator, paving the way for a resumption of Croatia's accession negotiations.

Macedonia, which has so far escaped the kind of violence that tore through other parts of the former Yugoslavia, applied for EU membership in March 2004. Following a positive report by the Commission, the European Council granted Macedonia candidate status in December 2005, largely in recognition of Macedonia's avoidance of civil war. In fact, Macedonia is a long way from membership, not least because of a bitter bilateral dispute with Greece, which has a province called Macedonia and, therefore, insists that the EU refer to its neighbor as the "former Yugoslav Republic of Macedonia." Macedonia also has a dispute with Bulgaria over contending interpretations of nineteenth- and twentieth-century history. As for the early twenty-first century, EU concerns about the political and economic situation in Macedonia preclude accession in the near future.

Turkey, for reasons of national identity and economic advantage, has long aspired to EU membership. Yet Turkey only became a serious contender in the late 1990s as the country stabilized politically and economically. Having applied for EU membership far earlier than any of the Central and Eastern European candidates, and having already signed an agreement for a customs union with the EU, Turkey pressed for participation in the round of accession negotiations slated to begin in 1998. The EU was in a quandary. On the one hand, Turkey was an economically underdeveloped country with a questionable human rights record and fragile political institutions (as recently as 1997, the army had helped to oust a democratically elected government). On the other hand, Turkey's European orientation and vocation were undeniable. Moreover, Turkey was a big emerging market, deserved support from the EU to help counter the rise of Muslim fundamentalism, and had assumed great strategic importance with respect to the Balkans, the Middle East, and parts of the former Soviet Union, all extremely volatile areas. Although EU governments had legitimate economic and political reasons to doubt Turkey's suitability for membership in the foreseeable future, many were motivated primarily by anti-Muslim prejudice and were fearful of the consequences of admitting a country such as Turkey, whose population of over 70 million would make it the EU's second-largest member state.[3]

Well aware of the EU's dilemma and discomfiture, Turkey knew exactly what buttons to press. "Will the future of the European Union be limited by religious and ethnic considerations, or will it be one that reaches out and boldly contributes to diversity and unity?" asked Turkey's foreign minister only days before the summit in December 1997 at which the European Council decided to open negotiations with certain applicant countries.[4] Apart from seizing the moral high ground, Turkey had a more pragmatic card to play: its ability to influence the negotiations on Cypriot accession through its suasion over the northern part of the island.

Although it decided not to invite Turkey to participate in the accession negotiations that were then about to begin, the European Council sought to reassure officials in Ankara that the EU's door was still open. In effect, the European Council put Turkey's application on hold, placing it behind all the other applications in the accession queue. Turkey retaliated by freezing its official ties with Brussels. More ominously, Turkey threatened to block progress on the reunification of Cyprus unless the EU reconsidered its candidacy.

A rapprochement between Greece and Turkey in the new decade, together with valiant Turkish efforts to meet the Copenhagen criteria, nevertheless kept Turkey's application at center stage. Turkey protested so vehemently against its exclusion from the enlargement process and strove so hard to improve its membership prospects that the European Council officially recognized it as a candidate country in December 1999. Yet Turkey was again outraged in October 2002 when the Commission recommended that the EU admit ten countries by 2004 while in Turkey's case offering merely to increase pre-accession assistance. In December 2002, having endorsed the Commission's recommendations on enlarging the EU, the European Council announced that it would decide by December 2004 whether to open accession negotiations with Turkey.

A change of government in Turkey in November 2002 greatly improved its prospects. Despite its Islamist-leaning stance, the new government of Prime Minister Recep Tayyip Erdoğan pushed through numerous economic and social reforms, cultivated closer relations with Greece, and moderated Turkey's position on Cyprus, which joined the EU in May 2004. Having a divided Cyprus as a member state would become a thorn in the side of the EU and a major impediment to harmonious EU-Turkey relations.

The Commission rewarded Erdoğan's reform and reconciliation efforts with a recommendation in October 2004 that the European Council agree to open accession negotiations with Turkey. The Commission did not suggest that the negotiations would be either short or trouble-free; on the contrary, it held out little hope of Turkish accession for at least a decade. France took a particularly hard line, acknowledging that negotiations would probably have to begin but pointing out that they might not necessarily end in full membership for Turkey. The political climate at the time was soured by growing tension over the assimilation (or nonassimilation) of Muslim minorities in Europe. Lurking behind the rhetoric of many conservative politicians in the EU was deep-seated concern about the social and cultural impact of Turkish membership, even if Turkey were to meet the political and economic criteria.

The European Council nevertheless agreed in December 2004 that accession negotiations would begin with Turkey. After much preliminary posturing, the talks opened in October 2005. The framework for the negotiations reflected the EU's doubts about Turkey's readiness for membership: "in the case of a serious and persistent breach in Turkey of the principles of liberty, democracy, respect for human rights and fundamental freedoms and the rule of law on which the Union is founded, the Commission will, on its own initiative or on the request of one-third of the Member States, recommend the suspension of the negotiations and propose the conditions for eventual resumption."[5]

Not surprisingly, the negotiations have not gone well. The main stumbling block has been Turkey's refusal to open its ports and airports to traffic from Cyprus, a basic EU demand. In December 2006, at the behest of the (Greek) Cypriot government, the EU blocked the opening of eight accession negotiation chapters because of the Cyprus issue. For its part, Turkey complained that the EU had not fulfilled its promise to end the trade embargo on the self-styled Turkish Republic of Northern Cyprus.

In its annual reviews of Turkey's candidacy, the Commission has acknowledged that Turkey is a functioning market economy that should be able to cope with competitive pressure and market forces within the EU, and that Turkey has made progress in aligning itself with the EU's legal order. Turkey has indeed made great strides forward. The process of Europeanization has helped the country move in the direction it wants to go in any case, despite the massive adjustment costs. Yet the political price of domestic Turkish reform is large and may be unsustainable, regardless of the government in power. As it is, Turkey's fiercely secular military and judiciary distrust the Islamist government, and the constitutional court even considered a case to ban the ruling Justice and Development Party. Had the court ruled in favor, the EU would have suspended the accession negotiations.

The advent to power of Sarkozy in France and Merkel in Germany, both adamantly opposed to Turkish accession, has been a huge setback for Ankara. Instead of full accession, Merkel and Sarkozy propose a "privileged partnership" for Turkey. Not surprisingly, public opinion in Turkey has turned decisively against EU membership. Most Turks, once enthusiastic about joining the EU, have concluded that there is no point in trying to join a club that does not want them as members. More troubling, there has been a strong nationalist backlash in Turkey against the EU, which most Turks now see as an anti-Turkish entity biased in favor of the Greek Cypriots.

For their part, most EU citizens recoil at the thought of Turkish membership, reflecting deep-rooted anti-Turkish and anti-Muslim prejudice. Europeans tend to see Turkey as culturally and religiously distinct, unstable and impoverished, and a potential drain on the EU budget. Turkey is indeed a poor country. Despite remarkable economic growth before the global recession of 2008–2009, Turkey's per capita GDP remains less than one-third that of the

EU. Nevertheless, Turkey's accession would benefit the EU in several ways: it would bring into the EU a rapidly developing economy; it would remove a roadblock in EU-NATO relations (Turkey has been impeding EU-NATO cooperation because of its dispute with Cyprus); it would enhance EU energy security; it would contribute greatly to the EU's military capacity; and it would show the world that the EU is an open, pluralistic entity and not a closed Christian club.

National governments are divided on the question of Turkish accession, both between and sometimes within themselves (such as in Germany's ruling coalition). There is a discernable though unofficial coalition of anti-Turkish states, led by Austria, France, and Germany. Herman Van Rompuy, the first elected European Council president, opposes Turkey's accession (otherwise Sarkozy and Merkel would not have supported him for the job). On the other side, Britain has consistently supported Turkey, a position that fuels suspicion in other member states that what Britain really wants is a wider and weaker EU.

Most EU governments, even those led by anti-Turkish politicians, seem satisfied with the status quo, which means keeping the negotiations open but without making much progress. That way, the EU can claim that it is not against Turkish accession, secure in the knowledge that Turkey will never join. The EU does not want to push Turkey away from the negotiating table, but would be happy if Turkey took the initiative and withdrew its membership application. In fact, the status quo is increasingly unsustainable. The people and government of Turkey know that the chances of EU accession are slim. According, conditionality—the EU's ability to leverage reform in Turkey—is rapidly waning.

Turkey could withdraw its application in one of two ways. Based on a rational reassessment of its strategy toward the EU, it could inform Brussels of its decision not to seek membership and request instead an institutionalized special relationship. The EU would be so relieved that it would probably shower Turkey with economic and other concessions. Alternatively, Turkey could walk away in anger and rupture its relations with the EU, to the detriment of the EU and of itself as well. Either way, an unsuccessful conclusion of Turkey's accession negotiations is undesirable. Nor is the option of negotiation without end tenable. The onus is on the EU to take seriously its responsibility toward Turkey, a country to which it promised long ago the prospect of full membership.

The Western Balkans

Making up for its failure to prevent or stop the fighting in the former Yugoslavia in the 1990s, the EU has become extremely active in military and civilian peacekeeping operations in the Western Balkans, encompassing Albania, Bosnia-Herzegovina, Kosovo, Montenegro, and Serbia. The EU is also the largest donor of development aid in the region, which it channels through the

Instrument for Pre-Accession Assistance. The EU sees the situation in the Western Balkans after the recent wars as being similar to the situation in Europe after World War II. Not surprisingly, the EU advocates the same solution: economic and political integration as the best means of promoting peace, stability, and prosperity.

The Stabilization and Association Process (SAP) is the framework for the EU's approach to the region. Under its auspices, the EU encourages economic, political, judicial, and administrative reform through the provision of financial aid, trade preferences, and technical advice. The EU and the countries of the Western Balkans launched the SAP at a summit in Zagreb, Croatia, in 2000, and strengthened it at a follow-on summit in Thessaloniki, Greece, in June 2003. The so-called Thessaloniki agenda now provides the overall framework for helping the countries of the Western Balkans meet the Copenhagen criteria and eventually join the EU. Indeed, the EU has repeatedly stated that "the future of the Western Balkans lies in the European Union," and sees the countries concerned as potential candidates.[6]

As part of the pre-accession process, the EU has concluded stabilization and association agreements with each country (except Kosovo). These agreements are analogous to the "Europe agreements" that the EU signed with the countries of Central and Eastern Europe in the 1990s and hold out the prospect of EU membership. The Instrument for Pre-Accession Assistance is an integral part of the Stabilization and Association Process.

In addition to the myriad challenges of economic and political reform, the countries of the Western Balkans are particularly hobbled by entrenched corruption and organized crime. The collapse of communism "created spectacular opportunities for corruption . . . [by creating] a vacuum that necessitated rewriting the rules of the economy and the state. Those in power in the early years could write those rules to benefit themselves."[7] Postcommunist elites in Albania, Bulgaria, and Romania certainly fit that description. The countries of the former Yugoslavia had a gentler transition from communism, but corruption is just as deep-rooted in many of them. On top of that, the Yugoslav wars of the 1990s were a gift to organized crime, which burrowed deep into the state apparatus in most of Yugoslavia's successor states.

Undoubtedly the EU's financial largesse and the lure of possible EU membership have had a marked effect on the conduct of most of the countries concerned. Thus the EU has helped Albania, which was a highly repressed, almost completely isolated communist country during the Cold War, make considerable progress after an extremely difficult period of postcommunist transition. EU assistance came in the form of extensive humanitarian and development programs and through generous trade preferences. Albania even applied for EU membership in April 2009, and EU foreign ministers recommended granting the country candidacy status in November 2009. Like Turkey, Albania is a majority-Muslim country; unlike Turkey, its population is small (just over 3 million). For that reason, Albania's accession, were it ever to happen, would not threaten the EU's cultural identity but would allow anti-Turkey and anti-Muslim Europeans to claim that they are not opposed to countries with predominantly Muslim populations joining the EU.

The other four countries in the region were all part of Yugoslavia before that country's violent breakup in the early 1990s (see Chapter 5). Serbia and Montenegro together formed the Federal Republic of Yugoslavia—the rump state of the old Socialist Federal Republic of Yugoslavia—from 1992 until 2003, when they reconstituted themselves as the State Union of Serbia and Montenegro. Montenegro became independent in June 2006.

Bosnia-Herzegovina was also a constituent republic of the old Yugoslavia until it declared independence in 1992. The war that followed was the bloodiest of the Yugoslavia wars of secession. The December 1995 Dayton Accords included a new constitution that organized the country along ethnic lines (Bosniac, Croat, and Serb). More than fifteen years after the Dayton peace agreement, Bosnia-Herzegovina is highly dysfunctional and does not have any prospect of joining the EU in the foreseeable future.

Kosovo was part of Serbia before breaking away, with NATO help, in 1999, in response to ethnic cleansing of Kosovo's Albanian (Muslim) majority by Serbian security forces. It then became a United Nations protectorate, before declaring independence in February 2008. It will be a long time before the question of Kosovo's sovereignty is satisfactorily resolved and before its level of economy and political development ever meets the standard required for EU entry.

Arguably the situation in the Western Balkans will never be normal until Serbia, historically the regional power and still a cultural beacon in southeastern Europe, joins the EU. Although the government submitted an application for EU membership in December 2009, Serbian opinion is divided on the issue. Many Serbs see the EU as an enemy that facilitated the breakup of the former Yugoslavia and supported NATO in its war against Serb forces in 1995 and again in 1999. Serbian nationalism, fed by resentment of the United States, NATO, and the EU, is rampant.

Nevertheless, the EU could take some credit for and comfort from the success of the pro-EU coalition in the Serbian general election of May 2008. The EU had signed a stabilization and association agreement with Serbia the previous month, but the Dutch government initially blocked its implementation (the Netherlands, whose soldiers failed to save Bosnian civilians from slaughter by Serbian forces in Srebrenica in 1995, adamantly opposed the normalization of relations with Serbia until the country cooperated fully with the International Criminal Tribunal for the former Yugoslavia, located in The Hague). For its part, Serbia harbors a huge grudge against those EU member states that have recognized the independence of Kosovo, which the vast majority of Serbs considers to be an integral part of Serbia. Before it can hope to join the

EU, Serbia and all of the EU's member states will have to accept Kosovo's independence. More fundamentally, Serbia will have to come to terms with its recent past and adopt a policy of reconciliation toward its neighbors, an important element of the integration process but one that is difficult to pursue in an atmosphere of unreconstructed Serbian nationalism.

The Eastern Partnership

The European Neighborhood Policy (ENP) is the vast organizational umbrella under which the EU conducts its relations with the countries of the "wider Europe"—the EU's neighbors to the south and east, running in an arc from Morocco to Russia, including everything in between (the Maghreb, parts of the Middle East, Turkey and the Balkans, and much of the former Soviet Union). Five countries under the ENP (Moldova, Ukraine, Armenia, Azerbaijan, and Georgia) form a subgroup called the Eastern Partnership, together with Belarus, which is in the wider Europe but is excluded from the ENP because of its human rights abuses.

Poland and Sweden proposed the Eastern Partnership in May 2008 at a time when France was emphasizing instead the importance of the EU's relations with the southern Mediterranean countries; the partnership was formally launched at a summit of leaders of all the participating countries in May 2009. The Eastern Partnership is a framework for relations between the EU and the participating countries with a view to promoting the rule of law, good governance, respect for human rights, protection of minorities, free market principles, and sustainable development (the usual list of EU external action objectives). Institutionally, the Eastern Partnership includes occasional meetings of heads of state and government, regular meetings of foreign ministers, and frequent meetings of national and European Commission officials.

The EU offers association agreements with each non-EU member of the Eastern Partnership, but without an explicit promise of eventual EU membership. Funding for Eastern Partnership activities comes from the financial instruments of the European Neighborhood Policy, within which the Eastern Partnership fits. With the possible exception of Ukraine, countries in the Eastern Partnership are well behind the countries of the Western Balkans in the EU accession queue. The EU likes to say that successive rounds of enlargement have brought the countries of the Eastern Partnership closer to the EU. In fact, enlargement has brought the EU closer to these countries.

Belarus is an unreconstructed European dictatorship that seems impervious to the pull of EU soft power and is many years away from membership. The EU has long imposed various sanctions on Belarus, but to little or no avail. Despite keeping Belarus out of the neighborhood policy, the EU reluctantly decided to bring Belarus into the Eastern Partnership in the hope of gaining some influence over the country.

Moldova, a small country wedged between Romania and Ukraine, is desperate to develop a close relationship with, and eventually join, the EU. The EU is eager to help Moldova, with which it signed a partnership and cooperation agreement as long ago as 1994. From the EU's point of view, Moldova is a model partner: susceptible to EU influence and willing to undertake difficult reforms. The only fly in the ointment is a so-called frozen conflict, a legacy of the bloody secession from Moldova of Transnistria, a small enclave along the border with Ukraine whose population is predominantly pro-Russian. The EU is trying to resolve the conflict. But although the EU has considerable leverage with Moldova, it lacks influence with Russia, whose support for Transnistria is the main obstacle to a settlement. Without a resolution of the Transnistria problem, Moldova has little prospect of EU membership.

Strategic considerations account for the high degree of EU interest in Ukraine, a big country (larger and more populous than France) that borders Russia and three EU member states. The EU signed a partnership and cooperation agreement with Ukraine in June 1994, only days before signing a similar agreement with Russia. The EU-Ukraine agreement became operational in March 1998, after extensive ratification delays on both sides. Yet Ukraine's failure to restructure its economy stymies Western investment in the country and threatens the political independence that Ukraine and the EU want, above all, to maintain. The situation in Ukraine became critical in November 2004 when mass demonstrations paralyzed the capital city following a disputed presidential election, and precipitated the so-called Orange Revolution. Acting as a counterpoint to Russia, the EU helped to broker the agreement to hold new elections at the end of the following month, which Viktor Yushchenko, the pro-Western candidate, won by a convincing margin.

EU relations with Ukraine improved following the Orange Revolution, but Ukraine remained divided between the pro-Russian eastern part of the country and the pro-European western part. The Ukrainian government was also bitterly divided, for personal rather than ideological reasons, between Victor Yushchenko and Yulia Tymoshenko, erstwhile allies in the Orange Revolution and the two most powerful Ukranian politicians. Given Russia's hypersensitivity about Ukraine's relations with Western organizations, the fragile state of Ukrainian politics, and the state of the Ukrainian economy, the EU treads warily in its dealings with Ukraine. Specifically, the EU is unwilling to state unequivocally that Ukraine has a good chance of joining the EU anytime soon.

Azerbaijan is an oil-rich country in the southern Caucasus bounded by the Caspian Sea. Corruption and organized crime are pervasive and political institutions are weak. Because of its wealth, Azerbaijan is not susceptible to EU leverage. The security situation in and around Azerbaijan has been tenuous since Nagorno-Karabakh, a predominantly ethnic Armenian enclave in the southwest of the country, unilaterally declared its independence in 1991

(Nagorno-Karabakh is not recognized internationally and remains constitutionally part of Azerbaijan). Fighting over Nagorno-Karabakh has cost thousands of lives and embittered relations between Armenia and Azerbaijan. A diplomatic rapprochement between erstwhile enemies Armenia and Turkey that began in 2009 may help to resolve the Nagorno-Karabakh situation, as Turkey is influential in the region and strongly supports Azerbaijan, a Turkic country. By contrast, the EU has little influence in the region. The participation of Armenia and Azerbaijan in the Eastern Partnership may help to improve their bilateral relationship and strengthen economic and political reforms in both countries. As far as EU membership is concerned, neither the EU nor Armenia and Azerbaijan are even thinking about it.

The EU's relations with Georgia briefly took center stage after the outbreak of war between Russia and Georgia in August 2008. President Sarkozy, in the European Council presidency at the time, immediately embarked on a peace mission and helped broker a cease-fire. The EU subsequently sent a monitoring mission to oversee the agreement, although Russia has denied the EU monitors entry to the breakaway (from Georgia) territories of Abkhazia and South Ossetia. While sympathizing with the plight of a small country (Georgia) that is being bullied by a much larger neighbor (Russia), most EU governments distrust Mikheil Saakashvili, Georgia's volatile leader, and worry about the weak foundations of Georgian democracy. Few governments would risk inflaming relations with Russia by bringing Georgia into the EU, a prospect that is remote in any case because of Georgia's political situation.

■ Relations with Other Countries of the Wider Europe

The European Neighborhood Policy does not include every country in the wider Europe. For instance, the countries of the Western Balkans as well as Russia and Turkey have special relationships with the EU and therefore are not included in the ENP. The Euro-Mediterranean Partnership, an association of the EU and sixteen southern Mediterranean countries that is now called the Union for the Mediterranean, is a pillar of the ENP. Participation in the ENP does not qualify those countries for eventual EU membership, not least because many of them are undisputedly not European. Some of the countries in the ENP, being vulnerable to economic collapse, political extremism, and religious fundamentalism, are a cause of acute concern to the EU. Accordingly, the EU uses the ENP to try to stabilize the vast region around itself.

Inevitably, the ENP speaks of promoting good governance, economic liberalism, respect for human rights, sustainable development, and social cohesion— sincere and admirable goals that are hardly realistic in all cases. The EU already has agreements of some kind with most of the countries in the region. The ENP provides an overarching framework for these agreements, sets priorities, and promises a series of action plans for each participant. The European Neighborhood Instrument, a fund to help implement the action plans, became active as part of the EU's financial perspective for the period 2007–2013.

Russia

EU-Russia relations are complicated and testy. Russia has difficulty dealing with the EU, partly because of the nature of European integration and partly because Russia is a revisionist power unhappy with the post–Cold War status quo. Russia resents the independence of countries that, not too long ago, were either part of the Soviet Union or under Soviet control. It especially resents those countries' membership in NATO and, to a lesser extent, in the EU. As a country that prizes national sovereignty, Russia finds the EU hard to fathom and has little patience with claims that the EU is a normative power. Russia especially resents the EU's efforts to lecture to it on issues such as democracy and human rights. Not surprisingly, Russia prefers to deal directly with the EU's member states, which have a better understanding of Russia's great-power approach to international relations.

Russia tolerates the EU because it has to, and negotiates with the EU to the extent that it must. Russia prefers to restrict the relationship to issues such as energy, trade, and migration, for which the EU has either exclusive or mixed competence. Yet political and economic factors are impossible to disentangle in the EU-Russia relationship. Politically, a stable Russia is essential for European security and for the success of the EU's neighborhood policy. Economically, the EU is Russia's main Western partner, and Russia provides a growing portion of the EU's energy needs. Without more trade and investment, especially when energy prices are low, Russia could stagnate politically and economically.

In 1989 the European Community concluded a trade and cooperation agreement with the Soviet Union, which was then on its last legs. As the situation there deteriorated, the European Council approved emergency food aid and an ambitious technical assistance program. Nevertheless, the Community's relations with the declining Soviet Union were tense as officials in Brussels protested against Soviet repression in the Baltic States in early 1991 and fretted about the apparent ascendancy of conservative Communists in the Kremlin.

The collapse of the Soviet Union in December 1991—coincidentally during the second day of the famous Maastricht summit—presented the Community with a major political and economic challenge. Germany, as a grudging host to several hundred thousand former Soviet troops in the eastern part of the country, urged the EU to pursue a positive, constructive policy toward Russia, the main successor state of the former Soviet Union. The EU duly reorganized its aid to Russia and other former Soviet republics in a program called Technical Assistance for the Commonwealth of Independent States (TACIS) and laid the foundations for a longer-term, more substantive relationship. This approach bore fruit in the partnership and cooperation agreement signed by Russia and the EU in June 1994. The EU's overall objectives were to bolster political and economic reform in Russia and win Russian support for—or at least acceptance of—EU enlargement in Central and Eastern Europe. However, a succession of trade disputes, coupled with Russia's brutality during Chechnya's secessionist war in 1995, held up ratification of the agreement and caused considerable tension in EU-Russia relations.

For Russia, struggling to come to terms with the Soviet Union's demise, resentful of the United States as the world's sole remaining superpower, and on the verge of economic collapse in 1998, relations with the EU assumed special importance. Only the EU could give Russia the economic assistance and market access that were indispensable for putting the country back on its feet. EU-Russia relations improved in the late 1990s, especially in terms of trade and aid. In return, Russia did not attempt to block EU enlargement. Moreover, without the EU's considerable economic assistance and political support, it is doubtful that Russia would have dropped its resistance to NATO enlargement.

Since then, EU-Russia relations have cooled considerably. The EU's new Central and Eastern European member states are understandably wary of Russia and irritated by what they see as the Western European countries' benign attitude toward their old nemesis. President Vladimir Putin's resumption and conduct of the war with Chechnya, without even the pretense of respect for human rights, became a major irritant in EU-Russia relations. Putin deeply resented his country's dependence on EU support and assistance.

The conduct of the biannual EU-Russia summits reflects the state of EU-Russia relations. Putin postponed the summit scheduled for November 2004 in The Hague, reportedly because of irritation with the Dutch presidency for criticizing Russia's handling of a hostage crisis the previous September and with continuing complaints in the EU about Russian human rights abuses in Chechnya. Postponement of the summit, and underlying tensions in EU-Russia relations, delayed the conclusion of agreements between the two sides on a number of important issues, such as foreign and security policy cooperation and collaboration on research and development. Since then, many summits have been perfunctory or unpleasant. At the May 2009 summit in Khabarovsk, in Russia's far east, President Dmitry Medvedev criticized the Eastern Partnership as hostile to Russia's interests, claiming that the initiative was really a partnership against Russia.

The EU has sought to reassure Russia about the Eastern Partnership and tried to tie the country into a web of bilateral and regional arrangements. In its dealings with the EU, however, Russia sees itself as a case apart from other Eastern European countries. Accordingly, it refused to participate in the European Neighborhood Policy. Instead, the EU and Russia agreed in May 2003 to create over the long term four "common spaces" for themselves, dealing with economics; freedom, security, and justice; external security; and research and education. Later, in November 2006, both sides adopted the "Northern Dimension," an initiative proposed by Finland as a regional approach to consolidating the common spaces. At the other end of the continent, several Eastern European countries, Russia, and Turkey are involved in the Black Sea Synergy, another regional initiative that began in 2007. Specific Black Sea partnerships focus on functional issues such as the environment and transport.

Russia generally views these initiatives as examples of EU procedural excess, preferring to limit its dealings with Brussels and measure the strength of the relationship by means of concrete achievements. Much to the EU's dismay, Russia has refused to renegotiate its partnership and cooperation agreement with the EU, the basic charter of the bilateral relationship.

Despite the existence of common spaces and regional forums, a number of bilateral disputes between Russia and some of the new Central and Eastern European member states have bedeviled EU-Russia relations. By far the greatest irritant in the relationship, however, is the apparent unreliability of Russian gas exports, upon which many European countries depend for home heating and other energy purposes. Supplies were interrupted on a number of occasions when Russia cut deliveries to Ukraine ostensibly over prices and payment but possibly for political reasons. The unpredictability of Russian gas supplies alarmed several European governments, but not enough to convince them to come together and adopt a common approach to Russia.

Russia was adept in any case at dealing directly with EU governments, often on the basis of a personal relationship between Putin and national leaders. Germany concluded a deal with Russia to supply gas via the Nord Stream pipeline in the Baltic Sea, bypassing other countries. As discussed in Chapter 15, the European Commission prefers an alternative arrangement in southern Europe that would reduce energy dependence on Russia by carrying gas to the EU from Azerbaijan through Turkey, thereby avoiding Russia altogether. The so-called Nabucco pipeline could be extended under the Caspian Sea to reach suppliers in Kazakhstan and Turkmenistan.

Russia's invasion of Georgia in August 2008 further complicated EU-Russia relations. While apparently welcoming President Sarkozy's peacemaking visits to Georgia at the height of the crisis, Russia has become increasingly suspicious of the EU monitoring mission and impatient with EU complaints about its recognition of Abkhazia and South Ossetia as independent states. More broadly, EU-Russia relations took about a year to recover from the shock of the Georgian war and return to their habitual state of mutual wariness.

The EU-Russia summit in Stockholm in November 2009 was the most constructive in several years. Medvedev pleased the EU by emphasizing Russia's concern about climate change and interest in reaching an agreement at the imminent Copenhagen Conference. More substantively, both sides emphasized their interest in the predictability and security of energy supplies from Russia to markets in the west. Shortly before the summit, the EU and Russia signed an enhanced early warning mechanism to help avoid renewed interruptions in the flow of gas.

Russia will likely remain a difficult neighbor and an unsatisfactory partner. Nevertheless, the EU and Russia share too many interests to risk a permanent rupture in their relationship. They are the two pillars of what Russia once called the common European home. Although leading Russian politicians occasionally remark that Russia might one day apply for EU membership, neither Russia nor the EU seriously considers that Russia will ever do so, or would ever be admitted. European integration may extend informally into Russia, but the geographical limits of the European Union lie at Russia's border.

The Union for the Mediterranean

The EU has always had a close relationship with neighboring Mediterranean countries. EU leaders adopted the Global Mediterranean Policy as long ago as 1972 to deepen and broaden the Community's involvement in the region. Yet the initiative sounded more impressive than it really was. The accession of Greece, Spain, and Portugal in the 1980s strengthened the Community's Mediterranean orientation but without tangible results.

In the late 1980s, southern Mediterranean countries worried about the external economic consequences of the internal market program and feared that massive financial transfers to Greece, Spain, and Portugal through the structural funds would further widen the economic divide between member and nonmember Mediterranean states. The EU's relations with most Mediterranean countries remained precarious. In October 1987 the Council rejected Morocco's application for EC membership on the self-evident grounds that Morocco was not a European country. The EC also complained about Morocco's poor human rights record. Morocco responded by freezing its agreement with the EC and jeopardizing a four-year fishing accord. The crisis ended only after the Council agreed to explore a wide-ranging free trade agreement with Morocco, possibly also including Algeria and Tunisia.

At the other end of the Mediterranean, political problems overshadowed the EC's economic relations with Israel, which are based on a 1975 free trade agreement that became fully operational in 1989. Israel wanted to upgrade its economic relations with the EU, its main trading partner, but political obstacles proved insurmountable. In particular, the EU was extremely critical of Israel's hard line in the Occupied Territories, and Israel objected to full EU participation in the Middle East peace process. Neighboring countries with which the EU had trade agreements dating from the 1970s—Syria, Egypt, Jordan, and Lebanon—also sought closer economic relations with the EU but objected to further EU trade concessions to Israel.

The Commission eventually came up with a typically ambitious proposal to establish a huge free trade area stretching from Morocco in the west to Turkey in the east; altogether it would embrace eleven Mediterranean countries (Algeria, Cyprus, Egypt, Israel, Jordan, Lebanon, Malta, Morocco, Syria, Tunisia, Turkey) and the autonomous Palestinian territories. Negotiations between the EU and the so-called MED 12 culminated in a declaration issued at a summit in Barcelona in November 1995. The Barcelona Declaration—the cornerstone of the EU's new Mediterranean policy—covered a wide range of issues beyond commercial relations. Chief among these were steps to enhance regional security and to strengthen cultural and educational ties.[8]

The success of the Barcelona Declaration depended on the EU's ability to promote regional development. The main vehicle for this was the proposed free trade area, due to be completed by 2010, which necessitated negotiating separate association agreements between the EU and the MED 12 and similar agreements among the MED 12 themselves. The association agreement between the EU and Syria, concluded in October 2004, completed the network of association agreements with the EU's partners in the Barcelona Process (Syria was the EU's most difficult and elusive partner). In the meantime, two of the original MED 12 (Cyprus and Malta) became EU members, and another (Turkey) became a candidate for membership.

The political volatility of the region and the degree of animosity between some of the Mediterranean states (Israel and Syria are officially at war with each other) stymied the EU's plans. Nor are relations between each of the Mediterranean countries and the EU on an equal footing. The apparent symmetry of the EU-Mediterranean relationship disguises a series of bilateral relations that range in their conduct from friendly to frosty and have made it impossible to achieve a large free trade area.

In 2004, the EU subsumed the Barcelona Process into the European Neighborhood Policy. By that time the EU's enlargement to the east had completely overshadowed the process. Occasional meetings among participants in the process failed to disguise the languid state of EU-MED relations. A Euro-Mediterranean summit in Barcelona in 2005, on the tenth anniversary of the summit that launched the Barcelona Process, was a lackluster affair. The EU appeared to have lost interest in its southern Mediterranean neighbors, many of which grew increasingly resentful of the EU's attitude of benign neglect.

Into this unsatisfactory situation strode Nicolas Sarkozy, first as a presidential candidate in 2006–2007, then as president of France. While campaigning for the presidency, Sarkozy lambasted the EU for its lack of attention to the Mediterranean region. Once elected, he decided to establish a Mediterranean Union encompassing the countries of the Mediterranean rim, excluding other EU member states. This was a typical Sarkozy initiative: well meaning but impulsive. The excluded EU members, especially Germany, which liked to be consulted about major European initiatives and suspected that it would be asked to foot the bill, immediately denounced Sarkozy's unilateralism. The Commission was equally alarmed, fearing that the proposed Mediterranean Union would completely undermine what was left of the Barcelona Process.

After some heated behind-the-scenes exchanges between Sarkozy and Merkel, what had been a unilateral French idea morphed into a Franco-German proposal not for a Mediterranean Union but for a *Union for the Mediterranean,* the subtle change of name being intended to allay concerns among EU member states and lower expectations among Mediterranean partners that the proposed union would resemble the *real* union—that is, the European Union. The European Council endorsed the idea in March 2008, paving the way for the launch of the Union for the Mediterranean at a grand summit in Paris in July 2008, attended by no fewer than forty-three monarchs, presidents, and prime ministers.

Participants in the summit agreed to transform the old Barcelona Process into the inelegantly named "Barcelona Process: Union for the Mediterranean," and to take over the work program of the existing process. Sprinkled with buzzwords such as "historic opportunity," "co-ownership" and "partnership," the joint declaration issued after the summit promised to revitalize efforts "to transform the Mediterranean into an area of peace, democracy, cooperation and prosperity." That was a tall order for a grouping that included countries with authoritarian regimes and dubious human rights records. The declaration announced a co-presidency (held on a rotating basis by an EU member and a non-EU member), regular meetings at ministerial and official levels, a small secretariat (about which the Commission was highly displeased), and biennial summits for the rejuvenated EU-Mediterranean Partnership. It also promised to launch "concrete projects, more visible to citizens," in areas such as transport and the environment.[9]

Following the excitement surrounding the inaugural Union for the Mediterranean summit, the spotlight moved to other EU initiatives and other parts of the European neighborhood. Typically, Sarkozy lost interest in his pet project, which disappeared under the weight of a relentless stream of other initiatives by the hyperactive French president. Most EU member states, especially those located far from the Mediterranean, were indifferent.

The Union for the Mediterranean seems destined to go the way of the old Barcelona Process, with lengthy periods of relative quiet punctuated by showy summits and occasional bursts of activity. Meanwhile, the Israeli-Palestinian conflict continues to cast a pall, blighting prospects for realizing the EU's regional ambitions. Overall, the Union for the Mediterranean does not do any harm and may even do some good. Yet it is difficult to avoid the conclusion that the EU could do better if only it could wean itself away from grandiose processes and programs.

◼ Trade Policy

The European Community came into existence in 1958 to facilitate trade and investment among its member states. From the outset, the Commission conducted bilateral and multilateral trade negotiations on behalf of the member states (trade policy—formally the Common Commercial Policy—is an original exclusive EU competence).

Over time, the EU and the global system have changed remarkably. Successive rounds of enlargement meant that the EC, and later the EU, acquired as members some of its largest trading partners (for example, the United Kingdom in 1973, Sweden in 1995, eight Central and Eastern European countries in 2004). Paradoxically, because of the growing size of the EU itself, the EU's relative weight as an external trader declined proportionately even as global trade exploded.

Trade and investment were key drivers of globalization, which in turn has accelerated global flows of trade and investment. Economic reform in China and later in India, the collapse of communism in Central and Eastern Europe, the disintegration of the Soviet Union, and the implosion of the apartheid regime in South Africa resulted in the international economic system becoming truly global. Membership in the General Agreement on Tariffs and Trade and its successor, the World Trade Organization, increased dramatically. A global manufacturing supply chain emerged with a resurgent China at its hub. International trade in services also exploded, with India being a major beneficiary.

The importance of trade policy cannot be overstated. Countries—or, in the case of the EU, a collection of countries—use trade policy to ensure that producers and consumers gain as much as possible through access to other countries' markets. Market access involves market opening, domestically as well as internationally. The global trading system is built on the basis of reciprocity. Companies, and the countries in which they are based, flourish by being competitive globally, not just regionally or domestically.

Adjustment to globalization can be painful. Millions of Chinese peasants have been released from economic enslavement through the provision of factory jobs, but at the cost of massive social dislocation and environmental degradation. In the West, millions of low-skilled manufacturing and service jobs have been lost to factories in China and warehouse-like offices in India, although consumers (including laid-off workers) have benefited from cheaper products and services. Social preferences such as generous welfare payments and high environmental standards are difficult to sustain in a highly integrated, global economic system that puts massive downward pressure on jobs and wages.

Under the circumstances, especially at a time of economic recession, it is difficult for governments to mobilize support for trade liberalization and resist pressure for protectionist measures. It is also difficult for the EU to ensure that high standards of workplace health and safety, child labor laws, animal welfare, and the like are respected abroad. What the EU sees as an insistence on minimal standards of human and animal rights, others see as an unacceptable intrusion into their domestic affairs and effort to impose barriers to trade.

The nature of the EU compounds these problems. Trade policy is an exclusive EU competence; governments know that they must negotiate and conclude international agreements as one. Nevertheless, the formulation of a common negotiating position involves reconciling strikingly different national priorities and preferences. Generally, the French are notoriously protectionist, whereas the British and Dutch champion free trade. Most countries are somewhere in between. Having been locked throughout the Cold War into a mercantilist system constructed by and for the benefit of the Soviet Union, the new Central and Eastern European member states generally favor an open international system and are more inclined than some of the older member states to reach agreement with the United States on contentious transatlantic trade issues. As in other policy areas, only more so, the Council of Ministers (and occasionally the European Council) attempt to reconcile divergent national interests and preferences.

National trade ministers do not restrict their work to their own capitals and to meetings in Brussels. On the contrary, they frequently participate in trade promotion missions outside the EU and in meetings with government ministers in non-EU member states, where they lobby on behalf of their own manufacturers and are lobbied by foreign governments with respect to EU trade policy. Nonmember states know that trade policy, though conducted by the Commission, is agreed upon in the Council, and that the Council can be lobbied through its constituent national ministers. Such lobbying is a fact of life in all areas of EU policy; trade is no exception.

The EU has a thick network of relationships with countries and groups of countries throughout the world, including agreements that range from minimal commitments on either side to intensive commitments covering a variety of issues. Although the EU's international agreements generally involve much more than trade, trade remains their core component.

The Political and Policymaking Context

Apart from sector- and case-specific disputes among national governments, two controversies have dominated the internal development of EU trade policy. One pertains to everyday interinstitutional relations, the other to the question of competence for trade policy given the emergence of new issues and the rapidly changing global trade agenda. Both are classic examples of the struggle between intergovernmentalism and supranationality in the EU system.

Interinstitutional Relations. The Treaty on the Functioning of the European Union states that the Council must approve Commission proposals to implement the Common Commercial Policy and must also approve Commission recommendations to open negotiations for agreements with third countries. Depending on the subject of the negotiations, the Council acts by either a qualified majority or unanimity. In addition, the treaty provides for "a special committee appointed by the Council to assist the Commission" with its negotiations "within the framework of such directives as the Council may issue to it." This is the well-known committee of national civil servants that meets regularly with Commission officials to approve the Commission's negotiating strategy and proposals. The name of the committee has changed over time as the number of the relevant treaty article has changed with successive rounds of reform. Originally it was the 113 Committee, then the 133 Committee (according to the Amsterdam Treaty); now it is the 207 Committee (according to the Lisbon Treaty).

The Commission has a love-hate relationship with the 207 Committee, whose presence behind the scenes ensures that Commission negotiators stick to the agreed-upon Council position. The committee's existence inherently strengthens the Commission's negotiating position because third countries know that the Commission has the committee's—and therefore the Council's—support. On the other hand, the committee's existence reduces the Commission's room for maneuver. Either way, the Article 207 regime means that the Commission is always involved in parallel sets of negotiations: with national governments to agree upon and (when necessary) adjust a negotiation position and with third countries to conclude a trade accord.

Inevitably the Commission tries to maximize its influence and frequently exceeds its negotiating brief. How much the Commission gets away with usually depends first and foremost on the political and economic importance of the negotiations. Other factors that determine the Commission's degree of flexibility in the conduct of external trade negotiations include:

- Complexity of the issues under discussion (the Commission has a long institutional memory and a high level of expertise).
- Stature of the trade policy commissioner and of the country currently holding the Council presidency.
- The Commission's willingness and ability to take initiatives, build coalitions of national governments, and mobilize interest groups.
- Timing of the negotiations and pressure (or nonpressure) for agreement; the involvement of various sectoral councils as well as the Foreign Affairs Council (which has overall authority for external relations).
- Busyness of the Commission's own political agenda.

Until implementation of the Lisbon Treaty, the EP was marginalized with respect to EU trade policy, the conduct of which was limited largely to the Commission and the Council. Nevertheless, the EP formed an international trade committee and frequently passed resolutions on—and sent delegations to—major trade negotiations. The Commission thought it prudent to keep the EP informed of trade policy developments.

As in many other respects, the EP emerged a winner in the Lisbon Treaty in the area of trade policy. In addition to extending the ordinary legislative procedure (codecision) to trade policy measures and strengthening the EP's role in ratifying trade agreements, the Lisbon Treaty obliges the Commission to inform the EP closely on the conduct of trade negotiations.

The Question of Competence. National governments started to dispute the extent of Community competence for trade relations once trade began to account for a larger share of GDP and as the international economic system grew more complex. When the original Rome Treaty was drafted, trade barriers consisted mostly of tariffs and quotas. Subsequently, regulatory barriers such as standards, conformity testing, certification, and product approval assumed paramount importance. At the same time, trade in goods lost its primacy to trade in services, and issues such as investment and the environment impinged more and more on the international trade agenda. The acceleration of technological change introduced new products (such as genetically modified organisms) and new processes (such as electronic commerce). Sometimes new products necessitated a reconfiguration of existing services (such as the impact of cell phones on the provision of telephone service).

The Commission consistently argued that the EU retained exclusive competence for trade relations regardless of these developments. There were frequent spats between the Council and the Commission in the 1980s, but matters came to a head during the final stages of the Uruguay Round of the GATT in the early 1990s. When governments questioned the Commission's competence to conclude agreements on trade in services and trade-related aspects of intellectual property rights, the Commission responded by requesting a ruling from the Court of Justice. Much to the Commission's surprise, the Court ruled in favor of the Council.

The Commission unsuccessfully attempted during the subsequent intergovernmental conference on treaty reform to extend the scope of Community competence to cover trade in services and intellectual property rights. By stipulating in the Amsterdam Treaty that the Council could decide in future by means of unanimity to extend trade policy competence, national governments effectively maintained the status quo.

The Commission had long complained to the Council that the existing treaty provisions made the EU a difficult trade partner. In the Commission's view, mixed or joint EU and national competence for new trade issues compounded the problem. For instance, in the WTO committee on trade in goods, the Commission alone represented the EU. In the services and intellectual property committees, the Commission and national officials negotiated jointly on behalf of the EU. Third countries may have found this strange, but they managed to come to terms with it. Similarly, third countries have long been reconciled to other peculiarities of EU trade policy and have learned to exploit them on occasion, for instance by lobbying the old 133 Committee before key negotiating sessions.

In a major breakthrough, national governments finally agreed in the Lisbon Treaty to do away with shared competence and therefore with mixed agreements in trade policy. Specifically, the Lisbon Treaty extended EU competence to all trade in services, trade-related intellectual property rights, and foreign direct investment. Reflecting national sensitivity on some of these issues, the treaty limits the use of qualified majority voting in the Council, calling for unanimity on agreements on services that "risk prejudicing the Union's cultural and linguistic diversity" and that "risk seriously disturbing the national organization of [social, education, and health services] and prejudicing the responsibility of Member States to deliver them."[10]

As in other policy areas, trade policy tends to be decided in the Council on the basis of consensus, although the possibility of voting undoubtedly helps national officials to reach an agreement. Provisions in the Lisbon Treaty for unanimity on certain trade policy issues may impede Council decisionmaking. Moreover, a consequence of doing away with mixed agreements is that national parliaments no longer have an opportunity to ratify trade accords, which, like EU agreements, are subject to ratification only by the EP. Critics of the EU claim that this widens the democratic deficit; defenders say that strengthening the role of the EP in trade policy (as in other areas) narrows the democratic deficit.

Development of Trade Policy

The Common Commercial Policy (CCP) is the external manifestation of the customs union, itself the foundation upon which the single market and monetary union were built. The common external tariff, established in July 1968 upon completion of the customs union, is a key regulatory instrument of the CCP. The EU's trade policy is reasonably open, with the exception of the agricultural and (for cultural reasons) audiovisual sectors. Apart from films and farm products, third countries complain most about limited market access for items such as textiles, clothing, and cars. The EU's average industrial tariff is declining to about 3 percent as a result of WTO commitments. Other trade-related concerns of third countries include:

- Impact of EU enlargement (concerns about trade diversion have been a feature of every EU enlargement).
- Impact of the EU's growing network of preferential and regional agreements on the multilateral system.
- Frequency and severity of EU antidumping actions in sensitive sectors such as electronics, steel, and textiles.
- Trade-restricting impact of EU health, safety, and environmental directives.

For its part, the EU

- Has always been willing to negotiate compensation for countries that encounter new or higher trade barriers in their dealings with the enlarged EU (although the Commission has not always conducted such negotiations with alacrity);
- Argues that there is no inconsistency between progressive multilateral liberalization and the conclusion of preferential trade agreements;
- Doggedly defends its recourse to antidumping measures under agreed-upon WTO rules; and
- Claims that its health and safety legislation is not politically inspired but is based on sound scientific advice or, more weakly, on "consumer preference."

In 2007, the EU strengthened its long-standing Market Access Strategy—intended to expose and tackle third-country trade barriers—and adopted the Market Access Partnership, "a new decentralized partnership between the Commission, Member States and business on the ground in Europe's most important export markets where local expertise makes trade barriers easier to identify and address."[11]

The Market Access Partnership is part of the Global Europe trade policy framework, launched with great fanfare in 2006. Global Europe sought to generate public and political support for globalization and refocused the priorities of EU trade policy on such goals as ensuring an open market for imports into the EU; improving market access for EU exporters, especially in the growing Chinese and other Asian markets, through targeted work to tackle individual trade barriers and the conclusion of bilateral and multilateral trade agreements; and action to improve the protection of intellectual property rights, which is essential for companies that have invested heavily in design and innovation.[12]

Peter Mandelson, trade commissioner during most of the first Barroso Commission, was the architect of the Global Europe initiative. An aggressive free-trader, Mandelson also attempted to reform the EU's antidumping rules. (Dumping is a form of predatory pricing whereby a manufacturer in one country sells a product in another country at a price either below the price it charges at home or below its production costs; antidumping duties are imposed against the country in which the export originates and are calculated to counteract the dumping margin.) Mandelson was generally reluctant to impose antidumping duties, seeing them as having become an instrument of protectionism and no longer a remedy for a specific injury. His proposed reform elicited a hostile response from producers and from a number of traditionally protectionist member states. Nicolas Sarkozy, the new French president, opposed the reform; José Manuel Barroso, beholden to Sarkozy for reappointment as Commission president, ensured that the idea went nowhere.

Sarkozy was fiercely critical of Mandelson's conduct of the Doha Round negotiations, fearing that the trade commissioner, who had little sympathy for the Common Agricultural Policy, was conceding too much to the EU's trading partners. Sarkozy was delighted when Mandelson resigned from the Commission in October 2008 in order to return to British politics. Mandelson's successor, Catherine Ashton, was less willing and able to stand up to French bullying (otherwise she would never have been appointed as the first High Representative for Foreign Affairs and Security under the Lisbon Treaty).

The World Trade Organization

For most of the post–World War II period, the General Agreement on Tariffs and Trade was the main forum for international trade liberalization. At the end of the Uruguay Round—the longest, most complicated, and most contentious round of multilateral trade liberalization negotiations held under the organization's auspices—the GATT's "contracting parties" agreed to establish a successor organization, the World Trade Organization, which has grown to over 150 members.

Substantively, the WTO encompasses not only the old GATT but also the General Agreement on Trade in Services (GATS) and the Trade-Related Aspects of Intellectual Property Rights (TRIPs) agreements, both of which were negotiated as part of the Uruguay Round and came into effect when the WTO became operational in January 1995. One of the WTO's most important innovations is the Dispute Settlement Body and Appellate Body to resolve disputes between contracting parties. This is a major improvement on the GATT system of dispute settlement, which, because it operated on the basis of unanimity, was weak and generally ineffective. The EU strongly supported establishing a new dispute settlement regime.

The EU and the United States are the WTO's heavyweight boxers. It used to be that, if they agreed among themselves, the EU and the United States could influence the WTO in their favor. In the past few years, however, a group of rapidly developing countries led informally by Brazil, India, and South Africa has challenged the preeminence of the EU and the United States in the WTO.

The EU has put its stamp on the WTO by taking an aggressive approach to procedural and institutional issues. For instance, the EU successfully insisted that "its candidate" become the WTO's first director-general and unsuccessfully insisted on two "EU seats" on the supposedly nonpartisan Appellate Body (the EU agreed to only one seat when the United States did likewise). In both cases, the EU thought of itself as acting not only in the EU's interests but also against US interests. Three of the five WTO directors have been European; none has been American.

The EU's approach to the WTO includes using the dispute settlement mechanism as a major trade policy instrument. The EU is the complainant far more often than it is the defendant. The EU has won some high-profile cases and lost a few as well. For instance, the EU lost a big case against its banana-import regime, which discriminated against larger, cheaper Latin American bananas in favor of more expensive, poorer-quality bananas from countries that were party to the EU's Cotonou Agreement (an aid and preferential trade program for former European colonies in Africa, the Caribbean, and the Pacific). The EU also lost a case brought by the United States against its ban on hormone-treated beef, because the ban was not based on scientific evidence (and therefore contravened international trade rules). Both cases caused considerable political upset in the EU.

The EU has been active helping aspiring members to join the WTO, and has been especially prominent in negotiating China's and Russia's membership. By contrast with the United States, which rejected China's candidacy outright until China lifted some well-documented trade barriers, the EU supported China's accession to the WTO as a means of encouraging economic reform by locking China into a rule-based organization. Critics contended that the EU also had selfish motives, that perhaps it hoped China would look more favorably on European exporters and investors. Nevertheless, the EU's support for China was not unconditional. Only when the EU and China concluded a bilateral agreement on WTO accession, allaying European concerns about financial services, public procurement, intellectual property rights, and other sensitive issues, did the EU rally wholeheartedly behind China's candidacy. The EU-China deal complemented a separate US-China agreement that finally paved the way for China's WTO membership in 2001.

The question of Russia's WTO membership has also divided the EU and the United States. Whereas the EU is sympathetic to Russia's application, the United States holds that Russia still has some way to go before it develops a market economy with a trade regime that complies with rigorous WTO rules. Without agreement between the EU and the United States, Russia is unlikely to be admitted to the WTO.

The EU participated fully in the WTO's work program for further multilateral liberalization, which includes unfinished GATT business as well as new initiatives. Key developments include:

- *Telecommunications:* The EU was in the forefront of efforts to reach a WTO agreement on the liberalization of global telecommunications markets. Sixty-nine countries (including the EU15) signed the agreement in February 1997. The agreement opened voice-telephony, electronic data transmissions, telex, and fax services to global competition and covered all means of service (cable, fiber optics, radio, and satellite). For the first time in a global accord, the agreement also included a commitment to basic competition policy principles. Implementation of the agreement, and the granting of temporary derogations for some countries, mirrored the calendar for the EU's own liberalization of telecommunications.

- *Information technology:* The EU and the United States sought the Information Technology Agreement (ITA) in order to eliminate tariffs on a host of electronic products, including telecommunications equipment, computers, computer chips, and software. After hectic negotiations, the EU15 and twelve other countries (including the United States) concluded the agreement in December 1996. The number of participants has grown since then to more than seventy, representing about 97 percent of world trade in information technology products.

- *Financial services:* The EU was instrumental in achieving an interim multilateral agreement on financial services in July 1995, despite US withdrawal from the talks because of dissatisfaction with the market-opening offers on the table, especially from emerging economies. The agreement promised foreign access (in varying degrees) to the banking, insurance, and securities sectors in more than ninety countries (covering 90 percent of all international financial business). The EU trumpeted its ability to lead the talks to a successful conclusion, regardless of the US walkout, as a major international achievement. The EU managed to translate the interim agreement into a permanent arrangement, which included the United States, in December 2007.

- *Foreign direct investment:* The EU has long taken the lead in calling for binding multilateral rules to cover foreign direct investment (FDI), and has been keen to negotiate a comprehensive multilateral agreement that would range from investment rules to environmental protection and sustainable development. However, the complexity and political sensitivity of many FDI-related issues have thwarted the Commission's initiatives to promote a global regime. The EU and other supporters of a multilateral agreement on FDI tried at the WTO ministerial meeting in Cancun in September 2003 to raise FDI as one of the so-called Singapore issues—the others are competition, transparency in government procurement, and trade facilitation—that many poor countries see as potential barriers to their development. These efforts failed again as a group of more than twenty developing countries united in opposition to them.

The best-known activity within the WTO is the ongoing negotiation of a successor to the Uruguay Round. The Commission was an early proponent of a new global agreement, but few other WTO players, including some EU member states, shared the Commission's enthusiasm. Post–Uruguay Round fatigue was still prevalent and the WTO already had plenty on its plate. Denied congressional authorization for "fast-track" trade talks, the US administration had little appetite for a new round either, as a commitment to begin such a round was not likely to win votes in the 2000 US presidential election.

The antiglobalization demonstrations at the WTO ministerial meeting in Seattle in December 1999 dampened whatever enthusiasm remained for a new round of negotiations, until the terrorist attacks on the United States in September 2001 galvanized governments to demonstrate a common commitment to economic globalization. Hence the launch of a new round of negotiations in Doha in November 2001, for which the US president received fast-track authority. In deference to the demands of the poorer countries, the new round of talks was officially called the Doha Development Round.

The EU has been criticized for using the new round to push the Singapore issues (investment, competition, transparency in government procurement, and trade facilitation), which are highly unpopular among developing countries. Not surprisingly, however, agriculture has become the biggest sticking point in the negotiations, with the EU once again defending the Common Agricultural Policy (see Chapter 12). A ministerial meeting in September 2003, held approximately halfway between the launch and the expected end of the round, broke down in acrimony over agriculture and the Singapore issues. Nor did the negotiators meet the deadline of January 2005 for completion of the round.

The EU is by no means the only or the worst culprit. The United States is also on the defensive on agricultural protection and subsidization, whereas countries such as Brazil, China, and India are aggressively promoting their own agricultural and nonagricultural interests. A renewed effort to make a breakthrough in the negotiations failed at a ministerial meeting in Geneva in July 2008, this time because of an impasse between India and the United States (the EU was pleased to be off the hook). Thereafter the round languished, despite pro forma calls in successive G20 summit communiqués for a successful conclusion of the negotiations. Domestic politics—the key determinant of trade policy—are not conducive in the EU or elsewhere to the kinds of concessions that completion of the Doha Round requires, not least because of the economic recession. Trade economists point out the benefits to the global economy of a successful round, politicians concur, but the negotiations remain deadlocked.

Relations with Asia

Asia is such a huge and heterogeneous region that it makes little sense to talk of a single EU-Asia relationship. Nevertheless, the EU pursues the same general objectives in Asia as it does elsewhere in its external action: peace and security; human rights, democracy, good governance, and rule of law; freer trade and investment; and international development. A particular challenge for the EU in its dealings with some countries in the region is their embrace of the so-called Asian model of modernization and development, which includes values and political ideas that are at odds with those of Western liberal democracy. Such differences, and the legacy of European colonialism in a large number of Asian countries, complicate the EU's dealings with the region.

For a long time the EU's involvement in Asia meant essentially EU efforts to open Japan's market and stem the flood of Japanese products into Western Europe. Nevertheless, the EU had long-standing relations with the Association of Southeast Asian Nations (ASEAN), which includes ten countries. The EU's interest in those countries was also primarily economic, especially in the 1980s, when fear of international competition from the so-called Asian Tigers swept across Western Europe.

The EU's growing interest in Asia from the mid-1990s was partly a reaction to renewed US economic interest in the region, notably through Washington's rejuvenation of the Asia Pacific Economic Cooperation (APEC) group, a loose association that spans the Pacific from Canada to Korea and includes the ASEAN countries. The EU's new approach manifested itself most obviously in an intensification of contacts with China. Like the United States, the EU appreciates China's huge economic and political impact, regionally and globally. Also like the United States, the EU hopes to shape China's reemergence as a great power in a mutually agreeable way. Finally, the EU is increasing its engagement with India, another emerging power. In addition to a thriving bilateral relationship with India, the EU has a relationship with the South Asian Association for Regional Cooperation (SAARC), an organization of eight countries, centered on India.

Asia-Europe Meeting. The Asia-Europe Meeting (ASEM) is a forum that brings together forty-five countries, encompassing almost the whole of Asia and Europe. ASEM consists of biennial summits, alternating between European and Asian locations, around which a growing network of public and private meetings revolves. The idea behind ASEM is to facilitate relatively free and informal exchanges of ideas and information on a range of economic, political, and security issues. However, the large number of participants and the sensitivity of some topics inevitably inhibit progress. For instance, a long-running dispute between the EU and ASEAN over the participation of Burma/ Myanmar, a country with an atrocious human rights record and against which the EU has imposed sanctions, overshadows the ASEM summits.

Indeed, the EU's Asia strategy is beset with disagreements with a number of countries over social policy, environmental issues, and human rights concerns. Nevertheless, the EU's dealings with ASEAN and with other countries in ASEM provide an opportunity to air such concerns and to deal with pressing global problems, such as the recession in the late 2000s.

The strategic framework for EU involvement in Asia is based on the Commission's Communication "Europe and Asia," adopted in 2001. Three years later, the EU set out to engage the countries of Asia in a deeper political and economic relationship when it adopted its first regional programming document for the region, covering the period 2005–2006; a second programming document covers the period 2007–2013. Through implementation of these programs, the EU seeks deeper involvement in Asia through closer bilateral and multilateral relations and activities covering more than one country, especially in the fields of trade, investment, education, and the environment. Publication of these documents highlights both the extent of EU involvement throughout Asia and the political and organizational challenges of dealing with such a fluid, dynamic, and distant part of the world.

Japan. Despite having suffered a serious economic slowdown in the late 1990s and early 2000s, and being hit by the global recession at the end of the decade, Japan remains an economic giant. Until recently, relations between the EU and Japan were almost exclusively economic. Japan's expanding trade surplus, especially in electronics and cars, greatly alarmed the EU in the 1990s. There were calls from European industry for retaliatory measures against alleged dumping of Japanese products and for EU efforts to break down supposed structural impediments to entry into the Japanese market. Commercial relations improved in the late 1990s following a drop in the number of Japanese cars entering the European market, thanks to an EC-Japan export-restraint agreement negotiated earlier in the decade. Largely because of the growth of production in Japanese-owned factories located in the EU, quotas under the auto agreement were rarely filled and the agreement did not have to be renewed.

Due partly to the impact of these Japanese "transplants," Japan's trade surplus with the EU fell sharply and the EU even made inroads into the Japanese marketplace. The resolution of two long-standing trade disputes between the EU and Japan in the late 1990s—one on Japan's insufficient music copyright protection, the other on Japan's discriminatory liquor taxes—improved relations further. Tension rose again during the Asian economic crisis when Japan resumed its export-led growth strategy with the assistance of a greatly depreciated yen. Hopes that the Asian crisis and the continuing deterioration of the Japanese economy would impel Japan to undertake fundamental structural reforms, upon which a more satisfactory relationship with the EU and its other trading partners could be built, were unavailing.

Nevertheless, Japan's protracted economic recession, an intensification of the EU-Japan dialogue over touchy trade and regulatory issues, and the widespread acceptance of Japanese transplants as legitimate EU enterprises have contributed to a marked improvement in EU-Japan relations. Compared to the late 1980s, when Europeans feared the encroachment of a seemingly unstoppable Japanese economic juggernaut, EU-Japan relations have become almost somnolent, despite occasional outbursts from EU politicians and businesspeople about high Japanese barriers to trade and investment and latent economic nationalism. The annual EU-Japan summits, held under the auspices of the 1991 EC-Japan Declaration, range far beyond trade and investment, covering climate change, science and technology, and other issues of mutual interest.

Today, the EU's difficulties with Japan look trifling compared with the challenges posed by China.

China. With its spectacular export-led economic growth and aggressive trade policy, China has replaced Japan as the EU's economic bogeyman. The EU's relationship with China goes back to the mid-1970s, when the two signed a trade and economic cooperation agreement, upgraded in 1985. The EC's cozy relationship with China came to an abrupt end in June 1989 when the Chinese government ruthlessly suppressed the pro-democracy student demonstrations in Tiananmen Square. The European Council condemned China's repression, suspended high-level bilateral meetings, postponed new cooperation projects, and cut existing programs. Pragmatism soon triumphed over principle and the EU decided gradually to normalize relations with China, although the conflict between upholding human rights and enhancing bilateral trade continues to trouble some national governments, especially over the issue of the arms embargo (a legacy of Tiananmen Square), which China has been pressing the EU to lift.

Despite the progressive intensification of contacts, which has blossomed into annual summits (usually held in November or December) and regular meetings at ministerial and official levels, EU-China relations remain troubled. Negotiations to reduce quotas and other barriers to trade have been difficult and prolonged. Although the EU was one of the earliest major trading partners to grant China fully unconditional most-favored-nation status (nondiscriminatory tariff access for China's goods and services), the EU resented continuing obstacles to European exports. For their part, the Chinese resented the frequent use by the EU of antidumping measures. China's disregard for intellectual property rights was another irritant in EU-China relations. Although China finally put intellectual property laws in place (thanks largely to US pressure), problems of enforcement remain.

The EU's interest in China still encompasses humanitarian and, more recently, environmental and climate change concerns. The EU wants to help China feed its huge population, make better use of its natural resources, reduce environmental damage, alleviate rural poverty, and address the global challenge of climate change (China has surpassed the United States in CO_2 emissions). The EU promotes these objectives through high-level contacts, direct financial and technical assistance, support for nongovernmental organizations working in China, and humanitarian aid through the European Community Humanitarian Office (ECHO).

Nevertheless, trade remains front and center in the EU-China relationship. China has a huge trade surplus with the EU. Although a WTO member, in many respects China does not seem to play by WTO rules. Like their US counterparts, European exporters are eager to break into the burgeoning domestic Chinese market but find the door at best half open. For foreign businesspeople,

China is a bewildering maze of hidden subsidies for domestic producers, state controls of certain economy activity, and unpredictable rules and regulations. Perhaps most disconcerting for exporters to China is that the country's currency is loosely pegged to the dollar. As the value of the dollar falls, European exporters find themselves priced out of the Chinese market, even if they can otherwise manage to get in.

Not surprisingly, Europeans are growing more resentful of China. Like others around the world, Europeans are torn between the obvious advantages and disadvantages of China's economic resurgence. As consumers, Europeans gain from cheap imports; as workers, they lose from factory closures. The tension between these conflicting experiences emerged in 2005, following a surge in imports from China and elsewhere in Asia of cheap clothes into the EU. European textile producers were in despair; consumers were either pleased or indifferent. Eventually the Commission negotiated an agreement whereby China would temporarily limit its exports of apparel to the EU, thereby defusing the tension, but without resolving the underlying problem.

At their November 2007 summit, the EU and China agreed to establish a high-level dialogue on economics and trade to try to tackle fundamental differences, as well as high-level dialogues on exchange rate and macroeconomic issues. These institutional arrangements have done little to strengthen the relationship. To the EU's dismay, China canceled the December 2008 summit because President Sarkozy had met the Dalai Lama, whom the Chinese regard as a dangerous subversive. The EU was incredulous that China would react so harshly to what, in European eyes, was a courtesy extended by the French head of state to a distinguished religious leader. The episode was a painful reminder of the different worldviews of the postnational EU and ultranationalistic China.

Overall, the EU's policy toward China is arguably too ambitious and unrealistic. It is difficult for the Commission to coordinate EU activities and national policies toward China, a country that is becoming adept at playing favorites among member states. Whereas the EU views China as an emerging global power, China views the EU as an important economic entity but as an insignificant political power. Deeply sovereignty-conscious, China has little sympathy for European efforts to share sovereignty or for the EU's emphasis on the importance of soft power. Together with the country's renowned prickliness and opacity, China's poor regard for the EU and strategic focus on the United States make the EU's laudable objectives toward China almost impossible to attain.

India. India was one of the first countries to establish diplomatic relations with the EC. Bilateral agreements for economic cooperation followed in 1973 and 1981. Relations were upgraded in December 1993 when the EU and India signed a wide-ranging cooperation agreement. This took the predictable form of calling for an intensification of trade and investment, better market access on both sides, and a political dialogue on issues of common concern. It also established an institutional structure along expected lines but went beyond the usual apparatus by including annual summit meetings.

Relations with the EU flourished as India liberalized its economy in the 1990s, developed its high-technology sector, and became a major player regionally and globally. The EU is now India's main trading partner and biggest investor. The EU and its member states are also the biggest contributors to India's development programs and biggest provider of humanitarian aid. In 2004 the Commission elevated the EU-India relationship to a strategic partnership, an impressive-sounding designation that would provide an added impetus for cooperation on a range of economic, development, and political issues. India's rapid economic rise, strong democratic values (despite religious and social impediments to pluralism), and de-escalation of tension with Pakistan make the country a favored EU interlocutor in the region.

Yet the relationship is not without difficulties and, in the case of the EU, deep frustration. India is a tough country with which to negotiate. The EU has sought a free trade agreement with India since 2007, which India has resisted because of EU demands relating to intellectual property rights, child labor laws, and environmental issues. As mentioned earlier in this chapter, India is a major player in the Doha Round negotiations of the WTO and, as the EU sees it, has impeded prospects of reaching an agreement. Moreover, India refuses to take an ambitious stand on tackling climate change, a cherished EU objective. Like China, only less so, India seems impervious to the EU's charms.

Relations with Latin America

Given the close cultural, historical, and social ties between Latin America on the one hand and Portugal and Spain on the other, relations between the EU and Latin America began to develop after the Iberian countries joined the EC in 1986. Yet it was only late in the 1990s, as democracy took hold throughout Latin America and the economic situation improved, that the EU took a sustained interest in the region. Not surprisingly, Portugal and Spain led the way. For instance, in December 1995, during Spain's presidency, the European Council endorsed the goal of strengthening EU–Latin America relations, and the EU and Mercosur, a common market embracing several South American countries, signed an agreement, the first ever between two customs unions.

Although EU trade with Latin America has risen since the late 1990s, Latin America's proportion of total EU trade has continued to decline. Nevertheless, Latin America is important to the EU, whose relations with the region are part of a broader strategy to raise its profile as a global actor. Latin America's traditionally close (although rocky) relationship with the United States adds an extra dimension to the EU's involvement in the region. Many Latin American countries see the EU as a potential counterweight to the United States, and the EU sees its involvement in Latin America as a way to assert itself politically vis-à-vis the United States. Yet both sides know that economic and geopolitical realities bind the countries of Latin America inexorably to the United States.

The EU has steadily intensified and institutionalized its dealings with Latin America, resulting in "a multi-layered inter-regionalism bringing together bilateral, plurilateral and inter-continental relationships."[13] Yet deep-rooted differences over EU agricultural protectionism and the EU's preferential trade agreements with some Caribbean countries have tested the relationship over time. Notwithstanding the seemingly harmonious development of EU–Latin American ties, the EU and Latin American countries, especially Brazil, are often at loggerheads in the Doha Round of global trade liberalization negotiations.

The EU's relationship with the Rio Group, a loose association of all the countries of Latin America as well as most Caribbean countries, provides an umbrella under which the EU deals with the region's constituent parts. The EU and the Rio Group hold biennial summits, such as in Madrid (during Spain's Council presidency) in May 2010. These summits are impressive affairs, attracting sixty or so heads of state and government. Inevitably, their substantive value is limited, as the broad theme of the Madrid summit would suggest ("Towards a New Stage in the Bi-Regional Partnership: Innovation and Technology for Sustainable Development and Social Inclusion"). Nevertheless, they have important symbolic value, as the United States notes with some annoyance.

On a day-to-day basis, the EU's relations with Latin America are based on a close association with the Central American countries; with the Andean Community; with Mercosur and its leading member, Brazil; and with two countries that do not fall within any of these groupings: Chile and Mexico.

Central America. The EU and the countries of Central America (Costa Rica, El Salvador, Guatemala, Honduras, Nicaragua, and Panama) have an unusually close relationship, a legacy of EU efforts through the so-called San José Dialogue to bring peace to the region in the mid-1980s, when many countries there were wracked by civil war. The EU has progressively strengthened its formal ties to the region, through which it aims to promote economic development partly by encouraging regional integration, notably through the establishment of the Central American Customs Union. In 2004, the EU and the Central American countries began the process of elevating their relationship to that of an association agreement. Given the asymmetries between both sides and the demands of the Central American countries for special treatment and extensive technical assistance, the association agreement has been difficult to negotiate.[14]

The Andean Community. The EU has long supported the process of Andean regional integration, which dates from the Andean Pact of 1969, originally consisting of Bolivia, Chile, Colombia, Ecuador, and Peru (Chile withdrew in 1976; Venezuela joined in 1973 but withdrew in 2006). The EU holds regular meetings with the Andean Community—the countries of the Andean Pact—on topics such as economic development, democracy and human rights, and the all-important fight against drugs. The EU and the Andean Community first concluded a formal agreement in 1983. It was upgraded in 1993 and again in December 2003, when the EU and the Andean Community signed a new political and cooperation agreement, which was intended to pave the way for an association agreement, including a free trade area.

Negotiation of the association agreement broke down in 2008. Since then, the EU has conducted a political dialogue with the Andean Community as a whole but has engaged in trade negotiations with individual countries (so far only Colombia, Ecuador, and Peru). The EU's problems with the Andean Community are not solely economic—the usual difficulties of negotiating an agreement in such an asymmetrical relationship—but are primarily political. Hugo Chavez, Venezuela's mercurial leader, is the fly in the ointment. Chavez took Venezuela out of the Andean Community and exercises a malign influence over Evo Morales, president of Bolivia, which remains in the community. At first, many Europeans found Chavez amusing and welcomed his virulent anti-Americanism. However, Chavez's nationalization of some foreign-owned companies has hurt Spanish and other European interests, and his reckless politics are raising regional tension. The EU has little leverage over Chavez, who sees the EU's activities in the region as neocolonial rather than benignly postmodern.

Mercosur and Brazil. Established in 1991, Mercosur (Mercado Común del Sur, or Southern Common Market) is a customs union whose members are Argentina, Brazil, Paraguay, and Uruguay. Venezuela signed an accession agreement in 2006 but is not yet a full member of the organization. The EU has supported Mercosur from the outset. The two signed an interregional cooperation agreement in 1995 as the basis for a free trade agreement, which has proved elusive due to protectionist proclivities on both sides. Much depends on Brazil, a regional giant that is also emerging as a global power in the WTO and the G20. Rivalry within Mercosur between Argentina and Brazil has stymied the organization and reduced the EU's interest in it. In the meantime, the EU has upgraded its relations with Brazil to a strategic partnership, complete with annual summits. The relationship is testy, with Brazil pushing for greater access to the EU market, especially for agricultural products.

Chile. Until the late 1980s, Chile was cut off from the international community because of its authoritarian, military regime. Since the restoration of democracy there, the EU has developed an unusually close relationship with Chile, culminating in an association agreement in November 2002, which includes a free trade agreement that entered into force the following year. In addition to trade, the association agreement covers political relations and development cooperation, and involves occasional summits and more regular ministerial and official meetings. Chile, a flourishing democracy and market economy, is the darling of the EU in Latin America.

Mexico. Mexico is one of the EU's most important trading partners in Latin America, and the EU is Mexico's second trading partner after the United States. Trade between the two sides immediately grew by 26 percent following implementation of a commercial agreement in 2000, but soon fell back again due to the global economic downturns at the beginning and end of the decade. The EU views Mexico as a key political interlocutor in the region. The EU-Mexico dialogue, held under the auspices of the 1997 partnership and cooperation agreement, covers a variety of social and political issues, including poverty, terrorism, drugs, human rights, democracy, migration, and regional affairs. The substance of the dialogue has improved markedly since 2000, when the federal elections resulted in the ouster of the oxymoronic Institutional Revolutionary Party, which had been in power for more than seventy years. In recognition of Mexico's importance in the region, in October 2008 the European Council upgraded the EU's relationship with Mexico to a strategic partnership.

Relations with Africa

Most African countries are party to the Cotonou Agreement, the centerpiece of the EU's development policy that provides assistance to nearly eighty African, Caribbean, and Pacific (ACP) countries. Covering the period 2000–2020, the Cotonou Agreement differs significantly from its predecessors, which were essentially preferential trade-and-aid programs uniformly applied to all applicable states. By contrast, the Cotonou Agreement includes three key goals: trade liberalization, regional and economic differentiation, and political conditionality (respect for human rights, democratic principles, and rule of law are essential elements of the agreement).

The growing emphasis on trade liberalization reflects an appreciation in the development community that free trade is the engine of economic growth and that poor countries are likely to benefit from progressive integration into the global economy. Globalization has helped to alleviate poverty on a massive scale in China and India. Why should this not happen in Africa as well? Accordingly, the Cotonou Agreement includes provisions for the adoption of trade policy in conformity with WTO rules and norms. Furthermore, the agreement emphasizes the importance of competition policy, protection of intellectual property rights, standardization, consumer protection, environmental protection, and the like.

The EU's desire to bring the Cotonou Agreement into the WTO regime also reflected sustained pressure from the United States and other trading partners to end EU trade preferences for such a large group of countries, which discriminated against other countries at a similar level of economic development. Indeed, the WTO ruled as long ago as 1993 that the EU's preferential trade arrangements with most developing countries were illegal. As well as promoting global economic integration for the Cotonou countries, the EU decided to abandon its all-embracing approach to the group and negotiate instead separate WTO-compliant economic cooperation and partnership agreements with subgroups of Cotonou countries. As it was, most Cotonou countries had little in common with each other. The Commission argued that geographical differentiation would improve the effectiveness of EU assistance and accelerate the integration of recipient countries into the global economy. Whether genuinely unconvinced by the Commission's arguments or simply afraid of the future, many Cotonou countries clung to the old framework and opposed what they saw as EU efforts to sunder supposed Cotonou solidarity.

In a major break from past conventions, the Cotonou Agreement differentiates not only among regions but also among countries on the basis of their level of development and ability to withstand global competition. It therefore called for the negotiation of several economic partnership agreements by the end of December 2007, when, in compliance with the WTO, the trade provisions of the Cotonou Agreement were due to expire. Promoting regional integration is central to the EU's external relations, based on the assumption that what is good for Europe must be good for other parts of the world.

The five regional groupings among African countries are:

- Central Africa
- East African Community
- Eastern and Southern Africa
- Southern African Development Community
- West Africa

The negotiations of the economic partnership agreements, which began in 2003, have not gone well. None was concluded by the stipulated deadline, although many ACP countries signed interim agreements with the EU in order to prevent disruption to their exports after the trade provisions of the Cotonou Agreement expired and in order to provide additional time to negotiate the comprehensive regional agreements. Distrust on the ACP side and irritation on the EU side best describe the state of play. Many of the ACP countries, lacking the administrative capacity to conduct complicated negotiations on highly technical issues such as rules of origin and trade defense measures, have complained about the EU's impatience and heavy-handedness. Many ACP countries have also resisted the EU's efforts to include in the agreements trade-related issues such as competition policy, the environment, and social policy.

Among African countries, Nigeria and South Africa are especially frustrated with the EU and are big enough to make their feelings known.

South Africa is a special case for the EU in a number of respects. Member states were divided on the question of sanctions against South Africa during the apartheid years, especially after the escalation of violence there in the mid-1980s. After the collapse of apartheid and the democratization of the country, South Africa became one of the few positive case studies for the EU's Common Foreign and Security Policy, as member states rallied in support of the new regime. Yet economic relations with the new South Africa were problematic because of the country's size and its peculiar status as both a developed and a developing country (depending on the sector). South Africa wanted to join the Lomé Convention (forerunner to the Cotonou Agreement), but the existing Lomé countries feared being crushed by South African competition and the EU feared a WTO challenge from non-Lomé trading partners. Accordingly, in 1997, South Africa became a "qualified member" of Lomé under a special protocol attached to the convention. Whereas South Africa enjoyed some benefits of Lomé membership, it was excluded from the convention's special trade regime.

South Africa is a qualified member of the Cotonou Agreement. EU–South Africa commercial relations are governed separately by a 1999 trade, development, and cooperation agreement. South Africa's situation has complicated negotiation of the economic partnership agreement between the EU and the Southern African Development Community (SADC), of which South Africa is the dominant member. Negotiations were suspended at the end of 2005 so that SADC could sort out within itself aspects of and linkages between the EU–South Africa trade, development, and cooperation agreement and the proposed EU-SADC economic partnership agreement. Although negotiations resumed in 2007 and an interim agreement was reached between the EU and several SADC countries, a final accord embracing the EU and SADC as a whole remains elusive.

Concerned about its strained relations with African countries as a result of the switch to economic partnership agreements, in 2005 the EU launched its Strategy for Africa with a view to developing "a comprehensive, integrated and long-term framework for its relations with the African continent."[15] The African Union, an organization of fifty-two African states loosely modeled on the EU, is the EU's interlocutor for the region as a whole. Portugal made relations with Africa a centerpiece of its Council presidency in 2007. Accordingly, European and African leaders launched the Africa-EU Strategic Partnership at the first EU-Africa Summit, held in Lisbon in December 2007. The summit resulted in a political declaration replete with language such as "co-ownership," "co-management," and "co-responsibility"; a joint EU-Africa strategy; and an action plan to achieve concrete results. The overall strategic partnership consists of eight functional strategic partnerships (the nomenclature is confusing):

- Peace and security
- Democratic governance and human rights
- Trade, regional integration, and infrastructure
- Millennium development goals
- Energy
- Climate change
- Migration, mobility, and employment
- Science, information society, and space

The elaborate framework of the Africa-EU Strategic Partnership cannot disguise underlying tension in the relationship. Britain and France, the foremost former colonial powers in Africa, are the main drivers of EU policy toward the region. Yet each is viewed differently by its former colonies, with Britain being regarded more favorably than France, whose record on democracy and human rights promotion in Africa is dubious, to say the least. Within the EU, many member states distrust French positions on Africa, seeing them as efforts to wrap French neocolonialism in the EU flag. The historical legacy of European imperialism in Africa therefore bedevils EU efforts to go beyond elaborate frameworks, strategies, and action plans and truly improve relations both among African countries and between them and the EU.

■ Development Cooperation and Humanitarian Aid

The EU prides itself on its generous support for developing countries around the world, ranging from food aid to technical advice to financial assistance. The EU and the member states collectively constitute the world's largest provider of development aid. Most countries have managed to meet their responsibilities as donors, even during and despite the onset of the 2008–2009 economic recession.

Governments incorporated the goal of "development cooperation" into the Maastricht Treaty in 1991. The EU's objectives in this area are to foster sustainable economic and social development in the world's poorer countries; encourage smooth and gradual integration of the poor countries into the global economy; campaign against global poverty; and promote democracy, rule of law, and respect for human rights. Among other things, the relevant treaty articles adjured governments to coordinate their own development policies with those of the EU.

The persistence of separate national development policies (some countries contribute more development assistance than the EU itself, and EU development assistance amounts to only about 25 percent of what the member states contribute altogether) is a reminder of the national governments' unwillingness to surrender policy instruments to the EU in the international sphere.

The Lisbon Treaty identified development cooperation as a policy area in which the EU shares competence with the member states, thereby giving the EU the authority "to carry out activities and conduct a common policy; however, the exercise of that competence shall not result in Member States being prevented from exercising theirs." According to the treaty, the development policies of the EU and the member states "shall complement and reinforce each other." The treaty also states that the reduction and eradication of poverty are the primary objective of the EU's development cooperation policy, a goal that must be respected when the EU implements policies likely to affect developing countries.

The fact that the European Development Fund (EDF), the main financial instrument for EU development assistance, is not part of the EU budget is another peculiarity of development policy. Keeping the EDF out of the EU budget maximizes governments' control over allocations from the fund but does not necessarily result in greater efficiency: intergovernmental negotiations to renew the EDF can be contentious and extend beyond the stipulated deadline, and lengthy national ratification procedures often delay implementation of the new agreements. Apart from the EDF, European Investment Bank loans to countries that have concluded cooperation agreements with the EU are an integral part of the EU's development policy.

The European Commission's role in development policy is complicated because responsibility for such a large policy area is spread among a number of commissioners and directorates-general (the most important Commission portfolios in that regard are foreign affairs, development, and trade). In order to improve the coordination of external action within the Commission, the commissioner for development policy works "in close cooperation with the High Representative/Vice-President in accordance with the treaties."[16] The Parliament's influence over development policy has increased over time, partly because many MEPs are deeply interested in the subject and partly for institutional reasons. Although the EDF is separate from the EU budget, the EP has a degree of control over other parts of the development budget; the EP must give its consent to development-related international agreements; and the ordinary legislative procedure is used to adopt "the measures necessary for the implementation of development cooperation policy, which may relate to multiannual cooperation programs with developing countries or programs with a thematic approach."

The Cotonou Agreement

Historically, the EU's development policy has centered on a succession of agreements with a large swath of African, Caribbean, and Pacific countries, all former colonies of EU member states (see Box 16.1). Since 2000, EU-ACP relations have been organized under the Cotonou Agreement (named after the capital city of Benin, where the agreement was signed). From the time of the first agreement to the current Cotonou partnership, the EU has enlarged to over four times its original size and the number of partnership ACP countries has increased from forty-six to seventy-nine. The nature and scope of the agreements have also changed, from a basic development assistance program, to a program combining development assistance and preferential access to the

Box 16.1 EU-ACP Agreements	
Yaoundé I	1964–1970
Yaoundé II	1970–1975
Lomé I	1975–1979
Lomé II	1980–1984
Lomé III	1985–1989
Lomé IVa	1990–1994
Lomé IVb	1995–1999
Cotonou	2000–2020

EU market, to a program that now emphasizes trade liberalization, political conditionality, and regional differentiation among the ACP states.

Regardless of its far-reaching reforms with respect to trade policy, the Cotonou Agreement commits the EU to continuing to help the ACP countries with debt reduction, balance-of-payments problems, structural reforms, and institutional development, as well as assistance for stabilization of export earnings, especially in the agricultural and mining sectors, subject to the recipient countries' commitment to trade liberalization and adherence to the political conditions of the agreement. In addition, the agreement stresses the importance of the private sector for economic growth and development, and the importance of involving civil society in the governance process.

The Cotonou Agreement lasts until 2020, when ideally it will not need to be renewed. Inevitably, most of the ACP countries will still need assistance, especially the least-developed. Some of the more economically advanced ACP countries, however, may be able to stand on their own feet by then.

The Generalized System of Preferences

Under the Generalized System of Preferences (GSP), the EU grants duty-free access for industrial goods and some agricultural produce from a number of developing countries. The EU introduced a new dimension to its GSP regime in the late 1990s by providing additional trade benefits to countries that meet core labor and environmental standards. Some GSP beneficiaries, such as Pakistan and Indonesia, have expressed concern about EU intrusion into their internal affairs and about EU conditionality regarding their continued eligibility for preferences. The EU argued that it was not limiting the GSP regime but was instead offering special incentives for developing countries to comply with internationally set social and environmental standards. However, a WTO ruling in 2004 upheld an Indian challenge to the EU's drugs scheme (which benefited textile exports from Pakistan, among others, in an effort to combat illegal drug production), saying that it was not based on clear, transparent, and nondiscriminatory criteria. In October 2004 the Commission adopted a new system to cover the period 2006–2015. The new scheme replaces the drugs, social, and environmental incentive schemes with a "GSP-plus" system, which offers additional benefits to "vulnerable" countries that accept various international conventions.

Everything but Arms

In February 2001 the EU launched a new development initiative when the Council adopted the so-called Everything but Arms (EBA) regulation, granting duty-free access to imports of all products from the least-developed countries (LDCs) without any quantitative restrictions except for arms and munitions. "Least-developed" is a United Nations category for countries that are particularly bad off; there are forty-nine LDCs altogether.

Only imports of bananas, rice, and sugar—highly sensitive products in the EU—were not fully liberalized immediately. The EU plans to keep the EBA regulation in place indefinitely rather than subjecting it to periodic renewal under the Generalized System of Preferences. This is the first time that the EU has used a country's level of development as a criterion for a particular development program (as opposed to historical ties to the EU, as in the case of the Cotonou Agreement). The initiative offers the LDC participants in the Cotonou Agreement, which includes the vast majority of the world's LDCs, a better preferential trade arrangement than does Cotonou, suggesting that Cotonou and the EBA are somewhat at cross-purposes with each other. For the first time also, non-ACP countries—the LDCs that are not party to the Cotonou Agreement— receive better treatment from the EU than do some ACP countries.

Humanitarian Aid

Apart from contractual development assistance agreements such as Cotonou, the EU dispenses large amounts of aid unilaterally. In 1992 the EU established the European Community Humanitarian Office to provide emergency humanitarian and food aid wherever needed around the world. ECHO now funds over 2,000 projects in nearly eighty countries on four continents. ECHO operates through a wide range of partners, including NGOs, which administer nearly 60 percent of ECHO funding, and UN agencies, which administer over 25 percent. ECHO's high dependence on NGOs reflects both a dearth of Commission officials on the ground and the Commission's frequent need to try to circumvent corrupt recipient governments. Ironically, the EU itself stands accused of major fraud and mismanagement in the conduct of ECHO affairs. The Lisbon Treaty introduced a specific legal basis for humanitarian aid and stressed that humanitarian aid operations would be conducted in compliance with the principles of international law, specifically with the principles of impartiality, neutrality, and nondiscrimination. The treaty also provided for the establishment of a voluntary European humanitarian aid corps (a rough equivalent of the US Peace Corps) to encourage young Europeans to contribute to the EU's aid operations.

◼ Notes

1. Chris Patten, *Not Quite the Diplomat: Home Truths About World Affairs* (London: Penguin, 2005), p. 153.

2. European Commission, "2005 Enlargement Strategy Paper," COM(2005)561 final, September 11, 2005.

3. On the Turkish case, see Ali Çarkoğlu and Barry Rubin, eds., *Turkey and the European Union: Domestic Politics, Economic Integration, and International Dynamics* (London: Cass, 2003); Esra LaGro and Knud Erik Jorgensen, eds., *Turkey and the European Union: Prospects for a Difficult Encounter* (Basingstoke: Palgrave Macmillan, 2005); and Meltem Müftüler-Baç and Yannis Stivachtis, eds., *Turkey–European Union Relations: Dilemmas, Opportunities, and Constraints* (Lanham: Lexington Books, 2008).

4. "Isn't Europe Ambitious Enough to Admit Turkey?" *International Herald Tribune*, December 10, 1997, p. 10.

5. Council of the European Union, "Negotiations Framework: Principles Governing Negotiations," Brussels, December 10, 2005.

6. See, for instance, Council of Ministers, press release, November 16, 2009, 2973rd Council meeting (General Affairs), p. 10.

7. Milada Anna Vachudova, "Corruption and Compliance in the EU's Post-Communist Members and Candidates," *Journal of Common Market Studies, Annual Review of the Eupean Union in 2008* (2009): 44.

8. European Commission, *1995 General Report* (Luxembourg: Office for Official Publications of the European Communities, 1996), point 926.

9. Council Presidency, "Joint Declaration of the Paris Summit for the Mediterranean," July 13, 2008, http://www.ue2008.fr/webdav/site/PFUE/shared/import/07/0713 _declaration_de_paris/Joint_declaration_of_the_Paris_summit_for_the_Mediterranean-EN.pdf.

10. On the question of trade policy competence, see Alasdair R. Young, *Extending European Cooperation: The European Union and the "New" International Trade Agenda* (Manchester: Manchester University Press, 2002); Stephen Woolcock, *The Potential Impact of the Lisbon Treaty on European Union External Trade Policy,* European Policy Analysis no. 8 (Stockholm: SIEPS, 2008).

11. European Commission, "Trade, Market Access," http://ec.europa.eu/trade/creating-opportunities/trade-topics/market-access/.

12. See European Commission, "Global Europe: EU Performance in the Global Economy," October 2008, http://trade.ec.europa.eu/doclib/docs/2008/october/tradoc_141196.pdf.

13. David Allen and Michael Smith, "Relations with the Rest of the World," *Journal of Common Market Studies* 46, *Annual Review of the European Union in 2008* (September 2009): 176.

14. See Council of the European Union, San José Dialogue meeting, Prague, May 14, 2009, joint communiqué, http://register.consilium.europa.eu/pdf/en/09/st09/st 09933.en09.pdf.

15. European Commission, "EU Strategy for Africa: Towards a Euro-African Act to Accelerate Africa's Development," COM(2005)489 final, December 10, 2005.

16. European Commission, "President Barroso Unveils His New Team," November 27, 2009, http://europa.eu/rapid/pressReleasesAction.do?reference=IP/09/1837& format=HTML&aged=0&language=EN&guiLanguage=en.

17 Internal and External Security

The EU is not a security organization along the lines of the North Atlantic Treaty Organization, but its activities have a major impact on regional and global security. In response to external security challenges, the EU has developed the Common Foreign and Security Policy. This is not a common policy like the Common Commercial Policy; it is a largely intergovernmental arrangement, notwithstanding the abolition of the old "pillar" system in the Lisbon Treaty. Despite the misleading nomenclature and the obvious constraints of intergovernmental cooperation, the CFSP has helped to raise the EU's profile as an international actor and to bolster security beyond the EU's borders. Tentative though it still is, the Common Security and Defense Policy (CSDP), an integral part of the CFSP, has given the EU a limited military capacity to intervene in trouble spots, especially close to home.

Instability on Europe's fringes could cause instability in the EU itself, not least because of the possible influx of refugees and asylum seekers. As it is, lack of economic opportunities in the "wider Europe" and beyond drives migration into the EU. Free movement of people among member states, a belated benefit of the single market program, necessitates the development of common asylum and immigration policies. Similarly, the opportunity for criminals (including terrorists) to exploit free movement within the EU necessitates close police and judicial cooperation. Hence the decision by EU leaders, enshrined in the Amsterdam Treaty, to establish the Area of Freedom, Security, and Justice (AFSJ). Putting that concept into practice has proved as difficult as developing the CFSP, for many of the same reasons, notably concerns about sovereignty, as well as discordant national philosophies and practices in the sensitive area of justice and home affairs (JHA).

It is easy to caricature the EU's plodding progress in the areas of internal and external security, including immigration, asylum, and the like. Given the political and historical constraints, however, the EU's record is impressive. Some advocates of deeper integration may wish otherwise, but the EU is not a state (let alone a superstate in the making) and cannot behave accordingly.

Even the Lisbon Treaty, which sharpens the EU's political profile and strengthens its policymaking capacity in the fields of internal and external security, does not endow the EU with the means necessary to become a state-like actor in such politically sensitive policy areas.

Nevertheless, the EU has considerable institutional and material potential to be more forceful and effective in the security realm, especially outside the EU itself. What is lacking, mostly, is political will, compounded by uncertainty over what exactly the EU is or should be. Even without wanting to become a statelike entity, and without diminishing the moral value of soft power, arguably the EU needs to have a hard edge in its international relations. Inadequate though the treaties may be, they are not the real reason why the EU continues to punch beneath its weight on the global stage.

■ Internal Security: The Area of Freedom, Security, and Justice

Cooperation among member states on justice and home affairs—a range of activities pertaining to asylum and immigration, control of external borders, and police and judicial cooperation—took off in the late 1980s with the launch of the single market program, which aimed to establish "an area without internal frontiers, in which the free movement of goods, persons, services and capital is ensured." Of the "four freedoms," free movement of people was the most problematic, because it implied the introduction of a host of difficult accompanying measures dealing with political asylum, immigration, and visas for nationals of nonmember states entering the Community and moving freely within it, as well as better police networks and external border measures directed against terrorism, drug smuggling, and other criminal activity. Such measures were mostly a new departure for the EU.

Buoyed by widespread enthusiasm for deeper integration and impatient with efforts to liberalize the free movement of people, five of the EU's founding member states—France, Germany, Belgium, the Netherlands, and Luxembourg— took the first step toward abolishing all frontier formalities among them when they signed an agreement in June 1985 in the town of Schengen in Luxembourg. The Schengen Agreement launched a lengthy series of negotiations to identify and implement the numerous measures necessary to abolish internal frontiers and establish a common external border around the signatory states. Major challenges included setting visa requirements, dealing with asylum applications, combating illegal immigration, improving police cooperation, and physically reconfiguring airports in order to segregate passengers traveling within the so-called Schengen area from those on other flights.[1]

Completion of the single market should have made Schengen redundant. But three member states—Britain (for reasons of history and national sovereignty), Ireland (because it wanted to keep a common travel area with Britain), and Denmark (because of the possible impact of free movement in the Community on long-standing free movement among Nordic countries)—did not subscribe fully to the call in the single market program for unrestricted travel. To be precise, they subscribed to the free movement of member state nationals, but not nationals of third countries. As it would have been impossible to distinguish between nationals of member and nonmember states without checks at intra-Community borders, Britain, Ireland, and Denmark insisted on keeping some frontier controls even after completion of the single market.

Italy, Greece, Portugal, and Spain (the remaining member states) wanted to join Schengen and resented their exclusion from it. Italy, the only founding member state not in the group, was especially miffed. Yet the Schengen states were reluctant to allow others into the fold until confident of those countries' willingness and ability to impose rigorous border checks. The Schengen states continued their preparations to establish an area inside the Community in which people could move freely without immigration controls, hoping that their example would encourage the other member states to participate as well, and hoping that Schengen would eventually be incorporated into the Community itself. Here was a striking example of differentiated integration led by a pioneer group of member states.

It took nearly five years for the Schengen states to conclude a convention (called Schengen II, signed in June 1990) to implement the measures necessary to ensure that "internal borders may be crossed at any point without any checks on persons being carried out." Key issues and features included:

- *Visas:* The convention aimed at harmonizing immigration law in order to devise a common list of third countries whose nationals needed a visa to enter the Schengen area and common rules for granting or denying visas, as well as agreement on a common visa stamp or sticker.
- *Illegal immigration:* Given the size and nature of the Schengen area's external borders, combating illegal entry posed a big challenge. Moreover, the expense of securing external borders would have to be shared by those countries (such as Belgium and the Netherlands) whose borders diminished or disappeared because they were subsumed into a large free travel area.
- *Asylum:* For historical reasons (memories of Jews fleeing Germany and being denied refuge in other European countries were still vivid), asylum was a particularly sensitive issue. There was little controversy about the definition of asylum or about how asylum seekers should be treated (member states had signed the relevant international agreements on the subject). The main challenge was to prevent an individual from submitting more than one asylum request in more than one country. Accordingly, the Schengen Convention included criteria to

determine which state should deal with which asylum application. It also outlined a system for tracking asylum seekers within the Schengen area.

- *Police cooperation:* There was already a high degree of cooperation among Schengen police forces, although mostly on a bilateral and informal basis. Media coverage of the Schengen negotiations occasionally raised the specter of a common European police force, but no government contemplated such a step. Nevertheless, intergovernmental cooperation would have to include a Community-wide system for exchanging information and intelligence (this was the genesis of Europol, the European police agency). Given the sensitivity surrounding police cooperation, especially at the operational level, provisions dealing with issues such as cross-border surveillance and "hot pursuit" were hedged with limitations and qualifications.
- *Judicial cooperation:* Negotiations about judicial cooperation contained the same pitfalls as those about police cooperation, although the convention contained a number of provisions to increase contacts and strengthen cooperation among judicial authorities, especially on the sensitive issue of extradition.
- *Information sharing:* The Schengen Convention included provision for the Schengen Information System (SIS), headquartered in Strasbourg and linking relevant databases in participating states. Access to the SIS at border posts and other locations would allow officials to retrieve information quickly on missing persons, arrest warrants, false passports, stolen vehicles, and so on. Without the SIS, Schengen simply could not function. Yet the development of the SIS further alarmed the sovereignty-conscious as well as civil libertarians. Strict privacy and confidentiality laws were put in place to govern the system's content and use.
- *Institutional structure:* The convention established an institutional arrangement (outside the Community framework) to manage its operation and future development, including an executive committee at the ministerial level, a central negotiating group of senior officials, and numerous working groups.

Work continued on implementing the Schengen Convention, to which Italy acceded in November 1990, Portugal and Spain in June 1991, and Greece in November 1992. Yet the convention took much longer than expected to come into operation, partly for political reasons and partly because of the technical difficulty of linking so many different national systems into the Schengen Information System. Thus, by the time the single market was to have been fully implemented, at the end of 1992, free movement of people was still a chimera even among the Schengen states. The Commission's efforts to achieve that goal within the EC itself were unavailing, notwithstanding successive European Council statements about the need to facilitate the free movement of people as part of the internal market.

From Maastricht to Amsterdam
Given the topicality of the policy area in the late 1980s and the desire of some countries, notably Germany, to strengthen the Community's competence in that regard (ultimately by bringing Schengen into the treaty), justice and home affairs was a major item on the agenda of the negotiations that resulted in the Maastricht Treaty. Yet doubts about free movement of people and difficulties surrounding the Schengen Convention did not bode well for the outcome. In the event, proponents of supranationalism, including the Commission, spent most of their political capital on issues such as monetary union and institutional reform rather than on the thorny area of justice and home affairs, which became a separate intergovernmental pillar (the third pillar) of the new EU.

Nevertheless, justice and home affairs issues were not rigidly segregated from the Community proper. Indeed, the establishment of Union citizenship reinforced the salience of justice and home affairs for the development of the EU as a whole (a new article asserted that "every citizen of the Union shall have the right to move and reside freely within the territory of the Member States"). Another new article gave the Council, acting unanimously on a proposal from the Commission, power to determine those countries whose nationals needed a visa in order to enter the territory of the EU, and to adopt measures for a uniform visa format. In the third pillar itself, member states agreed to act intergovernmentally "without prejudice to the powers of the European Community."

The bulk of the Maastricht Treaty's provisions for justice and home affairs were located in a new section at the end of the treaty, the first article of which listed nine areas of "common interest" subject to intergovernmental cooperation:

- Asylum
- Crossing of external borders
- Immigration
- Combating drug addiction
- Combating fraud on an international scale
- Judicial cooperation in civil matters
- Judicial cooperation in criminal matters
- Customs cooperation
- Police cooperation

Being closer to the core of national sovereignty, the last three areas were qualitatively different from the rest. Accordingly, they were not included in the *passerelle* (gateway) provision of the treaty that allowed for the transfer of third-pillar issues to the supranational first pillar. Although the *passerelle* provision was not used during the brief lifetime of the Maastricht Treaty before the reforms of the Amsterdam Treaty, the exclusion from it of police, customs, and most judicial cooperation suggested that governments would keep those areas in the intergovernmental third pillar, whatever the outcome of the next round of negotiations on treaty reform.

The Maastricht Treaty stipulated that the Commission would be "fully associated" with the work of the third pillar. The Commission received a nonexclusive right of initiative in the first six policies of common interest to member states, but no right of initiative in the remaining three areas. As for the European Parliament, the treaty used weak verbs such as "inform" and "consult" to describe its limited involvement in the third pillar. The Parliament's almost nonexistent role opened a democratic deficit in an important policy sphere at precisely the time when governments were advocating greater parliamentary oversight in EU affairs. The absence of the Court of Justice from the third pillar caused a similar "judicial deficit," although the treaty gave the Court authority to interpret the provisions of JHA conventions, subject to member state approval, on a case-by-case basis.

Even before implementation of the Maastricht Treaty, national ministers and officials busied themselves preparing a work program and an action plan, which the European Council endorsed in December 1993. But the sudden flurry of activity could not disguise the fact that the work program consisted mostly of old, repackaged items and that the action plan was condemned to inactivity as long as unanimity remained the norm. The EP immediately denounced the third pillar as an insult to the Community method and pressured the Commission to involve itself as aggressively as possible in JHA issues. Already reeling from the Maastricht ratification crisis, the Commission initially preferred a less confrontational approach. In an effort to move things along and establish its own credibility in an unfriendly intergovernmental environment, the Commission sent the Council general communications rather than a barrage of legislative proposals. Nevertheless, the Commission did not hesitate to take some legislative initiatives, which resulted, for example, in a regulation on a uniform format for visas (May 1995) and a regulation establishing a legally binding list of countries whose nationals needed a visa to enter the EU (September 1995).

Given the difficult history of cooperation on JHA, the cloak of confidentiality that shrouded Council deliberations on the subject, the imprecision of the new instruments, and the ability of governments to veto decisions, it is not surprising that there was little or no headway on most issues covered by the third pillar. Yet public support for EU-wide measures to combat illegal immigration and organized crime seemed high despite widespread antagonism during and after the Maastricht ratification crisis toward the EU and its institutions. Within the Schengen framework at least, despite differences of opinion and occasional political grandstanding, ministers and officials made some progress. In March 1995, the Schengen Convention finally became operational for seven of its signatory states (Italy and Greece needed to make additional adjustments; new member state Austria, which signed up in April 1995, also needed a lengthy transition period).

The fate of Europol, which occupied more time than any other third-pillar issue in the mid-1990s, demonstrated the continuing difficulty of making progress within the EU in the field of JHA. Although ministers reached political agreement in June 1993 to establish the new body, the necessary implementing convention became a major battleground in the war between supporters and opponents of supranationalism. Germany and the Benelux countries insisted on a role for the Court of Justice; Britain, supported to some extent by Denmark and (after January 1995) Sweden, fiercely resisted. In the meantime, in deference to public anxiety about transnational drug dealing, member states launched the Europol Drugs Unit in January 1994. The Drugs Unit did not undertake any operations itself but supported operations involving two or more countries by facilitating access to information, intelligence, and analysis. The unit's strengths were its highly sophisticated computer links and the discretion and personal contacts of its national liaison officers.

As the dispute over the Europol convention dragged on, governments progressively broadened the European Drugs Unit's scope to cover trafficking in stolen vehicles, illegal immigration, trafficking in human beings, and money laundering. In effect, the unit was Europol under a modified name (it lacked competence only for terrorism and other serious crimes such as kidnapping and arms trafficking). France wanted to resolve the Europol row during its Council presidency in early 1995 but failed to overcome British opposition to the Court's involvement in Europol's affairs. EU leaders finally reached a settlement in June 1996, when they agreed to allow the Court to give preliminary rulings on the interpretation of the Europol convention.

Public support for EU efforts to enhance internal security, together with disappointing progress to date on the third pillar, emboldened the Commission and like-minded governments in the run-up to the 1996–1997 intergovernmental conference that resulted in the Amsterdam Treaty. Nevertheless, preparations for the conference revealed deep divisions over how to strengthen and reorganize the EU's involvement in JHA. Not all governments favored extending EU competence over part of the third pillar or incorporating Schengen into the EU, albeit by means of flexible arrangements.

During the intergovernmental conference itself, Germany and the Benelux countries (supported by the Commission and the Parliament) advocated moving the first six areas of common interest listed in the third pillar into the supranational first pillar and bringing the corpus of rules and regulations that had accrued since the launch of the Schengen process in 1985 into the Community proper. Having joined Schengen in 1996, the Nordic member states did not demur (non-EU countries Iceland and Norway became associate members of Schengen), although Denmark insisted on an opt-out from those JHA provisions that were moved to the first pillar. Only Britain continued to object to a radical restructuring of treaty provisions for JHA, an objection that ended when the Labour Party came to power in May 1997. Nevertheless, like the Danish government, even the new British government insisted on an opt-out from the provisions that were moved to the first pillar.

The Amsterdam Treaty represented a huge leap forward for JHA as an EU policy area. It set a new objective for the EU: to become "an Area of Freedom, Security, and Justice . . . within a period of five years after the [treaty's] entry into force." The treaty included the wholesale transfer into the first pillar of responsibility for visas, asylum, immigration, and other policies related to the free movement of people; provisions for police cooperation and judicial cooperation on criminal matters remained within the third pillar. The treaty also included a flexibility clause allowing member states wanting to cooperate more closely to do so using EU institutions, procedures, and mechanisms. However, the flexibility clause included an "emergency brake": by invoking "important and stated reasons of national policy," a government could prevent the Council from voting to authorize closer cooperation.

In deference to governments that still had reservations about applying the traditional Community method of legislative decisionmaking to JHA policy areas, the new first-pillar provisions on asylum, immigration, external border controls, and the like were hedged with intergovernmental and other qualifications. During the time leading up to the establishment of the Area of Freedom, Security, and Justice, the Council would continue to act by unanimity, with the Commission having only a shared right of initiative and the EP being consulted only on proposed legislation. In other words, decisionmaking on the free movement of people remained essentially intergovernmental rather than supranational. After the transitional period, the Commission would acquire an exclusive right of initiative and the Council would decide whether to use the codecision procedure to enact legislation on the free movement of people—but the Council would make that decision unanimously. Finally, the role of the Court was still heavily restricted.

Determined to maintain control over its own borders, Britain won an opt-out from the treaty's new provisions on the free movement of people. Willing in principle to accept those provisions but constrained in practice by a desire to maintain a common travel area with Britain, Ireland also opted out. Although both countries could decide on a case-by-case basis to adopt legislation on JHA issues in the first pillar—in effect, they could selectively opt back in—they would not be able to prevent other member states from adopting such legislation. Because its hands were tied politically by earlier Maastricht Treaty opt-outs, the Danish government reluctantly opted out also from the JHA provisions of the Amsterdam Treaty, but could also opt back in on a case-by-case basis.

According to the Amsterdam Treaty, the purpose of the third pillar—now confined to police cooperation and judicial cooperation on criminal matters—was to give EU citizens "a high level of safety" within the putative AFSJ. The Commission gained the right of initiative (shared with member states) in all areas, and the EP gained the right to be consulted on most issues.

The Amsterdam Treaty included a range of new and revised third-pillar instruments:

- *Common positions:* Used to define the approach of the EU to a particular matter.
- *Framework decisions:* Used to approximate laws and regulations on third-pillar issues, framework decisions would bind countries as to the results to be achieved, but countries themselves could decide how to implement them. Governments more inclined toward closer cooperation hoped that framework decisions would replace conventions—often negotiated but rarely implemented—as the main third-pillar instrument.
- *Decisions:* As opposed to framework decisions, these could be used to achieve objectives other than by harmonizing member state laws and regulations.
- *Conventions:* Though they remained an option in the third pillar, conventions could enter into force once adopted by at least half of the member states.

In view of the Amsterdam Treaty's provisions for the AFSJ, including a flexibility clause for closer collaboration on JHA issues, there was no need to continue the Schengen Convention's separate existence. Accordingly, a protocol attached to the treaty provided for Schengen's incorporation into the EU framework with special provision for non–Schengen members Britain and Ireland to accept some or all of the 3,000 pages of the Schengen *acquis* (body of law). Having recently joined Schengen, Denmark was in the peculiar position of opting out of the JHA provisions into which Schengen was about to be folded. Denmark's situation was further complicated by the fact that non–EU members but fellow Nordic Union members Iceland and Norway remained fully associated with Schengen even after its incorporation into the EU. The inelegant solution to Denmark's dilemma was a clause in the "Danish protocol" stipulating that within six months of the Council taking a decision that built on the Schengen *acquis,* Denmark would decide whether to incorporate that decision into national law.

Building the Area of Freedom, Security, and Justice

EU leaders devoted their October 1999 summit in Tampere, Finland, to identifying the steps necessary for establishing the AFSJ, as called for in the Amsterdam Treaty. This was the first meeting of the European Council ever devoted exclusively to JHA. It symbolized the growing importance of that policy area for the EU and signaled the national leaders' political commitment to achieving real progress in the areas of asylum and immigration policy, border controls, and police and judicial cooperation.

The "communitarization" of aspects of JHA and the incorporation of Schengen into the EU saw the launch of a new formation of the Council of Ministers: the JHA Council. A special committee prepared JHA Council meetings dealing with third-pillar issues (under the Lisbon Treaty, which abolished the pillar system, this committee was renamed the Standing Committee on Internal Security). The Strategic Committee on Immigration, Frontiers, and Asylum prepared Council meetings on other JHA issues. The existence of special preparatory committees, separate from the Committee of Permanent Representatives, reflected the political sensitivity of JHA for most member states and the exceptional nature of this policy area in the decisionmaking process.

The Commission was also restructured as a result of the Amsterdam Treaty's provisions for JHA. The old JHA task force became a fully fledged and politically important directorate-general. The Commission became a more prominent player in the area of JHA, making good use of its new powers in the first-pillar part of the portfolio. The EP continued to complain about the democratic deficit with regard to JHA and used every opportunity that it had to muscle into the increasingly prominent policy area.

Differing national perspectives on JHA became more pronounced as the policy area grew in stature, especially following the political push provided by the Tampere summit. As "frontline" states on the eastern edge of the EU, Germany, Austria, and Italy wanted a single asylum and immigration policy, hoping perhaps for a tougher European-level regime than would be politically possible at the national level. Countries such as Britain, Denmark, and Ireland, more distant geographically from the EU's eastern border, were less interested in a common policy, preferring closer cooperation. France was primarily interested in establishing an EU-wide judicial area in which citizens would have equal access to agreed-upon standards of justice. France favored the harmonization of national laws for that purpose, whereas Britain and some other countries argued that mutual recognition was more practical and politically feasible.

In general, governments tended to take a restrictive position on JHA. Despite rhetoric to the contrary, their emphasis in the putative AFSJ was squarely on "security." Europeans fretted more and more about illegal immigrants crossing the Mediterranean or coming from Central and Eastern Europe. The war in Kosovo in 1999 triggered another exodus of Balkan refugees. Albania and Bosnia were becoming notorious as staging areas for the trafficking of drugs, people, and stolen property in the EU. The EU's citizens wanted more cooperation among national governments on JHA, but mostly to keep out undesirable illegal immigrants, asylum seekers, and refugees; to catch drug dealers and other criminals who exploited free movement across member states' borders; and to seal the EU's external borders as tightly as possible.

Legal immigration was another issue. The Lisbon strategy drew attention to the EU's chronic demographic and economic problems. As some member states (such as Germany) appreciated more than others, the EU needed an influx of highly skilled workers to fuel the knowledge economy. Yet there was widespread popular resistance to the idea of legal immigration, despite (or possibly because of) the fact that the EU had already become a multicultural immigrant society. Nor was it easy to make the case for large-scale legal immigration at a time when right-wing political parties were winning votes on anti-immigration platforms.

The terrorist attacks on the United States in September 2001 increased the political salience of JHA but focused attention further on the security aspect of it.[2] The fact that some of the planning for the attacks had taken place in Europe was an obvious cause of concern. The terrorist attacks in Madrid in March 2004 and London in July 2005 caused Europeans to fret even more about internal security. Accordingly, antiterrorism became a major focus of EU cooperation on JHA, with some attention being given also to the importance of integrating immigrants into their new countries rather than having them live apart in social and cultural (and sometimes actual) ghettoes.

The Impact of Enlargement

EU enlargement in 2004 had a profound impact on JHA. Many of the measures that member states adopted in the late 1990s and early 2000s with regard to asylum and immigration were intended to keep Central and Eastern European migrants out of the EU. With enlargement, the Central and Eastern Europeans would have every right to work throughout the EU. Austria and Germany, in particular, responded by pressing the other member states successfully for the right to maintain restrictions for a lengthy transitional period on the free movement of Central and Eastern Europeans even after their countries acceded to the EU, a move that undercut one of the key principles of European integration and arguably cast the Central and Eastern Europeans as second-class EU citizens. Only Britain, Ireland, and Sweden allowed Central and Eastern Europeans to work without restriction in their countries immediately after the 2004 enlargement.

Bulgaria and Romania were widely seen as problem countries with respect to the origin and transit of illegal immigrants into the EU. Yet given their status as candidate countries, member states had little option but to include them in the "white list" of countries whose citizens did not need a visa to enter the EU. Moreover, Romania was of special interest to Hungary because of the large Hungarian minority there (the Hungarian government did not want ethnic Hungarians in Romania to have to obtain a visa to visit their ancestral homeland once Romania entered the EU). Most of the EU15 again exercised their right under the accession treaties to restrict the free movement of Bulgarian and Romanian workers into their countries after the 2007 enlargement.

The prospect of Central and Eastern European enlargement focused EU attention especially on the control of external borders. The EU15 wanted to ensure that the candidate countries had the means to secure their eastern borders, even at the expense of severing long-standing connections between the candidate countries and their non-EU neighbors (Poland-Ukraine and Slovenia-Croatia are good examples). Thus, looming Central and Eastern European enlargement provided the main impetus for EU efforts to improve cooperation among governments on external border control.

The applicant countries struggled before enlargement to incorporate the Schengen *acquis* as part of their pre-accession strategies. Most lacked the administrative capacity and financial resources to do so. As a result, it looked at one point as if enlargement could delay the establishment of the AFSJ or as if the establishment of the AFSJ could delay enlargement. In the event, the EU provided considerable financial and technical assistance to the candidate countries to help them meet the requirements of membership in the area of JHA. Controls between the EU8 (the countries that joined in 2004) and the EU15 were eventually lifted in December 2007 for land and sea borders and in March 2008 for air borders. Border controls remain in place for Bulgaria, Cyprus, and Romania, pending a decision by the Council that those countries are ready to participate in the Schengen area.

Toward the Lisbon Treaty

The AFSJ was to have come into being in 2004, the same year as the EU's historic enlargement. The Commission launched a scoreboard in 2000 to monitor progress toward the 2004 AFSJ deadline. Updated twice a year, the scoreboard shadowed legislative proposals through the Council's decisionmaking machinery and outlined Commission plans for new proposals or other initiatives. The scoreboard showed mixed progress, especially on asylum and immigration policy. In December 2001, in a midterm review of the Tampere program, the Belgian presidency delivered an unusually hard-hitting report, criticizing governments for not doing enough to achieve a number of objectives in the field of JHA. Nevertheless, the Commission presented a positive appraisal of the Tampere program in June 2004.

Recognizing that establishing the AFSJ was a work in progress and not a definitive event, EU leaders agreed on a new program for JHA at their summit in The Hague in November 2004. Based on input from the Commission, European Parliament, relevant Council bodies, and national ministries, the so-called Hague program set objectives in all areas of JHA for the next five years. For example, it called for a common asylum system by 2010 (later extended to 2012). To facilitate decisionmaking and increase democratic accountability, governments agreed to use qualified majority voting and the codecision procedure in the areas of asylum and immigration (apart from legal immigration) as of January 2005; they were authorized to make such a decision under the terms of the Amsterdam Treaty.

Heightened popular concern about asylum, immigration, and transnational crime, together with institutional and political impediments to effective decisionmaking in these areas, brought JHA to the top of the agenda of the 2002–2003 Convention on the Future of Europe. The convention's working party on JHA advocated far-reaching reforms, including the abolition of the pillar structure, thereby bringing JHA under the umbrella of a unitary EU, and greater use of qualified majority voting in order to end legislative logjams. Nevertheless, the working group, as well as the convention as a whole, appreciated that unanimity would have to remain in use for decisionmaking in the most politically sensitive areas of police and judicial cooperation on criminal matters. The convention included these proposals in its Draft Constitutional Treaty.

The intergovernmental conference that followed incorporated most of the convention's proposals with respect to JHA into the Constitutional Treaty. Despite concerns expressed during the French referendum of May 2005 about the free movement of workers in the enlarged EU and the vulnerability of the EU's external borders, almost everything pertaining to JHA survived the defeat of the Constitutional Treaty and ended up in the Lisbon Treaty.

Perhaps the most significant institutional and policy changes in the Lisbon Treaty pertain to JHA (certainly the largest number of changes in the treaty relate to that area). The treaty states prominently and categorically that the EU "shall offer its citizens an area of freedom, security and justice without internal frontiers, in which the free movement of persons is ensured in conjunction with appropriate measures with respect to external border controls, asylum, immigration and the prevention and combating of crime." By abolishing the pillar structure in favor of a unitary EU, the treaty made almost every aspect of JHA subject to the ordinary legislative procedure (codecision), thereby greatly enhancing the role of the EP while also giving the Court of Justice more authority for judicial review. Since implementation of the Lisbon Treaty, the array of acts hitherto in use in the field of JHA is being replaced by laws and framework laws adopted using the ordinary legislative procedure.

The Lisbon Treaty provides for the establishment of the European Public Prosecutor's Office, intended to combat crimes affecting the financial interests of the EU. The Council may decide to establish the office only on the basis of unanimity, after obtaining the consent of the EP. The European Council may extend the powers of the Public Prosecutor's Office to include serious crime with a cross-border dimension. The treaty also clarifies the operational powers of Eurojust, a body established in 2002 to coordinate intra-EU efforts by investigators and prosecutors to fight organized crime.

In the field of judicial cooperation in criminal matters and criminal law, the Commission and the national governments continue to share the right of legislative initiative. However, governments may no longer act alone but only in a group of not less than one-quarter of the EU's membership, thereby reducing the number of separate national initiatives taken under the old system. The Constitutional Convention had proposed the use of qualified majority voting for decisions on judicial cooperation in criminal matters and criminal law, but the intergovernmental conference added an "emergency brake," which became part of the Lisbon Treaty. Accordingly, a government may refer to the European Council a proposal to which it is strongly opposed, thereby suspending the ordinary legislative procedure. The European Council then has four months either to restart the procedure or to ask the Commission or the group of countries that had drafted the proposal to submit a new one. If the European Council does not act, one-third of the member states may take up the proposal themselves through enhanced cooperation.

The Lisbon Treaty provides a limited role for national parliaments in monitoring the implementation of JHA policy and enables the Court to review member state compliance. It also retains the special arrangements for Britain and Ireland in the area of JHA and the Danish government's opt-outs.

The Stockholm Program

The collapse of the Constitutional Treaty and protracted ratification of the Lisbon Treaty took place during the time frame of the Hague program. As a result, the long-delayed implementation of the Lisbon Treaty coincided with the launch of a new, post-Hague program, this time called the Stockholm program in honor of the Swedish Council presidency in late 2009. Preparations for the Stockholm program began with the work of a ministerial-level advisory body established in 2007 to discuss and suggest possible objectives for a successor to the Hague program. The group submitted a final report to the JHA council in July 2008 calling for improvements in the areas of internal security; management of asylum, immigration, and external borders; civil protection; use of new technologies and information networks; and the external JHA dimension. After much deliberation, the Commission followed up, in June 2009, with a communication titled "An Area of Freedom, Security and Justice Serving the Citizen," which became the basis of the Stockholm program.[3]

The thrust of the Commission's approach was that citizens should be able to enjoy the benefits of European integration, notably movement without border controls throughout the Schengen area, in safety and security, despite the plethora of threats emanating from inside and outside the EU. To that end, the Commission set four general priorities:

- *"Europe of rights"*: Rights based on the Charter of Fundamental Rights, attached to the Lisbon Treaty.

- *"Europe of justice"*: Justice by facilitating people's access to the courts, so their rights can be enforced throughout the EU.
- *"Europe that protects"*: Protection by means of better cooperation in police matters and law enforcement and more secure borders around the EU.
- *"Europe of solidarity"*: Solidarity among member states on asylum and immigration issues, as well as partnership with non-EU countries.

As in other policy areas, the Commission advocated improving the quality of JHA legislation and closing the gap between its enactment at the EU level and implementation and enforcement at the national level. The Commission called for enhanced and comprehensive data protection, enforcement of mutual recognition of judgments, the creation of a police exchange program, establishment of procedural safeguards in criminal proceedings, and burden-sharing among member states in dealing with refugees and asylum seekers. Sensitive to public opinion on the still-unratified Lisbon Treaty, Commission president José Manuel Barroso was at pains to point out that the proposed strategy did not seek to "bring more power to the Commission or to the member states, but more power to the citizens."[4]

Not everyone was pleased with the Commission's approach. Civil liberties groups have long complained that the pendulum in JHA has swung too far in the direction of internal security and away from individual rights. Far from being mollified by the Commission's emphasis on the Charter of Fundamental Rights, the European Civil Liberties Network, a leading interest group, flatly opposed the Stockholm program, which it claimed "would extend militarized border controls, discriminatory immigration policies, mandatory and proactive surveillance regimes and an increasingly aggressive external security and defense policy." Believing that JHA in general constitutes "an attack on civil liberties and human rights," the interest group called "for active civil society engagement and opposition to dangerous authoritarian tendencies within the EU."[5]

Not least because of Europe's terrible experience with fascism and communism, most Europeans are acutely conscious of the need to protect civil liberties. At the same time, on a day-to-day basis they are concerned about cross-border crime, illegal immigration, and terrorism, all of which are on the rise and to which a response at the European and not only the national level seems appropriate. Rather than criticizing the EU for trampling on civil liberties in the area of JHA, public opinion in Europe seemed to want national governments and the EU to take a tougher stand on issues such as combating transnational crime and tightening external border control. Certainly, JHA ministers operated on that assumption when negotiating the Stockholm program in late 2009.

Indeed, the question of illegal immigration was uppermost in their minds due to a sharp rise in 2009 in the number of people, mostly from sub-Saharan

Africa, desperately trying to reach Europe's shores, many of whom drowned en route. The burden of intercepting and detaining these illegal immigrants fell disproportionately on Italy, Greece, Spain, Cyprus, and Malta. Italy incurred the wrath of civil liberties groups and the UN High Commissioner for Refugees in May 2009 when it sent about 500 immigrants back to Libya, the country from which they had set out on the last leg of their clandestine journey to Europe, without giving them the right to apply for asylum. Critics were especially alarmed because Libya is not a party to the Geneva Convention on refugee status. Taking a more diplomatic tack, Italy joined with Greece, Cyprus, and Malta in pressing successfully for a lengthy statement on illegal immigration to be included in the conclusions of the June 2009 meeting of the European Council, thereby raising the political salience of the issue.

The European Council called generally for "a determined European response based on firmness, solidarity and shared responsibility," and specifically for other countries to share Malta's burden by voluntarily taking in some of the asylum seekers being held there.[6] The European Council returned to the issue in October 2009, noting that the situation in the eastern Mediterranean had improved somewhat and welcoming the start of the "reinforced dialogue" on immigration with Turkey, a major transit country for people entering the EU illegally.[7] Intense public and political interest in the question of illegal immigration in late 2009 provided an additional incentive for the Swedish presidency to conclude the Stockholm program for AFSJ.

The European Council duly reached agreement in December 2009 on the new program, covering the period 2010–2014. As expected, the emphasis of the program was squarely on security, with EU leaders calling for the elaboration of an "internal security strategy," focusing on counterterrorism, border management, civil protection, and judicial cooperation in criminal matters.[8] The Commission began drafting proposals to flesh out the Stockholm program in early 2010.

JHA will continue to be a dynamic and rapidly developing area of EU activity, not least because implementation of the Lisbon Treaty has prompted a tidying-up exercise whereby existing JHA legislation is being consolidated and repackaged subject to the new decisionmaking rules, notably the use of the ordinary legislative procedure and qualified majority voting in the Council. The flurry of legislative activity is once again raising concerns by civil libertarians about the impact on people's rights of the growing JHA *acquis,* especially with regard to illegal immigration and antiterrorist measures. Under the Lisbon Treaty at least, legislating in the area of JHA is subject to better democratic scrutiny. Of course, the challenge of democratic control in such issues is not peculiar to the EU. It is always hard to strike the right balance between openness and the pursuit of greater security. It is harder still in an era of global terrorism.

■ External Security: Foreign and Defense Policy

As the EU became a leading international economic actor, its relatively weak political presence on the world stage appeared increasingly anomalous. An "economic giant but a political pygmy" is how some people described the European Community, just as they described the old West Germany. For reasons of symmetry, if nothing else, a common EU foreign policy seemed to make sense. More than that, however, a common foreign policy could enhance the collective security of the member states and help promote outside the EU their shared interests and objectives, such as strengthening democracy, the rule of law, and human rights, and preventing and resolving international conflicts. Just as member states could maximize their commercial clout in a common trade policy, so too might they be able to leverage their international influence in a common foreign policy.

Another motive for a common foreign policy is the ideology of European integration. Many advocates of ever closer union believe that the EU's destiny is to become a leading global power and that the member states must "speak with one voice" internationally (this is the metaphor most frequently used to describe the rationale for a common foreign policy in the EU). Related to this is the presumed importance of counterbalancing the United States, the world's sole superpower, in the global political system. Arguably, a unipolar world is inherently unstable, especially if the hegemon uses its power irresponsibly.

The nature of EU power, and the kind of international entity that the EU might eventually become, are contested. Although the decision to form or join the EU was, for all member states, a foreign policy decision, the appeal of European integration was partly that it encompassed a wide range of socioeconomic policies but did not encroach on traditional foreign and security policy. Moreover, to the extent that the EU would become a foreign policy actor by virtue of its economic weight, many people thought that it should rely exclusively on soft power (to attract and persuade) rather than acquiring hard power (to coerce and enforce).

Some people who want the EU to become a leading global power believe passionately that it should not develop a military capability but should remain a civilian power (as François Duchêne described it in 1972) or a normative power (as Ian Manners described it in 2002). According to Manners, just as the EU is highly distinctive in its character and composition, so it should remain a distinctive international actor. What the EU *is* (an exceptional political entity based on core values) determines what the EU *does and says*. Unlike most nation-states, which have a hard power component, the EU is a normative power that should project globally the values that define it domestically: a fundamental attachment to peace, liberty, democracy, rule of law, human rights, and fundamental freedoms.[9]

For others, military power is the sine qua non of statehood or, in the case of the EU, superstatehood. In order for the EU to become a truly effective international actor and to counterbalance the United States or other global powers, some proponents of ever closer union believe that it needs to develop a common defense policy and a credible military capability commensurate with its economic weight. Even if desirable, such a prospect seems remote. National sovereignty remains a formidable barrier to the development of a truly common foreign policy, let alone a common defense policy or a common army. Different national foreign policy interests, orientations, and traditions, which grow with each round of enlargement, are another obstacle to such a development. In addition, small member states are instinctively wary of the big member states' motives and tendencies when it comes to foreign and defense policy formulation, notwithstanding Germany's general reluctance since the end of World War II to assume an international political profile corresponding to its economic influence. In general, although all member states accept that closer foreign and defense policy cooperation is in their interests, the political hurdles remain high.

The possibility of a single EU seat in the United Nations Security Council illustrates the nature of the problem. If the EU wants to speak with one voice internationally, logically it should have one seat in the Security Council. But Britain and France, permanent Security Council members, are opposed to that idea. Nor do most other member states want to give up the prospect of occasionally sitting in the Security Council as nonpermanent members. Germany, less reticent recently about asserting itself internationally, is pressing for a seat of its own in the Security Council, to which Italy objects. In addition, Britain and France disagree strongly on many international issues (the US invasion of Iraq in 2003 and how to deal with African dictators are obvious examples).

Another illustration of the difficulty that member states have with respect to foreign policy is the recognition of Kosovo as a sovereign, independent state. Kosovo's declaration of independence from Serbia in February 2008 split the EU, with a minority of countries, notably those with close ties to Serbia or with possible secessionist problems of their own, refusing to recognize the new state. Given the difficulty that the EU had dealing with the Balkan wars of the 1990s, its failure to take a united position on Kosovo's independence was highly embarrassing.

From EPC to CFSP

Developing the CFSP and an EU military capability, however limited, has been a protracted process. It originated in the 1970s in European Political Cooperation, a procedure for coordinating national positions on international issues. EPC developed an elaborate administrative machinery, involving regular meetings of foreign ministers; meetings of the Political Committee (foreign ministries' political directors) to prepare and follow up on foreign ministers' meetings; and meetings of working groups (midlevel foreign ministry officials) to exchange views and prepare reports on a variety of geographical and functional issues, and of the group of European correspondents (junior foreign ministry officials) to liaise between foreign ministries and prepare meetings of the Political Committee. The Council presidency chaired EPC meetings at all levels. There was no voting; instead, lengthy negotiations in a search for consensus created informal pressures to agree. Consensus became one of the procedure's fundamental rules.

In the early 1980s, when the Community's external relations were every bit as problematic as its internal development, the procedural limits of EPC became obvious. The sudden heightening of tension between the United States and the Soviet Union in the late 1970s, after a decade of relatively benign relations, tested the Community's ability to act internationally. EPC proved an inadequate mechanism, especially in response to sudden crises. The 1985 intergovernmental conference on treaty reform presented a golden opportunity to strengthen EPC. Emphasizing the distinctiveness of EPC from other Community activities, the Political Committee discussed foreign and security policy in a separate working group. All governments agreed on the need to make the Community's external economic policy and their own foreign policies more consistent with each other. Other ideas included formalizing EPC in the Rome Treaty, providing a special secretariat for the process, and incorporating military and defense issues. Neutral Ireland shied away from going too far down the defense road, as did pacifist (though NATO member) Denmark and idiosyncratic (though also NATO member) Greece.

These discussions led to a separate section on EPC being included in the Single European Act. Procedural improvements included involving the Commission fully in EPC, ensuring that the European Parliament was "closely associated" with it; creating a mechanism for convening the Political Committee or the General Affairs Council on short notice; and establishing a special secretariat in Brussels. The Single European Act also stipulated that "the external policies of the EC and the policies agreed in Political Cooperation must be consistent" and charged the presidency and the Commission with ensuring such consistency. However, EPC was not subject to judicial review by the Court of Justice and remained largely intergovernmental—in effect a pillar separate from the Community.

Revolution in Central and Eastern Europe and the abrupt end of the Cold War brought security concerns to the top of the Community's agenda. Simultaneously, the Commission's leadership of the international aid effort in Central and Eastern Europe helped to narrow the conspicuous gap between foreign policy cooperation and the Community's external economic relations. With the imminence of German unification in 1990, there was near-unanimity among national governments and the Commission on the need to strengthen

European security at a potentially destabilizing time, boost the new EU's international standing, and bind external economic and political policymaking more closely together. Governments used the opportunity of the 1991 intergovernmental conference on political union to transform EPC into the CFSP.[10]

Iraq's invasion of Kuwait in August 1990 coincided with preparations for the intergovernmental conference. Despite having reacted promptly and forcefully within the limits of its ability to news of the Iraqi invasion, the Community soon came in for criticism, especially in the United States, for its inability to do more. To some extent the Community was a victim of its own success. Prevailing Europhoria and pervasive discussion of a putative CFSP had raised unrealizable expectations about the Community's capacity to take concerted international action, especially involving the use of force.

To the extent that some EU member states wanted to cooperate militarily during the Gulf crisis, the Western European Union provided a ready-made mechanism for doing so. The WEU also had considerable potential to facilitate Community defense cooperation, not least because the United States was not a member. With the Community's member states striving in 1991 for a common foreign and security policy as an element of political union and some of them eager to cooperate militarily in the Gulf, the WEU (which at that time comprised Britain, France, Germany, Italy, Belgium, the Netherlands, Luxembourg, Portugal, and Spain) was at the forefront of the debate.

As expected, negotiations about security and defense proved especially arduous during the 1991 intergovernmental conference. The outbreak of war in Yugoslavia in June of that year highlighted the difficulty of reconciling member states' notoriously discordant positions. Few countries supported establishing a full-fledged EU defense policy; neutral Ireland and pacifist Denmark were strongly opposed. Nevertheless, there was near-unanimity about at least establishing an EU defense identity and about using the WEU to do so. This suggestion led to difficult negotiations about the precise relationship among the EU, the WEU, and NATO. "Atlanticist" countries such as Britain, the Netherlands, and Portugal—staunch NATO supporters—were wary of forging too close a link between the EU and the WEU, fearing that such a development might weaken, or appear to weaken, the alliance with the United States. "Europeanist" countries—notably France—argued the contrary case, making the old point that a stronger European pillar would bolster NATO and the new point that with the end of the Cold War, Europe needed to develop its own defense organization because the United States was bound to reduce its military involvement on the continent. Germany sided instinctively with the Europeanists but, with Soviet troops still in the eastern part of the country, opted pragmatically for the Atlanticists.

Governments struck a compromise in the Maastricht Treaty between the two positions, allowing for "the eventual framing of a common defense policy, which might in time lead to a common defense." The unequivocal use of the word "defense" represented a new departure. The treaty also recognized the WEU as "an integral part of the development of the European Union" and authorized the Council, acting on the basis of unanimity, to ask the WEU "to elaborate and implement [the EU's] decisions and actions . . . which have defense implications."

A declaration attached to the treaty explained the member states' intention to "build up [the] WEU in stages as the defense component of the Union." The declaration also spelled out the WEU's relationship to NATO, citing the WEU's future development "as a means to strengthen the European pillar of the Atlantic Alliance." The treaty's language allowed both sides in the defense debate to claim victory. Yet a commitment in the treaty to review defense arrangements within five years hinted that the EU's defense identity would increasingly assume a Europeanist rather than an Atlanticist appearance.

More broadly, governments optimistically called in the Maastricht Treaty for consistency between the Community and the CFSP pillars of the new EU, and charged the Commission and the Council with achieving that goal. The treaty's CFSP provisions set out the policy's objectives, instruments, and decisionmaking procedures. The objectives—safeguarding common values, preserving peace and strengthening international security, promoting international cooperation, and the like—were uncontroversial. The instruments were of two kinds: *common positions* to establish cooperation on a day-to-day basis; and *joint actions* to allow member states to act together in concrete ways based on a Council decision as to the specific scope of such actions, the EU's objectives in carrying them out, and (if necessary) the duration, means, and procedures for their implementation.

The success of the CFSP would depend in large part on how these instruments were adopted. Some governments advocated the use of qualified majority voting; others insisted on unanimity for anything having to do with the CFSP. The treaty struck a clumsy compromise by providing for qualified majority voting for the implementation of joint actions, which the Council would first have to adopt on the basis of unanimity.

The treaty stipulated that the Commission would be fully associated with the work of the CFSP, although it would not have an exclusive right to submit proposals. The treaty contained a weaker commitment to involve the Parliament with the CFSP. Given that the CFSP occupied an intergovernmental pillar, there was no way of enforcing member state compliance with these or any other CFSP provisions.

From Maastricht to Amsterdam

The CFSP got off to a shaky start. Even before EU leaders put the finishing touches on the treaty at the Maastricht summit, there was a feeling among negotiators and observers that the treaty's foreign and security policy provisions were flawed. Accordingly, the treaty included specific provisions for a review of the CFSP in an intergovernmental conference that would start in 1996. Some officials may have hoped that such a review would give the CFSP a supranational character; most simply wanted to be able to iron out the CFSP's institutional and procedural wrinkles within a few years of the treaty becoming operational.

Even though implementation of the CFSP was delayed by the Maastricht ratification crisis, national governments and EU institutions lost little time preparing to put the treaty into effect. Meeting in Lisbon in June 1992, the European Council outlined EU policy toward certain countries or groups of countries and "domains within the security dimension" that could be subject to joint action.[11] Once the time came to adopt common positions and joint actions, however, there was considerable confusion among governments, the Council secretariat, and the Commission about the difference between the two instruments and the advisability of choosing one rather than the other in any given situation. In the meantime, governments seemed wedded to high-sounding but harmless declarations, which had been a disappointing feature of EPC.

Eventually the Council settled on a formula whereby common positions would be used to set out an agreed-upon approach to an issue and joint actions to make concrete commitments or undertake specific initiatives. The European Stability Pact, proposed by France as a means of resolving long-standing disputes among the countries of Central and Eastern Europe, became one of the EU's first joint actions in 1994. Most other joint actions and common positions were less clear-cut and less impressive. Even more striking were the joint actions and common positions that the EU might have taken but never did. The problem was both procedural and political. Despite possible recourse to qualified majority voting to implement joint actions, governments stuck doggedly to unanimity. Thus the consensus principle of EPC permeated the CFSP, thwarting effective decisionmaking and in some cases keeping worthy foreign and security policy issues off the EU's agenda.

Other challenges confronting the new CFSP ranged from the difficulty of setting up the CFSP unit in the Council secretariat, to the limitations of the Council presidency, to the tendency of governments to go it alone on issues of particular national interest. The problem with the CFSP unit was not administrative but cultural: officials seconded to it from national foreign ministries had a completely different outlook than their colleagues drawn from within the Council secretariat. Whereas the former had a national perspective, the latter had a European (although not necessarily a supranational) one. It took some time for the new unit to establish itself bureaucratically and for its mixed group of officials to begin to work harmoniously together.

The problem with the presidency was multifaceted: some presidencies threw themselves wholeheartedly behind the CFSP; others had different priorities. The Greek presidency in early 1994 distinguished itself by pursuing foreign policy interests that ran counter to the EU's own interests (notably by refusing to recognize the former Yugoslav Republic of Macedonia and imposing sanctions against it, in response to which the Commission took Greece—the Council presidency—before the Court of Justice). Lack of continuity due to the biannual presidential rotation inevitably affected the implementation of the CFSP and weakened the EU's external representation.

The procedural weaknesses of the CFSP and the member states' lack of political will were painfully evident during the Yugoslav debacle in the mid-1990s, discussed in Chapter 5. It was humiliating for the EU to have to depend on the United States to halt Serbia's aggression in Bosnia, and shameful for the EU to have done so little to avert the slaughter of thousands of Europeans in a far corner of the continent. The outbreak of war in the former Yugoslavia exposed deep foreign policy differences among national governments and demonstrated the limits of concerted EU action. The problem went far beyond procedural inadequacies. Clearly, national governments could not agree on a common EU interest and were extremely reluctant to share sovereignty in the highly sensitive areas of security and defense.

The Yugoslav debacle cast a pall over planning for the 1996–1997 intergovernmental conference that resulted in the Amsterdam Treaty. Obviously aware of the weakness of the CFSP, national governments had yet another chance to make major changes. Yet the lessons of Yugoslavia were not sufficient to overcome the governments' deep attachment to national sovereignty in the foreign policy field, nor did governments interpret them uniformly. Accordingly, at the outset of the conference there was consensus among governments only on what the CFSP-related negotiations should cover: instruments, decisionmaking, representation, planning and analysis, the budget, and the ever present issue of EU-WEU relations.

In an effort to improve the means available to make a success of the CFSP, the Amsterdam Treaty identified two new instruments and revised two existing instruments. The new instruments, to be adopted by the European Council, were *principles and guidelines,* to provide general political direction, and *common strategies,* to provide an umbrella under which the EU could act by setting out "the objectives, duration, and the means to be made available by the Union and the Member States" in areas of mutual interest. The revised instruments, to be adopted by the Council of Ministers by qualified majority voting (except those with military and defense implications), were *common positions,* to "define the approach of the Union to a particular matter of a geographical or thematic nature," and *joint actions,* to address specific situations requiring "operational action" by the member states.

As in the past, the clarity and effectiveness of these instruments would depend on the quality and capacity of the decisionmaking process. Also as in the past, few governments were willing to give up unanimity in all areas of the CFSP. Nevertheless, there was widespread acknowledgment during the conference of the need to provide greater scope for qualified majority voting and to allow a majority of member states to act on sensitive international issues even if a minority did not want to participate in such action. As a result, in addition to calling for greater use of qualified majority voting, the treaty incorporated two new decisionmaking formulas:

- *Constructive abstention:* As long as they did not constitute more than one-third of weighted votes in the Council, countries could abstain from a decision taken unanimously by the others.
- *Emergency brake:* Where decisions could be taken by qualified majority voting, a country could declare "for important and stated reasons of national policy" its opposition to a vote actually being taken. In that case, the Council could decide, by qualified majority vote, to refer the matter up to the European Council, which could in turn decide the matter unanimously. The presumption seemed to be that a reluctant government would succumb to peer pressure in the European Council and go along with the otherwise contested decision. In reality, if a minister felt strongly enough about an issue to pull the emergency brake in the first place, other ministers would be unlikely to vote the matter up to the European Council. Even if they did, the European Council would hardly be able to reach a unanimous decision.

These revised decisionmaking procedures looked more complicated than the original ones without necessarily being an improvement on them. Not only was the emergency brake a throwback to the Luxembourg Compromise, but also the codification of abstentionism and the introduction of various restrictions and qualifications seemed likely to reduce rather than enhance the effectiveness of the CFSP. The emergence of such an outcome reflected strong national sensitivities about foreign and security policy cooperation in the EU.

In response to the problems inherent in the rotating presidency, governments agreed to establish the permanent position of High Representative for CFSP. The High Representative would "contribute" to the formulation and implementation of policy and "assist" the work of the Council. These weak verbs showed how tentative some governments were about establishing the new position. The High Representative would work closely with the Council presidency; together with the Commission, the High Representative and the presidency would form a new troika to represent the EU in dealings with nonmember states. Lack of planning and analysis was generally seen as another of the main weaknesses of the CFSP. Accordingly, a declaration attached to the Amsterdam Treaty established the Policy Planning and Early Warning Unit in the Council secretariat, under the authority of the High Representative.

Under the Maastricht Treaty, governments could charge CFSP operations either to their own budgets or to the EU's budget. Not surprisingly, governments preferred to draw on the EU budget but were unwilling to pay the political price of scrutiny of CFSP operational expenses by the EP. For the Parliament, effectively shut out of the EU's intergovernmental pillars, such scrutiny provided a way to exert some influence over CFSP activities. Governments resolved the issue in the Amsterdam Treaty by agreeing that most CFSP operational expenditures were to be charged to the EU budget (the major exceptions were those with military implications), thereby acknowledging a role for the EP.

Collaboration between the EU and WEU, as envisioned in the Maastricht Treaty, had proceeded slowly and unspectacularly in the mid-1990s. Reflecting the nature of post–Cold War security challenges, in 1992 the WEU adopted the so-called Petersberg Declaration (named after the town outside Bonn where the declaration was adopted), which, among other things, included peacekeeping, humanitarian, and rescue missions in the organization's mandate. The WEU also established a planning cell to prepare troop deployments for Petersberg and other tasks and to act as an operation headquarters in the event of a crisis. In 1993 the WEU moved its headquarters from London to Brussels in order to be close to NATO and EU headquarters.

The asymmetry between EU and WEU membership became more marked in 1995 when three neutral states—Austria, Finland, and Sweden—joined the EU. The WEU responded to this and another asymmetry of the European security architecture, whereby not every European member of NATO was also a member of the WEU, by bringing everybody under the same roof through different kinds of affiliations, such as associate membership and observer status.

Defense-related negotiations at the 1996–1997 intergovernmental conference focused on whether to merge the EU and the WEU. In order to give greater substance and effectiveness to the EU's security and defense identity and strengthen the European pillar of NATO, a majority of governments wanted the EU and WEU to come together. Faced with strong opposition from Britain and Denmark, which opposed the militarization of the EU, and from the neutral countries, which remained opposed to participation in a military alliance, national governments agreed only to "the possibility of the integration of the WEU into the EU, should the European Council so decide."

The Amsterdam Treaty nevertheless included an important step with military implications: incorporation of the so-called Petersberg tasks into the EU (with the full support of the neutral countries), therefore raising the possibility of future EU peacekeeping operations. The NATO summit in Madrid in July 1997, held only a month after the EU summit in Amsterdam, where the intergovernmental conference came to an end, not only took a key decision about NATO enlargement (the admission of the Czech Republic, Hungary, and Poland) but also blessed the EU's efforts to develop a security and defense identity.

From Amsterdam to Lisbon

In June 1999, shortly after the Amsterdam Treaty came into effect, EU leaders selected Javier Solana to be the first High Representative for CFSP (he took up the position in October 1999). Solana, who remained in office for the next ten years, was an excellent choice. Patient, solicitous, and vastly experienced in international relations, he soon put his stamp on the CFSP. Solana was especially adept at working with successive presidencies and with the commissioner for external relations, a potential institutional rival, in an effort to forge a truly common EU position on international issues.

At the same time, the EU implemented other CFSP-related aspects of the Amsterdam Treaty, for instance by putting the Policy Planning and Early Warning Unit in place, within the Council secretariat and staffed by officials from the national governments, the Commission, and the Council secretariat itself. The unit set about monitoring international political developments, alerting the High Representative and the Council to impending crises, and suggesting possible action for the EU to take. Although governments were obliged to provide the unit with all relevant information, even of a confidential nature, it took some time for them to do so.

The EU adopted its first common strategies under the CFSP in 1999, when it also adopted twelve joint actions (mostly dealing with the Western Balkans) and twenty-two common positions. Thereafter the EU adopted few common strategies, which never became an important CFSP instrument (Solana soon complained that common strategies were too general to be effective), but adopted a steady stream of common positions and joint actions every year. The EU also produced scores of declarations and statements annually. The EU appointed special representatives to spearhead EU involvement in particular issues or regions, such as the Middle East peace process, the Great Lakes region in Africa, and Afghanistan and Pakistan. The EU regularly imposed sanctions such as arms embargoes, trade restrictions, or visa and travel bans under the auspices of the CFSP. Examples of common positions include the application of specific measures to combat terrorism (2006), action concerning restrictive measures against certain officials of Belarus (2008), and the renewal of restrictive measures against Burma/Myanmar (2009). Examples of joint actions include appointing a police mission in Afghanistan (2007), appointing a special representative in Kosovo (2008), and extending the monitoring mission in Georgia (2009).

The most striking CFSP development in the 2000s, however, has been in the area of defense policy and military capability.[12]

European Security and Defense Policy. Chastened by the EU's experience in Yugoslavia and cognizant of the waning interest of the United States in European security, British prime minister Tony Blair proposed developing an EU military capability in discussions with French president Jacques Chirac at a bilateral summit in St. Malo in December 1998. Like French presidents before and since, Chirac was highly receptive to a suggestion of that kind. France had always wanted Europe to be able to act militarily on its own. The need for such a capability became apparent in early 1999 when Serbia intensified attacks against the majority-Muslim (Albanian) population in Kosovo, a province of Serbia. Even if the EU had the will, it still lacked the means to act. Instead, the United States (in NATO's name) conducted an intensive air war against Serbian forces in Kosovo and military and government installations in the rest of Serbia, until the Serbian government capitulated in June 1999.

The short war over Kosovo was decisive in pushing the EU to develop the military means to conduct peacekeeping operations. Blair, Chirac, and other leaders were more determined than ever to ensure that, in future, the EU could resolve such a conflict on its own. Without doubt, "the Kosovo crisis reemphasized that the missing link in the EU's conflict management capabilities was the credible threat or the actual use of force in support of political and diplomatic efforts."[13]

Accordingly, the European Council, meeting in Cologne in June 1999, launched the European Security and Defense Policy (ESDP) as part of the CFSP. In order to be able to carry out the Petersberg tasks incorporated into the EU under the Amsterdam Treaty, the European Council declared that the EU "must have the capacity for autonomous action, backed up by credible military forces [and] the means to decide to use them."[14] Meeting in Helsinki six months later, the European Council set a "headline goal" for the ESDP: by 2003, member states should be able "to deploy in full [up to 60,000 troops] within 60 days . . . [and] sustain such a deployment for at least one year. . . . These forces should be militarily self-sustaining with the necessary command, control and intelligence capabilities, logistics, other combat support services, and additionally, as appropriate, air and naval elements."[15]

The European Council called on the Council of Ministers to establish by March 2000 a number of interim committees and bodies to get the ESDP up and running, including:

- *Political and Security Committee:* To replace the existing Political Committee and comprise senior national representatives, who would prepare meetings of foreign and defense ministers on CFSP and ESDP issues.
- *Military Committee:* To comprise senior military officers, who would advise and make recommendations to the Political and Security Committee on military matters and to direct the Military Staff.
- *Military Staff:* To comprise national military officials based in the Council secretariat, who would provide military expertise and support especially for the conduct of EU-led military crisis management operations.

Building on the momentum generated principally by Britain and France, progress on the ESDP continued apace in 2000, especially under the French presidency of the Council in the second half of the year. National governments held a capability commitment conference in Brussels in November—the first of what would become a series of conferences on military capacity building—at which they pledged forces to meet the Helsinki headline goal. A French presidency paper addressed some of the remaining political challenges confronting the ESDP, notably the precise operational relationship between the EU and NATO (covering EU access to NATO assets and permanent consultation arrangements) and the role of Turkey (a large NATO European country being kept at arm's length by the EU). As part of the package of reforms agreed to in the Nice Treaty, EU leaders decided to make permanent the CFSP and ESDP interim committees that were already operational and, in effect, to incorporate the WEU into the EU. Thus the rapid development of ESDP consolidated new organizational structures in Brussels—based in the permanent representations, the Council secretariat, and the Commission—and the national capitals. As a result, a sizable group of military and civilian officials began to work exclusively on EU security and defense issues.

Governments turned their attention as well to developing the nonmilitary component of international crisis management (police, rule of law, civilian administration, and civil protection). At its meeting in June 2000, the European Council welcomed the establishment and first meeting of the Committee for Civilian Aspects of Crisis Management, as well as the identification of priority targets for civilian aspects of crisis management and of specific targets for civilian police capabilities (by 2003 the member states were to provide a police force of up to 5,000 officers, including 1,000 deployable within thirty days; a team of judges, prosecutors, and other legal experts; a group of civilian administrators; and rapid response teams to assess emergency situations). The civilian crisis management committee would oversee the development and possible deployment of these resources.

Subsequent Developments. The terrorist attacks in the United States of September 11, 2001, gave a tremendous boost to the CFSP and the ESDP. Europe had long been wracked by terrorism, but of the homegrown variety. European governments realized that the September 2001 attacks typified a new kind of global security challenge to which they were not immune. The EU immediately issued a declaration under the CFSP condemning the attacks and held an extraordinary meeting of the European Council to express solidarity with the United States. The EU troika undertook several visits at the ministerial level to countries in Central Asia and the Middle East, firming up support for the fight against terrorism. The EU was instrumental, through the CFSP, in helping to broker the UN-backed agreement on political transition in Afghanistan, signed in Bonn in December 2001.

Militarily, by contrast, the EU was sidelined in the aftermath of September 11. The most significant collective European response came from NATO, not the EU, which in any case was still underequipped to play a military role. Not that the United States wanted or needed military assistance for the initial campaign against the Taliban in Afghanistan, which ended swiftly in November 2001. Like the Americans, however, the Europeans appreciated that the war against international terrorism would be a protracted affair.

Two developments ensuing directly from the events of September 11 were helpful and potentially harmful to the emergence of the ESDP. The helpful development was Germany's willingness finally to act militarily as a leading European power. Germany was constrained in that regard not only by history but also by politics: the governing coalition included the pacifist Green Party. In view of recent events in the Balkans and the terrorist attacks in the United States, only the most extreme pacifists could argue that military action was never justifiable or warranted. Germany may still have lacked the means to undertake major military operations around the world, but it no longer lacked the will to do so.

The potentially harmful development with respect to the ESDP was exposure of the rift within the EU between big and small countries, or more specifically between the "big three" (Britain, France, and Germany) and the rest, that lurked beneath the surface of security and defense cooperation. Traditionally, the smaller countries have brooded about the propensity of the big countries to dominate cooperation on security and defense policy. Their fears seemed justified in October 2001 when Blair, Chirac, and German chancellor Gerhard Schröder held informal talks on Afghanistan on the margins of a European Council meeting. The Belgian presidency and the Commission were particularly perturbed by this and by an invitation that Blair extended to Chirac and Schröder to continue their discussions some days later at a dinner in Downing Street, the prime minister's residence in London. The Belgians, Dutch, Italians, and Spanish kicked up such a fuss that Blair eventually invited them as well.

Though amusing, the diplomatic row over who was coming to dinner demonstrated the other countries' suspicion of the intentions of the big three. Far from undermining the ESDP, however, the incident may have helped each side to see the other's point of view. The majority of countries concluded that they had probably overreacted. After all, Britain, France, and Germany have considerable international political clout and the preponderance of military force in the EU. They did not propose acting alone, without regard to the other countries. Indeed, by clearing the air about the intentions of the big three, the incident may have helped pave the way for the diplomatic effort soon undertaken by Britain, France, and Germany on behalf of the EU to mediate the dispute with Iran over that country's nuclear capability.

Meanwhile, the ESDP continued to develop. The Political and Security Committee began to hold regular meetings with the North Atlantic Council (the political arm of NATO), and the EU and NATO military committees began to cooperate, however tentatively. In December 2002, the EU and NATO reached an agreement on the so-called Berlin-Plus arrangements for EU access to NATO assets during ESDP operations. In another important development, the EU's Joint Situation Center (SITCEN) opened in January 2003. Staffed by civilian and military officials, it provides early warning, monitoring, and assessment of looming crises; acts as an operational contact point; and provides facilities for ad hoc task forces.

A conference on capabilities improvement took place in November 2001 to try to rectify the deficiencies in the EU's "Force Catalogue." Nevertheless, a Belgian presidency announcement in December that year that the rapid reaction force was operational proved premature. As part of a continuous effort to build EU military capacity, in November 2004, defense ministers pledged up to 165,000 troops to make up a series of EU "battlegroups," each consisting of about 1,500 troops from one or more member states, deployable within ten days to help quell or contain international conflicts. At all times the EU keeps two battlegroups on standby at high readiness.

The EU took over most of the functions and bodies of the WEU in 2002, including the satellite center and the old WEU think tank, located in Paris, which became an autonomous EU agency under the CFSP. The renamed European Union Institute for Security Studies promotes research and debate on ESDP-related issues and acts as a forward studies unit for the High Representative. EU defense ministers also began to meet regularly in 2002 on the margins of the General Affairs Council.

The Impact of Iraq. By this time the situation in Iraq was dominating international affairs and about to convulse the EU. Influential elements within the US administration appear to have decided soon after the events of September 2001 to depose Saddam Hussein. Their intentions became clear in the latter part of 2002; a US invasion of Iraq seemed only a matter of time. Blair backed the United States unreservedly; Chirac and Schröder, who exploited the issue for electoral gain in September 2002, opposed it wholeheartedly. That divergence set the stage for a bitter altercation among member states (and soon-to-be member states) that seriously jeopardized recent progress on security and defense policy cooperation.

The extent of the disarray within the EU was plain for all to see when the leaders of five member states (Britain, Denmark, Italy, Portugal, and Spain) and three candidate countries (the Czech Republic, Hungary, and Poland) signed an open letter at the end of January 2003 expressing strong support for the United States. Chirac and Schröder were furious; Solana was embarrassed (he heard about the letter while listening to the radio). The following week, ten other Central and Eastern European countries (the other candidates plus Albania, Croatia, and Macedonia) issued a similar declaration of support for the United States, further infuriating Chirac and Schröder, who at least enjoyed the support of Belgium and Luxembourg.

Although a majority of governments may have supported the United States in the run-up to the war, a majority of Europeans seemed resolutely opposed to the venture. Massive public protests in London and Madrid in mid-February showed that Blair and José Maria Aznar, the Spanish prime minister, did not represent popular opinion in their views on the war. The divisions over Iraq were therefore deeply personal, with EU leaders holding entrenched positions for or against the imminent invasion.

EU leaders attempted to show unity at an extraordinary meeting of the European Council in mid-February 2003, on the eve of the US invasion, at which they produced an anodyne statement condemning Saddam Hussein and hoping that war could be avoided. Chirac soon shattered any pretense of EU accord when, at a press conference after the summit, he castigated the leaders of the soon-to-be Central and Eastern European member states, who had been present at the summit, for daring to take a position on Iraq contrary to his own. "Frankly, I believe that they behaved childishly," Chirac thundered, "as membership in the EU involves a measure of consideration for others, a degree of consultation . . . with the Union one proposes to enter."[16] Chirac's outburst was somewhat ironic because he liked to speak on behalf of the EU without consulting anybody else. Clearly, Chirac was worried about the impact of enlargement and frustrated by the refusal of other countries to follow his lead.

The Panglossian statements of Commission president Romano Prodi could not disguise the extent of the EU's disarray. After the mid-February summit, for example, Prodi declared that the EU now had "a message [to send] to the world: Europe is united and its voice must be heard."[17] Solana was more realistic, observing that "the EU still does not have a genuine common external policy, it has several. One day there is an agreement and the next day this is torn to shreds."[18]

The lowest point for the EU came in April 2003, about a month after the US invasion of Iraq, when Belgium, France, Germany, and Luxembourg held a summit to press ahead with their own plans for defense cooperation and announced afterward that they intended to establish a military headquarters in the Brussels suburb of Tervuren. It was as if the ESDP, put together so painstakingly over the previous five years, did not exist. Within a short time, however, the four countries realized that they had overreacted. A European military initiative without Britain, Europe's leading military power, simply did not make sense. For better or for worse, the EU would have to act together in the defense realm.

Despite having generated considerable bitterness among EU leaders, the crisis over Iraq did not derail the ESDP. Blair and Chirac even managed to smooth over their differences at a bilateral summit in February 2003, in the run-up to the war, in order to emphasize the importance of the ESDP and to commit more resources to it. Evidence that Iraq did not mean the end of the ESDP was readily apparent. The EU had begun a police mission in Bosnia in January 2003 and began its first military operation in March 2003 (taking over from NATO in Macedonia). In June 2003 the EU deployed a French-led peacekeeping mission, authorized by the UN Security Council, for three months in the Democratic Republic of Congo. This was the first EU military mission undertaken without recourse to NATO, and the first mission outside Europe. In December 2003, the European Council announced that the EU would consider fielding an EU military mission in Bosnia to replace the NATO Stabilization Force there. The EU eventually took over in November 2004, launching its biggest military operation to date, with over 7,000 troops. All of these operations took place despite highly visible sniping among national political leaders over the war in Iraq and its aftermath.

One of the most striking examples of the development of the ESDP after the war in Iraq was the presentation by Javier Solana of a European Security Strategy to EU leaders in June 2003. He called for an assertive EU foreign and security policy, including the possible use of military force, and identified three key threats to European security: terrorism, the proliferation of weapons of mass destruction, and failed states. In contrast to the position of the United States, the European Security Strategy, which EU leaders endorsed in December 2003, identified the UN Charter as the "fundamental framework" for international relations.[19] Strengthening the Charter was an EU priority.

Another noteworthy development was the progress made within NATO on accommodating the emerging ESDP. The Berlin-Plus arrangements for EU access to NATO assets have already been noted. Equally important was an agreement reached in December 2003 on the establishment of an EU planning unit within NATO's military headquarters outside Brussels. The French had initially wanted a full-fledged EU military headquarters, but having overplayed their hand during the Iraq crisis by pushing for a completely autonomous European defense force, they accepted the compromise pushed by Britain and acceptable to the United States, notwithstanding Washington's distrust of French intentions (see Chapter 18 for a discussion of the impact of the war in Iraq on EU-US relations).

In July 2004 the EU established the European Defense Agency, in Brussels, to help member states improve their military capacity and meet the EU's goals. Denmark is the sole EU member state not participating in the work of the agency; nonmember Norway participates without voting rights. The agency produced a "Long-Term Vision" report in October 2006, subsequently endorsed by national ministers, to guide defense planners as they attempt to match military capabilities with likely security threats and responses over the next twenty years.

The Lisbon Treaty. The CFSP and ESDP were high on the agenda of the Convention on the Future of Europe, which opened in February 2002. The convention and the ensuing intergovernmental conference presented an excellent opportunity to make further progress in these fields. Indeed, between the launch of the convention and the end of the intergovernmental conference in June 2004, the invasion of Iraq and its aftermath focused governments' attention on the importance of strengthening the CFSP and ESDP.

An obvious problem was the lack of coherence between the EU's external relations generally, conducted largely by the Commission, and the CFSP, run mostly by the Council, a problem personified by the awkward division of labor between the High Representative and the commissioner for external relations. There was little surprise or objection, therefore, when France and Germany proposed merging the two positions into a new, single position, that of EU foreign minister and Commission vice president. The EU foreign minister would chair the proposed Foreign Affairs Council and head the new External Action Service, an EU diplomatic service that would draw members from national ministries, the Council secretariat, and the Commission.

The convention endorsed the idea, and the intergovernmental conference wrote it into the Constitutional Treaty, which included a number of other innovations with respect to the CFSP and ESDP. All of these reforms survived in the Lisbon Treaty, with one notable exception: as part of the effort to appease critics who claimed that the Constitutional Treaty aimed to establish a statelike EU, national leaders decided in the aftermath of the treaty's rejection to drop the title "foreign minister" and revert to "High Representative" for the key new external relations position. Specifically, the new title was "High Representative of the Union for Foreign Affairs and Security Policy" (or, as Chris Patten called it, the "Even Higher Representative").[20]

Although the Lisbon Treaty did away with the pillar structure of the existing EU, the CFSP remained largely an intergovernmental arrangement with limited use of qualified majority voting, the EP kept at arm's length, and no right of judicial review. The Commission was centrally involved by virtue of the High Representative being also a Commission vice president, but the Commission did not have the same right of initiative as it had in other areas of EU policy.

The Lisbon Treaty streamlined the instruments available for the conduct of the CFSP, dropping "common strategies," "joint actions," and "common positions"—in use since the Amsterdam Treaty—in favor simply of "actions" and "positions." First, the European Council would define general CFSP principles and guidelines. Then the Foreign Affairs Council would define (1) actions to be undertaken, (2) positions to be taken, and (3) arrangements for the implementation of these actions and positions. In general the Foreign Affairs Council may act by qualified majority voting, but not when taking decisions having military or defense implications.

The Lisbon Treaty kept the "emergency brake" provision of the Amsterdam Treaty whereby, if a government declares that, for vital and stated reasons of national policy, it intends to oppose the adoption of a decision to be taken by qualified majority, a vote will not be taken. In that case, the High Representative would attempt to bring the government out of opposition. Failing that, the Council could, acting by a qualified majority, request that the matter be referred to the European Council for a decision by unanimity. The Lisbon Treaty also kept the existing provision for constructive abstention, allowing national governments to abstain from a decision being taken unanimously by the others, but revising it to say that the number of countries abstaining could not exceed one-third of the EU's membership and one-third of the EU's population.

An especially noteworthy innovation in the Lisbon Treaty—elaborated upon in a protocol—allows for a group of member states to participate in *permanent structured cooperation* within the Common Security and Defense Policy, as the European Security and Defense Policy is now called. The idea is that a number of countries, having the will and ability to organize militarily with a view to conducting peacemaking and peacekeeping operations in accordance with UN principles, could form a self-governing pioneer group. Other member states could join later. The group's council, made up of ministers of participating countries, could suspend a country that is no longer willing or able to meet the group's commitments. The High Representative would be fully involved in permanent structured cooperation.

The Constitutional Treaty's provisions for foreign, security, and defense policy, which made up almost 40 percent of the treaty's reforms, did not cause a stir during the French and Dutch referendum campaigns. By contrast, many opponents of the Lisbon Treaty in the two Irish referendums (June 2008 and October 2009) found fault specifically with the provisions for the CSDP, which some claimed would herald the emergence of an EU army and spell the end of Irish neutrality. Given that the treaty expressly stipulated that the CSDP "shall not prejudice the specific character of the security and defense policy of certain Member States"—meaning militarily neutral countries such as Ireland—and that the EU is far from ever forming its own army, such claims were disingenuous, to say the least. Sensitivity in Ireland to the CSDP, and the precariousness of the treaty during the two Irish referendum campaigns, stymied preparatory work in Brussels on the treaty's new foreign, security, and defense policy provisions.

■ Prospects for CFSP and CSDP

In the span of nearly twenty years and three major treaty changes, the EU has developed a commendable CFSP to complement its activities in the traditional areas of external economic relations. The development of the CFSP, personified for ten years (1999–2009) by Javier Solana, has undoubtedly raised the

EU's international profile and effectiveness. Yet the CFSP is limited by the nature of the EU and by the absence so far of a powerful military component. Without the credible threat of military force, the EU will always be reduced, when dealing with dictators and despots, to producing declarations full of "strong nouns, weak verbs."[21]

Considering member states' traditional reluctance to cooperate on security and defense policy in the framework of European integration, however, progress in this area has been remarkable since implementation of the Amsterdam Treaty in 1999. The objective of the ESDP was to make EU civilian and military resources rapidly available on a relatively limited scale for crisis management in international hot spots. The EU can claim some success, having launched twenty-two civilian and military missions (either separately or combined) since inception of the ESDP, twelve of which were ongoing at the beginning of 2010. On the whole, these missions—ranging from police and military missions in Macedonia (2003), to a rule of law mission in Iraq (2006), to a naval mission against piracy off the coast of Somalia (2009)—have been worthwhile and have benefited the people whose safety the EU has protected. It is difficult to imagine how opponents in Ireland and elsewhere of the EU's security and defense policy could oppose such activities.

The existence of the High Representative of the Union for Foreign Affairs and Security Policy—the improved-upon position that Solana held—is undoubtedly a step in the right direction. By virtue of being also the commissioner responsible for external relations, the High Representative is in a good position to ensure greater coherence and consistency between the Council and the Commission in the formulation and conduct of EU foreign, security, and defense policy. The High Representative heads the European External Action Service, set up soon after implementation of the Lisbon Treaty, whose existence also institutionalizes greater coordination between the two sides (Council and Commission) of EU external relations. The High Representative is also in charge of the more than 130 EU delegations (embassies and missions) around the world, staffed by the External Action Service and by Commission officials.

Welcome though they are, the Lisbon reforms may not go far enough to ensure the smooth functioning of the CFSP and have even institutionalized a new rivalry, this time between the position of High Representative and the newly configured European Council presidency. According to the Lisbon Treaty, "The President of the European Council shall, at his or her level and in that capacity, ensure the external representation of the Union on issues concerning its common foreign and security policy, without prejudice to the powers of the High Representative of the Union for Foreign Affairs and Security Policy." Accordingly, the EU has two new office holders charged with representing the EU externally. Just as the success of the CFSP depended to a great extent on the personal relationship between Solana and the commissioners for external relations during his tenure, it now depends on relations between the

High Representative and the European Council president. Although there is every reason to believe that Catherine Ashton, the first post-Lisbon High Representative, and Herman van Rompuy, the first elected European Council president, will get on famously together, the rivalry inherent in their positions is not a sound institutional arrangement. Nor will national leaders and the Commission president necessarily be willing to take a backseat when it comes to certain aspects of EU external representation.

The main problem for the CSDP, as for the ESDP before it, is that the EU is simply not doing enough to make the policy work, its rhetoric still exceeds reality, and its potential remains far greater than its willingness to act. The story of the ESDP is replete with capability commitment conferences in which member states made pledges that often went unfulfilled. Most EU countries are not spending enough on defense and get poor value for what little they do spend, not least because of the fragmentation of the European defense market.[22] Command and control, intelligence, strategic transport, training, logistics, and weapons are extremely expensive prerequisites for successful military intervention. Only a few member states, such as Britain, France, Spain, and the countries geographically closest to Russia (and formerly under Soviet control), seem to take defense seriously. Germany has made huge strides in recent years, but remains skittish about using military force (most Germans oppose their country's involvement in the war against Al-Qaida and the Taliban in Afghanistan). It is ironic that, having been cursed by German militarism for much of its recent history, Europe now needs Germany to be more muscular and militaristic in its foreign policy.

The main difficulty with the CSDP is fundamentally one of political will. The peoples and governments of Europe will pay more for defense, get better value for their money, and use their improved military capacity to the best possible effect if and when they believe that it is in their interest to do so. Thus far, their approach has been halfhearted. The EU's peacemaking and peacekeeping missions to date, while far better than doing nothing, have been underwhelming. EU battlegroups were declared fully operational in January 2007; none has been deployed as of early 2010. According to Anand Menon, perhaps the most significant ESDP missions were the ones *not* undertaken, such as in Congo in late 2008, when the EU declined to send troops at the behest of the UN, due to disagreements among member states.[23]

Strained relations between the EU and NATO, despite the fact that the majority of NATO members are also EU member states, also undermine the effectiveness of the CSDP. Different organizational cultures impede a close working relationship between the EU and NATO both in Brussels and in operations on the ground. Moreover, a bitter dispute between non-EU but NATO member Turkey and EU but non-NATO member Cyprus has injected itself into the EU-NATO relationship.

The most consequential EU mission so far has been in Bosnia-Herzegovina, an international protectorate still consumed by hatred among the Bosnian Muslims, Croats, and Serbs that has little prospect of ever standing on its own. The situation in Bosnia-Herzegovina may be intractable, but the EU seems incapable of thinking strategically about the future and devising a coherent approach to the country using the array of instruments at its disposal. Changes in the Lisbon Treaty may help the EU to deal more effectively with Bosnia-Herzegovina, but will not necessarily improve national governments' willingness to do so.

Laudable though they are, the EU's efforts to develop a credible and effective capacity to combat clear-cut cases of aggression around the world are likely to remain hobbled not only by tight defense budgets and weak political commitment, but also by different interests, traditions, and historical experiences among a growing number of member states.[24] Hence the potential importance of permanent structured cooperation, which would allow a small group of like-minded states to press ahead in security and defense policy. In order for it to have sufficient military muscle, Britain and France would have to be involved; in order for it to be a credible pioneer group for deeper European integration, Germany would also have to be involved. The problem is that these three countries rarely see eye to eye on where, when, and how the EU should intervene militarily to tackle an international crisis.

Yet the need for occasional EU armed involvement in a dangerous and messy world would seem to be obvious. It was the war in Kosovo in 1999 that finally impelled the EU to develop the means to carry out the Petersberg tasks (international crisis management). Despite having come so far in a relatively short time, the EU still has a long way to go before turning the CSDP into a credible means of projecting and applying military force, sometimes far from the EU's borders. Any doubts about the utility of such force could easily be dispelled by recalling the words of former external relations commissioner Chris Patten: "The people of the Western Balkans are our fellow Europeans. We cannot wash our hands of them. Let us remember the consequences of our refusal to get involved. The shattered ruins of Vukovar. The ghastly siege of Sarajevo. The charnel house of Srebrenica. The smoking villages of Kosovo. The European Union did not commit these crimes. But 200,000 or more fellow Europeans died in Bosnia and Herzegovina alone. As Europeans we cannot avoid a heavy share of responsibility for what happened."[25]

■ Notes

1. See Monica den Boer, ed., *Schengen: Judicial Cooperation and Policy Coordination* (Maastricht: European Institute for Public Administration, 1997).

2. See Monica den Boer and Jörg Monar, "Keynote Article: 11 September and the Challenge of Global Terrorism to the EU as a Security Actor," *Journal of Common Market Studies* 40, *Annual Review of the EU 2001/2002* (September 2002): 11–28.

3. European Commission, "An Area of Freedom, Security, and Justice Serving the Citizen: Wider Freedom in a Safer Environment," COM(2009)262, June 10, 2009.

4. Quoted in *Europolitics,* June 11, 2009.

5. From "The Stockholm Program: The Shape of Things to Come," *Statewatch Observatory,* November 26, 2009, http://www.statewatch.org/stockholm-programme .htm.

6. Brussels European Council, "Presidency Conclusions," June 18–19, 2009.

7. Brussels European Council, "Presidency Conclusions," October 29–30, 2009.

8. Brussels European Council, "Presidency Conclusions," December 10–11, 2009.

9. François Duchêne, "Europe's Role in World Peace," in Richard Mayne, ed., *Europe Tomorrow: Sixteen Europeans Look Ahead* (London: Fontana/Collins, 1972), pp. 32–47; Ian Manners, "Normative Power Europe: A Contradiction in Terms?" *Journal of Common Market Studies* 40, no. 2 (June 2002): 235–258.

10. See Elfride Regelsberger, Philippe de Schoutheete, and Wolfgang Wessels, eds., *Foreign Policy of the European Union: From EPC to CFSP and Beyond* (Boulder: Lynne Rienner, 1997); Martin Holland, *Common Foreign and Security Policy: The Record and Reforms* (London: Pinter, 1997); and Karen E. Smith, *The Making of European Union Foreign Policy* (New York: St. Martin's, 1998).

11. Lisbon European Council, "Presidency Conclusions," Bulletin EC 6-1992, point 1.2.4.

12. See Jolyon Howorth, *Security and Defense Policy in the EU* (Basingstoke: Palgrave, 2007).

13. Alistair J. K. Shepherd, "'A Milestone in the History of the EU:' Kosovo and the EU's International Role," *International Affairs* 85, no. 3 (2009): 516.

14. Cologne European Council, "Presidency Conclusions," Bulletin EC 6-1999.

15. Helsinki European Council, "Presidency Conclusions," Bulletin EC 12-1999.

16. Quoted in *European Report,* February 19, 2003, p. V.15.

17. Quoted in ibid., p. V.14.

18. Quoted in *European Report,* February 26, 2003, p. V.12.

19. Brussels European Council, "Presidency Conclusions," December 12, 2003.

20. Chris Patten, *Not Quite the Diplomat: Home Truths About Foreign Affairs* (London: Penguin, 2005).

21. Ibid., p. 152.

22. See Anand Menon, "Empowering Paradise? The ESDP at Ten," *International Affairs* 85, no. 2 (2009): 234–235.

23. Ibid., p. 237.

24. See Tom Hadden, *The Responsibility to Assist: EU Policy and Practice in Crisis-Management Operations Under European Security and Defence Policy* (Portland: Hart, 2009).

25. Chris Patten, "The Western Balkans: The Road to Europe," speech to European Affairs Committee of the Bundestag, Berlin, April 28, 2004, http://www.ear.eu .int/agency/main/agency-a1a2g3.htm.

18 EU-US Relations

Whenever transatlantic tension erupts, it is easy to forget that, historically, the United States consistently (and genuinely) supported European integration, largely for strategic reasons. The United States saw the European Community as an essential part of the post–World War II peace settlement and as an important contributor to the security of Western Europe during the Cold War. Thereafter it saw the European Union as indispensable for the security and stability of post–Cold War Europe. Throughout that time, the United States and the EU developed the world's largest and deepest economic relationship and a dynamic transatlantic economy. "For more than half a century, the United States and Europe have . . . been the main engines of global growth and wealth creation, leading the world in consumption, innovation, and competition, and accounting for a disproportionate share of global production, trade and investment."[1]

Despite its ups and downs, transatlantic economic relations remain fundamentally healthy and stable. By contrast with the structural problems inherent in EU (and US) relations with Asia, the EU-US trade balance reliably reflects growth rates and macroeconomic developments on both sides of the Atlantic. Yet friction between the world's two largest trading blocs often obscures the underlying soundness of transatlantic economic relations. Persistent trade disputes, spillover from domestic controversies, and rivalry on the world stage have dogged the economic dialogue between the United States and the EU.

Politically, the process of European integration was bound to contain the seeds of transatlantic discord, despite US support for ever closer union. Not surprisingly, mutual frustration and occasional unproductive rivalry have marked diplomatic relations between the EU and the United States. Deep cultural, philosophical, and foreign policy differences between the two sides became acute under the administration of President George W. Bush. Many Europeans deplored the resurgence of the religious right in the United States, the profound conservatism of much of American society, and the administration's apparent international adventurism and disdain for old allies and

567

partners. The inauguration of President Barack Obama, greeted enthusiastically throughout Europe, signaled a return toward a more moderate US position. Even under the Obama administration, however, strains in the transatlantic relationship have endured.

Nevertheless, Europe and the United States are bound together by more than commercial ties. For all the undoubted difficulties between them, they share fundamental political values, now under threat from Islamic fundamentalism. Europe and the United States have a common interest in bolstering democracy and stability in a deeply troubled world. Their global economic outlook is similarly aligned, even to the point of protecting their own agricultural interests at the risk of jeopardizing a new global trade agreement. Indeed, the current unease in transatlantic relations disguises a great degree of quiet cooperation between the EU and the United States on a range of bilateral and global issues.

■ Underlying Difficulties

Well before the deterioration in EU-US relations during the George W. Bush administration, it was popular in Europe to ascribe sour notes in the transatlantic relationship to American resentment of the emergence of a strong and united Europe and to the resulting decline in US influence on the continent. The truth is more complicated. The uneasy relationship between the United States and the EU is a result of a number of inherent asymmetries in their structure and outlook. Whereas the EU and the United States undoubtedly have far more in common with each other than with any other country or region, the devil, as always, is in the details.[2]

From the US perspective, the initial difficulties lay in the incremental, often untidy nature of European integration, which caused constant changes in the scope of the EU's agenda and in the character of its policymaking process. By contrast, bilateral, country-to-country relations were easier to comprehend and manage: both sides had a well-understood governmental structure and a readily identifiable set of issues. But in the case of the EU as it evolved over the years, who exactly had decisionmaking power, and where precisely was the boundary between Community and member state competence?

Understandably, the tenuous connection between the trade and commercial policies conducted by the EU and the geopolitical concerns of its member states made it difficult for the United States, a traditional nation-state, to achieve the normal trade-offs between political and economic goals. Despite early US support for European integration, the frustrations of dealing with this unnatural compartmentalization of political and economic policy soured many US policymakers on the EC and its institutional machinery. Increasing pressure on world agricultural markets as a result of subsidized exports from the

EU and the steady erosion of US agricultural exports to EU member states exacerbated the problems. Typically, disputes over European restrictions on agricultural imports—long the most visible element of the EU's international mandate—have been the biggest source of bilateral friction.

Other asymmetries have added to the difficulties of both sides in multilateral negotiations. The Commission's need to develop trade policy by negotiating with member states, a feature of the Common Commercial Policy, often results in lowest-common-denominator mandates that leave the Commission little room for maneuver. By the same token, the US administration's need to persuade Congress to accept the final package can leave an entire multilateral agreement in agonizing suspense for months or can lead to peculiar negotiating positions designed to placate a handful of powerful senators. Shifting boundaries between EU and member state competences have led to conflicting signals in important areas of trade policy.

Although the United States and the EU dominate the world trading system, their international and regional priorities are different. The United States has formidable trading interests to protect around the Pacific Rim, and its troubled relationship with Japan was for a long time at the center of its trade policy. The EU, by contrast, is primarily a regional power: the bulk of its trade is with its neighbors, and its links with Asia, especially Japan and China, are substantially weaker than those of the United States. Furthermore, successive enlargements have steadily brought the EU's most important regional trading partners into the fold and sapped the EU's energy for broader external relations, notwithstanding the EU's claims to the contrary.

The growing role of the EU as a political actor has undoubtedly added desirable depth to the relationship at a time when the simple verities of the Cold War were replaced by messy and nearly unmanageable regional breakdowns. However, this role brought with it new difficulties generated by incompatible expectations and capabilities on each side. For US policymakers, it was always easier to work with those European countries whose outlook and approach were similar to theirs and to rely on firm alliances with Britain, Germany, and others such as the Netherlands, ignoring opposition elsewhere in Europe. The development of the Common Foreign and Security Policy has made this traditional US strategy harder to pursue.

Inevitably, in moments of crisis, the United States tends to go back to its old friends and bypass the EU decisionmaking structures so painstakingly developed. This tendency is exacerbated by the fact that EU political clout does not extend much beyond the power of the purse. EU aid disbursements to the Western Balkans and, beyond that, the wider Europe, for example, dwarf those of the United States, yet the big decisions, such as on military intervention in trouble spots, remain the province of the nation-states. Whereas US development assistance has steadily declined in real terms during the postwar era, the United States remains the military power of last resort.

While a gross generalization, it also seems reasonable to observe that many Europeans are offended by the United States because of its military power and cultural influence. Perhaps frustrated by their own relative powerlessness on the international stage and operating as they do with a vision of Europe that is always slightly ahead of reality, EU officials often resent not being taken as seriously by Washington as they sometimes take themselves. Apart from having a legitimate complaint about America's international behavior, the EU tends to overreact to perceived (or real) American slights. Rampant anti-Americanism in Europe, although corrosive for the transatlantic relationship, is a powerful force in EU identity building. It is often easier for Europeans to articulate what they *are not* than what they *are*. Thus, Europeans are not moralistic, self-righteous, uncaring capitalists who devour the world's scarce resources and act unilaterally in their own selfish interests. In other words, according to this caricature, they are not Americans.

EU officials are not entirely free of such prejudice. Moreover, they like to complain that Americans are only dimly aware of the EU's existence. Certainly, most Americans know little about the EU, just as most Europeans know little about how the US government works. Nevertheless, academic study of the EU is as advanced in the United States as it is in Europe. As for US officials and businesspeople, those who deal with the EU regularly know well how it works and what it does; the US Mission to the EU and the EU Committee of the American Chamber of Commerce are among the most effective lobbyists in Brussels.

EU officials are especially irritated by what they see as the refusal of Americans who deal regularly with them to acknowledge the EU as a serious political actor. In their view, US officials are either unwilling to see the EU as a political equal or unable to comprehend the complexities of EU foreign, security, and defense policymaking. Indeed, many US officials are frustrated with the EU politically not because of the opacity of EU policymaking in those areas but because, more often than not, EU action fails to match EU rhetoric. Although Europeans may retort that Americans do not appreciate the difficulty of reaching a common EU position, Americans believe with some justification that the EU cannot expect to be taken seriously as a political entity as long as the results of its foreign, security, and defense policymaking efforts are so meager. The problem is not that US officials are unfamiliar with the intricacies of the CFSP, but that they are only too well aware of its procedural weaknesses, notwithstanding welcome changes in the Lisbon Treaty.

The United States is (and will remain for the foreseeable future) the world's sole superpower. As a result, US leaders, regardless of their political affiliation, are bound to view the world differently from their European counterparts, especially since the terrorist attacks of September 2001. The United States appreciates the EU's economic importance and weight but recognizes that the EU has only a limited foreign policy capacity. The United States wishes the EU well but has little patience for the procedural complexity of European integration, which even to many Europeans seems to have become an end in itself. Especially in view of the urgent challenges that it faces around the world, the United States unashamedly judges the EU by what it does, not by what it says.

To some extent, the problems and resentments inherent in transatlantic relations have been tempered (or at any rate muffled) by the growing mutual engagement that has resulted from the EU's increasing powers and mandate. Since the beginning of the 1990s, leaders on both sides have tried to speed this process by a series of ever more ambitious initiatives intended to increase EU-US cooperation and engagement across the board and to raise the profile of the relationship. These have been only partly successful. Through innumerable high-level meetings and rising piles of communiqués, they have created an aura of dynamism and progress and have provided political cover for some quiet compromises on especially touchy issues. They have been less success-ful in resolving either the persistent irritants in the trade field or the fundamen-tal differences in political priorities and social outlook that will continue to produce friction, especially in transatlantic trade, which increasingly is affected more by regulatory policy than by traditional protectionism.

■ The Course of EU-US Relations

Despite early US support for European unity, the development of European integration was bound to bring with it a degree of transatlantic tension. An economically strong Community caused a decline in US market share within the EC and in some third countries. Since the early 1960s, the United States and the EU have been embroiled in disputes over alleged protectionism and unfair practices in the international marketplace. Beginning with the so-called chicken and pasta wars, continuing with tit-for-tat restrictions on steel trade generated by domestic pressure to protect tottering industries, and culminating in a seemingly never-ending dispute over hormones in beef, the history of EU-US relations has been replete with issue-specific disputes even as transatlantic trade and investment flourished.

The changes that swept across Europe in the wake of the Single European Act offered the chance to breathe new life into transatlantic economic rela-tions. Initially, however, American reactions baffled and annoyed Community policymakers caught up in a vision of a Europe without borders. Businesspeo-ple and some policymakers in the United States, their opinions of the Commu-nity shaped by the Common Agricultural Policy as well as by limitless Euro-pean subsidies for "national champion" and "Eurochampion" industries such as Airbus, were unimpressed by the stated aims of the single market. They charged that the single market would bring about a "fortress Europe" in which the fruits of economic integration would be reserved for Europeans. Commission officials, perceiving themselves as the vanguard of a liberalizing force, were hurt and angry at this charge.

EU officials nevertheless responded to US criticism and addressed the international consequences of their decisions. As a practical matter, the structure of the proposed internal market would have made it difficult to deny its benefits to foreign economic actors, but US pressure made it necessary for the Commission to resist the temptation to try. Although rightly rejecting US demands for "a seat at the table," the Commission agreed to strengthen consultations with and develop greater institutional ties between US and European standards-setting bodies and to develop mutual recognition agreements that would allow manufacturers to sell in both European and foreign markets without the need for additional certification. Simultaneously, a second look at the single market program persuaded many US firms, especially those already established in Europe, that a fully integrated market presented more opportunity than threat. Ever eager to jump on the bandwagon, US business became a cheerleader for European deregulation and elimination of internal barriers, and seminars on "1992" became a cottage industry for US consulting firms.

At the same time, some of the institutional implications of the Single European Act, notably the increasing assertiveness and growing authority of the Commission and the emergence of the European Parliament as a potent political actor, were somewhat perturbing for the United States, where the name of the Commission itself evoked an unfavorable (and wholly unfair) image of all that was iniquitous about the EU: a bloated bureaucracy, an opaque administration, and an unaccountable authority. Who drafted proposals in the Commission? When were they circulated outside Commission headquarters? How could third countries express their points of view? The answers to those questions seemed to differ from one directorate-general to another. And the EP, notorious for its occasional bizarre resolution, reveled in taking the United States to task for real or imagined wrongdoing.

During the Cold War, a politically assertive EU might have challenged US hegemony in Europe and the superpower's global preeminence. But the member states never displayed a willingness, let alone ability, to form a political and military bloc that could rival the United States. At a time when Western Europe depended on US military protection, it would have been foolhardy for Western European countries to risk antagonizing the United States by challenging its ascendancy in the North Atlantic Treaty Organization—the French could afford to do so precisely because no other country would follow their lead. In the early 1970s, member states launched a process of foreign policy cooperation; a decade later, during a resurgence of Cold War tension, some sought to extend that process into the security domain. But the frosty US response, or some European governments' anticipation of a frosty response, helped restrict foreign policy cooperation among the member states to the "political and economic aspects" of security.

The political context of EU-US relations changed dramatically with the end of the Cold War.[3] The United States responded to the events in Central and Eastern Europe with a fundamental review of policy toward the continent. The essence of the "New Atlanticism" for the United States was a determination to preserve NATO regardless of the changes ahead, as well as recognition of the EU's importance as a political and economic anchor in post–Cold War Europe. The acceleration of reform in Central and Eastern Europe, and the Commission's ability to mobilize massive amounts of aid to help the process, further convinced the United States of the EU's political significance, especially as a crucial underpinning for a united Germany, which the United States strongly supported.

Given its newfound appreciation of the emerging EU's political importance, the United States accepted with alacrity a proposal by the Council presidency in early 1990 to formalize EU-US relations. The appeal for the United States of such an arrangement grew throughout the year as the Community responded to the collapse of communism in Central and Eastern Europe and the sudden inevitability of German reunification by calling for an intergovernmental conference on political union in addition to the previously scheduled conference on monetary union (the two conferences resulted in the Maastricht Treaty).

The Transatlantic Declaration, signed in Washington, D.C., in November 1990 by the US president and the presidents of the Council and Commission, nonetheless seemed long on rhetoric and short on substance. Among the reasons for a solid EC-US relationship, the declaration included a new factor: "the accelerating process by which the European Community is acquiring its own identity in economic and monetary matters, in foreign policy and in the domain of security." Yet apart from its general significance, the declaration's only tangible contribution to EC-US relations was a strengthened framework for regular consultations to enable both sides to "inform and consult each other on important matters of common interest, both political and economic, with a view to bringing their positions as close as possible, without prejudice to their respective independence."[4]

Changes in the political atmosphere, however, had little effect on the long-standing problems and tensions in the economic relationship. Soon after the Transatlantic Declaration was signed in Washington, D.C., the Uruguay Round negotiations of the General Agreement on Tariffs and Trade collapsed in Brussels over deep-seated transatlantic differences, with the United States and the EU accusing each other of never having been serious about a successful conclusion. The Europeans especially objected to what seemed like excessive and high-handed US demands for reform of the CAP at a time when the

Commission had not completed its own internal negotiations on this supremely touchy issue. Some in Europe interpreted the Community's stance as evidence of a newfound willingness to "stand up" to the United States. In fact, there was more of the old than the new in the European position, which resulted from a French veto of a last-minute compromise. For its part, the United States saw the failure of the Brussels talks as evidence of the Community's continuing intransigence and introversion.

What was less evident in the strife surrounding the final stages of the Uruguay Round negotiations was the extent to which it illustrated the duality of the economic relationship between the United States and the emerging EU: a continuing pattern of intractable disputes obscuring a far larger set of common interests vis-à-vis the rest of the world. Apart from agriculture, well-publicized spats between US and European negotiators over issues such as trade in services, intellectual property protection, and antidumping and subsidy rules suggested that the Uruguay Round was a struggle between titans with the rest of the world looking on. In fact, much of the force driving the talks came from the joint determination of the United States and the EU to restore the credibility of the GATT and drag the rest of the world into a liberalized trading system (most developing countries were by no means eager to open their domestic markets). A more muscular world trading regime would not only secure better market access for US and European exporters but could also contain transatlantic trade disputes that threatened to poison the broader economic and political relationship.

The emergence in May 1992 of a CAP reform package made possible the so-called Blair House agreement between the United States and the EU, which provided for a gradual reduction and limitation of agricultural subsidies. This, in turn, paved the way for the belated conclusion of the Uruguay Round and the birth of the World Trade Organization in 1995, which led to a respite in many long-running EU-US skirmishes. Some issues were subsumed into WTO commitments under the Blair House agreement; others, such as disputes over beef hormones and bananas, went temporarily on hold until they could be revived as WTO cases under more stringent dispute settlement rules.

New Transatlantic Initiatives

The Transatlantic Declaration appeared little more than a transitional measure pending the development of EU-US relations in the post-Maastricht period. Initially, the transition to a new political relationship with the EU proved difficult for the United States, which sometimes seemed alarmed, or at least discomfited, by the EU's rising political profile. On top of this, security and defense issues initially brought a new edge to transatlantic relations. Efforts by some member states during the intergovernmental conference to give the EU a security dimension and, ultimately, a military capability provoked an intemperate US response, with warnings from Washington about the dangers of undermining NATO. Rather than being representative of US policy toward European security in the post–Cold War period, however, this infamous outburst was a throwback to earlier Cold War ways.

The Europeans' apparent responsiveness to US demands in 1991 not to risk undermining NATO by developing an EU defense identity suggested that the United States continued to wield considerable diplomatic clout and that member states took seriously the implied threat of US military withdrawal from Europe. Indeed, member states drew back in the Maastricht Treaty from acquiring an independent defense capability for the EU and opted instead to use the Western European Union as a bridge between NATO and the EU. But their reasons for doing so were more diverse than simply succumbing to a US démarche. Regardless of Washington's position, governments could not agree among themselves so soon after the end of the Cold War about the form or content of an EU defense identity. Moreover, few were willing to surrender sovereignty in this area.[5]

The Maastricht Treaty's provisions on monetary union caused little surprise and no alarm in Washington. To the annoyance of EU politicians and officials, in the middle and late 1990s their US counterparts seemed indifferent or even hostile to monetary union. In fact, the United States was reasonably sanguine about it. Far from trying to thwart monetary union, most Americans who thought about the issue seemed more enthusiastic about the idea of a single currency than did the fabled European man in the street. At the same time, US officials appreciated that the launch of the euro would have important repercussions for transatlantic relations, though not immediately.

In other respects, the Maastricht Treaty altered the EU's policy scope and institutional framework in ways that were not uncongenial to the United States. The extension of Community competence in a variety of policy areas for the most part formalized the status quo. Institutional changes introduced in the treaty, together with a vogue for transparency, promised to make the decisionmaking process more open and amenable to outside influence. At the very least, the institutional provisions of the treaty did not require a radical reappraisal of the US foreign policy apparatus for dealing with European affairs.

The arrival of the Bill Clinton administration in 1993, headed by the first US president from the postwar generation, appeared initially to increase European ambivalence over relations with the United States. In fact, there was little in the early months of the new administration to suggest a turn away from Europe. Clinton's trade representative steered the United States through the final months of the Uruguay Round, and Clinton himself spearheaded a vigorous push to get congressional ratification of the results. However, Clinton's abrupt shift of attention to the North American Free Trade Agreement (NAFTA) and to the Pacific region rattled European leaders. The curious result of their anxiety was the sudden emergence in 1994 and 1995 of European calls for negotiation of a transatlantic free trade agreement. Its earliest advocates were not trade negotiators, who were exhausted after the Uruguay Round, but some of Europe's leading foreign and defense ministers.

The idea of a transatlantic free trade agreement was illusory. Under GATT rules, any such agreement would have to cover "substantially all trade." Negotiation of a free trade agreement would therefore require reopening all of the agricultural and other disputes that had plagued the Uruguay Round talks. This was hardly a recipe for greater transatlantic unity. The idea also raised worries among other WTO members that the United States and the EU would retreat to their own cozy condominium, creating the world's largest trading bloc and relegating the WTO to irrelevancy. Sensitive to such concerns and aware of the impossibility of negotiating a free trade agreement with the European Union, US officials made suitably encouraging, though vague, statements about the need for closer economic and political cooperation.

In the event, then–EU trade commissioner Leon Brittan proposed something at once less and more than a free trade agreement. The "transatlantic economic zone" was a highly flexible concept that would liberalize trade in certain areas while skipping over others. Its relation to existing WTO rules was ambiguous. US policymakers, more legalistic in their outlook, were uneasy about the haziness of the concept and reluctant to be dragged into bilateral free trade negotiations through the back door. Nevertheless, the United States signaled its willingness to go along with negotiation of a "transatlantic economic area" in the context of a broader bilateral effort to expand the Transatlantic Declaration of 1990 to include substantive cooperation under the existing consultation mechanisms.

Thus the second grand bilateral initiative, the New Transatlantic Agenda, was born. Following short but intensive negotiations, President Clinton and the presidents of the Council and the Commission signed the agenda in Madrid in December 1995.[6]

The new agenda was much more concrete than the old declaration. To the usual rhetoric about common values, it added broad areas in which the United States and the EU were to make joint efforts:

- Promoting peace, stability, democracy, and development.
- Responding to global challenges relating to issues such as the environment, terrorism, and international crime.
- Expanding world trade and promoting closer economic relations.
- Building "bridges" across the Atlantic in the cultural and educational domain.

The New Transatlantic Agenda further intensified the schedule of mandatory meetings established under the Transatlantic Declaration to include those of a "senior-level group" charged with the task of adding substance to the twice-yearly, and increasingly perfunctory, EU-US summits instituted under the declaration.

An accompanying action plan listed a number of short- and medium-term goals to achieve the agenda's objectives, ranging from the conclusion of issue-specific trade negotiations to closer educational cooperation. For the most part, the political game plan was heavily weighted with words such as "cooperate," "reinforce," and "pursue," reflecting the intractable nature and resistance to schematization of problems such as Bosnia, the Middle East, and the recurring crises in Africa. The few specifics referred mostly to participation in negotiations or conferences and implementation of various agreements already negotiated. Economic commitments were slightly more specific, covering both the multilateral issues of the day and continuing bilateral efforts.

Neither the New Transatlantic Agenda nor the action plan contained any reference to a free trade area. Instead, in addition to a host of promises to fulfill WTO commitments and strengthen the international system, the agenda and action plan called for a "New Transatlantic Marketplace" to be achieved by progressive reduction or elimination of bilateral trade barriers, stronger regulatory cooperation, and commitments to complete various negotiations then in progress. In short, the New Transatlantic Marketplace was less a radical departure from the past than an effort to breathe new life into a continuing process.

The New Transatlantic Agenda included one real innovation on the economic front: the Transatlantic Business Dialogue (TABD), which brought together senior corporate officials to help set an agenda for government negotiators. The TABD—the first truly transatlantic lobby—quickly showed its value in focusing the attention of trade negotiators on the bread-and-butter issues most important to those actually doing the trading; it placed a heavy emphasis on unglamorous but important tariff problems and standards, testing, and certification concerns. Successive EU-US summits called for transatlantic environmental, consumer, and labor dialogues, but these have had only mixed success. Indeed, the fortunes of the TABD fluctuated in the following years; the dialogue almost ceased in the early 2000s before coming back to life later in the decade, partly to try to offset the political problems then besetting the transatlantic relationship.

Beyond formalizing and making obligatory meetings among senior officials that had already been taking place on an ad hoc basis, the New Transatlantic Agenda cannot be said to have substantially improved transatlantic cooperation. Although later EU-US summits helped create pressure for progress on some issues, the increasingly frantic meeting schedule has not necessarily facilitated lasting progress on otherwise intractable problems. Even the combined pressure of regular EU-US summits, later scaled back to one a year, and the persistent nagging of the TABD could not spur negotiators to complete the initial round of talks on mutual recognition agreements in less than six years, let alone come to a real meeting of the minds on the correct approach to a problem country such as Iran.

The temptation to repackage the relationship returns periodically to US and EU officials, especially when relations appear to be under stress. In the late 1990s, tensions over a variety of political and economic issues were again on the rise. US ambivalence about European proposals for a broad new round of WTO negotiations increased European misgivings. In early 1998, therefore, Leon Brittan proposed to cap a long and brilliant career in the Commission with yet another bilateral initiative. This one, initially known as the New Transatlantic Marketplace (which had figured as one of the elements of the New Transatlantic Agenda of 1995), was carefully composed of elements, such as free trade in services, that both sides (particularly the EU) could presumably accept. It conspicuously did not include any proposals in the traditionally touchy area of agriculture.

The United States responded cautiously; the proposal met a much frostier reception in Europe. The French openly rejected the initiative on the grounds that it had not been vetted first by the Council. Others expressed concern about the advisability of some of the elements, especially efforts to achieve bilateral free trade in services at the expense of the multilateral process. As the Commission worked to finesse all these objections, the proposed New Transatlantic Marketplace was transmogrified and watered down into the Transatlantic Economic Partnership. Publicly unveiled at the May 1998 EU-US summit, the new initiative was worthy but anodyne. Its stated objective was the "intensification and extension of multilateral and bilateral cooperation." On the multilateral side, it affirmed that the EU and United States would cooperate to pursue a list of initiatives that for the most part were already under way in the WTO. On the bilateral side, the highlight was a promise to concentrate on "those barriers that really matter," especially regulatory barriers, with a nod to the efforts of the TABD. Following the New Transatlantic Agenda model, this rather general declaration was to be followed as soon as possible by a common action plan.

The next major initiative came during the administration of George W. Bush, when EU-US political relations were at an all-time low. The rift between Germany and the United States was especially deep and troubling. Gerhard Schröder, leader of the governing coalition in Berlin, narrowly won reelection in September 2002 by exploiting anti-Americanism and, especially, widespread hatred in Germany of President Bush. The US invasion of Iraq, in March 2003, brought anti-Americanism in Germany to the boil, put enormous strain on EU-US political relations, and divided the EU's member states among themselves.

The transatlantic economic relationship remained surprisingly buoyant at the time of the Iraq War, as both sides made every effort to insulate huge trade and investment flows from negative political feelings.[7] In an effort to prevent contamination of the transatlantic economic relationship and to repair German-US relations, Angela Merkel, who succeeded Schröder as chancellor in September 2005, set out to shore up transatlantic cooperation on trade and regulatory issues. Her initiative bore fruit in the Transatlantic Economic Council, launched by Bush, Merkel, and Commission president José Manuel Barroso at the EU-US summit in April 2007, during Germany's Council presidency. The Transatlantic Economic Council, which met for the first time in Washington, D.C., in November 2007, provides a platform for regular meetings among cabinet-level officials (relevant EU commissioners and US cabinet secretaries) to air a wide range of trade and regulatory concerns.

The EU-US High-Level Regulatory Cooperation Forum, established two years earlier, consists of senior officials from the Commission and US regulatory agencies who exchange views on regulatory procedures and issues. The forum meets more often (about twice a year) than does the Transatlantic Economic Council, to which it now reports. The Transatlantic Economic Council and the Regulatory Cooperation Forum provide opportunities for stakeholders—representatives of business, consumer, environmental, and other interests—to provide input, usually in sessions that follow closed-door meetings of the officials themselves.

These relatively new bodies serve a useful function and have a laudable goal: to reduce regulatory barriers to trade, remove persistent irritants in economic relations, and defuse potential aggravations before they escalate into open conflict. Topics under discussion in the council and the forum range from protecting intellectual property rights, to integrating financial markets, to encouraging investment; detailed negotiations have taken place on specific sectors such as pharmaceuticals, information and communication technology, and electrical equipment. Try as they might to soar above the fray, however, both bodies inevitably get bogged down in seemingly intractable problems.

A striking example is the EU's ban since 1997 on imports of chicken from the United States washed in chlorinated water. US and European food safety authorities have deemed that poultry covered by the ban is safe and the Commission has attempted to have the ban lifted. Stiff resistance from the EP, however, has tied the Commission's hands.[8] Frustrated by the EU's inaction and pressured by poultry producers eager for a share of the €2 billion spent annually on chicken imports into the EU, in October 2009 the US Trade Representative's office asked the WTO to establish a dispute settlement panel to hear the case.[9] The announcement of the US action coincided with a meeting in Washington, D.C., of the Transatlantic Economic Council and highlighted the inability of the council and the Regulatory Cooperation Forum to overcome relatively insignificant yet highly irritating disputes in the transatlantic economic relationship.

EU-US summits suffered the same fate. Far from providing an opportunity for the presidents of the United States, the European Council, and the

Commission to discuss high political issues of broad importance and concern, summit meetings frequently rehashed specific, long-standing disputes. President Clinton reportedly complained to his advisers: "Do I really have to talk about bananas again?"[10] President Bush, not known to be interested in the finer points of public policy, was thoroughly bored by EU-US summits. President Obama, by all accounts a policy wonk, was nonetheless uninterested in summits with his EU counterparts that failed to address substantive issues in transatlantic relations, and caused a stir in Europe when he declined to participate in a summit planned for Madrid in May 2010. The curse of the EU-US relationship, and of EU-US summits, may be the tendency of arcane economic disputes to predominate.

Nevertheless, the advent of the Obama administration presaged a dramatic improvement in transatlantic relations. The president's promise to close the prison camp in Guantanamo, launch a diplomatic initiative with Iran, and take climate change seriously was music to the ears of most Europeans. France and Germany had new, pro-American leaders (Sarkozy and Merkel, although Merkel was one of the few Europeans who seemed impervious to Obama's charm). Obama appeared more European than American in outlook. Yet even a cursory look at Obama's background and experience would have suggested that, of all recent US presidents, he had the least familiarity with Europe. Obama may have been a multilateralist at heart and been fascinated by the purpose and procedures of the EU, but he knew little about Europe and was arguably more interested in Russia, Asia, and Africa (and closer to home, Latin America).

European expectations were so high that Obama was bound to disappoint. Like previous US presidents, Obama looked to the EU for results and had little patience with procedural wrangling. Inevitably, European governments were bound to disappoint him, especially with respect to military assistance in Afghanistan. Europeans looked aghast as Obama became bogged down abroad in Afghanistan and at home in a debilitating effort to reform health care, which reminded Europeans of the superiority of their social market system. The onset of the financial crisis in the United States gave Europeans a brief opportunity to gloat before the tidal wave of foreclosures and failing banks swept all before it and the global recession set in. Obama and Merkel had a falling-out over how to respond to the crisis, with Obama advocating fiscal expansion and Merkel trying to rein in public spending. Obama seemed more European than American in his embrace of government intervention, but pursued such a policy out of necessity rather than conviction.

Monetary Union: A New Dimension in EU-US Relations
The launch of the euro entailed a major shift in the substance of the EU-US dialogue. A relationship forged in the slow-moving and compartmentalized world of trade disputes would have to evolve substantially to cope with fast-

breaking exchange rate fluctuations and international capital movements. The traditionally close relationship among Group of Seven (G7) finance ministers and central bankers (the G8 being a broader body), particularly between the United States and Britain, would also have to give way to a more complex and possibly less collegial interplay among the Eurogroup finance ministers, other EU finance ministers, the president of the European Central Bank and presidents of the non-eurozone central banks, and their US counterparts.

EU efforts to solve the conundrum of eurozone representation in global summits suggested that for the short term, decisionmaking on the EU side would be cumbersome and plagued by disputes over who would speak for whom. The risk was that European internal problems would irritate US policymakers and confirm them in their tendency to act alone rather than coordinate with the EU in finding solutions to future financial crises. The continuing role of member state finance ministries in providing International Monetary Fund resources and emergency financial assistance during crises, despite the existence of a monetary union among many of the member states, further complicated EU-US relations. As in the case of the CFSP, in times of crisis the United States was inclined to go back to its old friends for help rather than wait for the EU process to produce a response, much to the irritation of the smaller member states (both in and out of the eurozone) and the Commission.

As the euro acquired more weight on the world scene, the ECB and the US Federal Reserve learned to engage as equal partners. Their ability to work closely together became evident during the global financial crisis of 2007–2009. Indeed, the sight of the chairman of the Federal Reserve and the president of the ECB conferring during the crisis had a calming effect on jittery politicians and the markets. From the US point of view, however, the question of external representation of eurozone fiscal and economic policy is still unsatisfactory. As noted in Chapter 13, the US treasury secretary has multiple interlocutors in EU-US discussions, including the commissioner for economic and monetary affairs, the Eurogroup president, the Ecofin president, and various national finance ministers.

The financial crisis helped to bring about a realignment of international institutions, especially the IMF and the G8, to correspond with new global realities. The most significant development was the emergence of the more representative G20. Representatives of EU governments and institutions, accustomed to their overrepresentation in global institutions, are likely to face additional pressure to adjust. Whatever emerges on the global scene, informal contacts between the US Federal Reserve and the ECB, on the one hand, and the US Treasury and a shifting group of EU finance ministries, on the other, are likely to persist. In finance as in other policy areas, the EU and the United States are able to draw upon fifty years of experience and adjust again to the shifting nature of the relationship.

Transatlantic Security

In the early 1990s, the United States and its European allies resolved only temporarily the post–Cold War security dilemma of trying to maximize the EU's security identity and capability (the "Europeanist" position) and trying to maintain the status quo of US preeminence in NATO (the "Atlanticist" position). The Maastricht Treaty formula, whereby the WEU became both the prototypical defense arm of the EU and a vehicle through which the European pillar of NATO could be strengthened, was up for grabs at the 1996–1997 intergovernmental conference, which resulted in the Amsterdam Treaty. By that time, Clinton's political and military advisers had abandoned much of the previous administration's prickly resistance to the emergence of closer European cooperation within NATO and had obligingly stepped back to allow the EU's nascent CFSP to try to deal with the Yugoslav wars, a morass from which US diplomats instinctively recoiled. Paradoxically, by the mid-1990s the EU was almost uniformly Atlanticist, whereas the United States had become somewhat Europeanist. In other words, based especially on the lessons of Bosnia, erstwhile Europeanists (including the French) saw the necessity for a continuing US military presence in Europe, whereas the United States pressed its European allies to strengthen their own capability to confront security threats in Europe's backyard.

Agreement within NATO on an arrangement that would make the organization's assets available to European members for operations in which the United States did not want to participate demonstrated a new transatlantic consensus on European security and the US role in it. Of greater political importance in the aftermath of the Bosnian debacle was the outcome of the July 1997 NATO summit in Madrid, which endorsed the EU's development of a security and defense identity but asserted NATO's primacy. At the same time, EU leaders agreed in the Amsterdam Treaty to incorporate WEU peacekeeping tasks into the CFSP, thereby raising the possibility of future EU peacekeeping operations. This time there was no US diplomatic intervention (as there had been in 1991) to try to prevent a WEU-EU merger.

The Madrid NATO summit also endorsed the NATO membership applications of the Czech Republic, Poland, and Hungary. Yet the debate about NATO enlargement had angered many Europeans because of the US administration's apparently high-handed approach to one of the most important security issues in post–Cold War Europe. Essentially, the United States alone decided which Central and Eastern European countries would join NATO first and when they would do so. Related suggestions in the US Congress that EU membership was either a substitute for NATO membership or a consolation for those Central and Eastern European countries not initially admitted to NATO, together with criticism of the EU's slow enlargement process and arm's-length attitude toward Turkey, demonstrated serious misunderstanding in US political circles of the EU's nature and procedures. Although intensely irritating for

Europeans, US conduct of NATO enlargement and critical or erroneous comments about EU enlargement did not unravel the solid transatlantic consensus on the post–Cold War European security structure that seemed to exist at the end of the 1990s. That consensus seemed to fray only after the change of administration in the United States, when George W. Bush came to power.

Bush's inauguration in January 2001 ushered in a period of great difficulty in the transatlantic relationship. Bush knew little and cared less about the EU; those around him who knew anything about the EU were generally disdainful of it. The so-called neoconservatives, who provided the intellectual rationale for Bush's foreign policy, tended to dismiss the process of European integration as deeply flawed (after all, they valued national sovereignty above all else) and the outcome of European integration as derisory. They scoffed at the EU's economic sluggishness and foreign policy failings, especially in the Balkans in the late 1990s. In other words, they were ardent Euroskeptics.

Robert Kagan, a prominent neoconservative, touched a raw nerve in the EU with his book *Of Paradise and Power,* a stinging critique of the nature of European integration and what followed logically from it: the EU's multilateralist worldview.[11] According to Kagan, the EU engaged in endless negotiation in search of artful compromise because its member states, many of them former great powers, lacked the ability and had lost the will to do anything else. The United States, by contrast, was bound to act decisively and unilaterally in defense of its interests because it had the means and the determination to do so. In his view, the differences between the United States and the EU were historical, philosophical, and structural. They were also unbridgeable. As Kagan put it so pithily, America is from Mars, Europe from Venus.

Bush's abrupt dismissal of major international initiatives such as the Kyoto Protocol and International Criminal Court was consistent with a profoundly conservative outlook on the sanctity of national sovereignty as well as a socioeconomic philosophy that elevated narrowly perceived corporate interests above all else. The apparently selfish and sanctimonious outlook of Bush and those around him was bad enough for the Europeans; what made it extremely damaging for transatlantic relations and dangerous for the world as a whole was the administration's reaction to the terrorist attacks of September 2001 on the United States. The EU rallied in support of the United States in the aftermath of the attacks. Only diehard anti-Americans and fervent pacifists (sometimes one and the same thing) opposed the US war in Afghanistan. If anything, many European governments regretted that the United States had not at first accepted their offers of military assistance.

The successful efforts of key members of the US administration to exploit the terrorist attacks to press for an invasion of Iraq greatly exacerbated the deepening rift in transatlantic relations. Yet member states differed in their responses to America's march to war, which began in the summer of 2002 and became unstoppable by early 2003. Britain and France, long at loggerheads over policy toward Iraq, took diametrically opposite positions on the looming war. Britain (more precisely, Prime Minister Tony Blair) wholeheartedly supported the United States, while France refused to back a UN resolution intended to bless the imminent invasion. As noted earlier, German chancellor Schröder adamantly opposed the US war effort. The Italian and Spanish governments strongly supported the US position, as did almost all of the Central and Eastern European candidate states. That split prompted US defense secretary Donald Rumsfeld's infamous quip about the division between "old Europe" (France and Germany) and "new Europe" (the prospective member states).

For Rumsfeld and his ilk, the divisions in Europe over Iraq merely reinforced a tendency to dismiss the EU as irrelevant. Some Europeans fretted that the United States was attempting to set member states against each other and weaken the EU politically. In fact, the administration did not care enough about the EU to adopt such a strategy. Moreover, the EU seemed perfectly capable of tearing itself apart without US assistance. What really irritated EU officials and politicians was precisely that the Bush administration was so dismissive of them.

The nonexistence of weapons of mass destruction in Iraq (the ostensible justification for the war), US mishandling of the occupation, and apparent US indifference to the simmering Israeli-Palestinian conflict soon united Europeans in their condemnation of the United States. Most Europeans could not resist taking malicious pleasure in America's military misfortunes despite the suffering of the Iraqi people. Blair became more isolated in his own country and in the EU; Chirac grew more openly anti-American; and Schröder had little incentive to mend fences with Washington (not that he received any encouragement from the US administration to do so).

The fallout from Iraq also shattered the fragile transatlantic consensus on the emerging European Security and Defense Policy. Whereas the Clinton administration had accepted that an independent European military capability was compatible with NATO and ultimately in America's interest, the Bush administration was extremely skeptical, seeing it instead as a neo-Gaulist plot to undermine NATO and weaken the United States. Washington's distrust of European defense initiatives was tempered only by the administration's certainty that they were bound to fail. In the aftermath of the Iraq War, the French played into the administration's hands by reverting (unofficially) to an anti-American and anti-NATO rationale for the ESDP. Far from permanently dividing the EU, however, the war in Iraq may have emboldened member states to accelerate their plans for a common defense policy, although not necessarily for the reasons espoused by France.

Most Europeans were incredulous when they heard of Bush's election victory in November 2004: how could Americans give another four years in office to a president whose economic policies were so wrong and whose military adventures were so dangerous? For their part, many Americans wondered how Spanish voters could have caved in to terrorism and voted the Conservatives out of office after the Madrid bombings in March 2004. Clearly, there were gross misperceptions on both sides of the Atlantic: whereas many Europeans decried the American electorate's stupidity, many Americans decried the Spanish electorate's spinelessness. Such was the sorry state of transatlantic relations in the middle of the decade.

Nevertheless, the two sides could at least agree on the perils confronting them in an increasingly unstable world, if not on how best to respond internationally. The EU security strategy, endorsed by the European Council in December 2003 in the aftermath of the war in Iraq, identified the proliferation of weapons of mass destruction, the menace of failed states, and the spread of terrorism as the main threats confronting Europe (and the West). Acting on behalf of the EU and in the interest of the Unites States as well, Britain, France, and Germany—the three most influential member states—attempted in mid-decade, by applying diplomatic pressure and offering economic inducement, to convince Iran not to develop a nuclear weapons capability. The United States was skeptical of the Europeans' prospects but had little to offer when it came to dealing with Iran except the threat of war, a prospect uncongenial to most Americans, especially after the Iraq imbroglio.

One of the few bright spots in an otherwise gloomy EU-US relationship during the Bush presidency was the extent of cooperation between the two sides on measures to combat terrorism, ranging from visas to border controls to sharing intelligence. Although the US authorities have occasionally been high-handed in their pursuit of "homeland security," and despite the negative consequences of the US Patriot Act for trade and citizens' rights, EU officials have generally been understanding and cooperative in their approach to these issues. For example, the EU agreed to comply with US demands for information on passengers traveling to the United States, much to the chagrin of the EP, which took the Commission to task for its apparent violation of the EU data privacy directive. Europeans' horror at the attacks on the United States in September 2001, and the bombings in Madrid in March 2004 and London in July 2005, generated broad transatlantic agreement on specific measures to combat terrorism.

As noted earlier, Europeans rejoiced in Obama's election and looked forward to a renaissance in EU-US relations. On the security side, however, disputes over strategy and the commitment of troops to Afghanistan tarnished the reinvigorated transatlantic relationship. Vast differences in spending, commitment, and capabilities continued to divide the US and European allies within NATO and separate the United States from the EU. The Obama administration and the EU were generally in accord on issues such as dealing with Iran and ameliorating the Israeli-Palestinian conflict, but a wary public and Congress kept the administration in check. On one thing, at least, the United States wholeheartedly supported the EU: the development of the Common Security and Defense Policy. The United States also welcomed the institutional innovations in the Lisbon Treaty and looked forward to working with the standing European Council president and the High Representative for Foreign Affairs and Security. US misgivings about European efforts to develop a defense identity and capacity were long gone, but US doubts about the EU's ability to realize those efforts remained as entrenched as ever.

▓ Bound to Be Close

In looking at the long, complicated, and fractious relationship between the world's two greatest economic powers, it is clear that permanent harmony is neither achievable nor, perhaps, desirable. In most significant respects, the relationship remains sound. The overwhelming importance of the economic ties and the slow but definite growth of a strong institutional framework make it difficult to conceive of a major breakdown in EU-US relations. However, many of the most visible disputes between the two arise from real differences in social and political outlook. These are unlikely to yield to any grand initiatives; convergence, if it occurs, will happen incrementally and over time.

A recurring theme in EU-US economic dialogue has been the importance of regulatory cooperation, whereby the two sides try to find a common approach to thorny issues, thus eliminating disputes in advance. This is clearly a promising approach that has particular potential in areas where both sides are not already burdened with long-standing institutional differences. It would be a mistake to imagine, however, that true convergence is possible in regulating the economies of two societies with vastly different histories, geographies, demographics, and social philosophies.

One could argue that such an outcome is not even necessarily ideal. A single market is one of the guiding tenets of the EU, faced as it is with the challenge of fostering integration amid intractable linguistic and historical barriers. The United States, with a single language, a single currency covering its entire territory, and a singularly mobile population, has been much more willing to tolerate certain residual regulatory barriers. And in areas where it chooses to regulate, the United States has a federal regulatory apparatus far more powerful than anything most European governments would be willing to cede to Brussels. Under the circumstances, it is hard to argue that the benefits of eliminating remaining trade barriers from a relationship in which the overwhelming majority of trade already flows unhindered would be greater than the costs of trying to impose a "one-size-fits-all" economic regime, even if such a regime could be devised.

Accordingly, persistent efforts to make incremental progress on hard issues (such as agricultural trade), coupled with a willingness to live through occasional acrimonious rows in the WTO without paralyzing other important areas of cooperation, are likely to remain the preferred formula for managing the EU-US relationship. Periodic announcements of grand new initiatives are part of the picture and occasionally aid in achieving breakthroughs on particular issues. The risk, of course, is that an unending line of such initiatives will lead to "meeting fatigue" among policymakers and perhaps strain institutional resources with increasingly trivial processes such as "dialogues" among various social groups or redundant efforts to increase social and cultural exchanges. On balance, nevertheless, such initiatives appear to serve the important purpose of reaffirming that both sides still care about each other and that what they have in common far outweighs the remaining differences, irritating though they may be. As seen in the WTO, despite their differences, the United States and the EU are bound to remain close collaborators, not only because of the importance of their bilateral relationship but also because of the need to defend their common interests and approaches in a world where democratic values and functioning market economies remain largely ideals rather than realities.

▓ Notes

1. Joseph Quinlan, "The Shape of the Future: The Transatlantic Economy by 2025," policy brief (Washington, DC: German Marshall Fund of the United States, October 2008), p. 2.

2. See Thomas S. Mowle, *Allies at Odds? The United States and the European Union* (Basingstoke: Palgrave Macmillan, 2004); Jeffrey J. Anderson, G. John Ikenberry, and Thomas Risse, eds., *The End of the West? Crisis and Change in the Atlantic Order,* 2nd ed. (Ithaca: Cornell University Press, 2008).

3. See Michael Calingaert, *European Integration Revisited: Progress, Prospects, and US Interests* (Boulder: Westview, 1996), pp. 151–206; Kevin Featherstone and Roy H. Ginsberg, *The United States and the European Union in the 1990s: Partners in Transition* (New York: St. Martin's, 1996); and John Peterson, *Europe and America in the 1990s: The Prospects for Partnership,* 2nd ed. (London: Elgar, 1993).

4. US Department of State, "Declaration on US-EC Relations," November 11, 1990.

5. On the US démarche, see John Newhouse, "The Diplomatic Round: A Collective Nervous Breakdown," *New Yorker,* September 7, 1991, p. 92.

6. Bureau of Public Affairs, "The New Transatlantic Agenda and Joint EU-US Action Plan," *Department of State Dispatch* 6, no. 49 (December 3, 1995).

7. For an upbeat account of the state of transatlantic economic relations, see Joseph P. Quinlan, *Drifting Apart or Growing Together? The Primacy of the Transatlantic Economy* (Washington, DC: Center for Transatlantic Relations, 2003).

8. See European Parliament, http://www.europarl.europa.eu/sides/getDoc.do?type =IM-PRESS&reference=20080528IPR30273&language=EN.

9. See US Trade Representative, http://www.ustr.gov/about-us/press-office/press-releases/2009/october/united-states-requests-wto-panel-challenge-eu-rest.

10. Quoted in Bruce Stokes, "Balance of Payments: Transatlantic Bridge Building," *Congress Daily,* June 4, 2009.

11. Robert Kagan, *Of Paradise and Power: America and Europe in the New World Order* (New York: Knopf, 2003).

Acronyms

ACP	African, Caribbean, and Pacific
AFSJ	Area of Freedom, Security, and Justice
ALDE	Alliance of Liberals and Democrats for Europe
APEC	Asia Pacific Economic Cooperation
ASEAN	Association of Southeast Asian Nations
ASEM	Asia-Europe Meeting
Benelux	Belgium, the Netherlands, Luxembourg
BSE	bovine spongiform encephalopathy
CAP	Common Agricultural Policy
CCP	Common Commercial Policy
CE	European Conformity
CFI	Court of First Instance
CFSP	Common Foreign and Security Policy
CJD	Creutzfeld-Jakob disease
CMO	Common Market Organization
COPA	Committee of Professional Agricultural Organizations
CoR	Committee of the Regions
Coreper	Committee of Permanent Representatives
COSAC	Conférence des Organes Spécialisés dans les Affaires Communautaires et Européennes des Parlements de l'Union Européenne (Conference of Community and European Affairs Committees of Parliaments of the European Union)
CSDP	Common Security and Defense Policy
CTMO	Community Trademark Office
DG	directorate-general
EAFRD	European Agricultural Fund for Rural Development
EAGF	European Agricultural Guarantee Fund
EAGGF	European Agricultural Guarantee and Guidance Fund
EBA	Everything but Arms
EBRD	European Bank for Reconstruction and Development
EC	European Community
ECA	Court of Auditors
ECB	European Central Bank

ECHO	European Community Humanitarian Office
ECHR	European Convention for the Protection of Human Rights and Fundamental Freedoms
ECJ	European Court of Justice
Ecofin	Economic and Financial Affairs Council
ECR	European Conservatives and Reformists
ECSC	European Coal and Steel Community
EDC	European Defense Community
EDF	European Development Fund
EEA	European Economic Area
EEC	European Economic Community
EFD	Europe of Freedom and Democracy
EFTA	European Free Trade Association
EIB	European Investment Bank
EIF	European Investment Fund
EMI	European Monetary Institute
EMS	European Monetary System
EMU	Economic and Monetary Union
ENP	European Neighborhood Policy
EP	European Parliament
EPC	European Political Cooperation
EPP	European People's Party
EPP-ED	European People's Party–European Democrats
Erasmus	European Community Action Scheme for the Mobility of University Students
ERM II	exchange rate mechanism
ESC	Economic and Social Committee
ESDP	European Security and Defense Policy
ESPRIT	European Strategic Program for Research and Development in Information Technology
ETUC	European Trade Union Confederation
EU	European Union
Euratom	European Atomic Energy Community
Europol	European police agency
FDI	foreign direct investment
FSAP	Financial Services Action Plan
G4	Group of Four (Britain, France, Germany, and Italy)
G7	Group of Seven (leading industrial economies)
G8	Group of Eight (leading industrial economies)
G20	Group of Twenty (leading global economies)
GAC	General Affairs Council
GATS	General Agreement on Trade in Services

GATT	General Agreement on Tariffs and Trade
GDP	gross domestic product
GMO	genetically modified organism
GNI	gross national income
GSP	Generalized System of Preferences
GUE-NGL	European United Left–Nordic Green Left
IGC	intergovernmental conference
IMF	International Monetary Fund
IPCC	Intergovernmental Panel on Climate Change
ITA	Information Technology Agreement
JHA	justice and home affairs
LDCs	least-developed countries
LIFE	Financial Instrument for the Environment
Lingua	Action Program to Promote Foreign Language Competence in the European Community
MED	Mediterranean
MEP	member of the European Parliament
Mercosur	Mercado Común del Sur (Southern Common Market)
NAFTA	North American Free Trade Agreement
NATO	North Atlantic Treaty Organization
NGO	nongovernmental organization
OECD	Organization for Economic Cooperation and Development
OEEC	Organization for European Economic Cooperation
OLAF	Office européen de Lutte Anti-Fraude (European Anti-Fraud Office)
OMC	open method of coordination
OSCE	Organization for Security and Cooperation in Europe
PES	Party of European Socialists
QMV	qualified majority voting
R&D	research and development
REACH	Registration, Evaluation, Authorization, and Restriction of Chemicals
SAARC	South Asian Association for Regional Cooperation
SADC	Southern African Development Community
S&D	Socialists and Democrats
SAP	Stabilization and Association Process
SEA	Single European Act
SGP	Stability and Growth Pact
SIS	Schengen Information System
SITCEN	Joint Situation Center
SMEs	small and medium-sized enterprises
TABD	Transatlantic Business Dialogue

TACIS	Technical Assistance for the Commonwealth of Independent States
Tempus	Trans-European Mobility Scheme for University Students
TEN	trans-European network
TEN-E	trans-European energy network
TRIPs	Trade-Related Aspects of Intellectual Property Rights
UK	United Kingdom
UN	United Nations
US	United States
VAT	value-added tax
WEU	Western European Union
WTO	World Trade Organization

Bibliography

Acheson, Dean. *Present at the Creation: My Years in the State Department.* New York: Norton, 1969.

Andenas, M., and J. A. Usher. *The Treaty of Nice and Beyond: Enlargement and Constitutional Reform.* Portland: Hart, 2003.

Anderson, Jeffrey J., G. John Ikenberry, and Thomas Risse, eds. *The End of the West? Crisis and Change in the Atlantic Order.* 2nd ed. Ithaca: Cornell University Press, 2008.

Arnull, Anthony, *The European Union and Its Court of Justice.* 2nd ed. Oxford: Oxford University Press, 2006.

Atkin, Nocholas. *The Fifth French Republic.* Basingstoke: Palgrave Macmillan, 2005.

Bacon, Kelyn, ed. *European Community Law of State Aid.* Oxford: Oxford University Press, 2009.

Baimbridge, Mark, ed. *The 1975 Referendum on Europe.* Vol. 1, *Reflections of the Participants.* Exeter: Imprint Academic, 2006.

Baimbridge, Mark, Andrew Mullen, and Philip Whyman. *The 1975 Referendum on Europe.* Vol. 2, *Current Analysis and Lessons for the Future.* Exeter: Imprint Academic, 2006.

Bark, Dennis, and David Gress. *A History of West Germany.* Vol. 1, *1945–1963.* Oxford: Blackwell, 1989.

Baun, Michael. *An Imperfect Union: The Maastricht Treaty and the New Politics of European Integration.* Boulder: Westview, 1996.

———. *A Wider Europe: The Process and Politics of European Union Enlargement.* Lanham: Rowman and Littlefield, 2000.

Beach, Derek, and Colette Mazzucelli, eds. *Leadership in the Big Bangs of European Integration.* Basingstoke: Palgrave Macmillan, 2007.

Behrman, Greg. *The Most Noble Adventure: The Marshall Plan and the Reconstruction of Postwar Europe.* New York: Free Press, 2007.

Bellamy, Richard, and Alex Warleigh, eds. *Citizenship and Governance in the European Union.* London: Continuum, 2001.

Bergland, Sten, Joakim Ekman, Henri Vogt, and Frank Aarebrot. *The Making of the European Union: Foundations, Institutions, and Future Trends.* Northampton: Elgar, 2006.

Bieber, Roland, Jean-Paul Jacqué, and Joseph Weiler, eds. *An Ever Closer Union: A Critical Analysis of the Draft Treaty Establishing European Union.* European Perspectives Series. Luxembourg: Office for Official Publications of the European Community, 1985.

Bieber, Roland, and Jörg Monar, eds. *Justice and Home Affairs in the European Union.* Brussels: European Interuniversity Press, 1995.

Biscop, Sven, and Jan Joel Andersson, eds. *The EU and the European Security Strategy: Forging a Global Europe.* London: Routledge, 2008.

Bitsch, Marie-Thérèse. *Histoire de la construction européenne de 1945 à nos jours.* Brussels: Editions Complexe, 2004.

Buchan, David. *Energy and Climate Change: Europe at the Crossroads.* Oxford: Oxford University Press, 2009.

Buiter, Willem H., Giancarlo Corsetti, and Paolo A. Pesenti. *Financial Markets and European Monetary Cooperation: The Lessons of the 1992–93 Exchange Rate Mechanism Crisis.* Cambridge: Cambridge University Press, 2001.

Bullock, Alan. *The Life and Times of Ernest Bevin.* Vol. 3, *Ernest Bevin: Foreign Secretary, 1948–1951.* London: Heinemann, 1983.

Calingaert, Michael. *European Integration Revisited: Progress, Prospects, and US Interests.* Boulder: Westview, 1996.

Çarkoğlu, Ali, and Barry Rubin, eds. *Turkey and the European Union: Domestic Politics, Economic Integration, and International Dynamics.* London: Cass, 2003.

Cecchini, Paolo. *The European Challenge, 1992.* Aldershot: Wildwood, 1988.

Chang, Michele. *Monetary Integration in the European Union.* Basingstoke: Palgrave Macmillan, 2009.

Chryssochoou, Dimitris. *Democracy in the European Union.* New York: Tauris, 2000.

Cini, Michelle. *The European Commission: Leadership, Organisation, and Culture in the EU Administration.* Manchester: Manchester University Press, 1996.

Cini, Michelle, and Lee McGowan. *Competition Policy in the European Union.* 2nd ed. Basingstoke: Palgrave Macmillan, 2008.

Closa, Carlos, and Paul M. Heywood. *Spain and the European Union.* Basingstoke: Palgrave Macmillan, 2004.

Cockfield, Arthur. *The European Union: Creating the Single Market.* Chichester: Wiley, 1994.

Coen, David, and Jeremy Richardson, eds. *Lobbying the European Union: Institutions, Actors, and Issues.* Oxford: Oxford University Press, 2009.

Corbett, Richard, Francis Jacobs, and Michael Shackleton. *The European Parliament.* 7th ed. London: Harper, 2007.

Craig, Paul, and Gráinne de Burca. *EU Law: Text, Cases, and Materials.* 4th ed. Oxford: Oxford University Press, 2008.

Cremona, Marise, ed. *The Enlargement of the European Union.* Oxford: Oxford University Press, 2003.

Daddow, Oliver. *Harold Wilson and European Integration: Britain's Second Application to Join the EEC.* London: Routledge, 2002.

De Burca, Gráinne, and J. H. H. Weiler, eds. *The European Court of Justice.* Oxford: Oxford University Press, 2002.

de Gaulle, Charles. *Mémoires d'espoir.* Paris: Edition Omnibus, 1999.

De Ruyt, Jean. *L'Acte Unique Européen: Commentaire.* 2nd ed. Brussels: Editions de l'Université de Bruxelles, 1996.

Delors, Jacques. *Mémoires.* Paris: Plon, 2004.

Den Boer, Monica, ed. *Schengen: Judicial Cooperation and Policy Coordination.* Maastricht: European Institute for Public Administration, 1997.

Diez, Thomas, Mathias Albert, and Stephan Stetter, eds. *The European Union and Border Conflicts: The Power of Integration and Association.* Cambridge: Cambridge University Press, 2008.

Dinan, Desmond. *Europe Recast: A History of European Union.* Boulder: Lynne Rienner, 2004.

———. *Ever Closer Union? An Introduction to the European Community.* Boulder: Lynne Rienner, 1994.

Drake, Helen. *Jacques Delors: Perspectives on a European Leader.* London: Routledge, 2000.

Duchêne, François. *Jean Monnet: The First Statesman of Interdependence.* New York: Norton, 1994.

Dumoulin, Michel, ed. *Plans des temps de guerre pour l'Europe de l'après guerre, 1940–1947.* Brussels: Bruylant, 1995.

Dyson, Kenneth, ed. *The Euro at Ten: Europeanization, Power, and Convergence.* Oxford: Oxford University Press, 2008.

Dyson, Kenneth, and Kevin Featherstone. *The Road to Maastricht: Negotiating Economic and Monetary Union.* Oxford: Oxford University Press, 1998.

Egan, Michelle. *Constructing a European Market: Standards, Regulation, and Governance.* Oxford: Oxford University Press, 2001.

Egeberg, M., ed. *Multilevel Union Administration: The Transformation of Executive Politics in Europe.* Basingstoke: Palgrave Macmillan, 2006.

Eichengreen, Barry. *The European Economy Since 1945: Coordinated Capitalism and Beyond.* Princeton: Princeton University Press, 2007.

Endo, Ken. *The Presidency of the European Commission Under Jacques Delors: The Politics of Shared Leadership.* New York: St. Martin's, 1999.

Endow, Aparajita. *France, Germany, and the European Union: Maastricht and After.* Delhi: Aakar, 2005.

Eppink, Derek-Jan. *Life of a European Mandarin: Inside the Commission.* Tielt: Lannoo, 2008.

Eriksen, Erik Oddvar, John Erik Fossum, and Agustín José Meníndez, eds. *Developing a Constitution for Europe.* London: Routledge, 2004.

Feld, Werner. *West Germany and the European Community: Changing Interests and Competing Policy Objectives.* New York: Praeger, 1981.

Fella, Stefano. *New Labour and the European Union: Policy Strategy, Policy Transition, and the Amsterdam Treaty Negotiation.* Aldershot: Ashgate, 2000.

Fink, Carole, and Bernd Schaefer, eds. *Ostpolitik, 1969–1974: European and Global Responses.* Cambridge: Cambridge University Press, 2008.

Føllesdal, Andreas, and Peter Koslowski, eds. *Democracy and the European Union.* Berlin: Springer Verlag, 1997.

Fransen, Frederic J. *The Supranational Politics of Jean Monnet: Ideas and Origins of the European Community.* Westport: Greenwood, 2001.

Fursdon, Edward. *The European Defense Community: A History.* New York: St. Martin's, 1980.

Galloway, D. *The Treaty of Nice and Beyond: Reality and Illusions of Power in the EU.* Sheffield: Sheffield Academic, 2001.

Garzon, Isabelle. *Reforming the Common Agricultural Policy: History of a Paradigm Change.* Basingstoke: Palgrave Macmillan, 2007.

Gazzo, Marina, ed. *Towards European Union: From the "Crocodile" to the European Council in Milan.* 2 vols. Brussels: Agence Europe, 1985 and 1986.

George, Stephen. *An Awkward Partner: Britain in the European Community.* Oxford: Oxford University Press, 1990.

Gerbet, Pierre. *La Construction de l'Europe.* Paris: Imprimerie Nationale, 1999.

———. *La Genèse du Plan Schuman: Des origines à la déclaration du 9 mai 1950.* Lausanne: Centre de Recherches Européennes, Ecole des H.E.C., University of Lausanne, 1962.

Gilbert, Mark F. *Surpassing Realism: The Politics of European Integration Since 1945.* Lanham: Rowman and Littlefield, 2003.

Gillingham, John R. *Coal, Steel, and the Rebirth of Europe, 1945–1955: The Germans and French from Ruhr Conflict to Economic Community.* Cambridge: Cambridge University Press, 1991.

———. *European Integration, 1950–2003: Superstate or New Market Economy?* Cambridge: Cambridge University Press, 2003.

Gimbel, John. *The Origins of the Marshall Plan.* Stanford: Stanford University Press, 1976.

Grabbe, Heather. *The EU's Transformative Power: Europeanization Through Conditionality in Central and Eastern Europe.* Basingstoke: Palgrave Macmillan, 2006.

Griffiths, Richard. *Europe's First Constitution.* London: Federal Trust, 2001.

———, ed. *Explorations in OEEC History.* Paris: OECD Publishing, 1997.

Gstöhl, Sieglinde. *Reluctant Europeans: Norway, Sweden, and Switzerland in the Process of Integration.* Boulder: Lynne Rienner, 2002.

Hadden, Tom. *The Responsibility to Assist: EU Policy and Practice in Crisis-Management Operations Under European Security and Defence Policy.* Portland: Hart, 2009.

Hannay, David, ed. *Britain's Entry into the European Community: Report on the Negotiations of 1970–1972 by Sir Con O'Neill.* London: Routledge, 2000.

Hanrieder, Wolfram. *Germany, America, Europe: Forty Years of German Foreign Policy.* New Haven: Yale University Press, 1989.

Hantrais, Linda. *Social Policy in the European Union.* 3rd ed. Basingstoke: Palgrave 2007.

Hayes-Renshaw, Fiona, and Helen Wallace. *The Council of Ministers.* 2nd ed. Basingstoke: Palgrave Macmillan, 2006.

Hayward, Jack, ed. *Leaderless Europe.* Oxford: Oxford University Press, 2008.

Heisenberg, Dorothy. *The Mark of the Bundesbank: Germany's Role in European Monetary Cooperation.* Boulder: Lynne Rienner, 1999.

Henderson, Karen, ed. *Back to Europe: Central and Eastern Europe and the European Union.* London: Routledge, 1998.

Hill, Berkeley, and Sophia Davidova. *Understanding the Common Agricultural Policy.* London: Earthscan, 2010.

Hitchcock, William I. *The Struggle for Europe: The Turbulent History of a Divided Continent, 1945–2002.* New York: Doubleday, 2003.

Hix, Simon. *What's Wrong with the Europe Union and How to Fix It.* Cambridge: Polity, 2008.

Hogan, Michael. *The Marshall Plan: America, Britain, and the Reconstruction of Western Europe, 1947–1953.* Cambridge: Cambridge University Press, 1987.

Holland, Martin. *Common Foreign and Security Policy: The Record and Reforms.* London: Pinter, 1997.

Hooghe, Liesbet, ed. *Cohesion Policy and European Integration: Building Multi-Level Governance.* Oxford: Oxford University Press, 1996.

———. *The European Commission and the Integration of Europe: Images of Governance.* Cambridge: Cambridge University Press, 2001.

Hörber, Thomas. *The Foundations of Europe: European Integration Ideas in France, Germany, and Britain in the 1950s.* Wiesbaden: Vs Verlag, 2006.

Horne, Alastair. *Harold Macmillan.* Vol. 2. New York: Viking, 1989.

Hosli, Madeline O. *The Euro: A Concise Introduction to European Monetary Integration.* Boulder: Lynne Rienner, 2005.

Howorth, Jolyon. *Security and Defence Policy in the European Union.* Basingstoke: Palgrave Macmillan, 2007.

Howorth, Jolyon, and John T. S. Keeler. *Defending Europe: The EU, NATO, and the Quest for European Autonomy.* Basingstoke: Palgrave Macmillan, 2003.

Issing, Otmar. *The Birth of the Euro.* Cambridge: Cambridge University Press, 2009.

Jacoby, Wade. *The Enlargement of the European Union and NATO: Ordering from the Menu in Central Europe.* Cambridge: Cambridge University Press, 2006.

Jenkins, Roy. *European Diary, 1977–1981.* London: Collins, 1989.

———. *Life at the Centre.* London: Macmillan, 1991.

Joly, Marc. *Le Mythe Jean Monnet: Contribution à une sociologie historique de la construction européenne.* Paris: CNRS Science Politique, 2007.

Jouve, Edmond. *Le Général de Gaulle et la construction de l'Europe (1940–1966).* Paris: Librairie Générale de Droit et de Jurisprudence, R. Pichon et R. Durand-Auzias, 1967.

Judge, David, and David Earnshaw. *The European Parliament.* 2nd ed. Basingstoke: Palgrave Macmillan, 2008.

Judt, Tony. *Postwar: A History of Europe Since 1945.* London: Penguin, 2005.

Kagan, Robert. *Of Paradise and Power: America and Europe in the New World Order.* New York: Knopf, 2003.

Katz, Richard S., and Bernhard Wessels, eds. *The European Parliament, the National Parliaments, and European Integration.* Oxford: Oxford University Press, 1999.

Kenen, Peter B. *Economic and Monetary Union in Europe: Moving Beyond Maastricht.* Cambridge: Cambridge University Press, 1995.

Keohane, Robert O., and Stanley Hoffmann, eds. *The New European Community: Decisionmaking and Institutional Change.* Boulder: Westview, 1991.

Killick, John. *The United States and European Reconstruction, 1945–1960.* Chicago: Routledge, 2000.

Kolodziej, Edward. *French International Policy Under de Gaulle and Pompidou: The Politics of Grandeur.* Ithaca: Cornell University Press, 1974.

Kreppel, Amie. *The European Parliament and Supranational Party System: A Study in Institutional Development.* Cambridge: Cambridge University Press, 2002.

Kühnhardt, Ludger. *Crises in European Integration: Challenge and Response, 1945–2005.* New York: Berghahn, 2009.

Kusterer, Hermann. *Der Kanzler und der General.* Baden-Baden: Klett-Cotta, 1995.

LaGro, Esra, and Knud Erik Jorgensen, eds. *Turkey and the European Union: Prospects for a Difficult Encounter.* Basingstoke: Palgrave Macmillan, 2007.

Laursen, Finn, ed. *The Amsterdam Treaty: National Preference Formation, Interstate Bargaining, and Outcome.* Odense: Odense University Press, 2002.

———, ed. *The Ratification of the Maastricht Treaty: Issues, Debates, and Future Implications.* New York: Springer, 1994.

———, ed. *The Rise and Fall of the EU's Constitutional Treaty.* Leiden: Brill, 2008.

———, ed. *The Treaty of Nice: Actor Preferences, Bargaining, and Institutional Choice.* Leiden: Brill, 2006.

Laursen, Finn, and Sophie Vanhoonacker, eds. *The Intergovernmental Conference on Political Union.* Maastricht: European Institute of Public Administration, 1992.

Legoll, Paul. *Charles de Gaulle et Konrad Adenauer: La Cordiale entente.* Paris: Editions L'Harmattan, 2004.

Leonardi, Robert. *Cohesion Policy in the European Union: The Building of Europe.* Basingstoke: Palgrave Macmillan, 2005.

Libal, Michael. *Limits of Persuasion: Germany and the Yugoslav Crisis, 1991–1992.* Westport: Praeger, 1997.

Lipgens, Walter. *History of European Integration.* 2 vols. London: Oxford University Press, 1982 and 1986.

Loriaux, Michael. *European Union and the Deconstruction of the Rhineland Frontier.* Cambridge: Cambridge University Press, 2008.

Loth, W., ed. *Crises and Compromises: The European Project, 1963–1969.* Baden-Baden: Nomos, 2001.

Ludlow, N. Piers. *Dealing with Britain: The Six and the First UK Application to the EEC.* Cambridge: Cambridge University Press, 1997.

———. *The European Community and the Crises of the 1960s: The Gaullist Challenge.* London: Routledge, 2006.

———, ed. *European Integration and the Cold War: Ostpolitik-Westpolitik, 1965–1967.* London: Routledge, 2007.

Luif, P. *On the Road to Brussels: The Political Dimension of Austria's, Finland's, and Sweden's Road to Accession to the European Union.* Vienna: Austrian Institute for International Affairs, 1995.

Lundestad, Geir. *"Empire" by Integration: The United States and European Integration, 1945–1997.* Oxford: Oxford University Press, 1998.

Lynch, Frances. *France and the International Economy: From Vichy to the Treaty of Rome.* London: Routledge, 1997.

Lynch, Philip, Nanette Neuwahl, and G. Wyn Rees, eds. *Reforming the European Union: From Maastricht to Amsterdam.* London: Longman, 2000.

MacLennan, Julio Crespo. *Spain and the Process of European Integration, 1957–85.* Basingstoke: Palgrave Macmillan, 2001.

Mahan, Erin. *Kennedy, de Gaulle and Western Europe.* Basingstoke: Palgrave, 2003.

Mahant, Edelgard. *Birthmarks of Europe: The Origins of the European Community Reconsidered.* Aldershot: Ashgate, 2004.

Maier, Charles S. *The Marshall Plan and Germany: West German Development Within the Framework of the European Recovery Program.* New York: Berg, 1991.

Marjolin, Robert. *Architect of European Unity: Memoirs, 1911–1986.* London: Weidenfeld and Nicolson, 1989.

Marsh, David. *The Euro: The Politics of the New Global Currency.* New Haven: Yale University Press, 2009.

Maurer, Andreas, and Wolfgang Wessels, eds. *National Parliaments on Their Ways to Europe: Losers or Latecomers?* Baden-Baden: Nomos Verlag, 2001.

Mayhew, Alan. *Recreating Europe: The European Union's Policy Towards Central and Eastern Europe.* Cambridge: Cambridge University Press, 1998.

Mayne, Richard J. *The Recovery of Europe, 1945–1973.* Garden City: Anchor, 1973.

Mazzucelli, Colette. *France and Germany at Maastricht: Politics and Negotiations to Create the European Union.* New York: Garland, 1997.

McAllister, Richard. *European Union.* 2nd ed. London: Routledge, 2009.

McCormick, John. *Environmental Policy in the European Union.* Basingstoke: Palgrave, 2001.

Menon, Anand. *Europe: The State of the Union.* London: Atlantic, 2008.

Meny, Yves ed. *Adjusting to Europe: The Impact of the European Union on National Institutions and Policies.* London: Routledge, 1996.

Middlemass, Keith. *Orchestrating Europe: The Informal Politics of the European Union, 1973–95.* London: Fontana, 1995.

Miles, Lee, ed. *The European Union and the Nordic Countries.* New York: Routledge, 1996.

Milward, Alan S. *The European Rescue of the Nation-State.* 2nd ed. London: Routledge, 2000.

———. *The Reconstruction of Western Europe, 1945–51.* London: Methuen, 1984.

————. *The United Kingdom and the European Community.* Vol. 1, *The Rise and Fall of a National Strategy, 1945–1963.* London: Cass, 2002.

Milward, Alan S., et al. *The Frontier of National Sovereignty: History and Theory, 1945–1992.* London: Routledge, 1993.

Mioche, Philippe. *Le Plan Monnet: Genèse et élaboration, 1941–1947.* Paris: Publications de la Sorbonne, 1995.

Molle, Willem. *The Economics of European Integration: Theory, Practice, Policy.* 5th ed. Aldershot: Ashgate, 2006.

Monar, J., and W. Wessels, eds. *The European Union After the Treaty of Amsterdam.* London: Continuum, 2001.

Monnet, Jean. *Memoirs.* Garden City: Doubleday, 1978.

Moravscik, Andrew. *The Choice for Europe: Social Purpose and State Power from Messina to Maastricht.* Ithaca: Cornell University Press, 1998.

Morgan, Annette. *From Summit to Council: Evolution in the EEC.* London: Chatham, 1976.

Morgan, Roger. *West European Politics Since 1945: The Shaping of the European Community.* London: Batsford, 1972.

Morgan, Roger, and Caroline Bray. *Partners and Rivals in Western Europe: Britain, France, and Germany.* Brookfield, VT: Gower, 1986.

Mowle, Thomas S. *Allies at Odds? The United States and the European Union.* Basingstoke: Palgrave Macmillan, 2004.

Müftüler-Baç, Meltem, and Yannis Stivachtis, eds. *Turkey–European Union Relations: Dilemmas, Opportunities, and Constraints.* Lanham: Lexington Books, 2008.

Naurin, Daniel, and Helen Wallace, eds. *Unveiling the Council of the European Union: Games Governments Play in Brussels.* Basingstoke: Palgrave Macmillan, 2008.

Nelsen, Brent F., and Alexander Stubb, eds. *The European Union: Readings on the Theory and Practice of European Integration.* 3rd ed. Boulder: Lynne Rienner, 2003.

Neustadt, Richard. *Alliance Politics.* New York: Columbia University Press, 1970.

Nicholson, Frances, and Roger East. *From the Six to the Twelve: The Enlargement of the European Communities.* Chicago: St. James, 1987.

Norman, Peter. *Accidental Constitution: The Making of Europe's Constitutional Treaty.* 2nd ed. Brussels: EuroComment, 2005.

Nugent, Neill. *The European Commission.* Basingstoke, UK: Palgrave Macmillan, 2001.

————, ed. *European Union Enlargement.* Basingstoke: Palgrave Macmillan, 2004.

Nuttall, Simon J. *European Foreign Policy.* Oxford: Oxford University Press, 2000.

O'Brennan, John, and Tapio Raunio, eds. *National Parliaments Within the Enlarged European Union: From Victims of Integration to Competitive Actors?* London: Routledge, 2007.

Occhipinti, John D. *The Politics of EU Police Cooperation: Toward a European FBI?* Boulder: Lynne Rienner, 2003.

Padoa-Schioppa, Tommaso. *Efficiency, Stability, and Equity: A Strategy for the Evolution of the Economic System of the European Community.* Oxford: Oxford University Press, 1987.

Palayret, Jean-Marie, Helen Wallace, and Pascaline Winand, eds. *Visions, Votes, and Vetoes. The "Empty Chair" Crisis and the Luxembourg Compromise Forty Years On.* Brussels: Peter Lang, 2006.

Pallemaerts, Marc, and Albena Azmanova, eds. *The European Union and Sustainable Development: Internal and External Dimensions.* Brussels: VUB, 2006.

Papadimitriou, D. *Romania and the European Union: From Marginalization to Membership*. London: Routledge, 2008.

Parr, Helen. *British Policy Towards the European Community: Harold Wilson and Britain's World Role, 1964–1967*. London: Routledge, 2005.

Patel, Kiran, ed. *Fertile Ground for Europe? The History of European Integration and the Common Agricultural Policy Since 1945*. Baden-Baden: Nomos, 2009.

Patten, Chris. *Not Quite the Diplomat: Home Truths About Foreign Affairs*. London: Penguin, 2005.

Pattison de Menil, Lois. *Who Speaks for Europe? The Vision of Charles de Gaulle*. London: Macmillan, 1978.

Pelling, Henry. *Britain and the Marshall Plan*. New York: St. Martin's, 1988.

Perron, Régine. *Le Marché du charbon: Un enjeu entre l'Europe et les Etats-Unis de 1945 à 1958*. Paris: Publications de la Sorbonne, 1996.

Peterson, John. *Europe and America in the 1990s: The Prospects for Partnership*. 2nd ed. London: Elgar, 1993.

Petit, Michel, et al. *Agricultural Policy Formation in the European Community: The Birth of Milk Quotas and CAP Reform*. Amsterdam: Elsevier, 1987.

Pinder, John. *The European Community and Eastern Europe*. London: Royal Institute of International Affairs, 1991.

Pine, Melissa. *Harold Wilson and Europe: Pursuing Britain's Membership of the European Community*. London: Tauris Academic, 2008.

Poidevin, Raymond, ed. *Histoire des débuts de la construction européenne, Mars 1948–Mai 1950*. Brussels: Bruylant, 1986.

———. *Robert Schuman: Homme d'état, 1866–1963*. Paris: Imprimerie Nationale, 1986.

Pond, Elizabeth. *The Rebirth of Europe*. Washington, DC: Brookings Institution, 1999.

Priestley, Julian. *Six Battles That Shaped Europe's Parliament*. London: Harper, 2008.

Pryce, Roy, ed. *The Dynamics of European Union*. London: Croom Helm, 1987.

Quigley, Conor. *European State Aid Law and Policy*. 2nd ed. Portland: Hart, 2009.

Quinlan, Joseph P. *Drifting Apart or Growing Together? The Primacy of the Transatlantic Economy*. Washington, DC: Center for Transatlantic Relations, 2003.

Redmond, John, ed. *The 1995 Enlargement of the European Union*. Aldershot: Ashgate, 1997.

Rees, W., Philip Lynch, Nanette Neuwahl, and G. Wyn Rees, eds. *Reforming the European Union: From Maastricht to Amsterdam*. London: Longman, 2000.

Regelsberger, Elfride, Philippe de Schoutheete, and Wolfgang Wessels, eds. *Foreign Policy of the European Union: From EPC to CFSP and Beyond*. Boulder: Lynne Rienner, 1997.

Reif, Karlheinz, ed. *Ten European Elections: Campaigns and Results of the 1979/81 First Direct Elections to the European Parliament*. London: Gower, 1985.

Rittberger, Berthold. *Building Europe's Parliament: Democratic Representation Beyond the Nation State*. Oxford: Oxford University Press, 2007.

Rosengarten, Ulrich. *Die Genscher-Colombo-Initiative: Baustein für die Europäische Union*. Baden-Baden: Nomos, 2008.

Ross, George. *Jacques Delors and European Integration*. Oxford: Oxford University Press, 1995.

Rossbach, Niklas. *Heath, Nixon, and the Rebirth of the Special Relationship: Britain, the US, and the EC, 1969–74*. Basingstoke: Palgrave Macmillan, 2009.

Royo, Sebastian, and Paul Christopher Manuel, eds. *Spain and Portugal in the European Union: The First Fifteen Years*. London: Routledge, 2004.

Ruane, Kevin. *The Rise and Fall of the European Defence Community: Anglo-American Relations and the Crises of European Defence, 1950–55.* Basingstoke: Palgrave Macmillan, 2000.

Sabathil, Gerhard, Klemens Joos, and Bernd Kebler. *The European Commission: An Essential Guide to the Institution, the Procedures, and the Policies.* London: Kegan Page, 2008.

Sampedro, J. *The Enlargement of the European Community: Case Studies of Greece, Portugal, and Spain.* Atlantic Highlands, NJ: Humanities Press International, 1984.

Sbragia, Alberta, ed. *Euro-Politics: Institutions and Policymaking in the "New" European Community.* Washington, DC: Brookings Institution, 1992.

Schimmelfennig, Frank, and Ulrich Sedelmeier, eds. *The Europeanization of Central and Eastern Europe.* Ithaca: Cornell University Press, 2005.

Scully, Roger. *Becoming Europeans? Attitudes, Behaviour, and Socialization in the European Parliament.* Oxford: Oxford University Press, 2005.

Senden, L. *Soft Law in European Community Law.* Brookfield, VT: Hart, 2004.

Serra, Enrico, ed. *The Relaunching of Europe and the Treaties of Rome.* Baden-Baden: Nomos, 1989.

Sharp, M., and C. Shearman, *European Technological Collaboration.* London: Routledge and Kegan Paul, 1987.

Sharp, Margaret, Christopher Freeman, and William Walker. *Technology and the Future of Europe: Global Competition and the Environment in the 1990s.* New York: Pinter, 1991.

Shaw, Jo, ed. *The Convention on the Future of Europe: Working Towards an EU Constitution.* London: Federal Trust for Education and Research, 2003.

Sidjanski, Dusan. *The Federal Future of Europe: From the European Community to the European Union.* Ann Arbor: University of Michigan Press, 2000.

Simonian Haig. *The Privileged Partnership: Franco-German Relations in the European Community, 1969–1984.* Oxford: Clarendon, 1985.

Smith, Andy, ed. *Politics and the European Commission: Actors, Interdependence, Legitimacy.* London: Routledge, 2006.

Smith, Karen E. *European Foreign Policy in a Changing World.* Cambridge: Polity, 2003.

———. *The Making of European Union Foreign Policy.* New York: St. Martin's, 1998.

Smith, Michael L., and Peter M. R. Stirk, eds. *Making the New Europe: European Unity and the Second World War.* London: Pinter, 1993.

Spierenberg, Dirk, and Raymond Poidevin. *The History of the High Authority of the European Coal and Steel Community: Supranationality in Action.* London: Weidenfeld and Nicholson, 1994.

Staab, Andreas. *The European Union Explained: Institutions, Actors, Global Impact.* Bloomington: Indiana University Press, 2008.

Stevens, A., and H. Stevens. *Brussels Bureaucrats? The Administration of the European Union.* Basingstoke: Palgrave Macmillan, 2001.

Story, J., ed. *The New Europe: Politics, Government, and Economy Since 1945.* Oxford: Blackwell, 1993.

Strasser, Daniel. *The Finances of Europe.* 7th ed. Luxembourg: Office for Official Publications of the European Communities, 1992.

Stubb, Alexander. *Negotiating Flexibility in the European Union: Amsterdam, Nice, and Beyond.* Basingstoke: Palgrave Macmillan, 2003.

Svensson, Anna-Carin. *In the Service of the European Union: The Role of the Presidency in Negotiating the Amsterdam Treaty, 1995–1997.* Uppsala: Acta Universitatis, 2000.

Thatcher, Margaret. *The Downing Street Years*. New York: HarperCollins, 1993.

Tiersky, Ronald, ed. *Euro-Skepticism: A Reader*. Lanham: Rowman and Littlefield, 2001.

Torbiorn, Kjell M. *Destination Europe: The Political and Economic Growth of a Continent*. Manchester: Manchester University Press, 2003.

Tsalicoglou, Iacovos S. *Negotiating for Entry: The Accession of Greece to the European Community*. Hanover: Dartmouth Publishing Group, 1995.

Tsoukalis, Loukas. *The Politics and Economics of European Monetary Integration*. London: Allen and Unwin, 1977.

————. *What Kind of Europe?* Oxford: Oxford University Press, 2005.

Vachudova, Milada Anna. *Europe Undivided: Democracy, Leverage, and Integration After Communism*. Oxford: Oxford University Press, 2005.

Van der Harst, J. *Beyond the Customs Union: The European Community's Quest for Deepening, Widening, and Completion, 1969–1975*. Brussels: Bruylant, 2007.

Van Ypersele, Jacques. *The European Monetary System: Origins, Operation, and Outlook*. Chicago: St. James, 1985.

Vanthoor, Wim. *A Chronological History of the European Union, 1946–2001*. Northampton: Elgar, 2002.

Von der Groeben, Hans. *The European Community: The Formative Years: The Struggle to Establish the Common Market and the Political Union (1958–66)*. European Perspectives Series. Luxembourg: Office for Official Publications of the European Communities, 1985.

Wall, Irwin M. *The United States and the Making of Postwar France*. Cambridge: Cambridge University Press, 1991.

Wall, Stephen. *A Stranger in Europe*. Oxford: Oxford University Press, 2008.

Wallace, William, and I. Herreman, eds. *A Community of Twelve? The Impact of Further Enlargement on the European Communities*. Bruges: De Tempel, 1978.

Weigall, David, and Peter M. R. Stirk. *The Origins and Development of the European Community*. Leicester: Leicester University Press, 1992.

Willis, F. Roy, ed. *European Integration*. New York: New Viewpoints, 1975.

————. *France, Germany, and the New Europe, 1945–1967*. Palo Alto: Stanford University Press, 1968.

————. *The French in Germany, 1945–1949*. Stanford: Stanford University Press, 1962.

Wilson, Kevin, and Jan van der Dussen, eds. *The History of the Idea of Europe*. London: Routledge, 1995.

Young, Alasdair R. *Extending European Cooperation: The European Union and the "New" International Trade Agenda*. Manchester: Manchester University Press, 2002.

Young, John W. *Britain and European Unity, 1945–1999*. 2nd ed. Basingstoke: Palgrave Macmillan, 2000.

————. *France, the Cold War, and the Western Alliance, 1944–49: French Foreign Policy and Post-War Europe*. New York: St. Martin's, 1990.

Index

About the Book

In the years since the third edition of *Ever Closer Union* was published, the EU has seen the ratification and implementation of the Lisbon Treaty, further enlargement, key leadership changes, policy reforms, enduring Euroskepticism, an ever growing global role, and more—all of which is reflected in this fully revised and updated new edition. Unchanged, however, is the accessible, engaging nature of the text. Retaining its familiar three-part structure—history, institutions, and policies—*Ever Closer Union* clearly explains the complexities and vicissitudes of European integration from the 1950s to the present.

Desmond Dinan is professor of public policy and holds the *ad personam* Jean Monnet Chair at the School of Public Policy, George Mason University. His publications include *Europe Recast: A History of European Union* and *Encyclopedia of the European Union,* of which he is editor.